REFERENCE

AF701031

REFERENCE

KF 3941 .A68 G86 V. 1 The gun debate /

WITHDRAWN

REFERENCE

FASKEN LEARNING RESOURCE CENTER

9000089778

89778

Columbian Centinel.

Printed and published, on Wednesdays and Saturdays, by BENJAMIN RUSSELL, in State-Street, Boston, Massachusetts.

Whole No. 856.] SATURDAY, JUNE 2, 1792.

DEFINING DOCUMENTS IN AMERICAN HISTORY

The Gun Debate

REFERENCE
89778

DEFINING DOCUMENTS
IN AMERICAN HISTORY

The Gun Debate

Volume 1

Editor
Michael J. O'Neal

SALEM PRESS
A Division of EBSCO Information Services, Inc.
Ipswich, Massachusetts

GREY HOUSE PUBLISHING

Front page of a newspaper announcing the second Militia Act of 1792. (From the *Columbian Centinel.*)

Copyright © 2019 by EBSCO Information Services, Inc., and Grey House Publishing, Inc.

Defining Documents in American History: The Gun Debate, published by Grey House Publishing, Inc., Amenia, NY, under exclusive license from EBSCO Information Services, Inc.

All rights reserved. No part of this work may be used or reproduced in any manner whatsoever or transmitted in any form or by any means, electronic or mechanical, including photocopy, recording, or any information storage and retrieval system, without written permission from the copyright owner. For permissions requests, contact proprietary-publishing@ebsco.com.

∞ The paper used in these volumes conforms to the American National Standard for Permanence of Paper for Printed Library Materials, Z39.48 1992 (R2009).

Publisher's Cataloging-In-Publication Data
(Prepared by The Donohue Group, Inc.)

Names: O'Neal, Michael, 1949- editor.
Title: The gun debate / editor, Michael O'Neal, PhD.
Other Titles: Defining documents in American history (Salem Press)
Description: [First edition]. | Ipswich, Massachusetts : Salem Press, a division of EBSCO Information Services ; Amenia, NY : Grey House Publishing, [2019] | Includes bibliographical references and index.
Identifiers: ISBN 9781642650341 (set) | ISBN 9781642653205 (v. 1) | ISBN 9781642653212 (v. 2)
Subjects: LCSH: Firearms--Law and legislation--United States--Sources. | Gun control--United States--Sources.
Classification: LCC KF3941.A68 G86 2019 | DDC 363.3/3/0973/03--dc23

FIRST PRINTING
PRINTED IN THE UNITED STATES OF AMERICA

Contents

Volume 1

Volume 2

The Modern Court System Weighs In

Responses to the Debate

Appendixes

Publisher's Note

Defining Documents in American History series, produced by Salem Press, offers a closer look at important historical documents by pairing primary source documents on a broad range of subjects with essays written especially for the series by a diverse range of writers. This established series includes thirty titles that present documents selected to illuminate specific eras in American history—*The Emergence of Modern America* through the *1970s*, for example—or to explore significant themes and developments in American society—*Immigration & Immigrant Communities*; *Dissent & Protest*; *Environment & Conservation;* and *The Legacy of 9/11*.

This set, *Defining Documents in American History: The Gun Debate*, offers in-depth analysis of thirty-five documents, including speeches, court rulings, legal texts, blog posts, manifestos, and legislative acts.

The material is organized under four sections:

- The Constitution and Its Aftermath beginning with James Madison's *Federalist Papers;* House debates related to the Second Amendment; the Militia Acts of 1792; *Blackstone's Commentaries*: With Notes of Reference, to the Constitution and Laws, of the Federal Government of the United States; and of the Commonwealth of Virginia; and a discussion of guns entitled "All Guns Are Not Created Equal."
- As the Nation Expands includes a ongoing debate regarding the Consitution: A View of the Constitution of the United States; Familiar Exposition of the Constitution of the United States; and The General Principles of Constitutional Law in the United States of America. This section also includes an analysis of some signficant court rulings related to gun rights: *Johnson v. Tompkins, State v. Huntley, United States v. Cruikshank,* and *Presser v. Illinois*. Open carry ordinances come under scrutiny in Charter and Revised Ordinances of the City of Galveston, and All Ordinances.
- The Modern Court System Weighs In takes a look at a number of significant and often controversial rulings, including *United States v. Miller*; *United States v. Lopez*; *District of Columbia v. Heller*; *McDonald v. City of Chicago*; *Peruta v. County of San Diego*; and *Young v. Hawaii.*
- Responses to the Debate include legislative acts such as the National Firearms Act of 1934; Gun Control Act of 1968; Brady Handgun Violence Protection Act; Florida Legislation "Justifiable Use of Force" ("Stand Your Ground Law"); and Protection of Lawful Commerce in Arms Act, as well as a thought-provoking blog post: "An Honest Conversation about Guns."

In addition to the main documents and analyses, the set also includes an array of supplemental documents, including letters by the Antifederalist, Federal Farmer; an article on race and gun control; the Militia Act of 1903 (known as the Dick Act); discussions of the politics and policies of gun control; the Parkland Student Manifesto; and an article related to realties of the 3D printing of guns.

These documents provide a compelling view of what the ongoing debate surrounding guns and a well-regulated militia, as gun owners and advocates argue in favor of the protection of Second Amendment rights and those in favor of gun control argue for increased efforts to limit gun ownership in an effort to reduce gun violence and mass shootings.

Essay Format

Each Historical Document is supported by a critical essay, written by historians and teachers, that includes a Summary Overview, Defining Moment, About the Author, and Document Themes. An important feature of each essay is a close reading and analysis of the primary source that develops broader themes, such as the author's rhetorical purpose, social or class position, point of view, and other relevant issues..

Each section begins with a brief introduction that defines questions and problems underlying the subjects addressed in the historical documents. Each essay also includes a Additional Reading section for further research.

Appendixes

- **Chronological List** arranges all documents by year.
- **Web Resources** is an annotated list of websites that offer valuable supplemental resources.
- **Bibliography** lists helpful articles and books for further study.
- **Contributors**

Salem Press would like to extend its appreciation to all involved in the development and production of this work. The essays have been written and signed by scholars of history, humanities, and other disciplines related to the essays' topics. Without these expert contributions, a project of this nature would not be possible.

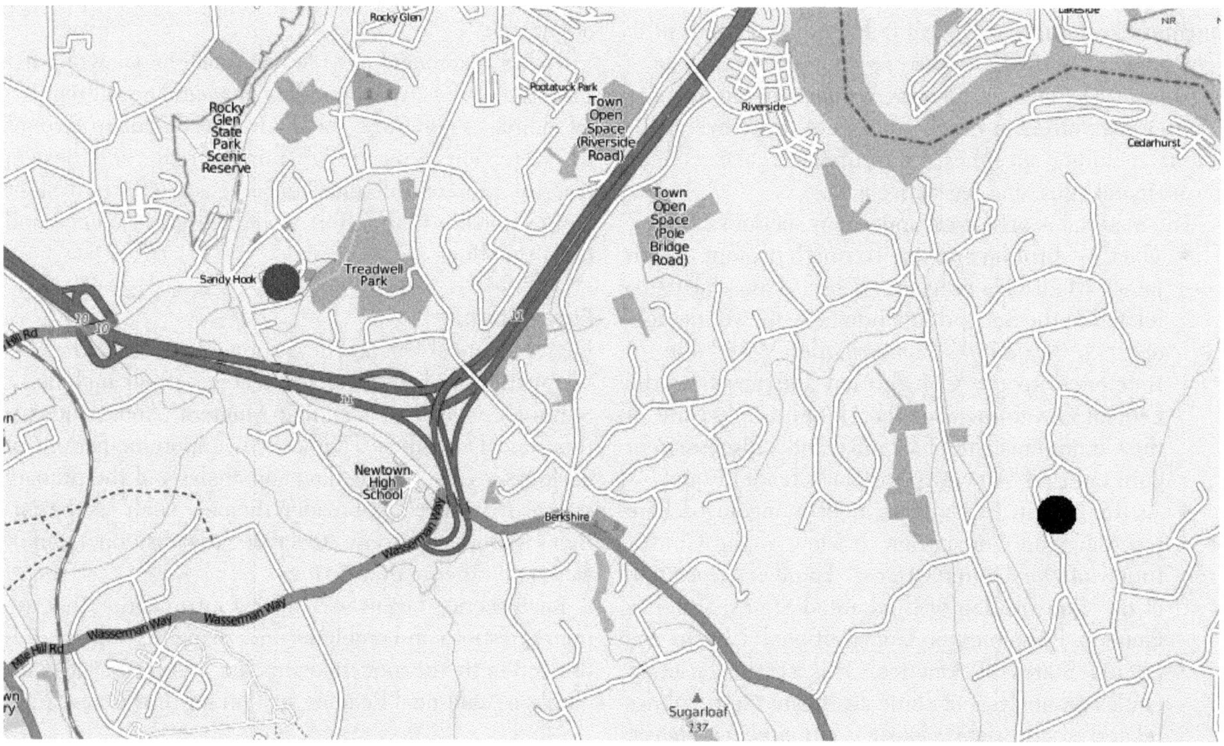

Map of Sandy Hook. The circle on the left is Sandy Hook Elementary School. The circle on the right is the Lanza household. (By Canadaolympic989.)

Editor's Introduction

On the morning of April 20, 1999, Dylan Klebold and Eric Harris, both seniors at Columbine High School near Denver, Colorado, entered the grounds of the school carrying a number of weapons, including an Intratec TEC-DC9 (a semi-automatic pistol), a Hi-Point 995 Carbine (a long gun with a shorter barrel than a rifle), a Savage 67H pump-action shotgun, and a Stevens 311D double-barreled sawed-off shotgun. Additionally, the pair brought nearly a hundred explosive devices to the school, and each was armed with knives. At about 11:19, the two began a shooting rampage that left twelve students and one teacher dead and twenty-one people wounded. The rampage ended when Klebold and Harris turned their guns on themselves at 12:08.

The nation was rightly horrified, and the story dominated the news cycle in the days and weeks that followed. Although there had been earlier instances of school shootings dating as far back as the nineteenth century, generally the number of fatalities was small—usually as few as none or one—and usually the shootings were the result of a dispute. The concept of a "mass shooting"—at a school, no less—was virtually unthinkable. The sheer mindless carnage of the Columbine shootings, however, sparked a national debate about a number of issues, including questions about what would motivate two young men to perpetrate such a horrific crime. Were they lashing out because they had been the victims of school bullying? What impact did violent video games and movies such as *Natural Born Killers* have on their mental state? Did they feel isolated and rejected because of school social cliques? To what extent was their state of mind distorted by the "Goth" subculture? All of these were thought to have played a role in motivating the Columbine killers. Disturbingly, a subculture of disaffected youth who refer to themselves as "Columbiners" take Klebold and Harris as role models in their obsession with violence and suicide.

One issue, however, dominated the discussion and analysis of the shootings: that of gun control and easy access to guns by people bent on committing crimes—not just garden-variety robberies and the like, but mass killings. The issue began to take on greater urgency in 2012 when, on December 14, a twenty-year-old man armed with his mother's Bushmaster XM15-E2S rifle took the lives of twenty children and six staff members at the Sandy Hook Elementary School in Newtown, Connecticut. On February 19, 2018, a nineteen-year-old former student at Marjory Stoneman Douglas High School in Parkland, Florida, killed seventeen people and injured seventeen others at the school, using a semi-automatic AR-15 rifle; this event sparked March for Our Lives, a protest by students in Washington, D.C., and other cities, when hundreds of thousands of students rallied to call for stricter gun control measures. Then on May 18, 2018, eight students and two teachers were killed and thirteen other were wounded at Santa Fe High School in Texas by a suspect armed with a Remington 870 shotgun and a .38 caliber revolver. Additionally, the suspect planted multiple improvised explosive devices around the school and its grounds, among them pressure cooker bombs, Molotov cocktails, pipe bombs, and propane tanks.

These events, however, were not the only ones that rekindled the gun debate. On April 16, 2007, thirty-three people were killed and twenty-three were injured at Virginia Tech University by a shooter armed with semi-automatic pistols. On June 17, 2015, a twenty-one-year-old white supremacist shot to death nine people attending a prayer service at the Emanuel African Methodist Church in Charleston, South Carolina, using a Glock 41 .45-caliber handgun. Terrorist shootings took place in San Bernadino, California, in 2015, leaving fourteen people dead; the weapons used included a DPMS Panther Arms A15 .223 caliber semi-automatic rifle; a Smith & Wesson M&P 15 .223 caliber semi-automatic rifle; a Llama 9mm semi-automatic pistol; and a Springfield XD 9mm semi-automatic pistol. A terrorist attack on a gay nightclub in Orlando, Florida, in 2016 left forty-nine people dead; the perpetrator was armed with a Sig Sauer MCX semi-automatic rifle and a Glock 17 semi-automatic pistol. On November 5, 2017, a twenty-six-year-old man shot twenty-six people to death and injured twenty others at the First Baptist Church in Sutherland Springs, Texas, using a Ruger AR-556 semi-automatic rifle. The shooter was prohibited from buying a firearm because of a domestic violence conviction while he was in the U.S. Air Force, but the Air Force failed to record the conviction in the FBI's National Crime Information Center database.

But the deadliest mass shooting in U.S. history occurred on October 1, 2017, when sixty-four-year-old Stephen Paddock opened fire on a crowd of people attending a music festival on the Las Vegas Strip in Nevada. Armed with twenty-four firearms, the gunman fired more than 1,100 rounds of ammunition, killing fifty-eight people and injuring 851. Meanwhile, on a daily basis, people are killed by criminals with guns in cities across the nation, with roughly 11,000 gun homicides taking place each year. In this context, many Americans decry the fact that there are almost as many guns as people in the United States. One estimate is that for every hundred people in the United States, there are nearly ninety guns; in second place is Switzerland, with half that many. In the United States, the murder rate each year is three for every 100,000 people—six times Canada's rate, thirty times Australia's rate.

The Gun Control Debate

Tragedies in which guns are involved have led to increased calls for strict gun regulation in the United States—regulations that mirror those of other developed countries with significantly lower rates of gun homicides. The debate is often impassioned. On the one hand, gun control advocates would like to see stringent laws passed regarding who can buy a gun, where guns can be sold, and what types of guns should be banned. Gun control advocates are likely to back a number of measures that they believe would curtail gun violence:

- Conducting more vigilant background checks on gun purchasers. It is estimated that more than 20 percent of guns are purchased without background checks.
- Requiring mandatory trigger locks.
- Ending immunity from lawsuits for gun manufacturers.
- Prohibiting domestic abusers who are subject to protection orders from purchasing guns.
- Tightening regulations having to do with "straw purchasers," that is, people who buy guns for others who cannot legally buy them, such as convicted felons.
- Banning bump stocks.
- Prohibiting people under the age of twenty-one from purchasing guns.
- Conducting background checks on first-time purchasers of ammunition.
- Developing "smart guns," or guns that can be fired only if a PIN is entered or if fired near a particular bracelet.
- Banning magazines that hold more than a specified number of rounds.

One issue that has attracted considerable attention is so-called bump stocks. These are gunstocks designed to make a semi-automatic firearm (that is, a firearm that fires a bullet each time the trigger is pulled but that also ejects a spent cartridge and reloads a new one) mimic the firing speed of a fully automatic weapon (that is, one that continues to fire as long as the trigger is held). Bump stocks, which are not thought to have any value for such activities as hunting and target shooting, increase the firing rate of a gun, potentially multiplying the number of victims in a mass shooting. Further, vocal gun control advocates would like to see a ban on the sale and ownership of all automatic and semi-automatic firearms—and even on all guns, period. On the other side of the debate are passionate gun owners who regard any attempt to regulate the sale or ownership of firearms as a violation of their constitutional rights. In this climate of extreme and entrenched positions, the federal government has found efforts to regulate firearms to be a seemingly insurmountable challenge.

The Second Amendment Debate

At the center of the debate over gun control is the Second Amendment to the U.S. Constitution, part of the Bill of Rights that protects the civil rights of all Americans. The Second Amendment reads: "A well regulated Militia, being necessary to the security of a free State, the right of the people to keep and bear Arms, shall not be infringed." These twenty-seven words have occasioned a considerable amount of ink to be spilled by constitutional scholars, jurists, gun enthusiasts, and gun opponents. The essence of the problem is that sharp disagreements exist as to what the Second Amendment actually says and what right it actually protects.

On one side of the debate are those who believe that the Second Amendment ensures that *individuals* have an unfettered right to own and carry guns. These individuals believe that any attempt to regulate the sale and ownership of guns, or to regulate the kinds of guns that can be legally sold and owned, constitutes an "infringement" of a fundamental constitutional right and represents the first step on a slippery slope to the government's confiscation of all guns. They tend to oppose all or most regulations, including background checks, registration of firearms, age requirements (for purchasing a gun), and concealed carry permits. They believe that the solution to the high homicide rate in the United States, and to the seemingly growing prevalence of school shootings, is an armed citizenry that can take action against a shooter. In reading the Second Amendment, they tend to focus on the second clause, "the right of the people to keep and bear Arms, shall not be infringed." They regard this right as absolute, enshrined in the amendment. Extremists in this camp are further committed to the belief that gun ownership on the part of citizens is an essential bulwark against government tyranny.

On the other side of the debate are those who passionately call for stricter regulation of guns, arguing that such regulations are not a violation of the Second Amendment. These individuals tend to focus less on the second clause of the Second Amendment and more on the first: "A well regulated Militia, being necessary to the security of a free state." In interpreting the Second Amendment, they tend to take a historical approach in an effort to determine what the framers of the Constitution actually meant. In their view, the right to "bear arms" is held by the state militias, which existed in the late eighteenth century in lieu of a large standing federal army. The notion was that any attack on the United States—by an Indian tribe, for example, or perhaps one of the European powers seeking to expand its empire in the New World—would need to be fended off by state militias. A militia might also be called into action to put down insurrection; George Washington, for example, called up the militia to put down the Whiskey Rebellion in 1791. Indeed, during the nineteenth century, a fair amount of jurisprudence dealt with the issue of defining the militias and their role.

A major turn took place, however, with the passage of the Militia Act of 1903, more formally, "An Act to promote the efficiency of the militia, and for other purposes." In essence, the 1903 act created the modern National Guard, and it codified the circumstances under which the National Guard could be federalized. The act states:

> That the militia shall consist of every able-bodied male citizen of the respective States, Territories, and the District of Columbia, and every able-bodied male of foreign birth who has declared his intention to become a citizen, who is more than eighteen and less than forty-five years of age, and shall be divided into two classes-the organized militia, to be known as the National Guard of the State, Territory, or District of Columbia, or by such other designations as may be given them by the laws of the respective States or Territories, and the remainder to be known as the Reserve Militia.

For gun control advocates, the creation of the National Guard in essence rendered the colonial-era militias obsolete. Accordingly, the Second Amendment does not give *individuals* a right to bear any and all arms under any and all circumstances. Rather, it extended the right to state militias at a time when such bodies of citizen-soldiers might have been necessary to protect the nation. They will note, for example, that the Militia Act of 1792 required militia members to report for duty with a musket, bayonet and belt, two spare flints, a cartridge box with twenty-four bullets, and a knapsack. Further, men who owned rifles were required to bring their own powder horn, a quarter pound of gunpowder, twenty rifle balls, and a shooting pouch. These requirements strongly suggest to gun control advocates that the framers intended to extend the right to "bear arms" to the militias, not to individuals. And they note that the framers, who lived at a time when guns by today's standards were primitive instruments, hard to load, and capable of firing perhaps three rounds a minute, if that, could not have envisioned guns capable of spraying hundreds of rounds a minute into a crowd of concert goers or school children.

Meanwhile, the bitter debate over the meaning of the Second Amendment has even entered the popular culture. In an episode of *The Simpsons* that aired in 1997, this comic exchange between Homer Simpson and his daughter Lisa captures in brief the essence of the debate:

> HOMER: But I have to have a gun! It's in the Constitution!
>
> LISA: Dad! The Second Amendment is just a remnant from revolutionary days. It has no meaning today!
>
> HOMER: You couldn't be more wrong, Lisa. If I didn't have this gun, the king of England could just walk in here anytime he wants and start shoving you around.

The current volume strives to provide a survey of the gun debate as it has played out from the end of the eighteenth century to 2018. It includes entries having to do with legislation, court decisions impacting the gun debate, and scholarly analyses of the Second Amendment and related issues. Equally as important, it includes the views of journalists and of ordinary citizens who have weighed in on the debate. The goal is to provide a comprehensive overview of the gun-control debate, with entries taking positions on both sides of the issue.

DEFINING DOCUMENTS
IN AMERICAN HISTORY

The Gun Debate

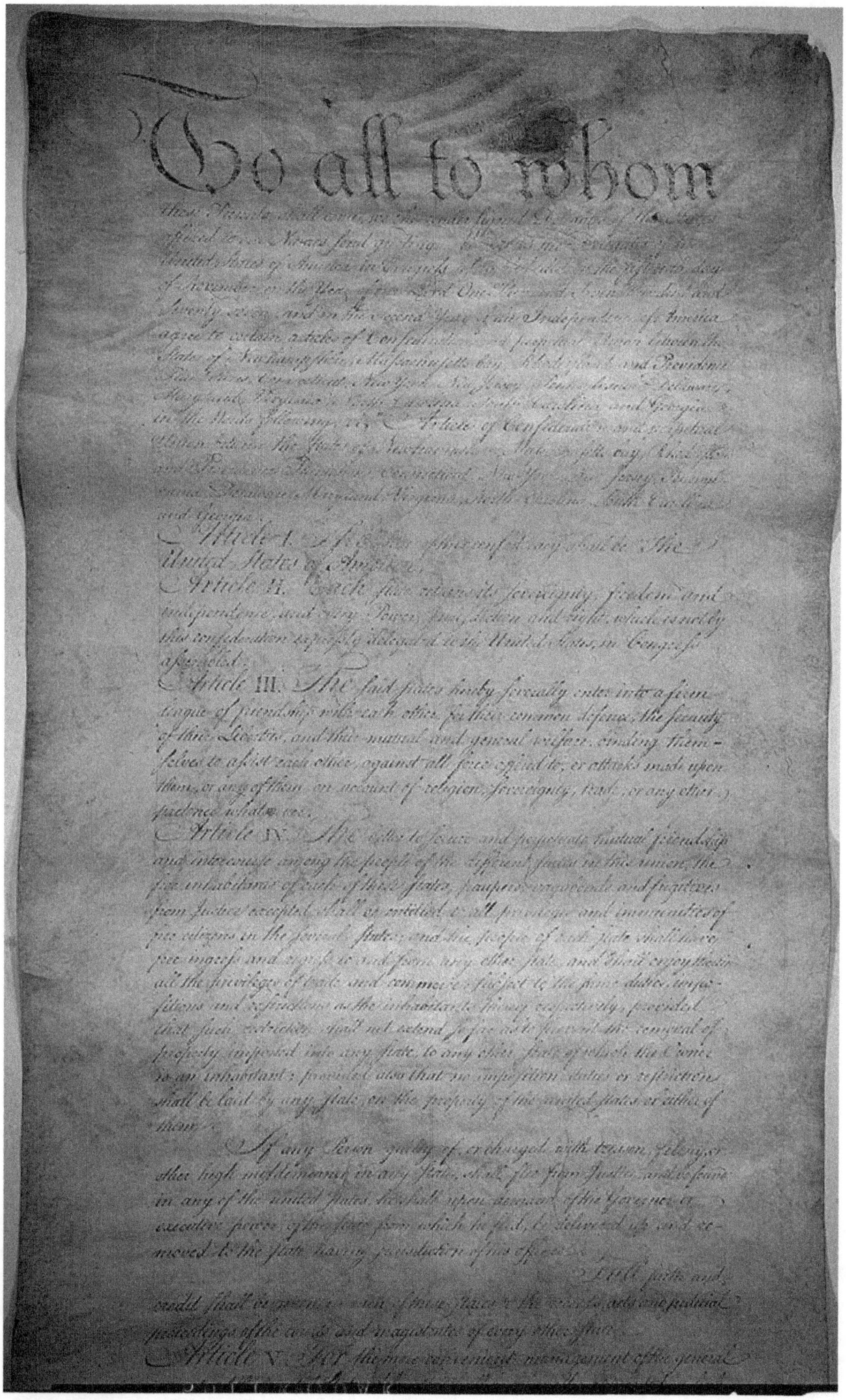

The Articles of Confederation: predecessor to the U.S. Constitution and drafted from Antifederalist principles.

The Constitution and Its Aftermath

"A well regulated Militia, being necessary to the security of a free State, the right of the people to keep and bear Arms, shall not be infringed."
—U.S. Constitution, Second Amendment

The intense debate surrounding guns and gun control measures might seem in the twenty-first century to have shallow roots in the context of highly publicized mass shootings, but the roots of the debate extend deep into the Anglo-American past. The framers of the Constitution, and those who participated in the debate over ratification of the Constitution in the late eighteenth century, struggled with the issue of the balance of power between the states and the national government. Opponents of the new Constitution, often referred to as the Antifederalists, were concerned that the Constitution gave the national government too much authority. A very real concern they had was that the national government would use its power and authority to trample on the rights of the states, and on the rights of individual citizens. Many of them lent their support to the Constitution only because of the promise that a bill of rights would later be included that would protect individual liberties.

It was James Madison, the "father" of the Constitution, who proposed a series of amendments that would be incorporated into the text of the newly ratified document. In the end, the Bill of Rights, which Madison largely wrote, was appended to the Constitution as the first ten amendments. The key amendment for the purposes of this volume is the Second Amendment, which reads: "A well regulated Militia, being necessary to the security of a free State, the right of the people to keep and bear Arms, shall not be infringed." Jurists, constitutional scholars, and even grammarians, have been left confused by this somewhat maddening formulation. They have fallen into two major camps. One focuses on the second clause of the amendment and argue that it affirms a pre-existing right of *individuals* to keep and bear arms. The other camp focuses on the first clause, insisting that the purpose of the amendment was to provide for and protect state militias.

Various historical documents shed light, however dim it may be, on these questions. In particular, Federalist Papers written by Alexander Hamilton and James Madison weigh in on the issue of the militia.

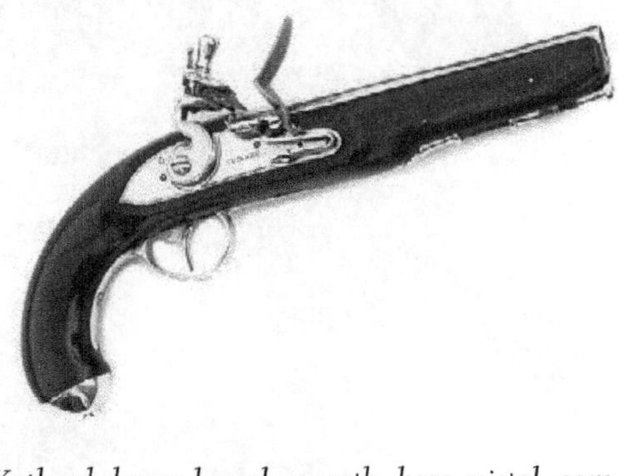

Ketland brass barrel smooth bore pistol common in Colonial America. (By Michael E. Cumpston.)

Students of constitutional history can also examine the congressional debate that took place with regard to the Bill of Rights generally and the Second Amendment in particular. The Militia Act of 1792 addressed the need for a federal fighting force to protect the nation from foreign enemies, but both sides in the twenty-first century debate use the Militia Act to support their contentions about the purpose of the Second Amendment. Those who support the "individual right" view of the Second Amendment often point to St. George Tucker, who, in his highly influential commentaries on *Blackstone's Commentaries* written very early in the nineteenth century, called the Second Amendment " the true palladium of liberty," adding that "the right of self defense is the first law of nature." More than two centuries later, opponents of gun control measures continue to echo Tucker's use of the word *palladium*, or safeguard. Additionally, modern writers have explored the roots and history of the Second Amendment, often reaching differing conclusions about what rights it extends and to whom it extends them. Any discussion of guns and gun control, however, must start with the historical record.

Ideals that helped to inspire the Second Amendment in part are symbolized by the minutemen. (By Aldaron.)

Federalist Papers 24 and 25

Author(s): Publius (Alexander Hamilton and John Jay)
Date: 1787
Genre: Essays

Summary Overview

The Federalist Papers were a series of eighty-five essays written by Alexander Hamilton, James Madison, and to a lesser extent, John Jay and published in various newspapers under the name Publius. The purpose to the essays was to influence public opinion with regard to the ratification of the new U.S. Constitution, which had been signed by the delegates to the Constitutional Convention in September. Federalist Papers 24 and 25 were both written by Hamilton; 24 appeared in the *Independent Journal* on December 19, 1787, while 25 appeared in the *New York Packet* on December 21. Both have an indirect bearing on the issue of the Second Amendment right to bear arms because of their discussion of maintaining a standing army and navy.

Defining Moment

On May 24, 1787, the Constitutional Convention was convened in Philadelphia. The express purpose of the Constitutional Convention was to amend the 1781 Articles of Confederation. The widespread perception was that the Articles of Confederation was a weak document that had led to conflict among the states and that granted too much power to the individual states and not enough to the federal government. Many of the convention's delegates arrived in Philadelphia with the intention not just of amending the articles but of creating an entirely new constitution. Among them was James Madison, who would ultimately be largely responsible for the language of the Bill of Rights, including the Second Amendment.

In the fall of 1787, debate ran high about the proposed new U.S. Constitution, which had been submitted to the states for ratification at the conclusion of the convention on September 17, 1787. Those who urged ratification, the Federalists, were put into the position of having to defend their views by the arguments of those who feared that the Constitution vested too much power in the federal government at the expense of the states. Alexander Hamilton, writing largely for a New York audience, notes that the American people faced a momentous choice about the form that their new government would take. Hamilton does not discuss the Second Amendment, which had not yet come into existence, but he takes up the issue of a standing army under the control of the federal government. At the time, many American citizens objected to the existence of a large standing army, believing that such an army would give the federal government the wherewithal to tyrannize over the states; it was this fear that contributed to the Second Amendment's right of "the people" to "keep and bear arms." Hamilton, in these two essays, counters this view.

On June 21, 1788, the Constitution was ratified when New Hampshire voted in its favor, and the new government began operations under the Constitution on March 4, 1789.

About the Author

Alexander Hamilton was born on January 11, although there is uncertainty about whether the year was 1755 or 1757. He was born in the West Indies, but moved to the U.S. mainland in 1772 to study at what is now Columbia University. He became involved in public life at an early age, serving as an artillery captain early in the Revolutionary War, then as a member of General George Washington's staff. Throughout the 1780s, he grew convinced that the national government had to be strengthened, a view he propounded in The Continentalist essays and later in the essays that would become known as the Federalist Papers. In 1783 he was appointed chair of a committee formed to plan for a peacetime army and navy. He served in Congress and was a delegate to the Constitutional Convention in 1787. Although he was not happy with the Constitution that was produced, he argued for its ratification in late 1787 and in 1788. He went on to become secretary of the treasury under President George Washington. In this position he steered the nation through the chaos occasioned by Revolutionary

John Jay, author of five of The Federalist Papers, later became the first Chief Justice of the United States. (By Gilbert Stuart.)

War debts. He also created the First Bank of the United States. In 1795 Hamilton left the treasury to practice law, but he continued to be active in Federalist politics, usually in opposition to James Madison and particularly Thomas Jefferson. Hamilton remains famous in the twenty-first century for having died as a result of a duel with Aaron Burr. The duel, occasioned by Hamilton's opposition to Burr during the latter's unsuccessful run for the governorship of New York, took place on July 11, 1804. Hamilton died the following day.

HISTORICAL DOCUMENT

Federalist 24: "The Powers Necessary to the Common Defense Further Considered"

To the People of the State of New York:

To THE powers proposed to be conferred upon the federal government, in respect to the creation and direction of the national forces, I have met with but one specific objection, which, if I understand it right, is this, that proper provision has not been made against the existence of standing armies in time of peace; an objection which, I shall now endeavor to show, rests on weak and unsubstantial foundations.

It has indeed been brought forward in the most vague and general form, supported only by bold assertions, without the appearance of argument; without even the sanction of theoretical opinions; in contradiction to the practice of other free nations, and to the general sense of America, as expressed in most of the existing constitutions. The proprietory of this remark will appear, the moment it is recollected that the objection under consideration turns upon a supposed necessity of restraining the LEGISLATIVE authority of the nation, in the article of military establishments; a principle unheard of, except in one or two of our State constitutions, and rejected in all the rest.

A stranger to our politics, who was to read our newspapers at the present juncture, without having previously inspected the plan reported by the convention, would be naturally led to one of two conclusions: either that it contained a positive injunction, that standing armies should be kept up in time of peace; or that it vested in the EXECUTIVE the whole power of levying troops, without subjecting his discretion, in any shape, to the control of the legislature.

If he came afterwards to peruse the plan itself, he would be surprised to discover, that neither the one nor the other was the case; that the whole power of raising armies was lodged in the LEGISLATURE, not in the EXECUTIVE; that this legislature was to be a popular body, consisting of the representatives of the people periodically elected; and that instead of the provision he had supposed in favor of standing armies, there was to be found, in respect to this object, an important qualification even of the legislative discretion, in that clause which forbids the appropriation of money for the support of an army for any longer period than two years a precaution which, upon a nearer view of it, will appear to be a great and real security against the keeping up of troops without evident necessity.

Disappointed in his first surmise, the person I have supposed would be apt to pursue his conjectures a little further. He would naturally say to himself, it is impossible that all this vehement and pathetic declamation can be without some colorable pretext. It must needs be that this people, so jealous of their liberties, have, in all the preceding models of the constitutions which they have established, inserted the most precise and rigid precautions on this point, the omission of which, in the new plan, has given birth to all this apprehension and clamor.

If, under this impression, he proceeded to pass in review the several State constitutions, how great would be his disappointment to find that TWO ONLY of them[1] contained an interdiction of standing armies in time of peace; that the other eleven had either observed a profound silence on the subject, or had in express terms admitted the right of the Legislature to authorize their existence.

Still, however he would be persuaded that there must be some plausible foundation for the cry raised on this head. He would never be able to imagine, while any source of information remained unexplored, that it was nothing more than an experiment upon the public credulity, dictated either by a deliberate intention to deceive, or by the overflowings of a zeal too intemperate to be ingenuous. It would probably occur to him, that he would be likely to find the precautions he was in search of in the primitive compact between the States. Here, at length, he would expect to meet with a solution of the enigma. No doubt, he would observe to himself, the existing Confederation must contain the most explicit provisions against military establishments in time of peace; and a departure from this model, in a favorite point, has occasioned the discontent which appears to influence these political champions.

If he should now apply himself to a careful and critical survey of the articles of Confederation, his astonishment would not only be increased, but would acquire a mixture of indignation, at the unexpected discovery, that these articles, instead of containing the prohibition he looked for, and though they had, with jealous circumspection, restricted the authority of the State legislatures in this particular, had not imposed a single restraint on that of the United States. If he happened to be a man of quick sensibility, or ardent temper, he could now no longer refrain from regarding these clamors as the dishonest artifices of a sinister and unprincipled opposition to a plan which ought at least to receive a fair and candid examination from all sincere lovers of their country! How else, he would say, could the authors of them have been tempted to vent such loud censures upon that plan, about a point in which it seems to have conformed itself to the general sense of America as declared in its different forms of government, and in which it has even superadded a new and powerful guard unknown to any of them? If, on the contrary, he happened to be a man of calm and dispassionate feelings, he would indulge a sigh for the frailty of human nature, and would lament, that in a matter so interesting to the happiness of millions, the true merits of the question should be perplexed and entangled by expedients so unfriendly to an impartial and right determination. Even such a man could hardly forbear remarking, that a conduct of this kind has too much the appearance of an intention to mislead the people by alarming their passions, rather than to convince them by arguments addressed to their understandings.

But however little this objection may be countenanced, even by precedents among ourselves, it may be satisfactory to take a nearer view of its intrinsic merits. From a close examination it will appear that restraints upon the discretion of the legislature in respect to military establishments in time of peace, would be improper to be imposed, and if imposed, from the necessities of society, would be unlikely to be observed.

Though a wide ocean separates the United States from Europe, yet there are various considerations that warn us against an excess of confidence or security. On one side of us, and stretching far into our rear, are growing settlements subject to the dominion of Britain. On the other side, and extending to meet the British settlements, are colonies and establishments subject to the dominion of Spain. This situation and the vicinity of the West India Islands, belonging to these two powers create between them, in respect to their American possessions and in relation to us, a common interest. The savage tribes on our Western frontier ought to be regarded as our natural enemies, their natural allies, because they have most to fear from us, and most to hope from them. The improvements in the art of navigation have, as to the facility of communication, rendered distant nations, in a great measure, neighbors. Britain and Spain are among the principal maritime powers of Europe. A future concert of views between these nations ought not to be regarded as improbable. The increasing remoteness of consanguinity is every day diminishing the force of the family compact between France and Spain. And politicians have ever with great reason considered the ties of blood as feeble and precarious links of political connection. These circumstances combined, admonish us not to be too sanguine in considering ourselves as entirely out of the reach of danger.

Previous to the Revolution, and ever since the peace, there has been a constant necessity for keeping small garrisons on our Western frontier. No person can doubt that these will continue to be indispensable, if it should only be against the ravages and depredations of the Indians. These garrisons must either be furnished by occasional detachments from the militia, or by permanent corps in the pay of the government. The first is impracticable; and if practicable, would be pernicious. The militia would not long, if at all, submit to be dragged from their occupations and families to perform that most disagreeable duty in times of profound peace. And if they could be prevailed upon or compelled to do it, the increased expense of a frequent rotation of service, and the loss of labor and disconcertion of the industrious pursuits of individuals, would form conclusive objections to the scheme. It would be as burdensome and injurious to the public as ruinous to private citizens. The latter resource of permanent corps in the pay of the government amounts to a standing army in time of peace; a small one, indeed, but not the less real for being small. Here is a simple view of the subject, that shows us at once the impropriety of a constitutional interdiction of such establishments, and the necessity of leaving the matter to the discretion and prudence of the legislature.

In proportion to our increase in strength, it is probable, nay, it may be said certain, that Britain and Spain would augment their military establishments in our neighborhood. If we should not be willing to be exposed, in a naked and defenseless condition, to their insults and encroachments, we should find it expedient to increase our frontier garrisons in some ratio to the force by which our Western settlements might be annoyed. There are, and will be, particular posts, the possession of which will include the command of large districts of territory, and facilitate future invasions of the remainder. It may be added that some of those posts will be keys to the trade with the Indian nations. Can any man think it would be wise to leave such posts in a situation to be at any instant seized by one or the other of two neighboring and formidable powers? To act this part would be to desert all the usual maxims of prudence and policy.

If we mean to be a commercial people, or even to be secure on our Atlantic side, we must endeavor, as soon as possible, to have a navy. To this purpose there must be dock-yards and arsenals; and for the defense of these, fortifications, and probably garrisons. When a nation has become so powerful by sea that it can protect its dock-yards by its fleets, this supersedes the necessity of garrisons for that purpose; but where naval establishments are in their infancy, moderate garrisons will, in all likelihood, be found an indispensable security against descents for the destruction of the arsenals and dock-yards, and sometimes of the fleet itself.

PUBLIUS.

[1] *This statement of the matter is taken from the printed collection of State constitutions. Pennsylvania and North Carolina are the two which contain the interdiction in these words: "As standing armies in time of peace are dangerous to liberty, THEY OUGHT NOT to be kept up." This is, in truth, rather a CAUTION than a PROHIBITION. New Hampshire, Massachusetts, Delaware, and Maryland have, in each of their bills of rights, a clause to this effect: "Standing armies are dangerous to liberty, and ought not to be raised or kept up WITHOUT THE CONSENT OF THE LEGISLATURE"; which is a formal admission of the authority of the Legislature. New York has no bills of rights, and her constitution says not a word about the matter. No bills of rights appear annexed to the constitutions of the other States, except the foregoing, and their constitutions are equally silent. I am told, however that one or two States have bills of rights which do not appear in this collection; but that those also recognize the right of the legislative authority in this respect.*

Federalist 25: "The Powers Necessary to the Common Defense Further Considered

To the People of the State of New York:

IT MAY perhaps be urged that the objects enumerated in the preceding number ought to be provided for by the State governments, under the direction of the Union. But this would be, in reality, an inversion of the primary principle of our political association, as it would in practice transfer the care of the common defense from the federal head to the individual members: a project oppressive to some States, dangerous to all, and baneful to the Confederacy.

The territories of Britain, Spain, and of the Indian nations in our neighborhood do not border on particular States, but encircle the Union from Maine to Georgia. The danger, though in different degrees, is therefore common. And the means of guarding against it ought, in like manner, to be the objects of common councils and of a common treasury. It happens that some States, from local situation, are more directly exposed. New York is of this class. Upon the plan of separate provisions, New York would have to sustain the whole weight of the establishments requisite to her immediate safety, and to the mediate or ultimate protection of her neighbors. This would neither be equitable as it respected New York nor safe as it respected the other States. Various inconveniences would attend such a system. The States, to whose lot it might fall to support the necessary establishments, would be as little able as willing, for a considerable time to come, to bear the burden of competent provisions. The security of all would thus be subjected to the parsimony, improvidence, or inability of a part. If the resources of such part becoming more abundant and extensive, its provisions should be proportionally enlarged, the other States would quickly take the alarm at seeing the whole military force of the Union in the hands of two or three of its members, and those probably amongst the most powerful. They would each choose to have some counterpoise, and pretenses could easily be contrived. In this situation, military establishments, nourished by mutual jealousy, would be apt to swell beyond their natural or proper size; and being at the separate disposal of the members, they would be engines for the abridgment or demolition of the national authority.

Reasons have been already given to induce a supposition that the State governments will too naturally be prone to a rivalship with that of the Union, the foundation of which will be the love of power; and that in any contest between the federal head and one of its members the people will be most apt to unite with their local government. If, in addition to this immense advantage, the ambition of the members should be stimulated by the separate and independent possession of military forces, it would afford too strong a temptation and too great a facility to them to make enterprises upon, and finally to subvert, the constitutional authority of the Union. On the other hand, the liberty of the people would be less safe in this state of things than in that which left the national forces in the hands of the national government. As far as an army may be considered as a dangerous weapon of power, it had better be in those hands of which the people are most likely to be jealous than in those of which they are least likely to be jealous. For it is a truth, which the experience of ages has attested, that the people are always most in danger when the means of injuring their rights are in the possession of those of whom they entertain the least suspicion.

The framers of the existing Confederation, fully aware of the danger to the Union from the separate possession of military forces by the States, have, in express terms, prohibited them from having either ships or troops, unless with the consent of Congress. The truth is, that the existence of a federal government and military establishments under State authority are not less at variance with each other than a due supply of the federal treasury and the system of quotas and requisitions.

There are other lights besides those already taken notice of, in which the impropriety of restraints on the discretion of the national legislature will be equally manifest. The design of the objection, which has been mentioned, is to preclude standing armies in time of peace, though we have never been informed how far it is designed the prohibition should extend; whether to raising armies as well as to KEEPING THEM UP in a season of tranquillity or not. If it be confined to the latter it will have no precise signification, and it will be ineffectual for the purpose intended. When armies are once raised what shall be denominated "keeping them up," contrary to the sense of the Constitution? What time shall be requisite to ascertain the violation? Shall it be a week, a month, a year? Or shall we say they may be continued as long as the danger which occasioned their being raised continues? This would be to admit that they might be kept up IN TIME OF PEACE, against threatening or impending danger, which would be at once to deviate from the literal meaning of the prohibition, and to introduce an extensive latitude of construction. Who shall judge of the continuance of the danger? This must undoubtedly be submitted to the national government, and the matter would then be brought to this issue, that the national government, to provide against apprehended danger, might in the first instance raise troops, and might afterwards keep them on foot as long as they supposed the peace or safety of the community was in any degree of jeopardy. It is easy to perceive that a discretion so latitudinary as this would afford ample room for eluding the force of the provision.

The supposed utility of a provision of this kind can only be founded on the supposed probability, or at least possibility, of a combination between the executive and the legislative, in some scheme of usurpation. Should this at any time happen, how easy would it be to fabricate pretenses of approaching danger! Indian hostilities, instigated by Spain or Britain, would always be at hand. Provocations to produce the desired appearances might even be given to some foreign power, and appeased again by timely concessions. If we can reasonably presume

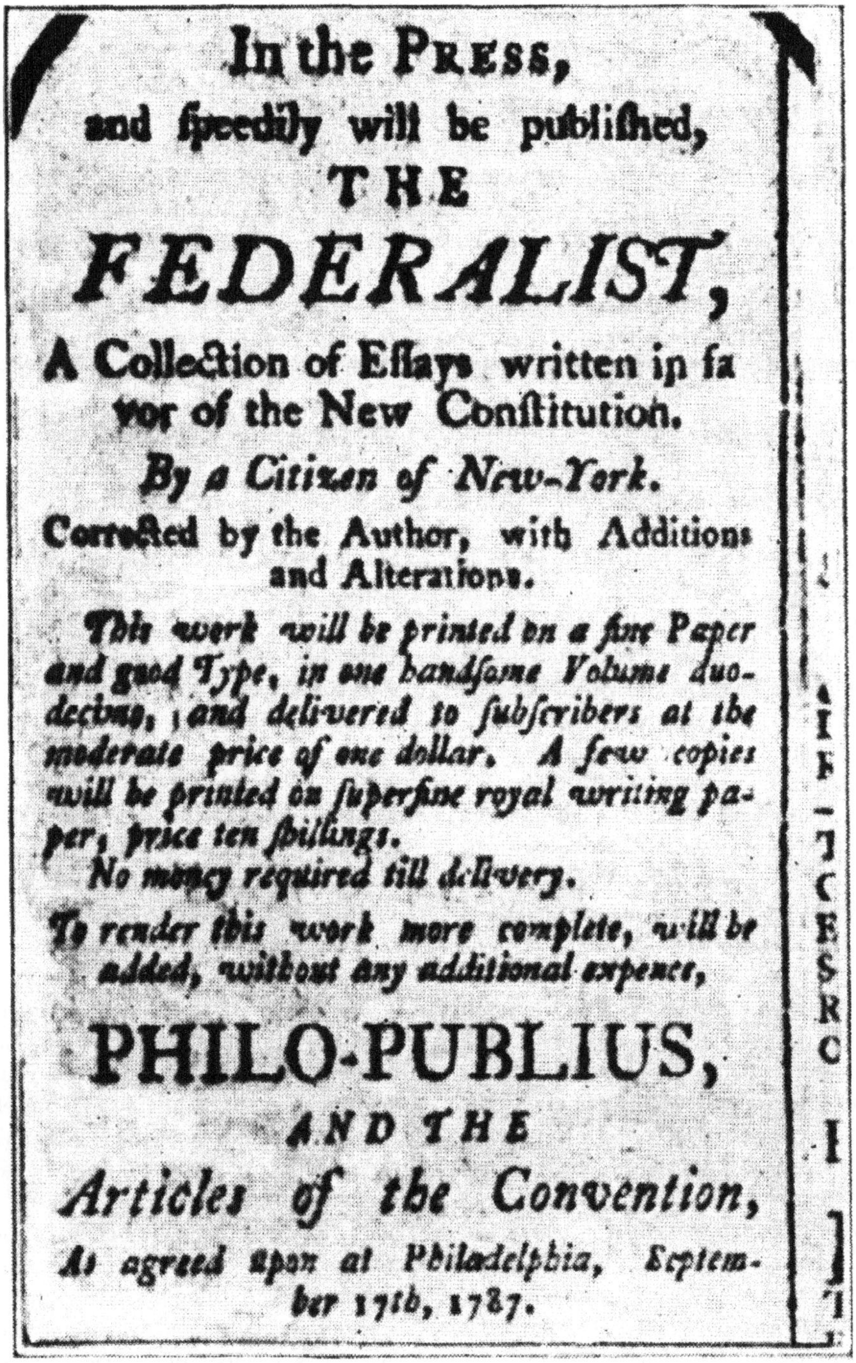

An advertisement for The Federalist, 1787, using the pseudonym "Philo-Publius."

such a combination to have been formed, and that the enterprise is warranted by a sufficient prospect of success, the army, when once raised, from whatever cause, or on whatever pretext, may be applied to the execution of the project.

If, to obviate this consequence, it should be resolved to extend the prohibition to the RAISING of armies in time of peace, the United States would then exhibit the most extraordinary spectacle which the world has yet seen, that of a nation incapacitated by its Constitution to prepare for defense, before it was actually invaded. As the ceremony of a formal denunciation of war has of late fallen into disuse, the presence of an enemy within our territories must be waited for, as the legal warrant to the government to begin its levies of men for the protection of the State. We must receive the blow, before we could even prepare to return it. All that kind of policy by which nations anticipate distant danger, and meet the gathering storm, must be abstained from, as contrary to the genuine maxims of a free government. We must expose our property and liberty to the mercy of foreign invaders, and invite them by our weakness to seize the naked and defenseless prey, because we are afraid that rulers, created by our choice, dependent on our will, might endanger that liberty, by an abuse of the means necessary to its preservation.

Here I expect we shall be told that the militia of the country is its natural bulwark, and would be at all times equal to the national defense. This doctrine, in substance, had like to have lost us our independence. It cost millions to the United States that might have been saved. The facts which, from our own experience, forbid a reliance of this kind, are too recent to permit us to be the dupes of such a suggestion. The steady operations of war against a regular and disciplined army can only be successfully conducted by a force of the same kind. Considerations of economy, not less than of stability and vigor, confirm this position. The American militia, in the course of the late war, have, by their valor on numerous occasions, erected eternal monuments to their fame; but the bravest of them feel and know that the liberty of their country could not have been established by their efforts alone, however great and valuable they were. War, like most other things, is a science to be acquired and perfected by diligence, by perserverance, by time, and by practice.

All violent policy, as it is contrary to the natural and experienced course of human affairs, defeats itself. Pennsylvania, at this instant, affords an example of the truth of this remark. The Bill of Rights of that State declares that standing armies are dangerous to liberty, and ought not to be kept up in time of peace. Pennsylvania, nevertheless, in a time of profound peace, from the existence of partial disorders in one or two of her counties, has resolved to raise a body of troops; and in all probability will keep them up as long as there is any appearance of danger to the public peace. The conduct of Massachusetts affords a lesson on the same subject, though on different ground. That State (without waiting for the sanction of Congress, as the articles of the Confederation require) was compelled to raise troops to quell a domestic insurrection, and still keeps a corps in pay to prevent a revival of the spirit of revolt. The particular constitution of Massachusetts opposed no obstacle to the measure; but the instance is still of use to instruct us that cases are likely to occur under our government, as well as under those of other nations, which will sometimes render a military force in time of peace essential to the security of the society, and that it is therefore improper in this respect to control the legislative discretion. It also teaches us, in its application to the United States, how little the rights of a feeble government are likely to be respected, even by its own constituents. And it teaches us, in addition to the rest, how unequal parchment provisions are to a struggle with public necessity.

It was a fundamental maxim of the Lacedaemonian commonwealth, that the post of admiral should not be conferred twice on the same person. The Peloponnesian confederates, having suffered a severe defeat at sea from the Athenians, demanded Lysander, who had before served with success in that capacity, to command the combined fleets. The Lacedaemonians, to gratify their allies, and yet preserve the semblance of an adherence to their ancient institutions, had recourse to the flimsy subterfuge of investing Lysander with the real power of admiral, under the nominal title of vice-admiral. This instance is selected from among a multitude that might be cited to confirm the truth already advanced and illustrated by domestic examples; which is, that nations pay little regard to rules and maxims calculated in their very nature to run counter to the necessities of society. Wise politicians will be cautious about fettering the government with restrictions that cannot be observed, because they know that every breach of the fundamental laws, though dictated by necessity, impairs that sacred reverence which ought to be maintained in the breast of rulers towards the constitution of a country, and forms a precedent for other breaches where the same plea of necessity does not exist at all, or is less urgent and palpable.

PUBLIUS.

Document Themes

In Federalist 24, Hamilton notes that he has met with criticism about "the creation and direction of the national forces." He comments that critics argue that "proper provision has not been made against the existence of standing armies in time of peace." He goes on to note that the proposed Constitution does not required the existence of a standing army, nor would the executive branch—the president—be given power to raise and direct such an army without the authority of the legislative branch—that is, Congress. He indicates that authority over a national military force would reside with the people through their congressional representatives. He also notes that legislative power over a national military force is limited by the purse, for the Constitution "forbids the appropriation of money for the support of an army for any longer period than two years." The essay then examines the need to maintain a national force in the face of continuing threats from England and Spain, both formidable maritime powers contending for empire in the New World. He notes that individual states, through their militias, would be unequal to the task of fending off incursions by foreign powers, as well as fending off the "ravages and depredations of the Indians."

Federalist 25 continues to counter criticisms of maintaining a standing army during peacetime. Hamilton takes up the question of whether the states rather than the federal government should provide military forces. He argues that turning this responsibility over to the states would undermine the very purpose of forming a federal union, noting that contributing to the common defense would be "oppressive to some States, dangerous to all, and baneful to the Confederacy." He notes that territories under the control of foreign nations surround the states, making the danger they pose a common one to all the states: "The territories of Britain, Spain, and of the Indian nations in our neighborhood do not border on particular States, but encircle the Union from Maine to Georgia. The danger, though in different degrees, is therefore common. And the means of guarding against it ought, in like manner, to be the objects of common councils and of a common treasury." Further, if New York, for example, were attacked (likely by French forces from Canada), the state would have no guarantee that other states would support it in repelling the attack. Hamilton concludes by commenting on the necessity of maintaining a standing military force in peacetime, for failing to do so would render the nation vulnerable to preemptive strikes by foreign nations. He cites as examples Pennsylvania and Massachusetts, which were required to raise armies to quell insurrections and then felt it necessary to maintain those armies to prevent further outbreaks of unrest.

Bibliography and Additional Reading

Allen, William B., and Kevin A. Cloonan, *The Federalist Papers: A Commentary*, 2nd ed. (New York: Peter Lang, 2004).

Brown, David W., "How Alexander Hamilton Solved America's Gun Problem—228 Years Ago," *The Week*, June 15, 2016, http://theweek.com/articles/629815/how-alexander-hamilton-solved-americas-gun-problem--228-years-ago.

Peacock, Anthony A., *How To Read The Federalist Papers* (Washington, D.C.: Heritage Foundation, 2010).

Scott, Kyle, *The Federalist Papers: A Reader's Guide* (New York: Bloomsbury Academic, 2013).

—*Michael J. O'Neal*

James Madison, Hamilton's major collaborator in the Federalist Papers, later President of the United States. (By John Vanderlyn.)

Federalist Paper 46: "The Influence of the State and Federal Governments Compared"

Author(s): Publius (James Madison)
Date: 1788
Genre: Essay

Summary Overview

Federalist Paper 46 was written by James Madison and published in the *New York Packet* newspaper on January 29, 1788. It was one of eighty-five essays written by Madison, Alexander Hamilton, and to a lesser extent, John Jay and published in various newspapers under the name Publius. The purpose to the essays was to influence public opinion with regard to the ratification of the new U.S. Constitution, which had been signed by the delegates to the Constitutional Convention in September. Madison's Federalist Paper on the issue of a standing army and the bearing of arms prefigures the Second Amendment to the Constitution, part of the Bill of Rights for which he was largely responsible.

Defining Moment

The Constitutional Convention was convened in Philadelphia on May 24, 1787, with the purpose of amending the 1781 Articles of Confederation. It was widely believed that the Articles of Confederation was a weak document that led to conflict among the states, granted too much power to the individual states, and left the federal government impotent in key ways. A number of the convention's delegates from the various states, however, arrived in Philadelphia with the intention not just of amending the articles but of creating an entirely new constitution. Among them was James Madison, who would ultimately be largely responsible for the language of the Bill of Rights, including the Second Amendment.

In the fall of 1787, debate about ratification of the proposed new U.S. Constitution, which had been submitted to the states at the conclusion of the convention on September 17, 1787, was heated. The "Federalists," who urged ratification, were put into the position of having to defend their views against those who feared that the new Constitution vested too much power in the federal government at the expense of the states. Federalists (and Antifederalists) published numerous essays in various newspapers throughout the states, arguing for or against ratification. Madison, one of the chief architects of the Constitution, emerged as a prominent political theorist, and his views of government are still invoked today. In Federalist 46, he examined the pressing question of the balance of power between the states and the federal government.

On June 21, 1788, the Constitution was ratified when New Hampshire voted in its favor, and the new government began operations under the Constitution on March 4, 1789.

About the Author

James Madison, who would go on to become the fourth president of the United States, is regarded as the "father" of the Constitution, particularly of the Bill of Rights. He was born on March 5, 1751, in Virginia. In 1771 he graduated from the College of New Jersey, now known as Princeton University. From an early age he was active in politics. In 1776 he was named a member of the First General Assembly of Virginia. In 1780 he was elected to the first of two nonconsecutive terms in the Continental Congress. In 1784 he returned to his native Virginia to take a seat in the Virginia House of Delegates. In the years that followed, he came to recognize that the Articles of Confederation, which dated from 1781, created a central government whose weakness could lead to disunion, rebellion, and even civil war. He thus began to agitate for a convention to draft a new Constitution.

Throughout the 1787 convention, Madison was a leading figure, and it is no exaggeration to say that his views of government, laid out in his notes and resolutions, provided the blueprint for the final document. After the new Constitution was submitted to the states for ratification, he joined with Alexander Hamilton (and to a lesser extent, John Jay) in writing a series of essays, published in various newspapers, that would become the "Federalist Papers." These essays made the case for ratification.

After the Constitution was ratified and the new federal government began operations, with George Washington as the first president, Madison, now a member of the House of Representatives, delivered on the promise of a bill of rights that several of the states had demanded in exchange for their ratification vote. He drafted the language of the Bill of Rights, including the Second Amendment, which Americans still rely on in the defense of their civil liberties. Madison remained a member of the House until 1797. He later served as secretary of state under Thomas Jefferson. Later still, on March 4, 1809, he took the oath of office as president. He went on to serve two terms, shepherding the nation through the War of 1812 with the British. Despite his poor health, he lived to the age of eighty-five, dying on June 28, 1836.

HISTORICAL DOCUMENT

To the People of New York:

RESUMING the subject of the last paper, I proceed to inquire whether the federal government or the State governments will have the advantage with regard to the predilection and support of the people. Notwithstanding the different modes in which they are appointed, we must consider both of them as substantially dependent on the great body of the citizens of the United States. I assume this position here as it respects the first, reserving the proofs for another place. The federal and State governments are in fact but different agents and trustees of the people, constituted with different powers, and designed for different purposes. The adversaries of the Constitution seem to have lost sight of the people altogether in their reasonings on this subject; and to have viewed these different establishments, not only as mutual rivals and enemies, but as uncontrolled by any common superior in their efforts to usurp the authorities of each other. These gentlemen must here be reminded of their error. They must be told that the ultimate authority, wherever the derivative may be found, resides in the people alone, and that it will not depend merely on the comparative ambition or address of the different governments, whether either, or which of them, will be able to enlarge its sphere of jurisdiction at the expense of the other.

Truth, no less than decency, requires that the event in every case should be supposed to depend on the sentiments and sanction of their common constituents. Many considerations, besides those suggested on a former occasion, seem to place it beyond doubt that the first and most natural attachment of the people will be to the governments of their respective States. Into the administration of these a greater number of individuals will expect to rise. From the gift of these a greater number of offices and emoluments will flow. By the superintending care of these, all the more domestic and personal interests of the people will be regulated and provided for. With the affairs of these, the people will be more familiarly and minutely conversant. And with the members of these, will a greater proportion of the people have the ties of personal acquaintance and friendship, and of family and party attachments; on the side of these, therefore, the popular bias may well be expected most strongly to incline. Experience speaks the same language in this case. The federal administration, though hitherto very defective in comparison with what may be hoped under a better system, had, during the war, and particularly whilst the independent fund of paper emissions was in credit, an activity and importance as great as it can well have in any future circumstances whatever. It was engaged, too, in a course of measures which had for their object the protection of everything that was dear, and the acquisition of everything that could be desirable to the people at large.

It was, nevertheless, invariably found, after the transient enthusiasm for the early Congresses was over, that the attention and attachment of the people were turned anew to their own particular governments; that the federal council was at no time the idol of popular favor; and that opposition to proposed enlargements of its powers and importance was the side usually taken by the men who wished to build their political consequence on the prepossessions of their fellow-citizens. If, therefore, as has been elsewhere remarked, the people should in future become more partial to the federal than to the State governments, the change can only result from such manifest and irresistible proofs of a better administration, as will overcome all their antecedent propensities. And in that case, the people ought not surely to be precluded from giving most of their confidence where they may discover it to be most due; but even in that case the State governments could have little to apprehend, because it is only within a certain sphere that the federal power can, in the nature of things, be advantageously administered. The remaining points on which I propose to compare the federal and State governments, are the disposition and the faculty they may respectively possess, to resist and frustrate the measures of each other. It has been already proved that the members of the federal will be more dependent on the members of the State governments, than the latter will be on the former.

It has appeared also, that the prepossessions of the people, on whom both will depend, will be more on the side of the State governments, than of the federal government. So far as the disposition of each towards the other may be influenced by these causes, the State governments must clearly have the advantage. But in a distinct and very important point of view, the advantage will lie on the same side. The prepossessions, which the members themselves will carry into the federal government, will generally be favorable to the States; whilst it will rarely happen, that the members of the State governments will carry into the public councils a bias in favor of the general government. A local spirit will infallibly prevail much more in the members of Congress, than a national spirit will prevail in the legislatures of the particular States.

Every one knows that a great proportion of the errors committed by the State legislatures proceeds from the disposition of the members to sacrifice the comprehensive and permanent interest of the State, to the particular and separate views of the counties or districts in which they reside. And if they do not sufficiently enlarge their policy to embrace the collective welfare of their particular State, how can it be imagined that they will make the aggregate prosperity of the Union, and the dignity and respectability of its government, the objects of their affections and consultations? For the same reason that the members of the State legislatures will be unlikely to attach themselves sufficiently to national objects, the members of the federal legislature will be likely to attach themselves too much to local objects. The States will be to the latter what counties and towns are to the former. Measures will too often be decided according to their probable effect, not on the national prosperity and happiness, but on the prejudices, interests, and pursuits of the governments and people of the individual States. What is the spirit that has in general characterized the proceedings of Congress? A perusal of their journals, as well as the candid acknowledgments of such as have had a seat in that assembly, will inform us, that the members have but too frequently displayed the character, rather of partisans of their respective States, than of impartial guardians of a common interest; that where on one occasion improper sacrifices have been made of local considerations, to the aggrandizement of the federal government, the great interests of the nation have suffered on a hundred, from an undue attention to the local prejudices, interests, and views of the particular States.

I mean not by these reflections to insinuate, that the new federal government will not embrace a more enlarged plan of policy than the existing government may have pursued; much less, that its views will be as confined as those of the State legislatures; but only that it will partake sufficiently of the spirit of both, to be disinclined to invade the rights of the individual States, or the preorgatives of their governments. The motives on the part of the State governments, to augment their prerogatives by defalcations from the federal government, will be overruled by no reciprocal predispositions in the members. Were it admitted, however, that the Federal government may feel an equal disposition with the State governments to extend its power beyond the due limits, the latter would still have the advantage in the means of defeating such encroachments. If an act of a particular State, though unfriendly to the national government, be generally popular in that State and should not too grossly violate the oaths of the State officers, it is executed immediately and, of course, by means on the spot and depending on the State alone. The opposition of the federal government, or the interposition of federal officers, would but inflame the zeal of all parties on the side of the State, and the evil could not be prevented or repaired, if at all, without the employment of means which must always be resorted to with reluctance and difficulty.

On the other hand, should an unwarrantable measure of the federal government be unpopular in particular

States, which would seldom fail to be the case, or even a warrantable measure be so, which may sometimes be the case, the means of opposition to it are powerful and at hand. The disquietude of the people; their repugnance and, perhaps, refusal to co-operate with the officers of the Union; the frowns of the executive magistracy of the State; the embarrassments created by legislative devices, which would often be added on such occasions, would oppose, in any State, difficulties not to be despised; would form, in a large State, very serious impediments; and where the sentiments of several adjoining States happened to be in unison, would present obstructions which the federal government would hardly be willing to encounter. But ambitious encroachments of the federal government, on the authority of the State governments, would not excite the opposition of a single State, or of a few States only. They would be signals of general alarm. Every government would espouse the common cause. A correspondence would be opened. Plans of resistance would be concerted. One spirit would animate and conduct the whole. The same combinations, in short, would result from an apprehension of the federal, as was produced by the dread of a foreign, yoke; and unless the projected innovations should be voluntarily renounced, the same appeal to a trial of force would be made in the one case as was made in the other. But what degree of madness could ever drive the federal government to such an extremity. In the contest with Great Britain, one part of the empire was employed against the other. The more numerous part invaded the rights of the less numerous part. The attempt was unjust and unwise; but it was not in speculation absolutely chimerical. But what would be the contest in the case we are supposing? Who would be the parties? A few representatives of the people would be opposed to the people themselves; or rather one set of representatives would be contending against thirteen sets of representatives, with the whole body of their common constituents on the side of the latter.

The only refuge left for those who prophesy the downfall of the State governments is the visionary supposition that the federal government may previously accumulate a military force for the projects of ambition. The reasonings contained in these papers must have been employed to little purpose indeed, if it could be necessary now to disprove the reality of this danger. That the people and the States should, for a sufficient period of time, elect an uninterupted succession of men ready to betray both; that the traitors should, throughout this period, uniformly and systematically pursue some fixed plan for the extension of the military establishment; that the governments and the people of the States should silently and patiently behold the gathering storm, and continue to supply the materials, until it should be prepared to burst on their own heads, must appear to every one more like the incoherent dreams of a delirious jealousy, or the misjudged exaggerations of a counterfeit zeal, than like the sober apprehensions of genuine patriotism.

Extravagant as the supposition is, let it however be made. Let a regular army, fully equal to the resources of the country, be formed; and let it be entirely at the devotion of the federal government; still it would not be going too far to say, that the State governments, with the people on their side, would be able to repel the danger. The highest number to which, according to the best computation, a standing army can be carried in any country, does not exceed one hundredth part of the whole number of souls; or one twenty-fifth part of the number able to bear arms. This proportion would not yield, in the United States, an army of more than twenty-five or thirty thousand men. To these would be opposed a militia amounting to near half a million of citizens with arms in their hands, officered by men chosen from among themselves, fighting for their common liberties, and united and conducted by governments possessing their affections and confidence. It may well be doubted, whether a militia thus circumstanced could ever be conquered by such a proportion of regular troops. Those who are best acquainted with the last successful resistance of this country against the British arms, will be most inclined to deny the possibility of it. Besides the advantage of being armed, which the Americans possess over the people of almost every other nation, the existence of subordinate governments, to which the people are attached, and by which the militia officers are appointed, forms a barrier against the enterprises of ambition, more insurmountable than any which a simple government of any form can admit of. Notwithstanding the military establishments in the several kingdoms of Europe, which are carried as far as the public resources will bear, the governments are afraid to trust the people with arms. And it is not certain, that with this aid alone they would not be able to shake off their yokes. But were the people to possess the additional advantages of local governments chosen by themselves, who could collect the national will and direct the national force, and of officers appointed out of the militia, by these governments, and attached both to them and to the militia, it may be affirmed with the greatest assurance, that the throne of every tyranny in Europe would be speedily overturned in spite of the legions which surround it.

Let us not insult the free and gallant citizens of America with the suspicion, that they would be less able to defend the rights of which they would be in actual possession, than the debased subjects of arbitrary power would be to rescue theirs from the hands of their oppressors. Let us rather no longer insult them with the supposition that they can ever reduce themselves to the necessity of making the experiment, by a blind and tame submission to the long train of insidious measures which must precede and produce it. The argument under the present head may be put into a very concise form, which appears altogether conclusive. Either the mode in which the federal government is to be constructed will render it sufficiently dependent on the people, or it will not. On the first supposition, it will be restrained by that dependence from forming schemes obnoxious to their constituents. On the other supposition, it will not possess the confidence of the people, and its schemes of usurpation will be easily defeated by the State governments, who will be supported by the people. On summing up the considerations stated in this and the last paper, they seem to amount to the most convincing evidence, that the powers proposed to be lodged in the federal government are as little formidable to those reserved to the individual States, as they are indispensably necessary to accomplish the purposes of the Union; and that all those alarms which have been sounded, of a meditated and consequential annihilation of the State governments, must, on the most favorable interpretation, be ascribed to the chimerical fears of the authors of them.

PUBLIUS.

Document Themes

Federalist 46 (along with 45) takes up the question of whether the people were more likely to support the federal government or the governments of their states. Madison notes that the state governments are closer to the people and their interests and concerns, and therefore are more likely to win popular support. For this reason, Madison argues that the federal government was unlikely to encroach on the authority of the states. At the same time, he argues that a stronger national government is needed as a counterweight to the parochial interests of the states: "Measures will too often be decided according to their probable effect, not on the national prosperity and happiness, but on the prejudices, interests, and pursuits of the governments and people of the individual States." Madison goes on to note that "should an unwarrantable measure of the federal government be unpopular in particular States, which would seldom fail to be the case, or even a warrantable measure be so, which may sometimes be the case, the means of opposition to it are powerful and at hand." Among these means is "the disquietude of the people."

Madison then turns to issues that have a bearing on the right to bear arms and what would evolve into the Second Amendment. "The only refuge left for those who prophesy the downfall of the State governments is the visionary supposition that the federal government may previously accumulate a military force for the projects of ambition." Madison scoffs at this fear, stating that it "must appear to every one more like the incoherent dreams of a delirious jealousy, or the misjudged exaggerations of a counterfeit zeal, than like the sober apprehensions of genuine patriotism." Madison then argues that the state governments would be equal to the task of repelling a military incursion by the federal government. He notes:

> The highest number to which, according to the best computation, a standing army can be carried in any country, does not exceed one hundredth part of the whole number of souls; or one twenty-fifth part of the number able to bear arms. This proportion would not yield, in the United States, an army of more than twenty-five or thirty thousand men. To these would be opposed a militia amounting to near half a million of citizens with arms in their hands

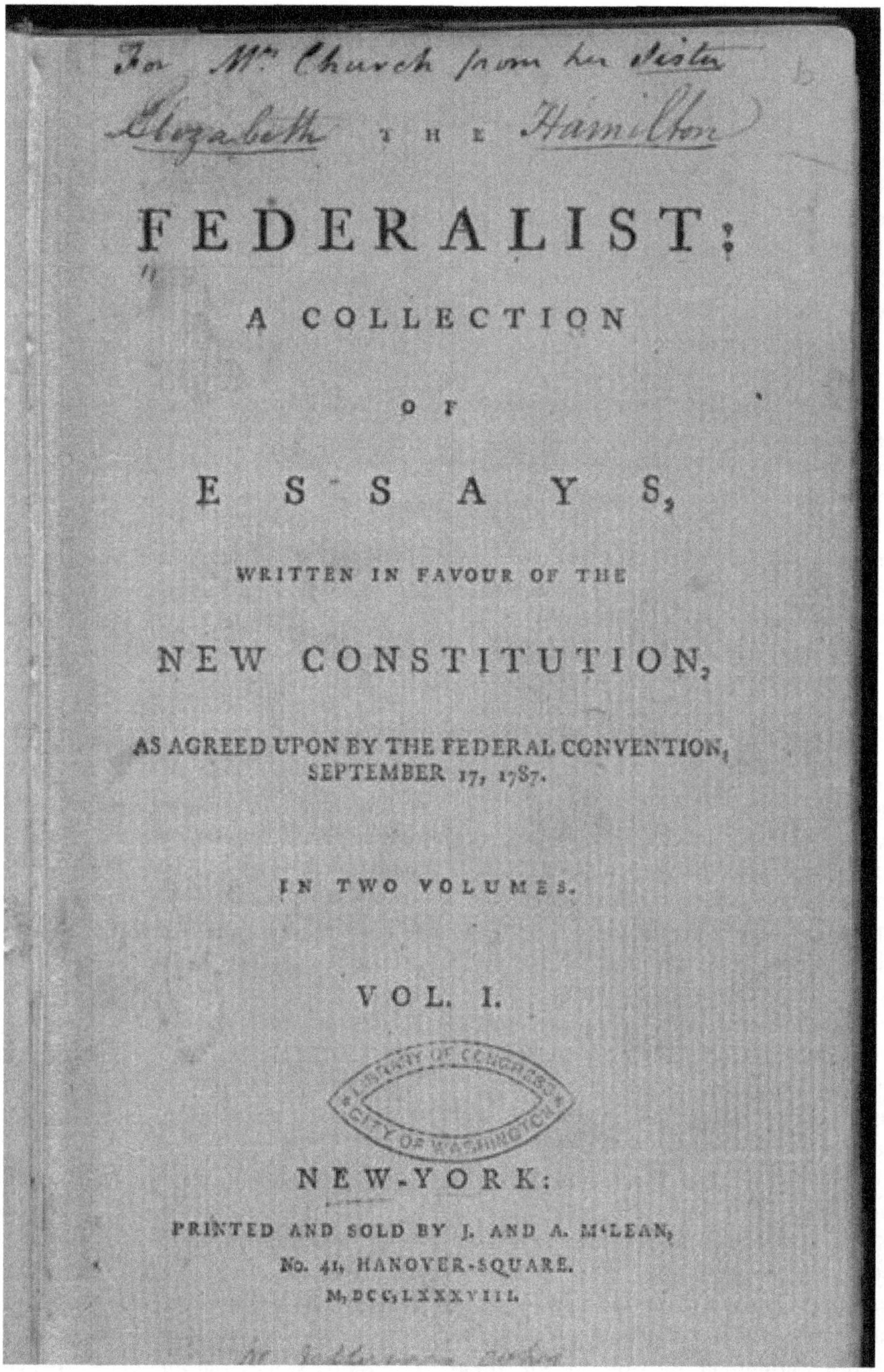

For Mrs Church from her Sister
Elizabeth Hamilton

THE

FEDERALIST:

A COLLECTION

OF

ESSAYS,

WRITTEN IN FAVOUR OF THE

NEW CONSTITUTION,

AS AGREED UPON BY THE FEDERAL CONVENTION, SEPTEMBER 17, 1787.

IN TWO VOLUMES.

VOL. I.

LIBRARY OF CONGRESS CITY OF WASHINGTON

NEW-YORK:

PRINTED AND SOLD BY J. AND A. M'LEAN, No. 41, HANOVER-SQUARE.

M,DCC,LXXXVIII.

Title page of Publius (pseudonym) [Alexander Hamilton, John Jay, James Madison] (1788) The Federalist: A Collection of Essays, Written in Favour of the New Constitution, as Agreed upon by the Federal Convention, September 17, 1787. *In Two Volumes. (1st ed.), New York, N.Y.: Printed and sold by J. and A. McLean, No. 41, Hanover-Square* OCLC: 642792893. *This copy is from the Rare Books and Special Collections Division of the Library of Congress.*

Put simply, the states would marshal more firepower than the federal government because of an armed citizenry. He calls attention to "the advantage of being armed, which the Americans possess over the people of almost every other nation." He goes on to state: "Notwithstanding the military establishments in the several kingdoms of Europe, which are carried as far as the public resources will bear, the governments are afraid to trust the people with arms"—in contrast to the United States.

In historical examinations of the Second Amendment, these passages are frequently invoked by gun rights advocates who regard Madison's words as strongly indicating that the framers of the Constitution were codifying an individual right to bear arms.

Additional Reading

Allen, William B., and Kevin A. Cloonan, *The Federalist Papers: A Commentary*, 2nd ed. (New York: Peter Lang, 2004).

Baron, Dennis, "Guns and Grammar: the Linguistics of the Second Amendment," University of Illinois English Department, https://www.english.illinois.edu/-people-/faculty/debaron/essays/guns.pdf

Brown, David W., "How Alexander Hamilton Solved America's Gun Problem—228 Years Ago," *The Week*, June 15, 2016, http://theweek.com/articles/629815/how-alexander-hamilton-solved-americas-gun-problem--228-years-ago

Dorf, Michael, "Federalist 46 and the Second Amendment," Dorf on Law website, February 21, 2018, http://www.dorfonlaw.org/2018/02/federalist-46-and-second-amendment.html

Peacock, Anthony A., *How To Read The Federalist Papers* (Washington, D.C.: Heritage Foundation, 2010).

Scott, Kyle, *The Federalist Papers: A Reader's Guide* (New York: Bloomsbury Academic, 2013).

Shalhope, Robert E., "The Ideological Origins of the Second Amendment," *Journal of American History*, Vol. 69 (1982): 599–614.

Tracinski, Robert, "How the Second Amendment Prevents Tyranny," *The Federalist*, March 22, 2018, http://thefederalist.com/2018/03/22/how-the-second-amendment-prevents-tyranny/

—*Michael J. O'Neal*

A 19th century depiction of young Elizabeth Zane's legendary feat of retrieving powder during the Revolutionary War. (Lithograph by Nagel and Weingaertne.)

House of Representatives Debate on the Second Amendment

Author(s): Various (including Elbridge Gerry)
Date: August 17, 1789
Genre: Debate

Summary Overview

In 1789, following the ratification of the new U.S. Constitution, the government opened for business on March 4 with the inauguration of President George Washington and the convening of Congress. That summer, the House of Representatives debated proposals pertaining to amendments to the Constitution. These amendments were not intended to affect the structure and operation of the federal government, but rather to safeguard the civil rights of the American people. These amendments were originally intended to be just that—amendments to the text of the Constitution. Ultimately, however, they were affixed to the Constitution as the Bill of Rights, the document's first ten amendments. One of the issues debated had to do with the militia and the right of Americans to bear arms.

Defining Moment

On May 25, 1787, the Constitutional Convention convened in Philadelphia, Pennsylvania, with the express purpose of revising the 1781 Articles of Confederation. As matters turned out, the framers scrapped the articles in favor of a new Constitution, one that strengthened the nation by giving the federal government more power. At the conclusion of the convention on September 17, the Constitution was submitted to the delegates for signing, then to the states for ratification. The Constitution was ratified on June 21, 1788, when New Hampshire became the ninth state to ratify it.

Meanwhile, on September 12, George Mason of Virginia, a primary author of the Virginia Bill of Rights, proposed the addition of a bill of rights to the Constitution, but his proposal was unanimously defeated. Nevertheless, supporters of ratification ("Federalists") agreed that the new Constitution would be more palatable to Antifederalists such as Thomas Jefferson, who feared a strong central government and its potential for tyranny, if the promise of a Bill of Rights was made clear. And they were right, for it is highly likely that the Constitution would not have been ratified without the expectation that a bill of rights would be appended.

Thus, on June 8, 1789, Representative James Madison, one of the Constitution's primary authors, introduced nine amendments in the House of Representatives; these amendments were initially intended to be incorporated into the main text of the Constitution. On July 28, a House select committee issued a report on Madison's proposals. From August 13 to August 24, members of the House of Representatives debated the various proposed amendments, including an amendment having to do with the right to bear arms. On September 24, ten amendments that would make up the Bill of Rights passed in the House; the following day the proposal passed in the Senate. The Bill of Rights underwent its own ratification process and became the first ten amendments to the Constitution on December 15, 1791, when Virginia ratified it. Oddly, it was not until 1939 that Connecticut, Georgia, and Massachusetts ratified the first ten amendments.

About the Author

No particular individual, of course, can be identified as the "author" of a debate recorded in the *Congressional Register.* However, one of the representatives who raised questions about what would become the Second Amendment was Elbridge Gerry of Massachusetts. Gerry was born in Marblehead, Massachusetts, on July 17, 1744, to a thriving mercantile family. He entered Harvard College in 1758; after graduation, he returned home to join the business. In the 1760s and 1770, he was acutely aware of the political developments that would lead to the Revolutionary War. He was elected to the second Continental Congress in December 1775, and would later be one of the signers of the Declaration of Independence.

He served in the Continental Congress until 1780, then again from 1783 to 1785.

Gerry was one of four delegates the Massachusetts legislature chose to take part in the 1787 Constitutional Convention, where he proved to be an active participant. During that summer, he began to worry that the proposed new constitution was creating a powerful national government that could trample on people's liberties and on the prerogatives of the states. The convention would adopt several of his proposals to limit the power of Congress, but he continued to regard the new document as flawed. Accordingly, he offered a motion to include a bill of rights and made other specific proposals designed to protect popular liberties, but the convention rejected his initiatives. Initially, he concluded that he could not support the new constitution as written, yet at the same time he feared that anarchy could result if the states failed to ratify it. He abandoned his initial call for a second convention and instead worked to garner support for amendments that would preserve liberties.

Gerry went on to serve in the House of Representatives from 1789 to 1793, and as a member of the House, he took part in the debates surrounding what would evolve into the Bill of Rights. In the years that followed, he was in and out of politics. He was elected governor of Massachusetts in 1810, in that capacity, backing a controversial redistricting plan that would give Republicans the advantage in state senatorial elections. In response, the press ran a cartoon of a salamander-shaped electoral district, giving rise to the word "gerrymandering," which still today refers to forming an irregularly shaped district designed to give an advantage to a political party or group.

On March 4, 1813, Gerry took the oath of office as the nation's fifth vice president, serving under James Madison. He died on November 23, 1814.

Aedanus Burke (June 16, 1743– March 30, 1802), who also contributed to the debates, was a judge and U.S. congressional representative from South Carolina. He was an Antifederalist, opposed to ratification of the new Constitution.

HISTORICAL DOCUMENT

The house went into a committee of the whole, on the subject of amendments. The 3d clause of the 4th proposition in the report was taken into consideration, being as follows; "A well regulated militia, composed of the body of the people, being the best security of a free state; the right of the people to keep and bear arms shall not be infringed, but no person, religiously scrupulous, shall be compelled to bear arms."

Mr. GERRY.

This declaration of rights, I take it, is intended to secure the people against the maladministration of the government; if we could suppose that in all cases the rights of the people would be attended to, the occasion for guards of this kind would be removed. Now I am apprehensive, sir, that this clause would give an opportunity to the people in power to destroy the constitution itself. They can declare who are those religiously scrupulous, and prevent them from bearing arms. What, sir, is the use of a militia? It is to prevent the establishment of a standing army, the bane of liberty. Now it must be evident, that under this provision, together with their other powers, congress could take such measures with respect to a militia, as make a standing army necessary. Whenever government mean to invade the rights and liberties of the people, they always attempt to destroy the militia, in order to raise an army upon their ruins. This was actually done by Great Britain at the commencement of the late revolution. They used every means in their power to prevent the establishment of an effective militia to the eastward. The assembly of Massachusetts, seeing the rapid progress that administration were making, to divest them of their inherent privileges, endeavored to counteract them by the organization of the militia, but they were always defeated by the influence of the crown.

Mr. SENEY

Wished to know what question there was before the committee, in order to ascertain the point upon which the gentleman was speaking?

Mr. GERRY

Replied, that he meant to make a motion, as he disapproved of the words as they stood. He then proceeded,

No attempts that they made, were successful, until they engaged in the struggle which emancipated them at once from their thralldom. Now, if we give a discretionary power to exclude those from militia duty who have religious scruples, we may as well make no provision on this head; for this reason he wished the words to be altered so as to be confined to persons belonging to a religious sect, scrupulous of bearing arms.

Mr. JACKSON

Did not expect that all the people of the United States would turn Quakers or Moravians, consequently one part would have to defend the other, in case of invasion; now this, in his opinion, was unjust, unless the constitution secured an equivalent, for this reason he moved to amend the clause, by inserting at the end of it "upon paying an equivalent to be established by law." Mr. SMITH, (of S. C.) Enquired what were the words used by the conventions respecting this amendment; if the gentleman would conform to what was proposed by Virginia and Carolina, he would second him: He thought they were to be excused provided they found a substitute.

Mr. JACKSON

Was willing to accommodate; he thought the expression was, "No one, religiously scrupulous of bearing arms, shall be compelled to render military service in person, upon paying an equivalent."

Mr. SHERMAN

Conceived it difficult to modify the clause and make it better. It is well-known that those who are religiously scrupulous of bearing arms, are equally scrupulous of getting substitutes or paying an equivalent; many of them would rather die than do either one or the other–but he did not see an absolute necessity for a clause of this kind. We do not live under an arbitrary government, said he, and the states respectively will have the government of the militia, unless when called into actual service; beside, it would not do to alter it so as to exclude the whole of any sect, because there are men amongst the quakers who will turn out, notwithstanding the religious principles of the society, and defend the cause of their country. Certainly it will be improper to prevent the exercise of such favorable dispositions, at least whilst it is the practice of nations to determine their contests by the slaughter of their citizens and subjects.

Mr. VINING

Hoped the clause would be suffered to remain as it stood, because he saw no use in it if it was amended so as to compel a man to find a substitute, which, with respect to the government, was the same as if the person himself turned out to fight.

Mr. STONE

Enquired what the words "Religiously scrupulous" had reference to, was it of bearing arms? If it was, it ought so to be expressed.

Mr. BENSON

Moved to have the words "But no person religiously scrupulous shall be compelled to bear arms" struck out. He would always leave it to the benevolence of the legislature—for, modify it, said he, as you please, it will be impossible to express it in such a manner as to clear it from ambiguity. No man can claim this indulgence of right. It may be a religious persuasion, but it is no natural right, and therefore ought to be left to the discretion of the government. If this stands part of the constitution, it will be a question before the judiciary, on every regulation you make with respect to the organization of the militia, whether it comports with this declaration or not? It is extremely injudicious to intermix matters of doubt with fundamentals. I have no reason to believe but the legislature will always possess humanity enough to indulge this class of citizens in a matter they are so desirous of, but they ought to be left to their discretion. The motion for striking out the whole clause being seconded, was put, and decided in the negative, 22 members voting for it, and 24 against it.

Mr. GERRY

Objected to the first part of the clause, on account of the uncertainty with which it is expressed: A well-regulated militia being the best security of a free state, admitted an idea that a standing army was a secondary one. It ought to read "a well regulated militia, trained to arms," in which case it would become the duty of the government to provide this security, and furnish a greater certainty of its being done. Mr. GERRY'S motion not being seconded, the question was put on the clause as reported, which being adopted,

Mr. BURKE
Proposed to add to the clause just agreed to, an amendment to the following effect: "A standing army of regular troops in time of peace, is dangerous to public liberty, and such shall not be raised or kept up in time of peace but from necessity, and for the security of the people, nor then without the consent of two-thirds of the members present of both houses, and in all cases the military shall be subordinate to the civil authority." This being seconded, Mr. VINING Asked whether this was to be considered as an addition to the last clause, or an amendment by itself? If the former, he would remind the gentleman the clause was decided; if the latter, it was improper to introduce new matter, as the house had referred the report specially to the committee of the whole.

Mr. BURKE
Feared that what with being trammelled in rules, and the apparent disposition of the committee, he should not be able to get them to consider any amendment; he submitted to such proceeding because he could not help himself.

SUPPLEMENTAL HISTORICAL DOCUMENT

A letter, attributed to either Richard Henry Lee and Melancton Smith, known as the Federal Farmer, and published in the Poughkeepsie Country Journal, considered some of the best writing of the Antifederalists and which became an important part of the debate surrounding the ratification of the U.S. constitution.

LETTER XVIII.

January 25, 1788.

Dear Sir,

I am persuaded, a federal head never was formed, that possessed half the powers which it could carry into full effect, altogether independently of the state or local governments, as the one, the convention has proposed, will possess. Should the state legislatures never meet, except merely for chusing federal senators and appointing electors, once in four and six years, the federal head may go on for ages to make all laws relative to the following subjects, and by its own courts, officers, and provisions, carry them into full effect, and to any extent it may deem for the general welfare; that is, for raising taxes, borrowing and coining monies, and for applying them — for forming and governing armies and navies, and for directing their operations — for regulating commerce with foreign nations, and among the several states, and with the Indian tribes — for regulating bankruptcies, weights and measures, post-offices and post-roads, and captures on land and water — for establishing a uniform rule of naturalization, and for promoting the progress of science and useful arts — for defining and punishing piracies and felonies committed on the high seas, the offences of counterfeiting the securities and current coin of the United States, and offences against the law of nations, and for regulating all maritime concerns — for organizing, arming and disciplining the militia (the respective states training them, and appointing the officers) — for calling them forth when wanted, and for governing them when in the service of the union — for the sole and exclusive government of a federal city or town, not exceeding ten miles square, and of places ceded for forts, magazines, arsenals, dock-yards, and other needful buildings — for granting letters of marque and reprisal, and making war — for regulating the times, places, and manner of holding elections for senators and representatives — for making and concluding all treaties, and carrying them into execution — for judicially deciding all questions arising on the constitution, laws, and treaties of the union, in law and equity, and questions arising on state laws also, where ambassadors, other public ministers, and consuls, where the United States, individual states, or a state, where citizens of different states, and where foreign states, or a foreign subject, are parties or party — for impeaching and trying federal officers — for deciding on elections, and for expelling members, &c. All these enumerated powers we must examine and contemplate in all their extent and various branches, and then reflect, that the federal head will have full power to make all laws whatever respecting them; and for carrying into full effect all powers vested in the union, in any department, or officers of it, by the constitution, in order to see the full extent of the federal powers, which will be supreme, and exercised by that head at pleasure, conforming to the few limitations mentioned in the constitution. Indeed, I conceive, it is impossible to see them in their full extent at present: we see vast undefined powers lodged in a weak organization, but cannot, by the enquiries of months and years, clearly discern them in all their numerous branches. These powers in feeble hands, must be tempting objects for ambition and a love of power and fame.

But, say the advocates, they are all necessary for forming an energetic federal government; all necessary in the hands of the union, for the common defence and general welfare. In these great points they appear to me to go from the end to the means, and from the means to the end, perpetually begging the question. I think in the course of these letters, I shall sufficiently prove, that some of these powers need not be lodged in the hands of the union — that others ought to be exercised under better checks, and in part, by the agency of the states-some I have already considered, some in my mind, are not liable to objections, and the others, I shall briefly notice in this closing letter.

The power to controul the military forces of the country, as well as the revenues of it, requires serious attention. Here again, I must premise, that a federal republic is a compound system, made up of constituent parts, each essential to the whole: we must then expect the real friends of such a system will always be very anxious for the security and preservation of each part, and to this end, that each constitutionally possess its natural portion of power and influence — and that it will constantly be an object of concern to them, to see one part armed at all points by the constitution, and in a manner destructive in the end, even of its own existence, and the others left constitutionally defenceless.

The military forces of a free country may be considered under three general descriptions — 1. The militia. 2. the navy — and 3. the regular troops — and the whole ought ever to be, and understood to be, in strict subordination to the civil authority; and that regular troops, and select corps, ought not to be kept up without evident necessity. Stipulations in the constitution to this effect, are perhaps, too general to be of much service, except merely to impress on the minds of the people and soldiery, that the military ought ever to be subject to the civil authority, &c. But particular attention, and many more definite stipulations, are highly necessary to render the military safe, and yet useful in a free government; and in a federal republic, where the people meet in distinct assemblies, many stipulations are necessary to keep a part from transgressing, which would be unnecessary checks against the whole met in one legislature, in one entire government. — A militia, when properly formed, are in fact the people themselves, and render regular troops in a great measure unnecessary. The powers to form and arm the militia, to appoint their officers, and to command their services, are very important; nor ought they in a confederated republic to be lodged, solely, in any one member of the government. First, the constitution ought to secure a genuine and guard against a select militia, by providing that the militia shall always be kept well organized, armed, and disciplined, and include, according to the past and general usuage of the states, all men capable of bearing arms; and that all regulations tending to render this general militia useless and defenceless, by establishing select corps of militia, or distinct bodies of military men, not having permanent interests and attachments in the community to be avoided. I am persuaded, I need not multiply words to convince you of the value and solidity of this principle, as it respects general liberty, and the duration of a free and mild government: having this principle well fixed by the constitution, then the federal head may prescribe a general uniform plan, on which the respective states shall form and train the militia, appoint their officers and solely manage them, except when called into the service of the union, and when called into that service, they may be commanded and governed by the union. This arrangement combines energy and safety in it; it places the sword in the hands of the solid interest of the community, and not in the hands of men destitute of property, of principle, or of attachment to the society and government, who often form the select corps of peace or ordinary establishments: by it, the militia are the people, immediately under the management of the state governments, but on a uniform federal plan, and called into the service, command, and government of the union, when necessary for the common defence and general tranquility. But, say gentlemen, the general militia are for the most part employed at home in their private concerns, cannot well be called out, or be depended upon; that we must have a select militia; that is, as I understand it, particular corps or bodies of young men, and of men who have but little to do at home, particularly armed and disciplined in some measure, at the public expence, and always ready to take the field. These corps, not much unlike regular troops, will ever produce an inattention to the general militia; and the consequence has ever been, and always must be, that the substantial men, having families and property, will generally be without arms, without knowing the use of them, and defenceless; whereas, to preserve liberty, it is essential that the whole body of the people always possess arms, and be taught alike, especially when young, how to use them; nor does it follow from this, that all promiscuously must go into actual service on every occasion. The mind that aims at a select militia, must be influenced by a truly anti-republican principle; and when we see many men disposed to practice upon it, whenever they can prevail, no wonder true republicans are for carefully guarding against it. As a farther check, it may be proper to add, that the militia of any state shall not remain in the service of the union, beyond a given period, without the express consent of the state legislature.

As to the navy, I do not see that it can have any connection with the local governments. The want of employment for it, and the want of monies in the hands of the union, must be its proper limitation. The laws for building or increasing it, as all the important laws mentioned in a former letter, touching military and money matters, may be checked by requiring the attendance of a large proportion of the representatives, and the consent of a large proportion of those present, to pass them as before mentioned.

By art. 1. sect. 8. "Congress shall have power to provide for organizing, arming, and disciplining the militia": power to provide for — does this imply any more than power to prescribe a general uniform plan? And must not the respective states pass laws (but in conformity to the plan) for forming and training the militia.

In the present state of mankind, and of conducting war, the government of every nation must have power to raise and keep up regular troops: the question is, how shall this power be lodged? In an entire government, as in Great-Britain, where the people assemble by their representatives in one legislature, there is no difficulty, it is of course properly lodged in that legislature: But in a confederated republic, where the organization consists of a federal head, and local governments, there is no one part in which it can be solely, and safely lodged. By art. 1. sect. 8. "congress shall have power to raise and support armies," &c.

By art. 1. sect. 10. "no state, without the consent of congress, shall keep troops, or ships of war, in time of peace." It seems fit the union should direct the raising of troops, and the union may do it in two ways; by requisitions on the states, or by direct taxes — the first is most conformable to the federal plan, and safest; and it may be improved, by giving the union power, by its own laws and officers, to raise the states quota that may neglect, and to charge it with the expence; and by giving a fixed quorum of the state legislatures power to disapprove the requisition. There would be less danger in this power to raise troops, could the state governments keep a proper controul over the purse and over the militia; but after all the precautions we can take, without evidently fettering the union too much, we must give a large accumulation of powers to it, in these and other respects. There is one check, which, I think, may be added with great propriety — that is, no land forces shall be kept up, but by legislative acts annually passed by congress, and no appropriation of monies for their support shall be for a longer term than one year. This is the constitutional practice in Great-Britain, and the reasons for such checks in the United States appear to be much stronger. We may also require that these acts be passed by a special majority, as before mentioned. There is another mode still more guarded, and which seems to be founded in the true spirit of a federal system: it seems proper to divide those powers we can with safety, lodge them in no one member of the government alone; yet substantially to preserve their use, and to ensure duration to the government, by modifying the exercise of them — it is to empower congress to raise troops by direct levies, not exceeding a given number, say 2000 in time of peace, and 12,000 in a time of war, and for such further troops as may be wanted, to raise them by requisitions qualified as before mentioned. By the above recited clause no state shall keep troops, &c. in time of peace — this clearly implies, it may do it in time of war: this must be on the principle, that the union cannot defend all parts of the republic, and suggests an idea very repugnant to the general tendency of the system proposed, which is to disarm the state governments: a state in a long war may collect forces sufficient to take the field against the neighbouring states. This clause was copied from the confederation, in which it was of more importance than in the plan proposed, because under this the separate states, probably, will have but small revenues. By article 1. section 8. congress shall have power to establish uniform laws on the subject of bankruptcies, throughout the United States. It is to be observed, that the separate states have ever been in possession of the power, and in the use of it, of making bankrupt laws, militia laws, and laws in some other cases, respecting which, the new constitution, when adopted, will give the union power to legislate, &c. — but no words are used by the constitution to exclude the jurisdiction of the several states, and whether they will be excluded or not, or whether they and the union will have concurrent jurisdiction or not, must be determined by inference; and from the nature of the subject; if the power, for instance, to make uniform laws on the subject of bankruptcies, is in its nature indivisible, or incapable of being exercised by two legislatures independently, or by one in aid of the other, then the states are excluded, and cannot legislate at all on the subject, even though the union should neglect or find it impracticable to establish uniform bankrupt laws. How far the union will find it practicable to do this, time only can fully determine. When we consider the extent of the country, and the very different ideas of the different parts in it, respecting credit, and the mode of making men's property liable for paying their debts, we may, I think, with some degree of certainty, conclude that the union never will be able to establish such laws; but if practicable, it does not appear to me, on further reflection, that the union ought to have the power; it does not appear to me to be a power properly incidental to a federal head, and, I believe, no one ever possessed it; it is a power that will immediately and extensively interfere with the internal police of the separate states, especially with their administering justice among their own citizens. By giving this power to the union, we greatly extend the jurisdiction of the federal judiciary, as all questions arising on bankrupt laws, being laws of the union, even between citizens of the same state, may be tried in the federal courts; and I think it may be shewn, that by the help of these laws, actions between citizens of different states, and the laws of the federal city, aided by no overstrained judicial fictions, almost all civil causes may be drawn into those courts. We must be sensible how cautious we ought to be in extending unnecessarily the jurisdiction of those courts for reasons I need not repeat. This article of power too, will considerably increase, in the hands of the union, an accumulation of powers, some of a federal and some of a unfederal nature, too large without it.

The constitution provides, that congress shall have the sole and exclusive government of what is called the federal city, a place not exceeding ten miles square, and of all places ceded for forts, dock-yards, &c. I believe this is a novel kind of provision in a federal republic; it is repugnant to the spirit of such a government, and must be founded in an apprehension of a hostile disposition between the federal head and the state governments; and it is not improbable, that the sudden retreat of congress from Philadelphia, first gave rise to it. — With this apprehension, we provide, the government of the union shall have secluded places, cities, and castles of defence, which no state laws whatever shall invade. When we attentively examine this provision in all its consequences, it opens to view scenes almost without bounds. A federal, or rather a national city, ten miles square, containing a hundred square miles, is about four times as large as London; and for forts, magazines, arsenals, dock-yards, and other needful buildings, congress may possess a number of places or towns in each state. It is true, congress cannot have them unless the state legislatures cede them; but when once ceded, they never can be recovered, and though the general temper of the legislatures may be averse to such cessions, yet many opportunities and advantages may be taken of particular times and circumstances of complying assemblies, and of particular parties, to obtain them. It is not improbable, that some considerable towns or places, in some intemperate moments, or influenced by anti-republican principles, will petition to be ceded for the purposes mentioned in the provision. There are men, and even towns, in the best republics, which are often fond of withdrawing from the government of them, whenever occasion shall present. The case is still stronger; if the provision in question holds out allurements to attempt to withdraw, the people of a state must ever be subject to state as well as federal taxes; but the federal city and places will be subject only to the latter, and to them by no fixed proportion; nor of the taxes raised in them, can the separate states demand any account of congress. — These doors opened for withdrawing from the state governments entirely, may, on other accounts, be very alluring and pleasing to those anti-republican men who prefer a place under the wings of courts.

If a federal town be necessary for the residence of congress and the public officers, it ought to be a small one, and the government of it fixed on republican and common law principles, carefully enumerated and established by the constitution. It is true, the states, when they shall cede places, may stipulate, that the laws and government of congress in them, shall always be formed on such principles; but it is easy to discern, that the stipulations of a state, or of the inhabitants of the place ceded, can be of but little avail against the power and gradual encroachments of the union. The principles ought to be established by the federal constitution, to which all the states are parties; but in no event can there be any need of so large a city and places for forts, &c. totally exempted from the laws and jurisdictions of the state governments. If I understand the constitution, the laws of congress, constitutionally made, will have complete and supreme jurisdiction to all federal purposes, on every inch of ground in the United States, and exclusive jurisdiction on the high seas, and this by the highest authority, the consent of the people. Suppose ten acres at West-Point shall be used as a fort of the union, or a sea port town as a dock-yard, the laws of the union in those places respecting the navy, forces of the union, and all federal objects, must prevail, be noticed by all judges and officers, and executed accordingly: and I can discern no one reason for excluding from these places, the operation of state laws, as to mere state purposes; for instance, for the collection of state taxes in them, recovering debts, deciding questions of property arising within them on state laws, punishing, by state laws, theft, trespasses, and offences committed in them by mere citizens against the state laws.

The city, and all the places in which the union shall have this exclusive jurisdiction, will be immediately under one entire government, that of the federal head; and be no part of any state, and consequently no part of the United States. The inhabitants of the federal city and places, will be as much exempt from the laws and controul of the state governments, as the people of Canada or Nova Scotia will be. Neither the laws of the states respecting taxes, the militia, crimes or property, will extend to them; nor is there a single stipulation in the constitution, that the inhabitants of this city, and these places, shall be governed by laws founded on principles of freedom. All questions, civil and criminal, arising on the laws of these places, which must be the laws of congress, must be decided in the federal courts; and also, all questions that may, by such judicial fictions as these courts may consider reasonable, be supposed to arise within this city, or any of these places, may be brought into these courts; and by a very common legal fiction, any personal contract may be supposed to have been made in any place. A contract made in Georgia may be supposed to have been made in the federal city, in Pennsylvania; the courts will admit the fiction, and not in these cases, make it a serious question, where it was in fact made. Every suit in which an inhabitant of a federal district may be a party, of course may be instituted in the federal courts — also, every suit in which it may be alledged, and not denied, that a party in it is an inhabitant of such a district — also, every suit to which a foreign state or subject, the union, a state, citizens of different states, in fact, or by reasonable legal fictions, may be a party or parties: And thus, by means of bankrupt laws, federal districts, &c. almost all judicial business, I apprehend may be carried into the federal courts, without essentially departing from the usual course of judicial proceedings. The courts in Great Britain have acquired their powers, and extended, very greatly, their jurisdictions by such fictions and suppositions as I have mentioned. The constitution, in these points, certainly involves in it principles, and almost hidden cases, which may unfold, and in time exhibit consequences we hardly think of. The power of naturalization, when viewed in connection with the judicial powers and cases, is, in my mind, of very doubtful extent. By the constitution itself, the citizens of each state will be naturalized citizens of every state, to the general purposes of instituting suits, claiming the benefits of the laws, &c. And in order to give the federal courts jurisdiction of an action, between citizens of the same state, in common acceptation, may not a court allow the plaintiff to say, he is a citizen of one state, and the defendant a citizen of another, without carrying legal fictions so far, by any means, as they have been carried by the courts of King's Bench and Exchequer, in order to bring causes within their cognizance — Further, the federal city and districts, will be totally distinct from any state, and a citizen of a state will not of course be a subject of any of them; and to avail himself of the privileges and immunities of them, must he not be naturalized by congress in them? and may not congress make any proportion of the citizens of the states naturalized subjects of the federal city and districts, and thereby entitle them to sue or defend, in all cases, in the federal courts? I have my doubts, and many sensible men, I find, have their doubts, on these points; and we ought to observe, they must be settled in the courts of law, by their rules, distinctions, and fictions. To avoid many of these intricacies and difficulties, and to avoid the undue and unnecessary extension of the federal judicial powers, it appears to me, that no federal districts ought to be allowed, and no federal city or town, except perhaps a small town, in which the government shall be republican, but in which congress shall have no jurisdiction over the inhabitants, but in common with the other inhabitants of the states. Can the union want, in such a town, any thing more than a right to the soil on which it may set its buildings, and extensive jurisdiction over the federal buildings, and property, its own members, officers, and servants in it? As to all federal objects, the union will have complete jurisdiction over them, of course any where, and every where. I still think, that no actions ought to be allowed to be brought in the federal courts, between citizens of different states, at least, unless the cause be of very considerable importance: that no action against a state government, by any citizen or foreigner, ought to be allowed, and no action, in which a foreign subject is party, at least, unless it be of very considerable importance, ought to be instituted in the federal courts — I confess, I can see no reason whatever, for a foreigner, or for citizens of different states, carrying sixpenny causes into the federal courts; I think the state courts will be found by experience, to be bottomed on better principles, and to administer justice better than the federal courts.

The difficulties and dangers I have supposed, will result from so large a federal city, and federal districts, from the extension of the federal judicial powers, &c. are not, I conceive, merely possible, but probable. I think, pernicious political consequences will follow from them, and from the federal city especially, for very obvious reasons, a few of which I will mention.

We must observe, that the citizens of a state will be subject to state as well as federal taxes, and the inhabitants of the federal city and districts, only to such taxes as congress may lay — We are not to suppose all our people are attached to free government, and the principles of the common law, but that many thousands of them will prefer a city governed, not on republican principles — This city, and the government of it, must indubitably take their tone from the characters of the men, who from the nature of its situation and institution, must collect there. This city will not be established for productive labour, for mercantile, or mechanic industry; but for the residence of government, its officers and attendants. If hereafter it should ever become a place of trade and industry, in the early periods of its existence, when its laws and government must receive their fixed tone, it must be a mere court, with its appendages, the executive, congress, the law courts, gentlemen of fortune and pleasure, with all the officers, attendants, suitors, expectants and dependants on the whole, however brilliant and honourable this collection may be, if we expect it will have any sincere attachments to simple and frugal republicanism, to that liberty and mild government, which is dear to the laborious part of a free people, we most assuredly deceive ourselves. This early collection will draw to it men from all parts of the country, of a like political description: we see them looking towards the place already.

Such a city, or town, containing a hundred square miles, must soon be the great, the visible, and dazzling centre, the mistress of fashions, and the fountain of politics. There may be a free or shackled press in this city, and the streams which may issue from it may overflow the country, and they will be poisonous or pure, as the fountain may be corrupt or not. But not to dwell on a subject that must give pain to the virtuous friends of freedom, I will only add, can a free and enlightened people create a common head so extensive, so prone to corruption and slavery, as this city probably will be, when they have it in their power to form one pure and chaste, frugal and republican.

Under the confederation congress has no power whereby to govern its own officers and servant[s]; a federal town, in which congress might have special jurisdiction, might be expedient; but under the new constitution, without a federal town, congress will have all necessary powers of course over its officers and servants; indeed it will have a complete system of powers to all the federal purposes mentioned in the constitution; so that the reason for a federal town under the confederation, will by no means exist under the constitution. — Even if a trial by jury should be admitted in the federal city, what man, with any state attachments or republican virtue about him, will submit to be tried by a jury of it.

I might observe more particularly upon several other parts of the constitution proposed; but it has been uniformly my object in examining a subject so extensive, and difficult in many parts to be illustrated, to avoid unimportant things, and not to dwell upon points not very material. The rule for apportioning requisitions on the states, having some time since been agreed to by eleven states, I have viewed as settled. The stipulation that congress, after twenty one years may prohibit the importation of slaves, is a point gained, if not so favourable as could be wished for. As monopolies in trade perhaps, can in no case be useful, it might not be amiss to provide expressly against them. I wish the power to repri[e]ve and pardon was more cautiously lodged, and under some limitations. I do not see why congress should be allowed to consent that a person may accept a present, office, or title of a foreign prince, &c. As to the state governments, as well as the federal, are essential parts of the system, why should not the oath taken by the officers be expressly to support the whole? As to debts due to and from the union, I think the constitution intends, on examining art. 4. sect. 8. and art. 6. that they shall stand on the same ground under the constitution as under the confederation. In the article respecting amendments, it is stipulated that no state shall ever be deprived of its equal vote in the senate without its consent; and that alterations may be made by the consent of three-fourths of the states. Stipulations to bind the majority of the people may serve one purpose, to prevent frequent motions for change; but these attempts to bind the majority, generally give occasion for breach of contract. The states all agreed about seven years ago, that the confederation should remain unaltered, unless every state should agree to alterations: but we now see it agreed by the convention, and four states, that the old confederacy shall be destroyed, and a new one, of nine states, be erected, if nine only shall come in. Had we agreed, that a majority should alter the confederation, a majority's agreeing would have bound the rest: but now we must break the old league, unless all the states agree to alter, or not proceed with adopting the constitution. Whether the adoption by nine states will not produce a nearly equal and dangerous division of the people for and against the constitution — whether the circumstances of the country were such as to justify the hazarding a probability of such a situation, I shall not undertake to determine. I shall leave it to be determined hereafter, whether nine states, under a new federal compact, can claim the benefits of any treaties made with a confederation of thirteen, under a distinct compact and form of existence — whether the new confederacy can recover debts due to the old confederacy, or the arrears of taxes due from the states excluded.

It has been well observed, that our country is extensive, and has no external enemies to press the parts together: that, therefore, their union must depend on strong internal ties. I differ with the gentlemen who make these observations only in this, they hold the ties ought to be strengthened by a considerable degree of internal consolidation; and my object is to form them and strengthen them, on pure federal principles. Whatever may be the fate of many valuable and necessary amendments in the constitution proposed, the ample discussion and respectable opposition it will receive, will have a good effect — they will operate to produce a mild and prudent administration, and to put the wheels of the whole system in motion on proper principles — they will evince, that true republican principles and attachments are still alive and formidable in this country. These, in view, I believe, even men quite disposed to make a bad use of the system, will long hesitate before they will resolve to do it. A majority from a view of our situation, and influenced by many considerations, may acquiese in the adoption of this constitution; but, it is evident, that a very great majority of the people of the United States think it, in many parts, an unnecessary and unadviseable departure from true republican and federal principles.

Document Themes

In the House debate over the proposed amendments to the Constitution, Elbridge Gerry repeatedly expressed reservations about the newly ratified document, fearing as it existed it gave too much power to the federal government. In the context of debates regarding the right to bear arms and the function of state militias, he asked the House specifically: "What, sir, is the use of a militia?" He went on to answer his own question: "It is to prevent the establishment of a standing army, the bane of liberty. Now it must be evident, that under this provision, together with their other powers, congress could take such measures with respect to a militia, as make a standing army necessary. Whenever government mean to invade the rights and liberties of the people, they always attempt to destroy the militia, in order to raise an army upon their ruins." As an example, he cites the efforts of Great Britain to disarm the colonists England at the start of the Revolutionary War. Clearly, Gerry was a strong proponent of state militias as a bulwark against usurpation of state authority on the part of a potentially oppressive national government.

Much of the remainder of the debate focused on who might be exempted from service in a militia. The concern was that members of certain religious sects, such as the Quakers, might have conscientious objects to serving in any military capacity. The proposal to provide such an exemption in the wording of the amendment was voted down out of concerns that it might be misused. As the representatives continued to struggle over the wording of the amendment, Aedanus Burke of South Carolina, an Antifederalist who would have been a strong proponent of state militias in lieu of a standing federal army, proposed the following wording:

> A standing army of regular troops in time of peace, is dangerous to public liberty, and such shall not be raised or kept up in time of peace but from necessity, and for the security of the people, nor then without the consent of two-thirds of the members present of both houses, and in all cases the military shall be subordinate to the civil authority.

It is clear from the House debate that the framers of the Constitution deeply distrusted the notion of a standing federal army in peacetime. In this context, the Second Amendment would ultimately begin with the words: "A well regulated Militia, being necessary to the security of a free State."

Additional Reading

Billias, George, *Elbridge Gerry: Founding Father and Republican Statesman* (New York: McGraw-Hill, 1976).

Bradsher, Greg, "A Founding Father in Dissent: Elbridge Gerry Helped Inspire Bill of Rights in His Opposition to the Constitution," *Prologue Magazine*, Vol. 38, no. 2 (Summer 2006), https://www.archives.gov/publications/prologue/2006/spring/gerry.html.

Conley, Patrick T., and John P. Kaminski, eds., *The Bill of Rights and the States: The Colonial and Revolutionary Origins of American Liberties* (Madison, WI: Conter for the Study of the American Constitution, 1992).

"The Debate over a Bill of Rights," Center for the Study of the American Constitution website, https://csac.history.wisc.edu/document-collections/constitutional-debates/bill-of-rights/.

Madison's Speech Proposing Amendments to the Constitution, June 8, 1789, Teaching American History.org, http://teachingamericanhistory.org/bor/madison_17890608/.

Report of the House Select Committee, July 28, 1789, Teaching American History.org, http://teachingamericanhistory.org/bor/houseselect_17890728/.

—Michael J. O'Neal

The Second Amendment to the U.S. Constitution

Author(s): James Madison
Date: 1791
Genre: Constitutional amendment

Summary Overview

The Second Amendment is part of the Bill of Rights, a group of ten provisions added to the U.S. Constitution to protect that the basic rights of Americans—in this case, to own and bear firearms. As such, it parallels such basic rights as freedom of speech, assembly, the press, and religion; protection from unlawful searches and seizures; the right to a jury trial, and protection from cruel and unusual punishments for crimes. The Second Amendment states that "the right of the people to keep and bear Arms, shall not be infringed," but since the amendment became part of the Constitution, sharp disagreement has existed over what right, specifically, it protects and who is protected, for the first clause of the amendment makes reference to a "well regulated Militia," suggesting that the amendment was meant to apply only to the statewide military units that existed at the time and not to individual citizens. The meaning and applicability of the Second Amendment lies at the heart of the ongoing debate over gun control. The debate rages in the twenty-first century in light of a number of highly publicized mass shootings, some of them in schools, at the hands of disturbed people who possessed an arsenal of firearms that would likely never be used for such legitimate purposes as hunting or target shooting—and that the framers of the Constitution could never have envisioned.

Defining Moment

From May 25 to September 17, 1787, the Constitutional Convention met in Philadelphia, Pennsylvania, with the initial purpose of revising the 1781 Articles of Confederation. In the end, the framers scrapped the articles in favor of a new Constitution, one that strengthened the nation by giving the federal government more sway. At the conclusion of the convention, the Constitution was submitted to the delegates for signing, then to the states. The Constitution was ratified on June 21, 1788, when New Hampshire became the ninth state to ratify it.

During the convention, on September 12, George Mason of Virginia, who had been a primary author of the Virginia Bill of Rights, proposed adding a bill of rights to the U.S. Constitution, but his proposal was unanimously defeated. It was not until later that the framers added the Bill of Rights, in large part to appease Antifederalists—figures such as Thomas Jefferson, who feared a strong central government and its potential for tyranny. The Constitution's supporters believed that the promise of a Bill of Rights would boost the likelihood that Antifederalists would support ratification. They were right, and it is highly likely that the Constitution would not have been ratified without the expectation that a bill of rights would be appended.

Accordingly, on June 8, 1789, Representative James Madison introduced nine amendments in the House of Representatives; these amendments were initially intended to be incorporated into the main text of the Constitution. After debate, on September 24, the ten amendments that would make up the Bill of Rights passed in the House; the following day the proposal passed in the Senate. The Bill of Rights was ratified on December 15, 1791, when Virginia was the eleventh state to ratify it. Oddly, it was not until 1939 that Connecticut, Georgia, and Massachusetts ratified the amendments.

About the Author

James Madison, who later became the fourth president of the United States, is regarded as the "father" of the Constitution, particularly of the Bill of Rights. He was born on March 5, 1751, in Virginia. In 1771 he graduated from the College of New Jersey, now known as Princeton University. From an early age he was active in politics. In 1776 he was named a member of the First General Assembly of Virginia, then in 1780 he was elected to the first of two nonconsecutive terms in the Continental Congress. In 1784 he returned to his native Virginia to take a seat in the Virginia House of Delegates. In the years that followed, he came to recognize that the 1781 Articles of Confederation created a central government whose weakness could lead to disunion, rebellion, and even civil war. He thus began to agitate for a convention to draft a new Constitution.

Throughout the 1787 Constitutional Convention, Madison was a leading figure, and it is no exaggeration to say that his views of government, laid out in his notes and resolutions, provided a blueprint for the final document. After the new Constitution was submitted to the states for ratification, he joined with Alexander Hamilton (and to a lesser extent, John Jay) in writing a series of essays, published in various newspapers, that made the case for ratification. Collectively, these essays would become the "Federalist Papers."

After the Constitution was ratified and the new federal government opened for business, with George Washington as the nation's first president, Madison, now a member of the House of Representatives, made good on the promise of a bill of rights that several of the states had demanded in exchange for their ratification vote. He drafted the language of the Bill of Rights, including the Second Amendment, which Americans still rely on in the defense of their civil liberties.

Madison remained a member of the House until 1797. He later served as secretary of state under Thomas Jefferson. Later still, on March 4, 1809, he took the oath of office as president. He went on to serve two terms, shepherding the nation through the War of 1812 with the British. Despite his poor health, he lived to the age of eighty-five, dying on June 28, 1836.

HISTORICAL DOCUMENT

A well regulated Militia, being necessary to the security of a free State, the right of the people to keep and bear Arms, shall not be infringed.

A well regulated Militia, being necessary to the security of a free State, the right of the people to keep and bear Arms, shall not be infringed.

The Second Amendment of the Bill of Rights. (By the 1st United States Congress.)

Document Themes

The phrasing of the Second Amendment has posed seemingly insurmountable problems for jurists, constitutional scholars, gun rights advocates, and gun control advocates. The amendment consists of two loosely connected clauses. The first, often called a "predicate clause," states that a "well regulated Militia" is "necessary to the security of a free State." The other, called an "operative clause," says that the "right of the people to keep and bear Arms, shall not be infringed." The problem is that the relationship between the two clauses is ambiguous, open to at least two major interpretations, and both of these interpretations can be supported by documents written in the framers' hands.

One interpretation is that the operative clause is the ruling one. This interpretation, held by proponents of gun rights, is often referred to as the "individual rights" interpretation. Under this interpretation, the Second Amendment grants *individuals* the right to keep and bear arms, with only very limited regulation. The notion at the time the amendment was adopted was that the citizenry needed firearms to defend themselves from various external threats and for purposes of hunting. The reference to the militia was merely an acknowledgment that any state's militia consisted of all able-bodied men who could be conscripted to stave off a threat—and who would be required to bring with them their personal firearms.

The competing interpretation is the "collective rights" theory. According to this view, the predicate clause takes on more significance, for it guaranteed the right of "the people" to own weapons only in connection with participation in state militias—which existed in part to prevent a strong federal government from running roughshod over the rights of the states. Proponents of this interpretation believe that the amendment has little to do with an individual's right to own firearms independent of statewide militia, with the result that they see the amendment as essentially obsolete, given that state militias have been rendered obsolescent by the formation of the National Guard under the terms of the Militia Act of 1903.

Until the two landmark decisions of 2008 and 2010, the Supreme Court's rare holdings on the Second Amendment had typically been narrowly drawn, leaving the broad Issues of gun control and the intent of the Second Amendment unresolved.

The Second Amendment to the U.S. Constitution states: "A well regulated militia being necessary to the security of a free state, the right of the people to keep and bear arms shall not be infringed." In comparison to other controversial constitutional guarantees, such as freedom of speech, the Supreme Court has had little to say about the Second Amendment. The Court has generally upheld criminal laws regarding firearms, but it has done so without attempting to establish a guiding interpretation of the amendment. Although the Court overturned two federal gun laws in two decisions during the 1990's, it did not rule on the laws as they pertained to the Second Amendment. Rather, in keeping with the Court's states' rights conservatism under Chief Justice William H. Rehnquist, the Court ruled on the laws as they pertained to the limits of the federal government's power to impose its laws on state and local authorities.

In *Printz v. United States* (1997), Jay Printz, the sheriff of Ravalli County, Montana, challenged a federal law that required him to perform background checks on people in his jurisdiction who sought to buy guns. The Court accepted his argument that the federal government may not compel the states to implement federal regulations, overturning the portion of the federal act that required local law enforcement agencies to conduct background checks. Before that, *United States v. Lopez* (1995) reached the Court after a student, Alfonso Lopez, was charged with violating the Gun-Free School Zones Act of 1990 when he carried a concealed handgun into a high school. The Court upheld an appellate ruling that the federal act exceeded the authority of Congress to legislate under the interstate commerce clause. To allow the act to stand, the Court wrote, would "require this Court to pile inference upon inference in a manner that would bid fair to convert congressional commerce clause authority to a general police power of the sort held only by the States." *Printz* and *Lopez* did not address the Second Amendment or rule on how it is to be interpreted. Nor is the controversy settled by a review of Court decisions touching on the Second Amendment.

In *United States v. Cruikshank* (1876), William Cruikshank, a member of the Ku Klux Klan, was tried in federal court for violating the federal civil rights laws protecting the African American victims of a murderous riot he led. The trial court found Cruikshank guilty of conspiring to deprive African Americans of their right to bear arms. The Supreme Court, however, ruled in favor of Cruikshank, arguing that the Second Amendment applied only to Congress and that people must look to local governments for protection against violations of their rights. The *Cruikshank* decision, like the *Slaughterhouse Cases* (1873), interpreted against use of the Fourteenth Amendment as a means to enforce the Bill of Rights at

Columbian Centinel.

Printed and published, on WEDNESDAYS and SATURDAYS, by BENJAMIN RUSSELL, in *State-Street*, BOSTON, MASSACHUSETTS.

Whole No. 856.] SATURDAY, JUNE 2, 1792. [No. 24, of vol. XVII.

LAWS of the UNITED STATES,

PUBLISHED

By Authority.

SECOND

CONGRESS *of the* UNITED STATES:

AT THE FIRST SESSION,

Begun and held at the City of Philadelphia, in the State of Pennsylvania, on Monday the twenty-fourth of October, one thousand seven hundred and ninety-one.

An ACT more effectually to provide for the National Defence by establishing an Uniform Militia throughout the United States.

BE *it enacted by the* SENATE *and* HOUSE *of* REPRESENTATIVES *of the United States of America in Congress assembled,* That each and every free able-bodied white male citizen of the respective states, resident therein, who is or shall be of the age of eighteen years, and under the age of forty-five years (except as is herein after excepted) shall severally and respectively be enrolled in the militia by the captain or commanding officer of the company, within whose bounds such citizen shall reside, and that within twelve months after the passing of this act.—And it shall at all times hereafter be the duty of every such captain or commanding officer of a company to enrol every

JONATHAN TRUMBULL, *Speaker of the House of Representatives.*

RICHARD HENRY LEE, *President pro tempore of the Senate.*

APPROVED, May eighth, 1792.

Go Washington,

President of the United States.

Deposited among the rolls in the office of the Secretary of State.

TH: JEFFERSON, *Secretary of State.*

An ACT relative to the compensations to certain Officers employed in the collection of the Duties of Impost and Tonnage.

Front page of a newspaper announcing the second Militia Act of 1792. (From the Columbian Centinel.*)*

the state and local level. This interpretation of the Fourteenth Amendment, however, was later abandoned in other decisions not relating to the Second Amendment.

The next major Second Amendment case was *Presser v. Illinois* (1886). Herman Presser led an armed group called the Lehr und Wehr Verein (Educational and Protective Association) on a march through the streets of Chicago. Presser argued that the Illinois law under which he was convicted was superseded by various provisions of federal law, including the Second Amendment. The Court upheld his conviction, arguing that to accept Presser's interpretations would amount to denying the rights of states to disperse mobs.

The Court in *United States v. Miller* (1939) upheld the federal regulation against a shotgun's having a barrel less than eighteen inches long, because the Court could see no evidence that such a weapon "was . . . ordinary military equipment or... could contribute to the common defense." The decision appeared to suggest that the majority of justices believed that the Second Amendment only guaranteed gun ownership and use when connected to service in the militia. The Court did not explicitly deny, however, that the Second Amendment might protect a personal right to own and use firearms for legal purposes.

A similar ambivalence can be inferred in *Cases v. United States* (1943), in which a lower court noted, "apparently . . . under the Second Amendment, the federal government can limit the keeping and bearing of arms by a single individual as well as by a group . . . but it cannot prohibit the possession or use of any weapon which has any reasonable relationship to the preservation or efficiency of a well-regulated militia." The Court made this observation, however, when declining to review a challenge to a provision of the Federal Firearms Act. In *Quilici v. Village of Morton Grove* (1983), the Court refused to review a Second Amendment case and let stand a decision upholding an ordinance in Morton Grove, Illinois, banning possession of handguns.

In an appeal from the U.S. District Court for the Northern District of Illinois, Eastern Division, the U.S. Court of Appeals for the Seventh Circuit in *Quilici v. Village of Morton Grove* (695 F.2d 261, 1982) affirmed the decision of the district court that the Village of Morton Grove's Ordinance No. 81-11, which prohibits the possession of handguns within the borders of the village, is constitutional. In the ordinance, Morton Grove officials declared that the availability of firearms increased the probability of gun-related deaths and injuries and that handguns are strongly related to the commission of such crimes as homicide, assault, and armed robbery, and are responsible for accidental injuries and deaths.

Victor Quilici began his challenge of the ordinance in state court, but at the instigation of Morton Grove, the case was shifted to the federal court system and combined with two additional challenges to the ordinance. The plaintiffs claimed that the ordinance violated article I, section 22 of the state constitution of Illinois, which states that, "Subject only to the police power, the right of the individual citizen to keep and bear arms shall not be infringed." In addition, the claim was made that the ordinance violated the Second, Ninth, and Fourteenth Amendments to the U.S. Constitution.

Morton Grove held that section 22 of the state constitution guaranteed the keeping of some, but not all, firearms. The court of appeals agreed with the district court that the police power in Illinois justifies limiting the right to keep and bear arms. The court argued, first, that the state constitution grants the right to keep and bear arms, but not specifically handguns, and second, that although the constitutional framers intended handguns to be among those firearms conditionally protected, they also intended that local governments could employ their police power to restrict or prohibit the possession of handguns.

In response to the appellants' argument that allowing municipalities to exercise the police power to enact dissimilar gun control laws would lead to an absurd situation involving a crazy quilt of various ordinances across the state, the court declared that the state constitution allows home rule charters for local governments, permitting them to govern their own affairs as they deem appropriate in a wide number of areas, including regulation for protection of the public health, safety, morals, and welfare, and to tax and assume debt. Whether a wise policy or not, municipalities may set their own standards regarding gun control because the state constitution only prohibits a ban on all firearms. As long as the Morton Grove ordinance does not prohibit all firearms, it does not violate the provisions of the state constitution. In addition, the court noted that there exists empirical evidence that such legislation may lower the number of accidents and deaths attributed to handguns. The court of appeals concurred with the district court's ruling that the ordinance is intended to preserve the health and safety of Morton Grove residents, is a valid exercise of the municipal police power, and does not violate any rights guaranteed by the state constitution.

As for the Second Amendment, the court of appeals noted that this provision of the national Constitution, according to *Presser v. Illinois* (1886), is applicable to the national Congress and not state legislatures. The appellants argued that, given the large number of provisions of the Bill of Rights that have been determined to apply to the states via the Fourteenth Amendment, the Second Amendment has been implicitly made applicable to the states along with other rights. The court rejected this argument, noting that the U.S. Supreme Court has explicitly rejected the assumption that the entire Bill of Rights now applies to the states. The court associated the right to bear arms with the preservation of state militias. Arguing that individually owned handguns are not military weapons, they concluded that the national Constitution does not protect a right to keep and bear handguns.

The appellants argued that the Morton Grove ordinance violates the Ninth Amendment to the U.S. Constitution, which states that, "The enumeration in the Constitution, of certain rights, shall not be construed to deny or disparage others retained by the people." Particular rights, if not explicitly mentioned in the Constitution, are not thereby excluded from protection, but remain viable against encroachment by the government. Among those rights considered so protected through the Ninth Amendment is self-protection and the ownership and carrying of firearms for that purpose. In his article "Beyond the Second Amendment: An Individual Right to Arms Viewed Through the Ninth Amendment" (1992), Nicholas Johnson argued that if the amendment is seen as a support for such things as "a right to engage in sodomy," "a right to wear long hair," and "protection against imprisonment in maximum security," it can be persuasively argued to protect a right to bear arms for self-defense. Even if the Second Amendment is interpreted to protect only a collective right of the states to maintain a militia, strong supporters of the right to keep and bear arms, such as Johnson, argue that the Ninth Amendment prevents the government from denying individuals the ability to defend themselves from others. Although the argument from natural rights to certain guarantees within the Ninth Amendment may be tenuous, Johnson argued that the de facto resistence of citizens to surrendering the right of self-protection may be a significant affirmation of such a right.

The appellants had in mind that unwritten, fundamental right to own or possess firearms. The court rejected this idea, indicating that the Supreme Court has never identified any specific right protected by this amendment. The court concluded that the Morton Grove ordinance banning handguns is a proper exercise of the police power that violates neither article I, section 22 of the Illinois state constitution nor the Second, Ninth, or Fourteenth Amendments to the U.S. Constitution.

One justice filed a dissenting opinion, raising the potential difficulty of a hodgepodge of local ordinances applicable not only to local residents but also to those traveling through the local area. Such ordinances, the judge argued, were an undue limitation on the right to travel and interfered with commerce. The judge focused on a basic constitutional right to protect home and family, believing that the ordinance violates the fundamental right to "privacy in the home," limited, according to the judge, only by private, noncommercial activities, as long as the general welfare is not endangered. He concluded that the prohibition on handgun possession is not necessary to protecting the public welfare.

Sklar v. Byrne (727 F.2d 633, 1984), a case that dealt with a Chicago, Illinois, ordinance prohibiting handgun registration after April 10, 1982, reinforced the state decision in the *Quilici v. Village of Morton Grove* (1981) case. Jerome Sklar, a handgun owner with a valid Illinois Firearms Identification Card, lived in Skokie, Illinois, when the Chicago ordinance was passed. Soon after April 10, 1982, Sklar moved to Chicago, where he discovered that the new law prevented him from registering his handgun. Therefore, he could not take the weapon with him to his new residence.

Sklar challenged the new firearms ordinance in court, arguing that Chicago had denied him the equal protection of the laws under the U.S. Constitution. Handgun owners living in Chicago before April 10, 1982, could maintain registration of their weapons, a right he was prevented from exercising. The U.S. District Court for the Northern District of Illinois ruled that the precedent affirmed in the *Quilici* decision required a conclusion that the Chicago ordinance did not violate Sklar's constitutional rights. In response to Sklar's claim that Chicago could have employed alternative and more effective means of protecting citizens from the damaging consequences of firearms, the court stated that it could not invalidate a law simply because judges concluded that other policies would result in better outcomes. Only if a law were judged "wholly arbitrary" could it face the possibility of invalidation. Because the city pursued a legitimate objective, limiting the right of registration to individuals who had registered their firearms by a certain date could be considered a nonarbitrary, and hence legitimate, exercise of government power.

The district court concluded that Sklar had not been denied equal protection under the U.S. Constitution. A policy-making body has the right to deal with a recognized harm piecemeal, and therefore the City of Chicago was not required to ban completely the registration of handguns. By passing an ordinance that limited handgun ownership to those already possessing a valid registration, "a notable first step toward limiting the havoc and mayhem caused by firearms could be made."

In his appeal to the U.S. Court of Appeals for the Seventh Circuit, Sklar argued that because he could not travel to Chicago without surrendering his weapon, the city ordinance also violated his right to travel freely. The Court of Appeals, upholding the lower court ruling, denied that the case involved any constitutional issue. Because the city council had concluded that the presence of firearms and ammunition were associated with crimes, deaths, and injuries in the city, it acted legitimately under the police power to protect the health and welfare of citizens.

Sklar further argued that the ordinance, by allowing some but not others to keep handguns, was arbitrary and unfair. The Court of Appeals rejected this argument, claiming that the grandfather clause allowing Chicago registrants to keep their handguns was a reasonable exception within the law. Although the city could have banned all handguns, the council had decided to make reasonable exceptions.

Sklar suggested that making a distinction based on qualifications for possessing a handgun constitutes a far more reasonable criterion for excluding some and not others from handgun registration. In a response similar to that given by the court of original jurisdiction, the Court of Appeals noted that the city council, as a political institution responding to many interests, could not be held to a standard of perfect consistency. A political body must be allowed the leeway to resolve a problem in the way it sees fit, which may mean only partial resolution of the difficulty. Provided that the city council devoted reasonable consideration to the question, the court should not impose its own substantive evaluation of what might constitute the best policy in a situation. More than 25 years later, the U.S. Supreme Court in *McDonald v. Chicago* (2010) ruled that the restrictions Chicago had instituted on the possession of firearms violated the Second Amendment guarantee of an individual right to possess firearms.

Early in the twenty-first century, the Supreme Court clarified two longstanding controversies concerning the interpretations of the Second Amendment. The first case, *District of Columbia v. Heller* (2008) was about a law in the nation's capital that made it impossible to legally own handguns and required rifles and shotguns to be kept "unloaded and disassembled or bound by a trigger lock." Dick Heller and five other resident of the city filed a lawsuit arguing that the restrictions violated their constitutional right to keep and bear arms.

In *Heller*, the Supreme Court agreed with their argument, voting 5-4 that the Second Amendment protects a personal right to self-defense in one's home. This right, moreover, is unconnected with service in the military. Writing for the majority, Justice Antonin Scalia explained that the amendment's prefatory clause announces a purpose, but that it does not limit the scope of the second clause, which is the operative clause. Chicago's handgun ban was unconstitutional because it prohibited an entire class of "arms" that Americans overwhelmingly chose for self-defense. Likewise, the trigger-lock requirement made it impossible for a citizen to prepared for an invasion into the home. But Scalia found that the right was not unlimited. The government, therefore, could reasonably prohibit felons and suspected terrorist from possessing firearms, and it could prohibit some dangerous weapons, such as machine guns. The decision did not specify whether lower courts should evaluate restrictions by strict scrutiny or by a lower standard of review.

The city of Chicago had a law similar to the one struck down in *Heller*, disallowing the registration of handguns. But the *Heller* decision applied only to laws enacted by the federal government and federal enclaves. Otis McDonald, a 76-year-old retired resident of the city, filed a lawsuit arguing that he should have the same rights as people living in the nation's capital. In the resulting case, *McDonald v. Chicago* (2010), the Court ruled 5-4 that the Second Amendment's protection (as defined in *Heller*) is incorporated by the Due Process Clause of the Fourteenth Amendment, thereby making it fully applicable to state and local governments. Writing a plurality opinion, Justice Samuel Alito based the ruling on the doctrine of "selective incorporation," which required the amendment to be either "fundamental" to the nation's "scheme of ordered liberty" or else "deeply rooted in the nation's history and tradition." Justice Clarence Thomas agreed with the outcome, but he wanted to base incorporation on the Privileges or Immunities Clause of the Fourteenth Amendment.

The National Rifle Association and other proponents of Second Amendment rights were delighted with the *Heller* and *McDonald* decisions, although they were disappointed that the Supreme Court had not specified that regulations of firearms would be judged according to the strict scrutiny standard. Wayne LaPierre, Vice President of the NRA, cautioned that the organization had "a lot of work ahead" in attempting to overturn gun restrictions that remained in place. As a result of the decisions, a number of cities revised their gun control measures. For example, three Illinois municipalities that had previously banned all handguns rescinded these bans. By 2012, lower federal courts had heard at least 80 different challenges to a large variety of gun control regulations. The courts found that most of these regulations were consistent with the right to keep and bear arms for self-protection and other lawful purposes.

SUPPLEMENTAL HISTORICAL DOCUMENT

"No, Salon, the U.S. Was Not 'Founded on Gun Control'"

by Charles W. Cooke, published in *National Review*, December 19, 2017.

"The U.S. was actually founded on gun control. . . . If you study your history, you'll see it." So begins the latest attempt to rewrite the republic's history, and thereby to achieve by revisionist "interpretation" what cannot be achieved via Article V.

The attempt was published in Salon, and one of its authors, Ed Asner, is a 9/11 truther. Given that, the quality of the work is about what you'd expect. Having proposed that Congress, the Supreme Court, and the majority of Americans "claim the Second Amendment is not simply about state militias but guarantees the unfettered right of everyone to own, carry, trade and eventually shoot someone with a gun"—ah, yes, the right to "eventually shoot someone with a gun," so beloved to those of us who can read—Asner and his co-author, Ed Weinberger, proceed to offer up the most comprehensively illiterate and most embarrassingly researched example within what is, alas, a growing genre. As an example of Second Amendment trutherism, this one will likely never be beaten.

We might start with the purely factual errors. Asner and Weinberger claim that "as written, the Second Amendment follows closely in meaning and in language previous state and national Constitutions—all of which explicitly refer to militias and not individuals." This is wrong. The Second Amendment was ratified in 1791, which is 15 years after Vermont's Bill of Rights, which held that "the people have a right to bear arms for the defence of themselves and the state"; 15 years after North Carolina's Bill of Rights, which proposed that "the people have a right to bear arms, for the defence of the State"; and a year after Pennsylvania's Declaration of Rights, which ensured that "the right of the citizens to bear arms in defence of themselves and the State shall not be questioned." It is also eleven years after Massachusetts confirmed that "the people have a right to keep and to bear arms for the common defence"—a plain statement that, like the others quoted, contains no references to a "militia," "explicit" or otherwise, but does mention "the people."

Asner and Weinberger also claim that Justice Scalia's "odd" take on the Second Amendment's grammar not only was incorrect, but was one that "nobody's ever heard of, then or since." His decision, they propose, ignored "200 years of precedent, historical context, the Framers' Intent." The ignorance or dishonesty that it must have taken to write these two sentences is, I must confess, beyond my ken. As Eugene Volokh has pointed out at length, the construction used in the Second Amendment was not peculiar for the era, but was in fact "commonplace." Here, for example, is a pre–Bill of Rights provision from New Hampshire's constitution, designed to protect the freedom of the press:

The Liberty of the Press is essential to the security of freedom in a state; it ought, therefore, to be inviolably preserved.

Moreover, the phrasing of the Second Amendment has been a topic of discussion since long before Justice Scalia's ancestors had even thought about emigrating to America. Most famously, Justice Thomas Cooley considered the question in his 1880 classic General Principles of Constitutional Law in the United States of America—

a book that was written, it should be noted, after the use of prefatory clauses had fallen out of fashion. "It may be supposed from the phraseology of this provision," Cooley wrote,

that the right to keep and bear arms was only guaranteed to the militia; but this would be an interpretation not warranted by the intent. The militia, as has been elsewhere explained, consists of those persons who, under the law, are liable to the performance of military duty, and are officered and enrolled for service when called upon. But the law may make provision for the enrolment of all who are fit to perform military duty, or of a small number only, or it may wholly omit to make any provision at all; and if the right were limited to those enrolled, the purpose of this guaranty might be defeated altogether by the action or neglect to act of the government it was meant to hold in check. The meaning of the provision undoubtedly is, that the people, from whom the militia must be taken, shall have the right to keep and bear arms, and they need no permission or regulation of law for the purpose. But this enables the government to have a well regulated militia; for to bear arms implies something more than the mere keeping; it implies the learning to handle and use them in a way that makes those who keep them ready for their efficient use; in other words, it implies the right to meet for voluntary discipline in arms, observing in doing so the laws of public order.

"Then or since," indeed.

As for the "Framers' intent" and the "historical context," both of these line up squarely on the side of what is, for good reason, described as the "Standard Model." It cannot be repeated often enough that the "odd" position in the debate over the Second Amendment is not the one taken by the Supreme Court, but the preposterous "collective right" theory that Asner, Weinberger, and a handful of other truthers have taken to peddling in the modern era. To "study the history," as Asner commands, is to discover this immediately, and thereby to realize the absurdity of the claims that the United States was "founded on gun control"; that our "American forefathers limited any and all freedoms when they clashed with public safety"; and that, ultimately, the Constitution was written because "the Founders were afraid of guns." It wasn't. They didn't. And they weren't. Rather, they understood that they had entrenched within the federal Constitution the principle that, as St. George Tucker put it in 1803,

The right of the people to keep and bear arms shall not be infringed. Amendments to C. U. S. Art.4, and this without any qualification as to their condition or degree, as is the case in the British government

Which meant, as William Rawle wrote in his seminal *A View of the Constitution of the United States of America*, that:

The prohibition is general. No clause in the Constitution could by any rule of construction be conceived to give to congress a power to disarm the people. Such a flagitious attempt could only be made under some general pretence by a state legislature.

Or, as outlined by Supreme Court Justice Joseph Story in his influential 1833 work, Commentaries on the Constitution,

The right of the citizens to keep and bear arms has justly been considered, as the palladium of the liberties of a republic; since it offers a strong moral check against the usurpations and arbitrary power of rulers; and it will generally, even if these are successful in the first instance, enable the people to resist and triumph over them.

Know who else wrote like this? James Madison, a man whom Asner and Weinberger inexplicably cast as a "scared' gun-controller. A quick reading of Federalist 46—in which Madison distinguished repeatedly between "the advantage of being armed, which the Americans possess over the people of almost every other nation" and "the existence of subordinate governments, to which the people are attached, and by which the militia officers are appointed"—should suffice to disabuse anybody of the first position. In Europe, Madison observed in the same document, "governments are afraid to trust the people with arms"; in America, those people had won independence, and they would do so again if it came to it. There is no way of squaring this document with the claim that Madison was either against the private ownership or arms per se, or that he wished it to be contingent upon militia service. (Those who are interested should also read this excellent explanation of how brazenly the pair is lying about Madison's "Preservation of Deer" bill.)

What about the Second Amendment's drafting history, confusion over which lies at the root of Asner and Weinberger's essay? Does what we know about that process show that we—along with every major commentator from the period—have made a dreadful historical mistake, and that the Second Amendment is in fact there to protect the individual right to join a state body over which the federal government had control? That, certainly, is the authors' contention: that the first draft of the amendment—which was rejected—indicates that the final version doesn't mean what it says.

This approach is a weak one in general. In what other context would we treat what a legislature started with as being more indicative of its will than what it finished with? But it also falls apart when one gets to the substance. As the debates over the Bill of Rights make clear, the question before the framers was not "Should we or shouldn't we have gun control?" but "How can we ensure that the federal government does not become a tyranny?" Along with a number of other drafters, Madison believed that the enumerated-powers doctrine would suffice to prevent any backsliding, and thus that no Bill of Rights was necessary—the theory being that if the federal government had only limited legal authority, it would have no real chance to exceed it. Madison had a point—indeed, intellectually, his approach was consistent. But, given the speed with which the British Empire's "salutary neglect" had been replaced by the Declaratory Act, and given the fear among many that the same thing could happen domestically, his argument did not satisfy everyone. And so a compromise was struck: The Constitution would be passed as it was, but it would be swiftly followed by a Bill of Rights, within which would lie a set of mechanisms to which the people might appeal should their national government cross the line.

Once again: There was no "gun control" contingent within the American founding generation. Not only had the right to bear arms been both a legal and practical fact within the colonies, but it was a British attempt at confiscation that had sparked the recent Revolution. There was, however, a contingent that remained terrified of the standing army for which the Constitution had provided, and which wanted assurances that the new government would not be permitted to supplant or to suppress the "militia," which, at the time, was considered synonymous with "the people." Within this context, there is no iteration of the Second Amendment that seems anything other than straightforward.

Here is the first draft that Asner and Weinberger consider so damning:

The right of the people to keep and bear arms shall not be infringed, a well-armed and well-regulated militia being the best security of a free country; but no person religiously scrupulous of bearing arms shall be compelled to render military service in person.

The conclusion that the pair draws from this evidence is incoherent. "Madison's intent," they propose, "could not be more obvious: his Second Amendment refers only to state militias." But the version they're using to make that claim—the first draft—does not actually refer to "state militas" anywhere; instead, it refers to "country." Indeed, it was only later that "country" was switched out for "state" in the explanatory provision. Amusingly enough, this supposedly damning draft is in fact clearer than the final one, in that it begins with the "right of the people," and only afterwards offers a justification that makes no mention of state militias. One can only assume that, had this wording survived, we'd have been spared a lot of sophistry.

Asner and Weinberger are not really investigating history, but trying to rewrite it.

Asner and Weinberger also imply that the final sentence within the draft—which would have protected any "person religiously scrupulous of bearing arms" from rendering military service—is in some way damning to the Standard Model's presumptions. But that is convincing only if one misunderstands both the contemporary environment and the drafting process. The "scrupulous" exemption in the initial draft echoed the language of the 1757 Pennsylvania Militia Act, which had confirmed for the state's Quakers and Mennonites that those "scrupling the use of arms" would not be forced into military service. Why did Madison tack this on to what eventually became the Second Amendment? Well, because his own state of Virginia had requested he do so. Effectively, the first draft of the amendment was a clumsy composite of the 17th and 19th items on Virginia's list of demands. That these two items didn't really belong together quickly became obvious, and the latter was thus removed without fanfare. As Justice Scalia noted in Heller, "the most natural interpretation of Madison's deleted text is that those opposed to carrying weapons for potential violent confrontation would not be 'compelled to render military service,' in which such carrying would be required." It is not that James Madison hoped to cast doubt upon the right to bear arms.

None of the aforementioned matters much, of course, because Asner and Weinberger are not really investigating history, but trying to rewrite it. Theirs is a piece designed to convince the already convinced that almost everyone has fallen for a hoax. It's hard work reversing much-beloved constitutional provisions, especially when they are built upon ideals that go back centuries. It's much easier to pretend that "people" doesn't mean "people," and "right" doesn't mean "right," and that Michael Bellesiles was right after all. The Truther Singularity is perhaps closer than I had thought.

Additional Reading

Charles, Patrick J., *Armed in America: A History of Gun Rights from Colonial Militias to Concealed Carry* (New York: Prometheus Books, 2018), Chapter 3, "American Constitutionalism and the Second Amendment."

Cornell, Saul, *A Well-Regulated Militia: The Founding Fathers and the Origins of Gun Control in America* (New York: Oxford University Press, 2006).

Spitzer, Robert J., *Guns across America: Reconciling Gun Rules and Rights* (New York: Oxford University Press, 2015).

———, *The Politics of Gun Control*, 5th ed. (Boulder, CO: Paradigm Publishers, 2012).

Winkler, Adam, "Scrutinizing the Second Amendment," *Michigan Law Review* 105 (2007): 683–733.

—Michael J. O'Neal

Militia Acts of 1792

Author(s): Various (Second United States Congress)
Date: 1792
Genre: Legislative act

Summary Overview

The Militia Acts of 1792 represented the efforts of Congress to bring some uniformity to the federal militia and thus make it a more effective military force. In 1789, President George Washington asked the legislature to draft a bill to that end. Congress finally took action after U.S. forces were defeated by Chief Little Turtle and the Miami confederacy of Native Americans in the fall of 1790. The bill was debated in late 1790 and early 1791, but again Congress dithered—until Little Turtle defeated another U.S. force in November 1791. Finally, a bill was submitted to Congress in early 1792 and signed into law by President Washington on May 2.

Defining Moment

The fledgling United States of America was able to defeat the British in the Revolutionary War through a combination of state militias and federal Continentals. But with the conclusion of the war, the Continental Army was essentially disbanded, and through the 1780s, the nation was vulnerable to attack both from foreign powers on its borders—the French in Canada, for example—and from Native American tribes. Distrust of a large standing federal military force ran high, for among Antifederalists and others, the fear was that large a peacetime federal army and navy could run roughshod over the rights of the states and of individuals. This fear in part prompted James Madison to include in the Bill of Rights the Second Amendment, which makes reference to a "well regulated Militia" and to the right of "the people" to "keep and bear arms."

The need for an effective federal fighting force had been articulated by Alexander Hamilton in Federalist Papers 24 and 25, written in 1787. That need became apparent in 1790 and 1791, when the Miami confederacy—an alliance of Algonquian-speaking tribes, including Shawnee, Delaware, Ottawa, Ojibwa, Potawatomi, and Miami peoples—raided settlements in the Northwest Territory under Little Turtle. Little Turtle first routed General Josiah Harmar, who led a force of poorly trained militia; he then defeated a force led by General Arthur St. Clair, who had been sent to build forts between Lake Erie and the Ohio River. It soon became apparent that Congress needed to act. After considerable debate, the House passed the bill by a narrow margin and sent it on to the Senate. President Washington signed the bill into law on May 2, 1792. On May 8 he signed a separate bill that included regulations that enforced uniformity among the state militias.

A further spur to action on the part of Congress was Shays' Rebellion, an armed uprising that took place in Massachusetts in 1786 and 1787. Led by Revolutionary War veteran Daniel Shays, some four thousand rebels protested various perceived injustices, prompting them to march on the U.S. armory at Springfield, Massachusetts, with a view to seizing the weapons and overthrowing the U.S. government. The federal government, under the Articles of Confederation, was unable to pay for a fighting force to quell the rebellion, which was eventually had to be put down by the Massachusetts militia and a privately funded local militia. Shays' Rebellion had a profound impact on George Washington, who saw it as indicative of the weakness of the post–Revolutionary War U.S. government. For his part, Washington would ultimately invoke the Militia Act when he called out the militia to the western counties of Pennsylvania to put down the Whiskey Rebellion of 1794—a rebellion that had been brewing since 1791, when farmers became angered by an excise tax imposed on whiskey.

About the Author

No individual was responsible for drafting the Militia Acts of 1792. The law was passed by the Second United States Congress, which sat from March 4, 1791 to March 4, 1793. The Speaker of the House was Jonathan Trumbull, Jr.; the president of the Senate was future president John Adams. One representative who had reservations about the original bill was Elbridge Gerry from Massachusetts, who was troubled that the act as written granted dangerous power to the president. Others who played a prominent role in the debate included Jonathan Sturges from Connecticut, who argued that the Constitution gave Congress only the authority to organize the militia but not call it out; Representative Thomas Sumter of South Carolina, who maintained that Congress should not meddle with the business of the states, including the designation of who should bear arms; and Representative Jeremiah Wadsworth of Connecticut, who countered that without congressional direction, any militia would be ineffective.

HISTORICAL DOCUMENT

Passed May 2, 1792,

Providing for the authority of the President to call out the Militia

Section 1. Be it enacted by the Senate and House of Representatives of the United States of America in Congress assembled, That whenever the United States shall be invaded, or be in imminent danger of invasion from any foreign nation or Indian tribe, it shall be lawful for the President of the United States, to call forth such number of the militia of the state or states most convenient to the place of danger or scene of action as he may judge necessary to repel such invasion, and to issue his orders for that purpose, to such officer or officers of the militia as he shall think proper; and in case of an insurrection in any state, against the government thereof, it shall be lawful for the President of the United States, on application of the legislature of such state, or of the executive (when the legislature cannot be convened) to call forth such number of the militia of any other state or states, as may be applied for, or as he may judge sufficient to suppress such insurrection.

Sec. 2. And be it further enacted, That whenever the laws of the United States shall be opposed or the execution thereof obstructed, in any state, by combinations too powerful to be suppressed by the ordinary course of judicial proceedings, or by the powers vested in the marshals by this act, the same being notified to the President of the United States, by an associate justice or the district judge, it shall be lawful for the President of the United States to call forth the militia of such state to suppress such combinations, and to cause the laws to be duly executed. And if the militia of a state, where such combinations may happen, shall refuse, or be insufficient to suppress the same, it shall be lawful for the President, if the legislature of the United States be not in session, to call forth and employ such numbers of the militia of any other state or states most convenient thereto, as may be necessary, and the use of militia, so to be called forth, may be continued, if necessary, until the expiration of thirty days after the commencement of the ensuing session.

Sec. 3. Provided always, and be it further enacted, That whenever it may be necessary, in the judgment of the President, to use the military force hereby directed to be called forth, the President shall forthwith, and previous thereto, by proclamation, command such insurgents to disperse, and retire peaceably to their respective abodes, within a limited time.

Sec. 4. And be it further enacted, That the militia employed in the service of the United States, shall receive the same pay and allowances, as the troops of the United States, who may be in service at the same time, or who were last in service, and shall be subject to the same rules and articles of war: And that no officer, non-commissioned officer or private of the militia shall be compelled to serve more than three months in any one year, nor more than in due rotation with every other able-bodied man of the same rank in the battalion to which be belongs.

Sec. 5. And be it further enacted, That every officer, non-commissioned officer or private of the militia, who shall fail to obey the orders of the President of the United States in any of the cases before recited, shall forfeit a sum not exceeding one year's pay, and not less than one month's pay, to be determined and adjudged by a court martial; and such officers shall, moreover, be liable to be cashiered by sentence of a court martial: and such non-commissioned officers and privates shall be liable to be imprisoned by the like sentence, or failure of payment of the fines adjudged against them, for the space of one calendar month for every five dollars of such fine.

Sec. 6. And be it further enacted, That court martial for the trial of militia be composed of militia officers only.

Sec. 7. And be it further enacted, That all fines to be assessed, as aforesaid, shall be certified by the presiding officer of the court martial before whom the same shall be assessed, to the marshal of the district, in which the delinquent shall reside, or to one of his deputies; and also the supervisor of the revenue of the same district, who shall record the said certificate in a book to be kept for that purpose. The said marshal or his deputy shall forthwith proceed to levy the said fines with costs, by distress and sale of the goods and chattels of the delinquent, which costs and manner of proceeding, with respect to the sale of the goods distrained, shall be agreeable to the laws of the state, in which the same shall be, in other cases of distress; and where any non-commissioned officer or private shall be adjudged to suffer imprisonment, there being no goods or chattels to be found, whereof to levy the said fines, the marshal of the district or his deputy may commit such delinquent to gaol, during the term, for which he shall be so adjudged to imprisonment, or until the fine shall be paid, in the same manner as other persons condemned to fine and imprisonment at the suit of the United States, may be committed.

Sec. 8. And be it further enacted, That the marshals and their deputies shall pay all such fines by them levied to the supervisor of the revenue, in the district in which they are collected, within two months after they shall have received the same, deducting therefrom five per centum, as a compensation for their trouble; and in case of failure, the same shall be recoverable by action of debt or information in any court of the United States, of the district, in which such fines shall be levied, having cognizance therefor, to be sued for, prosecuted and recovered, in the name of the supervisor of the district, with interest and costs.

Sec. 9. And be it further enacted, That the marshals of the several districts and deputies, shall have the same powers in executing the laws of the United States, as sheriffs, and their deputies in the several states have by law, in executing the laws of their respective states.

Sec. 10. And be it further enacted, That this act shall continue and be in force, for and during the term of two years, and from thence to the end of the next session of Congress thereafter, and no longer.

APPROVED, May 2, 1792.

The Militia Act of 1792, Passed May 8, 1792, providing federal standards for the organization of the Militia.

An ACT more effectually to provide for the National Defence, by establishing an Uniform Militia throughout the United States.

I. Be it enacted by the Senate and House of Representatives of the United States of America, in Congress assembled, That each and every free able-bodied white male citizen of the respective States, resident therein, who is or shall be of age of eighteen years, and under the age of forty-five years (except as is herein after excepted) shall severally and respectively be enrolled in the militia, by the Captain or Commanding Officer of the company, within whose bounds such citizen shall reside, and that within twelve months after the passing of this Act. And it shall at all time hereafter be the duty of every such Captain or Commanding Officer of a company, to enroll every such citizen as aforesaid, and also those who shall, from time to time, arrive at the age of 18 years, or being at the age of 18 years, and under the age of 45 years (except as before excepted) shall come to reside within his bounds; and shall without delay notify such citizen of the said enrollment, by the proper non-commissioned Officer of the company, by whom such notice may be proved. That every citizen, so enrolled and notified, shall, within six months thereafter, provide himself with a good musket or firelock, a sufficient bayonet and belt, two spare flints, and a knapsack, a pouch, with a box therein, to contain not less than twenty four cartridges, suited to the bore of his musket or firelock, each cartridge to contain a proper quantity of powder and ball; or with a good rifle, knapsack, shot-pouch, and powder-horn, twenty balls suited to the bore of his rifle, and a quarter of a pound of powder; and shall appear so armed, accoutred and provided, when called out to exercise or into service, except, that when called out on company days to exercise only, he may appear without a knapsack. That the commissioned Officers shall severally be armed with a sword or hanger, and espontoon; and that from and after five years from the passing of this Act, all muskets from arming the militia as is herein required, shall be of bores sufficient for balls of the eighteenth part of a pound; and every citizen so enrolled, and providing himself with the arms, ammunition and accoutrements, required as aforesaid, shall hold the same exempted from all suits, distresses, executions or sales, for debt or for the payment of taxes.

II. And be it further enacted, That the Vice-President of the United States, the Officers, judicial and executives, of the government of the United States; the members of both houses of Congress, and their respective officers; all custom house officers, with the clerks; all post officers, and stage-drivers who are employed in the care and conveyance of the mail of the post office of the United States; all Ferrymen employed at any ferry on the post road; all inspectors of exports; all pilots, all mariners actually employed in the sea service of any citizen or merchant within the United States; and all persons who now are or may be hereafter exempted by the laws of the respective states, shall be and are hereby exempted from militia duty, notwithstanding their being above the age of eighteen and under the age of forty-five years.

III. And be it further enacted, That within one year after the passing of the Act, the militia of the respective states shall be arranged into divisions, brigades, regiments, battalions, and companies, as the legislature of each state shall direct; and each division, brigade, and regiment, shall be numbered at the formation thereof; and a record made of such numbers of the Adjutant-General's office in the state; and when in the field, or in serviced in the state, such division, brigade, and regiment shall, respectively, take rank according to their numbers, reckoning the first and lowest number highest in rank. That if the same be convenient, each brigade shall consist of four regiments; each regiment or two battalions; each battalion of five companies; each company of sixty-four privates. That the said militia shall be officered by the respective states, as follows: To each division on Major-General, with two Aids-de-camp, with the rank of major; to each brigade, one brigadier-major, with the rank of a major; to each company, one captain, one lieutenant, one ensign, four serjeants, four corporals, one drummer, and one fifer and bugler. That there shall be a regimental staff, to consist of one adjutant, and one quartermaster, to rank as lieutenants; one paymaster; one surgeon, and one surgeon's mate; one serjeant-major; one drum- major, and one fife-major.

IV. And be it further enacted, That out of the militia enrolled as is herein directed, there shall be formed for each battalion, as least one company of grenadiers, light infantry or riflemen; and that each division there shall be, at least, one company of artillery, and one troop of horse: There shall be to each company of artillery, one captain, two lieutenants, four serjeants, four corporals, six gunners, six bombardiers, one drummer, and one fifer. The officers to be armed with a sword or hanger, a fusee, bayonet and belt, with a cartridge box to contain twelve cartridges; and each private of matoss shall furnish themselves with good horses of at least fourteen hands and an half high, and to be armed with a sword and pair of pistols, the holsters of which to be covered with bearskin caps. Each dragoon to furnish himself with a serviceable horse, at least fourteen hands and an half high, a good saddle, bridle, mail-pillion and valise, holster, and a best plate and crupper, a pair of boots and spurs; a pair of pistols, a sabre, and a cartouchbox to contain twelve cartridges for pistols. That each company of artillery and troop of house shall be formed of volunteers from the brigade, at the discretion of the Commander in Chief of the State, not exceeding one company of each to a regiment, nor more in number than one eleventh part of the infantry, and shall be uniformly clothed in raiments, to be furnished at their expense, the colour and fashion to be determined by the Brigadier commanding the brigade to which they belong.

V. And be it further enacted, That each battalion and regiment shall be provided with the state and regimental colours by the Field-Officers, and each company with a drum and fife or bugle-horn, by the commissioned officers of the company, in such manner as the legislature of the respective States shall direct.

VI. And be it further enacted, That there shall be an adjutant general appointed in each state, whose duty it shall be to distribute all orders for the Commander in Chief of the State to the several corps; to attend all publick reviews, when the Commander in Chief of the State shall review the militia, or any part thereof; to obey all orders from him relative to carrying into execution, and perfecting, the system of military discipline established by this Act; to furnish blank forms of different returns that may be required; and to explain the principles of which they should be made; to receive from the several officers of the different corps throughout the state, returns of the militia under their command, reporting the actual situation of their arms, accoutrements, and ammunition, their delinquencies, and every other thing which relates to the general advancement of good order and discipline: All which, the several officers of the division, brigades, regiments, and battalions are hereby required to make in the usual manner, so that the said adjutant general may be duly furnished therewith: From all which returns be shall make proper abstracts, and by the same annually before the Commander in Chief of the State.

VII. And be it further enacted, That the rules of discipline, approved and established by Congress, in their resolution of the twenty-ninth of March, 1779, shall be the rules of discipline so be observed by the militia throughout the United States, except such deviations from the said rules, as may be rendered necessary by the requisitions of the Act, or by some other unavoidable circumstances. It shall be the duty of the Commanding Officer as every muster, whether by battalion, regiment, or single company, to cause the militia to be exercised and trained, agreeably to the said rules of said discipline.

VIII. And be it further enacted, That all commissioned officers shall take rank according to the date of their commissions; and when two of the same grade bear an equal date, then their rank to be determined by lots, to be drawn by them before the Commanding officers of the brigade, regiment, battalion, company or detachment.

IX. And be it further enacted That if any person whether officer or solder, belonging to the militia of any state, and called out into the service of the United States, be wounded or disabled, while in actual service, he shall be taken care of an provided for at the publick expense.

X. And be it further enacted, That it shall be the duty of the brigade inspector, to attend the regimental and battalion meeting of the militia composing their several brigades, during the time of their being under arms, to inspect their arms, ammunition and accoutrements; superintend their exercise and maneuvres and introduce the system of military discipline before described, throughout the brigade, agreeable to law, and such orders as they shall from time to time receive from the commander in Chief of the State; to make returns to the adjutant general of the state at least once in every year, of the militia of the brigade to which he belongs, reporting therein the actual situation of the arms, accoutrement, and ammunition, of the several corps, and every other thing which, in his judgment, may relate to their government and general advancement of good order and military disciple; an adjutant general shall make a return of all militia of the state, to the Commander in Chief of the said state, and a duplicate of the same to the president of the United States.

And whereas sundry corps of artillery, cavalry and infantry now exist in several of the said states, which by the laws, customs, or usages thereof, have not been incorporated with, or subject to the general regulation of the militia.

XI. Be it enacted, That such corps retain their accustomed privileges subject, nevertheless, to all other duties required by this Act, in like manner with the other militias.

[Act of February 28, 1795, made small revisions in Sections 2, 4, 5, and 10 of Act of May 2, 1792. The 1795 act was the authority for ruling in *Houston v. Moore*, 1820. Other revisions were enacted April 18, 1814]

Sec. 2. And be it further enacted, That whenever the laws of the United States shall be opposed or the execution thereof obstructed, in any state, by combinations too powerful to be suppressed by the ordinary course of judicial proceedings, or by the powers vested in the marshals by this act, [words requiring notification by an associate justice or district judge were omitted in 1795 revision. The revision gave the President more authority] the same being notified to the President of the United States, by an associate justice or the district judge, it shall be lawful for the President of the United States to call forth the militia of such state to suppress such combinations, and to cause the laws to be duly executed. And if the militia of a state, where such combinations may happen, shall refuse, or be insufficient to suppress the same, it shall be lawful for the President, if the legislature of the United States be not in session, to call forth and employ such numbers of the militia of any other state or states most convenient thereto, as may be necessary, and the use of militia, so to be called forth, may be continued, if necessary, until the expiration of thirty days after the commencement of the ensuing session.

Sec. 4. And be it further enacted, That the militia employed in the service of the United States, shall receive the same pay and allowances, as the troops of the United States, [omitted in 1795: "who may be in service

An English Civil War manual of the New Model Army showing a part of the steps required to load and fire an earlier musket. The need to complete this difficult and potentially dangerous process as quickly as possible led to the creation of the military drill.

at the same time, or who were last in service, and shall be subject to the same rules and articles of war"]: And that no officer, non-commissioned officer or private of the militia shall be compelled to serve more than three months in any one year, nor more than in due rotation with every other able-bodied man of the same rank in the battalion to which be belongs.

Sec. 5. And be it further enacted, That every officer, non-commissioned officer or private of the militia, who shall fail to obey the orders of the President of the United States in any of the cases before recited, shall forfeit a sum not exceeding one year's pay, and not less than one month's pay, to be determined and adjudged by a court martial; and such officers shall, moreover, be liable to be cashiered by sentence of a court martial: [words added in 1795:] and be incapacitated from holding a commission in the militia, for a term not exceeding twelve months, at the discretion of the said court: and such non-commissioned officers and privates shall be liable to be imprisoned by the like sentence, or failure of payment of the fines adjudged against them, for the space of one calendar month for every five dollars of such fine.

Sec. 10. [revised to read:] And be it further enacted, That the act, intitled "Act to provide for calling forth the militia, to execute the laws of Union, suppress insurrections, and repel invasions," passed the second day of May one thousand seven hundred and ninety-two, shall be, and the same is hereby repealed.

APPROVED, February 28, 1795.

Document Themes

The core of the first Militia Act of 1792 is contained in the first two sections. These sections give to the U.S. president the authority to call up the militias of the states in the face of threats. Section 1 states that "whenever the United States shall be invaded, or be in imminent danger of invasion from any foreign nation or Indian tribe, it shall be lawful for the President of the United States, to call forth such number of the militia of the state or states most convenient to the place of danger or scene of action as he may judge necessary to repel such invasion." The state militias, then, constituted the defense force of the United States when the nation faced a foreign threat.

Section 2 turns to internal threats: "Whenever the laws of the United States shall be opposed or the execution thereof obstructed, in any state, by combinations too powerful to be suppressed by the ordinary course of judicial proceedings, or by the powers vested in the marshals by this act, the same being notified to the President of the United States, by an associate justice or the district judge, it shall be lawful for the President of the United States to call forth the militia of such state to suppress such combinations, and to cause the laws to be duly executed." Put simply, this section of the act authorizes the president to call up a state militia to put down rebellion or civil unrest.

The second Militia Act, enacted six days later, deals with the specifics of the militias. In effect, it was a conscription act, for it states that "each and every free able-bodied white male citizen of the respective States, resident therein, who is or shall be of age of eighteen years, and under the age of forty-five years (except as is herein after excepted) shall severally and respectively be enrolled in the militia." (This provision would be amended in 1862 to delete the reference to race and to raise the upper age limit to fifty-four.) Further, the act specified the weaponry that a member of the militia was required to provide for himself: "Every citizen, so enrolled and notified, shall, within six months thereafter, provide himself with a good musket or firelock, a sufficient bayonet and belt, two spare flints, and a knapsack, a pouch, with a box therein, to contain not less than twenty four cartridges, suited to the bore of his musket or firelock, each cartridge to contain a proper quantity of powder and ball; or with a good rifle, knapsack, shot-pouch, and powder-horn, twenty balls suited to the bore of his rifle, and a quarter of a pound of powder."

The Militia Acts of 1792 are frequently invoked by both sides of the Second Amendment/gun control debate. Gun rights advocates point out that *individuals* were in effect required to keep and bear arms, even if they were never called to service in the militia; gun control advocates counter that the right to "keep and bear Arms" existed only in the context of militia service.

Additional Reading

Finkelman, Paul, "A Well Regulated Militia: The Second Amendment in Historical Perspective," *Chicago-Kent Law Review* 76, no. 1 (October 2000): 195–236.

Gentile, Gian, Michael E. Linick, and Michael Shurkin, *The Evolution of U.S. Military Policy from the Constitution to the Present* (Santa Monica, CA: RAND Corporation, 2017), Chapter 2, "The Constitutional Moorings for the Evolution of U.S. Military Policy."

Halbrook, Stephen P., *The Founders' Second Amendment: Origins of the Right to Keep and Bear Arms* (Oakland, CA: The Independent Institute, 2008), Chapter 14.

Mahon, John K., *The American Militia: Decade of Decision 1789–1800* (Gainesville, FL: University of Florida Press, 1960.

———, *History of the Militia and the National Guard* (New York: Free Press, 1983).

Papers of the War Department, 1784–1800, http://wardepartmentpapers.org..

—Michael J. O'Neal

1781 drawing of American soldiers from the Yorktown campaign showing a black infantryman, on the far left, from the 1st Rhode Island Regiment, one of the regiments in the Continental Army having the largest majority of black patriot soldiers. An estimated 4% of the Continental Army was black. (By Jean-Baptiste-Antoine DeVerger).

SUPPLEMENTAL HISTORICAL DOCUMENT

Guns and Race

According to a 2013 Pew Research study, about 82 percent of gun owners are white and more than 74 percent are men, with a full 61 percent of gun owners being white men (a group that makes up 32 percent of the population). A 2015 Pew Research study also found that African Americans and Hispanics/Latinos are far more likely to support gun control, with only about 24 percent in either group believing it was more important to protect the Second Amendment than to control guns. Numerous statistics also indicate that gun ownership is highest where crime rates are lowest, such as in suburban and rural communities. In essence, it can be accurately stated that American gun owners are predominantly white men living in rural or suburban areas that typically have low levels of crime, population density, and racial diversity.

Researchers from Monash University in Australia took a look at statistics for gun ownership and political/cultural ideology in the United States and found that individuals who expressed "symbolic racism," defined as the tendency to believe in racial stereotypes (blacks are dangerous, blacks are lazy, etc.) are more likely to own guns. An interesting trend emerges, however, when African Americans take an interest in gun rights. When militant Black Power groups began encouraging members to carry guns for self-defense in the 1960s, white Americans embraced gun control, leading to then California Governor Ronald Reagan (despite defending gun-rights during his presidency) supporting the 1967 Mulford Act, which made it illegal to carry a loaded gun in public.

Researchers indicate that African Americans face a far greater risk of being victims of gun violence than the American population as a whole. African American males in their teens and early 20s are especially prone to suffer from gun violence. In 2000, it was estimated that while the overall homicide rate associated with firearms was 4 per 100,000 population, the rate for African American males was 27 per 100,000, nearly seven times as great.

"Black-on-black" violence remains a significant problem. In 2001, in homicides in which the offender could be identified, 94 percent of cases with white victims involved a white offender, and 86 percent with African American victims involved an African American offender. Black youths are considerably more likely to be threatened or shot with a firearm. The 2000 homicide rate per 100,000 population for blacks aged 15 to 24 was 41.8, but the rate for whites was 4.7.

In contrast to homicide, African Americans have a lower rate of suicide than do whites. Among white males in 2000, the suicide rate per 100,000 population was 12, but the rate among black males was 6. Comparable figures for white and black females were 6 and 1.7, respectively. The difference in rates between white and black youths is considerably smaller than the overall difference between whites and blacks. Data from 2000 indicate that among those aged 15 to 24, the white suicide rate was just 30 percent higher than the black rate. A somewhat higher percentage of African Americans in that age category used firearms (64 percent versus 57 percent). Gun control advocates point to the increasing availability of guns as one important factor in explaining the differences in homicide and suicide rates between blacks and the population as a whole. The African American population appears to have arrived at the same conclusion, for surveys indicate that African Americans support gun control at higher rates than whites.

Despite such data, gun rights advocates argue from a broader historical perspective. African Americans from the time of slavery to the present suffered from discrimination that, among other restrictions, prevented them from possessing firearms they could have used to defend themselves against racially motivated violence. They argue that despite Fourteenth Amendment (ratified in 1868) guarantees of equal protection under the law for all Americans, blacks were denied basic rights, particularly in the South, and thus were reduced to a status inferior to whites. Although in *United States v. Cruikshank* (1876) the Supreme Court refused to allow the national government to intervene to protect the rights of blacks to keep and bear arms, numerous tales are told of blacks who used firearms to protect themselves during the dark days of racial segregation and intimidation.

Lynchings of blacks by whites and other acts of intimidation led some blacks to acquire firearms for self-defense. Although at times blacks took collective action to arm themselves, southern states established legal policies intended to disarm them. Firearms laws did not ban the possession of guns, but made it more difficult for African Americans to acquire firearms. Gun rights advocates note that even during the height of nonviolent opposition to discrimination during the 1960s, some southern blacks decided to protect themselves by owning firearms. For instance, in 1964, a group of armed blacks in Jonesboro, Louisiana, formed the Deacons of Defense and Justice, vowing to resist any racist attacks. The organization established chapters in Louisiana, Mississippi, and Alabama to deter the violent attacks conducted against civil rights workers.

Gun rights advocates argue that today the crucial violence problem for African Americans cannot be solved by more stringent gun control efforts in the minority community, but rather by blacks exercising their right to keep and bear arms because government has demonstrated an inability to provide adequate protection. When applied to African Americans, gun rights supporters label gun control a racist policy, based on the long history of attempts to prevent blacks from exercising what is considered a basic civil right of self-defense. Gun control advocates respond to the claimed racist history of gun control measures by arguing that African Americans have suffered historically and are still experiencing the harmful effects of a society inundated with firearms. In any event, data indicate that blacks are at greater risk of being victims of firearm-related violence, and generally are more likely to support gun control measures.

A Pew Research Center poll conducted in 2015 indicated increasing support among African Americans for gun rights. The survey reported that 60 percent of blacks interviewed still supported gun control measures over gun rights, but that level of support represented a 14 percent decline from the 1993 finding that 74 percent of blacks interviewed supported gun control measures. The 2015 mass shooting at the Charleston, South Carolina, African Methodist Episcopal Church, in addition to well-publicized police shootings of Africans Americans has added to the increasing of government, especially the police, which is generally associated with support for gun rights and a belief in the need for self-protection.

Additional Reading

Carter, Gregg Lee. *The Gun Control Movement*. New York: Twayne, 1997.

Cottrol, Robert J. and Raymond T. Diamond. "The Second Amendment: Toward an Afro-Americanist Reconsideration." in David B. Kopel, ed., *Guns: Who Should Have Them*? Amherst, NY: Prometheus, 1995.

David Hemenway, *Private Guns, Public Health*. Ann Arbor, MI: University of Michigan Press, 2004.

Mzezewa, Tariro, and Jessica DiNapoli. "African-Americans Still Favor Gun Control But Views Are Shifting." *Reuters*. July 15, 2015.

Militia Act of 1903 (The Dick Act)

Author(s): Elihu Root, Charles F. Dick, and William Sanger
Date: 1903
Genre: Legislative act

Summary Overview

The Dick Act, or Militia Act, of 1903 repealed the Militia Act of 1792. The act revived state militias, or, as they had come to be called, National Guard units, based on voluntary recruitment and greater national government control over their organization and operation. The national army gained some control over the militia and was granted the authority to create a reserve force under its own supervision. Gun control advocates argue that the modern militia, beginning with the Dick Act, eliminated any notion of universal citizen membership in the militia and with it the claim that citizens in general have a right to bear arms as members of at least the "unorganized militia." Gun rights advocates contend that the National Guard as established under the Dick Act does not satisfy the constitutional reference to an organized militia.

Defining Moment

The Militia Act of 1792 never operated well in maintaining a militia force in each of the states. The inadequacies of American military preparedness during the Spanish American War of 1898 prompted Republican President William McKinley's secretary of war, Elihu Root, to begin an inquiry into possible strategies for modernizing and rationalizing the military organization. Noting that the militia system was still operating under the 111-year-old Militia Act and recognizing the value of an effective reserve system, Root asked Colonel William Sanger, inspector general of the New York National Guard, to investigate the citizen reserve systems in other nations. In 1900, following a tour of Europe, Sanger submitted a report on the English and Swiss systems.

Sanger developed the legislation in collaboration with Ohio Congressman Charles Dick, who was a major general in command of the Ohio National Guard, president of the National Guard Association, and chairman of the House Committee on the Militia. In 1902, Dick presented a plan to the annual meeting of the National Guard Association. Supporters of militia reform, including local militias, desired not only greater funds for state organizations, but also greater recognition for the militia's role in the national military system. Republican President Theodore Roosevelt strongly supported reform, as did the regular army.

Meanwhile, the War Department proposed its own reform bill, which included a measure that, although rejected, had a significant impact on the final version of the act. Section 24 of the failed reform bill would have mandated the creation of a national reserve force of up to 100,000 men with prior military service. This force would have had no relationship to any state. Although the House passed the bill, the Senate refused to concur. However, the Senate quickly passed the bill when Root agreed to withdraw Section 24. States' rights advocates, who had strongly opposed the national force, supported the revised bill even though it established significant national government supervision over the state militias. Not until after World War II did state militias protest expansion of national supervision, but by then such objections were too late to force a policy change.

About the Authors

Elihu Root (February 15, 1845–February 7, 1937) was an American lawyer and statesman who served as the Secretary of State under President Theodore Roosevelt and as Secretary of War under Roosevelt and President William McKinley. He moved frequently between high-level appointed government positions in Washington, D.C. and private-sector legal practice in New York City. For that reason, he is sometimes considered to be the prototype of the 20th century political "wise man," advising presidents on a range of foreign and domestic issues. He was elected by the state legislature as a U.S. Senator from New York and served one term, 1909–1915. Root was awarded the Nobel Peace Prize in 1912.

Charles F. Dick was born in Akron, Ohio to his parents, Gottlieb Dick (a Scots/German immigrant), and

Magdalena or "Lena" (Von Handel) Dick, who immigrated to the United States from Heidelberg, Germany. On June 30, 1881, Dick married Carrie May Peterson, the daughter of Dr. James Holman Peterson and Caroline Van Evera. They had five children: James, Lucius, Carl, Grace (Mrs. Edgar Williams) and Dorothy (Mrs. William Robinson). Dick was a Scottish Rite Mason, Odd Fellow, and Knight of Pythias.

William Sanger was born on May 21, 1853 in Brooklyn, New York City to Henry Sanger (1823-1888) and Mary E. Requa (1835-1910). He attended Brooklyn Polytechnic and then Harvard College, where he graduated with an A.B. in 1874. He received an LL.B. from Columbia University in 1878. He was a member of the New York State Assembly from 1895 to 1897. He married Mary Ethel Cleveland Dodge (1869-1952). Sanger served as the United States Assistant Secretary of War from 1901 to 1903. From 1911 to 1913 he served on the New York State Hospital Commission. He died on December 6, 1921 in Brooklyn, New York City. He was buried in Green-Wood Cemetery. His widow died in 1952.

HISTORICAL DOCUMENT

THE MILITIA ACT OF 1903.

BY LIEUTENANT-COLONEL JAMES PARKER, U.S.A., ACTING ASSISTANT ADJUTANT-GENERAL.

On January 21st, 1903, there was passed by Congress and approved by the President a law which, by adding greatly to the defensive power of the Republic, is destined to have a far-reaching effect on the future of the United States. By this law the National Government gains certain advantages which may be briefly summarized as follows:

First: A great improvement in the efficiency of the National Guard, which will result as a consequence of governmental supervision and aid, better arms and equipment, and more thorough training ;

Second: The placing of the National Guard, in an emergency, at the disposal of the general Government, whereby the President, in time of war, will be able to muster the whole of that force into the United States service, at twenty-four hours' notice, if necessary, to serve until the Volunteers are ready to take the field;

Third: The formation of a Corps of Reserve Officers, derived from sources outside of the Regular Army, but tested by examinations prescribed by the War Department, whose function in time of war will be to command our Volunteers.

I propose to state briefly the provisions of this Act.

The first section reiterates the law of 1793, that the militia shall consist of every able-bodied citizen between eighteen and forty-five, and divides the militia into two classes—the organized militia or National Guard, and the unorganized or reserve militia.

The third section defines the "organized militia "as the regularly enlisted, organized, and uniformed militia which shall hereafter participate in the annual militia appropriation (heretofore only one million a year). It gives the President authority to fix the minimum number of enlisted men in each company.

The fourth, fifth, sixth, and seventh sections give the President authority, in ease of invasion by a foreign power, rebellion, or when the laws of the Union cannot be executed with the other forces at his command, to call out " the militia " in such numbers as may be necessary. He may specify the period of service, not exceeding nine months ; and any officer or enlisted man who fails to present himself to the United States mustering officer, when so called out, may be court-martialled.

The thirteenth section provides for a free issue to the States of the new magazine rifles, carbines, and belts, in place of the old Springfield rifles, and for an exchange of ammunition.

The fourteenth section gives authority to the States to use a portion of the annual militia appropriation for the purpose of paying the National Guard while in camp.

The fifteenth and twenty-first sections provide that, whenever the National Guard and Regular Army shall have combined manoeuvres, the pay, subsistence, and transportation of the militia will come out of the Army appropriation, and not out of the militia appropriation. The militia will on such occasions also obtain ammunition for target practice without charge.

The eighteenth section provides that each State shall require every organization "not excused by the Governor" to have, during the calendar year, twenty-four drills and five days' field instruction, on penalty of forfeiture of the annual allotment of the State.

The nineteenth and twentieth sections provide for the detail of Army officers, to report to the Governor for duty with the militia.

The twenty-third section provides that any person who has served in the Regular Army or Volunteers or National Guard, or who has received instruction in military schools or colleges to which Army officers are detailed as instructors, is authorized to apply to the Secretary of War for a certificate that he is qualified as an officer of Volunteers; and that, on passing a stringent examination by an Army board, he shall be listed as such.

The sixteenth and twenty-third sections provide for the military instruction, at the United States Army Schools, of officers thus qualified for Volunteer commissions, or of officers of the National Guard, quarters and subsistence to be furnished by the United States.

Such are the main features of the Militia Act of 1903. While the execution of the law has been somewhat delayed, owing to the fact that a certain length of time was necessary to study and interpret its provisions, much has been accomplished already in carrying it into effect.

An inspection is now being made by Army officers to determine, in each State, the strength and efficiency of the militia. As there are, in the National Guard of 118,000 men and officers, over 2,300 companies, stationed in 1196 different towns, it may be readily understood that this inspection is a large undertaking. As soon as the reports from a State come in, showing the number of qualified militia, the necessary number of the new magazine guns and equipments are, upon the requisition of the Governor, shipped to replace the old arms. The War Department has definitely announced its intention, in future, to arm the National Guard with the best and latest arms and equipments. Congress has also appropriated, in the Army Appropriation Bill, $2,000,000 for the purchase of equipments and supplies sufficient to fully arm and equip all branches of the National Guard with the same arms and equipments as are used by the Army. Out of this sum will be obtained a new equipment of field-artillery, of the latest rapid-fire design.

The question of the pattern of uniform to be worn by the National Guard is a matter which, until acted upon by Congress, lies in the hands of the States. Accordingly, some of the States have adopted for their militia the uniform worn by the United States Army. This is not altogether relished by some of the regular soldiers, who would naturally prefer to preserve their identity. In view of the fact that the different corps in all services wear distinguishing marks, colors, or stripes, it is to be hoped that the States will agree upon some similar method of marking the distinction between the regular and the civilian soldier. The wearing of a broad stripe upon the arm has been suggested in this connection.

A uniform system of target practice, suited to the new arm and to the special needs of the National Guard, has been adopted. Under it reports will be published yearly at the Headquarters of the Army, showing the relative proficiency of the States. The States are arranging to comply faithfully with the requirement that, each year, every organization shall have at least twenty-four drills and five days' field service. Many of the States are desirous that the system of combined manoeuvres, in which both the Regular Army and the organized militia are to take part, shall be inaugurated this year, 1903, and the question of having such manoeuvres at Chickamauga, Georgia, Louisville, Kentucky, Fort Riley, Kansas, Fort Russell, Wyoming, and American Lake, near Tacoma, Washington, is now being considered. Most of the States are changing their laws so as to adopt the organization, uniform, regulations, system of reports, etc., of the Regular Army.

In general, the attitude of the States toward the new law is one of enthusiastic approval, as being a measure which will strengthen and protect the Republic, and which therefore deserves the support of patriotic men. The members of the National Guard have announced to the Inspectors, almost universally, that they are ready and anxious to serve the United States, whenever the call is made. In many States and Territories, the extra appropriations of this year have afforded an opportunity to greatly improve the equipment of the National Guard, as well as to increase the number of organizations and of men.

While, owing to lack of time and facilities, it has been impossible as yet to carry into effect those sections of the law providing for the instruction of officers of the

National Guard at the Service Schools at Fort Leavenworth and elsewhere, or for the examination of candidates for the eligible list of Volunteer officers, these matters are now under consideration by the General Staff; and in due time rules will be formulated for carrying into effect these most valuable provisions. And it is expected that under them a great advance will be made in the theoretical as well as practical instruction of our National Guard officers. It is believed that many young men who would not otherwise enter the National Guard will now do so, in order to obtain the training that will qualify them to compete for places on the War Department Roll of eligible Volunteer officers. A new and valuable element will thus enter the ranks, raising the standard of the personnel; and it is probable that in certain organizations, such as crack troops of cavalry, the theoretical instruction, in the hands of good commanders, will assume such proportions that such organizations will become, in fact, schools for officers. Thus we may expect a great increase in the number of elite regiments, companies, and troops of the National Guard.

The disposition to be made in time of war of this reserve corps of officers is a problem which may well evoke mature consideration. Where is the Government to place these Volunteer officers who have qualified themselves for commissions? Surely they will be used to officer United States Volunteer regiments, like those which did such magnificent work in the Philippines. For the State Volunteer regiments they are not available, since the appointment of officers of a State regiment lies in the hands of the Governor. And it is safe to presume that, in case of any future war, the United States will repeat, perhaps, on a larger scale, the plan of raising a contingent of United States Volunteers, the field officers to be largely drawn from the Regular Army, the lower grades from the officers of the Volunteer reserve. Such regiments, like the United States Volunteers of 1899, will be brought into shape in much less time than that consumed by the State Volunteer regiments. It is to be hoped, in such an event, the transfer of Regular officers to the Volunteers will leave vacancies which will be filled by their juniors, thus benefiting promotion in the regular army.

Now that we have a General Staff, charged with questions of future policy, it is probable that plans for the raising, organizing, equipping, and drilling of Volunteers will be worked out in detail, so that in no future war will arise such confusion as in 1898. In such plans, the corps of eligible Volunteer officers created by the Militia Act will occupy an important place.

In connection with the Militia Act, Congress has wisely passed a law for the detail, with full pay and allowances, of twenty retired officers as assistants in the instruction of the National Guard of the States. It is to be hoped this number will be so increased shortly as to permit of assigning one to each State and Territory. The increased pay which this duty brings will make it possible to select for this purpose from the ranks of the retired officers of the United States Army the very best material — officers of rank, experience, and efficiency. It often happens that the operation of the law retiring officers at the age of sixty-four places on the shelf men who are in the possession of their ripest powers. The retired list contains many Brigadiers-General and Colonels and other high ranking officers, who will bring to this task dignity, experience, and talent, and who will command the respect and admiration of the organized militia. It is to be expected that the functions of these officers will combine those of instructor and inspector of militia, and also of the confidential servant and adviser of both the Governor and the War Department.

The question of the minimum strength of companies of the organized militia presents some difficulties that as yet have prevented a satisfactory conclusion. It is, of course, desirable that the companies should not be too small; for otherwise the force lacks efficiency, and the organization is top-heavy and unduly expensive. It would be desirable that the minimum enlisted strength of the companies should be placed at the figure adopted, in peace, in the United States Army, sixty-five. But, while it may be easy to keep companies at this figure in large towns, in the smaller towns it is not, and the exclusion from the benefits of the militia appropriation of companies of less than sixty-five would disband many companies in localities where they are for local reasons needed by the States or Territories. It would also make the maintenance of a sufficient force of militia a difficult matter in some of our more sparsely inhabited States and Territories. This question will be perhaps settled by fixing a different standard for such communities.

Another difficult question is that of the physical examination that shall be required of the militia recruit. It is important, in case of the muster of the organized militia into the service of the United States, that the men thus mustered in shall be physically fit; otherwise the pension list will be unduly increased. But the United States cannot always in time of war wait until a physical examination is made of all the men before they shall be mustered in. Wars sometimes come suddenly and the troops may be needed at once. The medical examination of National Guard regiments in 1898 took, in some cases, two weeks. It would, therefore, be desirable that the National Guard should be composed only of men who have passed at entrance a physical examination akin to that of the Regular Army recruit. It is hoped that the States will see the necessity of carrying this rule into effect. In any case, it will probably be necessary, after muster into the United States service, that a physical examination be made by United States Surgeons, in order that all unsound men may be noted, and the pension lists thus protected.

Closely connected with the improvement of the National Guard is the question of the purchase by the general Government of camp sites for combined manoeuvres of the National Guard and Regulars, and of the purchase of rifle ranges. In 1901, Congress authorized the President to investigate the question of sites for the combined instruction of the Army and the National Guard, with a view of selecting and purchasing four. The essential features of such sites are that they should be in a central location, five or six miles square, with good transportation facilities, terrain suitable for movement of all arms, good water supply, with facilities for proper disposal of sewage, sandy, easily drained soil, and good locations for camps and rifle ranges. As, in order to carry out the ordinary regimental manoeuvre of the advance to the attack, a field having a length of at least 4,000 yards is required in these days of long-range arms, it may be seen how necessary such tracts are to the instruction of the Regular Army, not to speak of the National Guard. Our laws do not permit us to tramp uninvited over the farmer's fields, as they do in Europe; hence, like England, which has its Aldershot camp site, we must have tracts set apart for the purpose. It is to be hoped that we will shortly see the acquirement by the Government of several' such tracts and the carrying out of manoeuvres by the Army and National Guard on a large scale. The main difficulty is the expense. It is difficult for the Government to buy, in the more thickly settled States, land suitable for the purpose, in tracts of 20,000 to 30,000 acres, for less than $50 to $100 an acre.

Rifle ranges also are needed, not only for the National Guard, but also for the citizen population. To shoot well is a large part of the education of the soldier; and if the Government can arouse such an interest in shooting, in not only the organized but also the unorganized militia, that our male population shall be familiar with the accurate use of the rifle, we shall have gone far towards evening up the advantage the foreigner gains by his universal conscription. Much can be accomplished in this direction, if the United States will offer free the use of the military rifle on ranges to be established near our large towns. Such ranges would also be available for the instruction of the National Guard. Their cost would be little in comparison with the benefits to be obtained. The cost of sufficient target ranges and camp sites for the whole country will hardly exceed that of one or two new battle-ships.

To complete the intention of the law, legislation would seem to be required providing that the cost of maintenance of the horses of mounted officers and of cavalry troopers shall be defrayed by the United States, during encampments or field instruction. Another amendment in the law ardently desired by the National Guard, is a provision for a per diem allowance to men and officers attending the twenty-four drills a year required by the Act. The average militiaman, even though the sacrifice made may be considerable, receives no compensation for his services, except when in camp. It often happens that, in order to attend drills, the enlisted man has to travel a considerable distance, pay railroad fare, and sometimes in addition he is docked for wages on account of missing night work. Because of these and similar obstacles, in some communities it is difficult to obtain recruits of the stamp desired, and the militia service languishes. A much better state of discipline could be maintained if the services of these soldiers were not wholly gratuitous; and an allowance, say of one day's Regular Army pay for a private soldier (about 40 cents) per drill of two hours (coupled with a considerable fine for non-attendance)' would add much to the efficiency of the National Guard. When to this it is objected that such an expenditure would add largely to the cost of the National Guard, the reply is made that the United States may well afford an extra ten dollars or so per man per year. For the object of all military training is to produce a soldier for the emergency of war. Under this bill, the National Guardsman becomes at the outbreak of war virtually a United States soldier, having cost the Government annually about ten dollars, as against an annual outlay of five hundred dollars for each regular soldier. Surely, we can afford to spend a few extra dollars per man to make the National Guardsman a more efficient soldier in preparation for the time when every soldier is needed.

There seems to be an impression in some quarters that this Militia Act of 1903 weakens the power of the States over the militia, and is in some respects an attack on State sovereignty. Nothing could be farther from the facts. The bill is carefully drawn to preserve the authority of the Governors over their own troops, by " reserving to the States respectively the appointment of the officers and the authority of training the militia according to the discipline prescribed by Congress."* In time of peace, the National Guard of each State is thoroughly a State force, made more efficient for that purpose than ever before by the aid of the general Government. In time of war, the National Guard may be called into the United States service by the President, but this right is a constitutional right under the authority given Congress " to provide for calling forth the militia to execute the laws of the Union, to suppress insurrections and repel invasion."* The laws passed under this provision, by Congress, have from the earliest days of the Kepublic made every citizen of military age, whether in the organized militia or not, subject to military duty whenever called out by the United States. But, while the Militia Act of 1903 more clearly defines the rights and duties of the United States than before, and the organized militia must in future be ready to turn out at a moment's notice in case of war, there no longer seems to be the danger that (as was done in 1898) the militia regiments will be converted into United States Volunteer Regiments. The soldier who joins the National Guard now does so with the assurance that, in case of war, he will not be obliged to volunteer for a long period, but that, after a few weeks or months of service, the regiment will be returned again to the State from which it was borrowed.

The paramount value of the law of 1903 is that its passage enables us now, for the first time, to evolve a competent system of defence. In case of a great war, our principal reliance has always been, and will always be, on our Volunteer troops. But it takes time to raise, organize, clothe, and drill the Volunteers, and during this period of preparation we should, with only our small Regular Army ready for defence, be at the mercy of a powerful predatory enemy. But, under this law, the militia, supporting the Regulars, stand ready to save the country from the humiliation that is sure to overtake in modern wars a nation wholly unprepared. Under this law, the President is able to muster into the service of the United States, at once, and without the long delay made necessary in the case of the Volunteers, the whole National Guard, of 150,000 men, in brigades, regiments, and battalions, as they stand, fully armed and equipped, mobilized and ready for active service at six hours' notice, and ship them to the seaboard, or wherever they may be needed for the defence of the country. That the time will come when they will be needed cannot be doubted. The United States, a nation of nearly a hundred million people., is determined to exercise its legitimate influence in. the world's affairs. It cannot, with the blood of the American in its veins, adopt a Chinese policy of exclusion and isolation. And so war is foreordained. But we must remember that modern wars are not always preceded by a declaration of war and that the first notice of hostilities may be the landing of an Army on our shores, the sacking or burning of our seacoast towns. What we shall want in such an emergency is a first line of fairly well-trained troops, who will form a solid bulwark behind which our Volunteers may be got ready. This bulwark we are going to find in the Regular Army and the National Guard; well-trained men, good shots, accustomed to field service, proud of their record and of their organizations.

With such a line of defence protecting the country on the first outbreak of war, we shall be able to contemplate with more equanimity the possibility of being forced into war with a Power of the first order. It is to be expected that this eventuality will be taken into account by our new General Staff ; that they will draw up in preparation for war a complete plan for the formation of these Volunteers who are to relieve the militia; decide where the regiments shall be raised and who shall be their officers ; arrange for their prompt equipment and have all kinds of supplies stored near the places of mobilization — ammunition for their training, books and papers for their returns and records, tents for their encampments — so that there shall be no confusion, no disorder.

Enough has been said to demonstrate the importance of this measure to the country at large. As time goes on, its beneficent effects will be more and more evident, its scope made more farreaching. The country owes a debt of gratitude to General Charles Dick, Member of Congress from Ohio, to the Honorable Elihu Root, Secretary of War, and others, to whose persistent efforts the passage of this law is due. For, in a peace-loving nation, any measure that prepares for war tends to prevent war, since it tends to prevent aggression.

Document Themes

According to Elihu Root, the Dick Act would not simply replace state with national funds, but create an effective training ground for volunteer soldiers. The act required states to meet national standards to receive grant-in-aid funds. Funds were contingent upon a state having at least 100 militiamen for each senator and representative the state had in Congress. A state's militia units had to drill at least 24 times each year with at least two- thirds of its strength, and attend a five-day summer camp. Summer maneuvers had to be held jointly with regular troops, and could not occur unless federal inspectors certified that the militia was prepared. Federal inspections of all units were to be held annually and any deficiencies corrected. State governors were required to request additional arms before the War Department would provide them. Congressional appropriations for state militias increased from $3.5 million in 1903 to $5 million in 1908, while states collectively contributed from $5.8 to $9 million each year. The act succeeded in achieving one of its major objectives: to bring states with inadequate militia organizations up to national minimum standards.

Whatever anyone might argue about the purpose of state militias in opposing a possibly tyrannous national government, the Dick Act essentially placed militias (by 1903 commonly referred to as the National Guard) under federal control. Rather than representing a force potentially opposed to the national government, the National Guard and the regular army served as complementary organizations with a common objective. However, some gun rights advocates insist that if the National Guard, which they are not willing to equate with the militia as designated in the Constitution, is the first line of defense held in reserve, then another constitutionally protected force is the unorganized militia, potentially composed of all adult citizens armed with weapons they provide for themselves through the Second Amendment right to keep and bear arms. The practicality of such an interpretation does not matter so much to them as the asserted constitutional relationship between militia service and an individual's right to possess firearms.

Additional Reading

Mahon, John K. *History of the Militia and the National Guard.* New York: Macmillan, 1983.

Riker, William H. *Soldiers of the State: The Role of the National Guard in American Democracy.* Washington, DC: Public Affairs Press, 1957.

Poster shows an illustration of a well dressed young woman holding a firearm and carrying a container of gun powder around her neck. (By Hy S. Watson.)

Blackstone's *Commentaries*: With Notes of Reference, to the Constitution and Laws, of the Federal Government of the United States; and of the Commonwealth of Virginia

Author(s): St. George Tucker
Date: 1803
Genre: Legal commentary

Summary Overview

In the late eighteenth and early nineteenth centuries, St. George Tucker was a highly regarded lawyer and professor of law at the College of William and Mary in Virginia. In that capacity, he would have had thorough knowledge of Sir William Blackstone's *Commentaries on the Laws of England*, a highly influential legal text published in England in 1765–69. Still today, jurists refer to Blackstone's *Commentaries* in historical discussions of the law. In 1803, Tucker published an American edition of the *Commentaries*, based on his own commentaries and lectures he had prepared at the college. His five-volume commentary quickly became the leading treatise on American law. His comments on the Second Amendment to the Constitution are still quoted by those who oppose gun control measures.

Defining Moment

In the late eighteenth century, the principal legal text used in English-speaking countries was William Blackstone's four-volume *Commentaries on the Laws of England*. This text provided judges, lawyers, and students of the law with a thorough understanding of the principles of common law. St. George Tucker used the *Commentaries* as a primary text in his law classes, but he believed that the text had two major weaknesses. One was that in his view it accorded too much deference to the Crown and not enough to Parliament. The other was that, naturally enough, it did not take into account unique legal developments in the fledgling United States. Accordingly, he wrote marginal commentaries on Blackstone's text and read them to his classes; further, he wrote lectures about Virginia law, U.S. federal law, and comparisons of English and American law and political systems. After several of his friends urged him to publish his materials, he sold the copyright to his five-volume edition of Blackstone to a Philadelphia publishing firm for $4,000 (the equivalent of about $74,000 today). The volumes included Blackstone's original text, followed in each volume by Tucker's marginalia, lectures, and other writings on the volume's topics. The book quickly became the standard treatise on American law in the early decades of the nineteenth century. The U.S. Supreme Court frequently referred to it in the decades that followed, and still today, those who resist gun control efforts continue to quote from Tucker's comments on the Second Amendment.

About the Author

St. (pronounced SIN-gin) George Tucker was born near Port Royal, Bermuda, on July 10, 1752. At age nineteen he left for Virginia to study law at the College of William and Mary. He was admitted to the bar in 1774, but the American Revolution interrupted his efforts to practice the law, so he briefly returned to Bermuda to take a role in his father's trading business. Back in Virginia in 1777, he achieved financial independence functioning as his father's agent in Williamsburg. He also served an officer in the militia during the Revolutionary War, putting his fluency in French to good use in the Battle of Yorktown. After the war, he was finally able to practice law, which he did until 1788, when he took a position teaching law at the College of William and Mary. There is was frequently at odds with the college administration over his teaching methods, one of which was to conduct classes in his home. He also served as a judge on the Virginia General Court in Richmond. By the mid-1790s he had become an ardent opponent of slavery, and it was during these years that he compiled his commentaries on Blackstone, which were published in 1803. Tucker was also something of an inventor. He constructed the first bathroom in Williamsburg, complete with piped-in heated water, and he invented for his home an "earth closet" for waste disposal. He was an amateur astronomer, a poet, a gardener, and a charter member of the Society for the Promotion of Useful Knowledge in Williamsburg. He left the college in 1804 when he was appointed to a seat on the Virginia Court of Appeals. He became a U.S. District Court judge in Richmond in 1813, a position he held until 1825. He died on November 10, 1827.

HISTORICAL DOCUMENT

8. A well regulated militia being necessary to the security of a free state, the right of the people to keep, and bear arms, shall not be infringed.

Amendments to C.U.S. Art. 4.

This may be considered as the true palladium of liberty. … The right of self defense is the first law of nature: in most governments it has been the study of rulers to confine this right within the narrowest limits possible. Wherever standing armies are kept up, and the right of the people to keep and bear arms is, under any color or pretext whatsoever, prohibited, liberty, if not already annihilated, is on the brink of destruction. In England, the people have been disarmed, generally, under the specious pretext of preserving the game: a never failing lure to bring over the landed aristocracy to support any measure, under that mask, though calculated for very different purposes. True it is, their bill of rights seems at first view to counteract this policy: but the right of bearing arms is confined to protestants, and the words suitable to their condition and degree, have been interpreted to authorize the prohibition of keeping a gun or other engine for the destruction of game, to any farmer, or inferior tradesman, or other person not qualified to kill game. So that not one man in five hundred can keep a gun in his house without being subject to a penalty.

Document Themes

Tucker's commentary on the Second Amendment is regularly quoted by opponents of gun control. In particular, his description of the amendment as the "true palladium of liberty" has become almost a trademark among gun control opponents; *palladium* means "safeguard," and is derived from Pallas, the Greek goddess of wisdom, who protected Troy. Tucker goes on to affirm the "right of self defense," calling it the "first law of nature." He then notes that standing armies, combined with prohibitions on the right of the people to bear arms, lead liberty to the "brink of destruction." He refers specifically to England, where not even one person in five hundred is able to possess a gun without incurring a penalty. He notes that the pretext for disarming the populace was the preservation of game—but that this putative motive was nothing more than an effort to curry favor among the aristocracy, which controlled the forests and game preserves to the exclusion of common people.

Tucker acknowledges that England's bill of rights (an act of Parliament passed in 1689 under the formal title An Act Declaring the Rights and Liberties of the Subject and Settling the Succession of the Crown) would seem to counteract the policy of disarming the citizenry, but he further notes that in the context of the intense religious disputes of the time, the right of bearing arms applied only to Protestants and continued to prohibit ownership of firearms by farmers, any "inferior tradesman," or "other person not qualified to kill game." ("Qualified" persons typically were landowners and some leaseholders who had a license from the monarch.) Tucker is thus referring to the passage in the English Bill of Rights that states in a preamble that the previous monarch, the Catholic James II, had deprived Englishmen of their rights "By causing several good subjects being Protestants to be disarmed at the same time when papists were both armed and employed contrary to law." The right, then, that Parliament asserted was in the body of the document was "That the subjects which are Protestants may have arms for their defence suitable to their conditions and as allowed by law." In sum, Tucker's views on the Second Amendment seem to have supported the notion of an individual right to bear arms in self-defense and as a safeguard of personal liberties.

Additional Reading

Colonial Williamsburg website, "St. George Tucker," http://www.history.org/almanack/people/bios/biotuck.cfm.

Cullen, Charles T. *St. George Tucker and Law in Virginia, 1772–1804* (New York: Garland Publishing, 1987).

Douglas, Davison M., "St. George Tucker," *Encyclopedia Virginia*, 2017, https://www.encyclopediavirginia.org/Tucker_St_George_1752_x2013_1827.

Halbrook, Stephen P., "St. George Tucker's Second Amendment: Deconstructing 'the True Palladium of Liberty,'" *Tennessee Journal of Law and Policy* 3, no. 2 (2014): 1–36

Hobson, Charles F., ed. *St. George Tucker's Law Reports and Selected Papers, 1782–1825* (Chapel Hill, NC: University of North Carolina Press, 2013).

"Institute of Bill of Rights Law Symposium: St. George Tucker and His Influence on American Law" in the *William and Mary Law Review* 47, no. 4 (February 2006): 1111–1426.

—Michael J. O'Neal

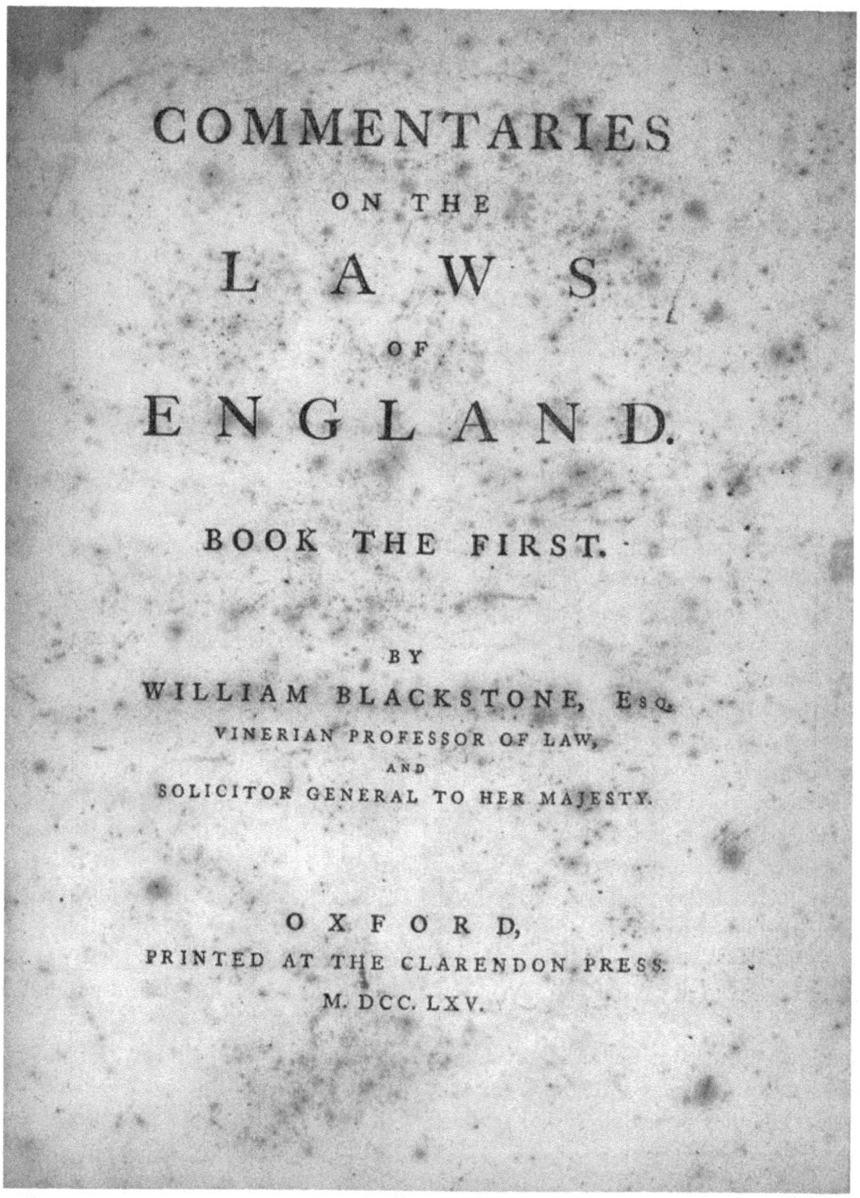

COMMENTARIES

ON THE

LAWS

OF

ENGLAND.

BOOK THE FIRST.

BY

WILLIAM BLACKSTONE, Esq.

VINERIAN PROFESSOR OF LAW,

AND

SOLICITOR GENERAL TO HER MAJESTY.

OXFORD,

PRINTED AT THE CLARENDON PRESS.

M. DCC. LXV.

The title page of the first book of William Blackstone's Commentaries on the Laws of England *(1st ed., 1765).*

Second Amendment Right to "Keep and Bear Arms"

Author(s): U.S. Senate's Subcommittee on the Constitution (chaired by Orrin Hatch)
Date: 1982
Genre: Senate committee report

Summary Overview

In 1982, the U.S. Senate's Subcommittee on the Constitution, a subcommittee of the Senate's Committee of the Judiciary, issued a report titled *The Right to Keep and Bear Arms*. The report consists primarily of essays written by prominent participants in the gun control debate. One of the essays, whose author is not identified, is titled "History: Second Amendment Right to 'Keep and Bear Arms.'" The essay provides an extensive overview of the historical roots of the Second Amendment to the U.S. Constitution, dating back to the ninth century. The essay examines the circumstances surrounding the passage of the Second Amendment, nineteenth- and twentieth-century jurisprudence pertaining to guns and gun control, and the views of early constitutional scholars. The author states: "The conclusion is thus inescapable that the history, concept, and wording of the second amendment to the Constitution of the United States, as well as its interpretation by every major commentator and court in the first half-century after its ratification, indicates that what is protected is an individual right of a private citizen to own and carry firearms in a peaceful manner."

Defining Moment

The Gun Control Act of 1968 could be considered the "defining moment" for the subcommittee's report. For many observers, the Gun Control Act was ripe for revision. That act, which established the Federal Firearms License system, focused on interstate commerce in firearms, requiring that the transfer of firearms across state lines be done only by licensed manufacturers, dealers, and importers. The passage of the law led to wider use of the term "Saturday Night Special" to refer to inexpensive imported handguns often used by urban criminals. These guns were not explicitly banned by the act (although the act repeatedly made reference to firearms "suitable for or readily adaptable to sporting purposes"), but many observers regarded this omission as a loophole that had to be closed.

The bill was prompted by the assassination of President John Kennedy in 1963, who was shot with a mail-order rifle; adding to the momentum behind the bill were the assassinations of Robert F. Kennedy and Martin Luther King, Jr., in 1968. In the years that followed passage of the bill, controversy about guns and gun ownership began to intensify, yet it was the perception of Congress, and specifically of the Senate Judiciary Committee and its Subcommittee on the Constitution, that the issue of Second Amendment rights had gone unstudied and had been in large part ignored by the federal court system. Dennis DeConcini, a member of the subcommittee, commented in a preface to *The Right to Keep and Bear Arms* that "our Supreme Court has but once touched on [the amendment's] meaning at the Federal level and that decision, now nearly a half-century old, is so ambiguous that any school of thought can find some support in it." (DeConcini is almost certainly referring to *United States v. Miller*, a 1939 Supreme Court case.)

In the same preface, DeConcini expressed his belief that Congress needed to amend the Gun Control Act of 1968, for rates of gun violence had *increased* significantly in the years after the act went into effect. It was in this context that Congress decided to survey the landscape with regard to rights granted under the Second Amendment.

About the Author

No particular author is identified for "History: Second Amendment Right to 'Keep and Bear Arms.'" The entire subcommittee report, however, was overseen by the subcommittee's chairman, Orrin G. Hatch, a Republican senator from Utah. Other members of the subcommittee included Strom Thurmond (a South Carolina Republican), Charles Grassley (an Iowa Republican), Patrick Leahy (a Vermont Democrat), and DeConcini (an Arizona Democrat).

Hatch was born on March 22, 1934, in Homestead Park, Pennsylvania. He graduated from Brigham Young University in 1959 with a degree in history. In 1962, he graduated from the University of Pittsburgh Law School. He was a practicing attorney, first in Pittsburgh (1963–69), then in Salt Lake City, Utah, until his election to the U.S. Senate in 1976. During his four decades in the Senate, Hatch was a consistent proponent of conservative positions and an unsuccessful candidate for the Republican nomination for president in 1999-2000. In 2017 he announced that he would not seek reelection in 2018.

97th Congress
2d Session

COMMITTEE PRINT

THE RIGHT TO KEEP AND BEAR ARMS

REPORT

OF THE

SUBCOMMITTEE ON THE CONSTITUTION

OF THE

COMMITTEE ON THE JUDICIARY

UNITED STATES SENATE

NINETY-SEVENTH CONGRESS

SECOND SESSION

FEBRUARY 1982

Printed for the use of the Committee on the Judiciary

U.S. GOVERNMENT PRINTING OFFICE
88-618 O WASHINGTON : 1982

For sale by the Superintendent of Documents, U. S. Government Printing Office
Washington, D.C. 20402(pg. II)

Senate Report on the right to Keep and Bear Arms

HISTORICAL DOCUMENT

Report of the Subcommittee on the Constitution of the Committee of the Judiciary, U.S. Senate, Ninety-seventy Congress, Second Session, February 1982.

The right to keep and bear arms as a part of English and American law antedates not only the Constitution, but also the discovery of firearms. Under the laws of Alfred the Great, whose reign began in 872 A.D., all English citizens from the nobility to the peasants were obliged to privately purchase weapons and be available for military duty.[1] This was in sharp contrast to the feudal system as it evolved in Europe, under which armament and military duties were concentrated in the nobility. The body of armed citizens were known as the "fyrd."

While a great many of the Saxon rights were abridged following the Norman conquest, the right and duty of arms possession was retained. Under the Assize of Arms of 1181, "the whole community of freemen" between the ages of 15 and 40 were required by law to possess certain arms, which were arranged in proportion to their possessions.[2] They were required twice a year to demonstrate to Royal officials that they were appropriately armed. In 1253, another Assize of Arms expanded the duty of armament to include not only freemen, but also villeins, who were the English equivalent of serfs. Now all "citizens, burgesses, free tenants, villeins and others from 15 to 60 years of age" were obliged-to be armed.[3] While on the Continent the villeins were regarded as little more than animals hungering for rebellion, the English legal system not only permitted, but affirmatively required them, to be armed.

The thirteenth century saw further definitions of this right as the long bow, a formidable armor-piercing weapon, became increasingly the mainstay of British national policy. In 1285, Edward I commanded that all persons comply with the earlier Assizes and added that "anyone else who can afford them shall keep bows and arrows."[4] The right of armament was subject only to narrow limitations. In 1279, it was ordered that those appearing in Parliament or other public assemblies "shall come without all force and armor, well and peaceably."[5] In 1328, the statute of Northampton ordered that no one use their arms in "affray of the peace, nor to go nor ride armed by day or by night in fairs, markets, nor in the presence of the justices or other ministers."[6] English courts construed this ban consistently with the general right of private armament as applying only to wearing of arms "accompanied with such circumstances as are apt to terrify the people."[7] In 1369, the King ordered that the sheriffs of London require all citizens "at leisure time on holidays" to "use in their recreation bowes and arrows" and to stop all other games which might distract them from this practice.[8]

The Tudor kings experimented with limits upon specialized weapons—mainly crossbows and the then-new firearms. These measures were not intended to disarm the citizenry, but on the contrary, to prevent their being diverted from longbow practice by (1) sport with other weapons which were considered less effective. Even these narrow measures were shortlived. In 1508, Henry VII limited shooting (but not possession) of crossbows to those with land worth 200 marks annual rental, but provided an exception for those who "shote owt of a howse for the lawefull defens of the same."[9] In 1511, Henry VIII increased the property requirement to 300 marks. He also expanded the requirement of longbow ownership, requiring all citizens to "use and exercyse shootyng in long-bowes, and also have a bowe and arrowes contynually" in the house.[10] Fathers were required by law to purchase bows and arrows for their sons between the age of 7 and 14 and to train them in longbow use.

In 1514 the ban on crossbows was extended to include firearms.[11] But in 1533, Henry reduced the property qualification to 100 pounds per year; in 1541 he limited it to possession of small firearms ("of the length of one hole yard" for some firearms and "thre quarters of a yarde" for othersl[12] and eventually he repealed the entire statute by proclamation.[13] The later Tudor monarchs continued the system and Elizabeth added to it by creating what came to be known as "train bands," selected portions of the citizenry chosen for special training. These trained bands were distinguished from the "militia," which term was first used during the Spanish Armada crisis to designate the entire of the armed citizenry.[14]

The militia continued to be a pivotal force in the English political system. The British historian Charles

Oman considers the existence of the armed citizenry to be a major reason for the moderation of monarchical rule in Great Britain; "More than once he [Henry VIII] had to restrain himself, when he discovered that the general feeling of his subjects was against him. . . . His 'gentlemen pensioners' and his yeomen of the guard were but a handful, and bills or bows were in every farm and cottage."[15]

When civil war broke out in 1642, the critical issue was whether the King or Parliament had the right to control the militia.[16] The aftermath of the civil war saw England in temporary control of a military government, which repeatedly dissolved Parliament and authorized its officers to "search for, and seize all arms" owned by Catholics, opponents of the government, "or any other person whom the commissioners had judged dangerous to the peace of this Common wealth."[17]

The military government ended with the restoration of Charles II. Charles in turn opened his reign with a variety of repressive legislation, expanding the definition of treason, establishing press censorship and ordering his supporters to form their own troops, "the officers to be numerous, disaffected persons watched and not allowed to assemble, and their arms seized."[18] In 1662, a Militia Act was enacted empowering officials "to search for and seize all arms in the custody or possession of any person or persons whom the said lieutenants or any two or more of their deputies shall judge dangerous to the peace of the kingdom."[19] Gunsmiths were ordered to deliver to the government lists of all purchasers.[20] These confiscations were continued under James II, who directed them particularly against the Irish population: "Although the country was infested by predatory bands, a Protestant gentleman could scarcely obtain permission to keep a brace of pistols." [21]

In 1668, the government of James was overturned in a peaceful uprising which came to be known as "The Glorious Revolution." Parliament resolved that James had abdicated and promulgated a Declaration of Rights, later enacted as the Bill of Rights. Before coronation, his successor William of Orange, was required to swear to respect these rights. The debates in the House of Commons over this Declaration of Rights focused largely upon the disarmament under the 1662 Militia Act. One member complained that "an act of Parliament was made to disarm all Englishmen, who the lieutenant should suspect, by day or night, by force or otherwise—this was done in Ireland for the sake of putting arms into Irish hands." The speech of another is summarized as "militia bill—power to disarm all England—now done in Ireland." A third complained "Arbitrary power exercised by the ministry. . . . Militia—imprisoning without reason; disarming—himself disarmed." Yet another summarized his complaints "Militia Act—an abominable thing to disarm the nation. . . ." [22]

The Bill of Rights, as drafted in the House of Commons, simply provided that "the acts concerning the militia are grievous to the subject" and that "it is necessary for the public Safety that the Subjects, which are Protestants, should provide and keep arms for the common defense; And that the Arms which have been seized, and taken from them, be restored." [23] The House of Lords changed this to make it a more positive declaration of an individual right under English law: "That the subjects which are Protestant may have arms for their defense suitable to their conditions and as allowed by law." [24] The only limitation was on ownership by Catholics, who at that time composed only a few percent of the British population and were subject to a wide variety of punitive legislation. The Parliament subsequently made clear what it meant by "suitable to their conditions and as allowed by law." The poorer citizens had been restricted from owning firearms, as well as traps and other commodities useful for hunting, by the 1671 Game Act. Following the Bill of Rights, Parliament reenacted that statute, leaving its operative parts unchanged with one exception—which removed the word "guns" from the list of items forbidden to the poorer citizens.[25] The right to keep and bear arms would henceforth belong to all English subjects, rich and poor alike.

In the colonies, availability of hunting and need for defense led to armament statutes comparable to those of the early Saxon times. In 1623, Virginia forbade its colonists to travel unless they were "well armed"; in 1631 it required colonists to engage in target practice on Sunday and to "bring their peeces to church. "[26] In 1658 it required every householder to have a functioning firearm within his house and in 1673 its laws provided that a citizen who claimed he was too poor to purchase a firearm would have one Purchased for him by the government, which would then require im to pay a reasonable price when able to do so.[27] In Massachusetts, the first session of the legislature ordered that not only freemen, but also indentured servants own firearms and in 1644 it imposed a stern 6 shilling fine upon any citizen who was not armed.[28]

When the British government began to increase its military presence in the colonies in the mid-eighteenth century, Massachusetts responded by calling upon its citizens to arm themselves in defense. One colonial newspaper argued that it was impossible to complain that his act was illegal since they were "British subjects, to whom the privilege of possessing arms is expressly recognized by the Bill of Rights" while another argued that this "is a natural right which the people have reserved to themselves, confirmed by the Bill of Rights, to keep arms for their own defense."[29] The newspaper cited Blackstone's commentaries on the laws of England, which had listed the "having and using arms for self preservation and defense" among the "absolute rights of individuals." The colonists felt they had an absolute right at common law to own firearms.

Together with freedom of the press, the right to keep and bear arms became one of the individual rights most prized by the colonists. When British troops seized a militia arsenal in September, 1774, and incorrect rumors that colonists had been killed spread through Massachusetts, 60,000 citizens took up arms.[30] A few months later, when Patrick Henry delivered his famed "Give me liberty or give me death" speech, he spoke in support of a proposition that a well regulated militia, composed of gentlemen and freemen, is the natural strength and only security of a free government. . . ." Throughout the following revolution, formal and informal units of armed citizens obstructed British communication, cut off foraging parties, and harassed the thinly stretched regular forces. When seven states adopted state "bills of rights" following the Declaration of Independence, each of those bills of rights provided either for protection of the concept of a militia or for an express right to keep and bear arms.[31]

Following the revolution but previous to the adoption of the Constitution, debates over militia proposals occupied a large part of the political scene. A variety of plans were put forth by figures ranging from George Washington to Baron von Steuben.[32] All of the proposals called for a general duty of all citizens to be armed, although some proposals (most notably von Steuben's) also emphasized a "select militia" which would be paid for its services and given special training. In this respect, this "select militia" was the successor of the "trained bands' and the predecessor of what is today the "national guard." In the debates over the Constitution, von Steuben's proposals were criticized as undemocratic. In Connecticut one writer complained of a proposal that "this looks too much like Baron von Steuben's militia, by which a standing army was meant and intended. "[33] In Pennsylvania, a delegate argued "Congress may give us a select militia which will, in fact, be a standing army—or Congress, afraid of a general militia, may say there will be no militia at all. When a select militia is formed, the people in general may be disarmed."[34] Richard Henry Lee, in his widely read pamphlet "Letters from the Federal Farmer to the Republican" worried that the people might be disarmed "by modeling the militia. Should one fifth or one eighth part of the people capable of bearing arms be made into a select militia, as has been proposed, and those the young and ardent parts of the community, possessed of little or no property, the former will answer all the purposes of an army, while the latter will be defenseless." He proposed that "the Constitution ought to secure a genuine, and guard against a select militia," adding that "to preserve liberty, it I is essential that the whole body of the people always possess arms / and be taught alike, especially when young, how to use them."[35]

The suspicion of select militia units expressed in these passages is a clear indication that the framers of the Constitution did not seek to guarantee a State right to maintain formed groups similar to the National Guard, but rather to protect the right of individual citizens to keep and bear arms. Lee, in particular, sat in the Senate which approved the Bill of Rights. He would hardly have meant the second amendment to apply only to the select militias he so feared and disliked.

Other figures of the period were of like mind. In the Virginia convention, George Mason, drafter of the Virginia Bill of Rights, accused the British of having plotted "to disarm the people—that was the best and most effective way to enslave them," while Patrick Henry observed that "The great object is that every man be armed" and "everyone who is able may have a gun."[36]

Nor were the antifederalist, to whom we owe credit for a Bill of Rights, alone on this account. Federalist arguments also provide a source of support for an individual rights view. Their arguments in favor of the proposed Constitution also relied heavily upon universal armament. The proposed Constitution had been heavily criticized for its failure to ban or even limit standing armies. Unable to deny this omission, the Constitution's supporters frequently argued to the people that the universal armament of Americans made such limitations unnecessary. A pamphlet written by Noah Webster, aimed at swaying Pennsylvania toward ratification, observed

> Before a standing army can rule, the people must be disarmed; as they are in almost every kingdom in Europe. The supreme power in America cannot enforce unjust laws by the sword, because the whole body of the people are armed, and constitute a force superior to any band of regular troops that can be, on any pretense, raised in the United States.[37]

In the Massachusetts convention, Sedgwick echoed the same thought, rhetorically asking if an oppressive army could be formed or "if raised, whether they could subdue a Nation of freemen, who know how to prize liberty, and who have arms in their hands?"[38] In Federalist Paper 46, Madison, later author of the Second Amendment, mentioned "The advantage of being armed, which the Americans possess over the people of all other countries" and that "notwithstanding the military establishments in the several kingdoms of Europe, which are carried as far as the public resources will bear, the governments are afraid to trust the people with arms."

A third and even more compelling case for an individual rights perspective on the Second Amendment comes from the State demands for a bill of rights. Numerous state ratifications called for adoption of a Bill of Rights as a part of the Constitution. The first such call came from a group of Pennsylvania delegates. Their proposals, which were not adopted but had a critical effect on future debates, proposed among other rights that "the people have a right to bear arms for the defense of themselves and their own state, or the United States, or for the purpose of killing game; and no law shall be passed for disarming the people or any of them, unless for crimes committed, or a real danger of public injury from individuals."[39] In Massachusetts, Sam Adams unsuccessfully pushed for a ratification conditioned on adoption of a Bill of Rights, beginning with a guarantee "That the said Constitution shall never be construed to authorize Congress to infringe the just liberty of the press or the rights of conscience; or to prevent the people of the United States who are peaceable citizens from keeping their own arms. . . ."[40] When New Hampshire gave the Constitution the ninth vote needed for its passing into effect, it called for adoption of a Bill of Rights which included the provision that "Congress shall never disarm any citizen unless such as are or have been in actual rebellion."[41] Virginia and North Carolina thereafter called for a provision "that the people have the right to keep and bear arms; that a well regulated militia composed of the body of the people trained to arms is the proper, natural and safe defense of a free state."[42]

When the first Congress convened for the purpose of drafting a Bill of Rights, it delegated the task to James Madison. Madison did not write upon a blank tablet. Instead, he obtained a pamphlet listing the State proposals for a Bill of Rights and sought to produce a briefer version incorporating all the vital proposals of these. His purpose was to incorporate, not distinguish by technical changes, proposals such as that of the Pennsylvania minority, Sam Adams, and the New Hampshire delegates. Madison proposed among other rights that:

> The right of the people to keep and bear arms shall not be infringed; a well armed and well regulated militia being the best security of a free country; but no person religiously scrupulous of bearing arms shall be compelled to render military service in person."[43]

In the House, this was initially modified so that the militia clause came before the proposal recognizing the right. The proposals for the Bill of Rights were then trimmed in the interests of brevity. The conscientious objector clause was removed following objections by Elbridge Gerry, who complained that future Congresses might abuse the exemption for the scrupulous to excuse everyone from militia service.

The proposal finally passed the House in its present form: "A well regulated militia, being necessary to the security of a free state, the right of the people to keep and bear arms, shall not be infringed." In this form it was submitted into the Senate, which passed it the following day. The Senate in the process indicated its intent that the right be an individual one, for private purposes, by rejecting an amendment which would have limited the keeping and bearing of arms to bearing "for the common defense." The earliest American constitutional commentators concurred in giving this broad reading to the amendment. When St. George Tucker, later Chief Justice of the Virginia Supreme Court, in 1803 published an edition of Blackstone annotated to American law, he followed Blackstone's citation of the right of the subject "of having arms suitable to their condition and degree, and such as are allowed by law" with a citation to the Second Amendment, "And this without any qualification as to their condition or degree, as is the case in the British government."[44] William Rawle's "View of the Constitution" published in Philadelphia in 1825 noted that under the Second Amendment

> The prohibition is general. No clause in the Constitution"" could by a rule of construction be conceived to give to 1 Congress a power to disarm the people. Such a flagitious attempt could only be made under some general pretense by a state legislature. But if in blind pursuit of inordinate power, either should attempt it, this amendment may be appealed to as a restraint on both."[45]

The Jefferson papers in the Library of Congress show that both Tucker and Rawle were friends of, and corresponded with Thomas Jefferson. This suggests that their assessment, as contemporaries of the Constitution's drafters, should be afforded special consideration.

Later commentators agreed with Tucker and Rawle. For instance, Joseph Story in his "Commentaries on the Constitution" considered the right to keep and bear arms as "the palladium of the liberties of the republic," which deterred tyranny and enabled the citizenry at large to overthrow it should it come to pass.[46]

Subsequent legislation in the Second Congress likewise supports the interpretation of the second amendment that creates an individual right. In the Militia Act of 1792, the second Congress defined "militia of the United States" to include almost every free adult male in the United States. These persons were obligated by law to possess a firearm and a minimum supply of ammunition and military equipment.[47] This statute, incidentally remained in effect into the early years of the present century as a legal requirement of gun ownership for most of the population of the United States. There can be little doubt from this that when the Congress and the people spoke of a "militia," they had reference to the traditional concept of the entire populace capable of bearing arms, and not to any formal group such as what is today called the National Guard. The purpose was to create an armed citizenry, such as the political theorists at the time considered essential to ward off tyranny. From this militia, appropriate measures might create a well regulated militia" of individuals trained in their duties and responsibilities as citizens and owners of firearms.

The Second Amendment as such was rarely litigated prior to the passage of the Fourteenth Amendment. Prior to that time, most courts accepted that the commands of the federal Bill of Rights did not apply to the states. Since there was no federal firearms legislation at this time, there was no legislation which was directly subject to the Second Amendment, if the accepted interpretations were followed. However, a broad variety of state legislation was struck down under state guarantees of the right to keep and bear arms and even in a few cases, under the Second Amendment, when it came before courts which considered the federal protections applicable to the states. Kentucky in 1813 enacted the first carrying concealed weapon statute in the United States; in 1822, the Kentucky Court of Appeals struck down the law as a violation of the state constitutional protection of the right to keep and bear arms: "And can there be entertained a reasonable doubt but the provisions of that act import a restraint on the right of the citizen to bear arms? The court apprehends it not. The right existed at the adoption of the Constitution; it then had no limit short of the moral power of the citizens to exercise it, and in fact consisted of nothing else but the liberty of the citizen to bear arms."[48] On the other hand, a similar measure was sustained in Indiana, not upon the grounds that a right to keep and bear arms did not apply, but rather upon the notion that a statute banning only concealed carrying still permitted the carrying of arms and merely regulated one possible way of carrying them.[49] A few years later, the Supreme Court of Alabama upheld a similar statute but added "We do not desire to be understood as maintaining, that in regulating the manner of wearing arms, the legislature has no other limit than its own discretion. A statute which, under the pretense of regulation, amounts to a destruction of that right, or which requires arms to be so borne as to render them wholly useless for the purpose of defense, would be clearly unconstitutional."[50] When the Arkansas Supreme Court in 1842 upheld a carrying concealed weapons statute, the chief justice explained that the statute would not "detract anything from the power of the people to defend their free state and the established institutions of the country. It prohibits only the wearing of certain arms concealed. This is simply a regulation as to the manner of bearing such arms as are specified," while the dissenting justice proclaimed "I deny that any just or free government upon earth has the power to disarm its citizens."[51]

Sometimes courts went farther. When in 1837, Georgia totally banned the sale of pistols (excepting the larger pistols "known and used as horsemen's pistols") and other weapons, the Georgia Supreme Court in *Nunn v. State* held the statute unconstitutional under the Second Amendment to the federal Constitution. The court held that the Bill of Rights protected natural rights which were fully as capable of infringement by states as by the federal government and that the Second Amendment provided "the right of the whole people, old and young, men, women and boys, and not militia only, to keep and bear arms of every description, and not merely such as are used by the militia, shall not be infringed, curtailed, or broken in on, in the slightest degree; and all this for the important end to be attained: the rearing up and qualifying of a well regulated militia, so vitally necessary to the security of a free state."[52] Prior to the Civil War, the Supreme Court of the United States likewise indicated that the privileges of citizenship included the individual right to own and carry firearms. In the notorious Dred Scott case, the court held that black Americans were not citizens and could not be made such by any state. This decision, which by striking down the Missouri Compromise did so much to bring on the Civil War, listed what the Supreme Court considered the rights of American citizens by way of illustrating what rights would have to be given to black Americans if the Court were to recognize them as full fledged citizens:

> It would give to persons of the negro race, who are recognized as citizens in any one state of the Union, the right to enter every other state, whenever they pleased. . . . and it would give them full liberty of speech in public and in private upon all subjects upon which its own citizens might meet; to hold public meetings upon political affairs, and to keep and carry arms wherever they went.[53]

Following the Civil War, the legislative efforts which gave us three amendments to the Constitution and our earliest civil rights acts likewise recognized the right to keep and bear arms as an existing constitutional right of the individual citizen and as a right specifically singled out as one protected by the civil rights acts and by the Fourteenth Amendment to the Constitution, against infringement by state authorities. Much of the reconstruction effort in the South had been hinged upon the creation of "black militias" composed of the armed and newly freed blacks, officered largely by black veterans of the Union Army. In the months after the Civil War, the existing southern governments struck at these units with the enactment of "black codes" which either outlawed gun ownership by blacks entirely, or imposed permit systems for them, and permitted the confiscation of firearms owned by blacks. When the Civil Rights Act of 1866 was debated members both of the Senate and the House referred to the disarmament of blacks as a major consideration.[54] Senator Trumbull cited provisions outlawing ownership of arms by blacks as among those which the Civil Rights Act would prevent; [55] Senator Sulsbury complained on the other hand that if the act were to be passed it would prevent his own state from enforcing a law banning gun ownership by individual free blacks.[56] Similar arguments were advanced during the debates over the "anti-KKK act"; its sponsor at one point explained that a section making it a federal crime to deprive a person of "arms or weapons he may have in his house or possession for the defense of his person, family or property" was "intended to enforce the well-known constitutional provisions guaranteeing the right in the citizen to 'keep and bear arms'."[57] Likewise, the debates over the Fourteenth Amendment Congress frequently referred to the Second Amendment as one of the rights which it intended to guarantee against state action. [58]

Following adoption of the Fourteenth Amendment, however, the Supreme Court held that that Amendment's prohibition against states depriving any persons of their federal "privileges and immunities" was to be given a narrow construction. In particular, the "privileges and immunities" under the Constitution would refer only to those rights which were not felt to exist as a process of natural right, but which were created solely by the Constitution. These might refer to rights such as voting in federal elections and of interstate travel, which would clearly not exist except by virtue of the existence of a federal government and which could not be said to be "natural rights."[59] This paradoxically meant that the rights which most persons would accept as the most important—those flowing from concepts of natural justice—were devalued at the expense of more technical rights. Thus when individuals were charged with having deprived black citizens of their right to freedom of assembly and to keep and bear arms, by violently breaking up a peaceable assembly of black citizens, the Supreme Court in *United States v. Cruikshank* [60] held that no indictment could be properly brought since the right "of bearing arms for a lawful purpose" is "not a right granted by the Constitution. Neither is it in any manner dependent upon that instrument for its existence." Nor, in the view of the Court, was the right to peacefully assemble a right protected by the Fourteenth Amendment: "The right of the people peaceably to assemble for lawful purposes existed long before the adoption of the Constitution of the United States. In fact, it is and has always been one of the attributes of citizenship under a free government. ... It was not, therefore, a right granted to the people by the Constitution." Thus the very importance of the rights protected by the First and Second Amendment was used as the basis for the argument that they did not apply to the states under the Fourteenth Amendment. In later opinions, chiefly *Presser v. Illinois* [61] and *Miller v. Texas*, [62] the Supreme Court adhered to the view. *Cruikshank* has clearly been superseded by twentieth century opinions which hold that portions of the Bill of Rights—and in particular the right to assembly with which Cruikshank dealt in addition to the Second Amendment—are binding upon the state governments. Given the legislative history of the Civil Rights Acts and the Fourteenth Amendment, and the more expanded views of incorporation which have become accepted in our own century, it is clear that the right to keep and bear arms was meant to be and should be protected under the civil rights statutes and the Fourteenth Amendment against infringement by officials acting under color of state law.

Within our own century, the only occasion upon which the Second Amendment has reached the Supreme Court came in *United States v. Miller*.[63] There, a prosecution for carrying a sawed off shotgun was dismissed before trial on Second Amendment grounds. In doing so, the court took no evidence as to the nature of the firearm or indeed any other factual matter. The Supreme Court reversed on procedural grounds, holding that the trial court could not take judicial notice of the relationship between a firearm and the Second Amendment, but must receive some manner of evidence. It did not formulate a test nor state precisely what relationship might be required. The court's statement that the amendment was adopted "to assure the continuation and render possible the effectiveness of such [militia] forces" and "must be interpreted and applied with that end in view," when combined with the court's statement that all constitutional sources "show plainly enough that the militia comprised all males physically capable of acting in concert for the common defense. . . . these men were expected to appear bearing arms supplied by themselves and of the kind in common use at the time," [64] suggests that at the very least private ownership by a person capable of self defense and using an ordinary privately owned firearm must be protected by the Second Amendment. What the Court did not do in *Miller* is even more striking: It did not suggest that the lower court take evidence on whether Miller belonged to the National Guard or a similar group. The hearing was to be on the nature of the firearm, not on the nature of its use; nor is there a single suggestion that National Guard status is relevant to the case.

The Second Amendment right to keep and bear arms therefore, is a right of the individual citizen to privately possess and carry in a peaceful manner firearms and similar arms. Such an "individual rights" interpretation is in full accord with the history of the right to keep and bear arms, as previously discussed. It is moreover in accord with contemporaneous statements and formulations of the right by such founders of this nation as Thomas Jefferson and Samuel Adams, and accurately reflects the majority of the proposals which led up to the Bill of Rights itself. A number of state constitutions, adopted prior to or contemporaneously with the federal Constitution and Bill of Rights, similarly provided for a right of the people to keep and bear arms. If in fact this language creates a right protecting the states only, there might be a reason for it to . be inserted in the federal Constitution but no reason for it to be inserted in state constitutions. State bills of rights necessarily protect only against action by the state, and by definition a state cannot infringe its own rights; to attempt to protect a right belonging to the state by inserting it in a limitation of the state's own powers would create an absurdity. The fact that the contemporaries of the framers did insert these words into several state constitutions would indicate clearly that they viewed the right as belonging to the individual citizen, thereby making it a right which could be infringed either by state or federal government and which must be protected against infringement by both.

Finally, the individual rights interpretation gives full meaning to the words chosen by the first Congress to reflect the right to keep and bear arms. The framers of the Bill of Rights consistently used the words "right of the people" to reflect individual rights—as when these words were used to recognize the "right of the people" to peaceably assemble, and the "right of the people" against unreasonable searches and seizures. They distinguished between the rights of the people and of the state in the Tenth Amendment. As discussed earlier, the "militia" itself referred to a concept of a universally armed people, not to any specifically organized unit. When the framers referred to the equivalent of our National Guard, they uniformly used the term "select militia" and distinguished this from "militia." Indeed, the debates over the Constitution constantly referred to organized militia units as a threat to freedom comparable to that of a standing army, and stressed that such organized units did not constitute, and indeed were philosophically opposed to, the concept of a militia.

That the National Guard is not the "Militia" referred to in the second amendment is even clearer today. Congress has organized the National Guard under its power to 'raise and support armies" and not its power to "Provide for organizing, arming and disciplining the Militia."[65] This Congress chose to do in the interests of organizing reserve military units which were not limited in deployment by the strictures of our power over the constitutional militia, which can be called forth only "to execute the laws of the Union, suppress insurrections and repel invasions." The modern National Guard was specifically intended to avoid status as the constitutional militia, a distinction recognized by 10 U.S.C. §311(a). The conclusion is thus inescapable that the history, concept, and wording of the second amendment to the Constitution of the United States, as well as its interpretation by every major commentator and court in the first half-century after its ratification, indicates that what is protected is an individual right of a private citizen to own and carry firearms in a peaceful manner.

REFERENCES

1. Charles Hollister, *Anglo-Saxon Military Institutions* 11-42 (Oxford University Press 1962); Francis Grose, *Military Antiquities Respecting a History of the British Army*, Vol. I at 1-2 (London, 1812).
2. Grose, supra, at 9-11; Bruce Lyon, *A Constitutional and Legal History of Medieval England* 273 (2d. ed. New York 1980).
3. J. J. Bagley and P. B. Rowley, *A Documentary History of England 1066-1540*, Vol. 1 at 155-56 (New York 1965).
4. Statute of Winchester (13 Edw. I c. 6). See Also Bagley and Rowley, supra at 158.
5. 7 Ed. I c. 2 (1279).
6. Statute of Northampton (2 Edw. Ill c. 3).
7. *Rex v. Knight*, 90 Eng. Rep. 330; 87 Eng. Rep. 75 (King's Bench, 1686).
8. E. G. Heath, *The Grey Goose Wing* 109 (London, 1971).
9. 19 Hen. VII c. 4 (1503).
10. 3 Hen. VIII c. 13 (1511).
11. 64 Hen. VIII c. 13 (1514).
12. 33 Hen. VIII c. 6 (1514).
13. Noel Perrin, *Giving Up the Gun* 59-60 (Boston,

1979).

14. Jim Hill, *The Minuteman in War and Peace* 26-27 (Harrisburg, 1968).
15. Charles Oman, *A History of the Art of War in the Sixteenth Century* 288 (New York, 1937).
16. William Blackstone, *Commentaries*, Vol. 2 at 412 (St. George Tucker, ed., Philadelphia 1803).
17. "An Act for Settling the Militia," *Ordinances and Acts of the Interregnum*, Vol. 2 1320 (London, HMSO 1911).
18. 8 Calendar of State Papers (Domestic), Charles II, No. 188, p. 150.
19. 14 Car. II c. 3 (1662).
20. Joyce Malcolm, *Disarmed: The Loss of the Right to Bear Arms in Restoration England*, at 11 (Mary Ingraham Bunting Institute, Radcliffe College 1980).
21. Thomas Macaulay, *The History of England from the Accession of Charles II*, Vol. II at 137 (London, 1856).
22. Phillip, Earl of Hardwicke, *Miscellaneous State Papers from 1501-1726*, vol. 2 at 407-17 (London, 1778).
23. J. R. Western, *Monarchy and Revolution: The English State in the 1680's*, at 339 (Totowa, N.J., 1972).
24. Journal of the House of Commons from December 26, 1688, to October 26, 1693, at 29. (London, 1742). The Bill of Rights was ultimately enacted in this form. 1Gul. and Mar., Sess. 2, c. 2 (1689).
25. Joyce Malcolm, supra, at 16.
26. William Hening, *The Statutes at Large: Being a Collection of All the Laws of Virginia from the First Session of the Legislature in 1619*, at pp. 127, 173-74 (New York, 1823).
27. Id.
28. William Brigham, *The Compact with the Charter and Laws of the Colony of New Plymouth*, 31, 76 (Boston, 1836).
29. Oliver Dickerson, ed., *Boston Under Military Rule*, 61, 79, (Boston, 1936).
30. Steven Patterson, *Political Parties in Revolutionary Massachusetts*, at 103 (Univ. of Wisconsin Press, 1973).
31. See Sprecher, *The Lost Amendment*, 51 A.B.A.J. 554, 665 (1965).
32. 32. The most extensive studies of these militia proposals are John McAuley Palmer, *Washington, Lincoln, Wilson: Three War Statesmen* (New York, 1930); Frederick Stern, *Citizen Army* (New York, 1957); John Mahon, *The American Militia: Decade of Decision 1789-1800* (Univ. of Florida, 1960).
33. Merrill Jensen, ed., *The Documentary of History of the Ratification of the Constitution*, vol. 3 at 378 (Madison, Wisc.).
34. Id., vol. 2 at 508.
35. Walter Bennett, ed., *Letters from the Federal Farmer to the Republican*, at 21, 22, 124 (Univ. of Alabama Press, 1975).
36. *Debates and other Proceedings of the Convention of Virginia, . . . taken in shorthand by David Robertson of Petersburg*, at 271, 275 (2d ed. Richmond, 1805).
37. Noah Webster, "An Examination into the Leading Principles of the Federal Constitution . . .," in Paul Ford, ed., *Pamphlets on the Constitution of the United States*, at 56 (New York, 1888).
38. Johnathan Elliott, ed., *Debates in the Several State Conventions on the Adoption of the Federal Constitution*, vol. 2 at 97 (2d ed., 1888).
39. Merrill Jensen, supra, vol. 2 at 597-98.
40. *Debates and Proceedings in the Convention of the Commonwealth of Massachusetts*, at 86-87 (Peirce & Hale, eds., Boston, 1850); 2 B. Schwartz, The Bill of Rights 675 (1971).
41. *Documents Illustrative of the Formation of the Union of the American States*, at 1026 (Washington, D.C.: GPO, 1927).
42. Id. at 1030.
43. *Annals of Congress* 434 (1789).
44. St. George Tucker, ed., *Blackstone's Commentaries*, Volume 1 at 143 n. 40, 41 (Philadelphia, 1803).
45. William Rawle, *A View of the Constitution* 125-6 (2d ed., Philadelphia, 1803).
46. Joseph Story, *Commentaries on the Constitution*, vol. 2 at 746 (1833).
47. Act of May 8, 1792; Second Cong., First Session,

ch. 33.

48. *Bliss v. Commonwealth*, 12 Ken. (2 Litt.) 90, 92 (1822).
49. *State v. Mitchell*, (3 Black.) 229.
50. *State v. Reid*, 1 Ala. 612, 35 Am. Dec. 44 (1840).
51. *State v. Buzzard*, 4 Ark. 18, 27, 36 (1842). The Arkansas Constitutional provision at issue was narrower than the second amendment, as it protected keeping and bearing arms "for the common defense." Id. at 34.
52. *Nunn v. State*, 1 Ga. 243, 251 (1846).
53. *Dred Scott v. Sandford*, 60 U.S. 691, 705.
54. The most comprehensive work in this field of constitutional law is Steven Halbrook, *The Jurisprudence of the Second and Fourteenth Amendments* (Institute for Humane Studies, Menlo Park, California, 1979), reprinted in 4 George Mason L. Rev. 1 (1981).
55. *Cong. Globe*, 39th Congress, 1st Sess., pt. 1, p. 474 (Jan. 29, 1866).
56. Id. at 478.
57. H.R. Rep. No. 37, 41st Cong., 3d sess., p. 3 (1871).
58. See generally Halbrook, supra, at 42-62.
59. *Slaughterhouse Cases*, 83 U.S. 36 (L873).
60. *United States v. Cruikshank*, 92 U.S. 542 (1876).
61. *Presser v. Illinois*, 116 U.S. 252 (1886).
62. *Miller v. Texas*, 153 U.S. 535 (1894).
63. *United States v. Miller*, 307 U.S. 175 (1939).
64. Id. at 178, 179.
65. H.R. Report No. 141, 73d Cong., 1st sess. at 2-5.

Document Themes

The author of "History: Second Amendment Right to 'Keep and Bear Arms'" offers a succinct but thorough examination of the Anglo-American roots of the Second Amendment and of interpretations of the amendment in the years following the ratification of the Constitution and the Bill of Rights. The author begins by touching on the laws of Alfred the Great in the ninth century, the impact of the Norman Conquest of Britain in the eleventh century, and the policies of the Tudor kings. Of course, at this point, firearms were not being regulated, but such weapons as longbows were subject to royal decree. It was not until the sixteenth century that firearms were first regulated in England. As political tensions in England grew, the issue of who controlled the militia—the king, or Parliament—bubbled to the surface, leading to disarmament of the citizenry under the 1662 Militia Act. In the wake of the Glorious Revolution in 1668, Parliament insisted that the new monarch, William of Orange, respect the rights of British citizens outlined in what came to be called the English Bill of Rights of 1689; one of the provisions of the English Bill of Rights was the right to bear arms.

Meanwhile, in the British colonies, ownership of firearms was commonplace, and colonists regarded their firearms as a bulwark against British tyranny. Several state constitutions affirmed a citizen's right to bear arms, and that right was further affirmed in the U.S. Constitution's Bill of Rights. The author marshals historical evidence in support of the view that the framers intended the Second Amendment to apply to the right of individuals to keep and bear arms.

The author then examines views of the Second Amendment held by nineteenth-century constitutional scholars, among them St. George Tucker, William Rawle, and Joseph Story. Further, the author examines critical nineteenth-century legal cases pertaining to firearms and firearm regulation. Many of these cases took up the issue of the militia and the seemingly ambiguous relationship between the "well regulated Militia" and "the right of the People to keep and bear Arms" of the Second Amendment. The author notes that in the twentieth century, the only Supreme Court case bearing on the Second Amendment was *United States v. Miller* (1939). The author concludes that "the Second Amendment right to keep and bear arms . . . is a right of the individual citizen to privately possess and carry in a peaceful manner firearms and similar arms. Such an 'individual rights' interpretation is in full accord with the history of the right to keep and bear arms."

Additional Readings

Charles, Patrick J., *Armed in America: A History of Gun Rights from Colonial Militias to Concealed Carry* (Amherst, NY: Prometheus Books, 2018).

Halbrook, Stephen P., *That Every Man Be Armed: The Evolution of a Constitutional Right*, rev. ed. (Albuquerque, NM: University of New Mexico Press, 2013).

Malcolm, Joyce Lee, *To Keep and Bear Arms: The Origins of an Anglo-American Right* (Cambridge, MA: Harvard University Press, 1996).

Saul Cornell, "St. George Tucker and the Second Amendment: Original Understandings and Modern Misunderstandings," *William and Mary Law Review*, 47, no. 4 (February 2006), 1123–55, http://scholarship.law.wm.edu/cgi/viewcontent.cgi?article=1231&context=wmlr&sei-redir=1

Vandercoy, David E., "The History of the Second Amendment," *Valparaiso University Law Review* 28, no. 3 (Spring 1994): 1007–39.

Yassky, David S., "The Second Amendment: Structure, History, and Constitutional Change," *Michigan Law Review* 99 (December 2000): 588–668.

Zimring, Franklin E., "Firearms and Federal Law: The Gun Control Act of 1968," *Journal of Legal Studies* 4 (January 1975): 133–98.

—*Michael J. O'Neal*

"All Guns Are Not Created Equal"

Author(s): Kevin M. Sweeney and Saul Cornell
Date: 2013
Genre: Article

Summary Overview

This article, first published in the *Chronicle of Higher Education*, was written by two historians whose purpose was to examine the meaning of the Second Amendment in the context of the types of armaments in use in the late eighteenth century. Their views run counter to those of other historians and legal scholars who argue that the Second Amendment affirms an individual right to keep and bear arms. Sweeney and Cornell, in contrast, argue that the Second Amendment was about the militia, not about personal self-defense, and in this regard they reject the conclusion reached by the U.S. Supreme Court in *District of Columbia v. Heller* (2008) that the Second Amendment protects a personal right to bear arms. They state, trenchantly, that the Court's ruling in *Heller* "makes sense only if you believe that Dirty Harry was the typical American in 1791."

Defining Moment

The defining moment of "All Guns Are Not Created Equal" would appear to be the U.S. Supreme Court's decision in *District of Columbia v. Heller*, a 2008 case ruling on the district's statute pertaining to the ownership of handguns in the home. That statute made it illegal to carry an unregistered firearm and prohibited the registration of handguns to be kept in the home. In effect, the statute amounted to a ban on handguns for most citizens. Dick Heller, who was authorized to carry a handgun while on duty as a special police officer at the Federal Judicial Center, was denied a license to keep a gun in his home. He filed suit against the city, arguing that the district's statute violated his rights under the Second Amendment. A district court dismissed his complaint, but the U.S. Court of Appeals for the District of Columbia reversed the ruling of the district court, ruling that the Second Amendment protects the right of an individual to keep a firearm in the home for self-defense. The district, hoping to preserve its gun ban, appealed to the U.S. Supreme Court, but the Court ruled in Heller's favor. The decision in *Heller* was written by Associate Justice Antonin Scalia, who extensively surveyed the historical record and concluded that the Second Amendment protects the right of individuals to arm themselves to defend their home. Sweeney and Cornell take issue with Scalia's analysis, citing other evidence that in their view refutes Scalia's conclusions.

About the Author

Kevin M. Sweeney earned a bachelor's degree at Williams College in 1972. He went on to earn a master's degree (1973), a master of philosophy degree (1975), and a Ph.D. (1986) from Yale University. Meanwhile, for nearly a decade, he worked in history museums. He joined the faculty of Amherst College in Massachusetts 1989, where he taught history and American Studies courses until his retirement. His area of specialization was colonial history, with emphasis on the material culture of early America.

One of the most prominent names in discussions of the Second Amendment is that of Saul Cornell, who occupies the Paul and Diane Guenther Chair in American history at Fordham University. He previously had been an assistant professor of history at the College of William and Mary and professor of history at Ohio State University. He is also a former director of the Second Amendment Research Center at the John Glenn Institute at Ohio State. He attended the University of Sussex in England before receiving a bachelor's degree in history from Amherst College in 1982. He went on to earn a master's degree (1985) and Ph.D. (1989) in history from the University of Pennsylvania. He is the author of numerous books and articles, including *The Other Founders: Anti-Federalism and the Dissenting Tradition in America* (1999), *Whose Right to Bear Arms Did the Second Amendment Protect?* (2000), and *A Well-Regulated Militia: The Founding Fathers and the Origins of Gun Control in America* (2006). He is also the co-author of many other publications, including the textbook *Visions of America: A History of the United States* (2009). Additionally, he has written a number of amicus curiae briefs in court cases involving the Second Amendment, including a brief he co-authored in *District of Columbia v. Heller.*

HISTORICAL DOCUMENT

"All Guns Are Not Created Equal"

Few debates in the recent past have been as contentious as the one surrounding the history of gun ownership. Once again, as the nation considers gun violence, gun rights, and gun regulation, we return to early America to shed light on the meaning of the Second Amendment.

When more than a decade ago the historian Michael A. Bellesiles wrote a controversial book claiming that Americans at the time of the Second Amendment's ratification owned few guns and were not particularly skilled at using them, he triggered a firestorm of controversy. That revisionist thesis was soon discredited for its dishonest use of historical evidence, leaving largely unchallenged the suspect counter-narrative put forth by some legal scholars and the National Rifle Association.

The latter mythical history, which the U.S. Supreme Court majority swallowed whole in *District of Columbia v. Heller* (2008) when it ruled that the "Second Amendment protects an individual right to possess a firearm," goes something like this: In early America, all adult males owned firearms; those privately owned guns armed the militia; the Second Amendment was meant to ensure an individual's right to own firearms for self-defense and as protection against tyranny. But the actual historical record is much more complicated—and more interesting.

Data from probate inventories, militia rolls, and colonial census returns reveal that private gun ownership was quite common during the 1600s, and though it declined in cities and along the coast during the later 1700s, it remained widespread in most rural areas. Generally, colonists preferred to own fowlers, Indian trade guns, and fusils (light muskets) well suited to birding, hunting, and pest control, and not heavier military-style muskets. Essentially these weapons were in purpose closer to a modern shotgun or a .22 rifle than an M-16 assault rifle. A distinct minority of colonists, mostly urban residents, owned pistols that had a limited range and limited military uses.

Self-defense was not the issue; national defense was.

During the second half of the 18th century, colonial governments and then revolutionary state governments concluded that lighter personal firearms were no longer adequate for soldiers in the field or militiamen at musters. Governments wanted their soldiers and militiamen armed like British Regulars, who carried the Brown Bess, a heavy, large-caliber smoothbore military musket that fired lead balls weighing about an ounce each and was equipped with a steel ramrod and 17-inch bayonet. But in New York, government reports show, some colonial militiamen were "so indigent" that they couldn't "purchase their proper arms," and in Georgia, "many" in the militia were "unable to purchase arms."

The shift in requirements created problems during the Revolutionary War. To deal with the problem, a number of states distributed to their militiamen thousands of publicly owned military muskets equipped with steel ramrods and bayonets, but inadequate supplies, losses, and wastage made the task of providing the desired type of firearms nearly impossible.

By the time the fighting had ended, state militias lacked adequate firearms, which became a continuing problem and source of discontent. In Virginia, the former wartime governor Thomas Jefferson wrote that the "law requires every militia-man to provide himself with arms usual in regular service," but that "in the lower parts of the country they are entirely disarmed. In the middle country a fourth or fifth part of them may have such firelocks as they had provided to destroy the noxious animals which infest their farms."

In Pennsylvania, militiamen remained dependent on publicly supplied muskets. Late in 1787, they protested when the state recalled their firearms to clean them and possibly redistribute them to exposed frontier counties. It is also telling that in 1786-87, the Massachusetts uprising that came to be known as Shays' Rebellion led to a climactic confrontation at the national arsenal in Springfield as both sides sought to control its store of 7,000 military muskets.

In the late 1780s, many state militias no longer appeared to be capable of ensuring what the Second Amendment would call the "security of a free State" without improved organization, better training, and thousands of publicly supplied military muskets with bayonets. Americans were not worried that agents of the new federal government would come, door to door, to take away their squirrel guns, trade guns, fowlers, and pistols. Nor was the problem that concerned them the disarmament of some imaginary "people's militia" or "civilian militia"—rhetorical terms found in the *Heller* decision that have no historical basis.

Instead, the very real danger was that the existing state militias would be disarmed by simple federal inaction.

Antifederalists such as George Mason wanted reassurance that, "in case the general government should neglect to arm and discipline the militia there should be an express declaration, that the state governments might arm and discipline them." It was in that context that the Second Amendment emerged and was ratified in 1791.

So what does all of that say about the current debate over the regulation of firearms and the meaning of the Second Amendment?

The first point is that, even in the 18th century, not all guns were created equal. Today all 18th-century muzzle-loading, single-shot firearms appear to be ineffective and antiquated. But members of the founding generation saw them differently, making distinctions concerning the size and use of firearms just as we do today.

Second, not all private arms—especially pistols—were militia arms, and not all militia arms were private arms, by the late 1700s.

Third, the assumption by the majority in *Heller* that the Second Amendment gave handguns constitutional protection because "the American people have considered the handgun to be the quintessential self-defense weapon" fails to meet the self-proclaimed standard of those jurists seeking to recover the Constitution's original meaning. According to the originalists, a document's words mean what the average rational man on the street thought they meant at the time. The ruling makes sense only if you believe that Dirty Harry was the typical American in 1791.

Fourth, despite Justice Anthony Kennedy's observation during oral arguments in *Heller* that the authors of the Second Amendment were worried about defending themselves against "grizzlies and things like that," references to hunting, in general, and bears, in particular, were rather rare in the debates over the Constitution and the Second Amendment. One could say they were almost as rare as encountering a grizzly bear east of the Ohio River. Protecting or banning firearms that would be the equivalent of today's shotguns and .22s was not really an issue at the time.

Finally, the Second Amendment really was about the militia. The need for it grew out of the Constitution's grant of power to the federal government for "organizing, arming, and disciplining" the state militias and the continuing need to equip them with military-style muskets.

The Second Amendment sought to reassure Antifederalists rhetorically, but not substantively. Critics and concerned state officials feared that actions or, more likely, inactions by the federal government would frustrate efforts to supply the nation's 13 state militias—the equivalent of today's National Guard—with the period's equivalent of the M-16. Self-defense was not the issue; national defense was.

Those who crafted and ratified the Second Amendment were dealing with very different issues from those we face today. We need to move our discussions about guns beyond claims rooted in a debate over securing military muskets to arm the militia. At the same time, it is useful to be aware that even in the 18th century, citizens and lawmakers made distinctions concerning the appropriate uses of different types of firearms.

Arms and the Man *masthead, incorporating previous titles* The Rifle *and* Shooting and Fishing. *(By National Rifle Association of America.)*

Document Themes

The authors stake out their position early on when they refer to the "mythical" history of the Second Amendment advanced by the National Rifle Association and others and "swallowed whole" by the U.S. Supreme Court in its decision in *District of Columbia v. Heller*, where the Court ruled that the "Second Amendment protects an individual right to possess a firearm." The authors argue that the matter is "more complicated" than the Supreme Court's analysis would suggest. They point out, first, that the weapons favored by the colonists tended to be lighter weapons most suitable for activities such as fowling and not the heavier muskets that would have been used by the militia, suggesting that the argument that colonists had to provide their own weapons when called up for militia duty fails to tell the entire story. Further, urban residents owned weapons, usually pistols, that were roughly equivalent to today's .22-caliber weapons, making them unsuitable for militia duty. The authors then state: "Self-defense was not the issue; national defense was."

In support of their view, Sweeney and Cornell point to evidence showing that "governments wanted their soldiers and militiamen armed like British Regulars, who carried the Brown Bess, a heavy, large-caliber smoothbore military musket that fired lead balls weighing about an ounce each and was equipped with a steel ramrod and 17-inch bayonet." During the Revolutionary War, these kinds of weapons were provided by the states, not by the individual militiamen. After the war, the militia in states like Pennsylvania relied on publically owned firearms. The fear among the states was not that the federal government would disarm them but rather that the federal government would, through inaction, fail to provide the weapons the militia needed. Many militiamen were frustrated that they were unable to purchase suitable weapons because of shortages. These considerations lead the authors to the conclusion that "not all private arms—especially pistols—were militia arms, and not all militia arms were private arms, by the late 1700s." Further, the authors conclude: "The Second Amendment really was about the militia. The need for it grew out of the Constitution's grant of power to the federal government for 'organizing, arming, and disciplining' the state militias and the continuing need to equip them with military-style muskets."

Additional Reading

Charles, Patrick J., *Armed in America: A History of Gun Rights from Colonial Militias to Concealed Carry* (Amherst, NY: Prometheus Books, 2018).

Epps, Garrett, "The Second Amendment Does Not Transcend All Others," *Atlantic*, March 8, 2018, https://www.theatlantic.com/politics/archive/2018/03/second-amendment-text-context/555101/.

Finkelman, Paul, "A Well Regulated Militia: The Second Amendment in Historical Perspective," *Chicago-Kent Law Review* 76, no. 1 (October 2000): 195–236.

Mondschein, Ken, "'A Well-Regulated Militia': The Medieval Origins of the Second Amendment," Medievalists.net, April 23, 2018, http://www.medievalists.net/2018/04/medieval-origins-of-the-second-amendment/.

Shusterman, Hoah, "What the Second Amendment Really Meant to the Founders," *Washington Post*, February 22, 2018, https://www.washingtonpost.com/.

Sullivan, William, "Is the Second Amendment for Just the Militia?," *American Thinker*, April 5, 2018, https://www.americanthinker.com/articles/2018/04/is_the_second_amendment_for_just_the_militia.html.

—*Michael J. O'Neal*

SUPPLEMENTAL HISTORICAL DOCUMENT

Public Safety and Recreational Firearms Use Protection Act

TITLE XI--FIREARMS

SEC. 110102. RESTRICTION ON MANUFACTURE, TRANSFER, AND POSSESSION OF CERTAIN SEMIAUTOMATIC ASSAULT WEAPONS.

(a) Restriction.--Section 922 of title 18, United States Code, is amended by adding at the end the following new subsection:

"(v)(1) It shall be unlawful for a person to manufacture, transfer, or possess a semiautomatic assault weapon.

"(2) Paragraph (1) shall not apply to the possession or transfer of any semiautomatic assault weapon otherwise lawfully possessed under Federal law on the date of the enactment of this subsection.

"(3) Paragraph (1) shall not apply to--

"(A) any of the firearms, or replicas or duplicates of the firearms, specified in Appendix A to this section, as such firearms were manufactured on October 1, 1993;

"(B) any firearm that--

"(i) is manually operated by bolt, pump, lever, or slide action;

"(ii) has been rendered permanently inoperable; or

"(iii) is an antique firearm;

"(C) any semiautomatic rifle that cannot accept a detachable magazine that holds more than 5 rounds of ammunition; or

"(D) any semiautomatic shotgun that cannot hold more than 5 rounds of ammunition in a fixed or detachable magazine.

The fact that a firearm is not listed in Appendix A shall not be construed to mean that paragraph (1) applies to such firearm. No firearm exempted by this subsection may be deleted from Appendix A so long as this subsection is in effect.

* * * * *

(c) Penalties.--

(1) Violation of section 922(v).--Section 924(a)(1)(B) of such title is amended by striking "or (q) of section 922" and inserting "(r), or (v) of section 922".

(2) Use or possession during crime of violence or drug trafficking crime.--Section 924(c)(1) of such title is amended in the first sentence by inserting ", or semiautomatic assault weapon," after "short-barreled shotgun,".

(d) Identification Markings for Semiautomatic Assault Weapons.--

Section 923(i) of such title is amended by adding at the end the following: "The serial number of any semiautomatic assault weapon manufactured after the date of the enactment of this sentence shall clearly show the date on which the weapon was manufactured.".

SEC. 110103. BAN OF LARGE CAPACITY AMMUNITION FEEDING DEVICES.

(a) Prohibition.--Section 922 of title 18, United States Code, as amended by section 110102(a), is amended by adding at the end the following new subsection:

"(w)(1) Except as provided in paragraph (2), it shall be unlawful for a person to transfer or possess a large capacity ammunition feeding device.

"(2) Paragraph (1) shall not apply to the possession or transfer of any large capacity ammunition feeding device otherwise lawfully possessed on or before the date of the enactment of this subsection.

"(3) This subsection shall not apply to--

"(A) the manufacture for, transfer to, or possession by the United States or a department or agency of the United States or a State or a department, agency, or political subdivision of a State, or a transfer to or possession by a law enforcement officer employed by such an entity for purposes of law enforcement (whether on or off duty);

"(B) the transfer to a licensee under title I of the Atomic Energy Act of 1954 for purposes of establishing and maintaining an on-site physical protection system and security organization required by Federal law, or possession by an employee or contractor of such licensee on-site for such purposes or off-site for purposes of licensee-authorized training or transportation of nuclear materials;

"(C) the possession, by an individual who is retired from service with a law enforcement agency and is not otherwise prohibited from receiving ammunition, of a large capacity ammunition feeding device transferred to the individual by the agency upon such retirement; or

"(D) the manufacture, transfer, or possession of any large capacity ammunition feeding device by a licensed manufacturer or licensed importer for the purposes of testing or experimentation authorized by the Secretary.".

"(4) If a person charged with violating paragraph (1) asserts that paragraph (1) does not apply to such person because of paragraph (2) or (3), the Government shall have the burden of proof to show that such paragraph (1) applies to such person. The lack of a serial number as described in section 923(i) of title 18, United States Code, shall be a presumption that the large capacity ammunition feeding device is not subject to the prohibition of possession in paragraph (1).".

* * * * *

SEC. 110104. STUDY BY ATTORNEY GENERAL.

(a) Study.--The Attorney General shall investigate and study the effect of this subtitle and the amendments made by this subtitle, and in particular shall determine their impact, if any, on violent and drug trafficking crime. The study shall be conducted over a period of 18 months, commencing 12 months after the date of enactment of this Act.

(b) Report.--Not later than 30 months after the date of enactment of this Act, the Attorney General shall prepare and submit to the Congress a report setting forth in detail the findings and determinations made in the study under subsection (a).

SEC. 110105. EFFECTIVE DATE.

This subtitle and the amendments made by this subtitle--

(1) shall take effect on the date of the enactment of this Act; and

(2) are repealed effective as of the date that is 10 years after that date.

Subtitle B--Youth Handgun Safety

SEC. 110201. PROHIBITION OF THE POSSESSION OF A HANDGUN OR AMMUNITION BY, OR THE PRIVATE TRANSFER OF A HANDGUN OR AMMUNITION TO, A JUVENILE.

(a) Offense.--Section 922 of title 18, United States Code, as amended by section 110103(a), is amended by adding at the end the following new subsection:

"(x)(1) It shall be unlawful for a person to sell, deliver, or otherwise transfer to a person who the transferor knows or has reasonable cause to believe is a juvenile--

"(A) a handgun; or

"(B) ammunition that is suitable for use only in a handgun.

"(2) It shall be unlawful for any person who is a juvenile to knowingly possess--

"(A) a handgun; or

"(B) ammunition that is suitable for use only in a handgun.

"(3) This subsection does not apply to--

"(A) a temporary transfer of a handgun or ammunition to a juvenile or to the possession or use of a handgun or ammunition by a juvenile if the handgun and ammunition are possessed and used by the juvenile--

"(i) in the course of employment, in the course of ranching or farming related to activities at the residence of the juvenile (or on property used for ranching or farming at which the juvenile, with the permission of the property owner or lessee, is performing activities related to the operation of the farm or ranch), target practice, hunting, or a course of instruction in the safe and lawful use of a handgun;

"(ii) with the prior written consent of the juvenile's parent or guardian who is not prohibited by Federal, State, or local law from possessing a firearm, except--

"(I) during transportation by the juvenile of an unloaded handgun in a locked container directly from the place of transfer to a place at which an activity described in clause (i) is to take place and transportation by the juvenile of that handgun, unloaded and in a locked container, directly from the place at which such an activity took place to the transferor; or

"(II) with respect to ranching or farming activities as described in clause (i), a juvenile may possess and use a handgun or ammunition with the prior written approval of the juvenile's parent or legal guardian and at the direction of an adult who is not prohibited by Federal, State or local law from possessing a firearm;

"(iii) the juvenile has the prior written consent in the juvenile's possession at all times when a handgun is in the possession of the juvenile; and "(iv) in accordance with State and local law;

"(B) a juvenile who is a member of the Armed Forces of the United States or the National Guard who possesses or is armed with a handgun in the line of duty;

"(C) a transfer by inheritance of title (but not possession) of a handgun or ammunition to a juvenile; or

"(D) the possession of a handgun or ammunition by a juvenile taken in defense of the juvenile or other persons against an intruder into the residence of the juvenile or a residence in which the juvenile is an invited guest.

"(4) A handgun or ammunition, the possession of which is transferred to a juvenile in circumstances in which the transferor is not in violation of this subsection shall not be subject to permanent confiscation by the Government if its possession by the juvenile subsequently becomes unlawful because of the conduct of the juvenile, but shall be returned to the lawful owner when such handgun or ammunition is no longer required by the Government for the purposes of investigation or prosecution.

"(5) For purposes of this subsection, the term 'juvenile' means a person who is less than 18 years of age.

"(6)(A) In a prosecution of a violation of this subsection, the court shall require the presence of a juvenile defendant's parent or legal guardian at all proceedings.

"(B) The court may use the contempt power to enforce subparagraph (A).

"(C) The court may excuse attendance of a parent or legal guardian of a juvenile defendant at a proceeding in a prosecution of a violation of this subsection for good cause shown.".

* * * * *

SEC. 110301. FIREARMS LICENSURE AND REGISTRATION TO REQUIRE A PHOTOGRAPH AND FINGERPRINTS.

(a) Firearms Licensure.--Section 923(a) of title 18, United States Code, is amended in the second sentence by inserting "and shall include a photograph and fingerprints of the applicant" before the period.

(b) Registration.--Section 5802 of the Internal Revenue Code of 1986 is amended by inserting after the first sentence the following: "An individual required to register under this section shall include a photograph and fingerprints of the individual with the initial application.".

SEC. 110302. COMPLIANCE WITH STATE AND LOCAL LAW AS A CONDITION TO LICENSE.

* * * * *

SEC. 110303. ACTION ON FIREARMS LICENSE APPLICATION.

Section 923(d)(2) of title 18, United States Code, is amended by striking "forty-five-day" and inserting "60-day".

SEC. 110304. INSPECTION OF FIREARMS LICENSEES' INVENTORY AND RECORDS.

Section 923(g)(1)(B)(ii) of title 18, United States Code, is amended to read as follows:

"(ii) for ensuring compliance with the record keeping requirements of this chapter--

"(I) not more than once during any 12-month period; or

"(II) at any time with respect to records relating to a firearm involved in a criminal investigation that is traced to the licensee.".

SEC. 110305. REPORTS OF THEFT OR LOSS OF FIREARMS.

Section 923(g) of title 18, United States Code, is amended by adding at the end the following new paragraph:

"(6) Each licensee shall report the theft or loss of a firearm from the licensee's inventory or collection, within 48 hours after the theft or loss is discovered, to the Secretary and to the appropriate local authorities.".

* * * * *

SEC. 110307. NOTIFICATION OF NAMES AND ADDRESSES OF FIREARMS LICENSEES.

Section 923 of title 18, United States Code, is amended by adding at the end the following new subsection:

"(1) The Secretary of the Treasury shall notify the chief law enforcement officer in the appropriate State and local jurisdictions of the names and addresses of all persons in the State to whom a firearms license is issued.".

Subtitle D--Domestic Violence

SEC. 110401. PROHIBITION AGAINST DISPOSAL OF FIREARMS TO, OR RECEIPT OF FIREARMS BY, PERSONS WHO HAVE COMMITTED DOMESTIC ABUSE.

(a) Intimate Partner Defined.--Section 921(a) of title 18, United States Code, as amended by section 110103(b), is amended by inserting at the end the following new paragraph:

"(32) The term 'intimate partner' means, with respect to a person, the spouse of the person, a former spouse of the person, an individual who is a parent of a child of the person, and an individual who cohabitates or has cohabited with the person.".

(b) Prohibition Against Disposal of Firearms.--Section 922(d) of title 18, United States Code, is amended--

(1) by striking "or" at the end of paragraph (6);

(2) by striking the period at the end of paragraph (7) and inserting "; or"; and

(3) by inserting after paragraph (7) the following new paragraph:

"(8) is subject to a court order that restrains such person from harassing, stalking, or threatening an intimate partner of such person or child of such intimate partner or person, or engaging in other conduct that would place an intimate partner in reasonable fear of bodily injury to the partner or child, except that this paragraph shall only apply to a court order that--

"(A) was issued after a hearing of which such person received actual notice, and at which such person had the opportunity to participate; and

"(B)(i) includes a finding that such person represents a credible threat to the physical safety of such intimate partner or child; or

"(ii) by its terms explicitly prohibits the use, attempted use, or threatened use of physical force against such intimate partner or child that would reasonably be expected to cause bodily injury.".

(c) Prohibition Against Receipt of Firearms.--Section 922(g) of title 18, United States Code, is amended--

(1) by striking "or" at the end of paragraph (6);

(2) by inserting "or" at the end of paragraph (7); and

(3) by inserting after paragraph (7) the following:

"(8) who is subject to a court order that--

"(A) was issued after a hearing of which such person received actual notice, and at which such person had an opportunity to participate;

"(B) restrains such person from harassing, stalking, or threatening an intimate partner of such person or child of such intimate partner or person, or engaging in other conduct that would place an intimate partner in reasonable fear of bodily injury to the partner or child; and

"(C)(i) includes a finding that such person represents a credible threat to the physical safety of such intimate partner or child; or

"(ii) by its terms explicitly prohibits the use, attempted use, or threatened use of physical force against such intimate partner or child that would reasonably be expected to cause bodily injury,".

(d) Storage of Firearms.--Section 926(a) of title 18, United States Code, is amended--

(1) by striking "and" at the end of paragraph (1);

(2) by striking the period at the end of paragraph (2) and inserting "; and"; and

(3) by inserting after paragraph (2) the following:

"(3) regulations providing for effective receipt and secure storage of firearms relinquished by or seized from persons described in subsection (d)(8) or (g)(8) of section 922.".

(e) Return of Firearms.--Section 924(d)(1) of title 18, United States Code, is amended by striking "the seized" and inserting "or lapse of or court termination of the restraining order to which he is subject, the seized or relinquished".

SEC. 110501. ENHANCED PENALTY FOR USE OF A SEMIAUTOMATIC FIREARM DURING A CRIME OF VIOLENCE OR A DRUG TRAFFICKING CRIME.

(a) Amendment to Sentencing Guidelines.--Pursuant to its authority under section 994 of title 28, United States Code, the United States Sentencing Commission shall amend its sentencing guidelines to provide an appropriate enhancement of the punishment for a crime of violence (as defined in section 924(c)(3) of title 18, United States Code) or a drug trafficking crime (as defined in section 924(c)(2) of title 18, United States Code) if a semiautomatic firearm is involved.

(b) Semiautomatic Firearm.--In subsection (a), "semiautomatic firearm" means any repeating firearm that utilizes a portion of the energy of a firing cartridge to extract the fired cartridge case and chamber the next round and that requires a separate pull of the trigger to fire each cartridge.

SEC. 110502. ENHANCED PENALTY FOR SECOND OFFENSE OF USING AN EXPLOSIVE TO COMMIT A FELONY.

Pursuant to its authority under section 994 of title 28, United States Code, the United States Sentencing Commission shall promulgate amendments to the sentencing guidelines to appropriately enhance penalties in a case in which a defendant convicted under section 844(h) of title 18, United States Code, has previously been convicted under that section.

SEC. 110503. SMUGGLING FIREARMS IN AID OF DRUG TRAFFICKING.

Section 924 of title 18, United States Code, as amended by section 60013, is amended by adding at the end the following new subsection:

"(j) A person who, with intent to engage in or to promote conduct that--

"(1) is punishable under the Controlled Substances Act (21 U.S.C. 801 et seq.), the Controlled Substances Import and Export Act (21 U.S.C. 951 et seq.), or the Maritime Drug Law Enforcement Act (46 U.S.C. App. 1901 et seq.);

"(2) violates any law of a State relating to any controlled substance (as defined in section 102 of the Controlled Substances Act, 21 U.S.C. 802); or

"(3) constitutes a crime of violence (as defined in subsection (c)(3),

smuggles or knowingly brings into the United States a firearm, or attempts to do so, shall be imprisoned not more than 10 years, fined under this title, or both.".

SEC. 110504. THEFT OF FIREARMS AND EXPLOSIVES.

(a) Firearms.--Section 924 of title 18, United States Code, as amended by section 110203(a), is amended by adding at the end the following new subsection:

"(k) A person who steals any firearm which is moving as, or is a part of, or which has moved in, interstate or foreign commerce shall be imprisoned for not more than 10 years, fined under this title, or both.".

(b) Explosives.--Section 844 of title 18, United States Code, is amended by adding at the end the following new subsection:

"(k) A person who steals any explosives materials which are moving as, or are a part of, or which have moved in, interstate or foreign commerce shall be imprisoned for not more than 10 years, fined under this title, or both.".

* * * * *

SEC. 110509. SUMMARY DESTRUCTION OF EXPLOSIVES SUBJECT TO FORFEITURE.

Section 844(c) of title 18, United States Code, is amended--

(1) by inserting "(1)" after "(c)"; and

(2) by adding at the end the following new paragraphs:

"(2) Notwithstanding paragraph (1), in the case of the seizure of any explosive materials for any offense for which the materials would be subject to forfeiture in which it would be impracticable or unsafe to remove the materials to a place of storage or would be unsafe to store them, the seizing officer may destroy the explosive materials forthwith. Any destruction under this paragraph shall be in the presence of at least 1 credible witness. The seizing officer shall make a report of the seizure and take samples as the Secretary may by regulation prescribe.

"(3) Within 60 days after any destruction made pursuant to paragraph (2), the owner of (including any person having an interest in) the property so destroyed may make application to the Secretary for reimbursement of the value of the property. If the claimant establishes to the satisfaction of the Secretary that--

"(A) the property has not been used or involved in a violation of law; or

"(B) any unlawful involvement or use of the property was without the claimant's knowledge, consent, or willful blindness,

the Secretary shall make an allowance to the claimant not exceeding the value of the property destroyed.".

* * * *

SEC. 110512. USING A FIREARM IN THE COMMISSION OF COUNTERFEITING OR FORGERY.

Pursuant to its authority under section 994 of title 28, United States Code, the United States Sentencing Commission shall amend its sentencing guidelines to provide an appropriate enhancement of the punishment for a defendant convicted of a felony under chapter 25 of title 18, United States Code, if the defendant used or carried a firearm (as defined in section 921(a)(3) of title 18, United States Code) during and in relation to the felony.

SEC. 110513. ENHANCED PENALTIES FOR FIREARMS POSSESSION BY VIOLENT FELONS AND SERIOUS DRUG OFFENDERS.

Pursuant to its authority under section 994 of title 28, United States Code, the United States Sentencing Commission shall amend its sentencing guidelines to--

(1) appropriately enhance penalties in cases in which a defendant convicted under section 922(g) of title 18, United States Code, has 1 prior conviction by any court referred to in section 922(g)(1) of title 18 for a violent felony (as defined in section 924(e)(2)(B) of that title) or a serious drug offense (as defined in section 924(e)(2)(A) of that title); and

(2) appropriately enhance penalties in cases in which such a defendant has 2 prior convictions for a violent felony (as so defined) or a serious drug offense (as so defined).

* * * *

SEC. 110517. INCREASED PENALTY FOR INTERSTATE GUN TRAFFICKING.

Section 924 of title 18, United States Code, as amended by section 110515(a), is amended by adding at the end the following new subsection:

"(m) A person who, with the intent to engage in conduct that constitutes a violation of section 922(a)(1)(A), travels from any State or foreign country into any other State and acquires, or attempts to acquire, a firearm in such other State in furtherance of such purpose shall be imprisoned for not more than 10 years.".

SEC. 110518. FIREARMS AND EXPLOSIVES CONSPIRACY.

(a) Firearms.--Section 924 of title 18, United States Code, as amended by section 110517(a), is amended by adding at the end the following new subsection:

"(n) A person who conspires to commit an offense under subsection (c) shall be imprisoned for not more than 20 years, fined under this title, or both; and if the firearm is a machinegun or destructive device, or is equipped with a firearm silencer or muffler, shall be imprisoned for any term of years or life.".

(b) Explosives.--Section 844 of title 18, United States Code, as amended by section 110515(b), is amended by adding at the end the following new subsection:

"(m) A person who conspires to commit an offense under subsection (h) shall be imprisoned for any term of years not exceeding 20, fined under this title, or both.

SEC. 110519. DEFINITION OF ARMOR PIERCING AMMUNITION.

Section 921(a)(17) of title 18, United States Code, is amended by revising subparagraph (B) and adding a new subparagraph (C) to read as follows:

"(B) The term 'armor piercing ammunition' means--

"(i) a projectile or projectile core which may be used in a handgun and which is constructed entirely (excluding the presence of traces of other substances) from one or a combination of tungsten alloys, steel, iron, brass, bronze, beryllium copper, or depleted uranium; or

"(ii) a full jacketed projectile larger than .22 caliber designed and intended for use in a handgun and whose jacket has a weight of more than 25 percent of the total weight of the projectile.

"(C) The term 'armor piercing ammunition' does not include shotgun shot required by Federal or State environmental or game regulations for hunting purposes, a frangible projectile designed for target shooting, a projectile which the Secretary finds is primarily intended to be used for sporting purposes, or any other projectile or projectile core which the Secretary finds is intended to be used for industrial purposes, including a charge used in an oil and gas well perforating device.".

As the Nation Expands

"No clause in the Constitution could by any rule of construction be conceived to give to congress a power to disarm the people."
—William Rawle, *A View of the Constitution of the United States*

When the year 1800 dawned, the government under the United States Constitution was just over a decade old. The fledgling nation was still feeling its way both internally and as a nation on the international stage. The Constitution had been ratified in 1788, and the Bill of Rights had been ratified in 1791, but the nation's citizens and leaders continued to struggle with the issue of the relationship between the states and the national government. In the twenty-first century, it is hard to imagine that throughout the seventeenth and eighteenth centuries, the entities that would become states were colonies, and that these colonies in large measure functioned independently from one another; in effect, each thought of itself in many ways as a separate nation. The people of Georgia, or South Carolina, where the plantation economy dominated and slavery was still a firmly rooted institution, did not see themselves as having much in common with New Yorkers, or Bostonians, and they feared domination by the larger, more populous, and more moneyed northern states. These cultural divisions were partially overcome in the debates over the new Constitution in the summer of 1787, and in the debates over the Bill of Rights in Congress in 1789, but tensions lingered, and it was up to the president, Congress, and the court system to in effect define the nation as a nation through its laws and its judicial interpretation of those laws.

Throughout the century, several treatises on constitutional law were published. These treatises were written by prominent constitutional scholars, and they were used in legal education programs throughout the nation. Still in the twenty-first century, they are quoted in judicial opinions and other contexts, for they provide modern readers with insight into how former generations viewed the provisions of the Constitution, including the Second Amendment. In 1800, and throughout the century, the United States was a frontier nation. Settlers expanded the nation westward from the narrow ribbon of land perched on the edge of the Atlantic Ocean. Their survival depended on their ability to defend themselves from Indian tribes that resented their encroachment, and from four-legged predators. They relied on hunting for much of their food. Further, the threat of foreign invasion was a constant as the nations of Europe had long jockeyed for empire in the New World.

In this context, the presence of armaments in the home was a matter taken for granted. Various of the legal treatises written during the century—by William Rawle, Joseph Story, John Pomeroy, and Thomas Cooley, among others—along with court decisions, affirmed an individual right of citizens to bear arms, although they emphasized that firearms could not be used in a manner that threatened peace and good order. Further, jurists and others continued to express distrust of large standing peacetime armies, leading them to comment on the function of militias in the nation's defense. A key case in the jurisprudence of the century, however, was *Presser v. Illinois*, a U.S. Supreme Court case that was among the first to maintain that the "right to keep and bear arms" was a collective right pertaining to militias, not an individual right.

At the same time, frontier towns—including many of the cattle towns whose names survive in legend as symbolic of the Old West—were becoming concerned about gunplay within their city limits. Accordingly, they passed ordinances that strongly prefigure the gun control proposals made in the twenty-first century, particularly as they pertain to "open carry" and "concealed carry" of firearms. The nation, however, would have to wait decades for substantive gun control legislation and for the judiciary to affirm its constitutionality.

David Higgins' idyl of the Tennessee mountains, At Piney Ridge. *Act III. Jack. "I have the right to kill you!" (By Strobridge Litho. Co., c1900.)*

A View of the Constitution of the United States

Author(s): William Rawle
Date: 1825
Genre: Constitutional interpreation

Summary Overview

First published in 1825, *A View of the Constitution of the United States* was the work of William Rawle, a prominent Philadelphia attorney in the early days of the Republic. During these years, the nation was struggling to arrive at an understanding of the workings of the U.S. Constitution and the Bill of Rights, including the Second Amendment. In this regard, Rawle joined a number of constitutional scholars in publishing his interpretation of the Constitution. His view of the Second Amendment is to a large degree consistent with that of other constitutional scholars during the nineteenth century in his assertion that the Second Amendment grants an individual right to bear arms. His work continues to be cited by jurists and by law students interested in understanding the evolution of American legal institutions in the early nineteenth century.

Defining Moment

No particular event took place that led to the publication of Rawle's treatise on constitutional law. During the 1820s, the United States was still very much a frontier nation, stretching from the Atlantic Ocean to roughly the western edge of the Mississippi River basin. As the wilderness was pushed back and tamed, firearms were a virtual necessity for settlers and farmers for hunting and for personal defense against predators, both of the four-legged and the two-legged kind. In this context, Rawle joined other scholars in tackling the issue of the meaning of the Second Amendment, in particular, to define what is meant by "keeping" and "bearing" arms and to clarify the ambiguous relationship between the two clauses of the amendment. In common with other scholars, he examined the issue of whether the amendment confirms the right of *individuals* to bear arms or whether it only grants to the states the right to maintain a militia for the common defense. And in common with most constitutional scholars in the nineteenth century, he came down on the "individual right" side of the question, arguing that the Second Amendment grants to individuals the right to bear arms independent of their participation in a state militia. Gun control opponents continue to quote the statements of many of these scholars, including Rawle, using their views in defense of the position that the Second Amendment affirms the right of individuals to keep and bear arms for personal use—and that the government oversteps its authority when it attempts to regulate firearms.

About the Author

William Rawle was born on April 28, 1759, in Philadelphia, Pennsylvania, and was reared in an affluent family after his father died and his mother was remarried. During the American Revolution, Rawle's stepfather, Samuel Shoemaker, a Quaker and former mayor of Philadelphia, remained loyal to Great Britain. After the war, he was convicted of treason, forcing him to flee to New York with his stepson. Rawle studied law in New York, then sailed for England to study law at the Middle Temple in London; while he was in England, he became frustrated by the nation's lack of social equality and its emphasis on rank and birth rather than merit. Accordingly, he returned to the United States. In 1783, he was admitted to the bar and founded a law firm in Philadelphia. That firm, now Rawle & Henderson, holds the distinction of being the oldest law firm in continuous practice in the United States. From 1791 to 1800, he served as the U.S. district attorney for Pennsylvania. He later served as counsel for the First Bank of the United States. Rawle was instrumental in creating a number of new U.S. institutions. He was the founder and first president of the Historical Society of Pennsylvania. A staunch abolitionist, he was among the first members of the Pennsylvania Abolition Society. He was a member of the American Philosophical Society, and for four decades he served as a trustee of the University of Pennsylvania. He died on April 12, 1836, in Philadelphia.

HISTORICAL DOCUMENT

In the second article, it is declared, that a *well regulated Militia is necessary to the security of a free state*; a proposition from which few will dissent. Although in actual war, the services of regular troops are confessedly more valuable; yet, while peace prevails, and in the commencement of a war before a regular force can be raised, the militia form the palladium of the country. They are ready to repel invasion, to suppress insurrection, and preserve the good order and peace of government. That they should be well regulated, is judiciously added. A disorderly militia is disgraceful to itself, and dangerous not to the enemy, but to its own country. The duty of the state government is, to adopt such regulations as will tend to make good soldiers with the least interruptions of the ordinary and useful occupations of civil life. In this all the Union has a strong and visible interest.

The corollary, from the first position, is, that the right of the people to keep and bear arms shall not be infringed.

The prohibition is general. No clause in the Constitution could by any rule of construction be conceived to give to congress a power to disarm the people. Such a flagitious attempt could only be made under some general pretence by a state legislature. But if in any blind pursuit of inordinate power, either should attempt it, this amendment may be appealed to as a restraint on both.

In most of the countries of Europe, this right does not seem to be denied, although it is allowed more, or less sparingly, according to circumstances. In England, a country which boasts so much of its freedom, the right was secured to Protestant subjects only, on the revolution of 1688; and it is cautiously described to be that of bearing arms for their defence, "suitable to their conditions, and as allowed by law." An arbitrary code for the preservation of game in that country has long disgraced them. A very small proportion of the people being permitted to kill it, though for their own subsistence; a gun or other instrument, used for that purpose by an unqualified person, may be seized and forfeited. Blackstone, in whom we regret that we cannot always trace the expanded principles of rational liberty, observes however, on this subject, that the prevention of popular insurrections and resistance to government by disarming the people, is oftener meant than avowed, by the makers of forest and game laws.

This right ought not, however, in any government, to be abused to the disturbance of the public peace.

An assemblage of persons with arms, for an unlawful purpose, is an indictable offence, and even the carrying of arms abroad by a single, individual, attended with circumstances giving just reason to fear that he purposes to make an unlawful use of them, would be sufficient cause to require him to give surety of the peace. If he refused he would be liable to imprisonments.

William Rawle (1759-1836) (By Benjamin West.)

Document Themes

Rawle first takes up the issue of the militia and its role in the defense of the nation. Like many early Americans, he was suspicious of a large standing federal army during peacetime. He concedes that a large national army might be necessary to repel an external threat, but he argues that the militia, at the "commencement of a war before a regular force can be raised," can serve as the "palladium," or safeguard, of the country; in his use of the word *palladium*, he echoes St. George Tucker, who used the word in his influential 1803 legal treatise, *Blackstone's Commentaries*. The state militias, he argues, "are ready to repel invasion, to suppress insurrection, and preserve the good order and peace of government."

Rawle goes on to argue that "the corollary, from the first position, is, that *the right of the people to keep and bear arms shall not be infringed*." He comments that the prohibition is "general," adding that "no clause in the Constitution could by any rule of construction be conceived to give to congress a power to disarm the people." The Second Amendment, then, can serve as a safeguard against the "blind pursuit of inordinate power."

Rawle then turns to the nations of Europe. He notes that the right to bear arms, while not denied, is granted "sparingly." Drawing on his experience in England, he calls attention to the 1689 English Bill of Rights, which granted to Protestants the right to keep and bear arms to defend themselves against Catholics, but he adds that the provision was "an arbitrary code for the preservation of game" for those who were allowed to hunt it, essentially the aristocracy. The purpose of the game laws, he believes, was in actuality the "prevention of popular insurrections and resistance to government by disarming the people."

Rawle concludes by taking up the issue of armed public disturbances, pointing out that the right to keep and bear arms cannot be "abused to the disturbance of the public peace." He goes on to maintain that "even the carrying of arms abroad by a single, individual, attended with circumstances giving just reason to fear that he purposes to make an unlawful use of them, would be sufficient cause to require him to give surety of the peace"—meaning that the individual would have to post a bond that would serve as a guarantee that he would keep the peace.

Additional Reading

Hardy, David T., "The Rise and Demise of the Collective Right Interpretation of the Second Amendment," *Cleveland State Law Review* 59 (2011): 315–59.

Kopel, David B., "The Second Amendment in the Nineteenth Century," *BYU Law Review* 4 (1998): 1359–1554.

Van Buskirk, Judith L., "William Rawle," *The Yale Biographical Dictionary of American Law*, ed. Roger K. Newman (New Haven, CT: Yale University Press, 2009), pp. 447–48.

Volokh, Eugene, "The Amazing Vanishing Second Amendment," *New York University Law Review* 73 (June 1998): 831–40.

—*Michael J. O'Neal*

Johnson v. Tompkins et al.

Author(s): Henry Baldwin (associate justice of the Supreme Court)
Date: 1833
Genre: Court decision (Third Circuit)

Summary Overview

Johnson v. Tompkins was a Third Circuit Court case in Pennsylvania; at the time, U.S. Supreme Court justices were required to "ride circuit," meaning that they functioned as the presiding judges at various locations within a geographical circuit. In this instance, the presiding judge was Henry Baldwin, an associate justice of the Supreme Court. Essentially, the case had to do with the property rights of slave owners. The court ruled that on questions pertaining to slaves, the same rules of evidence apply as in other cases having to do with the right of property. Further, the court ruled that a citizen of another state whose slave escapes into Pennsylvania may pursue him and seize him without warrant, using whatever force is necessary to return him to his place of bondage—and may do so without a warrant. If anyone opposes the slave owner, he may use force to repel the opposition, and no law enforcement officer may interfere. In the excerpt below, the court addresses the issue of armed force in the assertion of property rights.

Defining Moment

Article IV, section 2 of the U.S. Constitution states:

> No Person held to Service or Labour in one State, under the Laws thereof, escaping into another, shall, in Consequence of any Law or Regulation therein, be discharged from such Service or Labour, but shall be delivered up on Claim of the Party to whom such Service or Labour may be due.

On the basis of this provision of the Constitution, which affirmed the property rights of slave owners, the Fugitive Slave Act of 1793 passed. According to Article IV, section 3,

> when a person held to labor in any of the United States, or of the Territories on the Northwest or South of the river Ohio . . . shall escape into any other part of the said States or Territory, the person to whom such labor or service may be due . . . is hereby empowered to seize or arrest such fugitive from labor . . . and upon proof . . . before any Judge . . . it shall be the duty of such Judge . . . [to remove] the said fugitive from labor to the State or Territory from which he or she fled.

The act went on to specify a stiff fine for "any person who shall knowingly and willingly obstruct or hinder such claimant."

It was in this context that *Johnson v. Tompkins* arose. In 1822, a slave named Jack fled from New Jersey to Pennsylvania, where he was hired by John and Isachar Kenderdine. The plaintiff (Caleb Johnson) and others pursued Jack to Pennsylvania and the Kenderdine home, where they took steps to seize him. As the party was attempting to transport Jack, now in fetters, Kenderdine and a mob of locals attacked Johnson and his party. A melee ensued, leading to a thicket of legal complications involving fines, jailings, breaches of the peace, threats, rude conduct, and conflicting testimony—all of them having to do with Johnson's legal authority to reclaim Jack, and to do so on a Sunday. In cutting through the legalities (which included the rulings of one Judge Tompkins), the Court ruled that

> Jack is admitted to have been the slave of the plaintiff, who had by the constitution of the United States, and the act of February, 1793, a perfect right to take his slave within this state, at any time he pleased, to use any force necessary for the purpose, to detain him a reasonable time before taking him to any magistrate.

Thus, Johnson's property rights in Jack were affirmed. The relevance of the case to the gun debate was the court's assertion that Johnson could legally use whatever force was necessary to capture and return his slave.

About the Author

The decision in this case was written by Associate Justice Henry Baldwin, who was "riding" the Third Circuit in Pennsylvania in 1833. Baldwin was born on January 14, 1780, in New Haven, Connecticut. In 1797, at age seventeen, he received his bachelor's degree from Yale. After attending the Litchfield Law School in Connecticut (the nation's first-ever law school), he established a legal practice in Pittsburgh. From 1799 to 1801 he served as the deputy attorney general of Pennsylvania. Later, from 1817 to 1822, he served in the U.S. House of Representatives.

Baldwin was a strong supporter of Andrew Jackson in the latter's 1824 and 1828 presidential campaigns. Jackson tried to reward him by appointing him secretary of the treasury, but the appointment was blocked in the Senate. When a U.S. Supreme Court seat became vacant, Jackson turned to Baldwin, who joined the Court in 1830. Oddly, he considered resigning his position the very next year, and some historians believe that he was suffering from mental illness during this period, pointing in support of this view to a general incoherence in his views as a jurist and his lack of decorum on the bench. He stayed on the Court, however, until his death on April 21, 1844. He was the author of an 1837 legal treatise, *A General View of the Origin and Nature of the Constitution and Government of the United States: Deduced from the Political History and Condition of the Colonies and States.* In this treatise, he examined the two major schools of constitutional interpretation—an opposition that persists in the twenty-first century. One was the "strict constructionist," school, which requires a judge to apply the text of the Constitution exactly as it is written; the opposing view is that the Constitution is to be regarded as a flexible document open to interpretation. One of Baldwin's most significant cases was *Johnson v. Tompkins*, in which he expressed his abhorrence of slavery but felt compelled to apply the law as written.

HISTORICAL DOCUMENT

The nature of this case, its history, and the course of the argument, call on us to declare explicitly what is the effect of a constitutional protection or guarantee of any right, or the injunction of any duty. The twenty-sixth section of the bill of rights in the constitution of Pennsylvania, is in these words; "to guard against transgressions of the high powers we have delegated, we declare (we the people of Pennsylvania), that every thing in this article is excepted out of the general powers of government, and shall for ever remain inviolate." A higher power declares this constitution and the laws of the United States which shall be made in pursuance thereof, shall be the supreme laws of the land, and the judges in every state shall be bound thereby, any thing in the constitution or laws of any state to the contrary notwithstanding. An amendment of the constitution is of still higher authority, for it has the effect of controlling and repealing the express provisions of the constitution authorizing a power to be exercised, by a declaration that it shall not be construed to give such power. We have stated to you the various provisions of the constitution of the United States and its amendments, as well as that of this state; you see their authority and obligation to be supreme over any laws or regulations which are repugnant to them, or which violate, infringe or impair any right thereby secured; the conclusions which result are too obvious to be more than stated. Jack was the property of the plaintiff, who had a right to possess and protect his slave or servant, whom he had a right to seize and take away to his residence in New Jersey by force, if force was necessary, he had a right to secure him from escape, or rescue by any means not cruel or wantonly severe—he had a right to carry arms in defence of his property or person, and to use them, if either were assailed with such force, numbers or violence as made it necessary for the protection or safety of either; he had a right to come into the state and take Jack on Sunday, the act of taking him up and conveying him to the Billet was no breach of the peace, if not done by noise and disorder, occasioned by himself or his party—and their peaceable entry into the house of Mrs. Kenderdine was lawful and justifiable, for this purpose in doing these acts they were supported by laws which no human authority could shake or question. The power of the state was incompetent to impair the obligation of the contract of purchase from Rowley and Berrian, or to discharge Jack from the service of his master; he could not be impeded in the prosecution of his lawful pursuit, or restrained of his liberty, without the commission of an offence and process of law. Did they commit any breach of the peace? Joseph Kenderdine proves he was in the house when they entered and took Jack, he heard no noise, and did not see them enter—he informed his uncle of what had happened, came with him and his aunt to the wagon, but does not recollect what was said. Sarah Rakestraw testifies she heard Isachar ask them to prove their property, to which they replied, to stand off, and if he resisted they would blow him through—if this witness is credited, it shows the use of language rude and rough; but it did not amount to a breach of the peace without an offer to use an offensive weapon, or proof of some act done. Had such offer been made when Mr. Kenderdine was doing any act which interfered with their rights, they would have been justified in using as much force as was necessary to enable them to proceed in their lawful business—his demand of proof of property was unauthorized, if the law gave him this right he would also have the right to judge of its sufficiency; but he was acting in his own wrong in making the demand, and they were under no obligation, legal or moral, to exhibit their papers, and submit to an examination by him in the highway. A request, at a proper time and place, and under circumstances where there would be any probability of a candid and impartial attention to legal evidence, respect for the rights of property, or the laws of the land, would, if refused rudely, have indicated a disposition on the part of the Jerseymen extremely reprehensible, and put their refusal on a very different footing from that in which it appears by the evidence of Miss Rakestraw; though even in such ease they would not have been compelled by law to show their property or authority, yet rude conduct or language would have tended much to have palliated any excitement or violence which followed a refusal to accede to a proper request. On this subject there is much weight in the remark of the defendant's counsel, that there is a social law, a law of decent respect for the opinions of others, which ought not to be overlooked in the assertion of right—but it is most certainly a gross violation of this social law, to rudely demand as a right that which ought to be conceded only to courtesy of manner and propriety of time, place and circumstance.

The next act of the Jersey party which is complained of, is the threat to blow out the brains of Isachar Kenderdine, when he either had seized, or was about to seize one of their horses by the head, for the purpose of stopping them in the road, near the meetinghouse. At this time there was a crowd of some twenty or thirty about the wagon, and shortly after the plaintiff was struck in the head with a stone. Under such circumstances, a demand to prove property or to stop, was most unseasonable and improper, any attempt to stop them was unlawful, and would have justified the repelling such an attempt by as much force, and with such weapons as would be necessary to their safe passage to the Billet; what was said or done by them was no breach of the peace, or other offence, which in any manner justified their arrest or detention.

Document Themes

The bulk of Baldwin's much longer opinion in *Johnson v. Tompkins* is an effort to cut through all of the complexities bearing on Johnson's legal right to reclaim Jack and return him to New Jersey. The key portion of the decision as it pertains to the right to bear arms is this:

> Jack was the property of the plaintiff, who had a right to possess and protect his slave or servant, whom he had a right to seize and take away to his residence in New Jersey by force, if force was necessary, he had a right to secure him from escape, or rescue by any means not cruel or wantonly severe—he had a right to carry arms in defence of his property or person, and to use them, if either were assailed with such force, numbers or violence as made it necessary for the protection or safety of either.

Put simply, the court affirmed Johnson's right to bear—and use—arms in the assertion of his property rights. Later, Baldwin remarked:

> Under such circumstances, a demand to prove property or to stop [sic], was most unseasonable and improper, any attempt to stop them was unlawful, and would have justified the repelling such an attempt by as much force, and with such weapons as would be necessary to their safe passage to the Billet [where Johnson and his party were staying]; what was said or done by them was no breach of the peace, or other offence, which in any manner justified their arrest or detention.

Again, what is noteworthy is that the court did not question the plaintiff's right to use firearms in repelling the actions of the assemblage that attempted to stop him; use of such arms would not be considered a breach of the peace. The decision is representative of numerous decisions in lower courts during this era that left unquestioned the right of citizens to bear arms in defense of their person or property.

Additional Reading

Cushman, Clare, *The Supreme Court Justices: Illustrated Biographies, 1789–1995*, 2nd ed. (Supreme Court Historical Society, Congressional Quarterly Books, 2001).

Frank, John P., Leon Friedman, and Fred L. Israel, eds., *The Justices of the United States Supreme Court: Their Lives and Major Opinions* (Langhorne, PA: Chelsea House Publishers, 1995).

Seddig, Robert G., "Henry Baldwin," *The Oxford Companion to the Supreme Court of the United States*, edited by Kermit L. Hall (New York: Oxford University Press, 1992).

Swisher, Carl B., *The Taney Period, 1836–1864*. Vol. 5 of *History of the Supreme Court of the United States* (New York: Macmillan, 1974).

Urofsky, Melvin I., *The Supreme Court Justices: A Biographical Dictionary* (New York: Garland Publishing, 1994).

—*Michael J. O'Neal*

■ *Familiar Exposition of the Constitution of the United States*

Author(s): Joseph Story
Date: 1840
Genre: Book excerpt

Summary Overview

In the first half of the nineteenth century, Joseph Story's monumental three-volume *Commentaries on the Constitution of the United States*, first published in 1833, was the nation's most influential treatise on constitutional law. He abridged the *Commentaries* and published a popularized version of the treatise titled *Familiar Exposition of the Constitution of the United States* (1840). The first paragraph of the excerpt that follows was new to *Familiar Exposition*; the remainder of the excerpt appeared as is in the *Commentaries*. Story's commentary on the Second Amendment was largely consistent with nineteenth-century American jurisprudence in supporting the right of individuals to bear arms, although Story gives emphasis to the militia as a bulwark against government tyranny.

Defining Moment

Joseph Story was a major figure in American jurisprudence during the three decades he served on the U.S. Supreme Court and as a member of the faculty at Harvard Law School. In large measure, he helped shape the future of the United States as a commercial republic, but one with a strong central government. When he took his seat on the High Court in 1812, the chief issue facing the nation, and the Court, was the relative power of the federal government and the states. It was under the leadership of Chief Justice John Marshall, with Story's backing, that the Court greatly expanded the power of the federal government. While he argued for the supremacy of the national government, he also denounced states' rights in such landmark cases as *Martin v. Hunter's Lessee* (1816), writing that the Constitution was not created "by the states in their sovereign capacities, but emphatically, as the preamble of the constitution declared, by 'the people of the United States.'" Through this and other decisions, he tilted the balance of power from the states to the federal government. By the time Story wrote the *Commentaries* and the *Familiar Exposition*, he was on the faculty at Harvard, playing a key role in turning the law school into the nation's preeminent institution for legal education. His assertion that the Second Amendment protects an individual right to bear arms has been a key plank in the so-called Standard Model adopted by gun rights advocates. Although Story was a supporter of a strong central government, he was also a strong supporter of the liberties of "the people" as outlined in the Bill of Rights.

About the Author

Joseph Story was born on September 18, 1779, in Marblehead, Massachusetts. His father, Elisha Story, was one of the Sons of Liberty responsible for the Boston Tea Party. Story enrolled at Harvard in 1795, and after his graduation three years later, he returned to Marblehead to read law and was admitted to the bar in 1801. He was active in Democratic-Republican politics, serving three terms in the Massachusetts House of Representatives beginning in 1805; in 1808 he was elected to finish out an unexpired term in the U.S. House of Representatives.

After U.S. Supreme Court Justice William Cushing died in 1810, President James Madison turned to Story to fill the seat. Three days after the nomination in November 1811, Story was confirmed, and when he took his seat in February 1812, at age thirty-two, he became the youngest Supreme Court justice in the nation's history.

In the years that followed, he often used his position on the bench to denounce slavery. He remains best known in the twenty-first century for his decision in *United States v. Amistad* (1841), where he freed a "cargo" of Africans who had been illegally transported to Cuba as slaves before revolting against their captors. In his decision he maintained that the Africans were not "merchandise" but free individuals who had been kidnapped in contravention of international treaty. Their story was told in a major motion picture, Stephen Spielberg's *Amistad* (1997), in which Story was played by Supreme Court justice Harry Blackmun—the only known instance in which a Supreme Court justice has played the part of another Supreme Court justice in a film.

Story enjoyed a full career as a confidant of politicians, as a member of the Massachusetts Constitutional Convention, as a member of the board of trustees at Harvard, as president of a bank, and as a prolific legal scholar and writer. His health began to fail in the 1840s, and he died in Cambridge, Massachusetts on September 10, 1845.

HISTORICAL DOCUMENT

The next amendment is, "A well-regulated militia being necessary to the security of a free state, the right of the people to keep and bear arms shall not be infringed." One of the ordinary modes, by which tyrants accomplish their purposes without resistance, is, by disarming the people, and making it an offence to keep arms, and by substituting a regular army in the stead of a resort to the militia. The friends of a free government cannot be too watchful, to overcome the dangerous tendency of the public mind to sacrifice, for the sake of mere private convenience, this powerful check upon the designs of ambitious men.

The importance of this article will scarcely be doubted by any persons, who have duly reflected upon the subject. The militia is the natural defence of a free country against sudden foreign invasions, domestic insurrections, and domestic usurpations of power by rulers. It is against sound policy for a free people to keep up large military establishments and standing armies in time of peace, both from the enormous expenses, with which they are attended, and the facile means, which they afford to ambitious and unprincipled rulers, to subvert the government, or trample upon the rights of the people. The right of the citizens to keep and bear arms has justly been considered, as the palladium of the liberties of a republic; since it offers a strong moral check against the usurpation and arbitrary power of rulers; and will generally, even if these are successful in the first instance, enable the people to resist and triumph over them. And yet, though this truth would seem so clear, and the importance of a well regulated militia would seem so undeniable, it cannot be disguised, that among the American people there is a growing indifference to any system of militia discipline, and a strong disposition, from a sense of its burthens, to be rid of all regulations. How it is practicable to keep the people duly armed without some organization, it is difficult to see. There is certainly no small danger, that indifference may lead to disgust, and disgust to contempt; and thus gradually undermine all the protection intended by this clause of our national bill of rights. [fn1]

It would be well for Americans to reflect upon the passage in Tacitus, (Hist. IV. ch. 74): "Nam neque quies sine armis, neque arma, sine stipendiis, neque stipendia sine tributis, haberi queunt." Is there any escape from a large standing army, but in a well disciplined militia? There is much wholesome instruction on this subject in 1 Black. Comm. ch. 13, p. 408 to 417.

A similar provision in favour of protestants (for to them it is confined) is to be found in the bill of rights of 1688 [sic], it being declared, "that the subjects, which are protestants, may have arms for their defence suitable to their condition, and as allowed by law." But under various pretences the effect of this provision has been greatly narrowed; and it is at present in England more nominal than real, as a defensive privilege.

Document Themes

Story begins by sounding a theme that recurred throughout nineteenth-century examinations of the Second Amendment—the view that the right to bear arms serves as a safeguard against government tyranny:

> One of the ordinary modes, by which tyrants accomplish their purposes without resistance, is, by disarming the people, and making it an offence to keep arms, and by substituting a regular army in the stead of a resort to the militia. The friends of a free government cannot be too watchful, to overcome the dangerous tendency of the public mind to sacrifice, for the sake of mere private convenience, this powerful check upon the designs of ambitious men.

Here, Story expresses a commonly held view that a disarmed populace in a nation with a standing peacetime army rather than a militia is dangerous in allowing "ambitious men" and "tyrants" to pursue their "designs."

Story continues by taking up another common theme among nineteenth-century constitutional scholars: the role of the militia in the defense of the country: "The militia is the natural defence of a free country against sudden foreign invasions, domestic insurrections, and domestic usurpations of power by rulers." Again, it is noteworthy that he cites "usurpations of power by rulers" alongside of foreign invasions and insurrections as threats against which the Second Amendment guards. He goes on to comment that "the right of the citizens to keep and bear arms has justly been considered, as the palladium of the liberties of a republic; since it offers a strong moral check against the usurpation and arbitrary power of rulers; and will generally, even if these are successful in the first instance, enable the people to resist and triumph over them." His language echoes that of St. George Tucker, who used the word *palladium* ("safeguard") in *Blackstone's Commentaries* in 1803, and his phrase "moral check" would be echoed later in the century by constitutional scholar Thomas M. Cooley in *The General Principles of Constitutional Law in the United States of America.* This language strongly suggests that Story adhered to what would come to be called the "individual right" view of the Second Amendment.

Story is concerned about the possibility of the American people growing weary of "any system of military discipline." But he goes on to quote the ancient Roman historian Tacitus, who saw a well-regulated militia as a way to escape the need for a large standing army. He concludes by alluding to the English Bill of Rights and its granting of the right to bear arms to Protestants, though he notes that the restriction is a present "more nominal than real."

Additional Reading

Dunne, Gerald T., *Justice Joseph Story and the Rise of the Supreme Court* (New York: Simon & Schuster, 1970).

Hall, Kermit L., ed., *The Oxford Companion to the Supreme Court of the United States* (New York: Oxford University Press, 1992).

Horowitz, Valerie L., ed., *The Unsigned Essays of Supreme Court Justice Joseph Story: Early American Views of Law* (Clark, NJ: Lawbook Exchange, 2015).

Kopel, David B., "The Second Amendment in the Nineteenth Century," *BYU Law Review* 4 (1998): 1359–1554.

McClellan, James, *Joseph Story and the American Constitution: A Study in Political and Legal Thought, with Selected Writings* (Norman, OK: University of Oklahoma Press, 1971).

Presser, Stephen B., "Review: Resurrecting the Conservative Tradition in American Legal History," *Reviews in American History* 13, no. 4 (1985): 526–533.

—*Michael J. O'Neal*

State v. Huntly

Author(s): William Joseph Gaston
Date: 1843
Genre: North Carolina Supreme Court

Summary Overview

State v. Huntly is a case heard by the North Carolina Supreme Court in 1843. The case bore on the question of whether a citizen had to right to go about in public "armed with unusual and dangerous weapons." While the court affirmed the right of a citizen to carry about firearms for "any lawful purpose of business or amusement," he cannot do so in such a way as to "terrify and alarm" other people. The case is significant because it was one of the first cases in the United States to invoke the Statute of Northampton, an English law enacted in 1328 during the reign of King Edward III.

Defining Moment

The case turned on the actions of one Robert S. Huntly, who was tried and found guilty in the superior court of Anson County in North Carolina. The charge against him was that he armed himself with guns, knives, and "other dangerous and unusual weapons," then went about in public issuing threats, indicating that he would "beat, wound, kill and murder" one James H. Ratcliff. The result of his actions was that local citizens were "terrified" and the peace and dignity of the state were "endangered."

In ruling on the illegality of Huntly's actions, the Supreme Court of North Carolina would likely have been cognizant of statutes in various jurisdictions bearing on the issue of carrying arms in public. In 1736, for example, Virginia enacted a statute stating that a constable "may take away Arms from such who ride, or go, offensively armed, in Terror of the People." Another Virginia statute, this one dating to 1786, forbade citizens to "go nor ride armed by night or by day, in fairs or markets, or in other places, in terror of the Country."

In 1795 Massachusetts enacted a statute stating that justices of the peace should arrest "all affrayers, rioters, disturbers, or breakers of the peace, and such as shall ride or go armed offensive, to the fear or terrour of the good citizens of this Commonwealth." More generally, the court noted that appearing in public armed with dangerous weapons in a way that induces fear in others is an "offence at common law."

About the Author

The court's decision in *State v. Huntly* was written by Justice William Joseph Gaston. Gaston was born on September 19, 1778, in New Bern, North Carolina. He was the first student to enroll at Georgetown College, but he later attended the College of New Jersey (now Princeton University). He returned to New Bern to apprentice in the study of law, gaining admission to the bar in 1798. He engaged in private practice, but in 1800 he began to bounce around in the state and federal legislatures. That year, he was elected to the North Carolina Senate. He later served three terms in the North Carolina House of Representatives. In 1812 he returned to the state senate, but in 1813 he was elected to the U.S. House of Representatives, where he served until 1817. He returned to practicing law in New Bern, but again he answered the call of the state senate in 1818–19.

As a member of the Whig Party, Gaston was generally conservative and pro-business. In 1833, the state legislature elected Gaston to the state supreme court, where he issued significant rulings favorable to slaves and to African Americans generally. As a Catholic, he also worked to amend the state constitution, which had specified that the state's elected officials and civil servants had to be Protestants. In North Carolina, he is remembered as the author of the state song, "The Old North State." Gaston died in Raleigh, North Carolina, on January 23, 1844.

HISTORICAL DOCUMENT

IN THE SUPREME COURT

STATE vs. ROBERT S. HUNTLY.

June 1843-The offence of riding or going armed with unusual and dangerous weapons, to the terror of the people is an offence at common law, and is indictable in this State.

A man may, carry a gun for any lawful purpose of business or amusement; but he cannot go about with that or any other dangerous weapon, to terrify and alarm, and in such manner as naturally will terrify and alarm, a peaceful people.

The declarations of the defendant are admissible in evidence, on the part of the prosecution, as accompanying, explaining, and characterizing the acts charged.

Appeal from the Superior Court of Law of Anson county, at Spring Term, 1843, his Honor Judge SETTLE presiding.

The defendant was tried upon the following indictment, found in Anson Superior Court:

> The jurors for the State upon their oath present, that Robert S. Huntly, late of the county aforesaid, laborer, on the first day of September, in the present year, with force and arms, at and in the county aforesaid, did arm himself with pistols, guns, knives and other dangerous and unusual weapons and, being so armed, did go forth and exhibit himself openly, both in the day time and in the night, to the good citizens of Anson aforesaid, and in the said highway and before the citizens aforesaid, did openly and publicly declare a purpose and intent, one James H. Ratcliff and other good citizens of the State, then and there being in the peace of God and of the State, to beat, wound, kill and murder, which said purpose and intent, the said Robert S. Huntley, so openly armed and exposed and declaring, then and there had and entertained, by which said arming, exposure, exhibition and declarations of the said Robert S. Huntley, divers good citizens of the State were terrified, and the peace of the State endangered, to the evil example of all others in like cases offending, to the terror of the people, and against the peace and dignity of the State.

On the trial, it was insisted on the part of the defendant, that allowing all the facts charged in the indictment to be true, they constituted no offence for which the defendant could be punished as for a misdemeanor. His HONOR instructed the jury, that, if the facts charged in the indictment, were proven to their satisfaction, the defendant had been guilty, of a violation of the law, and that they ought to render their verdict accordingly. In the investigation before the jury it appeared, among other things, that the defendant was seen by several witnesses, and on divers occasions, riding upon the public highway, and upon the premises of James H. Ratcliff, (the person named in the indictment,) armed with a double barrelled gun, and on some of those occasions was heard to declare, that if "that if James H. Ratcliff did not surrender his negroes, he would kill him," at others, "if James H. Ratcliff did not give him his rights, he would kill him;" on some that "he had way laid the house of James H. Ratcliff in the night about day break, and if he had shewn himself he would have killed him, that he shewed himself once, but for too short a time to enable him to do so, and that he mistook another man for him, and was very near shooting him." On one occasion, that "he would kill James H. Ratcliff if he did not surrender his negroes, and that as for William Ratcliff, he was good for him any how, on sight, that there were four or five men whom he meant to kill." All these declarations were objected to by the defendant's counsel, but were received by the court, as accompanying, and qualifying, and explaining the defendant's riding about the county armed with a double barrelled gun. The jury having found the defendant guilty, his counsel moved for a new trial upon the grounds, first, that the declarations of the defendant before mentioned; were improperly received; secondly, because the judge should have told the jury, that supposing all the facts charged in the indictment to be true still the defendant was entitled to their verdict. The motion was overruled, and judgment having been pronounced, the defendant appealed.

Attorney General for the State.

Winston for the defendant.

GASTON, J. On the trial it was insisted by the defendant's counsel, and the judge was required so to instruct the jury, that if the facts charged in the indictment were all true, they nevertheless constituted in law no offence of which they could find the defendant guilty. His HONOR refused this prayer, and instructed the jury, that, it the facts charged were proved to their satisfaction, it was their duty to find him guilty. The same ground of defence has been taken here by way of a motion in arrest of judgment; but we are of opinion that in whatever form presented, it is not tenable.

The argument is, that the offence of riding or going about armed with unusual and dangerous weapons, to the terror of the people, was created by the statute of Northampton, 2nd Edward the 3d, ch. 3d, and that, whether this statute was or was not formerly in force in this State, it certainly has not been since the first of January, 1838, at which day it is declared in the Revised Statutes, (ch. 1st, sect. 2,) that the statutes of England or Great Britain shall cease to be of force and effect here. We have been accustomed to believe, that the statute referred to did not create this offence, but provided only special penalties and modes of proceeding, for its more effectual suppression, and of the correctness of this belief we can see no reason to doubt. All the elementary writers, who give us any information on the subject, concur in this representation, nor is there to be found in them, as far as we are aware of, a dictum or intimation to the contrary. Blackstone states, that "the offence of riding or going armed with dangerous or unusual weapons, is a crime against the public peace, by terrifying the good people of the land; and is particularly prohibited by the statute of Northampton, 2 Edward 3d, ch. 3d, upon pain of forfeiture of the arms and imprisonment during the Kings pleasure." 4 Bl. Com. 149. Hawkins, treating of offences against the public peace under the head of "Affrays," pointedly remarks, "but granting that no bare words in judgment of law carry in them so much terror as to amount to an affray, yet it seems certain that in some cases there may be an affray, where there is no actual violence, as where a man arms himself with dangerous and unusual weapons in such a manner, as will naturally cause a terror to the people; which is said to have been always an offence at common law and strictly prohibited by many statutes." Haw. P. C. B. 1, ch. 28, sect. 1. Burns and Tomlyns inform us, that, this term "Affray," is derived from the French word "effrayer" to affright and that anciently it meant no more, as where persons appeared with armour or weapons not usually worn, to the terror of others." Burn's Verbo "Affray". Dier do. It was declared by the Chief Justice in Sir John Knight's case, that the statute of Northampton was made in affirmance of the common law. 3 Mod. Rep. 117. And this is manifestly the doctrine of Coke, as will be found on comparing his observations on the word "Affray," which be defines (3d Just. 158,) "a public offence to the terror of the King's subjects, and so called because it affrighteth and maketh men afraid, and is enquirable in a leet as a common nuisance," with his reference immediately thereafter to this statute, and his subsequent comments on it (3d Inst. 160,) where he cites a record of the 29th year of Edward 1st, shewing, what had been considered the law then. Indeed, if those acts be deemed by the common law crimes and misdemeanors, which are in violation of the public rights and of the duties owing to the community in its social capacity, it is difficult to imagine any which more unequivocally deserve to be so considered than the acts charged upon this defendant. They attack directly that public order and sense of security, which it is one of the first objects of the common law, and ought to be of the law of all regulated societies, to preserve inviolate- and they lead almost necessarily to actual violence. Nor can, it for a moment be supposed, that such acts are less mischievous here or less the proper subjects of legal reprehension, than they wore in the country of our ancestors. The bill of rights in this State secures to every man indeed, the right to "bear arms for the defence of the State." While it secures to him a right of which he cannot be deprived, it holds forth the duty in execution of which that right is to be exercised. If he employ those arms, which he ought to wield for the safety and protection of his country, to the annoyance and terror and danger of its citizens, he deserves but the severer condemnation for the abuse of the high privilege, with which he has been invested.

It was objected below, and the objection has been also urged here, that the court erred in admitting evidence of the declarations of the defendant, set forth in the case, because those, or some of them at least, were acknowledgments of a different offence from that charged. But these declarations were clearly proper, because they accompanied, explained, and characterized the very acts charged. They were not received at all as admissions either of the offence under trial, or any other offence. They were constituent parts of that offence.

It has been remarked, that a double-barrelled gun or any other one, cannot in this country come under the description of "unusual weapons," for there is scarcely a man in the community who does not own and occasionally use guns of some sort. But we do not feel the force of this criticism. A gun is an "unusual weapon," wherewith to be armed and clad. No man amongst us carries it about with him, as one of his every day accoutrements-as a part of his dress-and never we trust will the day come when any deadly weapon will be worn or wielded in our peace loving and law-abiding State, as an appendage of manly equipment. But although a gun is an "unusual weapon," it is to be remembered that the carrying of a gun per se constitutes no offence. For any lawful purpose-either of business or amusement- the citizen is at perfect liberty to carry his gun. It is the wicked purpose-and the mischievous result-which essentially constitute the crime. He shall not carry about this or any other weapon of death to terrify and alarm, and in such manner as naturally will terrify and alarm, a peaceful people.

Our opinion is, that there is no error in the sentence below. This decision will be certified to the Superior Court of Anson accordingly.

PER CURIAM.

Ordered accordingly.

Document Themes

The court first noted that a person who goes about armed with "unusual and dangerous weapons, to the terror of the people" has committed an offense at common law. That said, the court also acknowledged that a citizen can go about armed for any lawful purpose of business or amusement, provided he does not breach the peace. Huntly argued that his actions—which consisted in large part of threats against Ratcliff—did not constitute an indictable offense, but the court rejected his argument. The court based its opinion in large part on historical precedent, specifically the Statute of Northampton, enacted in England in 1328. The statute states:

> Item, it is enacted, that no man great nor small, of what condition soever he be, except the king's servants in his presence, and his ministers in executing of the king's precepts, or of their office, and such as be in their company assisting them, and also [upon a cry made for arms to keep the peace, and the same in such places where such acts happen,] be so hardy to come before the King's justices, or other of the King's ministers doing their office, with force and arms, nor bring no force in affray of the peace, nor to go nor ride armed by night nor by day, in fairs, markets, nor in the presence of the justices or other ministers, nor in no part elsewhere.

Gaston notes that as of 1838, British law was declared no longer applicable in North Carolina, yet he indicates that a long legal tradition has imposed punishments on those who have disturbed the peace by wielding weapons in public in a threatening manner. Thus, he cites Sir William Blackstone, whose *Commentaries* (1765–69) on the law are still cited by jurists. According to Blackstone, "the offence of riding or going armed with dangerous or unusual weapons, is a crime against the public peace, by terrifying the good people of the land; and is particularly prohibited by the statute of Northampton." Gaston also cites eighteenth-century jurist William Hawkins, who commented on the word *affray* in the Statute of Northampton: "in some cases there may be an affray, where there is no actual violence, as where a man arms himself with dangerous and unusual weapons in such a manner, as will naturally cause a terror to the people; which is said to have been always an offence at common law and strictly prohibited by many statutes."

Gaston concludes:

> A gun is an "unusual weapon," wherewith to be armed and clad. No man amongst us carries it about with him, as one of his every day accoutrements—as a part of his dress—and never we trust will the day come when any deadly weapon will be worn or wielded in our peace loving and law-abiding State, as an appendage of manly equipment.

Accordingly, Gaston and the court upheld Huntly's conviction and sentence, concluding that Huntly "shall not carry about this or any other weapon of death to terrify and alarm, and in such manner as naturally will terrify and alarm, a peaceful people."

Additional Reading

Cornell, Saul, "The Right to Keep and Carry Arms in Anglo-American Law: Preserving Liberty and Keeping the Peace," *Law and Contemporary Problems* 80, no. 2 (2017): 11–54

Johnson, Nicholas J., David B. Kopel, George A. Mocsary, and Michael P. O'Shea, *Firearms Law and the Second Amendment: Regulation, Rights, and Policy* (Alphen aan den Rijn, Netherlands: Wolters Kluwer Law & Business, 2017).

Kopel, David, "English Legal History and the Right to Carry Arms," *Washington Post*, October 31, 2015, https://www.washingtonpost.com/news/volokh-conspiracy/wp/2015/10/31/wrenn-history/?utm_term=.a03d9a38c30b.

"William Joseph Gaston," *Dictionary of North Carolina Biography*, edited by William S. Powell (Chapel Hills, NC: University of North Carolina Press, 1979–1996).

—Michael J. O'Neal

"Crime Against Kansas"

Author(s): Charles Sumner
Date: 1856
Genre: Speech

Summary Overview

The following excerpt from Charles Sumner's "Crime against Kansas" speech is part of a lengthy address the Massachusetts senator delivered in the Old Senate Chamber in Washington, D.C., on May 19 and 20, 1856. His purpose in the speech was to address the issue of whether Kansas should be admitted to the Union as a slave state or a free state. The speech survives in American history not only for its content—Sumner was a passionate opponent of slavery—but also for one of its consequences. In the speech, Sumner berated Senator Andrew Butler, who was not present, for his pro-slavery stance. On May 22, Butler's cousin, Representative Preston Brooks, entered the Senate chamber bearing a heavy cane, which he used to severely beat Sumner. His fellow South Carolina representative, Laurence Keitt, waved a pistol to prevent others from intervening. The "caning of Senator Sumner" symbolized the high passions that surrounded the issue of slavery and hastened the onset of the Civil War. The following excerpt takes up the issue of the need for firearms by the citizens of Kansas.

Defining Moment

As the United States expanded westward, the question persistently arose as to whether new states would permit slavery. The Missouri Compromise of 1820 was effectively repealed by the Kansas-Nebraska Act of 1854, which was drafted by Senator Stephen A. Douglas of Illinois and Senator Andrew Butler of South Carolina and created the territories of Kansas and Nebraska. The 1854 act was noteworthy for granting voters of the new states the right to choose whether or not to allow slavery in their states. The result of the act was a series of violent confrontations along the border between the two territories. Usually referred to as "Bleeding Kansas" or "Bloody Kansas," the violence emerged from the political debate over whether slavery would be legal in the proposed state of Kansas. From 1854 to 1861, the region was rocked by electoral fraud, raids, assaults, murders, and even pitched battles between anti-slaver "Free-Staters" and pro-slavery "Border Ruffians" in Kansas and Missouri.

Senator Charles Sumner was a crusading antislavery Republican from Massachusetts. On the afternoon of May 19, 1856, he rose to his feet in the Senate and delivered a lengthy address in opposition to the view that Kansas should be admitted to the Union as a slave state. He had carefully prepared his address, which ran to 112 printed pages. Over two days, he spoke for five hours, a memorable feat, for he had memorized ever word of his speech. He singled out two Democratic senators as principal offenders in the push to extend slavery into Kansas. One was Stephen Douglas, whom Sumner described as a "noise-some, squat, and nameless animal . . . not a proper model for an American senator." But he particularly focused on Senator Andrew Butler of South Carolina, charging him with keeping "a mistress to whom he has made his vows, and who, though ugly to others, is always lovely to him; though polluted in the sight of the world, is chaste in his sight—I mean, the harlot, Slavery." Sumner was incensed by Butler's position that the people of Kansas should be deprived of their arms. He thus mounted a spirited defense of the need for citizens to retain their arms in the face of civil unrest and violence.

About the Author

Charles Sumner was born in Boston, Massachusetts on January 6, 1811. He graduated from Harvard University in 1830 and from the Harvard Law School in 1833. In 1834 he was admitted to the bar and began the practice of law in Boston. In 1846 he declined the Whig Party's nomination for election to Congress. An avid opponent of slavery, he was one of the founders of the Free Soil Party in 1848. That year, he ran for election to Congress on the Free Soil ticket, but his candidacy was unsuccessful. In 1851, however, he was elected to the Senate as a Free Soiler. Later, as a Republican, he successfully ran for reelection in 1857, 1863, and 1869, although he spent three years recovering from his injuries at the hand of Representative Preston Brooks and did not resume his duties in the Senate until 1859. He continued to serve in the Senate until his death in Washington, D.C., on March 11, 1874.

HISTORICAL DOCUMENT

"Crime Against Kansas"

Next comes the Remedy of Folly, which, indeed, is also a Remedy of Tyranny; but its Folly is so surpassing as to eclipse even its Tyranny. It does not proceed from the President. With this proposition he is not in any way chargeable. It comes from the Senator from South Carolina, who, at the close of a long speech, offered it as his single contribution to the adjustment of this question, and who thus far stands alone in its support. It might, therefore, fitly bear his name; but that which I now give to it is a more suggestive synonym.

This proposition, nakedly expressed, is that the people of Kansas should be deprived of their arms. That I may not do the least injustice to the Senator, I quote his precise words:

> "The President of the United States is under the highest and most solemn obligations to interpose; and if I were to indicate the manner in which he should interpose in Kansas, I would point out the old common law process. I would serve a warrant on Sharpe's rifles, and if Sharpe's rifles did not answer the summons, and come into court on a day certain, or if they resisted the sheriff, I would summon the posse comitatus, and would have Colonel Sumner'a regiment to be a part of that posse comitatus."

Really, sir, has it come to this? The rifle has ever been the companion of the pioneer, and, under God, his tutelary protector against the red man and. the beast of the forest. Never was this efficient weapon more needed in just self-defence, than now in Kansas, and at least one article in our National Constitution must be blotted out, before the complete right to it can in any way be impeached. And yet, such is the madness of the hour, that, in defiance of the solemn guarantee, embodied in the Amendments to the Constitution, that " the right of the people to keep and bear arms shall not be infringed," the people of Kansas have been arraigned for keeping and bearing them, and the Senator from South Carolina has had the face to say openly, on this floor, that they should be disarmed—of course, that the fanatics of Slavery, his allies and constituents, may meet no impediment. Sir, the Senator is venerable with years; he is reputed also to have worn at home, in the State which he represents, judicial honors; and he is placed here at the head of an important committee occupied particularly with questions of law; but neither his years nor his position, past or present, can give respectability to the demand he has made, or save him from indignant condemnation, when, to compass the wretched purposes of a wretched cause, he thus proposes to trample on one of the plainest provisions of constitutional liberty.

Lithograph of Preston Brooks' 1856 attack on Sumner; the artist depicts the faceless assailant bludgeoning Sumner. (*By John L. Magee.*)

Document Themes

Sumner begins the excerpt by referring to the "Folly" of Butler's solution to the Kansas-Nebraska question, although he amends the phrase "Remedy of Folly" to "Remedy of Tyranny." He alludes to the senator's words in a speech urging the U.S. president (Franklin Pierce) to intervene in the violent confrontations along the Kansas-Nebraska border. He states that he would issue a warrant on Sharpe's rifles. Sharpe's rifles, or Sharps rifles, were a new model of firearm that was being furnished to Kansas immigrants by the New England Emigrant Aid Company. The rifle was a self-priming breech loader that offered speed in firing and accuracy and was cited by no less a figure than abolitionist preacher Henry Ward Beecher as an effective weapon to use in the fight against slavery. The New England organization was accused by proslavery partisans of arming Kansans and thus fomenting violence, and in time, the phrase "Sharps rifles" became a slogan for the controversy and the violence it spawned. Congress even appointed a committee to learn how and when arms were being sent to Kansas, and state political conventions condemned the policy of sending arms to Kansas. Butler went on in his speech to indicate that if Sharpe's rifles did not respond to the warrant, he would form a posse to deal with the matter. Butler's reference to "Colonel Sumner" is likely to army colonel Edwin Vose Sumner, not to Charles Sumner.

Sumner goes on to point out the necessity of firearms for pioneers, who need them for protection against Indians and predatory animals. In particular, though, such weapons are needed for self-defense given the violence taking place in Kansas. Sumner then invokes the Second Amendment, commenting that the madness overtaking the issue of slavery threatens the right of the people to keep and bear arms. He asserts that the people of Kansas are asserting a constitutional right, yet they are being condemned for doing so. He concludes the excerpt by stating that people such as Butler, the "fanatics of Slavery," want to disarm Kansans so that they meet with no "impediment" in their efforts to expand slavery into Kansas.

Additional Readings

Boissoneault, Lorraine, "In the Congressional Fight over Slavery, Decorum Went out the Door," *Smithsonian.com*, February 10, 2017, https://www.smithsonianmag.com/history/tempers-ran-so-hot-congress-one-senator-was-nearly-beaten-death-180962111/

Pfau, Michael, "Time, Tropes, and Textuality: Reading Republicanism in Charles Sumner's 'Crime Against Kansas,'" *Rhetoric & Public Affairs*, Vol. 6, no. 3 (Fall 2003), pp. 385–413.

Pierson, Michael D., "'All Southern Society Is Assailed by the Foulest Charges': Charles Sumner's 'The Crime against Kansas' and the Escalation of Republican Anti-Slavery Rhetoric," *New England Quarterly*, Vol. 68, no. 4 (December 1995), pp. 531–57.

Sinha, Manisha, "The Caning of Charles Sumner: Slavery, Race, and Ideology in the Age of the Civil War," *Journal of the Early Republic*, Vol. 23 (Summer 2003), pp. 233–62.

Slusser, Daniel Lawrence, "In Defense of Southern Honor: Preston Brooks and the Attack on Charles Sumner," *The Forum: Journal of History*, Vol. 2, no. 1 (2010), pp. 98–110.

—*Michael J. O'Neal*

THE RACIST ROOTS OF GUN CONTROL

The historical record provides compelling evidence that racism underlies gun control laws—and not in any subtle way. Throughout much of American history, gun control was openly stated as a method for keeping blacks and Hispanics "in their place," and to quiet the racial fears of whites. This paper is intended to provide a brief summary of this unholy alliance of gun control and racism, and to suggest that gun control laws should be regarded as "suspect ideas," analogous to the "suspect classifications" theory of discrimination already part of the American legal system.

Racist arms laws predate the establishment of the United States. Starting in 1751, the French Black Code required Louisiana colonists to stop any blacks, and if necessary, beat "any black carrying any potential weapon, such as a cane." If a black refused to stop on demand, and was on horseback, the colonist was authorized to "shoot to kill."[1] Slave possession of firearms was a necessity at times in a frontier society, yet laws continued to be passed in an attempt to prohibit slaves or free blacks from possessing firearms, except under very restrictively controlled conditions.[2] Similarly, in the sixteenth century the colony of New Spain, terrified of black slave revolts, prohibited all blacks, free and slave, from carrying arms.[3]

In the Haitian Revolution of the 1790s, the slave population successfully threw off their French masters, but the Revolution degenerated into a race war, aggravating existing fears in the French Louisiana colony, and among whites in the slave states of the United States. When the first U. S. official arrived in New Orleans in 1803 to take charge of this new American possession, the planters sought to have the existing free black militia disarmed, and otherwise exclude "free blacks from positions in which they were required to bear arms," including such non-military functions as slave-catching crews. The New Orleans city government also stopped whites from teaching fencing to free blacks, and then, when free blacks sought to teach fencing, similarly prohibited their efforts as well.[4]

It is not surprising that the first North American English colonies, then the states of the new republic, remained in dread fear of armed blacks, for slave revolts against slave owners often degenerated into less selective forms of racial warfare. The perception that free blacks were sympathetic to the plight of their enslaved brothers, and the dangerous example that "a Negro could be free" also caused the slave states to pass laws designed to disarm all blacks, both slave and free. Unlike the gun control laws passed after the Civil War, these antebellum statutes were for blacks alone. In Maryland, these prohibitions went so far as to prohibit free blacks from owning dogs without a license, and authorizing any white to kill an unlicensed dog owned by a free black, for fear that blacks would use dogs as weapons. Mississippi went further, and prohibited any ownership of a dog by a black person.[5]

Understandably, restrictions on slave possession of arms go back a very long way. While arms restrictions on *free* blacks predate it, these restrictions increased dramatically after Nat Turner's Rebellion in 1831, a revolt that caused the South to become increasingly irrational in its fears.[6] Virginia's response to Turner's Rebellion prohibited free blacks "to keep or carry any firelock of any kind, any military weapon, or any powder or lead..." The existing laws under which free blacks were occasionally licensed to possess or carry arms was also repealed, making arms possession completely illegal for free blacks.[7] But even before this action by the Virginia Legislature, in the aftermath of Turner's Rebellion, the discovery that a free black family possessed lead shot for use as scale weights, without powder or weapon in which to fire it, was considered sufficient reason for a frenzied mob to discuss summary execution of the owner.[8] The analogy to the current hysteria where mere possession of ammunition in some states without a firearms license may lead to jail time, should be obvious.

One example of the increasing fear of armed blacks is the 1834 change to the Tennessee Constitution, where Article XI, 26 of the 1796 Tennessee Constitution was revised from: "That the freemen of this State have a right to keep and to bear arms for their common defence,"[9] to: "That the free *white* men of this State have a right to keep and to bear arms for their common defence."[10] [emphasis added] It is not clear what motivated this change, other than Turner's bloody insurrection. The year before, the Tennessee Supreme Court had recognized the right to bear arms as an individual guarantee, but there is nothing in that decision that touches on the subject of race.[11]

Other decisions during the antebellum period were unambiguous about the importance of race. In *State v. Huntly* (1843), the North Carolina Supreme Court had recognized that there was a right to carry arms guaranteed under the North Carolina Constitution, as long as such arms were carried in a manner not likely to frighten people.[12] The following year, the North Carolina Supreme Court made one of those decisions whose full significance would not appear until after the Civil War and passage of the Fourteenth Amendment. An 1840 statute provided:

> That if any free negro, mulatto, or free person of color, shall wear or carry about his or her person, or keep in his or her house, any shot gun, musket, rifle, pistol, sword, dagger or bowie-knife, unless he or she shall have obtained a licence therefor from the Court of Pleas and Quarter Sessions of his or her county, within one year preceding the wearing, keeping or carrying therefor, he or she shall be guilty of a misdemeanor, and may be indicted therefor.[13]

Elijah Newsom, "a free person of color," was indicted in Cumberland County in June of 1843 for carrying a shotgun without a license—at the very time the North Carolina Supreme Court was deciding *Huntly*. Newsom was convicted by a jury; but the trial judge directed a not guilty verdict, and the state appealed to the North Carolina Supreme Court. Newsom's attorney argued that the statute requiring free blacks to obtain a license to "keep and bear arms" was in violation of both the Second Amendment to the U. S. Constitution, and the North Carolina Constitution's similar guarantee of a right to keep and bear arms.[14] The North Carolina Supreme Court refused to accept that the Second Amendment was a limitation on state laws, but had to deal with the problem of the state constitutional guarantees, which had been used in the Huntly decision, the year before.

The 17th article of the 1776 North Carolina Constitution declared:

> That the people have a right to bear arms, for the defence of the State; and, as standing armies, in time of peace, are dangerous to liberty, they ought not to be kept up; and that the military should be kept under strict subordination to, and governed by, the civil power.[15]

The Court asserted that: "We cannot see that the act of 1840 is in conflict with it... The defendant is not indicted for carrying arms in defence of the State, nor does the act of 1840 prohibit him from so doing."[16] But in Huntly, the Court had acknowledged that the restrictive language "for the defence of the State" did not preclude an individual right.[17] The Court then attempted to justify the necessity of this law:

Its only object is to preserve the peace and safety of the community from being disturbed by an indiscriminate use, on ordinary occasions, by free men of color, of fire arms or other arms of an offensive character. Self preservation is the first law of nations, as it is of individuals.[18]

The North Carolina Supreme Court also sought to repudiate the idea that free blacks were protected by the North Carolina Constitution's Bill of Rights by pointing out that the Constitution excluded free blacks from voting, and therefore free blacks were not citizens. Unlike a number of other state constitutions with right to keep and bear arms provisions that limited this right only to citizens,[19] Article 17 guaranteed this right to the people—and try as hard as they might, it was difficult to argue that a "free person of color," in the words of the Court, was not one of "the people."

It is one of the great ironies that, in much the same way that the North Carolina Supreme Court recognized a right to bear arms in 1843—then a year later declared that free blacks were not included—the Georgia Supreme Court did likewise before the 1840s were out. The Georgia Supreme Court found in *Nunn v. State* (1846) that a statute prohibiting the sale of concealable handguns, sword-canes, and daggers violated the Second Amendment:

> The right of the whole people, old and young, men, women and boys, and not militia only, to keep and bear arms of every description, and not

> such merely as are used by the militia, shall not be infringed, curtailed, or broken in upon, in the smallest degree; and all of this for the important end to be attained: the rearing up and qualifying a well-regulated militia, so vitally necessary to the security of a free State. Our opinion is, that any law, State or Federal, is repugnant to the Constitution, and void, which contravenes this right, originally belonging to our forefathers, trampled under foot by Charles I. and his two wicked sons and successors, reestablished by the revolution of 1688, conveyed to this land of liberty by the colonists, and finally incorporated conspicuously in our own Magna Charta! And Lexington, Concord, Camden, River Raisin, Sandusky, and the laurel-crowned field of New Orleans, plead eloquently for this interpretation![20]

Finally, after this paean to liberty—in a state where much of the population remained enslaved, forbidden by law to possess arms of any sort—the Court defined the valid limits of laws restricting the bearing of arms:

> We are of the opinion, then, that so far as the act of 1837 seeks to suppress the practice of carrying certain weapons secretly, that it is valid, inasmuch as it does not deprive the citizen of his natural right of self-defence, or of his constitutional right to keep and bear arms. But that so much of it, as contains a prohibition against bearing arms openly, is in conflict with the Constitution, and void...[21]

"Citizen"? Within a single page, the Court had gone from "right of the whole people, old and young, men, women and boys" to the much more narrowly restrictive right of a "citizen." The motivation for this sudden narrowing of the right appeared two years later.

The decision *Cooper and Worsham v. Savannah* (1848) was not, principally, a right to keep and bear arms case. In 1839, the city of Savannah, Georgia, in an admitted effort "to prevent the increase of free persons of color in our city," had established a $100 per year tax on free blacks moving into Savannah from other parts of Georgia. Samuel Cooper and Hamilton Worsham, two "free persons of color," were convicted of failing to pay the tax, and were jailed.[22] On appeal, counsel for Cooper and Worsham argued that the ordinance establishing the tax was deficient in a number of technical areas; the assertion of most interest to us is, "In Georgia, free persons of color have constitutional rights..." Cooper and Worsham's counsel argued that these rights included writ of habeas corpus, right to own real estate, to be "subject to taxation," "[t]hey may sue and be sued," and cited a number of precedents under Georgia law in defense of their position.[23]

Justice Warner delivered the Court's opinion, most of which is irrelevant to the right to keep and bear arms, but one portion shows the fundamental relationship between citizenship, arms, and elections, and why gun control laws were an essential part of defining blacks as "non-citizens": "Free persons of color have never been recognized here as citizens; they are not entitled to bear arms, vote for members of the legislature, or to hold any civil office."[24] The Georgia Supreme Court did agree that the ordinance jailing Cooper and Worsham for non-payment was illegal, and ordered their release, but the comments of the Court made it clear that their brave words in *Nunn v. State* (1846) about "the right of the people," really only meant white people.

While settled parts of the South were in great fear of armed blacks, on the frontier, the concerns about Indian attack often forced relaxation of these rules. The 1798 Kentucky Comprehensive Act allowed slaves and free blacks on frontier plantations "to keep and use guns, powder, shot, and weapons, offensive and defensive." Unlike whites, however, a license was required for free blacks or slaves to carry weapons.[25]

The need for blacks to carry arms for self-defense included not only the problem of Indian attack, and the normal criminal attacks that anyone might worry about, but he additional hazard that free blacks were in danger of being kidnapped and sold into slavery.[26] A number of states, including Ohio, Indiana, Illinois, Michigan, and Wisconsin, passed laws specifically to prohibit kidnapping of free blacks, out of concern that the federal Fugitive Slave Laws would be used as cover for re-enslavement.[27]

The end of slavery in 1865 did not eliminate the problems of racist gun control laws; the various Black Codes adopted after the Civil War required blacks to obtain a license before carrying or possessing firearms or Bowie knives; these are sufficiently well-known that any reasonably complete history of the Reconstruction period mentions them. These restrictive gun laws played a part in the efforts of the Republicans to get the Fourteenth Amendment ratified, because it was difficult for night riders to generate the correct level of terror in a victim who was returning fire.[28] It does appear, however, that the requirement to treat blacks and whites equally before the law led to the adoption of restrictive firearms laws in the South that were equal in the letter of the law, but unequally enforced. It is clear that the vagrancy statutes adopted at roughly the same time, in 1866, were intended to be used against blacks, even though the language was race-neutral.[29]

The former states of the Confederacy, many of which had recognized the right to carry arms openly before the Civil War, developed a very sudden willingness to qualify that right. One especially absurd example, and one that includes strong evidence of the racist intentions behind gun control laws, is Texas.

In *Cockrum v. State* (1859), the Texas Supreme Court had recognized that there was a right to carry defensive arms, and that this right was protected under both the Second Amendment, and section 13 of the Texas Bill of Rights. The outer limit of the state's authority (in this case, attempting to discourage the carrying of Bowie knives), was that it could provide an enhanced penalty for manslaughters committed with Bowie knives.[30] Yet, by 1872, the Texas Supreme Court denied that there was any right to carry any weapon for self-defense under either the state or federal constitutions—and made no attempt to explain or justify why the *Cockrum* decision was no longer valid.[31]

What caused the dramatic change? The following excerpt from that same decision—so offensive that no one would dare make such an argument today—sheds some light on the racism that apparently caused the sudden perspective change:

> The law under consideration has been attacked upon the ground that it was contrary to public policy, and deprived the people of the necessary means of self- defense; that it was an innovation upon the customs and habits of the people, to which they would not peaceably submit... We will not say to what extent the early customs and habits of the people of this state should be respected and accommodated, where they may come in conflict with the ideas of intelligent and well-meaning legislators. *A portion of our system of laws, as well as our public morality, is derived from a people the most peculiar perhaps of any other in the history and derivation of its own system. Spain, at different periods of the world, was dominated over by the Carthagenians, the Romans, the Vandals, the Snovi, the Allani, the Visigoths, and Arabs; and to this day there are found in the Spanish codes traces of the laws and customs of each of these nations blended together in a system by no means to be compared with the sound philosophy and pure morality of the common law.*[32] [emphasis added]

This particular decision is more open than most as to its motivations, but throughout the South during this period, the existing precedents that recognized a right to open carry under state constitutional provisions were being narrowed, or simply ignored. Nor was the reasoning that led to these changes lost on judges in the North. In 1920, the Ohio Supreme Court upheld the conviction of a Mexican for concealed carry of a handgun--while asleep in his own bed. Justice Wanamaker's scathing dissent criticized the precedents cited by the majority in defense of this absurdity:

> I desire to give some special attention to some of the authorities cited, supreme court decisions from Alabama, Georgia, Arkansas, Kentucky, and one or two inferior court decisions from New York, which are given in support of the doctrines upheld by this court. The southern states have very largely furnished the precedents. It is only necessary to observe that the race issue there has extremely intensified a decisive purpose to entirely disarm the negro, and this policy is evident upon reading the opinions.[33]

While not relevant to the issue of racism, Justice Wanamaker's closing paragraphs capture well the biting wit and intelligence of this jurist, who was unfortunately, outnumbered on the bench:

> I hold that the laws of the state of Ohio should be so applied and so interpreted as to favor the law-abiding rather than the law-violating people. If this decision shall stand as the law of Ohio, a very large percentage of the good people of Ohio to-day are criminals, because they are daily committing criminal acts by having these weapons in their own homes for their own defense. The only safe course for them to pursue, instead of having the weapon concealed on or about their person, or under their pillow at night, is to hang the revolver on the wall and put below it a large placard with these words inscribed:

"The Ohio supreme court having decided that it is a crime to carry a concealed weapon on one's person in one's home, even in one's bed or bunk, this weapon is hung upon the wall that you may see it, and before you commit any burglary or assault, please, Mr. Burglar, hand me my gun."[34]

There are other examples of remarkable honesty from the state supreme courts on this subject, of which the finest is probably Florida Supreme Court Justice Buford's concurring opinion in *Watson v. Stone* (1941), in which a conviction for carrying a handgun without a permit was overturned, because the handgun was in the glove compartment of a car:

> I know something of the history of this legislation. The original Act of 1893 was passed when there was a great influx of negro laborers in this State drawn here for the purpose of working in turpentine and lumber camps. The same condition existed when the Act was amended in 1901 and the Act was passed for the purpose of disarming the negro laborers and to thereby reduce the unlawful homicides that were prevalent in turpentine and saw-mill camps and to give the white citizens in sparsely settled areas a better feeling of security. The statute was never intended to be applied to the white population and in practice has never been so applied.[35]

Today is not 1893, and when proponents of restrictive gun control insist that their motivations are colorblind, there is a possibility that they are telling the truth. Nonetheless, there are some rather interesting questions that should be asked today. The most obvious question is, "Why should a police chief or sheriff have any discretion in issuing a concealed handgun permit?" Here in California, even the state legislature's research arm--hardly a nest of pro-gunners--has admitted that the vast majority of permits to carry concealed handguns in California are issued to white males.[36] Even if overt racism is not an issue, an official may simply have more empathy with an applicant of a similar cultural background, and consequently be more able to relate to the applicant's concerns. As my wife pointedly reminded a police official when we applied for concealed weapon permits, "If more police chiefs were women, a lot more women would get permits, and be able to defend themselves from rapists."

Gun control advocates today are not so foolish as to openly promote racist laws, and so the question might be asked what relevance the racist past of gun control laws has. One concern is that the motivations for disarming blacks in the past are really not so different from the motivations for disarming law-abiding citizens today. In the last century, the official rhetoric in support of such laws was that "they" were too violent, too untrustworthy, to be allowed weapons. Today, the same elitist rhetoric regards law-abiding Americans in the same way, as child-like creatures in need of guidance from the government. In the last century, while never openly admitted, one of the goals of disarming blacks was to make them more willing to accept various forms of economic oppression, including the sharecropping system, in which free blacks were reduced to an economic state not dramatically superior to the conditions of slavery.

In the seventeenth century, the aristocratic power structure of colonial Virginia found itself confronting a similar challenge from lower class whites. These poor whites resented how the men who controlled the government used that power to concentrate wealth into a small number of hands. These wealthy feeders at the government trough would have disarmed poor whites if they could, but the threat of both Indian and pirate attack made this impractical; for all white men "were armed and had to be armed..." Instead, blacks, who had occupied a poorly defined status between indentured servant and slave, were reduced to hereditary chattel slavery, so that poor whites could be economically advantaged, without the upper class having to give up its privileges.[37]

Today, the forces that push for gun control seem to be heavily (though not exclusively) allied with political factions that are committed to dramatic increases in taxation on the middle class. While it would be hyperbole to compare higher taxes on the middle class to the suffering and deprivation of sharecropping or slavery, the analogy of disarming those whom you wish to economically disadvantage, has a certain worrisome validity to it.

Another point to consider is that in the American legal system, certain classifications of governmental discrimination are considered constitutionally suspect, and these "suspect classifications" (usually considered to be race and religion) come to a court hearing under a strong presumption of invalidity. The reason for these "suspect classifications" is because of the long history of governmental discrimination based on these classifications, and because these classifications often impinge on fundamental rights.[38]

In much the same way, gun control has historically been a tool of racism, and associated with racist attitudes about black violence. Similarly, many gun control laws impinge on that most fundamental of rights: self-defense. Racism is so intimately tied to the history of gun control in America that we should regard gun control aimed at law-abiding people as a "suspect idea," and require that the courts use the same demanding standards when reviewing the constitutionality of a gun control law, that they would use with respect to a law that discriminated based on race.

NOTES

1. Thomas N. Ingersoll, "Free Blacks in a Slave Society: New Orleans, 1718-1812", *William and Marry Quarterly*, 48:2 [April, 1991], 178-79.

2. Daniel H. Usner, Jr., *Indians, Settlers, & Slaves in a Frontier Exchange Economy: The Lower Mississippi Valley Before 1783*, (Chapel Hill, N.C.: University of North Carolina Press, 1992), 139, 165, 187.

3. Michael C. Meyer and William L. Sherman, *The Course of Mexican History*, 4th ed., (New York, Oxford University Press: 1991), 216.

4. Ingersoll, 192-200. Benjamin Quarles, *The Negro in the Making of America*, 3rd ed., (New York, Macmillan Publishing: 1987), 81.

5. Theodore Brantner Wilson, *The Black Codes of the South* (University of Alabama Press: 1965), 26-30.

6. Stanley Elkins, *Slavery*, (Chicago, University of Chicago Press: 1968), 220.

7. Eric Foner, ed., *Nat Turner*, (Englewood Cliffs, N.J., Prentice-Hall: 1971), 115.

8. Harriet Jacobs [Linda Brant], *Incidents in the Life of a Slave Girl_, (Boston: 1861), in Henry Louis Gates, Jr., ed., _The Classic Slave Narratives*, (New York, Penguin Books: 1987), 395-396.

9. Francis Newton Thorpe, *The Federal and State Constitutions, Colonial Charters, and Other Organic Laws of the States, Territories, and Colonies Now or Heretofore Forming The United States of America*, (Washington, Government Printing Office: 1909), reprinted (Grosse Pointe, Mich., Scholarly Press: n.d.), 6:3424.

10. Thorpe, 6:3428.

11. *Simpson v. State*, 5 Yerg. 356 (Tenn. 1833).

12. *State v. Huntly*, 3 Iredell 418, 422, 423 (N.C. 1843).

13. *State v. Newsom*, 5 Iredell 181, 27 N.C. 250 (1844).

14. *State v. Newsom*, 5 Iredell 181, 27 N.C. 250, 251 (1844).

15. Thorpe, 5:2788.

16. *State v. Newsom*, 5 Iredell 181, 27 N.C. 250, 254 (1844).

17. *State v. Huntly*, 3 Iredell 418, 422 (N.C. 1843).

18. *State v. Newsom*, 5 Iredell 181, 27 N.C. 250, 254 (1844).

19. Early state constitutions limiting the right to bear arms to citizens: Connecticut (1818), Kentucky (1792 & 1799), Maine (1819), Mississippi (1817), Pennsylvania (1790—but not the 1776 constitution), Republic of Texas (1838), State of Texas (1845).

20. *Nunn v. State*, 1 Ga. 243, 250, 251 (1846).

21. *Nunn v. State*, 1 Ga. 243, 250, 251 (1846).

22. *Cooper and Worsham v. Savannah*, 4 Ga. 68, 69 (1848).

23. *Cooper and Worsham v. Savannah*, 4 Ga. 68, 70, 71 (1848).

24. *Cooper and Worsham v. Savannah*, 4 Ga. 68, 72 (1848).

25. Juliet E. K. Walker, *Free Frank: A Black Pioneer on the Antebellum Frontier*, (Lexington, KY, University Press of Kentucky: 1983), 21. This is an inspiring biography of a slave who, through hard work moonlighting in the production of saltpeter (a basic ingredient of black powder) and land surveying, saved enough money to buy his wife, himself, and eventually all of his children and grandchildren out of slavery—while fighting against oppressive laws and vigorous racism. Most impressive of all, is that he did it without ever learning to read or write.

26. Walker, 73.

27. Stephen Middleton, *The Black Laws in the Old Northwest: A Documentary History*, (Westport, Conn., Greenwood Press: 1993), 27-32, 227-240, 309-314, 353-357, 403-404.

28. Michael Les Benedict,_*The Fruits of Victory: Alternatives to Restoring the Union*, 1865-1877, (New York, J.B. Lippincott Co.: 1975)

29. Foner, _Reconstruction_, 200-201.

30. *Cockrum v. State*, 24 Tex. 394, 401, 402, 403 (1859).

31. *English v. State*, 35 Tex. 473, 475 (1872).

32. *English v. State*, 35 Tex. 473, 479, 480 (1872).

33. *State v. Nieto*, 101 Ohio St. 409, 430, 130 N.E. 663 (1920).

34. *State v. Nieto*, 101 Ohio St. 409, 436, 130 N.E. 663 (1920).

35. *Watson v. Stone*, 4 So.2d 700, 703 (Fla. 1941).

36. Assembly Office of Research, _Smoking Gun: The Case For Concealed Weapon Permit Reform_, (Sacramento, State of California: 1986), 5.

37. Edmund S. Morgan, "Slavery and Freedom: The American Paradox," in Stanley N. Katz, John M. Murrin, and Douglas Greenberg, ed., *Colonial America: Essays in Politics and Social Development*, 4th ed., (New York: McGraw-Hill, Inc, 1993), 280.

38. Thomas G. Walker, "Suspect Classifications," *Oxford Companion to the Supreme Court of the United States*, (New York, Oxford University Press: 1992), 848.

An Introduction to the Constitutional Law of the United States

Author(s): John Norton Pomeroy
Date: 1875, originally published in 1868
Genre: Book excerpt

Summary Overview

John Norton Pomeroy was a prominent American lawyer, law professor, and legal writer. One of his chief works was *An Introduction to the Constitutional Law of the United States,* which went through nine editions from 1868 until 1886. His comments on the "right of the people to keep and bear arms" are often cited in historical overviews of the issue and are indicative of the way in which some legal scholars examined the issue in the nineteenth century. Pomeroy subscribes to the "individual right" to bear arms yet acknowledges that the government has the right to circumscribe that right in the interests of public safety.

Defining Moment

No particular event led to the publication of Pomeroy's treatise. However, it is noteworthy that the Civil War had ended just three years previously, and as a result of the war, several southern states modified their state constitutions in 1868, the year in which Pomeroy first published *Constitutional Law.* Texas, for example, retained a clause stating that every person had the "right to keep and bear arms in the lawful defence of himself of the State" but added "under such regulations as the legislature may prescribe."

North Carolina added to its constitution the words from the Second Amendment: "A well-regulated militia being necessary to the security of a free State." The state added that the right "shall not be infringed," but the state's constitution went on to comment that "as standing armies, in time of peace, are dangerous to liberty, they ought not to be kept up, and the military should be kept under strict subordination to, and governed by, the civil power." Florida affirmed the right of the people to bear arms but added "in defence of themselves and of the lawful authority of the state." South Carolina agreed with North Carolina in calling standing armies "dangerous to liberty" and added the words: "The people have a right to keep and bear arms for the common defence."

Mississippi amended its constitution to read: "All persons shall have a right to keep and bear arms for their defence." Georgia's constitution had already mirrored the Second Amendment, but the pertinent section added that "the general assembly shall have power to prescribe by law the manner in which arms may be borne." Finally, Arkansas's constitution read: "The citizens of this state shall have the right to keep and bear arms for their common defense."

In the years that followed, other states took up the issue of arms in public. In 1870, for example, Tennessee added to its constitution the words: "but the Legislature shall have power, by law, to regulate the wearing of arms with a view to prevent crime." Similarly, in 1875, Missouri added a provision stating that the right to bear arms is not "intended to justify the practice of wearing concealed weapons." It was in this context, as states and municipalities reexamined the issue of the right to keep and bear arms, that Pomeroy offered comments that affirmed the right but agreed that the right could be circumscribed for purposes of public safety.

About the Author

John Norton Pomeroy was born in Rochester, New York, on April 12, 1828. After graduating from Hamilton College in New York in 1847, he studied law by apprenticing in two law offices, gaining admission to the bar in 1851. He practiced law in Rochester, New York, until 1861, then tried, unsuccessfully, to establish a practice in New York City. In 1865, he took a position as professor of law and political science and dean of the law school at New York University, a position he held until 1871. Illness forced him to take a break from academia, though he worked in private practice until 1878, when he moved to California to take a position as a law professor at the Hastings College of Law at the University of California, the state's first law school; the school was so small that Pomeroy was its sole professor. He died in 1885 in San Francisco.

HISTORICAL DOCUMENT

1. The right of the people to keep and bear arms. The object of this clause is to secure a well-armed militia. It has always been the policy of free governments to dispense, as far as possible, with standing armies, and to rely for their defence, both against foreign invasion and domestic turbulence, upon the militia. Regular armies have always been associated with despotism. But a militia would be useless unless the citizens were enabled to exercise themselves in the use of warlike weapons. To preserve this privilege, and to secure to the people the ability to oppose themselves in military force against the usurpations of government, as well as against enemies from without, that government is forbidden by any law or proceeding to invade or destroy the right to keep and bear arms. But all such provisions, all such guaranties, must be construed with reference to their intent and design. This constitutional inhibition is certainly not violated by laws forbidding persons to carry dangerous or concealed weapons, or laws forbidding the accumulation of quantities of arms with the design to use them in a riotous or seditious manner. The clause is analogous to the one securing freedom of speech and of the press. Freedom, not license, is secured; the fair use, not the libellous abuse, is protected.

Document Themes

In common with many other jurists and legal writers in the eighteenth and nineteenth centuries, Pomeroy expresses suspicion of "standing armies." He notes that it has been the policy of free governments to do without standing armies for their defense; instead, they turn to the militia to drive off foreign invasions or to quell domestic disturbances.

He notes that regular armies have been regarded as an earmark of despotic government. He goes on to comment, though, that a militia would have little use if the citizens who made up the militia were unable to gain facility in the use of the weapons of war. Pomeroy then states that in order to preserve this privilege, and to resist the "usurpations of government" and foreign enemies, the government is prevented by law from passing any law or taking any steps to interfere with a person's right to keep and bear arms. Accordingly, Pomeroy would seem to subscribe to the "individual right" theory of the Second Amendment—that is, the view that the amendment extends the right to keep and bear arms to individuals, independent of their membership in a state militia.

Pomeroy goes on, however, to conceded that the right has to be understood in the context of its original "intent and design." Accordingly, the constitutional provision that inhibits the government from interfering with the right to bear arms is not violated by laws that forbid people from carrying dangerous or concealed weapons, or from amassing stockpiles of arms that could be used in a "riotous or seditious manner." He concludes by noting that the right to keep and bear arms is analogous to other constitutionally protected rights in protecting "freedom," but not "license," "fair use," not "abuse."

Additional Reading

Kopel, David B., "The Second Amendment in the Nineteenth Century," *BYU Law Review* 4 (1998): 1359–1554.

Leary, John C., "John Norton Pomeroy, 1828–1885: A Biographical Sketch," *Law Library Journal* 47 (1954): 138, https://heinonline.org/HOL/LandingPage?handle=hein.journals/llj47&div=24&id=&page=

Paludan, Phillip S., "John Norton Pomeroy, State Rights Nationalist," *American Journal of Legal History* 12, no. 4 (October, 1968): 275–93

Siegel, Stephen A., "Historicism in Late Nineteenth-Century Constitutional Thought," *Wisconsin Law Review* (1990): 1431–1547.

John Norton Pomeroy.

A political cartoon depicting the KKK and the Democratic Party as continuations of the Confederacy.

United States v. Cruikshank

Author(s): Morrison Remick Waite
Date: 1876
Genre: Court decision (Supreme Court)

Summary Overview

United States v. Cruikshank arose in the wake of the 1873 Colfax Massacre. On April 13 of that year, a group of armed whites in Colfax, Louisiana, killed a number of African American men during a political dispute. Some of the men were convicted of violating the 1870 and 1871 Enforcement Acts—laws intended to curb Ku Klux Klan violence by prohibiting conspiracies formed to deny the constitutional rights of any citizen. The men appealed. The U.S. Supreme Court sided with the defendants, holding that the rights they were alleged to have violated were not enforceable. The Court reasoned that the First Amendment right to assembly and the Second Amendment right to bear arms were intended to restrict the actions of the federal government; they did not apply to the states or private citizens. Further, the Fourteenth Amendment rights to Due Process and Equal Protection applied only to government actions, not to the actions of individuals. The case is significant, for it was the first Supreme Court ruling that included an analysis of the Second Amendment.

Defining Moment

After the Civil War, many Southern Democrats, most of them former slave owners, took steps to disenfranchise and restrict the rights of former slaves. To that end, white supremacist groups terrorized African Americans throughout the South. Matters came to a head in Louisiana in 1872 during that year's hotly contested governor's race; with violence threatened, President Ulysses S. Grant sent federal troops to ensure the safety of the Republican candidate and Republicans throughout the state. Many white southerners rebelled, forming a paramilitary force call the White League, which intimidated blacks and Republicans.

In April, an armed black militia group seized control of the local courthouse, fearing a Democratic takeover of the local government. Quickly, a mob of 150 whites, most of them former Confederate soldiers and members of the Ku Klux Klan and the White League, surrounded the courthouse. The two forces fired on each other until the black group was forced to surrender. As they were fleeing, the white mob shot to death between 60 and 150 of them, although some estimates range as high as 280. Ninety-seven members of the white mob were indicted, but just nine were ultimately charged with violating the Enforcement Acts of 1870 and 1871. Prosecutors believed that they would have a better chance of getting convictions of the men on *some* charge by bringing federal conspiracy charges rather than state murder charges. Their plan backfired when the U.S. Supreme Court overturned the convictions of the lower courts. The case had significant implications for the Reconstruction efforts of the federal government, for the case limited the ability of the federal government to prosecute crimes against African Americans.

About the Author

Chief Justice Morrison Remick Waite wrote the opinion for a unanimous Court. Waite was born on November 27, 1816, in Lyme Connecticut. After graduating from Yale University in 1837, he settled in Maumee City, Ohio, to study law. In 1848 he and his family moved to nearby Toledo, Ohio, where he established a successful law practice. His appointment as chief justice of the U.S. Supreme Court came as a surprise to virtually everyone, including Waite himself, for he had played little role in public affairs. He sat briefly on the Toledo city council and served a single term in the Ohio legislature. He ran for Congress twice, but was defeated both times. He was nominated to the Ohio Supreme Court in 1863, but he turned the appointment down. His most noteworthy public accomplishment was as a member of a delegation to adjudicate claims made by the United States against Great Britain for the latter's violation of neutrality during the Civil War. Waite and his colleagues won a $15.5 million award for the United States.

Waite was serving as president of the Ohio Constitutional Convention in 1873 when word reached him that Grant had nominated him as chief justice of the Supreme Court to fill the vacancy left by Salmon Chase. He was not the president's first choice; others turned down the nomination for various reasons or were rejected by the Senate. Grant turned to Waite, who did not carry any political baggage to Washington with him; he was unanimously confirmed by the Senate, and he took his seat in 1874.

Waite was one of the hardest working chief justices in U.S. history. Under his leadership, the Court decided nearly 3,500 cases; Waite himself wrote 872 opinions. Although his opinion in *United States v. Cruikshank* hamstrung the federal government's Reconstruction efforts, Waite was by no means hostile to African Americans and was in fact rather progressive. In *Strauder v. West Virginia* (1879), for example, he struck down all-white juries, and in the same year in *Neal v. Delaware* he ruled that state judges could not exclude African Americans from juries. Waite continued to carry a crushing workload on the Court until his death on March 23, 1888.

HISTORICAL DOCUMENT

United States v. Cruikshank

Syllabus

1. Citizens are the members of the political community to which they belong. They are the people who compose the community, and who, in their associated capacity, have established or submitted themselves to the dominion of a government for the promotion of their general welfare and the protection of their individual, as well as their collective, rights. The duty of a government to afford protection is limited always by the power it possesses for that purpose.

2. There is in our political system a government of each of the several States, and a Government of the United States. Each is distinct from the others, and has citizens of its own who owe it allegiance, and whose rights, within its jurisdiction, it must protect. The same person may be at the same time a citizen of the United States and a citizen of a State, but his rights of citizenship under one of those governments will be different from those he has under the other.

3. The Government of the United States, although it is, within the scope of its powers, supreme and beyond the States, can neither grant nor secure to its citizens rights or privileges which are not expressly or by implication placed under its jurisdiction. All that cannot be so granted or secured are left to the exclusive protection of the States.

4. The right of the people peaceably to assemble for lawful purposes, with the obligation on the part of the States to afford it protection, existed long before the adoption of the Constitution. The First Amendment to the Constitution, prohibiting Congress from abridging the right to assemble and petition, was not intended to limit the action of the State governments in respect to their own citizens, but to operate upon the National Government alone. It left the authority of the States unimpaired, added nothing to the already existing powers of the United States, and guaranteed the continuance of the right only against Congressional interference. The people, for their protection in the enjoyment of it, must therefore look to the States, where the power for that purpose was originally placed.

5. The right of the people peaceably to assemble for the purpose of petitioning Congress for a redress of grievances, or for anything else connected with the powers or duties of the National Government, is an attribute of national citizenship, and, as such, under the protection of and guaranteed by the United States. The very idea of a government republican in form implies that right, and an invasion of it presents a case within the sovereignty of the United States.

6. The right to bear arms is not granted by the Constitution; neither is it in any manner dependent upon that instrument for its existence. The Second Amendments means no more than that it shall not be infringed by Congress, and has no other effect than to restrict the powers of the National Government.

7. Sovereignty, for the protection of the rights of life

and personal liberty within the respective States, rests alone with the States.

8. The Fourteenth Amendment prohibits a State from depriving any person of life, liberty, or property without due process of law, and from denying to any person within its jurisdiction the equal protection of the laws, but it adds nothing to the rights of one citizen as against another. It simply furnishes an additional guaranty against any encroachment by the States upon the fundamental rights which belong to every citizen as a member of society. The duty of protecting all its citizens in the enjoyment of an equality of rights was originally assumed by the States, and it still remains there. The only obligation resting upon the United States is to see that the States do not deny the right. This the Amendment guarantees, but no more. The power of the National Government is limited to the enforcement of this guaranty.

9. In *Minor v. Happersett,* 21 Wall. 178, this Court decided that the Constitution of the United States has not conferred the right of suffrage upon anyone, and that the United States have no voters of their own creation in the States. In *United States v. Reese et al.,* it held that the Fifteenth Amendment has invested the citizens of the United States with a new constitutional right, which is exemption from discrimination in the exercise of the elective franchise on account of race, color, or previous condition of servitude. The right to vote in the States comes from the States; but the right of exemption from the prohibited discrimination comes from the United States. The first has not been granted or secured by the Constitution of the United States, but the last has been.

10. The counts of an indictment which charge the defendants with having banded and conspired to injure, oppress, threaten, and intimidate citizens of the United States of African descent, therein named, and which, in substance respectively allege that the defendants intended thereby to hinder and prevent such citizens in the free exercise and enjoyment of rights and privileges granted and secured to them in common with other good citizens by the Constitution and law of the United States, to hinder and prevent them in the free exercise of their right peacefully to assemble for lawful purposes, deprive them of their respective several lives and liberty of person without due process of law, prevent and hinder them in the free exercise and enjoyment of their several rights to the full and equal benefit of the law, prevent and hinder them in the free exercise and enjoyment of their several and respective rights to vote at any election to be thereafter by law had and held by the people in and of the State of Louisiana, or to put them in great fear of bodily harm and to injure and oppress them because, being and having been in all things qualified, they had voted at an election theretofore had and held according to law by the people of said State—do not present a case within the sixth section of the Enforcement Act of May 31, 1870 (16 Stat. 141). To bring a case within the operation of that statute, it must appear that the right the enjoyment of which the conspirators intended to hinder or prevent was one granted or secured by the Constitution or laws of the United States. If it does not so appear, the alleged offence is not indictable under any act of Congress.

11. The counts of an indictment which, in general language, charge the defendants with an intent to hinder and prevent citizens of the United States of African descent, therein named, in the free exercise and enjoyment of the rights, privileges, immunities, and protection granted and secured to them respectively as citizens of the United States, and of the State of Louisiana, because they were persons of African descent, and with the intent to hinder and prevent them in the several and free exercise and enjoyment of every, each, all, and singular the several rights and privileges granted and secured to them by the Constitution and laws of the United States do not specify any particular right the enjoyment of which the conspirators intended to hinder or prevent, are too vague and general, lack the certainty and precision required by the established rules of criminal pleading, and are therefore not good and sufficient in law.

12. In criminal cases prosecuted under the laws of the United States, the accused has the constitutional right "to be informed of the nature and cause of the accusation." The indictment must set forth the offence with clearness and all necessary certainty, to apprise the accused of the crime with which he stands charged, and every ingredient of which the offence is composed must be accurately and clearly alleged. It is an elementary principle of criminal pleading that, where the definition of an offence, whether it be at common law or by statute, includes generic terms, it is not sufficient that the indictment shall charge the offence in the same

generic terms as in the definition, but it must state the species—it must descend to particulars. The object of the indictment is first, to furnish the accused with such a description of the charge against him as will enable him to make his defence, and avail himself of his conviction or acquittal for protection against a further prosecution for the same cause, and, second, to inform the court of the facts alleged, so that it may decide whether they are sufficient in law to support a conviction if one should be had. For this, facts are to be stated, not conclusions of law alone. A crime is made up of acts and intent, and these must be set forth in the indictment with reasonable particularity of time, place, and circumstances.

13. By the act under which this indictment was found, the crime is made to consist in the unlawful combination with an intent to prevent the enjoyment of any right granted or secured by the Constitution, &c. All rights are not so granted or secured. Whether one is so or not is a question of law, to be decided by the court. The indictment should therefore state the particulars to inform the court as well as the accused. It must appear from the indictment that the acts charged will, if proved, support a conviction for the offence alleged. This was an indictment for conspiracy under the sixth section of the act of May 30, 1870, known as the Enforcement Act (16 Stat. 140), and consisted of thirty-two counts.

The *first* count was for banding together, with intent "unlawfully and feloniously to injure, oppress, threaten, and intimidate" two citizens of the United States, "of African descent and persons of color," "with the unlawful and felonious intent thereby" them

"to hinder and prevent in their respective free exercise and enjoyment of their lawful right and privilege to peaceably assemble together with each other and with other citizens of the said United States for a peaceable and lawful purpose."

The *second* avers an intent to hinder and prevent the exercise by the same persons of the "right to keep and bear arms for a lawful purpose."

The *third* avers an intent to deprive the same persons "of their respective several lives and liberty of person, without due process of law."

The *fourth* avers an intent to deprive the same persons of the

> "free exercise and enjoyment of the right and privilege to the full and equal benefit of all laws and proceedings for the security of persons and property"

enjoyed by white citizens.

The *fifth* avers an intent to hinder and prevent the same persons

> "in the exercise and enjoyment of the rights, privileges, immunities, and protection granted and secured to them respectively as citizens of the said United States, and as citizens of the said State of Louisiana, by reason of and for and on account of the race and color"

of the said persons.

The *sixth* avers an intent to hinder and prevent the same persons in

> "the free exercise and enjoyment of the several and respective right and privilege to vote at any election to be thereafter by law had and held by the people in and of the said State of Louisiana."

The *seventh* avers an intent "to put in great fear of bodily harm, injure, and oppress" the same persons, "because and for the reason" that, having the right to vote, they had voted.

The *eighth* avers an intent "to prevent and hinder" the same persons

> "in their several and respective free exercise and enjoyment of every, each, all, and singular and several rights and privileges granted and secured"

to them "by the Constitution and laws of the United States."

The next eight counts are a repetition of the first eight, except that, instead of the words "band together," the words "combine, conspire, and confederate together" are used. Three of the defendants were found guilty under the first sixteen counts, and not guilty under the remaining counts.

The parties thus convicted moved in arrest of judgment on the following grounds:

1. Because the matters and things set forth and charged in the several counts, one to sixteen inclusive, do not constitute offences against the laws of the United States, and do not come within the purview, true intent, and meaning of the act of Congress, approved 31st May, 1870, entitled *"An Act to enforce the right of citizens of the United States,"* &c.

2. Because the matters and things in the said indictment set forth and charged do not constitute offences cognizable in the Circuit Court, and do not come within its power and jurisdiction.

3. Because the offences created by the sixth section of the act of Congress referred to, and upon which section the aforesaid sixteen counts are based, are not constitutionally within the jurisdiction of the courts of the United States, and because the matters and things therein referred to are judicially cognizable by State tribunals only, and legislative action thereon is among the constitutionally reserved rights of the several States.

4. Because the said act, in so far as it creates offences and imposes penalties, is in violation of the Constitution of the United States, and an infringement of the rights of the several States and the people.

5. Because the eighth and sixteenth counts of the indictment are too vague, general, insufficient, and uncertain, to afford the accused proper notice to plead and prepare their defence, and set forth no specific offence under the law.

6. Because the verdict of the jury against the defendants is not warranted or supported by law.

On this motion, the opinions of the judges were divided, that of the presiding judge being that the several counts in question are not sufficient in law, and do not contain charges of criminal matter indictable under the laws of the United States, and that the motion in arrest of judgment should be granted. The case comes up at the instance of the United States, on certificate of this divisiOn of opinion.

Sect. 1 of the Enforcement Act declares that all citizens of the United States, otherwise qualified, shall be allowed to vote at all elections, without distinction of race, color, or previous servitude.

Sect. 2 provides that if, by the law of any State or Territory, a prerequisite to voting is necessary, equal opportunity for it shall be given to all, without distinction, &c., and any person charged with the duty of furnishing the prerequisite who refuses or knowingly omits to give full effect to this section shall be guilty of misdemeanor.

Sect. 3 provides that an offer of performance in respect to the prerequisite, when proved by affidavit of the claimant, shall be equivalent to performance, and any judge or inspector of election who refuses to accept it shall be guilty, &c.

Sect. 4 provides that any person who, by force, bribery, threats, intimidation, or other unlawful means, hinders, delays, prevents, or obstructs any citizen from qualifying himself to vote, or combines with others to do so, shall be guilty, &c.

Sect. 5 provides that any person who prevents, hinders, controls, or intimidates any person from exercising the right of suffrage, to whom it is secured by the Fifteenth Amendment, or attempts to do so, by bribery or threats of violence, or deprivation of property or employment, shall be guilty, &c.

The sixth section is as follows:

"That if two or more persons shall band or conspire together, or go in disguise upon the public highway, or upon the premises of another, with intent to violate any provisions of this act, or to injure, oppress, threaten, or intimidate any citizen with intent to prevent or hinder his free exercise and enjoyment of any right or privilege granted or secured to him by the Constitution or laws of the United States, or because of his having exercised the same, such persons shall be held guilty of felony, and, on conviction thereof, shall be fined or imprisoned, or both, at the discretion of the court—the fine not to exceed $5,000 and the imprisonment not to exceed ten years—and shall, moreover, be thereafter ineligible to, and disabled from holding, any office or place of honor, profit, or trust created by the Constitution or laws of the United States. "

MR. CHIEF JUSTICE WAITE delivered the opinion of the court.

This case comes here with a certificate by the judges of the Circuit Court for the District of Louisiana that they were divided in opinion upon a question which occurred at the hearing. It presents for our consideration an indictment containing sixteen counts, divided into two series of eight counts each, based upon sect. 6 of the Enforcement Act of May 31, 1870. That section is as follows:—

"That if two or more persons shall band or conspire together, or go in disguise upon the public highway, or upon the premises of another, with intent to violate any provision of this act, or to injure, oppress, threaten, or intimidate any citizen, with intent to prevent or hinder his free exercise and enjoyment of any right or privilege granted or secured to him by the Constitution or laws of the United States, or because of his having exercised the same, such persons shall be held guilty of felony, and, on conviction thereof, shall be fined or imprisoned, or both, at the discretion of the court—the fine not to exceed $5,000, and the imprisonment not to exceed ten years—and shall, moreover, be thereafter ineligible to, and disabled from holding, any office or place of honor, profit, or trust created by the Constitution or laws of the United States."

16 Stat. 141.

The question certified arose upon a motion in arrest of judgment after a verdict of guilty generally upon the whole sixteen counts, and is stated to be whether

"the said sixteen counts of said indictment are severally good and sufficient in law, and contain charges of criminal matter indictable under the laws of the United States."

The general charge in the first eight counts is that of "banding," and in the second eight that of "conspiring" together to injure, oppress, threaten, and intimidate Levi Nelson and Alexander Tillman, citizens of the United States, of African descent and persons of color, with the intent thereby to hinder and prevent them in their free exercise and enjoyment of rights and privileges "granted and secured" to them "in common with all other good citizens of the United States by the Constitution and laws of the United States."

The offences provided for by the statute in question do not consist in the mere "banding" or "conspiring" of two or more persons together, but in their banding or conspiring with the intent, or for any of the purposes, specified. To bring this case under the operation of the statute, therefore, it must appear that the right, the enjoyment of which the conspirators intended to hinder or prevent, was one granted or secured by the Constitution or laws of the United States. If it does not so appear, the criminal matter charged has not been made indictable by any act of Congress.

We have in our political system a government of the United States and a government of each of the several States. Each one of these governments is distinct from the others, and each has citizens of its own who owe it allegiance and whose rights, within its jurisdiction, it must protect. The same person may be at the same time a citizen of the United States and a citizen of a State, but his rights of citizenship under one of these governments will be different from those he has under the other.

Citizens are the members of the political community to which they belong. They are the people who compose the community, and who, in their associated capacity, have established or submitted themselves to the dominion of a government for the promotion of their general welfare and the protection of their individual as well as their collective rights. In the formation of a government, the people may confer upon it such powers as they choose. The government, when so formed, may, and when called upon should, exercise all the powers it has for the protection of the rights of its citizens and the people within its jurisdiction, but it can exercise no other. The duty of a government to afford protection is limited always by the power it possesses for that purpose.

Experience made the fact known to the people of the United States that they required a national government for national purposes. The separate governments of the separate States, bound together by the articles of confederation alone, were not sufficient for the promotion of the general welfare of the people in respect to foreign nations, or for their complete protection as citizens of the confederated States. For this reason, the people of the United States,

> "in order to form a more perfect union, establish justice, insure domestic tranquillity, provide for the common defence, promote the general welfare, and secure the blessings of liberty"

to themselves and their posterity (Const. Preamble), ordained and established the government of the United States, and defined its powers by a Constitution, which they adopted as its fundamental law, and made its rule of action.

The government thus established and defined is to some extent a government of the States in their political capacity. It is also, for certain purposes, a government of the people. Its powers are limited in number, but not in degree. Within the scope of its powers, as enumerated and defined, it is supreme, and above the States; but beyond, it has no existence. It was erected for special purposes, and endowed with all the powers necessary for its own preservation and the accomplishment of the ends its people had in view. It can neither grant nor secure to its citizens any right or privilege not expressly or by implication placed under its jurisdiction.

The people of the United States resident within any State are subject to two governments—one State and the other National—but there need be no conflict between the two. The powers which one possesses the other does not. They are established for different purposes, and have separate jurisdictions. Together, they make one whole, and furnish the people of the United States with a complete government, ample for the protection of all their rights at home and abroad. True, it may sometimes happen that a person is amenable to both jurisdictions for one and the same act. Thus, if a marshal of the United States is unlawfully resisted while executing the process of the courts within a State, and the resistance is accompanied by an assault on the officer, the sovereignty of the United States is violated by the resistance, and that of the State by the breach of peace in the assault. So, too, if one passes counterfeited coin of the United States within a State, it may be an offence against the United States and the State: the United States because it discredits the coin, and the State because of the fraud upon him to whom it is passed. This does not, however, necessarily imply that the two governments possess powers in common, or bring them into conflict with each other. It is the natural consequence of a citizenship which owes allegiance to two sovereignties and claims protection from both. The citizen cannot complain, because he has voluntarily submitted himself to such a form of government. He owes allegiance to the two departments, so to speak, and, within their respective spheres, must pay the penalties which each exacts for disobedience to its laws. In return, he can demand protection from each within its own jurisdiction.

The Government of the United States is one of delegated powers alone. Its authority is defined and limited by the Constitution. All powers not granted to it by that instrument are reserved to the States or the people. No rights can be acquired under the Constitution or laws of the United States, except such as the Government of the United States has the authority to grant or secure. All that cannot be so granted or secured are left under the protection of the States.

We now proceed to an examination of the indictment, to ascertain whether the several rights, which it is alleged the defendants intended to interfere with, are such as had been in law and in fact granted or secured by the

Constitution or laws of the United States.

The first and ninth counts state the intent of the defendants to have been to hinder and prevent the citizens named in the free exercise and enjoyment of their

> "lawful right and privilege to peaceably assemble together with each other and with other citizens of the United States for a peaceful and lawful purpose."

The right of the people peaceably to assemble for lawful purposes existed long before the adoption of the Constitution of the United States. In fact, it is, and always has been, one of the attributes of citizenship under a free government. It "derives its source," to use the language of Chief Justice Marshall in *Gibbons v. Ogden,* "from those laws whose authority is acknowledged by civilized man throughout the world." It is found wherever civilization exists. It was not, therefore, a right granted to the people by the Constitution. The Government of the United States, when established, found it in existence, with the obligation on the part of the States to afford it protection. As no direct power over it was granted to Congress, it remains, according to the ruling in *Gibbons v. Ogden,* subject to State jurisdiction.

Only such existing rights were committed by the people to the protection of Congress as came within the general scope of the authority granted to the national government.

The first amendment to the Constitution prohibits Congress from abridging "the right of the people to assemble and to petition the government for a redress of grievances." This, like the other amendments proposed and adopted at the same time, was not intended to limit the powers of the State governments in respect to their own citizens, but to operate upon the National Government alone. It is now too late to question the correctness of this construction. As was said by the late Chief Justice, in *Twitchell v. The Commonwealth,* "the scope and application of these amendments are no longer subjects of discussion here." They left the authority of the States just where they found it, and added nothing to the already existing powers of the United States.

The particular amendment now under consideration assumes the existence of the right of the people to assemble for lawful purposes, and protects it against encroachment by Congress. The right was not created by the amendment; neither was its continuance guaranteed, except as against congressional interference. For their protection in its enjoyment, therefore, the people must look to the States. The power for that purpose was originally placed there, and it has never been surrendered to the United States.

The right of the people peaceably to assemble for the purpose of petitioning Congress for a redress of grievances, or for any thing else connected with the powers or the duties of the national government, is an attribute of national citizenship, and, as such, under the protection of, and guaranteed by, the United States. The very idea of a government republican in form implies a right on the part of its citizens to meet peaceably for consultation in respect to public affairs and to petition for a redress of grievances. If it had been alleged in these counts that the object of the defendants was to prevent a meeting for such a purpose, the case would have been within the statute, and within the scope of the sovereignty of the United States. Such, however, is not the case. The offence, as stated in the indictment, will be made out, if it be shown that the object of the conspiracy was to prevent a meeting for any lawful purpose whatever.

The second and tenth counts are equally defective. The right there specified is that of "bearing arms for a lawful purpose." This is not a right granted by the Constitution. Neither is it in any manner dependent upon that instrument for its existence. The second amendment declares that it shall not be infringed, but this, as has been seen, means no more than that it shall not be infringed by Congress. This is one of the amendments that has no other effect than to restrict the powers of the national government, leaving the people to look for their protection against any violation by their fellow citizens of the rights it recognizes, to what is called, in *The City of New York v. Miln,* the "powers which relate to merely municipal legislation, or what was, perhaps, more properly called internal police," "not surrendered or restrained" by the Constitution of the United States.

The third and eleventh counts are even more objectionable. They charge the intent to have been to deprive the citizens named, they being in Louisiana, "of their respective several lives and liberty of person without due process of law." This is nothing else than alleging a conspiracy to falsely imprison or murder citizens of the United States, being within the territorial jurisdiction of the State of Louisiana. The rights of life and personal liberty are natural rights of man. "To secure these rights," says the Declaration of Independence, "governments are instituted among men, deriving their just powers from the consent of the governed." The very highest duty of the States, when they entered into the Union under the Constitution, was to protect all persons within their boundaries in the enjoyment of these "unalienable rights with which they were endowed by their Creator." Sovereignty, for this purpose, rests alone with the States. It is no more the duty or within the power of the United States to punish for a conspiracy to falsely imprison or murder within a State, than it would be to punish for false imprisonment or murder itself.

The Fourteenth Amendment prohibits a State from depriving any person of life, liberty, or property without due process of law, but this adds nothing to the rights of one citizen as against another. It simply furnishes an additional guaranty against any encroachment by the States upon the fundamental rights which belong to every citizen as a member of society. As was said by Mr. Justice Johnson, in *Bank of Columbia v. Okely,* it secures

> "the individual from the arbitrary exercise of the powers of government, unrestrained by the established principles of private rights and distributive justice."

These counts in the indictment do not call for the exercise of any of the powers conferred by this provision in the amendment.

The fourth and twelfth counts charge the intent to have been to prevent and hinder the citizens named, who were of African descent and persons of color, in

> "the free exercise and enjoyment of their several right and privilege to the full and equal benefit of all laws and proceedings, then and there, before that time, enacted or ordained by the said State of Louisiana and by the United States, and then and there, at that time, being in force in the said State and District of Louisiana aforesaid, for the security of their respective persons and property, then and there, at that time enjoyed at and within said State and District of Louisiana by white persons, being citizens of said State of Louisiana and the United States, for the protection of the persons and property of said white citizens."

There is no allegation that this was done because of the race or color of the persons conspired against. When stripped of its verbiage, the case as presented amounts to nothing more than that the defendants conspired to prevent certain citizens of the United States, being within the State of Louisiana, from enjoying the equal protection of the laws of the State and of the United States.

The Fourteenth Amendment prohibits a State from denying to any person within its jurisdiction the equal protection of the laws; but this provision does not, any more than the one which precedes it, and which we have just considered, add anything to the rights which one citizen has under the Constitution against another. The equality of the rights of citizens is a principle of republicanism. Every republican government is in duty bound to protect all its citizens in the enjoyment of this principle, if within its power. That duty was originally assumed by the States, and it still remains there. The only obligation resting upon the United States is to see that the States do not deny the right. This the amendment guarantees, but no more. The power of the national government is limited to the enforcement of this guaranty.

No question arises under the Civil Rights Act of April 9, 1866 (14 Stat. 27), which is intended for the protection of citizens of the United States in the enjoyment of certain rights, without discrimination on account of race, color, or previous condition of servitude, because, as has already been stated, it is nowhere alleged in these counts that the wrong contemplated against the rights of these citizens was on account of their race or color.

Another objection is made to these counts that they are too vague and uncertain. This will be considered hereafter, in connection with the same objection to other counts.

The sixth and fourteenth counts state the intent of the defendants to have been to hinder and prevent the citizens named, being of African descent, and colored,

"The Louisiana Murders—Gathering The Dead And Wounded." Published in Harper's Weekly *May 10, 1873, after the Colfax massacre in Colfax on April 13, 1873.*

> "in the free exercise and enjoyment of their several and respective right and privilege to vote at any election to be thereafter by law had and held by the people in and of the said State of Louisiana, or by the people of and in the parish of Grant aforesaid."

In *Minor v. Happersett,* we decided that the Constitution of the United States has not conferred the right of suffrage upon anyone, and that the United States have no voters of their own creation in the States. In *United States v. Reese et al., supra,* p. 92 U. S. 214, we hold that the Fifteenth Amendment has invested the citizens of the United States with a new constitutional right, which is, exemption from discrimination in the exercise of the elective franchise on account of race, color, or previous condition of servitude. From this, it appears that the right of suffrage is not a necessary attribute of national citizenship, but that exemption from discrimination in the exercise of that right on account of race, &c., is. The right to vote in the States comes from the States, but the right of exemption from the prohibited discrimination comes from the United States. The first has not been granted or secured by the Constitution of the United States, but the last has been.

Inasmuch, therefore, as it does not appear in these counts that the intent of the defendants was to prevent these parties from exercising their right to vote on account of their race, &c., it does not appear that it was their intent to interfere with any right granted or secured by the Constitution or laws of the United States. We may suspect that race was the cause of the hostility, but it is not so averred. This is material to a description of the substance of the offence, and cannot be supplied by implication. Everything essential must be charged positively, and not inferentially. The defect here is not in form, but in substance.

The seventh and fifteenth counts are no better than the sixth and fourteenth. The intent here charged is to put the parties named in great fear of bodily harm, and to injure and oppress them, because, being and having been in all things qualified, they had voted

> "at an election before that time had and held according to law by the people of the said State of Louisiana, in said State, to-wit, on the fourth day of November, A.D. 1872, and at divers other elections by the people of the State, also before that time had and held according to law."

There is nothing to show that the elections voted at were any other than State elections, or that the conspiracy was formed on account of the race of the parties against whom the conspirators were to act. The charge as made is really of nothing more than a conspiracy to commit a breach of the peace within a State. Certainly it will not be claimed that the United States have the power or are required to do mere police duly in the States. If a State cannot protect itself against domestic violence, the United States may, upon the call of the executive, when the legislature cannot be convened, lend their assistance for that purpose. This is a guaranty of the Constitution (art. 4, sect. 4), but it applies to no case like this.

We are therefore of the opinion that the first, second, third, fourth, sixth, seventh, ninth, tenth, eleventh, twelfth, fourteenth, and fifteenth counts do not contain charges of a criminal nature made indictable under the laws of the United States, and that consequently they are not good and sufficient in law. They do not show that it was the intent of the defendants, by their conspiracy, to hinder or prevent the enjoyment of any right granted or secured by the Constitution.

We come now to consider the fifth and thirteenth and the eighth and sixteenth counts, which may be brought together for that purpose. The intent charged in the fifth and thirteenth is

> "to hinder and prevent the parties in their respective free exercise and enjoyment of the rights, privileges, immunities, and protection granted and secured to them respectively as citizens of the United States, and as citizens of said State of Louisiana . . . for the reason that they, . . . being then and there citizens of said State and of the United States, were persons of African descent and race, and persons of color, and not white citizens thereof;"

and in the eighth and sixteenth, to hinder and prevent them

> "in their several and respective free exercise and enjoyment of every, each, all, and singular the several rights and privileges granted and secured to them by the Constitution and laws of the United States."

The same general statement of the rights to be interfered with is found in the fifth and thirteenth counts.

According to the view we take of these counts, the question is not whether it is enough, in general, to describe a statutory offence in the language of the statute, but whether the offence has here been described at all. The statute provides for the punishment of those who conspire

> "to injure, oppress, threaten, or intimidate any citizen, with intent to prevent or hinder his free exercise and enjoyment of any right or privilege granted or secured to him by the Constitution or laws of the United States."

These counts in the indictment charge, in substance that the intent in this case was to hinder and prevent these citizens in the free exercise and enjoyment of "every, each, all, and singular" the rights granted them by the Constitution, &c. There is no specification of any particular right. The language is broad enough to cover all.

In criminal cases, prosecuted under the laws of the United States, the accused has the constitutional right "to be informed of the nature and cause of the accusation." Amend. VI. In *United States v. Mills,* this was construed to mean that the indictment must set forth the offence "with clearness and all necessary certainty, to apprise the accused of the crime with which he stands charged;" and in *United States v. Cook,* that "every ingredient of which the offence is composed must be accurately and clearly alleged." It is an elementary principle of criminal pleading that, where the definition of an offence, whether it be at common law or by statute,

> "includes generic terms, it is not sufficient that the indictment shall charge the offence in the same generic terms as in the definition, but it must state the species—it must descend to particulars."

The object of the indictment is, first, to furnish the accused with such a description of the charge against him as will enable him to make his defence, and avail himself of his conviction or acquittal for protection against a further prosecution for the same cause; and, second, to inform the court of the facts alleged, so that it may decide whether they are sufficient in law to support a conviction, if one should be had. For this, facts are to be stated, not conclusions of law alone. A crime is made up of acts and intent; and these must be set forth in the indictment, with reasonable particularity of time, place, and circumstances.

It is a crime to steal goods and chattels, but an indictment would be bad that did not specify with some degree of certainty the articles stolen. This because the accused must be advised of the essential particulars of the charge against him, and the court must be able to decide whether the property taken was such as was the subject of larceny. So, too, it is in some States a crime for two or more persons to conspire to cheat and defraud another out of his property, but it has been held that an indictment for such an offence must contain allegations setting forth the means proposed to be used to accomplish the purpose. This because, to make such a purpose criminal, the conspiracy must be to cheat and defraud in a mode made criminal by statute; and, as all cheating and defrauding has not been made criminal, it is necessary for the indictment to state the means proposed, in order that the court may see that they are in fact illegal. In Maine, it is an offence for two or more to conspire with the intent unlawfully and wickedly to commit any crime punishable by imprisonment in the State prison (*State v. Roberts*), but we think it will hardly be claimed that an indictment would be good under this statute which charges the object of the conspiracy to have been "unlawfully and wickedly to commit each, every, all, and singular the crimes punishable by imprisonment in the State prison." All crimes are not so punishable. Whether a particular crime be such a one or not is a question of law. The accused has, therefore, the right to have a specification of the charge against him in this respect in order that he may decide whether he should present his defence by motion to quash, demurrer, or plea, and the court that it may determine whether the facts will sustain the indictment. So here, the crime is made to consist in the unlawful combination with an intent to prevent the enjoyment of any right granted or secured by the Constitution, &c. All rights are not so granted or secured. Whether one is so or not is a question of law, to be decided by the court, not the prosecutor. Therefore, the indictment should state the particulars, to inform the court as well as the accused. It must be made to appear—that is to say, appears from the indictment, without going further—that the acts charged will, if proved, support a conviction for the offence alleged.

But it is needless to pursue the argument further. The conclusion is irresistible that these counts are too vague and general. They lack the certainty and precision required by the established rules of criminal pleading. It follows that they are not good and sufficient in law. They are so defective that no judgment of conviction should be pronounced upon them.

The order of the Circuit Court arresting the judgment upon the verdict is, therefore, affirmed; and the cause remanded, with instructions to discharge the defendants.

Document Themes

The bulk of Chief Justice Waite's opinion in *United States v. Cruikshank* deals with the legalities surrounding the conspiracy charges brought against the defendants for their role in the Colfax Massacre. The defendants argued that the indictment against them was insufficient "Because the matters and things set forth and charged in the several counts, one to sixteen inclusive, do not constitute offences against the laws of the United States, and do not come within the purview, true intent, and meaning of the act of Congress." In this regard, the case in large part is a Fourteenth Amendment case, for the Court held that

> The Fourteenth Amendment prohibits a State from depriving any person of life, liberty, or property without due process of law, and from denying to any person within its jurisdiction the equal protection of the laws, but it adds nothing to the rights of one citizen as against another. It simply furnishes an additional guaranty against any encroachment by the States upon the fundamental rights which belong to every citizen as a member of society.

The effect of this holding was that, according to the Supreme Court, the federal government lacked the authority to prosecute *individuals* for violating the constitutional rights of other individuals. The Colfax Massacre was not perpetrated by a government entity. The defendants were members of a mob of private individuals, and while their actions were heinous, they were not a violation of the Fourteenth Amendment's guarantees of Due Process and Equal Protection of the laws.

The case, however, had implications for Second Amendment jurisprudence and the issue of gun rights, and it was the first Supreme Court case to examine the reach of the Second Amendment. In enumerating the counts against the defendants, the court notes that "The *second* avers an intent to hinder and prevent the exercise by the same persons of the 'right to keep and bear arms for a lawful purpose.'" In response, the Court reasoned that the second count is defective:

> The right there specified is that of "bearing arms for a lawful purpose." This is not a right granted by the Constitution. Neither is it in any manner dependent upon that instrument for its existence. The second amendment declares that it shall not be infringed, but this, as has been seen, means no more than that it shall not be infringed by Congress. This is one of the amendments that has no other effect than to restrict the powers of the national government, leaving the people to look for their protection against any violation by their fellow citizens of the rights it recognizes, to what is called, in The City of *New York v. Miln*, the "powers which relate to merely municipal legislation, or what was, perhaps, more properly called internal police," "not surrendered or restrained" by the Constitution of the United States.

Thus, the Court held that the Second Amendment did not prevent local officials from exercising their legal prerogative to disarm the African American citizens in their efforts to protect the state. The Court held that the Second Amendment was not "incorporated," which means that the amendment applied only to the actions of the federal government, not to state governments. This view would be sustained by the court system until 2010, when the Court incorporated the Second Amendment in the states in *McDonald v. City of Chicago*.

Additional Reading

Cornell, Saul. *A Well Regulated Militia: The Founding Fathers and the Origins of Gun Control in America* (New York: Oxford University Press, 2006).

Cottrol, Robert J., and Raymond T. Diamond., "The Second Amendment: Toward an Afro-Americanist Reconsideration," in *Guns: Who Should Have Them*, edited by David B. Kopel (Amherst, NY: Prometheus Books, 1995), pp. 127–57.

Lieber, David A. "The Cruikshank Redemption: The Enduring Rationale for Excluding the Second Amendment from the Court's Modern Incorporation Doctrine," *Journal of Criminal Law and Criminology*, Vol. 95, no. 3 (Spring 2005): pp. 1079–1125.

Stowell, Ethan T. "Top Gun: The Second Amendment, Self-Defense, and Private Property Exclusion," *Regent University Law Review*, Vol. 26 (2014): pp. 521–55.

—*Michael J. O'Neal*

Charter and Revised Ordinances of the City of Galveston, and All Ordinances in Force to October

Author(s): City of Galveston
Date: 1883
Genre: City ordinance

Summary Overview

In 1883, the port city of Galveston, Texas, compiled and published its city ordinances. Prominent among those ordinances were provisions restricting the carrying of arms in public. In this respect, Galveston was representative of a number of cities that placed restrictions on guns, and particularly the carrying of guns in public, during the nineteenth century. The policy of the city indicates that "gun control" is by no means an issue peculiar to the twenty-first century.

Defining Moment

No particular event took place that would have prompted Galveston to restrict the carrying of guns in public. What is significant is that during most of the nineteenth century, the island city of Galveston was a booming, progressive city, one that served as a gateway to the rest of Texas and points west. It was an architectural showplace. It was home to a large number of "firsts" in Texas: a customs house, a post office, a law firm, a private bank, an opera house, a telephone, a Catholic hospital, an orphanage, electric lights, a grocery store, a public library—the list is seemingly endless. In this environment, the city fathers would have been vigilant in keeping the peace, and to that end they restricted the carrying of firearms.

Galveston, however, was hardly unique in this regard. The popular conception of the frontier West is that of gunslingers and gunplay on the streets of dusty cattle towns with clapboard buildings. Emblematic of the Old West is a town such as Tombstone, Arizona, where the famous "Gunfight at the O.K. Corral" took place. The reality, however, is that Tombstone required visitors, when they entered the town to disarm. They could do so either at a hotel or at a lawman's office. This was by no means an uncommon practice in the West. Many of the famed cattle towns, such as Dodge City, Abilene, and Deadwood, had similar restrictions. Further, in earlier years, during the Founding era, cities such as Philadelphia, New York, and Boston had regulations prohibiting the firing of weapons within city limits. The Galveston ordinances are thus indicative of a history of firearms regulation in urban areas—in contrast to rural areas, where firearm regulation had long tended to be more lax.

About the Author

The *Charter and Revised Ordinances of the City of Galveston* would have had no particular author. The city government during the nineteenth century consisted of a mayor and city council. These elected representatives would have written and compiled the city's ordinances for publication.

Map of Galveston in 1871. (By Camille N. Drie.)

HISTORICAL DOCUMENT

REVISED ORDINANCES.
ARTICLE VI.
WEAPONS.
Sec 1:
Regulating the keeping and bearing of
Penalty for violation
Sec 2:
What constitutes a legal defense

SECTION 1. That any person carrying on or about his person, saddle or vehicle, within the corporate limits of the city of Galveston, any pistol, dirk, dagger, slung-shot, sword-cane, spear, brass knuckles, bowie knife, or any other kind of knife manufactured or sold for the purposes of offense or defense, or carried for purposes of offense or defense, unless he has reasonable ground for fearing an unlawful attack on his person, and that such attack shall be immediate and pressing, or unless having or carrying the same on or about his person for the lawful defense of the State of Texas, or the city of Galveston, as a militiaman in actual service, or as a peace officer or policeman, shall be fined in a sum of not less than twenty-five dollars, nor more than one hundred dollars, and in default of payment thereof shall be confined in the jail for a period of not less than ten days nor more than three months, and whilst so confined shall be required to work on the streets of said city, or any public work under the control of the city council, for the period of such confinement, and, in addition thereto, shall forfeit to the city the weapon or weapons so carried; *provided*, that this section shall not be so construed as to prohibit any person from keeping or bearing arms on his or her premises, or at his or her place of business, nor to prohibit sheriffs, their deputies, or other revenue officers, or other civil officers, from keeping or bearing arms whilst engaged in the discharge of their official duties, nor prohibit persons traveling through the city of Galveston from keeping or carrying arms with their baggage.

SEC. 2. That any person charged under the first section of this article, who may offer to prove, by way of defense, that he was in danger of an attack on his person, or unlawful interference with his property, shall be required to show that such danger was immediate and pressing, and was of such a nature as to alarm a person of ordinary courage, and that such weapon so carried was borne openly, and not concealed beneath the clothing; and if it shall appear that this danger had its origin in a difficulty first commenced by the accused, it shall not be considered as a legal defense.

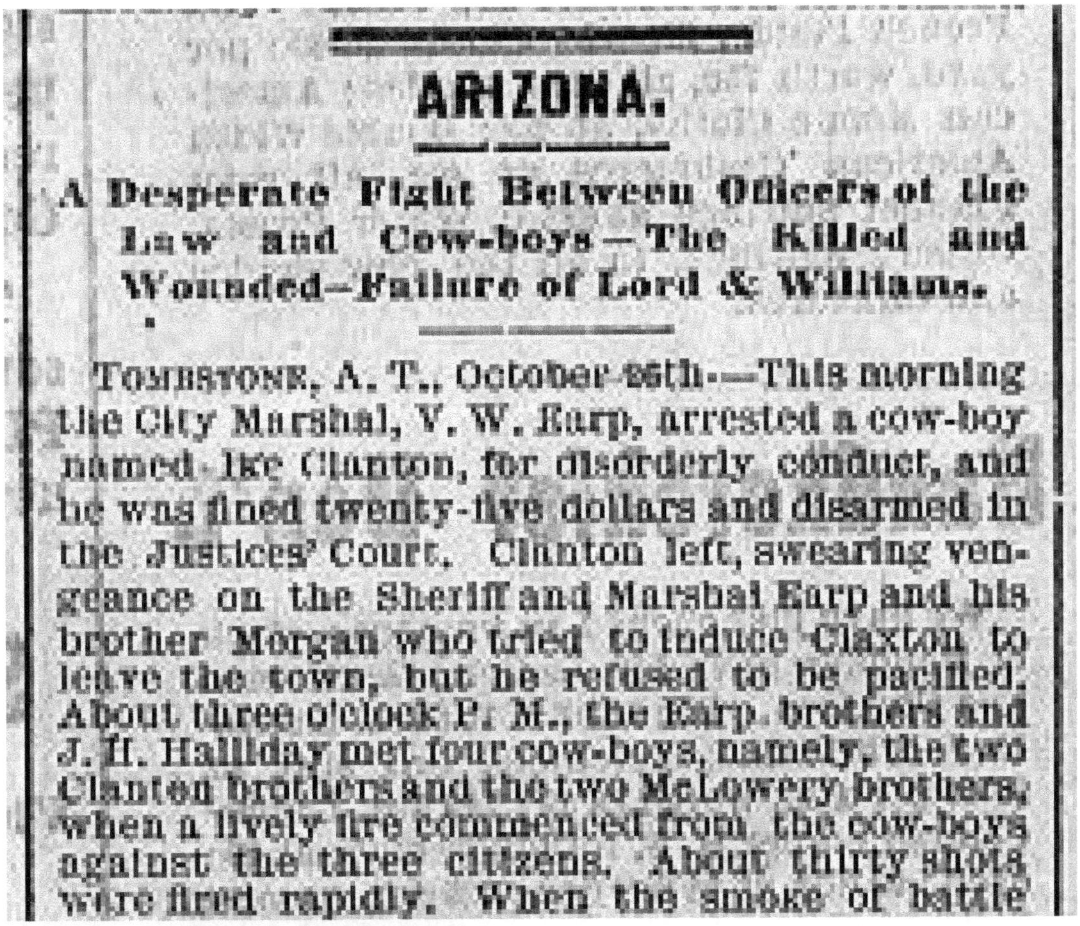

ARIZONA.

A Desperate Fight Between Officers of the Law and Cow-boys—The Killed and Wounded—Failure of Lord & Williams.

TOMBSTONE, A. T., October 26th.—This morning the City Marshal, V. W. Earp, arrested a cow-boy named Ike Clanton, for disorderly conduct, and he was fined twenty-five dollars and disarmed in the Justices' Court. Clanton left, swearing vengeance on the Sheriff and Marshal Earp and his brother Morgan who tried to induce Claxton to leave the town, but he refused to be pacified. About three o'clock P. M., the Earp brothers and J. H. Halliday met four cow-boys, namely, the two Clanton brothers and the two McLowery brothers, when a lively fire commenced from the cow-boys against the three citizens. About thirty shots were fired rapidly. When the smoke of battle

Newspaper coverage of the fight at the OK Corrall.

Wyatt Earp and Bat Masterson in 1876 as lawmen in Dodge City, Kansas.

Document Themes

Section 1 of the ordinance is clear. It states that a person cannot carry about a weapon, whether intended for offense or defense, with the city limits. Among the weapons prohibited are not only pistols but dirks, daggers, brass knuckles, slingshots, Bowie knives, spears, or sword-canes (canes that contain a blade). The ordinance makes two exceptions. One is that the person carrying the weapon has "reasonable grounds for fearing an unlawful attack on his person" and that the attack is immediate; thus, a person cannot carry a weapon about because of a vague or generalized fear that he or she might at some time in the future be attacked. A further exception includes law-enforcement officers in the performance of their duties, or a "militiaman" engaged in the defense of the state. The ordinance then specifies fines and potential jail sentences. The ordinance goes on to note that the law is not to be construed as prohibiting keeping a firearm in one's home or business. Section 2 specifies that a person charged with violation of the ordinance can offer as a defense the "he was in danger of an attack on his person, or unlawful interference with his property." Again, the person has to show that the danger was "immediate and pressing." Further, the weapon has to be "borne openly, and not concealed beneath the clothing." In this regard, the Galveston ordinance prefigures more modern debates about the carrying of concealed weapons. If the accused person commenced the "difficulty," he or she cannot assert this as a defense.

Additional Readings

Blocher, Joseph, "Firearm Localism," *Yale Law Journal* 123, no. 1 (October 2013), https://www.yalelawjournal.org/article/firearm-localism.

Charles, Patrick J. "Historical Thoughts on the Evolution of Firearms Regulations in the Late Nineteenth Century," Chapter 4 of *Bearing Arms: A History of Gun Rights from Colonial Militias to Concealed Carry* (Prometheus Books, 2017), http://wagv.org/wp-content/uploads/patrick-charles-evolution-of-firearms-regulations-in-the-late-nineteenth-century.pdf.

Cornell, Saul, "The Early American Origins of the Modern Gun Control Debate: The Right to Bear Arms, Firearms Regulation, and the Lessons of History," *Stanford Law and Policy Review* 17 (2006): 567–92.

Jancer, Matt, "Gun Control Is as Old as the Old West," *Smithsonian.com*, February 5, 2018, https://www.smithsonianmag.com/history/gun-control-old-west-180968013/.

Spitzer, Robert J. "Gun Laws Are as Old as Gun Ownership," American Constitution Society website, May 18, 2015, https://www.acslaw.org/acsblog/gun-laws-are-as-old-as-gun-ownership/.

—Michael J. O'Neal

SUPPLEMENTAL HISTORICAL DOCUMENT

Open Carry for All: *Heller* and Our Nineteenth-Century Second Amendment

INTRODUCTION

Since the Supreme Court's landmark decisions in *District of Columbia v. Heller* and *McDonald v. City of Chicago* announced that the Second Amendment guarantees an individual right to keep and bear arms and incorporated that right against the states, courts and scholars have struggled to determine the reach of those opinions. The past five years have witnessed dozens of challenges to state and federal gun regulations of all kinds, from bans on gun ranges, to laws preventing the sale of firearms to persons under twenty-one, to section 1983 suits in response to temporary disarmament. The most consequential cases in defining the contours of the Second Amendment, however, relate to the right to carry firearms outside the home. The issue is extraordinarily important to proponents and opponents of gun rights alike. For proponents, the only way to truly vindicate the right to self-defense is to allow law-abiding citizens to carry firearms on their person. According to opponents of gun rights, an individual right to carry would constitutionalize extreme behavior, allow for vigilantism, and undermine public safety.

The holdings of *Heller* and *McDonald* reached only the right to keep a handgun in the home, leaving the lower courts to sort out whether and how that right extends beyond the home. Provided with such minimal guidance, they have reached vastly different conclusions. Some have taken after *Heller*, conducting significant historical analysis to determine the extent of the Second Amendment right outside the home. Others have concentrated on tiers of scrutiny, weighing the benefits of the gun regulation at issue against its intrusion on the right to keep and bear arms. Others still have refused to extend the right outside the home absent further instruction from the Supreme Court.

This circuit split has led to a number of different conclusions about the right to carry outside the home. In *United States v. Masciandaro*, Judge Wilkinson stated that "[t]he whole matter [of the right to carry outside the home] strikes us as a vast terra incognita that courts should enter only upon necessity and only then by small degree." In a similar vein, the Court of Appeals of Maryland stated that "[i]f the Supreme Court . . . meant its [*Heller*] holding to extend beyond home possession, it will need to say so more plainly." Other courts have found that the right to carry must extend beyond the home, relying on the historical evidence presented in *Heller*, as well as on the case's dicta regarding the prime importance of self-defense, which they argue cannot be limited to the home. These courts have emphasized the need for states to allow some type of carry, but have not expressed a view on the constitutionality of one type of carry of weapons over another. A third group of courts has determined that although the Second Amendment may well extend beyond the home, particular regulations on the right to carry—for example, laws banning the concealed carry of weapons—do not infringe on the right. Two recent cases in the Second and Tenth Circuits have followed this model. Both of those opinions consulted extensive historical evidence regarding limitations on the right to carry in reaching their conclusions.

This Note, like the cases discussed above, attempts to understand the contours of the right to carry after *Heller* and *McDonald*. Like the panels of the Second and Tenth Circuits, I am particularly interested in what kind of carry of weapons, if any, the Second Amendment protects. I argue that *Heller* and *McDonald* have left little doubt that a historical analysis is the proper method for defining the right guaranteed by the Second Amendment. The Court's (and, for that matter, the dissents') use of history to determine the existence of an individual right to firearms suggests that elaboration of the extent of the right will require further expeditions into the past.

The history relied upon by the Supreme Court, particularly in *Heller*, and the way the Court reads the historical sources, compel two important conclusions about the right to carry weapons. First, the logic, interpretive choices, and dicta of *Heller* suggest that the right to keep and bear arms must extend beyond the home. Second, the right to carry weapons that is guaranteed by the Second Amendment is the right to carry weapons openly. Much of the history of the right to carry is difficult to decipher. Only one set of sources consulted by the Supreme Court speaks comprehensively and unequivocally on this question: antebellum state supreme court decisions. They find almost uniformly, in upholding state concealed weapons bans, that the right to keep and bear arms protects the right to carry weapons openly—and only openly—in self-defense. The particular rationale in those decisions—that the only way to carry weapons defensively is to carry them openly—may not jibe with modern sensibilities. But these opinions are still windows, according to the *Heller* Court, into the historical understanding of the Second Amendment. Our modern right should reflect this understanding, meaning that the logical outgrowth of *Heller* would be a regime in which the concealed carry of firearms could be banned, but the open carry of the same weapons could not.

Such a holding would not sit well with either the opponents or proponents of the individual right to keep and bear arms. Opponents see open carry as the worst of the pro-gun movement—a practice aimed more at provocation and showmanship than at any legitimate safety goal. Meanwhile, many proponents of gun rights recognize how unusual and fear-inducing open carry is in many situations, and how much many Americans prefer to carry weapons concealed. They worry that a constitutional right limited to open carry would prevent many law-abiding citizens from carrying weapons due to the stigma of carrying openly. Still, even if this result is impractical and unpopular, it is the most loyal reading of *Heller*. And because the Court has committed to an originalist methodology for the Second Amendment, complaints about open carry's lack of agreement with modern practice ought to have very little sway.

This Note proceeds in three Parts. Part I summarizes the holdings of *Heller* and *McDonald* with an eye to what they suggest about the right to carry. It also surveys current state laws regarding the right to carry. Part II examines historical evidence from the periods deemed crucial by *Heller* and *McDonald* to determine how it illuminates the original understanding of the right to carry. This Part notes the lack of clear evidence from the Founding era regarding the right to carry—a sharp contrast with the nineteenth-century case law, which concentrates heavily on the carry of weapons. Part III explores the implications of this historical analysis. It argues that the early nineteenth-century case law, which the *Heller* Court stated was critical to determining the public understanding of the right to carry, leaves little doubt that the Second Amendment was understood at that time to guarantee the right to carry outside the home, but only a right to do so openly. It also discusses other possible readings of the history provided by courts and scholars, and why they comport less well with this evidence. Finally, the Note concludes with a recognition that the Supreme Court may well avoid the finding compelled by this history, and it ties this possible, perhaps even likely, avoidance of an open carry regime to some of *Heller*'s shortcomings.

I. HELLER, MCDONALD, AND THE STATE OF GUN RIGHTS IN AMERICA

Heller and *McDonald* upended Second Amendment jurisprudence by holding that the Amendment guarantees an individual right to keep and bear arms, and that this individual right is incorporated by the Fourteenth Amendment. These cases have been analyzed and debated in detail in academic literature, an exercise I will not replicate in this Note. Instead, I will focus more narrowly on their application to the right to carry weapons outside the home. To supplement this analysis, I will also offer in this Part a short summary of the contemporary legal landscape of right to carry laws in the United States, in order to provide readers with the backdrop against which this legal battle will play out.

This Part and the next focus heavily on the history of the Second Amendment when discussing the right to carry arms beyond the home. *Heller* and *McDonald* made clear that originalism is the proper method for assessing the constitutionality of laws challenged under the Second Amendment. The majority and the dissents in *Heller* rested their conflicting arguments upon the history of the right to keep and bear arms, and the majority in *McDonald* once again performed a substantial historical inquiry on the question of incorporation. Scholars on the left and right have questioned that choice of methodology as well as the way in which the Court employed it, but there can be little doubt after *Heller* and *McDonald* that defining the Second Amendment right is a task that requires historical analysis. This Note, without endorsing this methodology, operates within it.

A. *Heller, McDonald,* and the Right to Carry

Heller conclusively established that the Second Amendment guarantees an individual right to keep and bear arms. The Court held that the Amendment did not bestow a new privilege, but simply codified a "pre-existing" right. Analyzing the structure of the Amendment, the Court determined that the "operative clause," which states that "the right of the people to keep and bear Arms shall not be infringed," was not controlled by "the prefatory clause," which refers to a "well regulated Militia." Having thus brushed aside the possibility that the prefatory clause might have limited the guarantee to some sort of collective or hybrid right, the Court then examined the language of the operative clause. The majority determined that it bestows an individual right to keep and bear arms.

An individual right to keep and bear arms might be guaranteed for any number of reasons, and the Court determined that the Second Amendment grants "the individual right to possess and carry weapons in case of confrontation." It came to this conclusion upon finding "[t]his meaning . . . strongly confirmed by the historical background of the Second Amendment." The Court stated that although the prefatory clause indicated that preserving the militia was key to the right's codification, self-defense "was the central component of the right itself."

Just how far the right to bear arms for self-defense stretches was not made clear in *Heller*. The Court's language indicating that the Second Amendment protects "the individual right to possess and carry weapons in case of confrontation" would seem to require some right to carry outside of the home. Without any right to carry outside the home at all, many (indeed, perhaps most) confrontations would occur outside the protection of the Amendment. Consequently, many commentators have argued that the only way to read *Heller* is as a guarantee of some right to carry a weapon anywhere a confrontation may occur. Furthermore, at least one court has argued that the Supreme Court's reference to "self-defense and hunting" as purposes for bearing arms in *Heller* suggests that the right to carry firearms outside the home in order to hunt game is guaranteed.

There are certain sections of *Heller*, however, that so clearly limit its holding to the home that it is premature to read the decision as a definitive guarantee of the right to carry. For example, the majority brushed aside a statute cited by Justice Breyer's dissent that regulated the use of guns on streets or in taverns, because it dealt with guns outside the home. And in validating the right to keep a handgun in the home, the Court stated that whatever the Second Amendment might protect more broadly, it "surely elevates above all other interests the right of law-abiding, responsible citizens to use arms in defense of hearth and home." The Court is best seen as purposefully using broad language to define the right but also making explicit efforts to prevent *Heller* from reaching the right to carry.

One further reason to question *Heller*'s reach with regard to the right to carry is the Court's explicit approval of certain contemporary gun regulations. Indeed, the most significant limits that the *Heller* Court places on the Second Amendment right are carve-outs that seem aimed at rescuing common and widely accepted laws. After its exhaustive historical analysis, the Court provided the following checks on the right it had just excavated:

> Although we do not undertake an exhaustive historical analysis today of the full scope of the Second Amendment, nothing in our opinion should be taken to cast doubt on longstanding prohibitions on the possession of firearms by felons and the mentally ill, or laws forbidding the carrying of firearms in sensitive places such as schools and government buildings, or laws imposing conditions and qualifications on the commercial sale of arms.

Conservative critics of the *Heller* opinion have argued that regulations involving felons, the mentally ill, and sensitive places have no Founding-era analogues. The Court supplemented this limitation on who could own guns with a further restriction on what types of weapons were protected. The majority limited the right to weapons "in common use at the time," essentially legitimizing existing (or recently existing) bans on machine guns and certain assault weapons.

Most important for understanding *Heller*'s lessons for the right to carry, however, was the opinion's statement about the concealed carry of weapons. After confirming the existence of the individual right, the first limitation the Court placed on it was the Court's recognition of the validity of concealed weapons bans: "For example, the majority of the 19th-century courts to consider the question held that prohibitions on carrying concealed weapons were lawful under the Second Amendment or state analogues." While this is not an explicit acknowledgement that bans on concealed carry are constitutional, it is about as close as dictum can get. Justice Scalia thus used the very same nineteenth-century opinions on which he relied to validate the right to limit its application to concealed carry. *Heller*, then, clearly gestures at a right to carry firearms outside the home, but also acknowledges significant limitations on it.

The Court would follow a similar script in *McDonald*. In this follow-up case, theplurality reaffirmed the key holdings of *Heller* that individual self-defense was "'the central component' of the Second Amendment right," and that the right applied "most notably for self-defense within the home." It further held that the right to keep and bear arms was incorporated against the states by the Fourteenth Amendment's Due Process Clause because it "is fundamental to our scheme of ordered liberty" and "deeply rooted in this Nation's history and tradition."

Like *Heller*, *McDonald* does not directly address whether there is a constitutional right to carry firearms outside the home. The Court's opinions—the plurality, concurrences, and dissents—do suggest, however, that it has begun to grapple with this issue. First, portions of the plurality opinion hint that the right to keep and bear arms is not limited to self-defense in the home. More directly, Justice Stevens's dissent acknowledges that *Heller* contains "the possibility of a more expansive arms-bearing right, one that would travel with the individual to an extent into public places as 'in case of confrontation.'" Justice Stevens, doubtless hoping to stave off this interpretation in future cases, then explained why, in his view, the case for recognizing a right to possess firearms is "heightened in the home," and why "[t]he historical case for regulation is likewise stronger outside [of it]." Even as Justice Stevens tried to limit the right to carry, it is worth noting that *McDonald* omits *Heller*'s discussion of limits on concealed carry despite repeating nearly all of *Heller*'s other limitations of the Second Amendment right.

Taken together, the two opinions begin to paint a picture of how the Court might examine restrictions on the right to carry. While the Court certainly limited the holdings of the opinions, the broad language it used is impossible to ignore. After all, if the Second Amendment guarantees "the individual right to possess and carry weapons in case of confrontation," surely that right cannot exist solely in the home. Confrontations can occur anywhere, and if the Second Amendment is truly meant to protect an individual who is being confronted, it ought to extend to locations outside of the home as well. There is the beginning of a scholarly consensus on this point, as well as a small number of judicial opinions that make the same argument.

B. The Current Gun Regulation Landscape

The timing of *Heller* and *McDonald* was not coincidental. The cases were decided against the backdrop of an extraordinary wave of gun rights scholarship over the previous three decades and an accompanying change in the firearm laws of many states. Because the decisions were so wrapped up with contemporary political and legal movements, some scholars have argued forcefully that *Heller* and *McDonald* are not in fact originalist decisions, but instead examples of popular constitutionalism. This shifting Second Amendment landscape is important not only in the influence it might have had upon the Court's recent decisions, but also for the effect those decisions will have on contemporary gun laws. Thus, in order to gauge the real-world effect that *Heller* and *McDonald* may have on the right to carry, we must understand the regulations that Americans currently face.

State regulations on the carry of weapons fall into a few general categories. The vast majority of these statutes deal with concealed carry; while open carry is sometimes permitted in these states, nearly all of the laws focus on the right to carry a concealed weapon. The most restrictive laws, often called "no carry" restrictions, currently exist only in the District of Columbia. People living in Washington, D.C., are not able to apply for permits to carry weapons—any carry simply is not allowed. At the other extreme, four states—Alaska, Arizona, Vermont, and Wyoming—do not require permits at all, and any resident can carry a weapon openly or concealed, subject only to federal gun laws concerning type of weapon, sale to felons, and other similar restrictions.

The vast majority of states, meanwhile, issue permits to those wishing to carry concealed weapons. Most of these concealed carry laws were passed in the 1990s, and some, in addition to allowing concealed carry with a permit, also allow for open carry for the purposes of self-defense. There is a crucial divide in these laws between those that issue permits essentially automatically to anyone who applies and those that employ a measure of discretion. The majority of states fall into the former category, often called "shall issue," giving states and municipalities no choice but to issue a permit so long as the person is not a felon, a domestic violence offender, or seriously mentally ill. Nine states are "may issue" states, requiring good character, good reason, or both, as judged by state or local officials, to carry a weapon. How these laws are enforced varies considerably by state, but in most "may issue" states, the rules are exceedingly strict, and few licenses are issued.

In the discussion of the right to carry that follows, this brief summary of current gun laws is worth keeping in mind. In over eighty percent of states, the right to either concealed or open carry is available to most people in most places. Most of these states have chosen to protect the right to concealed carry while only some have done the same for open carry. Any decision guaranteeing a right to carry would be felt most acutely in Washington, D.C., and the "may issue" states, where stringent restrictions on the right to carry are in force. But a decision specifying that open carry must be protected would also force changes in the "shall issue" states that currently allow only the right to concealed carry. Thus, the Supreme Court could issue a decision that does not change the status quo (by finding that there is no right to carry outside the home) or it could force dozens of states and countless municipalities to change their laws (by requiring protection for open carry).

II. THE RIGHT TO CARRY IN THE FOUNDING ERA AND THE NINETEENTH CENTURY

If the underlying logic of *Heller* and *McDonald* suggests that there is a right to carry, the natural next question is what kind of carry the opinions contemplate. Because, beyond *Heller*'s dictum regarding concealed carry bans, the opinions provide little clue of what a right to carry might entail, it is necessary to follow their lead and examine the historical understanding of the Second Amendment and its state analogues at and after the Founding. This Part follows the path forged by *Heller*, examining in turn the "preexisting" English right to keep and bear arms, the legal commentary relied upon by the Framers, Founding-era laws, and nineteenth-century state court cases that the Court used to determine the original meaning of the Second Amendment.

Perhaps the most striking aspect of the Founding-era sources is how little they say about the right to carry. Laws regulating firearms were far from rare before and at the time of the Founding. Yet few laws explicitly addressed the carry of weapons. Similarly, the two most prominent legal commentators around the time of the Founding—William Blackstone and his principal American interpreter, St. George Tucker—did not write directly about the right to carry. Still, these laws and commentaries remain useful because of the window they provide into two issues that the Founding generation clearly did think about when it came to firearms: self-defense and public safety. These two principles animated much of the writing and legislating at the time of the Founding, and they both underlie any discussion of the right to carry. After all, a robust right to carry is justified by the need for personal self-defense, whereas a circumscribed right finds its rationale in enhancing public safety. Thus, while Founding-era laws and legal commentaries themselves say little about weapons outside the home, the interests they address are crucial to any understanding of the right to carry.

Furthermore, *Heller* teaches us that historical inquiry into the Second Amendment must not end in the eighteenth century. Following its lead, this Part also looks beyond the Founding-era sources to the nineteenth-century case law. *Heller* stated that these later sources can clarify "the public understanding of a legal text in the period after its enactment or ratification," and that examining later sources is a "critical tool of constitutional interpretation." Just as the nineteenth-century sources provided crucial support for the Court's conclusion in *Heller* that there was an individual right to keep and bear arms, so too these sources give the clearest picture of the right to carry in the time period the Court has deemed relevant for understanding the meaning of the Second Amendment.

Unlike in the Founding era, states did indeed attempt to ban the carry of certain weapons during the nineteenth century, and courts were forced to define the contours of the right to carry in deciding these cases. While the rulings were not entirely uniform, a clear pattern emerges from these cases: states were allowed to ban the concealed carry of weapons but not their open carry. This was not an arbitrary choice—instead, the dichotomy between open and concealed carry underscored antebellum understandings of permissible self-defense and public safety. Just as the nineteenth-century cases proved "critical" to the determination that the Second Amendment protects an individual right, so too are they critical to further explicating that right. And they ultimately suggest that open carry, but not concealed carry, is constitutionally protected.

A. The English Right

The Second Amendment traces its origins to a provision of the English Bill of Rights that read: "[T]he subjects which are Protestants may have Arms for their Defence suitable to their Conditions and as allowed by Law." The text of the English right is less broad than the Second Amendment, and there is general scholarly consensus that the English right was less expansive in practice than its American analogue. Indeed, there is some disagreement as to whether the English provision guaranteed an individual right at all, but the *Heller* majority concluded that it did. Still, Hellerindicates that the English right was held against the Crown, and there is little indication in the majority opinion that the pre-existing right guaranteed the ability to carry a weapon outside the home in case of confrontation.

B. Legal Commentators at the Founding

Throughout the past two decades, legal scholars have argued vociferously about the views of important legal commentators at the time of the Founding. In particular, the statements of William Blackstone and St. George Tucker have been analyzed exhaustively by academics looking for clues about how the English jurist and the foremost Founding-era American expert on his work understood the right to keep and bear arms. While the scholarship remains deeply divided, the Supreme Court in *Heller* found Blackstone and Tucker to support a robust right to individual self-defense. This interpretation may well have significant consequences for the right to carry outside the home. If Blackstone and Tucker understood the right to keep and bear arms as guaranteeing individuals a right to protect themselves from public and private violence, then they could also be marshaled to support a right to carry outside the home to vindicate that guarantee.

1. Blackstone's *Commentaries*

In *Heller*, the Supreme Court declared that William Blackstone's *Commentaries on the Laws of England* "constituted the preeminent authority on English law for the founding generation." Blackstone situated the right to bear arms within his larger discussion of the rights and liberties of Englishmen. He began this discussion by describing three absolute rights: the right to "personal security," the right to "personal liberty," and the right to "private property." Because these rights would provide little protection of their own, Blackstone laid out five "auxiliary subordinate rights," which functioned to protect these three primary rights. The "fifth and last" of these auxiliary rights, he explained, was

> that of having arms for their defence, suitable to their condition and degree, and such as are allowed by law. Which is also declared by the same statute 1 W. & M. st. 2. c. 2. [the English Bill of Rights] and is indeed a public allowance, under due restrictions, of the natural right of resistance and self-preservation, when the sanctions of society and laws are found insufficient to restrain the violence of oppression.

Some scholars have interpreted this and other passages to mean that Blackstone understood that the right to keep and bear arms guarantees an individual right to self-defense. Others have vehemently disagreed with this interpretation, claiming that Blackstone's Commentaries contained two different English Enlightenment conceptions of self-defense: the civil and political right to self-defense and the natural right to personal self-defense.

This second group argues that this passage dealt with the public right of English subjects to resort to arms if all other manners of peaceful redress have failed. Meanwhile, early Americans understood the right to personal self-defense as a common law question, which Blackstone and Tucker discussed in a different section of their treatises. In his section on common law crimes, Blackstone noted numerous English limitations on the carrying of weapons, which has led some scholars to suggest that Blackstone would have favored strong regulations on the right to carry due to its common law pedigree. Blackstone's most notable comment on a limitation on the right to carry weapons was his paraphrasing of the Statute of Northampton, a 1328 law that allowed no person except the King's minions doing their official duties to "ride armed by night nor by day, in Fairs, Markets, nor in the presence of the Justices or other Ministers, nor in no part elsewhere, upon pain to forfeit their Armour to the King, and their Bodies to Prison at the King's pleasure." He approvingly compared this law to the Laws of Solon in Athens that had barred men from walking in public in full armor, and New York even reproduced it as an example of affray in a guide for common law judges.

The Court in *Heller* did not make the distinction between political and common law self-defense drawn by Cornell, Miller, and Charles. Instead, the Court saw Blackstone as simply guaranteeing one right, "understood [at the Founding] to be an individual right protecting against both public and private violence." By framing its discussion of Blackstone around the passage discussing the political right to self-defense, the Court may have limited the use of Blackstone's common law. If indeed there was only one right to self-defense articulated by Blackstone—as the *Heller* Court seemed to imply—a future decision on the right to carry might also emphasize Blackstone's discussion of self-defense over his common law-inspired focus on laws that aim to protect public safety.

2. St. George Tucker

St. George Tucker, America's first Blackstone scholar, has engendered equally contentious disagreement among contemporary scholars regarding his views of the Second Amendment. Tucker both included his own annotations on Blackstone in the edition of the Commentaries he edited and wrote a series of unpublished lectures on the nature of the Second Amendment. The Supreme Court in *Heller* found that these writings supported an individual right to self-defense, though, as with Blackstone, many scholars have alleged that the Court oversimplified Tucker's views.

C. Founding-Era Constitutions and Laws

While discussion of the proper role of firearms is omnipresent in contemporary society, the Founding generation did not share our fascination. Less than one-third of the states guaranteed a right to bear arms in their constitutions in 1789. Gun ownership was widespread, and while gun regulation was minor by modern standards, it was still commonplace. Colonies, states, and cities were known to require gun ownership for militia service, prohibit the discharge of guns in populous areas, regulate the storage of powder, and sometimes even bar the storage of loaded weapons.

It appears, however, that there were no direct statutory bans on the carry of arms. This leaves courts and scholars with a series of laws that regulated the discharge, storage, and aggressive use of firearms, as well as laws that disarmed people who were considered untrustworthy in some capacity. None of these laws closely tracks current restrictions on the right to carry, which limits their usefulness. Still, they remain quite important for two reasons. First, of course, is that they are the evidence we have from the Founding era. As disappointing as it may be that they are not more helpful, they form the base of the historical record for the era that *Heller* has established as all-important for a Second Amendment inquiry. Second, these sources show that even if the Founders did not regulate the carry of weapons, they engaged in significant gun regulation to protect public safety.

These laws, then, are open to two conflicting interpretations that will profoundly affect the debate over the constitutionality of limits on the carry of weapons. On the one hand, courts can point to the dearth of laws regulating the carry of weapons and argue that these laws did not exist because it was understood at the time that they infringed on an accepted right to carry. How could the Framers have clearly understood that proscribing the carry of weapons was permissible if there is not a single example of a law that did so? Alternatively, states regulated firearms for the sake of public safety rather robustly, making clear that limits on the right to keep and bear arms were well established and accepted. One scholar claims that these policies are best seen as time, place, and manner restrictions that made using a firearm more difficult in order to prevent serious hazards. Limiting the open carry of weapons may not have been an imperative for any number of reasons, such as the lack of danger caused by weapons that could not quickly be reloaded, the relative lack of large urban areas, or, relatedly, the need to carry weapons in rural areas for hunting or protection. Courts could find that the lack of regulation was not due to a constitutional imperative but instead simply prudent lawmaking in a time when public safety would not be significantly enhanced by limiting the ability to carry weapons. The history provides no clear answer, but given that this core disagreement will likely be crucial to any evaluation of the right to carry, these Founding-era laws remain important to any examination of that right.

1. State Constitutions

Between the Declaration of Independence in 1776 and the ratification of the Bill of Rights in 1791, just four states adopted provisions analogous to the Second Amendment in their own constitutions. These provisions are important because they provide a contemporary view of how Revolutionary-era Americans conceived of the right to keep and bear arms. Unfortunately, however, the small number of state provisions offers a rather limited perspective. Furthermore, the formulations, as the *Heller* Court noted, differed subtly but significantly by state. Pennsylvania and Vermont both seemed to contemplate an individual right, stating that "the people have a right to bear arms for the defence of themselves and the state." Massachusetts, which guaranteed "a right to keep and to bear arms for the common defense," and North Carolina, which protected only the right to bear arms "for the defence of the State," appeared to enshrine a more collective understanding. Justice Scalia interpreted these state constitutions together as protective of an individual right to bear arms for defensive purposes. As with much of the Court's opinion, its analysis would seem to hold whether the defensive purpose exists in the home or outside of it.

The Court also pointed to Thomas Jefferson's failed addition to the Virginia Declaration of Rights, which read: "No freeman shall ever be debarred the use of arms [within his own land or tenements]." Justice Scalia used this language to buttress his view that the Second Amendment protects the right to bear arms within the home. Of course, that same failed provision—though its failure would seem to limit its force for any proposition—implicates more protection for firearms in and around the home than away from it. This could prove one piece of Revolutionary-era evidence that a court could use to distinguish *Heller*'s homebound ruling from a case involving right to carry outside of the home. Still, the different emphases of the Founding-era state constitutional provisions make it difficult to draw any meaningful conclusions about the Founders' views on the right to carry.

2. Gun Laws that Promoted Public Safety

Laws regulating the use and storage of firearms in the Founding era, while far from ubiquitous, were enacted across the colonies and states in the late eighteenth century. Similarly to today, the laws concentrated on cities and towns, where the danger from gun violence and fire from powder storage posed the greatest threat. States and municipalities also passed time, place, and manner restrictions on the use of firearms. None of these laws regulated the right to carry explicitly, and none were ever challenged as violating the Second Amendment or state analogues.

Most pertinent to the right to carry were the numerous colonial and early American derivatives of the Statute of Northampton, the 1328 English statute that became a fixture of the common law. The wording of the individual laws varied by state and legal treatise, but the statute was generally imported into colonial and state law in a manner resembling its original decree that no one should "go nor ride armed by night nor by day in Fairs, Markets, nor in the presence of the Justices or other Ministers, nor in no part elsewhere." Some prohibited going "armed offensively," perhaps implying a more aggressive form of conduct, while others referred to causing "terror" in bystanders.

As previously noted, the statute and its implications for the Second Amendment are fiercely debated in the scholarship. In general, the disagreement pits those who read it more literally—and therefore as a significant limit on the right to carry—against those who instead focus on aggressive use and the intent to frighten, minimizing its applicability where a firearm is simply being carried.

Scholars are correct to place great emphasis on the meaning of these statutes. Read broadly, they grant wide authority to officials to prevent the carrying of weapons, especially their open carry. Construed more narrowly, they would allow the proscription of open carry only if the carrier were engaged in some sort of particularly aggressive activity or was actively trying to scare those around him. Thus, their implications are enormous for the legality of the right to carry in twenty-first century America. Unfortunately, as with much of the Founding-era source material, the correct interpretation is far from clear.

Also related to restrictions to the right to carry were laws that prevented individuals from using firearms in urban areas. The largest cities in revolutionary America—Boston, New York, and Philadelphia—all prohibited the shooting of guns within city limits. Pennsylvania and New York extended these laws to all other cities in the colony, and Delaware also prevented the discharge of firearms in built-up areas except on "days of public rejoicing." Massachusetts banned the shooting of guns on Boston Neck (the only land access to colonial Boston), while Pennsylvania prevented the use of firearms on public highways, though it specified that the laws barred only the discharge and not the open carry of those arms. And a 1790 Ohio law prevented the firing of guns within a quarter mile of any building or between sunset and sunrise.

The second provision of this Ohio law was quite typical—colonial and early American state governments regularly proscribed firing guns after dark. These widespread bans largely developed because discharging weapons in quick succession was the typical way of warning of an impending attack. As a result, firing guns for other purposes was frequently barred. Connecticut, Georgia, and New Hampshire all banned shooting guns after dark in the colonial period, and Rhode Island, after an accidental death in 1731, banned firing guns in towns at night. North Carolina passed a law preventing hunting after dark in 1774.

Cities also limited the right to keep and bear arms to enhance public safety through statutes meant to reduce the risk of fire. Cities large—Boston, New York, and Philadelphia, for example—and small often restricted the storage and transport of loaded weapons. These laws took many forms: from limiting powder that could be kept in the home (and as a result the number of possible shots that an inhabitant could fire), to forcing gunpowder to be stored in particular parts of a home, to even preventing, as Massachusetts did in 1783, the storage of loaded firearms.

While none of these laws expressly implicated the right to carry, they showed a robust willingness on the part of state and local officials to limit firearm use in order to enhance public safety. None ever appears to have raised any concern about violating the right to keep and bear arms. And in particular, the emphasis on preventing the use of firearms in cities and after dark shows a recognition that the right to bear arms could be limited in scenarios in which its exercise causes more harm than good. Perhaps courts might regard limits on the right to carry as modern-day equivalents passed in the same spirit. For example, a law barring the carry of weapons in a high-crime city or in particular public places might be justified as an appropriate limit on the Second Amendment due to the great harm the carry of weapons can do to the public and the police in such circumstances. These colonial laws might suggest, then, that the right to bear arms would have an inherent balancing of cost and benefit built into it. Still, it is worth noting that the Founding-era laws addressed the use, and not the carry, of firearms, and so they provide no direct support for upholding a ban on the right to carry.

3. The Founding Era as a Whole

A dearth of regulations directly related to the right to carry during the late eighteenth century makes it difficult to glean too much from the era's history. States did, as discussed above, frequently regulate firearms for the sake of public safety, making clear that limits on the right to keep and bear arms were well established and accepted. Those state statutes that codified a version of the Statute of Northampton seem to provide a broad police power to the state, but their meaning is fiercely contested. Furthermore, it appears that not a single law was, at any point in the eighteenth century, struck down by a court as violating a state law right to keep and bear arms. At the same time, none of the Founding-era laws explicitly banned the carry of arms, and some even made exceptions for it. The result is a lack of clarity as to the meaning of the status of the right to carry at the time of the Founding.

D. The Antebellum Period

This opacity of Founding-era views of the right to carry stands in contrast with the far more consistent interpretations during the first half of the nineteenth century. TheHeller Court relied heavily on case law from this period, which was comparatively voluminous and almost uniform in its interpretation of the Second Amendment and its state analogues. *Heller's*use of this case law remains among its more controversial techniques, but there is little reason to think the Court will discard this "critical tool" for interpreting the public understanding of the Second Amendment in the immediate aftermath of its ratification. And with regard to the right to carry, this case law is particularly important: it provides the only clear and detailed discussions of the right to carry in the source material consulted by *Heller*. The cases, while differing subtly in their discussion of the right to carry, point decisively toward a robust right to carry weapons openly for self-defense but no right at all to carry such weapons concealed. Indeed, these cases are notable for their understanding of the right to keep and bear arms as not encompassing concealed carry. Thus, a faithful reading of the most telling source material on the right to carry should lead courts to the conclusion that *Heller's* conception of the Second Amendment protects open, but not concealed, carry.

Beginning in the years immediately after the end of the War of 1812 and continuing through the Jacksonian era, American culture—especially in the backcountry of the West and South—became more individualistic and more aggressive. Explanations for the transformation—from the constant violence of slavery, to the culture of the Scots-Irish, to the presence of large numbers of young, single men—differ, but historians are largely uniform in their recognition of the growing presence of violence in early nineteenth-century Appalachia. In response to this culture of violence, states began to, among other measures, regulate the carry of weapons. These restrictions were in turn challenged in state supreme courts, occasionally under the Second Amendment, though usually under the Second Amendment's variously worded state analogues. While these challenges were more successful in some states than others, courts generally upheld bans on concealed weapons but often overturned those on open carry.

Attempts to curb the increased violence began with anti-dueling measures, aimed at this ritual of formal, organized violence. But more than any other contributor to homicides, it was the carrying of concealed weapons—pistols and knives both—that allowed ordinary arguments to escalate into fatal encounters at a moment's notice. In addition to safety grounds, legislators banning concealed weapons also justified the laws as preventing dishonorable acts. In their understanding, those who relied on concealed weapons could not possibly be interested in self-defense, but instead must have an improper, aggressive motive. This view allowed lawmakers like New York Governor DeWitt Clinton to pitch bans on concealed carry in populist terms, arguing that the cowardly practice endangered "an essential right of every free citizen." Still, lawmakers knew their weapons bans would be unpopular, and constitutional challenges soon followed.

Between 1822 and 1850, eight western and southern states faced challenges to statutes, or in one case a common law court ruling, which limited the right to carry. Of these cases, just one produced a holding that protected the right to concealed carry—and that holding was soon overturned by state constitutional amendment. And just one state supreme court gave its legislature nearly no limits in its regulation of the carry of arms. Six state high courts affirmed the state's right to ban concealed carry, but held that bans on open carry would run afoul of the right to keep and bear arms. Thus, six out of eight of the courts reaching this question found constitutional significance in the distinction between open and concealed carry, determining that the need for self-defense required open carry while the interest in public safety allowed states to ban concealed carry.

Kentucky was the first state to ban the carry of concealed weapons, and the first state to hear a challenge to the law in its highest court. This was no surprise, given that Kentucky was, according to historian Clayton Cramer, "at or near the center of a back country culture of violence" in early nineteenth-century America. The Kentucky Court of Appeals, in *Bliss v. Commonwealth*, found that the state's concealed weapons ban violated the Second Amendment analogue in the Kentucky Constitution. The legislature voiced its displeasure with the court's decision, and Kentucky subsequently amended its constitution to allow bans on concealed weapons.

The Kentucky Court of Appeals would prove an outlier, not a trailblazer, in its treatment of concealed weapons bans. So too would the Arkansas Supreme Court in its approval of a ban on the carry of all weapons. In *State v. Buzzard*, the court provided the era's most permissive view of limitations on the carry of weapons:

I have come to the conclusion that the Legislature possesses competent powers to prescribe, by law, that any and all arms, kept or borne by individuals, shall be so kept and borne as not to injure or endanger the private rights of others, distur[b] the peace or domestic tranquility, or in any manner endanger the free institutions of this State or the United States; and that no enactment on this subject, which neither directly nor indirectly so operates as to impair or render inefficient the means provided by the Constitution for the defense of the State, can be adjudged invalid on the ground that it is repugnant to the Constitution.

It is difficult to find a firmer statement of a state's ability to regulate the right to carry for private purposes. Buzzard envisioned a right to keep and bear arms that was violated only when a challenged regulation impaired the defense of the state. This interpretation would also stand apart from those offered by other state courts of the era.

Most states that heard challenges to laws regulating the carry of weapons instead distinguished between open and concealed carry. They found open carry protected by the Second Amendment or the state analogue, while determining that concealed carry could be banned. In each case, courts emphasized that concealed carry did not vindicate the interests of legitimate self-defense that underscored the right to keep and bear arms. The earliest of these cases, the Indiana Supreme Court's 1833 decision in *State v. Mitchell*, provides no reasoning at all, simply stating in a one sentence opinion: "IT was held in this case, that the statute of 1831, prohibiting all persons, except travelers, from wearing or carrying concealed weapons, is not unconstitutional." Subsequent courts would offer more substantial justifications. For example, in the 1840 case of *State v. Reid*, Alabama's highest court ruled that a concealed weapons ban was constitutional, while a ban on open carry would not be. According to the court, "it is only when carried openly, that [weapons] can be efficiently used for defence." Carrying concealed weapons did not fit within the state's constitutional allowance that a person could keep and bear arms "for the purposes of defending himself and the State" because, for purposes of self-protection in moments of immediate danger, the court found that "there can be no necessity for concealing the weapon." And, tellingly, the court rejected an argument that open carry and concealed carry were functionally identical, and that it mattered not which one was allowed and which was barred.

That same year, the Tennessee Supreme Court upheld the state's concealed weapons ban. Finding that "the right to bear arms in defence of themselves is coupled with the right to bear them in defence of the State," and that arms used in defense of the state "must necessarily be borne openly," the court held that only the open carry of weapons could be protected by Tennessee's Second Amendment analogue. Concealed carry was simply not contemplated by the state constitution. Six years later, the Georgia Supreme Court similarly found that a ban on the open carry of guns and knives was too great an imposition on the Second Amendment, but that the state's concealed weapons law was permissible. The court noted that the proscription of concealed carry "does not deprive the citizen of his natural right of self-defence, or of his constitutional right to keep and bear arms," while "a prohibition against bearing arms openly, is in conflict with the Constitution, and void." In *Heller*, Justice Scalia noted with approval the interpretation adopted by the Georgia Supreme Court in Nunn, which makes the Georgia court's distinction between open and concealed carry all the more consequential.

Shortly thereafter, in *State v. Chandler*, the Louisiana Supreme Court seized on the same divide between open and concealed carry, and ruled that the state could ban concealed carry. Chandler, while similar to Reid and Nunn, provided a more complete statement of the importance of the concealed/open divide in the culture of Jacksonian America. Explaining the constitutionality of the state's concealed weapons ban, the court wrote:

The act of the 25th of March, 1813, makes it a misdemeanor to be "found with a concealed weapon, such as a dirk, dagger, knife, pistol, or any other deadly weapon concealed in his bosom, coat, or any other place about him, that does not appear in full open view." This law became absolutely necessary to counteract a vicious state of society, growing out of the habit of carrying concealed weapons, and to prevent bloodshed and assassinations committed upon unsuspecting persons. It interfered with no man's right to carry arms (to use its words) "in full open view," which places men upon an equality. This is the right guaranteed by the Constitution of the United States, and which is calculated to incite men to a manly and noble defence of themselves, if necessary, and of their country, without any tendency to secret advantages and unmanly assassinations.

Just a few years earlier, the North Carolina Supreme Court had upheld the conviction of a man for arming himself with dangerous and unusual weapons, stating: "[I]t is to be remembered that the carrying of a gun per se constitutes no offence. For any lawful purpose—either of business or amusement—the citizen is at perfect liberty to carry his gun. It is the wicked purpose—and the mischievous result—which essentially constitute the crime." These cases illustrate that early nineteenth-century legislatures and courts were not merely indulging policy preferences by proscribing concealed, but not open, carry. Their understanding of the right to keep and bear arms did not include concealed carry, which simply could not, in their minds, be utilized for legitimate self-defense. It was a tool of the sneaky and the dishonorable, and its protection could not possibly be intended by their state constitutions.

E. The Fourteenth Amendment and the Right to Carry

When the Supreme Court determined that the Second Amendment was incorporated against the states in *McDonald*, it incorporated the right as understood in 1866, not as understood in 1791. This raises the possibility that the Second Amendment could mean something different when applied to state laws than it means when applied to federal laws. This distinction made no difference in *Heller* and *McDonald* because the Court found that the 1791 and the 1866 understandings of the Second Amendment both guaranteed an individual right. But that uniformity might not remain in a case involving the right to carry. Indeed, the Court described the post-Civil War Second Amendment right in *McDonald* as one that was no longer associated with the militia but instead intended to ensure the right to self-defense of the freedmen. It is not difficult to imagine a more robust right to carry as part of this later understanding.

The question of whether the Second Amendment meant something different in 1866 than in 1791, and whether that difference should lead to different rights against the state and federal governments, is a complex question that is outside to scope of this Note. Instead of attempting to address it in detail, I will make two small observations. First, the Supreme Court and academic scholars have advanced strong evidence from the ratification debates of the Fourteenth Amendment that at least some congressmen intended the Amendment to provide freedmen with the right to armed self-defense against the widespread violence to which they were subjected. A court could read this evidence independently of the Founding-era sources in order to determine the constitutionality of state restrictions on the right to carry. Second, courts and scholars that have evaluated state laws challenged under the Second Amendment have, generally speaking, continued to consult Founding-era history, either at the expense of or in addition to Reconstruction understandings of the Second Amendment. Because of the remaining prevalence of the Founding- and antebellum-era sources in these authorities, I will not devote space in this Note to addressing whether courts should use the Reconstruction understanding of the Second Amendment when evaluating state laws. Nor will I address the differences that this approach might yield. It remains, however, an important unresolved issue in Second Amendment scholarship, and one that I hope commentators will address in the future.

III. IMPLICATIONS FOR AN ORIGINALIST RIGHT TO CARRY

The history discussed in Part II, and the Court's reading of that history in *Heller* and *McDonald*, does not offer a clear answer on the contours of the right to carry. This is unsurprising–after all, the Second Amendment-related historical material in those opinions and this Note have been vociferously debated in legal scholarship for decades. Still, *Heller* and *McDonald*, by revealing the Supreme Court's view of which sources matter and how they should be read, provide a blueprint for how the Court would address a case involving the right to carry. This Part argues that fidelity to Hellerrequires that courts protect the open carry of firearms but allow for restrictions on concealed carry. This theory has not been advanced in the Second Amendment scholarship, but it most accurately captures the understanding of the right to keep and bear arms in the only sources used in *Heller* that contain any significant discussion of the right to carry. This interpretation may prove unpopular with most camps in the Second Amendment discussion, but that does not alter its descriptive force.

After laying out the argument for the constitutional significance of open carry, this Part addresses two alternative interpretations of the original understanding of the Second Amendment. First, I examine the argument against any right to carry outside the home at all. While a colorable argument can be made for this position, it would both require a retreat from *Heller* and diminish the importance of the nineteenth-century sources relied upon substantially by the Court. Next, I discuss what one scholar has described as the "alternative outlet" theory, which posits that some right to carry must be allowed, but that the government is free to choose whether that carry is open or concealed. While this argument is convenient for modern-day sensibilities regarding the right to carry, it does not conform to the nineteenth-century understanding of the Second Amendment and its analogues embraced by the HellerCourt. As a result, courts would be wrong to embrace it.

A. The Right to Carry Openly (and Not Concealed)

The argument for a Second Amendment that guarantees the right to carry, but to carry only openly, is straightforward and grounded in fidelity to *Heller*. As we have seen, in that case, the Supreme Court consulted a range of sources—material on the English right, Founding-era legal authorities, Founding-era statutes, and nineteenth-century state court cases. Evaluating the same sources reveals that the material regarding the English right and the Founding era provides little to no help in discerning the historical right to carry. The Founding era certainly provides some examples of laws regulating firearms for public safety as well as discussions of the importance of self-defense, but the eighteenth-century authorities simply do not speak to the question of the right to carry. The Court's nineteenth-century sources, however, concentrate heavily on the right to carry, and speak with what is close to a single voice on what the Second Amendment protected: the right to carry weapons openly for personal self-defense. *Heller* determined that these cases were a "critical tool" for understanding the historical public meaning of the Second Amendment, and using them as such leads to the conclusion that only open carry should be constitutionally protected.

Regardless of what we think about their reasoning today, antebellum courts did not randomly choose open carry over concealed carry. As discussed above, their understanding of the right to carry for self-defense explicitly encompassed a view that the two were different, and that only open carry was protected. Antebellum state courts explicitly valorized the type of self-defense guaranteed by open carry and rejected what they saw as the deficiencies of concealed carry. The Alabama Supreme Court in *State v. Reid* reasoned that "it is difficult to conceive" of why someone interested in self-protection would have an interest to carry concealed instead of openly." It held, quite unequivocally, that "it is only when carried openly, that [weapons] can be efficiently used for defence." In *State v. Chandler*, the Louisiana Supreme Court agreed, holding that the right to carry openly "is the right guaranteed by the Constitution of the United States, and which is calculated to incite men to a manly and noble defence of themselves, if necessary, and of their country, without any tendency to secret advantages and unmanly assassinations." Concealed carry bans simply did not implicate the right to keep and bear arms, because they were entirely outside of its protection. The Georgia Supreme Court found that a concealed weapons ban did not "deprive the citizen of his natural right of self-defense, or of his constitutional right to bear arms. But that so much of it, as contains a prohibition against bearing arms openly, is in conflict with the Constitution, and void . . . ." These cases do not speak with the equivocal language of either and or when describing open and concealed carry. Instead, they clearly embody a Jacksonian understanding of the right to self-defense as requiring the visible carry of weapons that would prevent unexpected, unmanly violence.

When contemporary commentators and courts claim that it does not matter what kind of carry is protected, they set aside this antebellum understanding of self-defense in favor of a modern conception that does not align with the case law on which Hellerrested much of its holding. Their desire to do so is understandable. Concealed carry and open carry no longer hold the same significance that they did in the nineteenth century. Today, open carry, as Eugene Volokh points out, intimidates those around the carrier and makes the carrier appear unreasonable to many—factors that may discourage some from carrying openly. This may well be true. And yet, so too, the need for gun ownership for self-defense has changed enormously since the antebellum era. Unlike two hundred years ago, every American lives within the jurisdiction of a local law enforcement agency, there are no skirmishes with the European powers or Indians on the frontier, and dangerous wild animals pose no threat to most people. But just as those largely outdated threats mattered greatly to the Court's opinion in *Heller*, so too the arguably outdated understanding of the proper mode for self-defense ought to carry weight in the Court's consideration of the right to carry.

One further factor also counsels in favor of unequal treatment for concealed and open carry: the long pedigree of concealed weapons bans. The *Heller* Court recognized this pedigree, specifically citing concealed weapons bans when explaining that the right to bear arms could be limited in certain ways. More generally, it also noted that its holding should not "cast doubt on longstanding prohibitions." These statements by the majority further demonstrate that the equivalence drawn by contemporary scholars between open and concealed carry does not comport with the Court's approach to the history in *Heller*.

Two circuit courts have recently issued opinions that conform at least in some way to this conception of the right to keep and bear arms. Most directly, in *Peterson v. Martinez*, the Tenth Circuit upheld a Colorado law that limited concealed carry licenses to state residents. In its decision, the court canvassed much of the same antebellum case law analyzed in *Heller* and in Section II.D above, as well as Second Amendment scholarship, and found a "long history of concealed carry restrictions in this country." Because of *Heller*'s warning about respecting longstanding prohibitions, and because concealed weapons bans have just such a pedigree, the court found that the Second Amendment did not invalidate the concealed weapons ban. The plaintiff waived his challenge to Denver's ban on the open carry of firearms, and so the court did not reach the question of whether Colorado's concealed and Denver's open carry bans acted together to effectively deprive non-residents of any right to carry weapons. If it had, it might have had occasion to find that banning the open carry of weapons runs afoul of the Second Amendment, even as concealed carry bans remain constitutional.

The Second Circuit, in upholding New York State's very strict concealed carry licensing regime, was less definitive than the Tenth Circuit in its reading of *Heller*. Still, its opinion leaves open the possibility of an open-carry-only view of the Second Amendment. In *Kachalsky v. County of Westchester*, the court agreed with the Fourth Circuit that the application of *Heller* beyond the home was a "vast terra incognita." It nonetheless stated that a faithful reading of *Heller* "suggests . . . that the Amendment must have some application in the very different context of the public possession of firearms." This acknowledgement set the Second Circuit apart from the Fourth Circuit and the Maryland Court of Appeals, as discussed below. Still, the court found the history of regulation of the right to carry too indeterminate to support the plaintiffs' argument that the state could not bar both concealed and open carry of firearms. It also found that New York's lack of a total ban on the carry of firearms fell within the mainstream of gun regulations. Then, using an intermediate level of scrutiny, the court upheld the law. It is difficult to tease out a clear distinction in the Second Circuit's opinion between concealed and open carry. But the court's reliance on numerous historical concealed weapons bans from New York and elsewhere shows that the court recognized the disparate treatment the two methods have received over the years. Perhaps if it had been forced to explore more fully how the Second Amendment applies outside the home, it would have used that history to find the protection extended to the open carry of firearms.

Unsurprisingly, the possibility of a right to open, but not concealed, carry has garnered little support from either side of the gun debate. There is little doubt that brandishing a weapon in most situations causes great alarm to the surrounding population. For gun control advocates, open carry could not be worse: it combines the danger of guns with the public terror of observing them regularly. Meanwhile, because carrying openly is outside of mainstream practice and inspires discomfort and sometimes panic or terror, many gun rights advocates have also tried to sidestep a constitutional rule that would protect only a right to open carry. Nonetheless, if the *Heller* Court is to be taken at its word that the Second Amendment ought to be interpreted by its original understanding, and that the nineteenth-century cases are crucial to explaining that understanding, then any inconvenience posed by a constitutionalized open carry should not prevent the Court from staying loyal to its methodology.

B. Alternative Interpretations of the Right to Carry

Although the historical evidence best supports a right to carry only openly outside the home, two other prominent interpretations have emerged in judicial opinions and legal scholarship since *Heller*. Those opposed to extending *Heller* beyond the home have attempted to argue that the history supports no right to carry at all—that Hellershould essentially be confined to its facts and protect the right to carry weapons only in the home. Meanwhile, scholars more receptive to gun rights have argued that the history supports the right to carry, but that the method of carry is not implicated by the Second Amendment. States, then, can choose how to best protect the right. This position, which has been described as the "alternative outlet" theory because it requires either open or concealed carry as an "outlet" for the right to carry, has been accepted by at least one lower court, and perhaps another. Neither of these positions, however, can be easily justified by *Heller* and its sources.

1. No Right to Carry

One way for the Supreme Court to avoid constitutionalizing open carry would be to rule that there is no right to carry weapons outside the home at all. This would confine *Heller* and *McDonald* to their holdings: that there is an individual right to possess a handgun in the home. This theory arguably finds some support in laws at the time of the Founding, as well as a broad reading of the common law's embrace of the Statute of Northampton. This limited reading of *Heller* runs into one key problem: the logic of *Heller* itself seems to extend beyond the home, based both on the way the right to self-defense is described and the case law that the Court used to recognize an individual right.

The strongest argument for the absence of any right to carry is simple but intuitive: there are no examples from the Founding era of anyone espousing the concept of a general right to carry, while there are many examples of limiting gun use for public safety reasons. As noted in Section II.C, gun regulation at the time of the Founding was relatively common, and there are no records of any challenges to any of those gun laws using states' Second Amendment analogues. If the Second Amendment and its state analogues protected a robust right to carry, one would expect to see some evidence in defenses to gun charges in the Founding era, but there appears to be none. Perhaps its absence lends credence to Patrick Charles's recent scholarship on the important role of the Statute of Northampton in the common law of colonies and states in the early Republic. This argument, historically grounded and well sourced, provides the strongest case for *Heller* and *McDonald* being confined to the home.

Some courts, without delving into the history discussed in this Note, have seemed to embrace this limited conception of the right to keep and bear arms. For example, in *United States v. Masciandaro*, which dealt with the right to carry a handgun in a national park, the Fourth Circuit found that the Second Amendment was not implicated. Judge Niemeyer, writing only for himself, claimed that "a plausible reading" of *Heller* would require the Second Amendment to apply outside the home in some capacity. But Judge Wilkinson, writing for the court, refused to venture outside the home at all. Maryland's highest court made a similar ruling in *Williams v. State*, upholding a conviction for carrying a handgun in public without a permit. The court reasoned that "[i]f the Supreme Court . . . meant its [*Heller*] holding to extend beyond home possession, it will need to say so more plainly."

This limited conception of the Second Amendment right is difficult to square with the logic of the Court's decision in *Heller*, which appears to foreclose a regime that allows no right to carry. *Heller* guarantees "the individual right to possess and carry weapons in case of confrontation." While not entirely definitive, this statement seems to require a right to carry outside the home of some kind. A substantial number, perhaps the majority, of potential confrontations are likely to occur away from the home. If the right to carry arms were confined to an individual's property, the right to carry in case of confrontation would be stripped of much of its use.

This reading of *Heller*—as requiring some right to carry—is certainly the most dominant in the academic analysis. Some lower courts have also roundly rejected a total ban on the right to carry. Most notably, Judge Posner, writing for a divided panel in *Moore v. Madigan*, held that the Second Amendment must include the right to carry arms outside the home, striking down Illinois's blanket ban on all carry of guns. Judge Posner declined to revisit the history discussed in *Heller*, noting only that "[t]he Supreme Court has decided that the amendment confers a right to bear arms for self-defense, which is as important outside the home as inside." The Seventh Circuit's decision seems to flow naturally from *Heller*'s reasoning, and fits into the scholarly consensus. While there is a defensible historical case to be made for limiting the Second Amendment right to the home, *Heller* appears to foreclose that interpretation, and to require some right to carry.

2. The Alternative Outlet Theory

Alan Gura, a prominent gun rights litigator and the victorious attorney in *Heller*, has been a principal exponent of the argument that some form of carry must be permitted, but it does not matter which one. James Bishop, taking his cue from the reasoning of a California district court, has named this the "alternative outlet doctrine." This conception of the right to carry relies on one of two options: sidestepping the history of regulation of open and concealed carry, or reading the case law in such a way as to minimize its emphasis on the difference between the two. Different scholars have adopted each of these approaches, but neither can be reconciled with *Heller*.

The first method is to recognize that the history points toward a right to open carry only, but to reject such a finding as impractical. The most prominent advocate of this compromise is Eugene Volokh. He acknowledges that the case law points toward a history of upholding concealed carry bans while protecting open carry. But because cultural norms have changed, he believes that "social pressure" will prevent most Americans from carrying openly, and those who carry concealed do not now pose the danger that nineteenth-century courts thought they did. Volokh worries that because of the stigma against open carry, a Second Amendment right that protected only open carry would deter many law-abiding citizens from carrying weapons at all. Meanwhile, James Bishop, after canvassing the largely opaque empirical data, argues that concealed carry offers the least dangerous and least costly outlet for the right to carry.

Michael O'Shea has advanced a more ambitious and historically grounded approach to undergird the alternative outlet theory. He reads the antebellum case law as focused not on the divide between open and concealed carry, but instead on presumptive versus non-presumptive carry. That distinction rests on whether most individuals are allowed to carry defensive weapons most of the time (presumptive carry), or whether they need to provide special justification in order to carry (non-presumptive carry). Those state courts that recognized a right to carry openly were, according to O'Shea, in fact recognizing a right to carry weapons presumptively, and the method was of secondary importance. He argues that what mattered to the majority of state high courts in the antebellum period was that the right to carry not be abridged or outlawed entirely. Concealed weapons bans were permissible, but only because open carry was allowed. For O'Shea, then, the key question in the right to carry debate is whether states must recognize presumptive carry—the method of the carry itself is of secondary importance. This theory supports what O'Shea sees as Gura's "functional" approach: what matters is the right to carry presumptively, and the method itself should not be constitutionalized.

One federal appeals court, adding yet another divergent interpretation of the right to carry in the lower courts, explicitly adopted this approach. In *Peruta v. County of San Diego*, the Ninth Circuit accepted the plaintiff's alternative outlet argument. It examined in detail much of the same historical evidence explored in this Note. The majority then stated that the nineteenth century case law stands not for the legality of open carry, but instead for the need for legal carry outside the home of some kind. Adopting O'Shea's presumptive carry model, the court stated: "California, through its legislative scheme, has taken a different course than most nineteenth-century state legislatures, expressing a preference for concealed rather than open carry ... California's favoring concealed carry over open carry does not offend the Constitution, so long as it allows one of the two." The

Ninth Circuit reversed a grant of summary judgment in favor of San Diego County and remanded the case, all but assuring that California's regulatory scheme—a general prohibition on open carry combined with difficult to obtain "may issue" concealed carry permits—will be overturned. The opinion stands as the only explicit invocation of the alternative outlet theory by a circuit court. Were this interpretation to take hold, it might well render the question of open versus concealed carry largely moot.

In spite of Volokh's practical focus and O'Shea's creative presumptive carry argument, the centrality of open carry to the originalist inquiry of the right to self-defense is not so easy to dispatch. As discussed in Section III.A, the nineteenth-century courts did not exalt open carry simply because it was convenient. Nor because it was just one way of carrying presumptively, otherwise no different from concealed carry. Instead, the distinction between open and concealed carry was crucial to their understanding of what proper self-defense entailed. For them, the right to keep and bear arms did not protect the carry of concealed weapons. Self-defense inherently required the open carry of weapons, because someone who concealed a weapon must surely have some sort of aggressive or sneaky intent.

At the conclusion of his majority opinion in *Heller*, Justice Scalia admonishes those who disagree with him with the following statement:

Undoubtedly some think that the Second Amendment is outmoded in a society where our standing army is the pride of our Nation, where well-trained police forces provide personal security, and where gun violence is a serious problem. That is perhaps debatable, but what is not debatable is that it is not the role of this Court to pronounce the Second Amendment extinct.

These closing lines offer a combative testament that the Court will not bow to modern sensibilities at the expense of its interpretation of the original meaning of the Second Amendment. For the purposes of the original meaning of the Second Amendment, the nineteenth-century understanding of the right to carry matters, *Heller* tells us. Modern attempts to disregard the era's emphasis on the importance of carrying openly in order to make gun rights more palatable simply do not comport with how the Court approached the Second Amendment in *Heller*. Just as the Court refused to mollify those who wished to use one modern understanding of the value of the right to bear arms to limit its contemporary application, so too the Court should, in fidelity to *Heller*, reject those who wish to erase the connection between self-defense and open carry in the nineteenth century case law.

CONCLUSION

This Note has argued that *Heller* and *McDonald*, and especially *Heller*, compel the conclusion that the Second Amendment protects the right to carry openly outside the home. The Court's methodology in *Heller* and its reliance on the nineteenth-century case law suggest that there must be some right to carry, and that open carry, not concealed carry, is protected by the Second Amendment. It is surely no accident, however, that no court has fully embraced this approach. Such a holding would be drastic, out of sync with contemporary norms, and could generate enormous public outcry. As a result, there is a reasonably good chance that the Supreme Court will, in future cases, find a way around such a result in favor of a more popular policy.

One way that the Court could affirm a personal right to self-defense without constitutionalizing open carry would be to evaluate the right to self-defense through a wider frame. Any originalist inquiry, by necessity, picks a given level of specificity at which to examine historical sources. In the future, the Supreme Court could remain at the quite narrow level it utilized in *Heller* when it found that historic laws regulating guns did not provide sufficient basis to allow Washington, D.C., to prevent residents from keeping guns in their homes. According to the Court, the public safety laws cited by Justice Breyer in dissent were about specific issues like the storage of powder, and therefore inapposite to the safety of a loaded weapon. A similarly narrow reading of the antebellum case law should lead the Court to find that only open carry is constitutionally protected. But by widening its scope, and instead finding that the nineteenth-century case law stands only for the existence of an individual right and nothing more, the Court could then fashion that right as it saw fit—as requiring an alternative outlet, for example.

A second way the Supreme Court might escape enshrining a right to open carry would be to simply insert a historical reasoning into a case otherwise reliant on history. The Court would have a particularly good model for such a maneuver: *Heller* itself. As has been noted by disgruntled gun rights supporters, *Heller*'s statement that its holding should not affect laws disarming felons and the mentally ill or laws preventing guns in sensitive places lacks significant historical support. And the Court cited a 1998 opinion of Justice Ginsburg's which itself cited the 1990 edition of Black's Law Dictionary to determine the meaning of "bear arms." More fundamentally, Washington, D.C.'s handgun ban posed something of a problem for the majority in *Heller*, seeing as the framers of the Second Amendment undoubtedly had long guns in mind in 1791. To avoid this problem, the *Heller* Court determined that because handguns were the overwhelming choice of modern-day Americans for use in self-defense, they should receive protection under the Second Amendment.

This was a puzzling move for an originalist opinion. After all, *Heller* is premised in no small part on a rejection of using modern norms at the expense of historical understanding. And yet, the Court had no trouble making these thoroughly modern accommodations, lending support to those scholars who argue that *Heller* is in fact a product of popular constitutionalism, and not originalism at all. It is not difficult to imagine a similarly a historical accommodation for the modern preference for concealed carry, perhaps premised on Volokh's claim that the unpopularity of open carry would prevent it from truly vindicating the right to self-defense or on O'Shea's presumptive carry argument.

Still, even while recognizing the potential for an unprincipled retreat from *Heller*'s reasoning, this Note takes the Supreme Court at its word. For the right to carry, the most consequential choice the Court made in *Heller* was to place such a strong emphasis on nineteenth-century case law. These cases do indeed seem to require an individual right, as *Heller* stated. But they also protect only open carry, and for reasons tied to cultural factors not present at the Founding itself. *Heller*, then, has used post-Founding history to create a Second Amendment that reflects the sensibility of the Jacksonian frontier, not that of the eighteenth-century Enlightenment. This strange result is what *Heller* gave us. Following its methodology leads to an embrace of open carry and a rejection of both a strong public safety-oriented limitation on the right to carry and the alternative outlet theory. This is a result that is unlikely to please most anyone, and perhaps the Court will avoid it. But we should not mistake such a choice for anything but an unprincipled path of convenience. Given *Heller*'s reliance on modernity-accommodating carve-outs, however, perhaps we should prepare ourselves for just such an unsatisfying and unprincipled resolution for the right to carry weapons outside the home.

■ *Presser v. Illinois*

Author(s): William B. Woods
Date: 1886
Genre: Court decision (Supreme Court)

Summary Overview

Presser v. Illinois is a U.S. Supreme Court case argued in November 1885 and decided on January 4, 1886. The case is significant because the High Court held that the Second Amendment's "right to bear Arms" pertained to state militias and to the service of citizens in those militias. Further, the Court held that the Second Amendment restrained the federal government, not the states; accordingly, states could enact statutes that would seem to stand in opposition to the Second Amendment. *Presser v. Illinois* proved to be a landmark case, one cited in future Supreme Court decisions in support of the view that the Second Amendment did not confer an individual right to bear arms but rather codified a collective right of the states to form and maintain militias.

Defining Moment

Herman Presser was the leader of a paramilitary group called Lehr and Wehr Verein, which translates from German roughly as Teaching and Defense (or Resistance) Association. At the time, Illinois law prohibited armed paramilitary organizations from drilling or parading without a license from the governor: "It shall not be lawful for any body of men whatever other than the regular organized volunteer militia of this state and the troops of the United States to associate themselves together as a military company or organization, or to drill or parade with arms in any city or town of this state without the license of the Governor thereof."

Presser was indicted for leading a group of four hundred of his followers armed with rifles in a parade through the streets of Chicago. He was convicted and sentenced to pay a fine of $10. After the Illinois Supreme Court upheld his conviction, he appealed to the U.S. Supreme Court, arguing that the Illinois law usurped the powers of Congress over militias, as outlined in Article I of the Constitution.

The High Court rejected this claim, holding that Illinois was well within its rights to enact a statute restricting the activities of an organization such as Presser's and that the Second Amendment did not apply to the states. In this regard, the Court reaffirmed its holding in *United States v. Cruikshank* (1876) that the Second Amendment was not "incorporated," meaning that the amendment applied only to the federal government, not to state governments—a position the Court would hold until 2010, in the case of *McDonald v. City of Chicago.*

About the Author

The Court's opinion in *Presser v. Illinois* was written by Associate Justice William B. Woods. Woods was born on August 3, 1924, in Newark, Ohio. He attended Western Reserve College for three years before transferring to Yale University, where he completed his bachelor's degree in 1845.

He returned to Newark, where he read law with a local attorney, with whom he established a law practice after he was admitted to the bar in 1847. He entered public service in 1856, when he was elected mayor of Newark; two years later he was elected to the Ohio House of Representatives, where he became Speaker of the House.

In 1862 Woods joined the Union army and would go on to take part in campaigns at Shiloh and Vicksburg; he left the army in 1866 with the rank of major general. Rather than returning north, however, he remained in Bentonville, Alabama, where he established a law practice; he was elected Chancellor of the Middle Chancery Division of Alabama in 1868. The following year, President Ulysses S. Grant appointed Woods to the Fifth U.S. Circuit Court.

In 1880, President Rutherford B. Hayes nominated him to the U.S. Supreme Court. When he was confirmed on January 5, 1881, he became the first Supreme Court justice from a former Confederate state since 1853. He served on the Court until his death on May 14, 1887.

HISTORICAL DOCUMENT

Syllabus

The doctrine that statutes constitutional in part only will be upheld as to what is constitutional if it can he separated from the unconstitutional provisions reasserted.

A state statute providing that all able-bodied male citizens of the state between eighteen and forty-five, except those exempted, shall be subject to military duty, and shall he enrolled and designated as the state militia, and prohibiting all bodies of men other than the regularly organized volunteer militia of the state and the troops of the United States from associating together as military organizations or drilling or parading with arms in any city of the state without license from the governor as to these provisions is constitutional, and does not infringe the laws of the United States, and it is sustained as to them, although the act contains other provisions, separable from the foregoing, which it was contended infringed upon the powers vested in the United States by the Constitution or upon laws enacted by Congress in pursuance thereof.

The provision in the Second Amendment to the Constitution, that "The right of the people to keep and bear arms shall not be infringed" is a limitation only on the power of Congress and the national government, and not of the states. But in view of the fact that all citizens capable of bearing arms constitute the reserved military force of the national government as well as in view of its general powers, the states cannot prohibit the people from keeping and bearing arms so as to deprive the United States of their rightful resource for maintaining the public security.

The provision in the Fourteenth Amendment to the Constitution that "No state shall make or enforce any law which shall abridge the privileges or immunities of citizens of the United States" does not prevent a state from passing such laws to regulate the privileges and immunities of its own citizens as do not abridge their privileges and immunities as citizens of the United States.

Unless restrained by their own constitutions, state legislatures may enact statutes to control and regulate all organizations, drilling, and parading of military bodies and associations except those which are authorized by the militia laws of the United States.

Herman Presser, the plaintiff in error, was indicted on September 24, 1879, in the Criminal Court of Cook County, Illinois, far a violation of the following sections of Art. XI of the Military Code of that state, Act of May 28, 1879, Laws of 1879, 192.

> "§ 5. It shall not be lawful for any body of men whatever other than the regular organized volunteer militia of this state and the troops of the United States to associate themselves together as a military company or organization, or to drill or parade with arms in any city or town of this state without the license of the Governor thereof, which license may at any time be revoked, *and provided further* that students in educational institutions where military science is a part of the course of instruction may, with the consent of the Governor, drill and parade with arms in public under the superintendence of their instructors, and may take part in any regimental or brigade encampment under command of their military instructor, and while so encamped shall be governed by the provisions of this act. They shall be entitled only to transportation and subsistence, and shall report and be subject to the commandant of such encampment, *provided* that nothing herein contained shall be construed so as to prevent benevolent or social organizations from wearing swords."

> "§ 6. Whoever offends against the provisions of the preceding section or belongs to or parades with any such unauthorized body of men with arms shall be punished by a fine not exceeding the sum of ten dollars ($10), or by imprisonment in the common jail for a term not exceeding six months, or both."

The indictment charged in substance that Presser, on September 24, 1879, in the County of Cook, in the State of Illinois,

> "did unlawfully belong to and did parade and drill in the City of Chicago with an unauthorized body of men with arms who had associated themselves together as a military company and organization without having a license from the governor, and not being a part of or belonging to 'the regular organized volunteer militia' of the State of Illinois or the troops of the United States."

A motion to quash the indictment was overruled. Presser then pleaded not guilty, and, both parties having waived a jury, the case was tried by the court, which found Presser guilty and sentenced him to pay a fine of $10.

The bill of exceptions taken upon the trial set out all the evidence, from which it appeared that Presser was thirty-one years old, a citizen of the United States and of the State of Illinois, and a voter; that he belonged to a society called the "Lehr und Wehr Verein," a corporation organized April 16, 1875, in due form, under chapter 32, Revised Statutes of Illinois, called the "General Incorporation Laws of Illinois," "for the purpose," as expressed by its certificate of association,

> "of improving the mental and bodily condition of its members so as to qualify them for the duties of citizens of a republic. Its members shall therefore obtain, in the meetings of the association, a knowledge of our laws and political economy, and shall also be instructed in military and gymnastic exercises;"

that Presser, in December, 1879, marched at the head of said company, about four hundred in number, in the streets of the City of Chicago, he riding on horseback and in command; that the company was armed with rifles, and Presser with a cavalry sword; that the company had no license from the Governor of Illinois to drill or parade as a part of the militia of the state, and was not a part of the regular organized militia of the state, nor a part of troops of the United States, and had no organization under the militia law of the United States. The evidence showed no other facts. Exceptions were reserved to the ruling of the court upon the motion to quash the indictment, to the finding of guilty, and to the judgment thereon. The case was taken to the Supreme Court of Illinois, where the judgment was affirmed. Thereupon Presser brought the present writ of error for a review of the judgment of affirmance.

MR. JUSTICE WOODS delivered the opinion of the Court. After stating the facts in the language reported above, he continued:

The position of the plaintiff in error in this Court was that the entire statute under which he was convicted was invalid and void because its enactment was the exercise of a power by the Legislature of Illinois forbidden to the states by the Constitution of the United States. The clauses of the Constitution of the United States referred to in the assignments of error were as follows:

> "Art. I, sec. 8. The Congress shall have power . . . to raise and support armies; . . . to provide for calling forth the militia to execute the laws of the union, suppress insurrections, and repel invasions; to provide for organizing, arming, and disciplining the militia, and for governing such part of them as may be employed in the service of the United States, reserving to the states, respectively, the appointment of the officers, and the authority of training the militia, according to the discipline prescribed by Congress; . . . to make all laws which shall be necessary and proper, for carrying into execution the foregoing powers," &c.

> "Art. I, sec. 10. No state shall, without the consent of Congress, keep troops . . . in time of peace."

> "Art. II of Amendments. A well regulated militia being necessary to the security of a free state, the right of the people to keep and bear arms shall not be infringed."

The plaintiff in error also contended that the enactment of the 5th and 6th sections of Article XI of the Military Code was forbidden by subdivision 3 of section 9, Art. I, which declares "No bill of attainder or *ex post facto* law shall be passed," and by Art. XIV of Amendments, which provides that

> "No state shall make or enforce any law which shall abridge the privileges or immunities of citizens of

the United States, nor shall any state deprive any person of life, liberty, or property without due process of law."

The first contention of counsel for plaintiff in error is that the Congress of the United States having, by virtue of the provisions of Article I of section 8, above quoted, passed the Act of May 8, 1792, entitled "An act more effectually to provide for the national defense by establishing an uniform militia throughout the United States," 1 Stat. 271, the Act of February 28, 1795, "to provide for calling forth the militia to execute the laws of the union, suppress insurrections, and repel invasions," 1 Stat. 424, and the Act of July 22, 1861, "to authorize the employment of volunteers to aid in enforcing the laws and protecting public property," 12 Stat. 268, and other subsequent acts, now forming "Title 16, The Militia," of the Revised Statutes of the United States, the Legislature of Illinois had no power to pass the act approved May 28, 1879, "to provide for the organization of the state militia," entitled the Military Code of Illinois, under the provisions of which (sections 5 and 6 of Article XI) the plaintiff in error was indicted.

The argument in support of this contention is that the power of organizing, arming, and disciplining the militia being confided by the Constitution to Congress, when it acts upon the subject, and passes a law to carry into effect the constitutional provision, such action excludes the power of legislation by the state on the same subject.

It is further argued that the whole scope and object of the Military Code of Illinois is in conflict with that of the law of Congress. It is said that the object of the act of Congress is to provide for organizing, arming, and disciplining all the able-bodied male citizens of the states, respectively, between certain ages, that they may be ready at all times to respond to the call of the nation to enforce its laws, suppress insurrection, and repel invasion, and thereby avoid the necessity for maintaining a large standing army, with which liberty can never be safe, and that, on the other hand, the effect if not object of the Illinois statute is to prevent such organizing, arming, and disciplining of the militia.

The plaintiff in error insists that the act of Congress requires absolutely all able-bodied citizens of the state, between certain ages, to be enrolled in the militia; that the act of Illinois makes the enrollment dependent on the necessity for the use of troops to execute the laws and suppress insurrections, and then leaves it discretionary with the governor by proclamation to require such enrollment; that the act of Congress requires the entire enrolled militia of the state, with a few exemptions made by it and which may be made by state laws, to be formed into companies, battalions, regiments, brigades, and divisions; that every man shall be armed and supplied with ammunition; provides a system of discipline and field exercises for companies, regiments, &c., and subjects the entire militia of the state to the call of the President to enforce the laws, suppress insurrection, or repel invasion, and provides for the punishment of the militia officers and men who refuse obedience to his orders. On the other hand, it is said that the state law makes it unlawful for any of its able-bodied citizens, except eight thousand, called the "Illinois National Guard," to associate themselves together as a military company or to drill or parade with arms without the license of the governor, and declares that no military company shall leave the state with arms and equipments without his consent; that even the eight thousand men styled the "Illinois National Guard" are not enrolled or organized as required by the act of Congress, nor are they subject to the call of the President, but they constitute a military force sworn to serve in the military service of the state, to obey the orders of the governor, and not to leave the state without his consent, and that, if the state act is valid, the national act providing for organizing, arming, and disciplining the militia is of no force in the State of Illinois, for the Illinois act, so far from being in harmony with the act of Congress, is an insurmountable obstacle to its execution.

We have not found it necessary to consider or decide the question thus raised as to the validity of the entire Military Code of Illinois, for, in our opinion, the sections under which the plaintiff in error was convicted may be valid even if the other sections of the act were invalid. For it is a settled rule "that statutes that are constitutional in part only will be upheld so far as they are not in conflict with the Constitution, provided the allowed and prohibited parts are separable."

We are of opinion that this rule is applicable in this

case. The first two sections of Article I of the Military Code provide that all able-bodied male citizens of the state between the ages of 18 and 45 years, except those exempted, shall be subject to military duty, and be designated the "Illinois state Militia," and declare how they shall be enrolled and under what circumstances. The residue of the Code, except the two sections on which the indictment against the plaintiff in error is based, provides for a volunteer active militia, to consist of not more than eight thousand officers and men, declares how it shall be enlisted and brigaded, and the term of service of its officers and men; provides for brigade generals and their staffs, for the organization of the requisite battalions and companies and the election of company officers; provides for inspections, parades, and encampments, arms and armories, rifle practice, and courts-martial; provides for the pay of the officers and men, for medical service, regimental bands, books of instructions and maps; contains provisions for levying and collecting a military fund by taxation, and directs how it shall be expended, and appropriates $25,000 out of the Treasury, in advance of the collection of the military fund, to be used for the purposes specified in the Military Code.

It is plain from this statement of the substance of the Military Code that the two sections upon which the indictment against the plaintiff in error is based may be separated from the residue of the Code and stand upon their own independent provisions. These sections might have been left out of the Military Code and put in an act by themselves, and the act thus constituted and the residue of the Military Code would have been coherent and sensible acts. If it be conceded that the entire Military Code, except these sections, is unconstitutional and invalid for the reasons stated by the plaintiff in error, these sections are separable, and, put in an act by themselves, could not be considered as forbidden by the clauses of the Constitution having reference to the militia or to the clause forbidding the states, without the consent of Congress, to keep troops in time of peace. There is no such connection between the sections which prohibit any body of men, other than the organized militia of the state and the troops of the United States, from associating as a military company and drilling with arms in any city or Town of the state, and the sections which provide for the enrollment and organization of the state militia, as makes it impossible to declare one, without declaring both, invalid.

This view disposes of the objection to the judgment of the Supreme Court of Illinois, which judgment was in effect that the legislation on which the indictment is based is not invalid by reason of the provisions of the Constitution of the United States which vest Congress with power to raise and support armies, and to provide for calling out, organizing, arming, and disciplining the militia, and governing such part of them as may be employed in the service of the United States, and that provision which declares that "no state shall, without the consent of Congress, . . . keep troops . . . in time of peace."

We are next to inquire whether the 5th and 6th sections of Article XI of the Military Code are in violation of the other provisions of the Constitution of the United States relied on by the plaintiff in error. The first of these is the Second Amendment, which declares: "A well regulated militia being necessary to the security of a free state, the right of the people to keep and bear arms shall not be infringed."

We think it clear that the sections under consideration, which only forbid bodies of men to associate together as military organizations, or to drill or parade with arms in cities and towns unless authorized by law, do not infringe the right of the people to keep and bear arms. But a conclusive answer to the contention that this amendment prohibits the legislation in question lies in the fact that the amendment is a limitation only upon the power of Congress and the national government, and not upon that of the state. It was so held by this Court in the case of *United States v. Cruikshank,* in which THE CHIEF JUSTICE, in delivering the judgment of the Court, said that the right of the people to keep and bear arms

> "is not a right granted by the Constitution. Neither is it in any manner dependent upon that instrument for its existence. The Second Amendment declares that it shall not be infringed, but this, as has been seen, means no more than that it shall not be infringed by Congress. This is one of the amendments that has no other effect than to restrict the powers of the national government, leaving the people to look for their protection

against any violation by their fellow citizens of the rights it recognizes to what is called in *City of New York v. Miln,* 11 Pet. 102, 36 U. S. 139, the 'powers which relate to merely municipal legislation, or what was perhaps more properly called internal police,' 'not surrendered or restrained' by the Constitution of the United States."

It is undoubtedly true that all citizens capable of bearing arms constitute the reserved military force or reserve militia of the United States as well as of the states, and, in view of this prerogative of the general government, as well as of its general powers, the states cannot, even laying the constitutional provision in question out of view, prohibit the people from keeping and bearing arms so as to deprive the United States of their rightful resource for maintaining the public security, and disable the people from performing their duty to the general government. But as already stated, we think it clear that the sections under consideration do not have this effect.

The plaintiff in error next insists that the sections of the Military Code of Illinois under which he was indicted are an invasion of that clause of the first section of the Fourteenth Amendment to the Constitution of the United States which declares "No state shall make or enforce any law which shall abridge the privileges or immunities of citizens of the United States." It is only the privileges and immunities of citizens of the United States that the clause relied on was intended to protect. A state may pass laws to regulate the privileges and immunities of its own citizens, provided that in so doing it does not abridge their privileges and immunities as citizens of the United States. The inquiry is therefore pertinent what privilege or immunity of a citizen of the United States is abridged by sections 5 and 6 of Article XI of the Military Code of Illinois?

The plaintiff in error was not a member of the organized volunteer militia of the State of Illinois, nor did he belong to the troops of the United States or to any organization under the militia law of the United States. On the contrary, the fact that he did not belong to the organized militia or the troops of the United States was an ingredient in the offense for which he was convicted and sentenced. The question is therefore had he a right as a citizen of the United States, in disobedience of the state law, to associate with others as a military company and to drill and parade with arms in the towns and cities of the state? If the plaintiff in error has any such privilege, he must be able to point to the provision of the Constitution or statutes of the United States by which it is conferred. For, as was said by this Court in *United States v. Cruikshank,* the government of the United States, although it is

> "within the scope of its powers supreme and above the states, . . . can neither grant nor secure to its citizens any right or privilege not expressly or by implication placed under its jurisdiction. . . . All that cannot be so granted or so secured are left to the exclusive protection of the state."

We have not been referred to any statute of the United States which confers upon the plaintiff in error the privilege which he asserts. The only clause in the Constitution which upon any pretense could be said to have any relation whatever to his right to associate with others as a military company is found in the First Amendment, which declares that

> "Congress shall make no laws . . . abridging . . . the right of the people peaceably to assemble and to petition the government for a redress of grievances."

This is a right which it was held in *United States v. Cruikshank,* above cited, was an attribute of national citizenship, and, as such, under the protection of and guaranteed by the United States. But it was held in the same case that the right peaceably to assemble was not protected by the clause referred to unless the purpose of the assembly was to petition the government for a redress of grievances.

The right voluntarily to associate together as a military company or organization or to drill or parade with arms without and independent of an act of Congress or law of the state authorizing the same is not an attribute of national citizenship. Military organization and military drill and parade under arms are subjects especially under the control of the government of every country. They cannot be claimed as a right independent of law. Under our political system, they are subject to the regulation and control of the state and federal governments, acting in due regard to their respective prerogatives and powers. The Constitution and laws of the United States will be searched in vain for any support to the view that these rights are privileges and immunities of citizens of the United States independent of some specific legislation on the subject.

It cannot be successfully questioned that the state governments, unless restrained by their own constitutions, have the power to regulate or prohibit associations and meetings of the people, except in the case of peaceable assemblies to perform the duties or exercise the privileges of citizens of the United States, and have also the power to control and regulate the organization, drilling, and parading of military bodies and associations, except when such bodies or associations, are authorized by the militia laws of the United States. The exercise of this power by the states is necessary to the public peace, safety, and good order. To deny the power would be to deny the right of the state to disperse assemblages organized for sedition and treason, and the right to suppress armed mobs bent on riot and rapine.

In the case of *New York v. Miln,* this Court said:

> "We choose rather to plant ourselves on what we consider impregnable positions. They are these: that a state has the same undeniable and unlimited jurisdiction over all persons and things within its territorial limits as any foreign nation where that jurisdiction is not surrendered or restrained by the Constitution of the United States; that by virtue of this, it is not only the right but the bounden and solemn duty of a state to advance the safety, happiness, and prosperity of its people and to provide for its general welfare by any and every act of legislation which it may deem to be conducive to these ends where the power over the particular subject or the manner of its exercise is not surrendered or restrained in the manner just stated," namely by the Constitution and laws of the United States. These considerations and authorities sustain the power exercised by the Legislature of Illinois in the enactment of sections 5 and 6 of Article XI of the Military Code.

The argument of the plaintiff in error that the legislation mentioned deprives him of either life, liberty, or property without due process of law, or that it is a bill of attainder or *ex post facto* law is so clearly untenable as to require no discussion.

It is next contended by the plaintiff in error that sections 5 and 6 of Article XI of the Military Code, under which he was indicted, are in conflict with the acts of Congress for the organization of the militia. But this position is based on what seems to us to be an unwarranted construction of the sections referred to. It is clear that their object was to forbid voluntary military associations, unauthorized by law, from organizing or drilling and parading with arms in the cities or towns of the state, and not to interfere with the organization, arming and drilling of the militia under the authority of the acts of Congress. If the object and effect of the sections were in irreconcilable conflict with the acts of Congress, they would, of course, be invalid. But it is a rule of construction that a statute must be interpreted so as, if possible, to make it consistent with the Constitution and the paramount law. If we yielded to this contention of the plaintiff in error, we should render the sections invalid by giving them a strained construction, which would make them antagonistic to the law of Congress. We cannot attribute to the legislature, unless compelled to do so by its plain words, a purpose to pass an act in conflict with an act of Congress on a subject over which Congress is given authority by the Constitution of the United States. We are therefore of opinion that, fairly construed, the sections of the Military Code referred to do not conflict with the laws of Congress on the subject of the militia.

The plaintiff in error further insists that the organization of the Lehr und Wehr Verein as a corporate body under the general corporation law of the State of Illinois was in effect a license from the governor within the meaning of section 5 of Article XI of the Military Code, and that such corporate body fell within the exception of the same section "of students in educational institutions where military science is a part of the course of instruction."

In respect to these points, we have to say that they present no federal question. It is not, therefore, our province to consider or decide them.

All the federal questions presented by the record were rightly decided by the Supreme Court of Illinois.

Judgment affirmed.

Lehr & Wehr Verein poster.

Document Themes

Presser v. Illinois has a bearing on two issues. One has to do with the "incorporation doctrine." This is the constitutional doctrine through which the first ten amendments to the Constitution—the Bill of Rights—are made applicable in the states through the Due Process clause of the Fourteenth Amendment (1868). Woods writes: "It cannot be successfully questioned that the state governments, unless restrained by their own constitutions, have the power to regulate or prohibit associations and meetings of the people." Then, quoting an earlier case, *New York v. Miln* (1837), he notes that "a state has the same undeniable and unlimited jurisdiction over all persons and things within its territorial limits as any foreign nation where that jurisdiction is not surrendered or restrained by the Constitution of the United States; that by virtue of this, it is not only the right but the bounden and solemn duty of a state to advance the safety, happiness, and prosperity of its people and to provide for its general welfare by any and every act of legislation which it may deem to be conducive to these ends where the power over the particular subject or the manner of its exercise is not surrendered or restrained in the manner just stated." Accordingly, the argument that the state of Illinois had usurped the authority of the federal government in prohibiting paramilitary organizations from parade while exercising a Second Amendment right to bear arms was invalid.

The other issue involves the relationship between the citizenry, the militia, and the right to bear arms. Woods quotes from *United States v. Cruikshank*, stating that the right of the people to keep and bear arms "is not a right granted by the Constitution. Neither is it in any manner dependent upon that instrument for its existence. The Second Amendment declares that it shall not be infringed, but this, as has been seen, means no more than that it shall not be infringed by Congress. This is one of the amendments that has no other effect than to restrict the powers of the national government. . . ." The key passage from the opinion then is this:

> It is undoubtedly true that all citizens capable of bearing arms constitute the reserved military force or reserve militia of the United States as well as of the states, and, in view of this prerogative of the general government, as well as of its general powers, the states cannot, even laying the constitutional provision in question out of view, prohibit the people from keeping and bearing arms so as to deprive the United States of their rightful resource for maintaining the public security, and disable the people from performing their duty to the general government. But as already stated, we think it clear that the sections under consideration do not have this effect.

The conclusion that jurists and scholars have drawn is that the Court was asserting the principal that the right "to keep and bear Arms" is to be read in the context of service in the militia, not as an assertion of an individual right.

Additional Reading

Carter, Gregg Lee, *The Gun Control Movement* (New York: Twayne, 1997).

Cottrol, Robert J., "*Presser v. Illinois,*" in *The Oxford Guide to United States Supreme Court Decisions*, edited by Kermit L. Hall (New York: Oxford University Press, 1999), p. 244.

Halbrook, Stephen P., "The Right of Workers to Assemble and to Bear Arms: *Presser v. Illinois*, One of the Last Holdouts Against Application of the Bill of Rights to the States," *University of Detroit Mercy Law Review*, Vol 76 (Summer 1999): 943–89.

Spitzer, Robert J., *Gun Control: A Documentary and Reference Guide* (Westport, CT: Greenwood Press, 2009).

Story, Allan C., ed., *Presser v. State of Illinois* U.S. Supreme Court Transcript of Record with Supporting Pleadings (Detroit, MI: Gale, 2011).

—Michael J. O'Neal

The General Principles of Constitutional Law in the United States of America

Author(s): Thomas M. Cooley and Andrew C. McLaughlin
Date: 1898
Genre: Treatise

Summary Overview

The General Principles of Constitutional Law in the United States of America was first published in 1880; a third edition was published in 1898. The treatise was originally written by Thomas M. Cooley, who died in 1898, so preparation of the third edition was turned over to Andrew C. McLaughlin. Cooley was a prominent jurist in Michigan, as well as a legal writer whose work continues to be cited in discussions of constitutional law as it was understood in the nineteenth century. In *General Principles*, Cooley examines each of the amendments of the Bill of Rights, including, of course, the Second Amendment. In common with other scholars of the period, he attempts to specify what right the amendment granted and to whom it was granted.

Defining Moment

No particular event took place that led to the publication of Cooley's remarks on the Second Amendment. Throughout the nineteenth century, numerous legal scholars tackled the issue of the meaning of the amendment. They made efforts to define precisely what was meant by "keeping" and "bearing" arms, and they tried to clarify the relationship between the two clauses of the amendment, the first referring to a "well regulated Militia," the second specifying that the right to keep and bear arms "shall not be infringed." These legal scholars, in various treatises on constitutional law that were used in law schools, took up the issue of whether the amendment grants *individuals* the right to bear arms or whether it grants to states the right to maintain a militia for the common defense.

In general, scholars such as Cooley came down on the "individual right" side of the issue—that is, they argued that the Second Amendment grants to individuals the right to bear arms independent of their participation in a state militia. The statements of many of these scholars continue to be quoted by gun control opponents, who argue that American frontier traditions, combined with legal scholarship, grant to the individual the right to own firearms and that the government oversteps its constitutional authority when it passes gun control legislation.

About the Author

Thomas McIntyre Cooley was born on January 26, 1824, in Attica, New York. In 1842 he began studying law as an apprentice in New York. The following year, he moved to Adrian, Michigan, where he continued his apprenticeship in the study of law and, in 1846, was admitted to the Michigan bar. He built a small legal practice while becoming active in a number of other pursuits.

He was an opponent of slavery; he edited pro-Democratic newspapers; and he founded the Michigan branch of the Free Soil Party, although he changed his party affiliation to Republican in 1856. He went on to compile Michigan's statutes and worked as a reporter for the Michigan Supreme Court. He began his career as an educator when he moved to Ann Arbor, Michigan, in 1859 to become one of the first professors at the University of Michigan Law School. He served on the faculty of the law school until 1884; from 1871 to 1883, he served as dean of the law school. Meanwhile, in 1864 he was elected to the Supreme Court of Michigan and served as its chief justice for two decades.

Cooley's first major publication was *A Treatise on the Constitutional Limitations Which Rest Upon the Legislative Power of the States of the American Union* (1868), followed by *A Treatise on the Law of Torts or the Wrongs Which Arise Independently of Contract* (1878). *The General Principles of Constitutional Law in the United States of America* was first published in 1880.

Cooley might have gained an appointment to the U.S. Supreme Court, but he left the Republican Party to support Grover Cleveland for the presidency. Cleveland rewarded him for his support by nominating him as chairman of the Interstate Commerce Commission, a federal agency that Cooley in essence helped create. He died on September 12, 1898, in Ann Arbor. The Thomas M. Cooley Law School in Lansing, Michigan, was founded in his honor in 1972; since 2014, the law school has been affiliated with Western Michigan University.

HISTORICAL DOCUMENT

The General Principles of Constitutional Law in the United States of America

By the Second Amendment to the Constitution it is declared that "a well regulated militia being necessary to the security of a free State, the right of the people to keep and bear arms shall not be infringed."

The amendment, like most other provisions in the Constitution, has a history. It was adopted with some modification and enlargement from the English Bill of Eights of 1688, where it stood as a protest against arbitrary action of the overturned dynasty in disarming the people, and as a pledge of the new rulers that this tyrannical action should cease. The right declared was meant to be a strong moral check against the usurpation and arbitrary power of rulers, and as a necessary and efficient means of regaining rights when temporarily overturned by usurpation,

The Rigid is General.—It may be supposed from the phraseology of this provision that the right to keep and bear arms was only guaranteed to the militia; but this would be an interpretation not warranted by the intent. The militia, as has been elsewhere explained, consists of those persons who, under the law, are liable to the performance of military duty, and are officered and enrolled for service when called upon. But the law may make provision for the enrolment of all who are fit to perform military duty, or of a small number only, or it may wholly omit to make any provision at all; and if the right were limited to those enrolled, the purpose of this guaranty might be defeated altogether by the action or neglect to act of the government it was meant to hold in check. The meaning of the provision undoubtedly is, that the people, from whom the militia must be taken, shall have the right to keep and bear arms, and they need no permission or regulation of law for the purpose. But this enables the government to have a well regulated militia; for to bear arms implies something more than the mere keeping; it implies the learning to handle and use them in a way that makes those who keep them ready for their efficient use; in other words, it implies the right to meet for voluntary discipline in arms, observing in doing so the laws of public order.

Standing Army.—A further purpose of this amendment is, to preclude any necessity or reasonable excuse for keeping up a standing army. A standing army is condemned by the traditions and sentiments of the people, as being as dangerous to the liberties of the people as the general preparation of the people for the defence of their institutions with arms is preservative of them.

What Arms may be kept.—The arms intended by the Constitution are such as are suitable for the general defence of the community against invasion or oppression, and the secret carrying of those suited merely to deadly individual encounters may be prohibited.

THE

GENERAL PRINCIPLES

OF

CONSTITUTIONAL LAW

IN THE

UNITED STATES OF AMERICA.

BY

THOMAS M. COOLEY, LL.D.,

AUTHOR OF "CONSTITUTIONAL LIMITATIONS," ETC.

MERRITT KING, ITHACA, N.Y. Attorney & Counselor at Law, APR 18 1880

BOSTON:

LITTLE, BROWN, AND COMPANY.

1880.

PREFACE.

THE manual which follows has been prepared for the use of students in law schools and other institutions of learning. The design has been to present succinctly the general principles of constitutional law, whether they pertain to the federal system, or to the state system, or to both. Formerly, the structure of the federal constitutional government was so distinct from that of the States, that each might usefully be examined and discussed apart from the other; but the points of contact and dependence have been so largely increased by the recent amendments to the federal Constitution that a different course is now deemed advisable. Some general principles of constitutional law, which formerly were left exclusively to state protection, are now brought within the purview of the federal power, and any useful presentation of them must show the part they take in federal as well as state government. An attempt has been made to do this in the following pages.

The reader will soon discover that mere theories have received very little attention, and that the principles stated are those which have been settled, judicially or otherwise, in the practical working of the government.

THOMAS M. COOLEY.

UNIVERSITY OF MICHIGAN, ANN ARBOR,
March, 1880.

through the publication of false charges; but when the occasion is proper for petition, good motives in presenting it will be presumed, and the fact that it contains false and injurious aspersions of character will not make out a right of action, but malice in the petitioner must be established also.[1] The petition must be for something within the authority of the person or body addressed to grant, or must in good faith be supposed to be;[2] and when it is, it will be protected while circulating for signatures, as well as after it has been presented.[3] But if a false charge is merely put in the form of a petition, without the intent to present it, it is not within the privilege.[4]

SECTION IV. — THE RIGHT TO KEEP AND BEAR ARMS.

The Constitution. — By the second amendment to the Constitution it is declared that, "a well-regulated militia being necessary to the security of a free state, the right of the people to keep and bear arms shall not be infringed."

The amendment, like most other provisions in the Constitution, has a history. It was adopted with some modification and enlargement from the English Bill of Rights of 1688, where it stood as a protest against arbitrary action of the overturned dynasty in disarming the people, and as a pledge of the new rulers that this tyrannical action should cease. The right declared was meant to be a strong moral check against the usurpation and arbitrary power of rulers, and as a necessary and efficient means of regaining rights when temporarily overturned by usurpation.[5]

[1] Gray *v.* Pentland, 2 S. & R. (Penn.) 23; Howard *v.* Thompson, 21 Wend. (N. Y.) 319.

[2] See Fairman *v.* Ives, 5 B. & Ald. 642.

[3] Vanderzee *v.* McGregor, 12 Wend. (N. Y.) 545.

[4] State *v.* Burnham, 9 N. H. 34.

[5] 1 Tuck. Bl. Com., App. 300.

The Right is General. — It might be supposed from the phraseology of this provision that the right to keep and bear arms was only guaranteed to the militia; but this would be an interpretation not warranted by the intent. The militia, as has been elsewhere explained, consists of those persons who, under the law, are liable to the performance of military duty, and are officered and enrolled for service when called upon. But the law may make provision for the enrolment of all who are fit to perform military duty, or of a small number only, or it may wholly omit to make any provision at all; and if the right were limited to those enrolled, the purpose of this guaranty might be defeated altogether by the action or neglect to act of the government it was meant to hold in check. The meaning of the provision undoubtedly is, that the people, from whom the militia must be taken, shall have the right to keep and bear arms; and they need no permission or regulation of law for the purpose. But this enables the government to have a well-regulated militia; for to bear arms implies something more than the mere keeping; it implies the learning to handle and use them in a way that makes those who keep them ready for their efficient use; in other words, it implies the right to meet for voluntary discipline in arms, observing in doing so the laws of public order.

Standing Army. — A further purpose of this amendment is, to preclude any necessity or reasonable excuse for keeping up a standing army. A standing army is condemned by the traditions and sentiments of the people, as being as dangerous to the liberties of the people as the general preparation of the people for the defence of their institutions with arms is preservative of them.

What Arms may be kept. — The arms intended by the Constitution are such as are suitable for the general defence of the community against invasion or oppression, and the secret carrying of those suited merely to deadly individual encounters may be prohibited.[1]

Section V. — Freedom of Speech and of the Press.

The Constitution. — The first amendment to the Constitution further provides that Congress shall make no law abridging the freedom of speech or of the press. What is first noticeable in this provision is that it undertakes to give no rights, but it recognizes the rights mentioned as something known, understood, and existing, and it forbids any law of Congress that shall abridge them. We are thus referred for an understanding of the protection to the pre-existing law; and this must either have been the common law, or the existing statutes of the States. The statutes, however, will be found to be nearly silent on this important subject, and the common law must be our guide.

Freedom of the Press. — De Lolme, who wrote upon the Constitution of England just before the meeting of the Constitutional Convention, and who undertook to gather from the common law the meaning of this among other principles of liberty, has expressed his conclusion thus: "The liberty of the press as established in England consists in this, that neither the courts of justice, nor any other judges whatever, are authorized to take notice of writings intended for the press, but are confined to those which are actually printed, and must in these cases proceed by the trial by jury."[2] Mr. Justice Blackstone adopted this view as undoubtedly correct,[3] and in this country it has been accepted as expressing the views of those who framed and adopted this amendment.[4] If it

[1] Andrews v. State, 3 Heisk. 165, found also with notes in 1 Green's Cr. Rep. 466, and 8 Am. Rep. 8.

[2] De Lolme, Const. of Eng., ch. 10.

[3] 4 Bl. Com. 151.

[4] Rawle on Const., ch. 10; 2 Kent, 17; Story on Const., § 1889; Commonwealth v. Blanding, 3 Pick. (Mass.) 304, 313.

Document Themes

Cooley struck a number of themes that were common in nineteenth-century jurisprudence as it pertained to the Second Amendment and the right to bear arms. After quoting the amendment, he notes that it derived from the 1689 English Bill of Rights, commenting that the purpose of the provision in both bills of rights was to resist the arbitrary actions of government in disarming people. Cooley goes on to remark that the assertion of the right to bear arms served as a "moral check" on "usurpation" of arbitrary power and as a means of "regaining rights" when they have been abrogated by rulers.

Cooley then takes up the issue of the militia, asserting that the right to bear arms is "general." He then asserts that "it might be supposed from the phraseology of this provision that the right to keep and bear arms was only guaranteed to the militia; but this would be an interpretation not warranted by the intent." He points out that the militia can be defined narrowly or even be neglected by the federal government. This would defeat the purpose of the amendment, which is to hold the government in check. He reasons that "the meaning of the provision undoubtedly is, that the people, from whom the militia must be taken, shall have the right to keep and bear arms; and they need no permission or regulation of law for the purpose." Put differently, if the state is going to call up a person to serve in a militia, and if the person so called is to provide his own weapons, ammunition, and the like, then clearly the person must enjoy the right to own firearms, and this right exists even in the absence of service in the militia when the militia is not mustered.

Cooley goes on to comment on the arms that may be kept. He notes that the Constitution's intent was that people could keep arms that were suitable "for the general defence of the community against invasion or oppression." Accordingly, the government may prohibit any weapon that is suited "merely to deadly individual encounters." The statement would clearly have a bearing on the issue of whether the government can place limits on the right of people to carry arms, whether openly or concealed.

Additional Reading

Carrington, Paul D., "The Constitutional Law Scholarship of Thomas McIntyre Cooley," *American Journal of Legal History* 41 (1997): 368–99.

Jones, Alan, "Thomas M. Cooley and the Michigan Supreme Court: 1865–1885," *American Journal of Legal History* 10 (1966): 97–121.

Knowlton, Jerome C., "Thomas McIntyre Cooley," *Michigan Law Review* 5 (March 1907): 309–25.

Kopel, David B., "The Second Amendment in the Nineteenth Century," *BYU Law Review* 4 (1998): 1359–1554.

Michigan Law: University of Michigan, "Thomas M. Cooley," *History and Traditions*, http://www.law.umich.edu/historyandtraditions/faculty/Faculty_Lists/Alpha_Faculty/Pages/Cooley_ThomasM.aspx.

Mocsary, George A., "Explaining Away the Obvious: The Infeasibility of Characterizing the Second Amendment as a Nonindividual Right," *Fordham Law Review* 76 (2008): 2113–75.

—*Michael J. O'Neal*

FASKEN LEARNING RESOURCE CENTER
9000089778

REFERENCE

KF 3941 .A68 G86 V. 1 The gun debate /

89779

REFERENCE

KF The gun debate /
3941
.A68
G86
V. 2

WITHDRAWN

REFERENCE

FASKEN LEARNING RESOURCE CENTER

9000089779

89779

DEFINING DOCUMENTS IN AMERICAN HISTORY

The Gun Debate

89779

DEFINING DOCUMENTS
IN AMERICAN HISTORY

The Gun Debate

Volume 2

Editor

Michael J. O'Neal

SALEM PRESS
A Division of EBSCO Information Services, Inc.
Ipswich, Massachusetts

GREY HOUSE PUBLISHING

Front page of a newspaper announcing the second Militia Act of 1792. (From the *Columbian Centinel.*)

Copyright © 2019 by EBSCO Information Services, Inc., and Grey House Publishing, Inc.

Defining Documents in American History: The Gun Debate, published by Grey House Publishing, Inc., Amenia, NY, under exclusive license from EBSCO Information Services, Inc.

All rights reserved. No part of this work may be used or reproduced in any manner whatsoever or transmitted in any form or by any means, electronic or mechanical, including photocopy, recording, or any information storage and retrieval system, without written permission from the copyright owner. For permissions requests, contact proprietarypublishing@ebsco.com.

∞ The paper used in these volumes conforms to the American National Standard for Permanence of Paper for Printed Library Materials, Z39.48 1992 (R2009).

Publisher's Cataloging-In-Publication Data
(Prepared by The Donohue Group, Inc.)

Names: O'Neal, Michael, 1949- editor.
Title: The gun debate / editor, Michael O'Neal, PhD.
Other Titles: Defining documents in American history (Salem Press)
Description: [First edition]. | Ipswich, Massachusetts : Salem Press, a division of EBSCO Information Services ; Amenia, NY : Grey House Publishing, [2019] | Includes bibliographical references and index.
Identifiers: ISBN 9781642650341 (set) | ISBN 9781642653205 (v. 1) | ISBN 9781642653212 (v. 2)
Subjects: LCSH: Firearms--Law and legislation--United States--Sources. | Gun control--United States--Sources.
Classification: LCC KF3941.A68 G86 2019 | DDC 363.3/3/0973/03--dc23

FIRST PRINTING
PRINTED IN THE UNITED STATES OF AMERICA

Contents

Volume 1

Volume 2

The Modern Court System Weighs In

Responses to the Debate

Appendixes

The Modern Court System Weighs In

"In the absence of any evidence tending to show that possession or use of a 'shotgun having a barrel of less than eighteen inches in length' at this time has some reasonable relationship to the preservation or efficiency of a well regulated militia, we cannot say that the Second Amendment guarantees the right to keep and bear such an instrument."
—United States v. Miller (1939)

In the wake of the gun violence that appeared to be growing increasingly prevalent during Prohibition and the Roaring Twenties, Congress in 1934 passed the National Firearms Act, the first federal law to regulate firearms. The law required those engaged in the business of selling firearms to register with Internal Revenue and pay transfer taxes on firearms. The weapons themselves had to be registered, and certain types of "gangster" weapons, including Tommy guns and sawed-off shotguns, were made illegal. In 1939 the U.S. Supreme Court, in *United States v. Miller*, held that the law did not violate the Second Amendment and thus affirmed the constitutionality of the law. The case is significant because, for the first time, the High Court upheld the right of the government to impose restrictions on the scope and meaning of the Second Amendment's right to bear arms.

United States v. Miller would be the most consequential Supreme Court case bearing on the Second Amendment until *District of Columbia v. Heller* in 2008. Meanwhile, in an effort to curb what appeared to be a rising tide of gun violence, various measures had been passed at the local and federal level, including the Gun Control Act of 1968. Debates about Second Amendment rights were intensifying, with organizations such as the National Rifle Association taking an increasingly hard line in opposition to gun regulations. In this context, the court system was called on to weigh in on the issue of gun rights, leading to several significant U.S. Supreme Court cases, along with cases heard in lower appellate courts.

Some of these cases had to do with local gun bans. Landmark cases include *District of Columbia v. Heller* (2008) and *McDonald v. Chicago* (2010); in these cases, the Court invalidated local statutes banning handgun ownership. *United States v. Lopez* (1995) examined the issue of the Gun-Free School Zones Act and the complex relationship between gun control and the Commerce Clause of the Constitution; the case serves as a reminder that the federal government is limited in its powers by the explicit constitutional provisions. The Ninth Circuit U.S. Court of Appeals took up the issue of carrying concealed weapons in *Peruta v. County of San Diego* (2016), holding "that the Second Amendment does not protect, in any degree, the carrying of concealed firearms by members of the general public." The same appellate court adjudicated the issue of "open carry" of firearms in 2018 in *Young v. Hawaii*, concluding: "We are persuaded, therefore, that the right to carry a firearm openly for self-defense falls within the core of the Second Amendment."

Chapter 15A.—FIREARMS

Sec.
1132. Definitions.
1132a. Importers, manufacturers, and dealers in firearms to register with collector of internal revenue; tax.
1132b. Tax on firearms transferred; stamps; refund.
1132c. Transfer of firearms; order, form; retransfer.
1132d. Registration of firearms; presumption from failure to register.
1132e. Receiving or possessing firearm unlawfully transferred.
1132f. Seizure and forfeiture of firearms; disposition.
1132g. Identification number as mark; removal or change of mark; evidence.
1132h. Importers, manufacturers, and dealers; records.
1132i. Importation of firearms.
1132j. Transportation in interstate commerce.
1132k. Rules and regulations.
1132l. Transfers excepted.
1132m. Offenses; penalties.
1132n. Exemption from revenue taxes.
1132o. Separability of provisions.
1132p. Effective date.
1132q. Citation of chapter.

Section 1132. Definitions. For the purposes of sections 1132 to 1132q—

(a) The term "firearm" means a shotgun or rifle having a barrel of less than eighteen inches in length, or any other weapon, except a pistol or revolver, from which a shot is discharged by an explosive if such weapon is capable of being concealed on the person, or a machine gun, and includes a muffler or silencer for any firearm whether or not such firearm is included within the foregoing definition.

(b) The term "machine gun" means any weapon which shoots, or is designed to shoot, automatically or semiautomatically, more than one shot, without manual reloading, by a single function of the trigger.

(c) The term "person" includes a partnership, company, association, or corporation, as well as a natural person.

(d) The term "continental United States" means the States of the United States and the District of Columbia.

(e) The term "importer" means any person who imports or brings firearms into the continental United States for sale.

(f) The term "manufacturer" means any person who is engaged within the continental United States in the manufacture of firearms, or who otherwise produces therein any firearm for sale or disposition.

(g) The term "dealer" means any person not a manufacturer or importer engaged within the continental United States in the business of selling firearms. The term "dealer" shall include wholesalers, pawnbrokers, and dealers in used firearms.

(h) The term "interstate commerce" means transportation from any State or Territory or District, or any insular possession of the United States (including the Philippine Islands), to any other State or to the District of Columbia.

(i) The term "Commissioner" means the Commissioner of Internal Revenue.

(j) The term "Secretary" means the Secretary of the Treasury.

(k) The term "to transfer" or "transferred" shall include to sell, assign, pledge, lease, loan, give away, or otherwise dispose of. (June 26, 1934, c. 757, § 1, 48 Stat. 1236.)

§ 1132a. Importers, manufacturers and dealers in firearms to register with collector of internal revenue; tax. (a) Within fifteen days after the thirtieth day after June 26, 1934, or upon first engaging in business, and thereafter on or before the 1st day of July of each year, every importer, manufacturer, and dealer in firearms shall register with the collector of internal revenue for each district in which such business is to be carried on his name or style, principal place of business, and places of business in such district, and pay a special tax at the following rates: Importers or manufacturers, $500 a year; dealers, other than pawnbrokers, $200 a year; pawnbrokers, $300 a year. Where the tax is payable on the 1st day of July in any year it shall be computed for one year; where the tax is payable on any other day it shall be computed proportionately from the 1st day of the month in which the liability to the tax accrued to the 1st day of July following.

(b) It shall be unlawful for any person required to register under the provisions of this section to import, manufacture, or deal in firearms without having registered and paid the tax imposed by this section. (June 26, 1934, c. 757, § 2, 48 Stat. 1237.)

§ 1132b. Tax on firearms transferred; stamps; refund. (a) There shall be levied, collected, and paid upon firearms transferred in the continental United States a tax at the rate of $200 for each firearm, such tax to be paid by the transferor, and to be represented by appropriate stamps to be provided by the Commissioner, with the approval of the Secretary; and the stamps herein provided shall be affixed to the order for such firearm, hereinafter provided for. The tax imposed by this section shall be in addition to any import duty imposed on such firearm.

(b) All provisions of law (including those relating to special taxes, to the assessment, collection, remission, and refund of internal-revenue taxes, to the engraving, issuance, sale, accountability, cancelation, and distribution of tax-paid stamps provided for in the internal-revenue laws, and to penalties) applicable with respect to the taxes imposed by sections 1040 and 1383 of this title, and all other provisions of the internal-revenue laws shall, insofar as not inconsistent with the provisions of sections 1132 to 1132q of this chapter, be applicable with respect to the taxes imposed by sections 1132 to 1132q of this chapter.

(c) Under such rules and regulations as the Commissioner, with the approval of the Secretary, may prescribe, and upon proof of the exportation of any firearm to any foreign country (whether exported as part of another article or not) with respect to which the transfer tax under this section has been paid by the manufacturer, the Commissioner shall refund to the manufacturer the amount of the tax so paid, or, if the manufacturer waives all claim for the amount to be refunded, the refund shall be made to the exporter. (June 26, 1934, c. 757, § 3, 48 Stat. 1237.)

§ 1132c. Transfer of firearms; order, form; retransfer. (a) It shall be unlawful for any person to transfer a firearm except in pursuance of a written order from the person seeking to obtain such article, on an application form issued in blank in duplicate for that purpose by the Commissioner. Such order shall identify the applicant by such means of identification as may be prescribed by regulations under sections 1132 to 1132q: *Provided*, That, if the applicant is an individual, such identification shall include fingerprints and a photograph thereof.

(b) The Commissioner, with the approval of the Secretary, shall cause suitable forms to be prepared for the purposes above mentioned, and shall cause the same to be distributed to collectors of internal revenue.

(c) Every person so transferring a firearm shall set forth in each copy of such order the manufacturer's number or other mark identifying such firearm, and shall forward a copy of such order to the Commissioner. The original thereof with stamps affixed, shall be returned to the applicant.

(d) No person shall transfer a firearm which has previously been transferred on or after the thirtieth day after June 26, 1934, unless such person, in addition to complying with subsection (c), transfers therewith the stamp-affixed order provided for in this section for each such prior transfer, in compliance with such regulations as may be prescribed under sections 1132 to 1132q for proof of payment of all taxes on such firearms.

(e) If the transfer of a firearm is exempted from the provisions of sections 1132 to 1132q as provided in section 1132*l*, the person transferring such firearm shall notify the Commissioner of the name and address of the applicant, the number or other mark identifying such firearm, and the date of its transfer, and shall file with the Commissioner such documents in proof thereof as the Commissioner may by regulations prescribe.

§ 1132d TITLE 26.—INTERNAL REVENUE Page 1136

(f) Importers, manufacturers, and dealers who have registered and paid the tax as provided for in section 1132a (a) shall not be required to conform to the provisions of this section with respect to transactions in firearms with dealers or manufacturers if such dealers or manufacturers have registered and have paid such tax, but shall keep such records and make such reports regarding such transactions as may be prescribed by regulations under sections 1132 to 1132q. (June 26, 1934, c. 757, § 4, 48 Stat. 1237.)

§ 1132d. Registration of firearms; presumption from failure to register. (a) Within sixty days after the thirtieth day after June 26, 1934, every person possessing a firearm shall register, with the collector of the district in which he resides, the number or other mark identifying such firearm, together with his name, address, place where such firearm is usually kept, and place of business or employment, and, if such person is other than a natural person, the name and home address of an executive officer thereof: *Provided*, That no person shall be required to register under this section with respect to any firearm acquired after the thirtieth day after June 26, 1934, and in conformity with the provisions of sections 1132 to 1132q.

(b) Whenever on trial for a violation of section 1132e the defendant is shown to have or to have had possession of such firearm at any time after such period of sixty days without having registered as required by this section, such possession shall create a presumption that such firearm came into the possession of the defendant subsequent to the thirtieth day after June 26, 1934, but this presumption shall not be conclusive. (June 26, 1934, c. 757, § 5, 48 Stat. 1238.)

§ 1132e. Receiving or possessing firearm unlawfully transferred. It shall be unlawful for any person to receive or possess any firearm which has at any time been transferred in violation of section 1132b or 1132c. (June 26, 1934, c. 757, § 6, 48 Stat. 1238.)

§ 1132f. Seizure and forfeiture of firearms; disposition. (a) Any firearm which has at any time been transferred in violation of the provisions of sections 1132 to 1132q shall be subject to seizure and forfeiture, and (except as provided in subsection (b)) all the provisions of internal-revenue laws relating to searches, seizures, and forfeiture of unstamped articles are extended to and made to apply to the articles taxed under sections 1132 to 1132q, and the persons to whom sections 1132 to 1132q apply.

(b) In the case of the forfeiture of any firearm by reason of a violation of sections 1132 to 1132q: No notice of public sale shall be required; no such firearm shall be sold at public sale; if such firearm is in the possession of any officer of the United States except the Secretary, such officer shall deliver the firearm to the Secretary; and the Secretary may order such firearm destroyed or may sell such firearm to any State, Territory, or possession (including the Philippine Islands), or political subdivision thereof, or the District of Columbia, or retain it for the use of the Treasury Department or transfer it without charge to any Executive department or independent establishment of the Government for use by it. (June 26, 1934, c. 757, § 7, 48 Stat. 1238.)

§ 1132g. Identification number as mark; removal or change of mark; evidence. (a) Each manufacturer and importer of a firearm shall identify it with a number or other identification mark approved by the Commissioner, such number or mark to be stamped or otherwise placed thereon in a manner approved by the Commissioner.

(b) It shall be unlawful for anyone to obliterate, remove, change, or alter such number or other identification mark. Whenever on trial for a violation of this subsection the defendant is shown to have or to have had possession of any firearm upon which such number or mark shall have been obliterated, removed, changed, or altered, such possession shall be deemed sufficient evidence to authorize conviction, unless the defendant explains such possession to the satisfaction of the jury. (June 26, 1934, c. 757, § 8, 48 Stat. 1239.)

§ 1132h. Importers, manufacturers and dealers; records. Importers, manufacturers, and dealers shall keep such books and records and render such returns in relation to the transactions in firearms specified in sections 1132 to 1132q as the Commissioner, with the approval of the Secretary, may by regulations require. (June 26, 1934, c. 757, § 9, 48 Stat. 1239.)

§ 1132i. Importation of firearms. (a) No firearm shall be imported or brought into the United States or any territory under its control or jurisdiction (including the Philippine Islands), except that, under regulations prescribed by the Secretary, any firearm may be so imported or brought in when (1) the purpose thereof is shown to be lawful, and (2) such firearm is unique or of a type which cannot be obtained within the United States or such territory.

(b) It shall be unlawful (1) fraudulently or knowingly to import or bring any firearm into the United States or any territory under its control or jurisdiction (including the Philippine Islands), in violation of the provisions of sections 1132 to 1132q; or (2) knowingly to assist in so doing; or (3) to receive, conceal, buy, sell, or in any manner facilitate the transportation, concealment, or sale of any such firearm after being imported or brought in, knowing the same to have been imported or brought in contrary to law. Whenever on trial for a violation of this section the defendant is shown to have or to have had possession of such firearm, such possession shall be deemed sufficient evidence to authorize conviction unless the defendant explains such possession to the satisfaction of the jury. (June 26, 1934, c. 757, § 10, 48 Stat. 1239.)

§ 1132j. Transportation in interstate commerce. It shall be unlawful for any person who is required to register as provided in section 1132d and who shall not have so registered, or any other person who has not in his possession a stamped-affixed order as provided in section 1132c of this title, to ship, carry, or deliver any firearm in interstate commerce. (June 26, 1934, c. 757, § 11, 48 Stat. 1239.)

§ 1132k. Rules and regulations. The Commissioner, with the approval of the Secretary, shall prescribe such rules and regulations as may be necessary for carrying the provisions of sections 1132 to 1132q into effect. (June 26, 1934, c. 757, § 12, 48 Stat. 1240.)

§ 1132l. Transfers excepted. Sections 1132 to 1132q of this title shall not apply to the transfer of firearms (1) to the United States Government, any State, Territory, or possession of the United States, or to any political subdivision thereof, or to the District of Columbia; (2) to any peace officer or any Federal officer designated by regulations of the Commissioner; (3) to the transfer of any firearm which is unserviceable and which is transferred as a curiosity or ornament. (June 26, 1934, c. 757, § 13, 48 Stat. 1240.)

§ 1132m. Offenses; penalties. Any person who violates or fails to comply with any of the requirements of sections 1132 to 1132q shall, upon conviction, be fined not more than $2,000 or be imprisoned for not more than five years, or both, in the discretion of the court. (June 26, 1934, c. 757, § 14, 48 Stat. 1240.)

§ 1132n. Exemption from revenue taxes. The taxes imposed by section 1120 (a) of this title and by section 610 of the Revenue Act of 1932 (June 6, 1932, chapter 209, 47 Statutes 264), shall not apply to any firearm on which the tax provided by section 1132b of this title has been paid. (June 26, 1934, c. 757, § 15, 48 Stat. 1240.)

"Section 610 of the Revenue Act of 1932", referred to in the text of this section, is set out in note under section 1481 of this title.

§ 1132o. Separability of provisions. If any provision of sections 1132 to 1132q, or the application thereof to any person or circumstance, is held invalid, the remainder of sections 1132 to 1132q, and the application of such provision to other persons or circumstances, shall not be affected thereby. (June 26, 1934, c. 757, § 16, 48 Stat. 1240.)

§ 1132p. Effective date. Sections 1132 to 1132q shall take effect on the thirtieth day after June 26, 1934. (June 26, 1934, c. 757, § 17, 48 Stat. 1240.)

§ 1132q. Citation of chapter. This chapter (sections 1132 to 1132q) may be cited as the "National Firearms Act." (June 26, 1934, c. 757, § 18, 48 Stat. 1240.)

Chapter 16.—SAFE-DEPOSIT BOXES

Section 1134. Tax. (a) There shall be imposed a tax equivalent to 10 per centum of the amount collected on or after June 21, 1932, for the use after such date of any safe deposit box, such tax to be paid by the person paying for the use of the safe deposit box.

(b) For the purposes of this section any vault, safe, box, or other receptacle, of not more than 40 cubic feet capacity, used for the safekeeping or storage of jewelry, plate, money, specie, bullion, stocks, bonds, securities, valuable papers of any kind, or other valuable personal property, shall be regarded as a safe deposit box.

(c) Every person making any collections specified in subsection (a) shall collect the amount of tax imposed by such subsection from the person paying for the use of the safe deposit box, and shall on or before the last day of each month make a return, under oath, for the preceding month, and pay the tax imposed by subsection (a), to the collector for the district in which is located his principal place of business, or, if he has no principal place of business in the United States, then to the collector at Baltimore, Maryland. Such returns shall contain such information and be made in such manner as the Commissioner, with the approval of the Secretary, may by regulations prescribe. (June 6, 1932, c. 209, § 741, 47 Stat. 276.)

§ 1135. Payment of tax. The tax imposed by this chapter shall, without assessment by the Commissioner or notice from the collector, be due and payable to the collector at the time fixed for filing the return. If the tax is not paid when due, there shall be added, as part of the tax, interest at the rate of 1 per centum a month from the time the tax became due until paid. (June 6, 1932, c. 209, § 771, 47 Stat. 277.)

§ 1136. Refunds and credits. (a) Credit or refund of any overpayment of tax imposed by this chapter may be allowed to the person who collected the tax and paid it to the United States if such person establishes, to the satisfaction of the Commissioner, under such regulations as the Commissioner with the approval of the Secretary may prescribe, that he has repaid the amount of such tax to the person from whom he collected it, or obtained the consent of such person to the allowance of such credit or refund.

(b) Any person entitled to refund of tax under this chapter paid, or collected and paid, to the United States by him may take credit therefor against taxes due upon any monthly return.

(c) Any person making a refund of any payment on which tax under this chapter has been collected, may repay therewith the amount of tax collected on such payment, and the amount of tax so repaid may be credited against the tax under any subsequent return. (June 6, 1932, c. 209, § 772, 47 Stat. 277.)

§ 1137. Regulations. The Commissioner, with the approval of the Secretary, shall prescribe and publish all needful rules and regulations for the enforcement of this chapter. (June 6, 1932, c. 209, § 773, 47 Stat. 278.)

§ 1138. Applicability of administrative provisions. All provisions of law (including penalties) applicable in respect of the taxes imposed by subchapter A of chapter 8, shall, insofar as applicable and not inconsistent with this chapter, be applicable in respect of the tax imposed by this chapter. (June 6, 1932, c. 209, § 774, 47 Stat. 278.)

93859°—35——72

Chapter 17.—CIRCULATION OTHER THAN OF NATIONAL BANKS

Section 1140. Rate of tax—(a) Average circulation outstanding. There shall be levied, collected, and paid—

(1) Entire circulation. A tax of one-twelfth of 1 per centum each month upon the average amount of circulation issued by any bank, association, corporation, company, or person, including as circulation all certified checks and all notes and other obligations calculated or intended to circulate or to be used as money, but not including that in the vault of the bank, or redeemed and on deposit for said bank; and

(2) Circulation exceeding 90% of capital. An additional tax of one-sixth of 1 per centum each month upon the average amount of such circulation, issued as aforesaid, beyond the amount of 90 per centum of the capital of any such bank, association, corporation, company, or person.

In the case of banks with branches, the tax herein provided shall be assessed upon the circulation of each branch severally, and the amount of capital of each branch shall be considered to be the amount allotted to it. (R. S. § 3408.)

(b) Circulation paid out—(1) Own circulation. Every person, firm, association other than national bank associations, and every corporation, State bank, or State banking association, shall pay a tax of 10 per centum on the amount of their own notes used for circulation and paid out by them. (Feb. 8, 1875, c. 36, § 19, 18 Stat. 311.)

(2) Other circulation. Every such person, firm, association, corporation, State bank, or State banking association, and also every national banking association, shall pay a like tax of 10 per centum on the amount of notes of any person, firm, association other than a national banking association, or of any corporation, State bank, or State banking association, or of any town, city, or municipal corporation, used for circulation and paid out by them. (Feb. 8, 1875, c. 36, § 20, 18 Stat. 311.)

§ 1141. Exemption from tax—(a) Circulation reduced to not over five per centum of capital. Whenever the outstanding circulation of any bank, association, corporation, company, or person is reduced to an amount not exceeding 5 per centum of the chartered or declared capital existing at the time the same was issued, said circulation shall be free from taxation; and

(b) Circulation under redemption in whole. Whenever any bank which has ceased to issue notes for circulation deposits in the Treasury of the United States, in lawful money, the amount of its outstanding circulation, to be redeemed at par, under such regulations as the Secretary shall prescribe, it shall be

Sale of Firearms IRS

United States v. Miller

Author(s): James Clark McReynolds (Justice of the Supreme Court)
Date: 1939
Genre: Court decision (Supreme Court)

Summary Overview

United States v. Miller was the U.S. Supreme Court's most significant case bearing on the meaning of the Second Amendment until *District of Columbia v. Heller* in 2008. The High Court asserted that the federal government had the right to control certain types of weapons, including such "gangster" weapons as sawed-off shotguns and "Tommy guns" (a submachine gun that took its name from its inventor, John T. Thompson). The case is significant because for the first time the High Court upheld the government's right to impose restrictions on the scope and meaning of the Second Amendment's right to bear arms.

Defining Moment

The Prohibition era of the 1920s and early 1930s were a chaotic time in America, marked by the rise of mobsters and criminal enterprises that often relied on unrestricted firepower to protect their interests. Out of this chaos came the National Firearms Act of 1934, the first federal law that dealt with the regulation of firearms. The law required that anyone engaged in the business of selling certain types of firearms had to register with the agency that would become the Internal Revenue Service and pay taxes on the transfer of firearms. Further, the law required that the weapons themselves be registered. A chief purpose to the act was to protect the public from highly dangerous weapons that had become prevalent in gangland wars. Among these weapons were machine guns, sawed-off shotguns (that is, shotguns with a barrel less than eighteen inches long), silencers, bazookas, bombs, and grenades. The intention of the statute was to prevent these weapons from being acquired and used by criminals.

United States v. Miller arose when two men, Jack Miller and Frank Layton, were indicted under the law for transporting an unregistered sawed-off shotgun across state lines (from Oklahoma to Arkansas). The two men challenged the constitutionality of the law, argument that the law violated their Second Amendment right to keep and bear arms and represented a usurpation of state police power by the federal government. The Court ruled against the two men and upheld the constitutionality of the National Firearms Act.

About the Author

Justice James Clark McReynolds, the author of the Supreme Court's opinion in the case of *United States v. Miller*, was born on February 3, 1862, in Elkton, Kentucky, where he was raised on a plantation. After graduating from Vanderbilt University, he studied law at the University of Virginia. Returning to Tennessee, he practiced law. In 1896 he made an unsuccessful run for Congress. Then in 1900 he began a three-year-stint as an adjunct law professor at Vanderbilt. In 1903, President Theodore Roosevelt appointed him to the position of assistant attorney general for the Antitrust Division of the Department of Justice, a position he held until 1907. He returned to the practice of law, this time in New York, but in 1913 President Woodrow Wilson appointed him attorney general of the United States. The following year, Wilson nominated him to the U.S. Supreme Court, where he served as an associate justice until 1941, often opposing the Progressive and New Deal legislation of President Franklin D. Roosevelt. He died on August 24, 1946. McReynolds, of a prickly temperament, was not a particularly popular justice. He refused to converse with the liberal Justice John Clarke, and because of his anti-Semitism, he refused to speak to Justices Louis Brandeis and Benjamin Cardozo.

HISTORICAL DOCUMENT

United States v. Miller (307 U.S. 174)

Argued: March 30, 1939

Decided: May 15, 1939

Syllabus

The National Firearms Act, as applied to one indicted for transporting in interstate commerce a 12-gauge shotgun with a barrel less than 18 inches long without having registered it and without having in his possession a stamp-affixed written order for it, as required by the Act, held:

1. Not unconstitutional as an invasion of the reserved powers of the States. Citing *Sonzinsky v. United States*, 300 U.S. 506, and Narcotic Act cases.P. 177.

2. Not violative of the Second Amendment of the Federal Constitution. P. 178.

The Court cannot take judicial notice that a shotgun having a barrel less than 18 inches long has today any reasonable relation to the preservation or efficiency of a well regulated militia, and therefore cannot say that the Second Amendment guarantees to the citizen the right to keep and bear such a weapon.

APPEAL under the Criminal Appeals Act from a judgment sustaining a demurrer to an indictment for violation of the National Firearms Act. [p175]

Opinion

Mr. Justice McReynolds delivered the opinion of the Court.

An indictment in the District Court, Western District Arkansas, charged that Jack Miller and Frank Layton did unlawfully, knowingly, willfully, and feloniously transport in interstate commerce from the town of Claremore in the State of Oklahoma to the town of Siloam Springs in the State of Arkansas a certain firearm, to-wit, a double barrel 12-gauge Stevens shotgun having a barrel less than 18 inches in length, bearing identification number 76230, said defendants, at the time of so transporting said firearm in interstate commerce as aforesaid, not having registered said firearm as required by Section 1132d of Title 26, United States Code (Act of June 26, 1934, c. 737, Sec. 4 [§ 5], 48 Stat. 1237), and not having in their possession a stamp-affixed written order for said firearm as provided by Section 1132c, Title 2, United States Code (June 26, 1934, c. 737, Sec. 4, 48 Stat. 1237) and the regulations issued under authority of the said Act of Congress known as the "National Firearms Act," approved June 26, 1934, contrary to the form of the statute in such case made and provided, and against the peace and dignity of the United States. [n1]

A duly interposed demurrer alleged: the National Firearms Act is not a revenue measure, but an attempt to usurp police power reserved to the States, and is therefore unconstitutional. Also, it offends the inhibition of the Second Amendment to the Constitution—"A well regulated Militia, being necessary to the security of a free State, the right of people to keep and bear Arms, shall not be infringed."

The District Court held that section eleven of the Act violates the Second Amendment. It accordingly sustained the demurrer and quashed the indictment.

The cause is here by direct appeal.

Considering *Sonzinsky v. United States* (1937), 300 U.S. 506, 513, and what was ruled in sundry causes arising [p178] under the Harrison Narcotic Act [n2]—*United States v. JinFuey Moy* (1916), 241 U.S. 394, *United States v. Doremus* (1919), 249 U.S. 86, 94; *Linder v. United States* (1925), 268 U.S. 5; *Alston v. United States* (1927), 274 U.S. 289; *Nigro v. United States* (1928), 276 U.S. 332—the objection that the Act usurps police power reserved to the States is plainly untenable.

In the absence of any evidence tending to show that possession or use of a "shotgun having a barrel of less than eighteen inches in length" at this time has some reasonable relationship to the preservation or efficiency of a well regulated militia, we cannot say that the Second Amendment guarantees the right to keep and bear such an instrument. Certainly it is not within judicial notice that this weapon is any part of the ordinary military equipment, or that its use could contribute to the common defense.

The Constitution, as originally adopted, granted to the Congress power—

> "To provide for calling forth the Militia to execute the Laws of the Union, suppress Insurrections and repel Invasions; To provide for organizing, arming, and disciplining, the Militia, and for governing such Part of them as may be employed in the Service of the United States, reserving to the States respectively, the Appointment of the Officers, and the Authority of training the Militia according to the discipline prescribed by Congress."

With obvious purpose to assure the continuation and render possible the effectiveness of such forces, the declaration and guarantee of the Second Amendment were made. It must be interpreted and applied with that end in view.

The Militia which the States were expected to maintain and train is set in contrast with Troops which they were forbidden to keep without the consent of Congress. The sentiment of the time strongly disfavored standing armies; the common view was that adequate defense of country and laws could be secured through the Militia—civilians primarily, soldiers on occasion.

The signification attributed to the term Militia appears from the debates in the Convention, the history and legislation of Colonies and States, and the writings of approved commentators. These show plainly enough that the Militia comprised all males physically capable of acting in concert for the common defense. "A body of citizens enrolled for military discipline." And further, that ordinarily, when called for service these men were expected to appear bearing arms supplied by themselves and of the kind in common use at the time.

Blackstone's Commentaries, Vol. 2, Ch. 13, p. 409 points out "that king Alfred first settled a national militia in this kingdom," and traces the subsequent development and use of such forces.

Adam Smith's *Wealth of Nations*, Book V, Ch. 1, contains an extended account of the Militia. It is there said: "Men of republican principles have been jealous of a standing army as dangerous to liberty."

> "In a militia, the character of the labourer, artificer, or tradesman, predominates over that of the soldier: in a standing army, that of the soldier predominates over every other character, and in this distinction seems to consist the essential difference between those two different species of military force."

"The American Colonies in the 17th Century," Osgood, Vol. 1, ch. XIII, affirms in reference to the early system of defense in New England—

> "In all the colonies, as in England, the militia system was based on the principle of the assize of arms. This implied the general obligation of all adult male inhabitants to possess arms, and, with certain exceptions, to cooperate in the work of defence.
>
> The possession of arms also implied the possession of ammunition, and the authorities paid quite as much attention to the latter as to the former.
>
> A year later [1632] it was ordered that any single man who had not furnished himself with arms might be put out to service, and this became a permanent part of the legislation of the colony [Massachusetts]."

Also,

> "Clauses intended to insure the possession of arms and ammunition by all who were subject to military service appear in all the important enactments concerning military affairs. Fines were the penalty for delinquency, whether of towns or individuals. According to the usage of the times, the infantry of Massachusetts consisted of pikemen and musketeers. The law, as enacted in 1649 and thereafter, provided that each of the former should be armed with a pike, corselet, head-piece, sword, and knapsack. The musketeer should carry a "good fixed musket," not under bastard musket bore, not less than three feet, nine inches, nor more than four feet three inches in length, a priming wire,

scourer, and mould, a sword, rest, bandoleers, one pound of powder, twenty bullets, and two fathoms of match. The law also required that two-thirds of each company should be musketeers."

The General Court of Massachusetts, January Session 1784, provided for the organization and government of the Militia. It directed that the Train Band should "contain all able bodied men, from sixteen to forty years of age, and the Alarm List, all other men under sixty years of age, . . ." Also,

"That every noncommissioned officer and private soldier of the said militia not under the controul of parents, masters or guardians, and being of sufficient ability therefor in the judgment of the Selectmen of the town in which he shall dwell, shall equip himself, and be constantly provided with a good fire arm etc."

By an Act passed April 4, 1786, the New York Legislature directed:

"That every able-bodied Male Person, being a Citizen of this State, or of any of the United States, and residing in this State, (except such Persons as are hereinafter excepted) and who are of the Age of Sixteen, and under the Age of Forty-five Years, shall, by the Captain or commanding Officer of the Beat in which such Citizens shall reside, within four Months after the passing of this Act, be enrolled in the Company of such Beat. . . . That every Citizen so enrolled and notified shall, within three Months thereafter, provide himself, at his own Expense, with a good Musket or Firelock, a sufficient Bayonet and Belt, a Pouch with a Box therein to contain not less than Twenty-four Cartridges suited to the Bore of his Musket or Firelock, each Cartridge containing a proper Quantity of Powder and Ball, two spare Flints, a Blanket and Knapsack; . . .

The General Assembly of Virginia, October, 1785, (12 Hening's Statutes) declared,

"The defense and safety of the commonwealth depend upon having its citizens properly armed and taught the knowledge of military duty."

It further provided for organization and control of the Militia, and directed that "All free male persons between the ages of eighteen and fifty years," with certain exceptions, "shall be inrolled or formed into companies." "There shall be a private muster of every company once in two months."

Also that

"Every officer and soldier shall appear at his respective muster-field on the day appointed, by eleven o'clock in the forenoon, armed, equipped, and accoutred, as follows: . . . every non-commissioned officer and private with a good, clean musket carrying an ounce ball, and three feet eight inches long in the barrel, with a good bayonet and iron ramrod well fitted thereto, a cartridge box properly made, to contain and secure twenty cartridges fitted to his musket, a good knapsack and canteen, and moreover, each non-commissioned officer and private shall have at every muster one pound of good [p182] powder, and four pounds of lead, including twenty blind cartridges, and each serjeant shall have a pair of moulds fit to cast balls for their respective companies, to be purchased by the commanding officer out of the monies arising on delinquencies. Provided, That the militia of the counties westward of the Blue Ridge, and the counties below adjoining thereto, shall not be obliged to be armed with muskets, but may have good rifles with proper accoutrements, in lieu thereof. And every of the said officers, non-commissioned officers, and privates, shall constantly keep the aforesaid arms, accoutrements, and ammunition ready to be produced whenever called for by his commanding officer. If any private shall make it appear to the satisfaction of the court hereafter to be appointed for trying delinquencies under this act that he is so poor that he cannot purchase the arms herein required, such court shall cause them to be purchased out of the money arising from delinquents."

General John Taliaferro Thompson holding the Thompson Sub Machine Gun M1921.

Most if not all of the States have adopted provisions touching the right to keep and bear arms. Differences in the language employed in these have naturally led to somewhat variant conclusions concerning the scope of the right guaranteed. But none of them seems to afford any material support for the challenged ruling of the court below.

In the margin, some of the more important opinions and comments by writers are cited.

We are unable to accept the conclusion of the court below, and the challenged judgment must be reversed. The cause will be remanded for further proceedings.

MR. JUSTICE DOUGLAS took no part in the consideration or decision of this cause.

1. Act of June 26, 1934, c. 757, 48 Stat. 1236-1240, 26 U.S.C. § 1132.

That for the purposes of this Act—

(a) The term "firearm" means a shotgun or rifle having a barrel of less than eighteen inches in length, or any other weapon, except a pistol or revolver, from which a shot is discharged by an explosive if such weapon is capable of being concealed on the person, or a machine gun, and includes a muffler or silencer for any firearm whether or not such firearm is included within the foregoing definition [The Act of April 10, 1936, c. 169, 49 Stat. 1192 added the words], but does not include any rifle which is within the foregoing provisions solely by reason of the length of its barrel if the caliber of such rifle is .22 or smaller and if its barrel is sixteen inches or more in length.

Sec. 3. (a) There shall be levied, collected, and paid upon firearms transferred in the continental United States a tax at the rate of $200 for each firearm, such tax to be paid by the transferor, and to be represented by appropriate stamps to be provided by the Commissioner, with the approval of the Secretary, and the stamps herein provided shall be affixed to the order for such firearm, hereinafter provided for. The tax imposed by this section shall be in addition to any import duty imposed on such firearm.

Sec. 4. (a) It shall be unlawful for any person to transfer a firearm except in pursuance of a written order from the person seeking to obtain such article, on an application form issued in blank in duplicate for that purpose by the Commissioner. Such order shall identify the applicant by such means of identification as may be prescribed by regulations under this Act: Provided, That, if the applicant is an individual, such identification shall include fingerprints and a photograph thereof.

(c) Every person so transferring a firearm shall set forth in each copy of such order the manufacturer's number or other mark identifying such firearm, and shall forward a copy of such order to the Commissioner. The original thereof, with stamps affixed, shall be returned to the applicant.

(d) No person shall transfer a firearm which has previously been transferred on or after the effective date of this Act, unless such person, in addition to complying with subsection (c), transfers therewith the stamp-affixed order provided for in this section for each such prior transfer, in compliance with such regulations as may be prescribed under this Act for proof of payment of all taxes on such firearms.

Sec. 5. (a) Within sixty days after the effective date of this Act every person possessing a firearm shall register, with the collector of the district in which he resides, the number or other mark identifying such firearm, together with his name, address, place where such firearm is usually kept, and place of business or employment, and, if such person is other than a natural person, the name and home address of an executive officer thereof: Provided, That no person shall be required to register under this section with respect to any firearm acquired after the effective date of, and in conformity with the provisions of, this Act.

Sec. 6. It shall be unlawful for any person to receive or possess any firearm which has at any time been transferred in violation of section 3 or 4 of this Act.

Sec. 11. It shall be unlawful for any person who is required to register as provided in section 5 hereof and who shall not have so registered, or any other person who has not in his possession a stamp-affixed order as provided in section 4 hereof, to ship, carry, or deliver any firearm in interstate commerce.

Sec. 12. The Commissioner, with the approval of the Secretary, shall prescribe such rules and regulations as may be necessary for carrying the provisions of this Act into effect.

Sec. 14. Any person who violates or fails to comply with any of the requirements of this Act shall, upon conviction, be fined not more than $2,000 or be imprisoned for not more than five years, or both, in the discretion of the court.

Sec. 16. If any provision of this Act, or the application thereof to any person or circumstance, is held invalid, the remainder of the Act, and the application of such provision to other persons or circumstances, shall not be affected thereby.

Sec. 18. This Act may be cited as the "National Firearms Act."

2. Act December 17, 1914, c. 1, 38 Stat. 785; February 24, 1919, c. 18, 40 Stat. 1057.

3. Concerning The Militia—Presser v. Illinois, 116 U.S. 252; Robertson v. Baldwin, 165 U.S. 275; Fife v. State, 31 Ark. 455; Jeffers v. Fair, 33 Ga. 347; Salina v. Blaksley, 72 Kan. 230; 83 P. 619; People v. Brown, 253 Mich. 537; 235 N.W. 245; Aymette v. State, 2 Humphr. (Tenn.) 154; State v. Duke, 42 Texas 455; State v. Workman, 35 W.Va. 367; 14 S.E. 9; Cooley's Constitutional Limitations, Vol. 1, p. 729; Story on The Constitution, 5th Ed., Vol. 2, p. 646; Encyclopaedia of the Social Sciences, Vol. X, p. 471, 474.

[CHAPTER 850]

June 30, 1938
[S. 3]
[Public, No. 785]

AN ACT

To regulate commerce in firearms.

Federal Firearms Act.
Definitions.

Be it enacted by the Senate and House of Representatives of the United States of America in Congress assembled, That as used in this Act—

"Person."

(1) The term "person" includes an individual, partnership, association, or corporation.

"Interstate or foreign commerce."

(2) The term "interstate or foreign commerce" means commerce between any State, Territory, or possession (including the Philippine Islands but not including the Canal Zone), or the District of Columbia, and any place outside thereof; or between points within the same State, Territory, or possession (including the Philippine Islands but not including the Canal Zone), or the District of Columbia, but through any place outside thereof; or within any Territory or possession or the District of Columbia.

"Firearm."

(3) The term "firearm" means any weapon, by whatever name known, which is designed to expel a projectile or projectiles by the action of an explosive and a firearm muffler or firearm silencer, or any part or parts of such weapon.

"Manufacturer."

(4) The term "manufacturer" means any person engaged in the manufacture or importation of firearms, or ammunition or cartridge cases, primers, bullets, or propellent powder for purposes of sale or distribution; and the term "licensed manufacturer" means any such person licensed under the provisions of this Act.

"Dealer."

(5) The term "dealer" means any person engaged in the business of selling firearms or ammunition or cartridge cases, primers, bullets or propellent powder, at wholesale or retail, or any person engaged in the business of repairing such firearms or of manufacturing or fitting special barrels, stocks, trigger mechanisms, or breach [1] mechanisms to firearms, and the term "licensed dealer" means any such person licensed under the provisions of this Act.

"Licensed dealer."

"Crime of violence."

(6) The term "crime of violence" means murder, manslaughter, rape, mayhem, kidnaping, burglary, housebreaking; assault with intent to kill, commit rape, or rob; assault with a dangerous weapon, or assault with intent to commit any offense punishable by imprisonment for more than one year.

"Fugitive from justice."

(7) The term "fugitive from justice" means any person who has fled from any State, Territory, the District of Columbia, or possession of the United States to avoid prosecution for a crime of violence or to avoid giving testimony in any criminal proceeding.

"Ammunition."

(8) The term "ammunition" shall include all pistol or revolver ammunition except .22-caliber rim-fire ammunition.

Unlawful acts.
Transportation, etc., of firearms or ammunition without license.

SEC. 2. (a) It shall be unlawful for any manufacturer or dealer, except a manufacturer or dealer having a license issued under the provisions of this Act, to transport, ship, or receive any firearm or ammunition in interstate or foreign commerce.

Knowingly receiving same.

(b) It shall be unlawful for any person to receive any firearm or ammunition transported or shipped in interstate or foreign commerce in violation of subdivision (a) of this section, knowing or having reasonable cause to believe such firearms or ammunition to have been transported or shipped in violation of subdivision (a) of this section.

Shipment to person under indictment, etc.

(d) It shall be unlawful for any person to ship, transport, or cause to be shipped or transported in interstate or foreign commerce any firearm or ammunition to any person knowing or having reasonable cause to believe that such person is under indictment or has been convicted in any court of the United States, the several States, Territories, possessions (including the Philippine Islands), or the District of Columbia of a crime of violence or is a fugutive [1] from justice.

Shipment by person under indictment, etc.

(e) It shall be unlawful for any person who is under indictment or who has been convicted of a crime of violence or who is a fugutive [1] from justice to ship, transport, or cause to be shipped or transported in interstate or foreign commerce any firearm or ammunition.

Receipt by person convicted of crime of violence, etc.

(f) It shall be unlawful for any person who has been convicted of a crime of violence or is a fugutive [1] from justice to receive any firearm or ammunition which has been shipped or transported in interstate or foreign commerce, and the possession of a firearm or ammunition by any such person shall be presumptive evidence that such firearm or ammunition was shipped or transported or received, as the case may be, by such person in violation of this Act.

Transportation of stolen firearms, etc.

(g) It shall be unlawful for any person to transport or ship or cause to be transported or shipped in interstate or foreign commerce any stolen firearm or ammunition, knowing, or having reasonable cause to believe, same to have been stolen.

Traffic in stolen firearms.

(h) It shall be unlawful for any person to receive, conceal, store, barter, sell, or dispose of any firearm or ammunition or to pledge or accept as security for a loan any firearm or ammunition moving in or which is a part of interstate or foreign commerce, and which while so moving or constituting such part has been stolen, knowing, or having reasonable cause to believe the same to have been stolen.

Transportation of firearms from which serial number has been removed.

(i) It shall be unlawful for any person to transport, ship, or knowingly receive in interstate or foreign commerce any firearm from which the manufacturer's serial number has been removed, obliterated, or altered, and the possession of any such firearm shall be presumptive evidence that such firearm was transported, shipped, or received, as the case may be, by the possessor in violation of this Act.

Licenses, application, fee.

SEC. 3. (a) Any manufacturer or dealer desiring a license to transport, ship, or receive firearms or ammunition in interstate or foreign commerce shall make application to the Secretary of the Treasury, who shall prescribe by rules and regulations the information to be contained in such application. The applicant shall, if a manufacturer, pay a fee of $25 per annum and, if a dealer, shall pay a fee of $1 per annum.

Issuance.

(b) Upon payment of the prescribed fee, the Secretary of the Treasury shall issue to such applicant a license which shall entitle the licensee to transport, ship, and receive firearms and ammunition in interstate and foreign commerce unless and until the license is suspended or revoked in accordance with the provisions of this Act: *Provided*, That no license shall be issued to any applicant within two years after the revocation of a previous license.

Proviso. Issuance after revocation.

Revocation on conviction of licensee.

(c) Whenever any licensee is convicted of a violation of any of the provisions of this Act, it shall be the duty of the clerk of the court to notify the Secretary of the Treasury within forty-eight hours after such conviction and said Secretary shall revoke such license: *Provided*, That in the case of appeal from such conviction the licensee may furnish a bond in the amount of $1,000, and upon receipt of such bond acceptable to the Secretary of the Treasury he may permit the licensee to continue business during the period of the appeal, or should the licensee refuse or neglect to furnish such bond, the Secre-

Proviso. Temporary continuance; bond.

[1] So in original.

tary of the Treasury shall suspend such license until he is notified by the clerk of the court of last appeal as to the final disposition of the case.

Dealers' records.

(d) Licensed dealers shall maintain such permanent records of importation, shipment, and other disposal of firearms and ammunition as the Secretary of the Treasury shall prescribe.

Exemptions.

Federal, State governments, agencies, etc.

Banks, carriers, etc.

Research laboratories.

Proviso.
Exemptions granted by Secretary of Treasury.

Antiques, curios, etc.

Shipments to designated institutions or persons.

Military training, etc.

SEC. 4. The provisions of this Act shall not apply with respect to the transportation, shipment, receipt, or importation of any firearm, or ammunition, sold or shipped to, or issued for the use of, (1) the United States or any department, independent establishment, or agency thereof; (2) any State, Territory, or possession, or the District of Columbia, or any department, independent establishment, agency, or any political subdivision thereof; (3) any duly commissioned officer or agent of the United States, a State, Territory, or possession, or the District of Columbia, or any political subdivision thereof; (4) or to any bank, public carrier, express, or armored-truck company organized and operating in good faith for the transportation of money and valuables; (5) or to any research laboratory designated by the Secretary of the Treasury: *Provided*, That such bank, public carriers, express, and armored-truck companies are granted exemption by the Secretary of the Treasury; nor to the transportation, shipment, or receipt of any antique or unserviceable firearms, or ammunition, possessed and held as curios or museum pieces: *Provided*, That nothing herein contained shall be construed to prevent shipments of firearms and ammunition to institutions, organizations, or persons to whom such firearms and ammunition may be lawfully delivered by the Secretary of War, nor to prevent the transportation of such firearms and ammunition so delivered by their lawful possessors while they are engaged in military training or in competitions.

Penalty provisions.

SEC. 5. Any person violating any of the provisions of this Act or any rules and regulations promulgated hereunder, or who makes any statement in applying for the license or exemption provided for in this Act, knowing such statement to be false, shall, upon conviction thereof, be fined not more than $2,000, or imprisoned for not more than five years, or both.

Effective date.

SEC. 6. This Act shall take effect thirty days after its enactment.

Rules and regulations.

SEC. 7. The Secretary of the Treasury may prescribe such rules and regulations as he deems necessary to carry out the provisions of this Act.

Separability of provisions.

SEC. 8. Should any section or subsection of this Act be declared unconstitutional, the remaining portion of the Act shall remain in full force and effect.

Short title.

SEC. 9. This Act may be cited as the Federal Firearms Act.

Approved, June 30, 1938.

[CHAPTER 851]

June 30, 1938
[S. 1131]
[Public, No. 786]

AN ACT

To amend the part of the Act entitled "An Act making appropriations for the naval service for the fiscal year ending June 30, 1921, and for other purposes", approved June 4, 1920, relating to the conservation, care, custody, protection, and operation of the naval petroleum and oil-shale reserves.

Naval petroleum reserves.
41 Stat. 813.
34 U. S. C. § 524.

Be it enacted by the Senate and House of Representatives of the United States of America in Congress assembled, That the part of the Act entitled "An Act making appropriations for the naval service for the fiscal year ending June 30, 1921, and for other purposes", approved June 4, 1920 (41 Stat. 813), relating to the conservation, care, custody, protection, and operation of the naval petroleum and

Federal Firearms Act 1938

Document Themes

Justice McReynolds, writing for a unanimous Court, immediately addressed the Second Amendment issue in his written opinion:

> In the absence of any evidence tending to show that possession or use of a "shotgun having a barrel of less than eighteen inches in length" at this time has some reasonable relationship to the preservation or efficiency of a well regulated militia, we cannot say that the Second Amendment guarantees the right to keep and bear such an instrument. Certainly it is not within judicial notice that this weapon is any part of the ordinary military equipment, or that its use could contribute to the common defense.

McReynolds went on to cite the Constitution, which gave Congress the power to call up the militia "to execute the Laws of the Union, suppress Insurrections and repel Invasions." It further granted to Congress the authority "to provide for organizing, arming, and disciplining, the Militia." He then concluded:

> With obvious purpose to assure the continuation and render possible the effectiveness of such forces, the declaration and guarantee of the Second Amendment were made. It must be interpreted and applied with that end in view.

This was a crucial comment in the history of Second Amendment jurisprudence: that the Second Amendment has to be interpreted in the context of ensuring the effectiveness of the militia, not as a guarantee of an individual's right to bear arms.

McReynolds went on to examine at some length historical legal doctrines pertaining to militias. He noted, for example, the distrust of large standing armies at the time, accompanied by the belief that the citizen-soldiers of state militias were equal to answering the threats of invasion or insurrection. He makes reference to the debates about the amendment at the Constitutional Convention, noting that the militia "comprised all males physically capable of acting in concert for the common defense" and "that ordinarily, when called for service these men were expected to appear bearing arms supplied by themselves and of the kind in common use at the time." He invokes *Blackstone's Commentaries on the Laws of England*, which dated back to the eighteenth century, and Adam Smith's *On the Wealth of Nations* (1776), both of which comment on militias. He also cites *The American Colonies in the 17th Century*, an early twentieth-century work that referred, significantly, to "the general obligation of all adult male inhabitants to possess arms, and, with certain exceptions, to cooperate in the work of defence."

McReynolds further notes: "Clauses intended to insure the possession of arms and ammunition by all who were subject to military service appear in all the important enactments concerning military affairs." McReynolds then cites New York, Massachusetts, and Virginia statutes that required men to provide their own armaments when they were summoned for militia duty. He points out, for example, that in Virginia: "Every officer and soldier shall appear at his respective muster-field on the day appointed, by eleven o'clock in the forenoon, armed, equipped, and accoutered." The Virginia statute then goes on to specify in great detail the arms and equipment that a militiaman was expected to provide. For the Supreme Court, the requirements contained in states laws bearing on the arms that a member of the militia had personally to provide strongly suggest that the Second Amendment applies to militias, not to individuals.

Additional Reading

Cornell, Saul. *A Well-Regulated Militia: The Found Fathers and the Origins of Gun Control in America*. (New York: Oxford University Press, 2006).

Frye, Brian L., "The Peculiar Story of United States v. Miller," *NYU Journal of Law & Liberty* 3, no. 1 (2008): 48–82.

Levy, Robert A., and William H. Mellor. "Gun Owners' Rights," in *The Dirty Dozen: How Twelve Supreme Court Cases Radically Expanded Government and Eroded Freedom* (New York: Sentinel), Chapter 6, pp. 107–126.

Spitzer, Robert J., *The Politics of Gun Control*, 5th ed. (Boulder, CO: Paradigm Publishers, 2012).

—*Michael J. O'Neal*

Colt's new Police Positive. (An advertisement from 1905.)

United States v. Lopez

Author(s): William Rehnquist (Chief Justice of the Supreme Court)
Date: April 26, 1995
Genre: Court decision (Supreme Court)

Summary Overview

In this case, the Supreme Court ruled, for the first time since 1936, that a federal statute was unconstitutional because Congress had overstepped its authority to regulate interstate commerce.

Defining Moment

Responding to crime in the schools, Congress in 1990 passed the Gun-Free School Zones Act, making it a federal crime to possess guns within one thousand feet of any school. More than forty states already had similar laws. After Alfonso Lopez, Jr., a high school student in San Antonio, Texas, was arrested for taking a .38-caliber handgun to school, he was tried under federal law because federal penalties were greater than they would have been under state law. The federal court of appeals, however, ruled that the 1990 statute was unconstitutional, referring to it as a "singular incursion by the federal government into territory long occupied by the states." The federal government appealed the case to the Supreme Court.

The issue of the case was the nature of federalism. Not since 1936, in *Carter v. Carter Coal Company*, had the Court overturned a statute because it exceeded federal prerogative to regulate commerce. In fact, in *Garcia v. San Antonio Metropolitan Transit Authority* (1985) the Court had ruled that the scope of the federal authority to regulate commerce was a question to be decided entirely by the political process rather than by the courts. The *Garcia* precedent was usually applauded by liberals and denounced by conservatives, but few on either side expected it to be soon overturned.

In *United States v. Lopez*, however, the Court ruled 5 to 4 that the 1990 statute did exceed Congress's authority under the commerce clause. Writing the majority opinion, Chief Justice William H. Rehnquist noted that possession of guns near a school had nothing to do with interstate commerce and that such an issue is traditionally a concern of local police power. As a principle, Rehnquist argued that Congress could regulate only "those activities that have a substantial relationship to interstate commerce." The four dissenters argued that guns in schools interfere with education and thus affect interstate commerce by damaging the national economy. Even more, they expressed deep concern that the decision would create "uncertainty" about the validity of many federal laws on the books.

AUTHENTICATED U.S. GOVERNMENT INFORMATION GPO

II

105TH CONGRESS
2D SESSION

S. 1917

To prevent children from injuring themselves and others with firearms.

IN THE SENATE OF THE UNITED STATES

APRIL 2, 1998

Mr. DURBIN (for himself, Mr. CHAFEE, Mr. REED, and Mrs. BOXER) introduced the following bill; which was read twice and referred to the Committee on the Judiciary

---

A BILL

To prevent children from injuring themselves and others with firearms.

Be it enacted by the Senate and House of Representatives of the United States of America in Congress assembled,

SECTION 1. SHORT TITLE.

This Act may be cited as the "Child Firearm Access Prevention Act".

SEC. 2. CHILDREN AND FIREARMS SAFETY.

(a) SECURE GUN STORAGE OR SAFETY DEVICE.—Section 921(a) of title 18, United States Code, is amended by adding at the end the following:

"(34) The term 'secure gun storage or safety device' means—

"(A) a device that, when installed on a firearm, prevents the firearm from being operated without first deactivating or removing the device;

"(B) a device incorporated into the design of the firearm that prevents the operation of the firearm by anyone not having access to the device; or

"(C) a safe, gun safe, gun case, lock box, or other device that is designed to be or can be used to store a firearm and that can be unlocked only by means of a key, a combination, or other similar means.".

(b) Prohibition and Penalties.—Section 922 of title 18, United States Code, is amended by adding at the end the following:

"(y) Prohibition Against Giving Juveniles Access to Certain Firearms.—

"(1) Definition of juvenile.—In this subsection, the term 'juvenile' means an individual who has not attained the age of 18 years.

"(2) Prohibition.—Except as provided in paragraph (3), any person that—

"(A) keeps a loaded firearm, or an unloaded firearm and ammunition for the firearm,

3

any of which has been shipped or transported in interstate or foreign commerce or otherwise substantially affects interstate or foreign commerce, within any premise that is under the custody or control of that person; and

"(B) knows, or reasonably should know, that a juvenile is capable of gaining access to the firearm without the permission of the parent or legal guardian of the juvenile;

shall, if a juvenile obtains access to the firearm and thereby causes death or bodily injury to the juvenile or to any other person, or exhibits the firearm either in a public place, or in violation of subsection (q), be imprisoned not more than 1 year, fined not more than $10,000, or both.

"(3) EXCEPTIONS.—Paragraph (2) does not apply if—

"(A) the person uses a secure gun storage or safety device for the firearm;

"(B) the person is a peace officer, a member of the Armed Forces, or a member of the National Guard, and the juvenile obtains the firearm during, or incidental to, the performance of the official duties of the person in that capacity;

4

"(C) the juvenile obtains, or obtains and discharges, the firearm in a lawful act of self-defense or defense of 1 or more other persons; or

"(D) the person has no reasonable expectation, based on objective facts and circumstances, that a juvenile is likely to be present on the premises on which the firearm is kept.".

(c) ROLE OF LICENSED FIREARMS DEALERS.—Section 926 of title 18, United States Code, is amended by adding at the end the following:

"(d) The Secretary shall ensure that a copy of section 922(y) appears on the form required to be obtained by a licensed dealer from a prospective transferee of a firearm.".

(d) NO EFFECT ON STATE LAW.—Nothing in this section or the amendments made by this section shall be construed to preempt any provision of the law of any State, the purpose of which is to prevent children from injuring themselves or others with firearms.

○

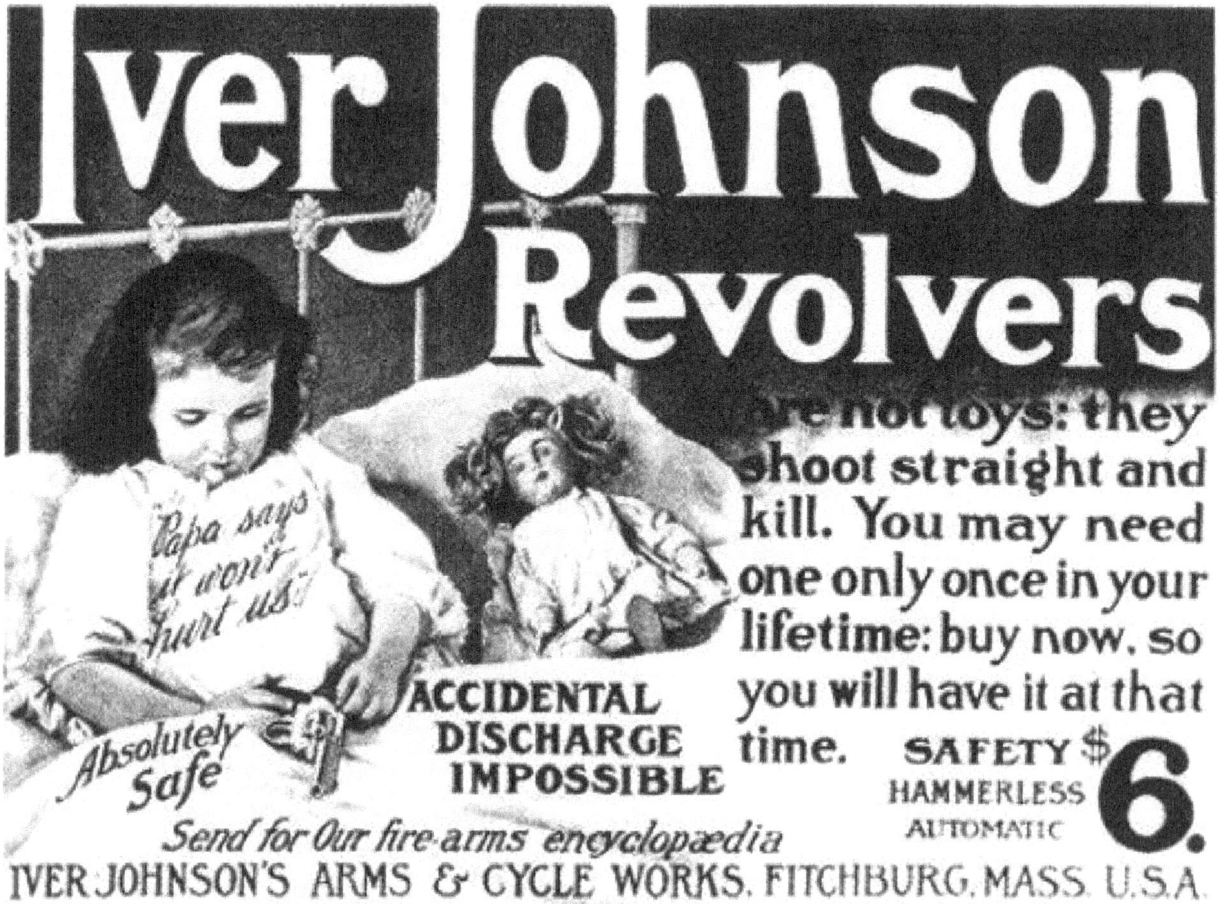

This revolver (and thus this advertisement) was only produced until 1906

HISTORICAL DOCUMENT

UNITED STATES V. LOPEZ

514 U.S. 549 (1995)
OCTOBER TERM, 1994
Syllabus
UNITED STATES v. LOPEZ
CERTIORARI TO THE UNITED STATES COURT OF APPEALS FOR THE FIFTH CIRCUIT
No. 93-1260. Argued November 8, 1994-Decided April 26, 1995

After respondent, then a 12th-grade student, carried a concealed handgun into his high school, he was charged with violating the Gun-Free School Zones Act of 1990, which forbids "any individual knowingly to possess a firearm at a place that [he] knows ... is a school zone," 18 U. S. C. § 922(q)(I)(A). The District Court denied his motion to dismiss the indictment, concluding that § 922(q) is a constitutional exercise of Congress' power to regulate activities in and affecting commerce. In reversing, the Court of Appeals held that, in light of what it characterized as insufficient congressional findings and legislative history, § 922(q) is invalid as beyond Congress' power under the Commerce Clause.

Held: The Act exceeds Congress' Commerce Clause authority. First, although this Court has upheld a wide variety of congressional Acts regulating intrastate economic activity that substantially affected interstate commerce, the possession of a gun in a local school zone is in no sense an economic activity that might, through repetition elsewhere, have such a substantial effect on interstate commerce. Section 922(q) is a criminal statute that by its terms has nothing to do with "commerce" or any sort of economic enterprise, however broadly those terms are defined. Nor is it an essential part of a larger regulation of economic activity, in which the regulatory scheme could be undercut unless the intrastate activity were regulated. It cannot, therefore, be sustained under the Court's cases upholding regulations of activities that arise out of or are connected with a commercial transaction, which, viewed in the aggregate, substantially affects interstate commerce. Second, § 922(q) contains no jurisdictional element that would ensure, through case-by-case inquiry, that the firearms possession in question has the requisite nexus with interstate commerce. Respondent was a local student at a local school; there is no indication that he had recently moved in interstate commerce, and there is no requirement that his possession of the firearm have any concrete tie to interstate commerce. To uphold the Government's contention that § 922(q) is justified because firearms possession in a local school zone does indeed substantially affect interstate commerce would require this Court to pile inference upon inference in a manner that would bid fair to convert congressional Commerce Clause authority to a general police power of the sort held only by the States. Pp. 552-568.

2 F.3d 1342, affirmed.

REHNQUIST, C. J., delivered the opinion of the Court, in which O'CONNOR, SCALIA, KENNEDY, and THOMAS, JJ., joined. KENNEDY, J., filed a concurring opinion, in which O'CONNOR, J., joined, *post*, p. 568. THOMAS, J., filed a concurring opinion, *post*, p. 584. STEVENS, J., *post*, p. 602, and SOUTER, J., *post*, p. 603, filed dissenting opinions. BREYER, J., filed a dissenting opinion, in which STEVENS, SOUTER, and GINSBURG, JJ., joined, *post*, p. 615.

In the Gun-Free School Zones Act of 1990, Congress made it a federal offense "for any individual knowingly to possess a firearm at a place that the individual knows, or has reasonable cause to believe, is a school zone." 18 U. S. C. § 922(q)(1)(A) (1988 ed., Supp. V). The Act neither regulates a commercial activity nor contains a requirement that the possession be connected in any way to interstate commerce. We hold that the Act exceeds the authority of Congress "[t]o regulate Commerce ... among the several States .... " U.S. Const., Art. I, § 8, cl. 3.

On March 10, 1992, respondent, who was then a 12th-grade student, arrived at Edison High School in San Antonio, Texas, carrying a concealed .38-caliber handgun and five bullets. Acting upon an anonymous tip, school authorities confronted respondent, who admitted that he was carrying the weapon. He was arrested and charged under Texas law with firearm possession on school premises. See Tex. Penal Code Ann. § 46.03(a)

(1) (Supp. 1994). The next day, the state charges were dismissed after federal agents charged respondent by complaint with violating the Gun-Free School Zones Act of 1990. 18 U. S. C. § 922(q)(1)(A) (1988 ed., Supp. V).1

A federal grand jury indicted respondent on one count of knowing possession of a firearm at a school zone, in violation of § 922(q). Respondent moved to dismiss his federal indictment on the ground that § 922(q) "is unconstitutional as it is beyond the power of Congress to legislate control over our public schools." The District Court denied the motion, concluding that § 922(q) "is a constitutional exercise of Congress' well-defined power to regulate activities in and affecting commerce, and the 'business' of elementary, middle and high schools ... affects interstate commerce." App. to Pet. for Cert. 55a. Respondent waived his right to a jury trial. The District Court conducted a bench trial, found him guilty of violating § 922(q), and sentenced him to six months' imprisonment and two years' supervised release.

On appeal, respondent challenged his conviction based on his claim that § 922(q) exceeded Congress' power to legislate under the Commerce Clause. The Court of Appeals for the Fifth Circuit agreed and reversed respondent's conviction. It held that, in light of what it characterized as insufficient congressional findings and legislative history, "section 922(q), in the full reach of its terms, is invalid as beyond the power of Congress under the Commerce Clause." 2 F.3d 1342, 1367-1368 (1993). Because of the importance of the issue, we granted certiorari, 511 U. S. 1029 (1994), and we now affirm.

We start with first principles. The Constitution creates a Federal Government of enumerated powers. See Art. I, § 8.As James Madison wrote: "The powers delegated by the proposed Constitution to the federal government are few and defined. Those which are to remain in the State governments are numerous and indefinite." The Federalist No. 45, pp. 292-293 (C. Rossiter ed. 1961). This constitutionally mandated division of authority "was adopted by the Framers to ensure protection of our fundamental liberties." *Gregory* v. *Ashcroft*, 501 U. S. 452, 458 (1991) (internal quotation marks omitted). "Just as the separation and independence of the coordinate branches of the Federal Government serve to prevent the accumulation of excessive power in anyone branch, a healthy balance of power between the States and the Federal Government will reduce the risk of tyranny and abuse from either front." *Ibid.* cl. 3. The Court, through Chief Justice Marshall, first defined the nature of Congress' commerce power in *Gibbons* v. *Ogden*, 9 Wheat. 1, 189-190 (1824):

> "Commerce, undoubtedly, is traffic, but it is something more: it is intercourse. It describes the commercial intercourse between nations, and parts of nations, in all its branches, and is regulated by prescribing rules for carrying on that intercourse."

The commerce power "is the power to regulate; that is, to prescribe the rule by which commerce is to be governed. This power, like all others vested in congress, is complete in itself, may be exercised to its utmost extent, and acknowledges no limitations, other than are prescribed in the constitution." *Id.*, at 196. The *Gibbons* Court, however, acknowledged that limitations on the commerce power are inherent in the very language of the Commerce Clause.

> "It is not intended to say that these words comprehend that commerce, which is completely internal, which is carried on between man and man in a State, or between different parts of the same State, and which does not extend to or affect other States. Such a power would be inconvenient, and is certainly unnecessary.
>
> "Comprehensive as the word 'among' is, it may very properly be restricted to that commerce which concerns more States than one .... The enumeration presupposes something not enumerated; and that something, if we regard the language, or the subject of the sentence, must be the exclusively internal commerce of a State." *Id.*, at 194-195.

For nearly a century thereafter, the Court's Commerce Clause decisions dealt but rarely with the extent of Congress' power, and almost entirely with the Commerce Clause as a limit on state legislation that discriminated against interstate commerce. See, *e. g.*, *Veazie* v. *Moor*, 14 How. 568, 573-575 (1853) (upholding a state-created steamboat monopoly because it involved regulation of wholly internal commerce); *Kidd* v. *Pearson,* 128 U. S. 1, 17, 20-22 (1888) (upholding a state prohibition on the manufacture of intoxicating liquor because the commerce power "does not comprehend the purely internal domestic commerce of a State which is carried on between man and man within a State or between different parts of the same State"); see also L. Tribe, American Constitutional Law 306 (2d ed. 1988). Under this line of precedent, the Court held that certain categories of activity such as "production," "manufacturing," and "mining" were within the province of state governments, and thus were beyond the power of Congress under the Commerce Clause. See *Wickard* v. *Filburn,* 317 U. S. 111, 121 (1942) (describing development of Commerce Clause jurisprudence).

In 1887, Congress enacted the Interstate Commerce Act, 24 Stat. 379, and in 1890, Congress enacted the Sherman Antitrust Act, 26 Stat. 209, as amended, 15 U. S. C. § 1 *et seq.* These laws ushered in a new era of federal regulation under the commerce power. When cases involving these laws first reached this Court, we imported from our negative Commerce Clause cases the approach that Congress could not regulate activities such as "production," "manufacturing," and "mining." See, *e. g., United States* v. *E. C. Knight Co.,* 156 U. S. 1, 12 (1895) ("Commerce succeeds to manufacture, and is not part of it"); *Carter* v. *Carter Coal Co.,* 298 U. S. 238, 304 (1936) ("Mining brings the subject matter of commerce into existence. Commerce disposes of it"). Simultaneously, however, the Court held that, where the interstate and intrastate aspects of commerce were so mingled together that full regulation of interstate commerce required incidental regulation of intrastate commerce, the Commerce Clause authorized such regulation. See, *e. g., Shreveport Rate Cases,* 234 U. S. 342(1914).

In *A. L. A. Schechter Poultry Corp.* v. *United States,* 295 U. S. 495, 550 (1935), the Court struck down regulations that fixed the hours and wages of individuals employed by an intrastate business because the activity being regulated related to interstate commerce only indirectly. In doing so, the Court characterized the distinction between direct and indirect effects of intrastate transactions upon interstate commerce as "a fundamental one, essential to the maintenance of our constitutional system." *Id.,* at 548. Activities that affected interstate commerce directly were within Congress' power; activities that affected interstate commerce indirectly were beyond Congress' reach. *Id.,* at 546. The justification for this formal distinction was rooted in the fear that otherwise "there would be virtually no limit to the federal power and for all practical purposes we should have a completely centralized government." *Id.,* at 548.

Two years later, in the watershed case of *NLRB* v. *Jones & Laughlin Steel Corp.,* 301 U. S. 1 (1937), the Court upheld the National Labor Relations Act against a Commerce Clause challenge, and in the process, departed from the distinction between "direct" and "indirect" effects on interstate commerce. *Id.,* at 36-38 ("The question [of the scope of Congress' power] is necessarily one of degree"). The Court held that intrastate activities that "have such a close and substantial relation to interstate commerce that their control is essential or appropriate to protect that commerce from burdens and obstructions" are within Congress' power to regulate. *Id.,* at 37.

In *United States* v. *Darby,* 312 U. S. 100 (1941), the Court upheld the Fair Labor Standards Act, stating:

> "The power of Congress over interstate commerce is not confined to the regulation of commerce among the states. It extends to those activities intrastate which so affect interstate commerce or the exercise of the power of Congress over it as to make regulation of them appropriate means to the attainment of a legitimate end, the exercise of the granted power of Congress to regulate interstate commerce." *Id.,* at 118. See also *United States* v. *Wrightwood Dairy Co.,* 315 U. S. 110, 119 (1942) (the commerce power "extends to those intrastate activities which in a substantial way interfere with or obstruct the exercise of the granted power").

In *Wickard* v. *Filburn,* the Court upheld the application of amendments to the Agricultural Adjustment Act of 1938 to the production and consumption of homegrown wheat. 317 U. S., at 128-129. The *Wickard* Court explicitly rejected earlier distinctions between direct and indirect effects on interstate commerce, stating:

> "[E]ven if appellee's activity be local and though it may not be regarded as commerce, it may still, whatever its nature, be reached by Congress if it exerts a substantial economic effect on interstate commerce, and this irrespective of whether such effect is what might at some earlier time have been defined as 'direct' or 'indirect.'" *Id.*, at 125.

The *Wickard* Court emphasized that although Filburn's own contribution to the demand for wheat may have been trivial by itself, that was not "enough to remove him from the scope of federal regulation where, as here, his contribution, taken together with that of many others similarly situated, is far from trivial." *Id.*, at 127-128.

Jones & Laughlin Steel, Darby, and *Wickard* ushered in an era of Commerce Clause jurisprudence that greatly expanded the previously defined authority of Congress under that Clause. In part, this was a recognition of the great changes that had occurred in the way business was carried on in this country. Enterprises that had once been local or at most regional in nature had become national in scope. But the doctrinal change also reflected a view that earlier Commerce Clause cases artificially had constrained the authority of Congress to regulate interstate commerce.

But even these modern-era precedents which have expanded congressional power under the Commerce Clause confirm that this power is subject to outer limits. In *Jones & Laughlin Steel,* the Court warned that the scope of the interstate commerce power "must be considered in the light of our dual system of government and may not be extended so as to embrace effects upon interstate commerce so indirect and remote that to embrace them, in view of our complex society, would effectually obliterate the distinction between what is national and what is local and create a completely centralized government." 301 U. S., at 37; see also *Darby, supra,* at 119-120 (Congress may regulate intrastate activity that has a "substantial effect" on interstate commerce); *Wickard, supra,* at 125 (Congress may regulate activity that "exerts a substantial economic effect on interstate commerce"). Since that time, the Court has heeded that warning and undertaken to decide whether a rational basis existed for concluding that a regulated activity sufficiently affected interstate commerce. See, *e. g., Hodel* v. *Virginia Surface Mining & Reclamation Assn., Inc.,* 452 U. S. 264, 276-280 (1981); *Perez* v. *United States,* 402 U. S. 146, 155-156 (1971); *Katzenbach* v. *McClung,* 379 U. S. 294, 299-301 (1964); *Heart of Atlanta Motel, Inc.* v. *United States,* 379 U. S. 241, 252-253 (1964).2

Similarly, in *Maryland v. Wirtz,* 392 U. S. 183 (1968), the Court reaffirmed that "the power to regulate commerce, though broad indeed, has limits" that "[t]he Court has ample power" to enforce. *Id.*, at 196, overruled on other grounds, *National League of Cities* v. *Usery,* 426 U. S. 833 (1976), overruled by *Garcia* v. *San Antonio Metropolitan Transit Authority,* 469 U. S. 528 (1985). In response to the dissent's warnings that the Court was powerless to enforce the limitations on Congress' commerce powers because "[a]ll activities affecting commerce, even in the minutest degree, *[Wickard],* may be regulated and controlled by Congress," 392 U. S., at 204 (Douglas, J., dissenting), the *Wirtz* Court replied that the dissent had misread precedent as "[n]either here nor in *Wickard* has the Court declared that Congress may use a relatively trivial impact on commerce as an excuse for broad general regulation of state or private activities," *id.*, at 197, n. 27. Rather, "[t]he Court has said only that where *a general regulatory statute bears a substantial relation to commerce,* the *de minimis* character of individual instances arising under that statute is of no consequence." *Ibid.* (first emphasis added).

Consistent with this structure, we have identified three broad categories of activity that Congress may regulate under its commerce power. *Perez, supra,* at 150; see also *Hodel, supra,* at 276-277. First, Congress may regulate the use of the channels of interstate commerce. See, *e. g., Darby,* 312 U. S., at 114; *Heart of Atlanta Motel, supra,* at 256 (" '[T]he authority of Congress to keep the channels of interstate commerce free from immoral and injurious uses has been frequently sustained, and is no longer open to question'" (quoting *Caminetti* v. *United States,* 242 U. S. 470, 491 (1917))). Second, Congress is empowered to regulate and protect the instrumentalities of interstate commerce, or persons or things in interstate commerce, even though the threat may come only from intrastate activities. See, *e. g., Shreveport Rate Cases,* 234 U. S. 342 (1914); *Southern R. Co.* v. *United States,* 222 U. S. 20 (1911) (upholding amendments to Safety Appliance Act as applied to vehicles used in intrastate commerce); *Perez, supra,* at 150 ("[F]or example, the destruction of an aircraft (18 U. S. C. § 32), or ... thefts from interstate shipments (18 U. S. C. § 659)"). Finally, Congress' commerce authority includes the power to regulate those activities having a substantial relation to interstate commerce, *Jones & Laughlin Steel,* 301 U. S., at 37, i. e., those activities that substantially affect interstate commerce, *Wirtz, supra,* at 196, n. 27.

Within this final category, admittedly, our case law has not been clear whether an activity must "affect" or "substantially affect" interstate commerce in order to be within Congress' power to regulate it under the Commerce Clause. Compare *Preseault* v. *ICC,* 494 U. S. 1, 17 (1990), with *Wirtz, supra,* at 196, n. 27 (the Court has never declared that "Congress may use a relatively trivial impact on commerce as an excuse for broad general regulation of state or private activities"). We conclude, consistent with the great weight of our case law, that the proper test requires an analysis of whether the regulated activity "substantially affects" interstate commerce.

We now turn to consider the power of Congress, in the light of this framework, to enact § 922(q). The first two categories of authority may be quickly disposed of: § 922(q) is not a regulation of the use of the channels of interstate commerce, nor is it an attempt to prohibit the interstate transportation of a commodity through the channels of commerce; nor can § 922(q) be justified as a regulation by which Congress has sought to protect an instrumentality of interstate commerce or a thing in interstate commerce. Thus, if § 922(q) is to be sustained, it must be under the third category as a regulation of an activity that substantially affects interstate commerce.

First, we have upheld a wide variety of congressional Acts regulating intrastate economic activity where we have concluded that the activity substantially affected interstate commerce. Examples include the regulation of intrastate coal mining; *Hodel, supra,* intrastate extortionate credit transactions, *Perez, supra,* restaurants utilizing substantial interstate supplies, *McClung, supra,* inns and hotels catering to interstate guests, *Heart of Atlanta Motel, supra,* and production and consumption of home-grown wheat, *Wickard* v. *Filburn,* 317 U. S. 111 (1942). These examples are by no means exhaustive, but the pattern is clear. Where economic activity substantially affects interstate commerce, legislation regulating that activity will be sustained.

Even *Wickard,* which is perhaps the most far reaching example of Commerce Clause authority over intrastate activity, involved economic activity in a way that the possession of a gun in a school zone does not. Roscoe Filburn operated a small farm in Ohio, on which, in the year involved, he raised 23 acres of wheat. It was his practice to sow winter wheat in the fall, and after harvesting it in July to sell a portion of the crop, to feed part of it to poultry and livestock on the farm, to use some in making flour for home consumption, and to keep the remainder for seeding future crops. The Secretary of Agriculture assessed a penalty against him under the Agricultural Adjustment Act of 1938 because he harvested about 12 acres more wheat than his allotment under the Act permitted. The Act was designed to regulate the volume of wheat moving in interstate and foreign commerce in order to avoid surpluses and shortages, and concomitant fluctuation in wheat prices, which had previously obtained. The Court said, in an opinion sustaining the application of the Act to Filburn's activity:

> "One of the primary purposes of the Act in question was to increase the market price of wheat and to that end to limit the volume thereof that could affect the market. It can hardly be denied that a factor of such volume and variability as home-consumed wheat would have a substantial influence on price and market conditions. This may arise because being in marketable condition such wheat overhangs the market and, if induced by rising prices, tends to flow into the market and check price increases. But if we assume that it is never marketed, it supplies a need of the man who grew it which would otherwise be reflected by purchases in the open market. Home-grown wheat in this sense competes with wheat in commerce." 317 U. S., at 128.

Section 922(q) is a criminal statute that by its terms has nothing to do with "commerce" or any sort of economic enterprise, however broadly one might define those terms.3 Section 922(q) is not an essential part of a larger regulation of economic activity, in which the regulatory scheme could be undercut unless the intrastate activity were regulated. It cannot, therefore, be sustained under our cases upholding regulations of activities that arise out of or are connected with a commercial transaction, which viewed in the aggregate, substantially affects interstate commerce.

Second, § 922(q) contains no jurisdictional element which would ensure, through case-by-case inquiry, that the firearm possession in question affects interstate commerce. For example, in *United States* v. *Bass,* 404 U. S. 336 (1971), the Court interpreted former 18 U. S. C. § 1202(a), which made it a crime for a felon to "receiv[e], posses[s], or transpor[t] in commerce or affecting commerce ... any firearm." 404 U. S., at 337. The Court interpreted the possession component of § 1202(a) to require an additional nexus to interstate commerce both because the statute was ambiguous and because "unless Congress conveys its purpose clearly, it will not be deemed to have significantly changed the federal-state balance." *Id.,* at 349. The *Bass* Court set aside the conviction because, although the Government had demonstrated that Bass had possessed a firearm, it had failed "to show the requisite nexus with interstate commerce." *Id.,* at 347. The Court thus interpreted the statute to reserve the constitutional question whether Congress could regulate, without more, the "mere possession" of firearms. See *id.,* at 339, n. 4; see also *United States* v. *Five Gambling Devices,* 346 U. S. 441, 448 (1953) (plurality opinion) ("The principle is old and deeply imbedded in our jurisprudence that this Court will construe a statute in a manner that requires decision of serious constitutional questions only if the statutory language leaves no reasonable alternative"). Unlike the statute in *Bass,* § 922(q) has no express jurisdictional element which might limit its reach to a discrete set of firearm possessions that additionally have an explicit connection with or effect on interstate commerce.

Although as part of our independent evaluation of constitutionality under the Commerce Clause we of course consider legislative findings, and indeed even congressional committee findings, regarding effect on interstate commerce, see, *e. g., Preseault* v. *ICC,* 494 U. S., at 17, the Government concedes that "[n]either the statute nor its legislative history contain[s] express congressional findings regarding the effects upon interstate commerce of gun possession in a school zone." Brief for United States 5-6. We agree with the Government that Congress normally is not required to make formal findings as to the substantial burdens that an activity has on interstate commerce. See *McClung,* 379 U. S., at 304; see also *Perez,* 402 U. S., at 156 ("Congress need [not] make particularized findings in order to legislate"). But to the extent that congressional findings would enable us to evaluate the legislative judgment that the activity in question substantially affected interstate commerce, even though no such substantial effect was visible to the naked eye, they are lacking here.4

The Government argues that Congress has accumulated institutional expertise regarding the regulation of firearms through previous enactments. Cf. *Fullilove* v. *Klutznick,* 448 U. S. 448, 503 (1980) (Powell, J., concurring). We agree, however, with the Fifth Circuit that importation of previous findings to justify § 922(q) is especially inappropriate here because the "prior federal enactments or Congressional findings [do not] speak to the subject matter of section 922(q) or its relationship to interstate commerce. Indeed, section 922(q) plows thoroughly new ground and represents a sharp break with the long-standing pattern of federal firearms legislation." 2 F. 3d, at 1366.

The Government's essential contention, *in fine,* is that we may determine here that § 922(q) is valid because possession of a firearm in a local school zone does indeed substantially affect interstate commerce. Brief for United States 17. The Government argues that possession of a firearm in a school zone may result in violent crime and that violent crime can be expected to affect the functioning of the national economy in two ways. First, the costs of violent crime are substantial, and, through the mechanism of insurance, those costs are spread throughout the population. See *United States* v. *Evans,* 928 F.2d 858, 862 (CA9 1991). Second, violent crime reduces the willingness of individuals to travel to areas within the country that are perceived to be unsafe. Cf. *Heart of Atlanta Motel,* 379 U. S., at 253. The Government also argues that the presence of guns in schools poses a substantial threat to the educational process by threatening the learning environment. A handicapped educational process, in turn, will result in a less productive citizenry. That, in turn, would have an adverse effect on the Nation's economic well-being. As a result, the

Government argues that Congress could rationally have concluded that § 922(q) substantially affects interstate commerce.

We pause to consider the implications of the Government's arguments. The Government admits, under its "costs of crime" reasoning, that Congress could regulate not only all violent crime, but all activities that might lead to violent crime, regardless of how tenuously they relate to interstate commerce. See Tr. of Oral Arg. 8-9. Similarly, under the Government's "national productivity" reasoning, Congress could regulate any activity that it found was related to the economic productivity of individual citizens: family law (including marriage, divorce, and child custody), for example. Under the theories that the Government presents in support of § 922(q), it is difficult to perceive any limitation on federal power, even in areas such as criminal law enforcement or education where States historically have been sovereign. Thus, if we were to accept the Government's arguments, we are hard pressed to posit any activity by an individual that Congress is without power to regulate.

Although JUSTICE BREYER argues that acceptance of the Government's rationales would not authorize a general federal police power, he is unable to identify any activity that the States may regulate but Congress may not. JUSTICE BREYER posits that there might be some limitations on Congress' commerce power, such as family law or certain aspects of education. *Post,* at 624. These suggested limitations, when viewed in light of the dissent's expansive analysis, are devoid of substance.

JUSTICE BREYER focuses, for the most part, on the threat that firearm possession in and near schools poses to the educational process and the potential economic consequences flowing from that threat. *Post,* at 619-624. Specifically, the dissent reasons that (1) gun-related violence is a serious problem; (2) that problem, in turn, has an adverse effect on classroom learning; and (3) that adverse effect on classroom learning, in turn, represents a substantial threat to trade and commerce. *Post,* at 623. This analysis would be equally applicable, if not more so, to subjects such as family law and direct regulation of education.

For instance, if Congress can, pursuant to its Commerce Clause power, regulate activities that adversely affect the learning environment, then, *a fortiori,* it also can regulate the educational process directly. Congress could determine that a school's curriculum has a "significant" effect on the extent of classroom learning. As a result, Congress could mandate a federal curriculum for local elementary and secondary schools because what is taught in local schools has a significant "effect on classroom learning," cf. *ibid.*, and that, in turn, has a substantial effect on interstate commerce.

JUSTICE BREYER rejects our reading of precedent and argues that "Congress ... could rationally conclude that schools fall on the commercial side of the line." *Post,* at 629. Again, JUSTICE BREYER'S rationale lacks any real limits because, depending on the level of generality, any activity can be looked upon as commercial. Under the dissent's rationale, Congress could just as easily look at child rearing as "fall[ing] on the commercial side of the line" because it provides a "valuable service-namely, to equip [children] with the skills they need to survive in life and, more specifically, in the workplace." *Ibid.* We do not doubt that Congress has authority under the Commerce Clause to regulate numerous commercial activities that substantially affect interstate commerce and also affect the educational process. That authority, though broad, does not include the authority to regulate each and every aspect of local schools.

Admittedly, a determination whether an intrastate activity is commercial or noncommercial may in some cases result in legal uncertainty. But, so long as Congress' authority is limited to those powers enumerated in the Constitution, and so long as those enumerated powers are interpreted as having judicially enforceable outer limits, congressional legislation under the Commerce Clause always will engender "legal uncertainty." *Post,* at 630. As Chief Justice Marshall stated in *McCulloch* v. *Maryland,* 4 Wheat. 316 (1819):

> "Th[e] [federal] government is acknowledged by all to be one of enumerated powers. The principle, that it can exercise only the powers granted to it ... is now universally admitted. But the question respecting the extent of the powers actually granted, is perpetually arising, and will probably continue to arise, as long as our system shall exist." *Id.*, at 405.

See also *Gibbons* v. *Ogden,* 9 Wheat., at 195 ("The enumeration presupposes something not enumerated"). The Constitution mandates this uncertainty by withholding from Congress a plenary police power that would authorize enactment of every type of legislation. See Art. I, § 8. Congress has operated within this framework of legal uncertainty ever since this Court determined that it was the Judiciary's duty "to say what the law is." *Marbury* v. *Madison,* 1 Cranch 137, 177 (1803) (Marshall, C. J.). Any possible benefit from eliminating this "legal uncertainty" would be at the expense of the Constitution's system of enumerated powers.

In *Jones* & *Laughlin Steel,* 301 U. S., at 37, we held that the question of congressional power under the Commerce Clause "is necessarily one of degree." To the same effect is the concurring opinion of Justice Cardozo in *Schechter Poultry*:

> "There is a view of causation that would obliterate the distinction between what is national and what is local in the activities of commerce. Motion at the outer rim is communicated perceptibly, though minutely, to recording instruments at the center. A society such as ours 'is an elastic medium which transmits all tremors throughout its territory; the only question is of their size.'" 295 U. S., at 554 (quoting *United States* v. *A. L. A. Schechter Poultry Corp.,* 76 F.2d 617, 624 (CA2 1935) (L. Hand, J., concurring)).

These are not precise formulations, and in the nature of things they cannot be. But we think they point the way to a correct decision of this case. The possession of a gun in a local school zone is in no sense an economic activity that might, through repetition elsewhere, substantially affect any sort of interstate commerce. Respondent was a local student at a local school; there is no indication that he had recently moved in interstate commerce, and there is no requirement that his possession of the firearm have any concrete tie to interstate commerce.

To uphold the Government's contentions here, we would have to pile inference upon inference in a manner that would bid fair to convert congressional authority under the Commerce Clause to a general police power of the sort retained by the States. Admittedly, some of our prior cases have taken long steps down that road, giving great deference to congressional action. See *supra,* at 556-558. The broad language in these opinions has suggested the possibility of additional expansion, but we decline here to proceed any further. To do so would require us to conclude that the Constitution's enumeration of powers does not presuppose something not enumerated, cf. *Gibbons* v. *Ogden, supra,* at 195, and that there never will be a distinction between what is truly national and what is truly local, cf. *Jones* & *Laughlin Steel, supra,* at 30. This we are unwilling to do.

For the foregoing reasons the judgment of the Court of Appeals is

Affirmed.

Section 1702(b)(5) of Pub. L. 101-647 states: "Federal, State, and local authorities are encouraged to cause signs to be posted around school zones giving warning of prohibition of the possession of firearms in a school zone." (By Marcus Quigmire.)

Document Themes

The *Lopez* decision had many possible implications for the future relationship between the federal government and the states. In concluding that Congress had gone further than the commerce clause allowed, the Court opened the door for additional restrictions on the powers of the national government. Since such an important decision was based on a 5-4 vote, the significance of *Lopez* as a precedent largely depended on the future membership of the Court; therefore, the decision appeared to increase the stakes of the presidential election of 1996.

Further Reading

Powell, H. Jefferson. "Enumerated Means and Unlimited Ends." *Michigan Law Review* 94, no. 3 (December, 1995): 651-673.

Regan, Donald H. "How to Think About the Federal Commerce Power and Incidentally Rewrite *United States v. Lopez*." *Michigan Law Review* 94, no. 3 (December, 1995): 554-614.

Smith, Richard W. "Interpreting the Constitution from Inside the Jury Box: Affecting Interstate Commerce as an Element of the Crime." *Washington and Lee Law Review* 55, no. 2 (Spring, 1998): 615-658.

Vile, John R. *A Companion to the United States Constitution and Its Amendments*. 3d ed. Westport, Conn.: Praeger, 2001.

—*Thomas Tandy Lewis*

District of Columbia v. Heller

Author(s): Antonin Scalia (Justice of the Supreme Court)
Date: 2008
Genre: Court decision (Supreme Court)

Summary Overview

District of Columbia v. Heller is a landmark U.S. Supreme Court case that represented the first time the Court enforced a claim made under the Second Amendment and the first time the Court clearly severed the ownership of firearms from service in the militia. The opinion of the Court was sharply divided, with four justices joining Justice Antonin Scalia in his ruling that "the District's ban on handgun possession in the home violates the Second Amendment, as does its prohibition against rendering any lawful firearm in the home operable for the purpose of immediate self-defense." Four justices dissented.

Defining Moment

The Supreme Court issued its decision in the context of public perceptions that violent crime, particularly crime committed with handguns, was on the rise in the United States. The municipal code of the District of Columbia made it illegal to carry an unregistered firearm; additionally, it prohibited the registration of handguns to be kept in the home, although the city's chief of police could issue a one-year license for a handgun. Any owner of a lawfully registered firearm had to keep it unloaded and disassembled, or affix to it a trigger lock, if the gun was kept in the home.

The case found its way into the court system when Dick Heller, a special police officer who was authorized to carry a gun while he was on duty at the Federal Judicial Center, applied for, but was denied, a license to keep his gun in his home. Accordingly, he filed suit against the city, seeking an injunction against enforcement of the statute, arguing that it violated his Second Amendment right to keep a working firearm in his home without a license.

After a district court dismissed his complaint, the U.S. Court of Appeals for the District of Columbia reversed, ruling that the Second Amendment protects the right of an individual to keep a firearm in the home for self-defense. The district, hoping to preserve its gun ban, then appealed to the U.S. Supreme Court, which ruled in Heller's favor. In his opinion, Justice Scalia relied heavily on historical and textual arguments to endorse the view that the Second Amendment protects the right of individuals to arm themselves to defend their home.

About the Author

Justice Antonin Scalia was born on March 11, 1936, in Trenton, New Jersey, although when he was a young child, the family moved to Queens, New York. In 1957 he completed a bachelor's degree at Georgetown University, and in 1960 he graduated as class valedictorian from Harvard Law School. He entered private practice as a commercial law attorney in 1961, but his interest in the academic aspects of the law drew him to a faculty position at the University of Virginia law school in 1967.

He entered government service in 1971, when he was appointed general counsel for the Office of Telecommunications Policy by President Richard Nixon. In 1974 he was confirmed as the assistant attorney general for the Office of Legal Counsel. In 1977 he returned to academia, taking a position teaching law at the University of Chicago, a position he held until 1982, when President Ronald Reagan appointed him to the U.S. District Court of Appeals for the District of Columbia. Then, in 1986, Reagan appointed him to a vacant seat on the U.S. Supreme Court. His nomination was unanimously confirmed.

Scalia was known as a strict constructionist, meaning that he placed great emphasis on his interpretation of the original meaning of the text of the Constitution, including the Second Amendment. Both on the circuit court and on the Supreme Court, he was also known for his witty, erudite, and sometimes humorous written opinions, as well as for his scathing rebukes of his fellow justices when he believed their views were misguided.

Scalia died in his sleep of natural causes; his body was discovered on the morning of February 13, 2016.

HISTORICAL DOCUMENT

DISTRICT OF COLUMBIA, et al., PETITIONERS v. DICK ANTHONY HELLER

[June 26, 2008]

Justice Scalia delivered the opinion of the Court.

We consider whether a District of Columbia prohibition on the possession of usable handguns in the home violates the Second Amendment to the Constitution.

I

The District of Columbia generally prohibits the possession of handguns. It is a crime to carry an unregistered firearm, and the registration of handguns is prohibited. Wholly apart from that prohibition, no person may carry a handgun without a license, but the chief of police may issue licenses for 1-year periods. District of Columbia law also requires residents to keep their lawfully owned firearms, such as registered long guns, "unloaded and dissembled or bound by a trigger lock or similar device" unless they are located in a place of business or are being used for lawful recreational activities.

Respondent Dick Heller is a D. C. special police officer authorized to carry a handgun while on duty at the Federal Judicial Center. He applied for a registration certificate for a handgun that he wished to keep at home, but the District refused. He thereafter filed a lawsuit in the Federal District Court for the District of Columbia seeking, on Second Amendment grounds, to enjoin the city from enforcing the bar on the registration of handguns, the licensing requirement insofar as it prohibits the carrying of a firearm in the home without a license, and the trigger-lock requirement insofar as it prohibits the use of "functional firearms within the home." The District Court dismissed respondent's complaint. The Court of Appeals for the District of Columbia Circuit, construing his complaint as seeking the right to render a firearm operable and carry it about his home in that condition only when necessary for self-defense, reversed. It held that the Second Amendment protects an individual right to possess firearms and that the city's total ban on handguns, as well as its requirement that firearms in the home be kept nonfunctional even when necessary for self-defense, violated that right. The Court of Appeals directed the District Court to enter summary judgment for respondent.

* * * * *

II

We turn first to the meaning of the Second Amendment.

A

The Second Amendment provides: "A well regulated Militia, being necessary to the security of a free State, the right of the people to keep and bear Arms, shall not be infringed." In interpreting this text, we are guided by the principle that "[t]he Constitution was written to be understood by the voters; its words and phrases were used in their normal and ordinary as distinguished from technical meaning." Normal meaning may of course include an idiomatic meaning, but it excludes secret or technical meanings that would not have been known to ordinary citizens in the founding generation.

The two sides in this case have set out very different interpretations of the Amendment. Petitioners and today's dissenting Justices believe that it protects only the right to possess and carry a firearm in connection with militia service. Respondent argues that it protects an individual right to possess a firearm unconnected with service in a militia, and to use that arm for traditionally lawful purposes, such as self-defense within the home.

The Second Amendment is naturally divided into two parts: its prefatory clause and its operative clause. The former does not limit the latter grammatically, but rather announces a purpose. The Amendment could be rephrased, "Because a well regulated Militia is necessary to the security of a free State, the right of the people to keep and bear Arms shall not be infringed." Although this structure of the Second Amendment is unique in our Constitution, other legal documents of the founding era, particularly individual-rights provisions of state constitutions, commonly included a prefatory statement of purpose.

Logic demands that there be a link between the stated purpose and the command. The Second Amendment would be nonsensical if it read, "A well regulated Militia, being necessary to the security of a free State, the right of the people to petition for redress of grievances shall not be infringed." That requirement of logical connection may cause a prefatory clause to resolve an ambiguity in the operative clause ("The separation of church and state being an important objective, the teachings of canons shall have no place in our jurisprudence." The preface makes clear that the operative clause refers not to canons of interpretation but to clergymen.) But apart from that clarifying function, a prefatory clause does not limit or expand the scope of the operative clause. . . . Therefore, while we will begin our textual analysis with the operative clause, we will return to the prefatory clause to ensure that our reading of the operative clause is consistent with the announced purpose.

1. Operative Clause.

a. "Right of the People." The first salient feature of the operative clause is that it codifies a "right of the people." The unamended Constitution and the Bill of Rights use the phrase "right of the people" two other times, in the First Amendment's Assembly-and-Petition Clause and in the Fourth Amendment's Search-and-Seizure Clause. The Ninth Amendment uses very similar terminology ("The enumeration in the Constitution, of certain rights, shall not be construed to deny or disparage others retained by the people"). All three of these instances unambiguously refer to individual rights, not "collective" rights, or rights that may be exercised only through participation in some corporate body.

Three provisions of the Constitution refer to "the people" in a context other than "rights"—the famous preamble ("We the people"), §2 of Article I (providing that "the people" will choose members of the House), and the Tenth Amendment (providing that those powers not given the Federal Government remain with "the States" or "the people"). Those provisions arguably refer to "the people" acting collectively—but they deal with the exercise or reservation of powers, not rights. Nowhere else in the Constitution does a "right" attributed to "the people" refer to anything other than an individual right.

What is more, in all six other provisions of the Constitution that mention "the people," the term unambiguously refers to all members of the political community, not an unspecified subset. As we said in *United States* v. *Verdugo-Urquidez*:

" '[T]he people' seems to have been a term of art employed in select parts of the Constitution... . [Its uses] sugges[t] that 'the people' protected by the Fourth Amendment, and by the First and Second Amendments, and to whom rights and powers are reserved in the Ninth and Tenth Amendments, refers to a class of persons who are part of a national community or who have otherwise developed sufficient connection with this country to be considered part of that community."

This contrasts markedly with the phrase "the militia" in the prefatory clause. As we will describe below, the "militia" in colonial America consisted of a subset of "the people"—those who were male, able bodied, and within a certain age range. Reading the Second Amendment as protecting only the right to "keep and bear Arms" in an organized militia therefore fits poorly with the operative clause's description of the holder of that right as "the people."

We start therefore with a strong presumption that the Second Amendment right is exercised individually and belongs to all Americans.

b. "Keep and bear Arms." We move now from the holder of the right—"the people"—to the substance of the right: "to keep and bear Arms."

Before addressing the verbs "keep" and "bear," we interpret their object: "Arms." The 18th-century meaning is no different from the meaning today. The 1773 edition of Samuel Johnson's dictionary defined "arms" as "weapons of offence, or armour of defence." Timothy Cunningham's important 1771 legal dictionary defined "arms" as "any thing that a man wears for his defence, or takes into his hands, or useth in wrath to cast at or strike another." . . . The term was applied, then as now, to weapons that were not specifically designed for military use and were not employed in a military capacity. For instance, Cunningham's legal dictionary gave as an example of usage: "Servants and labourers shall use bows and arrows on *Sundays*, &c. and not bear other arms." Although one founding-era thesaurus limited "arms" (as opposed to "weapons") to "instruments of offence *generally* made use of in war," even that source stated that all firearms constituted "arms."

Some have made the argument, bordering on the frivolous, that only those arms in existence in the 18th century are protected by the Second Amendment. We do not interpret constitutional rights that way. Just as the First Amendment protects modern forms of communications, and the Fourth Amendment applies to modern forms of search, the Second Amendment extends, prima facie, to all instruments that constitute bearable arms, even those that were not in existence at the time of the founding.

We turn to the phrases "keep arms" and "bear arms." Johnson defined "keep" as, most relevantly, "[t]o retain; not to lose," and "[t]o have in custody." Johnson 1095. Webster defined it as "[t]o hold; to retain in one's power or possession." No party has apprised us of an idiomatic meaning of "keep Arms." Thus, the most natural reading of "keep Arms" in the Second Amendment is to "have weapons."

The phrase "keep arms" was not prevalent in the written documents of the founding period that we have found, but there are a few examples, all of which favor viewing the right to "keep Arms" as an individual right unconnected with militia service. William Blackstone, for example, wrote that Catholics convicted of not attending service in the Church of England suffered certain penalties, one of which was that they were not permitted to "keep arms in their houses." Petitioners point to militia laws of the founding period that required militia members to "keep" arms in connection with militia service, and they conclude from this that the phrase "keep Arms" has a militia-related connotation. This is rather like saying that, since there are many statutes that authorize aggrieved employees to "file complaints" with federal agencies, the phrase "file complaints" has an employment-related connotation. "Keep arms" was simply a common way of referring to possessing arms, for militiamen *and everyone else*.

At the time of the founding, as now, to "bear" meant to "carry." When used with "arms," however, the term has a meaning that refers to carrying for a particular purpose—confrontation. In *Muscarello* v. *United States*, 524 U. S. 125 (1998), in the course of analyzing the meaning of "carries a firearm" in a federal criminal statute, Justice Ginsburg wrote that "[s]urely a most familiar meaning is, as the Constitution's Second Amendment ... indicate[s]: 'wear, bear, or carry ... upon the person or in the clothing or in a pocket, for the purpose ... of being armed and ready for offensive or defensive action in a case of conflict with another person.' " We think that Justice Ginsburg accurately captured the natural meaning of "bear arms." Although the phrase implies that the carrying of the weapon is for the purpose of "offensive or defensive action," it in no way connotes participation in a structured military organization.

From our review of founding-era sources, we conclude that this natural meaning was also the meaning that "bear arms" had in the 18th century. In numerous instances, "bear arms" was unambiguously used to refer to the carrying of weapons outside of an organized militia. The most prominent examples are those most relevant to the Second Amendment: Nine state constitutional provisions written in the 18th century or the first two decades of the 19th, which enshrined a right of citizens to "bear arms in defense of themselves and the state" or "bear arms in defense of himself and the state." It is clear from those formulations that "bear arms" did not refer only to carrying a weapon in an organized military unit. Justice James Wilson interpreted the Pennsylvania Constitution's arms-bearing right, for example, as a recognition of the natural right of defense "of one's person or house"—what he called the law of "self preservation." That was also the interpretation of those state constitutional provisions adopted by pre-Civil War state courts. These provisions demonstrate—again, in the most analogous linguistic context—that "bear arms" was not limited to the carrying of arms in a militia.

The phrase "bear Arms" also had at the time of the founding an idiomatic meaning that was significantly different from its natural meaning: "to serve as a soldier, do military service, fight" or "to wage war." But it *unequivocally* bore that idiomatic meaning only when followed by the preposition "against," which was in turn followed by the target of the hostilities. (That is how, for example, our Declaration of Independence ¶28, used the phrase: "He has constrained our fellow Citizens taken Captive on the high Seas to bear Arms against their Country ... .") Every example given by petitioners' *amici* for the idiomatic meaning of "bear arms" from the founding period either includes the preposition "against" or is not clearly idiomatic. Without the preposition, "bear arms" normally meant (as it continues to mean today) what Justice Ginsburg's opinion in *Muscarello* said.

In any event, the meaning of "bear arms" that petitioners and Justice Stevens propose is *not even* the (sometimes) idiomatic meaning. Rather, they manufacture a hybrid definition, whereby "bear arms" connotes the actual carrying of arms (and therefore is not really an idiom) but only in the service of an organized militia. No dictionary has ever adopted that definition, and we have been apprised of no source that indicates that it carried that meaning at the time of the founding. But it is easy to see why petitioners and the dissent are driven to the hybrid definition. Giving "bear Arms" its idiomatic meaning would cause the protected right to consist of the right to be a soldier or to wage war—an absurdity that no commentator has ever endorsed. Worse still, the phrase "keep and bear Arms" would be incoherent. The word "Arms" would have two different meanings at once: "weapons" (as the object of "keep") and (as the object of "bear") one-half of an idiom. It would be rather like saying "He filled and kicked the bucket" to mean "He filled the bucket and died." Grotesque.

Petitioners justify their limitation of "bear arms" to the military context by pointing out the unremarkable fact that it was often used in that context—the same mistake they made with respect to "keep arms." It is especially unremarkable that the phrase was often used in a military context in the federal legal sources (such as records of congressional debate) that have been the focus of petitioners' inquiry. Those sources would have had little occasion to use it *except* in discussions about the standing army and the militia. And the phrases used primarily in those military discussions include not only "bear arms" but also "carry arms," "possess arms," and "have arms"—though no one thinks that those *other* phrases also had special military meanings. The common references to those "fit to bear arms" in congressional discussions about the militia are matched by use of the same phrase in the few nonmilitary federal contexts where the concept would be relevant. Other legal sources frequently used "bear arms" in nonmilitary contexts. Cunningham's legal dictionary, cited above, gave as an example of its usage a sentence unrelated to military affairs ("Servants and labourers shall use bows and arrows on *Sundays*, &c. and not bear other arms"). And if one looks beyond legal sources, "bear arms" was frequently used in nonmilitary contexts. …

Justice Stevens points to a study by *amici* supposedly showing that the phrase "bear arms" was most frequently used in the military context. Of course, as we have said, the fact that the phrase was commonly used in a particular context does not show that it is limited to that context, and, in any event, we have given many sources where the phrase was used in nonmilitary contexts. Moreover, the study's collection appears to include (who knows how many times) the idiomatic phrase "bear arms against," which is irrelevant. The *amici* also dismiss examples such as " 'bear arms … for the purpose of killing game' " because those uses are "expressly qualified." (Justice Stevens uses the same excuse for dismissing the state constitutional provisions analogous to the Second Amendment that identify private-use purposes for which the individual right can be asserted.) That analysis is faulty. A purposive qualifying phrase that contradicts the word or phrase it modifies is unknown this side of the looking glass (except, apparently, in some courses on Linguistics). If "bear arms" means, as we think, simply the carrying of arms, a modifier can limit the purpose of the carriage ("for the purpose of self-defense" or "to make war against the King"). But if "bear arms" means, as the petitioners and the dissent think, the carrying of arms only for military purposes, one simply cannot add "for the purpose of killing game." The right "to carry arms in the militia for the purpose of killing game" is worthy of the mad hatter. Thus, these purposive qualifying phrases positively establish that "to bear arms" is not limited to military use.

Justice Stevens places great weight on James Madison's inclusion of a conscientious-objector clause in his original draft of the Second Amendment: "but no person religiously scrupulous of bearing arms, shall be compelled to render military service in person." He argues that this clause establishes that the drafters of the Second Amendment intended "bear Arms" to refer only to military service. It is always perilous to derive the meaning of an adopted provision from another provision deleted in the drafting process. In any case, what Justice Stevens would conclude from the deleted provision does not follow. It was not meant to exempt from military service those who objected to going to war but had no scruples about personal gunfights. Quakers opposed the use of arms not just for militia service, but for any violent purpose whatsoever—so much so that Quaker frontiersmen were forbidden to use arms to defend their families, even though "[i]n such circumstances the temptation to seize a hunting rifle or knife in self-defense ... must sometimes have been almost overwhelming." The Pennsylvania Militia Act of 1757 exempted from service those *"scrupling the use of arms"*—a phrase that no one contends had an idiomatic meaning. Thus, the most natural interpretation of Madison's deleted text is that those opposed to carrying weapons for potential violent confrontation would not be "compelled to render military service," in which such carrying would be required.

Finally, Justice Stevens suggests that "keep and bear Arms" was some sort of term of art, presumably akin to "hue and cry" or "cease and desist." (This suggestion usefully evades the problem that there is no evidence whatsoever to support a military reading of "keep arms.") Justice Stevens believes that the unitary meaning of "keep and bear Arms" is established by the Second Amendment's calling it a "right" (singular) rather than "rights" (plural). There is nothing to this. State constitutions of the founding period routinely grouped multiple (related) guarantees under a singular "right," and the First Amendment protects the "right [singular] of the people peaceably to assemble, and to petition the Government for a redress of grievances." And even if "keep and bear Arms" were a unitary phrase, we find no evidence that it bore a military meaning. Although the phrase was not at all common (which would be unusual for a term of art), we have found instances of its use with a clearly nonmilitary connotation. In a 1780 debate in the House of Lords, for example, Lord Richmond described an order to disarm private citizens (not militia members) as "a violation of the constitutional right of Protestant subjects to keep and bear arms for their own defense." 49 The London Magazine or Gentleman's Monthly Intelligencer 467 (1780). In response, another member of Parliament referred to "the right of bearing arms for personal defence," making clear that no special military meaning for "keep and bear arms" was intended in the discussion.

c. Meaning of the Operative Clause. Putting all of these textual elements together, we find that they guarantee the individual right to possess and carry weapons in case of confrontation. This meaning is strongly confirmed by the historical background of the Second Amendment. We look to this because it has always been widely understood that the Second Amendment, like the First and Fourth Amendments, codified a *pre-existing* right. The very text of the Second Amendment implicitly recognizes the pre-existence of the right and declares only that it "shall not be infringed." As we said in *United States* v. *Cruikshank*, "[t]his is not a right granted by the Constitution. Neither is it in any manner dependent upon that instrument for its existence. The Second amendment declares that it shall not be infringed ... ."

Between the Restoration and the Glorious Revolution, the Stuart Kings Charles II and James II succeeded in using select militias loyal to them to suppress political dissidents, in part by disarming their opponents. Under the auspices of the 1671 Game Act, for example, the Catholic James II had ordered general disarmaments of regions home to his Protestant enemies. These experiences caused Englishmen to be extremely wary of concentrated military forces run by the state and to be jealous of their arms. They accordingly obtained an assurance from William and Mary, in the Declaration of Right (which was codified as the English Bill of Rights), that Protestants would never be disarmed: "That the subjects which are Protestants may have arms for their defense suitable to their conditions and as allowed by law." This right has long been understood to be the predecessor to our Second Amendment. It was clearly an individual right, having nothing whatever to do with service in a militia. To be sure, it was an individual right not available to the whole population, given that it was restricted to Protestants, and like all written English rights it was held only against the Crown, not Parliament. But it was secured to them as individuals, according to "libertarian political principles," not as members of a fighting force.

By the time of the founding, the right to have arms had become fundamental for English subjects. Blackstone, whose works, we have said, "constituted the preeminent authority on English law for the founding generation," cited the arms provision of the Bill of Rights as one of the fundamental rights of Englishmen. His description of it cannot possibly be thought to tie it to militia or military service. It was, he said, "the natural right of resistance and self-preservation," and "the right of having and using arms for self-preservation and defence." Other contemporary authorities concurred. Thus, the right secured in

1689 as a result of the Stuarts' abuses was by the time of the founding understood to be an individual right protecting against both public and private violence.

And, of course, what the Stuarts had tried to do to their political enemies, George III had tried to do to the colonists. In the tumultuous decades of the 1760's and 1770's, the Crown began to disarm the inhabitants of the most rebellious areas. That provoked polemical reactions by Americans invoking their rights as Englishmen to keep arms. A New York article of April 1769 said that "[i]t is a natural right which the people have reserved to themselves, confirmed by the Bill of Rights, to keep arms for their own defence." They understood the right to enable individuals to defend themselves. As the most important early American edition of Blackstone's Commentaries (by the law professor and former Antifederalist St. George Tucker) made clear in the notes to the description of the arms right, Americans understood the "right of self-preservation" as permitting a citizen to "repe[l] force by force" when "the intervention of society in his behalf, may be too late to prevent an injury."

There seems to us no doubt, on the basis of both text and history, that the Second Amendment conferred an individual right to keep and bear arms. Of course the right was not unlimited, just as the First Amendment's right of free speech was not. Thus, we do not read the Second Amendment to protect the right of citizens to carry arms for *any sort* of confrontation, just as we do not read the First Amendment to protect the right of citizens to speak for *any purpose*. Before turning to limitations upon the individual right, however, we must determine whether the prefatory clause of the Second Amendment comports with our interpretation of the operative clause.

2. Prefatory Clause.

The prefatory clause reads: "A well regulated Militia, being necessary to the security of a free State … ."

a. "Well-Regulated Militia." In *United States* v. *Miller*, we explained that "the Militia comprised all males physically capable of acting in concert for the common defense." That definition comports with founding-era sources. …

Petitioners take a seemingly narrower view of the militia, stating that "[m]ilitias are the state- and congressionally-regulated military forces described in the Militia Clauses (art. I, §8, cls. 15–16)." Although we agree with petitioners' interpretive assumption that "militia" means the same thing in Article I and the Second Amendment, we believe that petitioners identify the wrong thing, namely, the organized militia. Unlike armies and navies, which Congress is given the power to create ("to raise … Armies"; "to provide … a Navy," Art. I, §8, cls. 12–13), the militia is assumed by Article I already to be *in existence*. Congress is given the power to "provide for calling forth the militia," §8, cl. 15; and the power not to create, but to "organiz[e]" it—and not to organize "a" militia, which is what one would expect if the militia were to be a federal creation, but to organize "the" militia, connoting a body already in existence, *ibid.*, cl. 16. This is fully consistent with the ordinary definition of the militia as all able-bodied men. From that pool, Congress has plenary power to organize the units that will make up an effective fighting force. That is what Congress did in the first militia Act, which specified that "each and every free able-bodied white male citizen of the respective states, resident therein, who is or shall be of the age of eighteen years, and under the age of forty-five years (except as is herein after excepted) shall severally and respectively be enrolled in the militia." To be sure, Congress need not conscript every able-bodied man into the militia, because nothing in Article I suggests that in exercising its power to organize, discipline, and arm the militia, Congress must focus upon the entire body. Although the militia consists of all able-bodied men, the federally organized militia may consist of a subset of them.

Finally, the adjective "well-regulated" implies nothing more than the imposition of proper discipline and training. …

b. "Security of a Free State." The phrase "security of a free state" meant "security of a free polity," not security of each of the several States as the dissent below argued. Joseph Story wrote in his treatise on the Constitution that "the word 'state' is used in various senses [and in] its most enlarged sense, it means the people composing a particular nation or community." It is true that the term "State" elsewhere in the Constitution refers to individual States, but the phrase "security of a free state" and close variations seem to have been terms of art in 18th-century political discourse, meaning a " 'free country' " or free polity. Moreover, the other instances of "state" in the Constitution are typically accompanied by modifiers making clear that the reference is to the several States—"each state," "several states," "any state," "that state," "particular states," "one state," "no state." And the presence of the term "foreign state" in Article I and Article III shows that the word "state" did not have a single meaning in the Constitution.

There are many reasons why the militia was thought to be "necessary to the security of a free state." First, of course, it is useful in repelling invasions and suppressing insurrections. Second, it renders large standing armies unnecessary—an argument that Alexander Hamilton made in favor of federal control over the militia. Third, when the able-bodied men of a nation are trained in arms and organized, they are better able to resist tyranny.

3. Relationship between Prefatory Clause and Operative Clause

We reach the question, then: Does the preface fit with an operative clause that creates an individual right to keep and bear arms? It fits perfectly, once one knows the history that the founding generation knew and that we have described above. That history showed that the way tyrants had eliminated a militia consisting of all the able-bodied men was not by banning the militia but simply by taking away the people's arms, enabling a select militia or standing army to suppress political opponents. This is what had occurred in England that prompted codification of the right to have arms in the English Bill of Rights.

The debate with respect to the right to keep and bear arms, as with other guarantees in the Bill of Rights, was not over whether it was desirable (all agreed that it was) but over whether it needed to be codified in the Constitution. During the 1788 ratification debates, the fear that the federal government would disarm the people in order to impose rule through a standing army or select militia was pervasive in Antifederalist rhetoric. John Smilie, for example, worried not only that Congress's "command of the militia" could be used to create a "select militia," or to have "no militia at all," but also, as a separate concern, that "[w]hen a select militia is formed; the people in general may be disarmed." Federalists responded that because Congress was given no power to abridge the ancient right of individuals to keep and bear arms, such a force could never oppress the people. It was understood across the political spectrum that the right helped to secure the ideal of a citizen militia, which might be necessary to oppose an oppressive military force if the constitutional order broke down.

It is therefore entirely sensible that the Second Amendment's prefatory clause announces the purpose for which the right was codified: to prevent elimination of the militia. The prefatory clause does not suggest that preserving the militia was the only reason Americans valued the ancient right; most undoubtedly thought it even more important for self-defense and hunting. But the threat that the new Federal Government would destroy the citizens' militia by taking away their arms was the reason that right—unlike some other English rights—was codified in a written Constitution. Justice Breyer's assertion that individual self-defense is merely a "subsidiary interest" of the right to keep and bear arms, is profoundly mistaken. He bases that assertion solely upon the prologue—but that can only show that self-defense had little to do with the right's *codification;* it was the *central component* of the right itself.

Besides ignoring the historical reality that the Second Amendment was not intended to lay down a "novel principl[e]" but rather codified a right "inherited from our English ancestors," petitioners' interpretation does not even achieve the narrower purpose that prompted codification of the right. If, as they believe, the Second Amendment right is no more than the right to keep and use weapons as a member of an organized militia—if, that is, the *organized* militia is the sole institutional beneficiary of the Second Amendment's guarantee—it does not assure the existence of a "citizens' militia" as a safeguard against tyranny. For Congress retains plenary authority to organize the militia, which must include the authority to say who will belong to the organized force. That is why the first Militia Act's requirement that only whites enroll caused States to amend their militia laws to exclude free blacks. Thus, if petitioners are correct, the Second Amendment protects citizens' right to use a gun in an organization from which Congress has plenary authority to exclude them. It guarantees a select militia of the sort the Stuart kings found useful, but not the people's militia that was the concern of the founding generation.

B

Our interpretation is confirmed by analogous arms-bearing rights in state constitutions that preceded and immediately followed adoption of the Second Amendment. Four States adopted analogues to the Federal Second Amendment in the period between independence and the ratification of the Bill of Rights. Two of them—Pennsylvania and Vermont—clearly adopted individual rights unconnected to militia service. Pennsylvania's Declaration of Rights of 1776 said: "That the people have a right to bear arms *for the defence of themselves*, and the state … ." In 1777, Vermont adopted the identical provision, except for inconsequential differences in punctuation and capitalization.

North Carolina also codified a right to bear arms in 1776: "That the people have a right to bear arms, for the defence of the State … ." This could plausibly be read to support only a right to bear arms in a militia—but that is a peculiar way to make the point in a constitution that elsewhere repeatedly mentions the militia explicitly. Many colonial statutes required individual arms-bearing for public-safety reasons—such as the 1770 Georgia law that "for the security and *defence of this province* from internal dangers and insurrections" required those men who qualified for militia duty individually "to carry fire arms" "to places of public worship." That broad public-safety understanding was the connotation given to the North Carolina right by that State's Supreme Court in 1843.

The 1780 Massachusetts Constitution presented another variation on the theme: "The people have a right to keep and to bear arms for the common defence… ." Once again, if one gives narrow meaning to the phrase "common defence" this can be thought to limit the right to the bearing of arms in a state-organized military force. But once again the State's highest court thought otherwise. Writing for the court in an 1825 libel case, Chief Justice Parker wrote: "The liberty of the press was to be unrestrained, but he who used it was to be responsible in cases of its abuse; like the right to keep fire arms, which does not protect him who uses them for annoyance or destruction." The analogy makes no sense if firearms could not be used for any individual purpose at all. (19th-century courts never read "common defence" to limit the use of weapons to militia service).

We therefore believe that the most likely reading of all four of these pre-Second Amendment state constitutional provisions is that they secured an individual right to bear arms for defensive purposes. Other States did not include rights to bear arms in their pre-1789 constitutions—although in Virginia a Second Amendment analogue was proposed (unsuccessfully) by Thomas Jefferson. (It read: "No freeman shall ever be debarred the use of arms [within his own lands or tenements]."

Between 1789 and 1820, nine States adopted Second Amendment analogues. Four of them—Kentucky, Ohio, Indiana, and Missouri—referred to the right of the people to "bear arms in defence of themselves and the State." Another three States—Mississippi, Connecticut, and Alabama—used the even more individualistic phrasing that each citizen has the "right to bear arms in defence of himself and the State." Finally, two States—Tennessee and Maine—used the "common defence" language of Massachusetts. That of the nine state constitutional protections for the right to bear arms enacted immediately after 1789 at least seven unequivocally protected an individual citizen's right to self-defense is strong evidence that that is how the founding generation conceived of the right. And with one possible exception that we discuss in Part II–D–2, 19th-century courts and commentators interpreted these state constitutional provisions to protect an individual right to use arms for self-defense.

The historical narrative that petitioners must endorse would thus treat the Federal Second Amendment as an odd outlier, protecting a right unknown in state constitutions or at English common law, based on little more than an overreading of the prefatory clause.

C

Justice Stevens relies on the drafting history of the Second Amendment—the various proposals in the state conventions and the debates in Congress. It is dubious to rely on such history to interpret a text that was widely understood to codify a pre-existing right, rather than to fashion a new one. But even assuming that this legislative history is relevant, Justice Stevens flatly misreads the historical record.

It is true, as Justice Stevens says, that there was concern that the Federal Government would abolish the institution of the state militia. That concern found expression, however, *not* in the various Second Amendment precursors proposed in the State conventions, but in separate structural provisions that would have given the States concurrent and seemingly nonpre-emptible authority to organize, discipline, and arm the militia when the Federal Government failed to do so. The Second Amendment precursors, by contrast, referred to the individual English right already codified in two (and probably four) State constitutions. The Federalist-dominated first Congress chose to reject virtually all major structural revisions favored by the Antifederalists, including the proposed militia amendments. Rather, it adopted primarily the popular and uncontroversial (though, in the Federalists' view, unnecessary) individual-rights amendments. The Second Amendment right, protecting only individuals' liberty to keep and carry arms, did nothing to assuage Antifederalists' concerns about federal control of the militia.

Justice Stevens thinks it significant that the Virginia, New York, and North Carolina Second Amendment proposals were "embedded … within a group of principles that are distinctly military in meaning," such as statements about the danger of standing armies. But so was the highly influential minority proposal in Pennsylvania, yet that proposal, with its reference to hunting, plainly referred to an individual right. Other than that erroneous point, Justice Stevens has brought forward absolutely no evidence that those proposals conferred only a right to carry arms in a militia. By contrast, New Hampshire's proposal, the Pennsylvania minority's proposal, and Samuel Adams' proposal in Massachusetts unequivocally referred to individual rights, as did two state constitutional provisions at the time. Justice Stevens' view thus relies on the proposition, unsupported by any evidence, that different people of the founding period had vastly different conceptions of the right to keep and bear arms. That simply does not comport with our longstanding view that the Bill of Rights codified venerable, widely understood liberties.

D

We now address how the Second Amendment was interpreted from immediately after its ratification through the end of the 19th century. Before proceeding, however, we take issue with Justice Stevens' equating of these sources with postenactment legislative history, a comparison that betrays a fundamental misunderstanding of a court's interpretive task. "Legislative history," of course, refers to the pre-enactment statements of those who drafted or voted for a law; it is considered persuasive by some, not because they reflect the general understanding of the disputed terms, but because the legislators who heard or read those statements presumably voted with that understanding. "Postenactment legislative history," a deprecatory contradiction in terms, refers to statements of those who drafted or voted for the law that are made after its enactment and hence could have had no effect on the congressional vote. It most certainly does not refer to the examination of a variety of legal and other sources to determine *the public understanding* of a legal text in the period after its enactment or ratification. That sort of inquiry is a critical tool of constitutional interpretation. As we will show, virtually all interpreters of the Second Amendment in the century after its enactment interpreted the amendment as we do.

1. Post-ratification Commentary

Three important founding-era legal scholars interpreted the Second Amendment in published writings. All three understood it to protect an individual right unconnected with militia service.

St. George Tucker's version of *Blackstone's Commentaries*, as we explained above, conceived of the Blackstonian arms right as necessary for self-defense. He equated that right, absent the religious and class-based restrictions, with the Second Amendment. In Note D, entitled, "View of the Constitution of the United States," Tucker elaborated on the Second Amendment: "This may be considered as the true palladium of liberty … . The right to self-defence is the first law of nature: in most governments it has been the study of rulers to confine the right within the narrowest limits possible. Wherever standing armies are kept up, and the right of the people to keep and bear arms is, under any colour or pretext whatsoever, prohibited, liberty, if not already annihilated, is on the brink of destruction." He believed that the English game laws had abridged the right by prohibiting "keeping a gun or other engine for the destruction of game." He later grouped the right with some of the individual rights included in the First Amendment and said that if "a law be passed by congress, prohibiting" any of those rights, it would "be the province of the judiciary to pronounce whether any such act were constitutional, or not; and if not, to acquit the accused … ." It is unlikely that Tucker was referring to a person's being "accused" of violating a law making it a crime to bear arms in a state militia.

In 1825, William Rawle, a prominent lawyer who had been a member of the Pennsylvania Assembly that ratified the Bill of Rights, published an influential treatise, which analyzed the Second Amendment as follows:

> "The first [principle] is a declaration that a well regulated militia is necessary to the security of a free state; a proposition from which few will dissent… .
>
> "The corollary, from the first position is, that the right of the people to keep and bear arms shall not be infringed.
>
> "The prohibition is general. No clause in the constitution could by any rule of construction be conceived to give to congress a power to disarm the people. Such a flagitious attempt could only be made under some general pretence by a state legislature. But if in any blind pursuit of inordinate power, either should attempt it, this amendment may be appealed to as a restraint on both."

Like Tucker, Rawle regarded the English game laws as violating the right codified in the Second Amendment. Rawle clearly differentiated between the people's right to bear arms and their service in a militia: "In a people permitted and accustomed to bear arms, we have the rudiments of a militia, which properly consists of armed citizens, divided into military bands, and instructed at least in part, in the use of arms for the purposes of war." Rawle further said that the Second Amendment right ought not "be abused to the disturbance of the public peace," such as by assembling with other armed individuals "for an unlawful purpose"—statements that make no sense if the right does not extend to *any* individual purpose.

Joseph Story published his famous *Commentaries on the Constitution of the United States* in 1833. Justice Stevens suggests that "[t]here is not so much as a whisper" in Story's explanation of the Second Amendment that favors the individual-rights view. That is wrong. Story explained that the English Bill of Rights had also included a "right to bear arms," a right that, as we have discussed, had nothing to do with militia service. He then equated the English right with the Second Amendment:

> "§1891. A similar provision [to the Second Amendment] in favour of protestants (for to them it is confined) is to be found in the bill of rights of 1688, it being declared, 'that the subjects, which are protestants, may have arms for their defence suitable to their condition, and as allowed by law.' But under various pretences the effect of this provision has been greatly narrowed; and it is at present in England more nominal than real, as a defensive privilege." (Footnotes omitted.)

This comparison to the Declaration of Right would not make sense if the Second Amendment right was the right to use a gun in a militia, which was plainly not what the English right protected. As the Tennessee Supreme Court recognized 38 years after Story wrote his Commentaries, "[t]he passage from Story, shows clearly that this right was intended … and was guaranteed to, and to be exercised and enjoyed by the citizen as such, and not by him as a soldier, or in defense solely of his political rights." Story's *Commentaries* also cite as support Tucker and Rawle, both of whom clearly viewed the right as unconnected to militia service. See 3 Story §1890, n. 2; §1891, n. 3. In addition, in a shorter 1840 work Story wrote: "One of the ordinary modes, by which tyrants accomplish their purposes without resistance, is, by disarming the people, and making it an offence to keep arms, and by substituting a regular army in the stead of a resort to the militia."

Antislavery advocates routinely invoked the right to bear arms for self-defense. Joel Tiffany, for example, citing Blackstone's description of the right, wrote that "the right to keep and bear arms, also implies the right to use them if necessary in self defence; without this right to use the guaranty would have hardly been worth the paper it consumed." In his famous Senate speech about the 1856 "Bleeding Kansas" conflict, Charles Sumner proclaimed:

> "The rifle has ever been the companion of the pioneer and, under God, his tutelary protector against the red man and the beast of the forest. Never was this efficient weapon more needed in just self-defence, than now in Kansas, and at least one article in our National Constitution must be blotted out, before the complete right to it can in any way be impeached. And yet such is the madness of the hour, that, in defiance of the solemn guarantee, embodied in the Amendments to the Constitution, that 'the right of the people to keep and bear arms shall not be infringed,' the people of Kansas have been arraigned for keeping and bearing them, and the Senator from South Carolina has had the face to say openly, on this floor, that they should be disarmed—of course, that the fanatics of Slavery, his allies and constituents, may meet no impediment." The Crime Against Kansas, May 19–20, 1856, in *American Speeches: Political Oratory from the Revolution to the Civil War* 553, 606–607 (2006).

We have found only one early 19th-century commentator who clearly conditioned the right to keep and bear arms upon service in the militia—and he recognized that the prevailing view was to the contrary. "The provision of the constitution, declaring the right of the people to keep and bear arms, &c. was probably intended to apply to the right of the people to bear arms for such [militia-related] purposes only, and not to prevent congress or the legislatures of the different states from enacting laws to prevent the citizens from always going armed. A different construction however has been given to it."

2. Pre-Civil War Case Law

The 19th-century cases that interpreted the Second Amendment universally support an individual right unconnected to militia service. In *Houston* v. *Moore*, this Court held that States have concurrent power over the militia, at least where not pre-empted by Congress. Agreeing in dissent that States could "organize, discipline, and arm" the militia in the absence of conflicting federal regulation, Justice Story said that the Second Amendment "may not, perhaps, be thought to have any important bearing on this point. If it have, it confirms and illustrates, rather than impugns the reasoning already suggested." Of course, if the Amendment simply "protect[ed] the right of the people of each of the several States to maintain a well-regulated militia," it would have enormous and obvious bearing on the point. But the Court and Story derived the States' power over the militia from the nonexclusive nature of federal power, not from the Second Amendment, whose preamble merely "confirms and illustrates" the importance of the militia. Even clearer was Justice Baldwin. In the famous fugitive-slave case of *Johnson v. Thomkins*, Baldwin, sitting as a circuit judge, cited both the Second Amendment and the Pennsylvania analogue for his conclusion that a citizen has "a right to carry arms in defence of his property or person, and to use them, if either were assailed with such force, numbers or violence as made it necessary for the protection or safety of either."

Many early 19th-century state cases indicated that the Second Amendment right to bear arms was an individual right unconnected to militia service, though subject to certain restrictions. A Virginia case in 1824 holding that the Constitution did not extend to free blacks explained that "numerous restrictions imposed on [blacks] in our Statute Book, many of which are inconsistent with the letter and spirit of the Constitution, both of this State and of the United States as respects the free whites, demonstrate, that, here, those instruments have not been considered to extend equally to both classes of our population. We will only instance the restriction upon the migration of free blacks into this State, and upon their right to bear arms." The claim was obviously not that blacks were prevented from carrying guns in the militia. See also *Waters* v. *State*, (because free blacks were treated as a "dangerous population," "laws have been passed to prevent their migration into this State; to make it unlawful for them to bear arms; to guard even their religious assemblages with peculiar watchfulness"). An 1829 decision by the Supreme Court of Michigan said: "The constitution of the United States also grants to the citizen the right to keep and bear arms. But the grant of this privilege cannot be construed into the right in him who keeps a gun to destroy his neighbor. No rights are intended to be granted by the constitution for an unlawful or unjustifiable purpose." It is not possible to read this as discussing anything other than an individual right unconnected to militia service. If it did have to do with militia service, the limitation upon it would not be any "unlawful or unjustifiable purpose," but any nonmilitary purpose whatsoever.

In the Georgia Supreme Court construed the Second Amendment as protecting the "*natural* right of self-defence" and therefore struck down a ban on carrying pistols openly. Its opinion perfectly captured the way in which the operative clause of the Second Amendment furthers the purpose announced in the prefatory clause, in continuity with the English right:

> "The right of the whole people, old and young, men, women and boys, and not militia only, to keep and bear *arms* of every description, and not *such* merely as are used by the *militia,* shall not be *infringed,* curtailed, or broken in upon, in the smallest degree; and all this for the important end to be attained: the rearing up and qualifying a well-regulated militia, so vitally necessary to the security of a free State. Our opinion is, that any law, State or Federal, is repugnant to the Constitution, and void, which contravenes this *right,* originally belonging to our forefathers, trampled under foot by Charles I. and his two wicked sons and successors, re-established by the revolution of 1688, conveyed to this land of liberty by the colonists, and finally incorporated conspicuously in our own Magna Charta!"

Likewise, in *State* v. *Chandler*, the Louisiana Supreme Court held that citizens had a right to carry arms openly: "This is the right guaranteed by the Constitution of the United States, and which is calculated to incite men to a manly and noble defence of themselves, if necessary, and of their country, without any tendency to secret advantages and unmanly assassinations."

Those who believe that the Second Amendment preserves only a militia-centered right place great reliance on the Tennessee Supreme Court's 1840 decision in *Aymette* v. *State*. The case does not stand for that broad proposition; in fact, the case does not mention the word "militia" at all, except in its quoting of the Second Amendment. *Aymette* held that the state constitutional guarantee of the right to "bear" arms did not prohibit the banning of concealed weapons. The opinion first recognized that both the state right and the federal right were descendents of the 1689 English right, but (erroneously, and contrary to virtually all other authorities) read that right to refer only to "protect[ion of] the public liberty" and "keep[ing] in awe those in power," at 158. The court then adopted a sort of middle position, whereby citizens were permitted to carry arms openly, unconnected with any service in a formal militia, but were given the right to use them only for the military purpose of banding together to oppose tyranny. This odd reading of the right is, to be sure, not the one we adopt—but it is not petitioners' reading either. More importantly, seven years earlier the Tennessee Supreme Court had treated the state constitutional provision as conferring a right "of all the free citizens of the State to keep and bear arms for their defence," and 21 years later the court held that the "keep" portion of the state constitutional right included the right to personal self-defense: "[T]he right to keep arms involves, necessarily, the right to use such arms for all the ordinary purposes, and in all the ordinary modes usual in the country, and to which arms are adapted, limited by the duties of a good citizen in times of peace."

3. Post-Civil War Legislation.

In the aftermath of the Civil War, there was an outpouring of discussion of the Second Amendment in Congress and in public discourse, as people debated whether and how to secure constitutional rights for newly free slaves Since those discussions took place 75 years after the ratification of the Second Amendment, they do not provide as much insight into its original meaning as earlier sources. Yet those born and educated in the early 19th century faced a widespread effort to limit arms ownership by a large number of citizens; their understanding of the origins and continuing significance of the Amendment is instructive.

Blacks were routinely disarmed by Southern States after the Civil War. Those who opposed these injustices frequently stated that they infringed blacks' constitutional right to keep and bear arms. Needless to say, the claim was not that blacks were being prohibited from carrying arms in an organized state militia. A Report of the Commission of the Freedmen's Bureau in 1866 stated plainly: "[T]he civil law [of Kentucky] prohibits the colored man from bearing arms. . . . Their arms are taken from them by the civil authorities… . Thus, the right of the people to keep and bear arms as provided in the Constitution is *infringed*." A joint congressional Report decried:

> "in some parts of [South Carolina], armed parties are, without proper authority, engaged in seizing all fire-arms found in the hands of the freemen. Such conduct is in clear and direct violation of their personal rights as guaranteed by the Constitution of the United States, which declares that 'the right of the people to keep and bear arms shall not be infringed.' The freedmen of South Carolina have shown by their peaceful and orderly conduct that they can safely be trusted with fire-arms, and they need them to kill game for subsistence, and to protect their crops from destruction by birds and animals." Joint Comm. on Reconstruction, H. R. Rep. No. 30, 39th Cong., 1st Sess., pt. 2, p. 229 (1866) (Proposed Circular of Brigadier General R. Saxton).
>
> The view expressed in these statements was widely reported and was apparently widely held. For example, an editorial in *The Loyal Georgian* (Augusta) on February 3, 1866, assured blacks that "[a]ll men, without distinction of color, have the right to keep and bear arms to defend their homes, families or themselves."

Congress enacted the Freedmen's Bureau Act on July 16, 1866. Section 14 stated:

> "[T]he right ... to have full and equal benefit of all laws and proceedings concerning personal liberty, personal security, and the acquisition, enjoyment, and disposition of estate, real and personal, including the constitutional right to bear arms, shall be secured to and enjoyed by all the citizens ... without respect to race or color, or previous condition of slavery.... "

The understanding that the Second Amendment gave freed blacks the right to keep and bear arms was reflected in congressional discussion of the bill, with even an opponent of it saying that the founding generation "were for every man bearing his arms about him and keeping them in his house, his castle, for his own defense."

Similar discussion attended the passage of the Civil Rights Act of 1871 and the Fourteenth Amendment. For example, Representative Butler said of the Act: "Section eight is intended to enforce the well-known constitutional provision guaranteeing the right of the citizen to 'keep and bear arms,' and provides that whoever shall take away, by force or violence, or by threats and intimidation, the arms and weapons which any person may have for his defense, shall be deemed guilty of larceny of the same." With respect to the proposed Amendment, Senator Pomeroy described as one of the three "indispensable" "safeguards of liberty ... under the Constitution" a man's "right to bear arms for the defense of himself and family and his homestead." Representative Nye thought the Fourteenth Amendment unnecessary because "[a]s citizens of the United States [blacks] have equal right to protection, and to keep and bear arms for self-defense."

It was plainly the understanding in the post-Civil War Congress that the Second Amendment protected an individual right to use arms for self-defense.

4. Post-Civil War Commentators.

Every late-19th-century legal scholar that we have read interpreted the Second Amendment to secure an individual right unconnected with militia service. The most famous was the judge and professor Thomas Cooley, who wrote a massively popular 1868 *Treatise on Constitutional Limitations*. Concerning the Second Amendment it said:

> "Among the other defences to personal liberty should be mentioned the right of the people to keep and bear arms.... The alternative to a standing army is 'a well-regulated militia,' but this cannot exist unless the people are trained to bearing arms. How far it is in the power of the legislature to regulate this right, we shall not undertake to say, as happily there has been very little occasion to discuss that subject by the courts."

That Cooley understood the right not as connected to militia service, but as securing the militia by ensuring a populace familiar with arms, is made even clearer in his 1880 work, *General Principles of Constitutional Law*. The

Second Amendment, he said, "was adopted with some modification and enlargement from the English Bill of Rights of 1688, where it stood as a protest against arbitrary action of the overturned dynasty in disarming the people." In a section entitled "The Right in General," he continued:

> "It might be supposed from the phraseology of this provision that the right to keep and bear arms was only guaranteed to the militia; but this would be an interpretation not warranted by the intent. The militia, as has been elsewhere explained, consists of those persons who, under the law, are liable to the performance of military duty, and are officered and enrolled for service when called upon. But the law may make provision for the enrolment of all who are fit to perform military duty, or of a small number only, or it may wholly omit to make any provision at all; and if the right were limited to those enrolled, the purpose of this guaranty might be defeated altogether by the action or neglect to act of the government it was meant to hold in check. The meaning of the provision undoubtedly is, that the people, from whom the militia must be taken, shall have the right to keep and bear arms; and they need no permission or regulation of law for the purpose. But this enables government to have a well-regulated militia; for to bear arms implies something more than the mere keeping; it implies the learning to handle and use them in a way that makes those who keep them ready for their efficient use; in other words, it implies the right to meet for voluntary discipline in arms, observing in doing so the laws of public order."

All other post-Civil War 19th-century sources we have found concurred with Cooley. One example from each decade will convey the general flavor:

> "[The purpose of the Second Amendment is] to secure a well-armed militia. . . . But a militia would be useless unless the citizens were enabled to exercise themselves in the use of warlike weapons. To preserve this privilege, and to secure to the people the ability to oppose themselves in military force against the usurpations of government, as well as against enemies from without, that government is forbidden by any law or proceeding to invade or destroy the right to keep and bear arms. . . . The clause is analogous to the one securing the freedom of speech and of the press. Freedom, not license, is secured; the fair use, not the libellous abuse, is protected." J. Pomeroy, *An Introduction to the Constitutional Law of the United States* 152–153 (1868) (hereinafter Pomeroy).

> "As the Constitution of the United States, and the constitutions of several of the states, in terms more or less comprehensive, declare the right of the people to keep and bear arms, it has been a subject of grave discussion, in some of the state courts, whether a statute prohibiting persons, when not on a journey, or as travellers, from *wearing or carrying concealed weapons*, be constitutional. There has been a great difference of opinion on the question.

> "Some general knowledge of firearms is important to the public welfare; because it would be impossible, in case of war, to organize promptly an efficient force of volunteers unless the people had some familiarity with weapons of war. The Constitution secures the right of the people to keep and bear arms. No doubt, a citizen who keeps a gun or pistol under judicious precautions, practices in safe places the use of it, and in due time teaches his sons to do the same, exercises his individual right. No doubt, a person whose residence or duties involve peculiar peril may keep a pistol for prudent self-defence."

> "The right to bear arms has always been the distinctive privilege of freemen. Aside from any necessity of self-protection to the person, it represents among all nations power coupled with the exercise of a certain jurisdiction. . . . [I]t was not necessary that the right to bear arms should be granted in the Constitution, for it had always existed."

E

We now ask whether any of our precedents forecloses the conclusions we have reached about the meaning of the Second Amendment.

United States v. *Cruikshank*, in the course of vacating the convictions of members of a white mob for depriving blacks of their right to keep and bear arms, held that the Second Amendment does not by its own force apply to anyone other than the Federal Government. The opinion explained that the right "is not a right granted by the Constitution [or] in any manner dependent upon that instrument for its existence. The second amendment ... means no more than that it shall not be infringed by Congress." States, we said, were free to restrict or protect the right under their police powers. The limited discussion of the Second Amendment in *Cruikshank* supports, if anything, the individual-rights interpretation. There was no claim in *Cruikshank* that the victims had been deprived of their right to carry arms in a militia; indeed, the Governor had disbanded the local militia unit the year before the mob's attack. We described the right protected by the Second Amendment as " 'bearing arms for a lawful purpose' " and said that "the people [must] look for their protection against any violation by their fellow-citizens of the rights it recognizes" to the States' police power. That discussion makes little sense if it is only a right to bear arms in a state militia.

Presser v. *Illinois* held that the right to keep and bear arms was not violated by a law that forbade "bodies of men to associate together as military organizations, or to drill or parade with arms in cities and towns unless authorized by law." This does not refute the individual-rights interpretation of the Amendment; no one supporting that interpretation has contended that States may not ban such groups. Justice Stevens presses *Presser* into service to support his view that the right to bear arms is limited to service in the militia by joining *Presser*'s brief discussion of the Second Amendment with a later portion of the opinion making the seemingly relevant (to the Second Amendment) point that the plaintiff was not a member of the state militia. Unfortunately for Justice Stevens' argument, that later portion deals with the *Fourteenth Amendment;* it was the *Fourteenth Amendment* to which the plaintiff's nonmembership in the militia was relevant. Thus, Justice Stevens' statement that *Presser* "suggested that... nothing in the Constitution protected the use of arms outside the context of a militia," is simply wrong. *Presser* said nothing about the Second Amendment's meaning or scope, beyond the fact that it does not prevent the prohibition of private paramilitary organizations.

Justice Stevens places overwhelming reliance upon this Court's decision in *United States* v. *Miller*, "[H]undreds of judges," we are told, "have relied on the view of the amendment we endorsed there," and "[e]ven if the textual and historical arguments on both side of the issue were evenly balanced, respect for the well-settled views of all of our predecessors on this Court, and for the rule of law itself ... would prevent most jurists from endorsing such a dramatic upheaval in the law." And what is, according to Justice Stevens, the holding of *Miller* that demands such obeisance? That the Second Amendment "protects the right to keep and bear arms for certain military purposes, but that it does not curtail the legislature's power to regulate the nonmilitary use and ownership of weapons."

Nothing so clearly demonstrates the weakness of Justice Stevens' case. *Miller* did not hold that and cannot possibly be read to have held that. The judgment in the case upheld against a Second Amendment challenge two men's federal convictions for transporting an unregistered short-barreled shotgun in interstate commerce, in violation of the National Firearms Act. It is entirely clear that the Court's basis for saying that the Second Amendment did not apply was *not* that the defendants were "bear[ing] arms" not "for ... military purposes" but for "nonmilitary use." Rather, it was that the *type of weapon at issue* was not eligible for Second Amendment protection: "In the absence of any evidence tending to show that the possession or use of a [short-barreled shotgun] at this time has some reasonable relationship to the preservation or efficiency of a well regulated militia, we cannot say that the Second Amendment guarantees the right to keep and bear *such an instrument.*" "Certainly," the Court continued, "it is not within judicial notice that this weapon is any part of the ordinary military equipment or that its use could contribute to the common defense." Beyond that, the opinion provided no explanation of the content of the right.

This holding is not only consistent with, but positively suggests, that the Second Amendment confers an individual right to keep and bear arms (though only arms that "have some reasonable relationship to the preservation or efficiency of a well regulated militia"). Had the Court believed that the Second Amendment protects only those serving in the militia, it would have been odd to examine the character of the weapon rather than simply note that the two crooks were not militiamen. Justice Stevens can say again and again that *Miller* did "not turn on the difference between muskets and sawed-off shotguns, it turned, rather, on the basic difference between the military and nonmilitary use and possession of guns," but the words of the opinion prove otherwise. The most Justice Stevens can plausibly claim for *Miller* is that it declined to decide the nature of the Second Amendment right, despite the Solicitor General's argument (made in the alternative) that the right was collective. *Miller* stands only for the proposition that the Second Amendment right, whatever its nature, extends only to certain types of weapons.

It is particularly wrongheaded to read *Miller* for more than what it said, because the case did not even purport to be a thorough examination of the Second Amendment. Justice Stevens claims that the opinion reached its conclusion "[a]fter reviewing many of the same sources that are discussed at greater length by the Court today." Not many, which was not entirely the Court's fault. The respondent made no appearance in the case, neither filing a brief nor appearing at oral argument; the Court heard from no one but the Government (reason enough, one would think, not to make that case the beginning and the end of this Court's consideration of the Second Amendment). The Government's brief spent two pages discussing English legal sources, concluding "that at least the carrying of weapons without lawful occasion or excuse was always a crime" and that (because of the class-based restrictions and the prohibition on terrorizing people with dangerous or unusual weapons) "the early English law did not guarantee an unrestricted right to bear arms." It then went on to rely primarily on the discussion of the English right to bear arms in *Aymette* v. *State* for the proposition that the only uses of arms protected by the Second Amendment are those that relate to the militia, not self-defense. The final section of the brief recognized that "some courts have said that the right to bear arms includes the right of the individual to have them for the protection of his person and property," and launched an alternative argument that "weapons which are commonly used by criminals," such as sawed-off shotguns, are not protected. The Government's *Miller* brief thus provided scant discussion of the history of the Second Amendment—and the Court was presented with no counterdiscussion. As for the text of the Court's opinion itself, that discusses *none* of the history of the Second Amendment. It assumes from the prologue that the Amendment was designed to preserve the militia, and then reviews some historical materials dealing with the nature of the militia, and in particular with the nature of the arms their members were expected to possess, *id.*, at 178–182. Not a word *(not a word)*about the history of the Second Amendment. This is the mighty rock upon which the dissent rests its case.

We may as well consider at this point (for we will have to consider eventually) *what* types of weapons *Miller* permits. Read in isolation, *Miller*'s phrase "part of ordinary military equipment" could mean that only those weapons useful in warfare are protected. That would be a startling reading of the opinion, since it would mean that the National Firearms Act's restrictions on machineguns (not challenged in *Miller*) might be unconstitutional, machineguns being useful in warfare in 1939. We think that *Miller*'s "ordinary military equipment" language must be read in tandem with what comes after: "[O]rdinarily when called for [militia] service [able-bodied] men were expected to appear bearing arms supplied by themselves and of the kind in common use at the time." The traditional militia was formed from a pool of men bringing arms "in common use at the time" for lawful purposes like self-defense. "In the colonial and revolutionary war era, [small-arms] weapons used by militiamen and weapons used in defense of person and home were one and the same." Indeed, that is precisely the way in which the Second Amendment's operative clause furthers the purpose announced in its preface. We therefore read *Miller* to say only that the Second Amendment does not protect those weapons not typically possessed by law-abiding citizens for lawful purposes, such as short-barreled shotguns. That accords with the historical understanding of the scope of the right, see Part III.

We conclude that nothing in our precedents forecloses our adoption of the original understanding of the Second Amendment. It should be unsurprising that such a significant matter has been for so long judicially unresolved. For most of our history, the Bill of Rights was not thought applicable to the States, and the Federal Government did not significantly regulate the possession of firearms by law-abiding citizens. Other provisions of the Bill of Rights have similarly remained unilluminated for lengthy periods. This Court first held a law to violate the First Amendment's guarantee of freedom of speech in 1931, almost 150 years after the Amendment was ratified, and it was not until after World War II that we held a law invalid under the Establishment Clause. Even a question as basic as the scope of proscribable libel was not addressed by this Court until 1964, nearly two centuries after the founding. It is demonstrably not true that, as Justice Stevens claims, "for most of our history, the invalidity of Second-Amendment-based objections to firearms regulations has been well settled and uncontroversial." For most of our history the question did not present itself.

III

Like most rights, the right secured by the Second Amendment is not unlimited. From Blackstone through the 19th-century cases, commentators and courts routinely explained that the right was not a right to keep and carry any weapon whatsoever in any manner whatsoever and for whatever purpose. For example, the majority of the 19th-century courts to consider the question held that prohibitions on carrying concealed weapons were lawful under the Second Amendment or state analogues. Although we do not undertake an exhaustive historical analysis today of the full scope of the Second Amendment, nothing in our opinion should be taken to cast doubt on longstanding prohibitions on the possession of firearms by felons and the mentally ill, or laws forbidding the carrying of firearms in sensitive places such as schools and government buildings, or laws imposing conditions and qualifications on the commercial sale of arms.

We also recognize another important limitation on the right to keep and carry arms. *Miller* said, as we have explained, that the sorts of weapons protected were those "in common use at the time." We think that limitation is fairly supported by the historical tradition of prohibiting the carrying of "dangerous and unusual weapons."

It may be objected that if weapons that are most useful in military service—M-16 rifles and the like—may be banned, then the Second Amendment right is completely detached from the prefatory clause. But as we have said, the conception of the militia at the time of the Second Amendment's ratification was the body of all citizens capable of military service, who would bring the sorts of lawful weapons that they possessed at home to militia duty. It may well be true today that a militia, to be as effective as militias in the 18th century, would require sophisticated arms that are highly unusual in society at large. Indeed, it may be true that no amount of small arms could be useful against modern-day bombers and tanks. But the fact that modern developments have limited the degree of fit between the prefatory clause and the protected right cannot change our interpretation of the right.

IV

We turn finally to the law at issue here. As we have said, the law totally bans handgun possession in the home. It also requires that any lawful firearm in the home be disassembled or bound by a trigger lock at all times, rendering it inoperable.

As the quotations earlier in this opinion demonstrate, the inherent right of self-defense has been central to the Second Amendment right. The handgun ban amounts to a prohibition of an entire class of "arms" that is overwhelmingly chosen by American society for that lawful purpose. The prohibition extends, moreover, to the home, where the need for defense of self, family, and property is most acute. Under any of the standards of scrutiny that we have applied to enumerated constitutional rights, banning from the home "the most preferred firearm in the nation to 'keep' and use for protection of one's home and family," would fail constitutional muster.

Few laws in the history of our Nation have come close to the severe restriction of the District's handgun ban. And some of those few have been struck down. In *Nunn v. State*, the Georgia Supreme Court struck down a prohibition on carrying pistols openly (even though it upheld a prohibition on carrying concealed weapons). In *Andrews*

v. *State*, the Tennessee Supreme Court likewise held that a statute that forbade openly carrying a pistol "publicly or privately, without regard to time or place, or circumstances," violated the state constitutional provision (which the court equated with the Second Amendment). That was so even though the statute did not restrict the carrying of long guns.

It is no answer to say, as petitioners do, that it is permissible to ban the possession of handguns so long as the possession of other firearms (*i.e.*, long guns) is allowed. It is enough to note, as we have observed, that the American people have considered the handgun to be the quintessential self-defense weapon. There are many reasons that a citizen may prefer a handgun for home defense: It is easier to store in a location that is readily accessible in an emergency; it cannot easily be redirected or wrestled away by an attacker; it is easier to use for those without the upper-body strength to lift and aim a long gun; it can be pointed at a burglar with one hand while the other hand dials the police. Whatever the reason, handguns are the most popular weapon chosen by Americans for self-defense in the home, and a complete prohibition of their use is invalid.

We must also address the District's requirement (as applied to respondent's handgun) that firearms in the home be rendered and kept inoperable at all times. This makes it impossible for citizens to use them for the core lawful purpose of self-defense and is hence unconstitutional. The District argues that we should interpret this element of the statute to contain an exception for self-defense. But we think that is precluded by the unequivocal text, and by the presence of certain other enumerated exceptions: "Except for law enforcement personnel … , each registrant shall keep any firearm in his possession unloaded and disassembled or bound by a trigger lock or similar device unless such firearm is kept at his place of business, or while being used for lawful recreational purposes within the District of Columbia." The nonexistence of a self-defense exception is also suggested by the D. C. Court of Appeals' statement that the statute forbids residents to use firearms to stop intruders.

Apart from his challenge to the handgun ban and the trigger-lock requirement respondent asked the District Court to enjoin petitioners from enforcing the separate licensing requirement "in such a manner as to forbid the carrying of a firearm within one's home or possessed land without a license." The Court of Appeals did not invalidate the licensing requirement, but held only that the District "may not prevent [a handgun] from being moved throughout one's house." It then ordered the District Court to enter summary judgment "consistent with [respondent's] prayer for relief." Before this Court petitioners have stated that "if the handgun ban is struck down and respondent registers a handgun, he could obtain a license, assuming he is not otherwise disqualified," by which they apparently mean if he is not a felon and is not insane. Respondent conceded at oral argument that he does not "have a problem with … licensing" and that the District's law is permissible so long as it is "not enforced in an arbitrary and capricious manner." We therefore assume that petitioners' issuance of a license will satisfy respondent's prayer for relief and do not address the licensing requirement.

Justice Breyer has devoted most of his separate dissent to the handgun ban. He says that, even assuming the Second Amendment is a personal guarantee of the right to bear arms, the District's prohibition is valid. He first tries to establish this by founding-era historical precedent, pointing to various restrictive laws in the colonial period. These demonstrate, in his view, that the District's law "imposes a burden upon gun owners that seems proportionately no greater than restrictions in existence at the time the Second Amendment was adopted." Of the laws he cites, only one offers even marginal support for his assertion. A 1783 Massachusetts law forbade the residents of Boston to "take into" or "receive into" "any Dwelling House, Stable, Barn, Out-house, Ware-house, Store, Shop or other Building" loaded firearms, and permitted the seizure of any loaded firearms that "shall be found" there. That statute's text and its prologue, which makes clear that the purpose of the prohibition was to eliminate the danger to firefighters posed by the "depositing of loaded Arms" in buildings, give reason to doubt that colonial Boston authorities would have enforced that general prohibition against someone who temporarily loaded a firearm to confront an intruder (despite the law's application in that case). In any case, we would not stake our interpretation of the Second Amendment upon a single law, in effect in a single city, that contradicts the overwhelming weight of other evidence regarding the right to keep and bear arms for defense of the home. The other laws Justice Breyer cites are gunpowder-storage laws that he concedes did not clearly prohibit loaded weapons, but required only that excess gunpowder be kept in a special container or on the top floor of the home. Nothing about those fire-safety laws undermines our analysis; they do not remotely burden the right of self-defense as much as an absolute ban on handguns. Nor, correspondingly, does our analysis suggest the invalidity of laws regulating the storage of firearms to prevent accidents.

Justice Breyer points to other founding-era laws that he says "restricted the firing of guns within the city limits to at least some degree" in Boston, Philadelphia and New York. Those laws provide no support for the severe restriction in the present case. The New York law levied a fine of 20 shillings on anyone who fired a gun in certain places (including houses) on New Year's Eve and the first two days of January, and was aimed at preventing the "great Damages ... frequently done on [those days] by persons going House to House, with Guns and other Firearms and being often intoxicated with Liquor." It is inconceivable that this law would have been enforced against a person exercising his right to self-defense on New Year's Day against such drunken hooligans. The Pennsylvania law to which Justice Breyer refers levied a fine of 5 shillings on one who fired a gun or set off fireworks in Philadelphia without first obtaining a license from the governor. Given Justice Wilson's explanation that the right to self-defense with arms was protected by the Pennsylvania Constitution, it is unlikely that this law (which in any event amounted to at most a licensing regime) would have been enforced against a person who used firearms for self-defense. Justice Breyer cites a Rhode Island law that simply levied a 5-shilling fine on those who fired guns in *streets* and *taverns*, a law obviously inapplicable to this case. Finally, Justice Breyer points to a Massachusetts law similar to the Pennsylvania law, prohibiting "discharg[ing] any Gun or Pistol charged with Shot or Ball in the Town of *Boston*." It is again implausible that this would have been enforced against a citizen acting in self-defense, particularly given its preambulatory reference to "the *indiscreet* firing of Guns."

A broader point about the laws that Justice Breyer cites: All of them punished the discharge (or loading) of guns with a small fine and forfeiture of the weapon (or in a few cases a very brief stay in the local jail), not with significant criminal penalties. They are akin to modern penalties for minor public-safety infractions like speeding or jaywalking. And although such public-safety laws may not contain exceptions for self-defense, it is inconceivable that the threat of a jaywalking ticket would deter someone from disregarding a "Do Not Walk" sign in order to flee an attacker, or that the Government would enforce those laws under such circumstances. Likewise, we do not think that a law imposing a 5-shilling fine and forfeiture of the gun would have prevented a person in the founding era from using a gun to protect himself or his family from violence, or that if he did so the law would be enforced against him. The District law, by contrast, far from imposing a minor fine, threatens citizens with a year in prison (five years for a second violation) for even obtaining a gun in the first place.

Justice Breyer moves on to make a broad jurisprudential point: He criticizes us for declining to establish a level of scrutiny for evaluating Second Amendment restrictions. He proposes, explicitly at least, none of the traditionally expressed levels (strict scrutiny, intermediate scrutiny, rational basis), but rather a judge-empowering "interest-balancing inquiry" that "asks whether the statute burdens a protected interest in a way or to an extent that is out of proportion to the statute's salutary effects upon other important governmental interests." After an exhaustive discussion of the arguments for and against gun control, Justice Breyer arrives at his interest-balanced answer: because handgun violence is a problem, because the law is limited to an urban area, and because there were somewhat similar restrictions in the founding period (a false proposition that we have already discussed), the interest-balancing inquiry results in the constitutionality of the handgun ban. QED.

We know of no other enumerated constitutional right whose core protection has been subjected to a freestanding "interest-balancing" approach. The very enumeration of the right takes out of the hands of government—even the Third Branch of Government—the power to decide on a case-by-case basis whether the right is *really worth* insisting upon. A constitutional guarantee subject to future judges' assessments of its usefulness is no constitutional guarantee at all. Constitutional rights are enshrined with the scope they were understood to have when the people adopted them, whether or not future legislatures or (yes) even future judges think that scope too broad. We would not apply an "interest-balancing" approach to the prohibition of a peaceful neo-Nazi march through Skokie. The First Amendment contains the freedom-of-speech guarantee that the people ratified, which included exceptions for obscenity, libel, and disclosure of state secrets, but not for the expression of extremely unpopular and wrong-headed views. The Second Amendment is no different. Like the First, it is the very *product*of an interest-balancing by the people—which Justice Breyer would now conduct for them anew. And whatever else it leaves to future evaluation, it surely elevates above all other interests the right of law-abiding, responsible citizens to use arms in defense of hearth and home.

Justice Breyer chides us for leaving so many applications of the right to keep and bear arms in doubt, and for not providing extensive historical justification for those regulations of the right that we describe as permissible. But since this case represents this Court's first in-depth examination of the Second Amendment, one should not expect it to clarify the entire field, any more than *Reynolds* v. *United States*, our first in-depth Free Exercise Clause case, left that area in a state of utter certainty. And there will be time enough to expound upon the historical justifications for the exceptions we have mentioned if and when those exceptions come before us.

In sum, we hold that the District's ban on handgun possession in the home violates the Second Amendment, as does its prohibition against rendering any lawful firearm in the home operable for the purpose of immediate self-defense. Assuming that Heller is not disqualified from the exercise of Second Amendment rights, the District must permit him to register his handgun and must issue him a license to carry it in the home.

* * * * *

We are aware of the problem of handgun violence in this country, and we take seriously the concerns raised by the many *amici* who believe that prohibition of handgun ownership is a solution. The Constitution leaves the District of Columbia a variety of tools for combating that problem, including some measures regulating handguns. But the enshrinement of constitutional rights necessarily takes certain policy choices off the table. These include the absolute prohibition of handguns held and used for self-defense in the home. Undoubtedly some think that the Second Amendment is outmoded in a society where our standing army is the pride of our Nation, where well-trained police forces provide personal security, and where gun violence is a serious problem. That is perhaps debatable, but what is not debatable is that it is not the role of this Court to pronounce the Second Amendment extinct.

We affirm the judgment of the Court of Appeals.

It is so ordered.

SUPPLEMENTAL HISTORICAL DOCUMENT

The *District of Columbia v. Heller* Decision

In 2003, Dick Anthony Heller and other plaintiffs challenged the District of Columbia's decades-old laws banning possession of handguns and requiring firearms in the home to be stored locked or disassembled. After the D.C. Circuit Court of Appeals ruled the laws unconstitutional under the Second Amendment[1]—the only time a federal appellate court had ever invalidated a gun law on Second Amendment grounds—the U.S. Supreme Court agreed to hear the case. This set the stage for the Court's first ruling on the Second Amendment in almost 70 years.

The Court's Holding: The Supreme Court issued its historic decision in *District of Columbia v. Heller* on June 26, 2008.[2] In a 5-4 ruling written by Justice Antonin Scalia, the Court held that the Second Amendment confers an individual right to possess firearms unrelated to service in a well-regulated state militia. The Court struck down the District's ban on handgun possession, finding that "the inherent right of self-defense has been central to the Second Amendment" and that handguns are "overwhelmingly chosen by American society" for self-defense in the home, "where the need for defense of self, family, and property is most acute."[3] The Court also struck down the District's requirement that firearms in the home be stored unloaded and disassembled or bound by a trigger lock or similar device, because the law contained no exception for self-defense.

An Abrupt About-Face From Prior Precedent:

The Court's ruling in *District of Columbia v. Heller* represents a radical departure from the Court's previous interpretation of the Second Amendment in *United States v. Miller*, 307 U.S. 174 (1939). In the *Miller* case, the Court stated, in a unanimous decision, that the "obvious purpose" of the Second Amendment was to "assure the continuation and render possible the effectiveness of" the state militia, and the Amendment "must be interpreted and applied with that end in view."[4] In reliance on Miller, hundreds of lower federal and state appellate courts have rejected Second Amendment challenges to our nation's gun laws over the last seven decades.[5]

1. *Parker v. District of Columbia*, 478 F.3d 370 (D.C. Cir. 2007).

2. *District of Columbia v. Heller*, 128 S. Ct. 2783 (2008).

3. Id. at 2817.

4. *United States v. Miller*, 307 U.S. 174, 178 (1939).

5. The Heller Court dismissed the Miller case as not "a thorough examination" of the Second Amendment, and limited Miller to the proposition that "the Second Amendment does not protect those weapons not typically possessed by law-abiding citizens for lawful purposes, such as short-barreled shotguns." Heller, supra note 2, at 2814.

The Right is Not Unlimited:

Although the Heller decision establishes a new individual right to "keep and bear arms," the opinion makes clear that the right is not unlimited, and should not be understood as "a right to keep and carry any weapon whatsoever in any manner whatsoever and for whatever purpose."[6] The Court provides examples of gun laws that it deems "presumptively lawful" under the Second Amendment, including those which:

• Prohibit the possession of firearms by felons and the mentally ill;

• Forbid firearm possession in sensitive places such as schools and
government buildings;

• Impose conditions on the commercial sale of firearms.

The Court makes clear that this list is not exhaustive.[7] The Court also concludes that the Second Amendment is consistent with laws banning "dangerous and unusual weapons" not "in common use at the time," such as M-16 rifles and other firearms that are most useful in military service.[8] Finally, the Court declares that its analysis should not be read to suggest "the invalidity of laws regulating the storage of firearms to prevent accidents."[9]

The Standard of Review:

The *Heller* decision fails to articulate a legal standard of review, or test, to be applied in evaluating other laws under the Second Amendment. Thus, the decision provides little guidance to lower courts or legislators, creating new uncertainty in this area and inviting litigation.[10]

The Second Amendment Applies Only to the Federal Government:

Because Heller considered laws of the District of Columbia (a federal enclave), the Court stated that the question of whether the Second Amendment applies to the states is "a question not presented by this case."[11] While the Heller Court did not rule on whether the Second Amendment applies to state or local governments, the Court did note its earlier decisions holding that "the Second Amendment applies only to the Federal Government."[12] These decisions remain the law of the land.

6. Id. at 2816.
7. Id. at 2817 n. 26.
8. Id. at 2817.
9. Id. at 2820.
10. Immediately after the Heller decision was issued, the gun lobby filed suits challenging handgun possession bans in San Francisco, Chicago and other Illinois communities. The San Francisco prohibition applies only to public housing.
11. Heller, supra note 2, at 2813 n. 23.
12. Id., citing *Miller v. Texas*, 153 U.S. 535, 538 (1894); *Presser v. Illinois*, 116 U.S. 252, 265 (1886); and *United States v. Cruikshank*, 92 U.S. 542 (1876).

What the Decision Means for Our Nation's Gun Laws

While the *Heller* decision leaves many questions unanswered, one thing is clear: Gun regulation is alive and well in the United States. Elected officials and community leaders can feel confident that most common sense gun laws will be upheld. A strong legislative record—including facts regarding the problem sought to be addressed and the reasons why the proposed law is an appropriate response—is critical to maximizing the likelihood that a gun law will be affirmed by the courts.

Given our nation's tragic epidemic of gun violence, elected officials should have no difficulty describing the problem. The undisputed facts show:

- More than 30,000 Americans die from firearm-related injuries each year—an average of 80 deaths each day[13]—and nearly 70,000 others are treated for gunshot wounds.[14]

- Young people up to 24 years of age constitute over 40% of all firearm deaths and non-fatal injuries each year.[15] The number of children and teens in America killed by guns in 2005 would fill 120 public school classrooms of 25 students each.[16]

- On average, 46 gun suicides were committed each day for the years 1999-2005. During that time, over 5,300 people in the United States died from unintentional shootings.[17]

13. U.S. Department of Health and Human Services, Centers for Disease Control and Prevention, National Center for Injury Prevention and Control, Web-Based Injury Statistics Query & Reporting System (WISQARS), WISQARS Injury Mortality Reports, 1999-2005 (2008), at http://webappa.cdc.gov/sasweb/ncipc/mortrate10_sy.html.
14. U.S. Department of Health and Human Services, Centers for Disease Control and Prevention, National Center for Injury Prevention and Control, Web-Based Injury Statistics Query & Reporting System (WISQARS), WISQARS Nonfatal Injury Reports (2008), at http://webappa.cdc.gov/sasweb/ncipc/nfirates2001.html.
15. Id.; WISQARS Injury Mortality Reports, 1999-2005, supra note 13.
16. Id.
17. Id.

Following the Heller decision, we must redouble our efforts at the state and local levels to promote effective, commonsense laws as a means to reduce the growing gun violence epidemic in our country.

- • The U.S. has the highest rate of firearm deaths among 25 high-income nations.[18]

- Guns are used to commit nearly 400,000 crimes every year and nearly

- 70% of all murders in the U.S. are committed with a firearm.[19]

- Medical costs related to gun violence are estimated at $2.3 billion annually, half of which are borne by American taxpayers.[20]

Factoring in all the direct and indirect medical, legal and societal costs, the annual cost of gun violence in our nation amounts to $100 billion.[21]

Fortunately, a variety of common sense regulatory options exist to address this national crisis. Many jurisdictions across the country already have adopted laws to require background checks on all gun purchasers; to ensure that guns are not sold to criminals and other prohibited purchasers; to prohibit the sale of military-style weapons (such as assault weapons and 50 caliber rifles); to require gun owners to obtain a license and register their firearms; to regulate guns as a consumer product; and to regulate firearms dealers through licensing and other requirements. Legal Community Against Violence (LCAV) believes that these types of laws and many others should be upheld as consistent with the Supreme Court's holding in the Heller case.

18. Wendy Cukier and Victor W. Sidel, The Global Gun Epidemic: From Saturday Night Specials to AK47s, 17 (2006).

19. U.S. Department of Justice, Bureau of Justice Statistics, Key Facts at a Glance: Crimes Committed with Firearms, 1973-2006, at http://www.ojp.usdoj.gov/bjs/glance/tables/guncrimetab.htm.

20. Philip Cook et al., The Medical Costs of Gunshot Injuries in the United States, 282 JAMA 447 (Aug. 4, 1999).

21. Philip J. Cook and Jens Ludwig, Gun Violence: The Real Costs 115 (2000).

SUPREME COURT OF THE UNITED STATES

No. 07–290

DISTRICT OF COLUMBIA, ET AL., PETITIONERS *v.* DICK ANTHONY HELLER

ON WRIT OF CERTIORARI TO THE UNITED STATES COURT OF APPEALS FOR THE DISTRICT OF COLUMBIA CIRCUIT

[June 26, 2008]

JUSTICE STEVENS, with whom JUSTICE SOUTER, JUSTICE GINSBURG, and JUSTICE BREYER join, dissenting.

The question presented by this case is not whether the Second Amendment protects a "collective right" or an "individual right." Surely it protects a right that can be enforced by individuals. But a conclusion that the Second Amendment protects an individual right does not tell us anything about the scope of that right.

Guns are used to hunt, for self-defense, to commit crimes, for sporting activities, and to perform military duties. The Second Amendment plainly does not protect the right to use a gun to rob a bank; it is equally clear that it *does* encompass the right to use weapons for certain military purposes. Whether it also protects the right to possess and use guns for nonmilitary purposes like hunting and personal self-defense is the question presented by this case. The text of the Amendment, its history, and our decision in *United States* v. *Miller*, 307 U. S. 174 (1939), provide a clear answer to that question.

The Second Amendment was adopted to protect the right of the people of each of the several States to maintain a well-regulated militia. It was a response to concerns raised during the ratification of the Constitution that the power of Congress to disarm the state militias and create a national standing army posed an intolerable threat to the sovereignty of the several States. Neither the text of the Amendment nor the arguments advanced by its proponents evidenced the slightest interest in limiting any legislature's authority to regulate private civilian uses of firearms. Specifically, there is no indication that the Framers of the Amendment intended to enshrine the common-law right of self-defense in the Constitution.

In 1934, Congress enacted the National Firearms Act, the first major federal firearms law.[1] Sustaining an indictment under the Act, this Court held that, "[i]n the absence of any evidence tending to show that possession or use of a 'shotgun having a barrel of less than eighteen inches in length' at this time has some reasonable relationship to the preservation or efficiency of a well regulated militia, we cannot say that the Second Amendment guarantees the right to keep and bear such an instrument." *Miller*, 307 U. S., at 178. The view of the Amendment we took in *Miller*—that it protects the right to keep and bear arms for certain military purposes, but that it does not curtail the Legislature's power to regulate the nonmilitary use and ownership of weapons—is both the most natural reading of the Amendment's text and the interpretation most faithful to the history of its adoption.

Since our decision in *Miller,* hundreds of judges have relied on the view of the Amendment we endorsed there;[2]

---

[1] There was some limited congressional activity earlier: A 10% federal excise tax on firearms was passed as part of the Revenue Act of 1918, 40 Stat. 1057, and in 1927 a statute was enacted prohibiting the shipment of handguns, revolvers, and other concealable weapons through the United States mails. Ch. 75, 44 Stat. 1059–1060 (hereinafter 1927 Act).

[2] Until the Fifth Circuit's decision in *United States* v. *Emerson,* 270 F. 3d 203 (2001), every Court of Appeals to consider the question had understood *Miller* to hold that the Second Amendment does not protect the right to possess and use guns for purely private, civilian purposes. See, *e.g., United States* v. *Haney,* 264 F. 3d 1161, 1164–1166 (CA10 2001); *United States* v. *Napier,* 233 F. 3d 394, 402–404 (CA6 2000);

we ourselves affirmed it in 1980. See *Lewis* v. *United States,* 445 U. S. 55, 65–66, n. 8 (1980).[3] No new evidence has surfaced since 1980 supporting the view that the Amendment was intended to curtail the power of Congress to regulate civilian use or misuse of weapons. Indeed, a review of the drafting history of the Amendment demonstrates that its Framers *rejected* proposals that would have broadened its coverage to include such uses.

The opinion the Court announces today fails to identify any new evidence supporting the view that the Amendment was intended to limit the power of Congress to regulate civilian uses of weapons. Unable to point to any such evidence, the Court stakes its holding on a strained and

---

Gillespie v. *Indianapolis,* 185 F. 3d 693, 710–711 (CA7 1999); *United States* v. *Scanio,* No. 97–1584, 1998 WL 802060, *2 (CA2, Nov. 12, 1998) (unpublished opinion); *United States* v. *Wright,* 117 F. 3d 1265, 1271–1274 (CA11 1997); *United States* v. *Rybar,* 103 F. 3d 273, 285–286 (CA3 1996); *Hickman* v. *Block,* 81 F. 3d 98, 100–103 (CA9 1996); *United States* v. *Hale,* 978 F. 2d 1016, 1018–1020 (CA8 1992); *Thomas* v. *City Council of Portland,* 730 F. 2d 41, 42 (CA1 1984) *(per curiam); United States* v. *Johnson,* 497 F. 2d 548, 550 (CA4 1974) *(per curiam); United States* v. *Johnson,* 441 F. 2d 1134, 1136 (CA5 1971); see also *Sandidge* v. *United States,* 520 A. 2d 1057, 1058–1059 (DC App. 1987). And a number of courts have remained firm in their prior positions, even after considering *Emerson.* See, *e.g., United States* v. *Lippman,* 369 F. 3d 1039, 1043–1045 (CA8 2004); *United States* v. *Parker,* 362 F. 3d 1279, 1282–1284 (CA10 2004); *United States* v. *Jackubowski,* 63 Fed. Appx. 959, 961 (CA7 2003) (unpublished opinion); *Silveira* v. *Lockyer,* 312 F. 3d 1052, 1060–1066 (CA9 2002); *United States* v. *Milheron,* 231 F. Supp. 2d 376, 378 (Me. 2002); *Bach* v. *Pataki,* 289 F. Supp. 2d 217, 224–226 (NDNY 2003); *United States* v. *Smith,* 56 M. J. 711, 716 (C. A. Armed Forces 2001).

[3] Our discussion in *Lewis* was brief but significant. Upholding a conviction for receipt of a firearm by a felon, we wrote: "These legislative restrictions on the use of firearms are neither based upon constitutionally suspect criteria, nor do they entrench upon any constitutionally protected liberties. See *United States* v. *Miller,* 307 U. S. 174, 178 (1939) (the Second Amendment guarantees no right to keep and bear a firearm that does not have 'some reasonable relationship to the preservation or efficiency of a well regulated militia')." 445 U. S., at 65, n. 8.

unpersuasive reading of the Amendment's text; significantly different provisions in the 1689 English Bill of Rights, and in various 19th-century State Constitutions; postenactment commentary that was available to the Court when it decided *Miller;* and, ultimately, a feeble attempt to distinguish *Miller* that places more emphasis on the Court's decisional process than on the reasoning in the opinion itself.

Even if the textual and historical arguments on both sides of the issue were evenly balanced, respect for the well-settled views of all of our predecessors on this Court, and for the rule of law itself, see *Mitchell* v. *W. T. Grant Co.,* 416 U. S. 600, 636 (1974) (Stewart, J., dissenting), would prevent most jurists from endorsing such a dramatic upheaval in the law.[4] As Justice Cardozo observed years ago, the "labor of judges would be increased almost to the breaking point if every past decision could be reopened in every case, and one could not lay one's own

---

[4] See *Vasquez* v. *Hillery,* 474 U. S. 254, 265, 266 (1986) ("*[Stare decisis]* permits society to presume that bedrock principles are founded in the law rather than in the proclivities of individuals, and thereby contributes to the integrity of our constitutional system of government, both in appearance and in fact. While *stare decisis* is not an inexorable command, the careful observer will discern that any detours from the straight path of *stare decisis* in our past have occurred for articulable reasons, and only when the Court has felt obliged 'to bring its opinions into agreement with experience and with facts newly ascertained.' *Burnet* v. *Coronado Oil & Gas Co.,* 285 U. S. 393, 412 (1932) (Brandeis, J., dissenting)"); *Pollock* v. *Farmers' Loan & Trust Co.*, 157 U. S. 429, 652 (1895) (White, J., dissenting) ("The fundamental conception of a judicial body is that of one hedged about by precedents which are binding on the court without regard to the personality of its members. Break down this belief in judicial continuity and let it be felt that on great constitutional questions this Court is to depart from the settled conclusions of its predecessors, and to determine them all according to the mere opinion of those who temporarily fill its bench, and our Constitution will, in my judgment, be bereft of value and become a most dangerous instrument to the rights and liberties of the people").

course of bricks on the secure foundation of the courses laid by others who had gone before him." The Nature of the Judicial Process 149 (1921).

In this dissent I shall first explain why our decision in *Miller* was faithful to the text of the Second Amendment and the purposes revealed in its drafting history. I shall then comment on the postratification history of the Amendment, which makes abundantly clear that the Amendment should not be interpreted as limiting the authority of Congress to regulate the use or possession of firearms for purely civilian purposes.

I

The text of the Second Amendment is brief. It provides: "A well regulated Militia, being necessary to the security of a free State, the right of the people to keep and bear Arms, shall not be infringed."

Three portions of that text merit special focus: the introductory language defining the Amendment's purpose, the class of persons encompassed within its reach, and the unitary nature of the right that it protects.

"A well regulated Militia, being necessary to the security of a free State"

The preamble to the Second Amendment makes three important points. It identifies the preservation of the militia as the Amendment's purpose; it explains that the militia is necessary to the security of a free State; and it recognizes that the militia must be "well regulated." In all three respects it is comparable to provisions in several State Declarations of Rights that were adopted roughly contemporaneously with the Declaration of Independence.[5]

---

[5]The Virginia Declaration of Rights ¶13 (1776), provided: "That a well-regulated militia, composed of the body of the people, trained to arms, is the proper, natural, and safe defence of a free State; that Standing Armies, in time of peace, should be avoided, as dangerous to

Document Themes

The Court majority joined with Justice Scalia in overturning the handgun ban in the District of Columbia and in severing the ownership of weapons from service in a militia. He begins his detailed analysis of the case, and of the Second Amendment, first by examining the "prefatory clause" of the amendment, which referenced the militia, then by examining the "operative clause," which references the right to bear arms. After conducting a wide-ranging review of the text of the Second Amendment and the historical record surrounding it, Scalia concludes that the amendment supports an individual right to bear arms.

In Scalia's view, the operative clause—"the right of the people to keep and bear Arms, shall not be infringed"—is controlling. He argues that "the people" refers to the entire community, not to a specific group such as the militia. He also argues extensively that "the right of the people" was a preexisting right, not a right that was granted by the amendment. Congress, in effect, was simply codifying an existing right, not creating a new one.

Scalia then examines the prefatory clause, which says: a "well regulated Militia, being necessary to the security of a free State." He argues that the clause refers to the necessity of a well trained militia in denying Congress the power to "infringe" the right of individuals to keep and bear arms. He notes that the reason for codifying the prefatory clause was not only "to ensure the preservation of a well-regulated militia" but also to preserve the right to bear arms "for self-defense and hunting."

Scalia goes on to cite scholars, court decisions, and legislators who support the individual right theory. He extensively disputes views expressed by Justice John Paul Stevens in his dissent from the majority. Stevens relied on the 1939 case *United States v. Miller* to argue that the legislature can regulate the nonmilitary use and ownership of weapons. In Scalia's view, *Miller* does precisely the opposite: It "positively suggests, that the Second Amendment confers an individual right to keep and bear arms." Scalia acknowledges that Second Amendment rights are not absolute; he agrees that lawful regulatory measure might include prohibitions against carrying concealed weapons; allowing felons and the mentally ill to own weapons; and forbidding the carrying of firearms in sensitive places such as schools and government buildings. Scalia also acknowledges the serious problem of handgun violence, but he asserts that "the enshrinement of constitutional rights necessarily takes certain policy choices off the table."

In this landmark ruling the Supreme Court held that the Second Amendment protected the right of individuals to keep guns and other weapons that are appropriate for traditionally legal purposes, especially self-defense in one's home. The decision did not apply to regulations at the state and local level.

Before the *Heller* decision, there had been much debate about whether the Second Amendment protected the right of individuals to "keep and bear" firearms for personal use, or whether it simply authorized the states to institute laws and regulations for the maintenance of "a well-regulated militia." The Supreme Court's major precedent, *U.S. v. Miller* (1939), appeared to give some support for the second understanding of the amendment. In addition to this controversy, constitutional scholars disagreed about which restrictions were consistent with the expression "shall not be infringed."

In 1975, Washington, D.C., a federal enclave, enacted legislation with two contested provisions: first, almost all residents were prohibited from keeping handguns anywhere in the city, and second, residents were required to keep all legally owned firearms unloaded and either dissembled or bound by a trigger lock, thereby requiring time to make them operable.

Dick A. Heller, a special police officer in the District, was authorized to carry a handgun while on duty at the Federal Judicial Center. But when he applied for a license to keep a handgun at his home, the District rejected the request. In February 2003, Heller filed a suit, on Second Amendment grounds, challenging the constitutionality of the city's ban on the possession of handguns in the home and also challenging the trigger-lock requirement, which made it almost impossible to keep a firearm ready-to-use for self-defense in the home. The U.S. District Court dismissed the suit, but the D.C. Circuit reversed the dismissal and ruled in favor of Heller's two contentions.

The defendants petitioned the U.S. Supreme Court for a *writ of certiorari*, and on November 20, 2007, the Court agreed to review the case. Because of its controversial nature, sixty-seven groups filed *amici curiae* (friends of the court) briefs, with forty-seven urging the Court to affirm the ruling. A majority of the members of Congress signed a brief that opposed the city's ban on handguns. Republican candidate for president, John McCain, also signed the brief, but the Democratic candidate, Barack Obama, did not do so. Following oral hearings, the five more conservative members of the Court voted to uphold the D.C. Circuit's ruling. The four more liberal Justices disagreed.

Writing for the majority, Justice Antonin Scalia asserts that the Second Amendment's first clause announces its primary purpose, and that the term "militia" refers to the "body of all citizens capable of military service." The second, or operative, clause, moreover, has the expression, "right of the people," thereby connoting a right of individual citizens. The wording of the Amendment must interpreted as ordinary citizens would have understood it at the time of its ratification—including the common-law right to self-defense in one's home. Within this perspective, the District had violated the Constitution when it prohibited an entire class of "arms" that the great majority of Americans choose for the lawful purpose of self-defense. In addition, the trigger-lock requirement was unconstitutional because it prevented citizens from being prepared for self-defense if an intruder were to enter without warning.

Scalia recognizes, nevertheless, that the Second Amendment does not provide an unlimited right "to keep and carry any weapon whatsoever in any manner whatsoever and for whatever purpose." The ruling does not affect "longstanding prohibitions on the possession of firearms by felons and the mentally ill, or laws forbidding the carrying of firearms in sensitive places such as schools and government buildings, or laws imposing conditions and qualifications on the commercial sale of arms." Although Scalia did not address the level of judicial review for deciding future cases, he documents that the right to keep and bear arms was considered a "fundamental right" in the late eighteenth century; therefore, restrictions on the right require more than simply a "rational basis." This suggested that the standard for review would be either "strict scrutiny" or "intermediate scrutiny."

In a strong dissent, Justice John Paul Stevens argues that the Second Amendment touches only on state military service, and that the framers would have expressly referred to an individual right if that was what was intended. In a more conciliatory dissent, Justice Stephen Breyer's insists that the premise of the individual-rights position does not make the District's restrictions unconstitutional. Advocating an "interest-balancing approach," he found the restrictions provided reasonable means of limiting the harm often caused by the careless and irresponsible use of firearms in homes. When the Second Amendment was instituted, moreover, some cities had nuisance laws providing punishment for imprudent usage of guns and also fire-safety laws forbidding the storage of gunpowder. Accusing the majority of demonstrating "a lack of respect" for the Court's well-settled precedents, Breyer insisted that the Second Amendment did not guarantee any right of persons "to keep loaded handguns in the house in crime-ridden urban areas."

Constitutional scholar Lawrence Tribe has predicted "that *Heller* will persist as a landmark opinion of the Roberts Court." Proponents of strict gun regulation regret that the decision prohibits the enactment restrictions similar to the District of Columbia's law of 1975. In contrast, many advocates of the right to own and use firearms are appalled that Scalia's opinion endorsed the majority of traditional regulations. Five years after *Heller,* lower courts had heard over eighty challenges to gun control laws, and very few of these restrictions were found to be unconstitutional. The District of Columbia revised its regulations of firearms in order to conform to the Supreme Court's decision. The new law disallowed a number of specific weapons, including semi-automatic pistols that were bottom loaded. Dick Heller filed a lawsuit challenging this particular provision. On March 26, 2010, the D.C. District Court ruled against him, finding that the revised regulations respected "the core Second Amendment right to use arms for the purpose of self-defense in the home."

Additional Reading

Cornell, Saul, and Nathan Kozuskanich, eds., *The Second Amendment on Trial: Critical Essays on District of Columbia v. Heller* (Amherst, MA: University of Massachusetts Press, 2013).

District of Columbia v. Heller Oral Argument, C-SPAN, March 18, 2008, https://www.c-span.org/video/?204466-1/district-columbia-v-heller-oral-argument.

Malcolm, Joyce Lee, "The Supreme Court and the Uses of History: *District of Columbia v. Heller*," *UCLA Law Review*, 56 (2009): 1377–98.

Posner, Richard A., "In Defense of Looseness," *New Republic*, August 27, 2008, https://newrepublic.com/article/62124/defense-looseness.

Solum, Lawrence B., "*District of Columbia v. Heller* and Originalism," *Northwestern University Law Review*, 103, no. 2 (2009): 923–82.

—Michael J. O'Neal

McDonald v. City of Chicago

Author(s): Samuel Alito (lead opinion)
Date: 2010
Genre: Court decision (Supreme Court)

Summary Overview

McDonald v. City of Chicago was a landmark U.S. Supreme Court case that followed closely on the heels of another key Supreme Court case, *District of Columbia v. Heller* (2008). The *Heller* court struck down a District of Columbia handgun ban as an unconstitutional violation of the Second Amendment right to bear arms—the first time the High Court had specifically endorsed such a right independent of membership in a lawful militia. However, the *Heller* court left open the question of whether the right to arm oneself applied not just against federal action but against state and local action. In *McDonald*, the Court ruled that it did and that Chicago's firearms laws (and those of nearby Oak Park, Illinois), which were similar to those of the District of Columbia, violated the plaintiffs' constitutional rights.

Defining Moment

The District of Columbia enacted a relatively strict handgun ban that the plaintiff challenged in court. The case, *District of Columbia v. Heller*, made its way to the U.S. Supreme Court, which ruled that the district's statute was an unconstitutional violation of the plaintiff's Second Amendment right to keep and bear arms. The Court, however, left one important question open: whether the Second Amendment supplied a safeguard against actions by just the federal government, or whether it applied to the actions of state and local governments as well. The Fourteenth Amendment, added to the Constitution in 1868 primarily to protect the rights of freedmen in the wake of the Civil War, initially applied strictly to the actions of the federal government. However, over the course of the following century, the direction of Supreme Court jurisprudence was "incorporation," meaning that the Court made the Bill of Rights applicable at the level of the states through the Due Process and Equal Protection clauses of the Fourteenth Amendment. Put simply, the issue was this: The Second Amendment prohibits the federal government from taking action that would deprive "the people" of the "right to keep and bear Arms," but nothing prevented states and municipalities from doing so. The Court remained silent on this issue up through the *Heller* decision, but that changed with *McDonald*.

The city of Chicago enacted a handgun ban that was similar to that of the District of Columbia. Otis McDonald, an elderly resident of the crime-ridden Morgan Park neighborhood of Chicago, wanted to purchase a handgun for self-defense but was unable to do so because of Chicago's ban on the ownership of handguns. Joined by three other plaintiffs, he challenged the ban in federal district court, arguing that the Second Amendment should be interpreted to limit state and municipal action as it applied to gun ownership. The Court of Appeals for the Seventh Circuit affirmed the judgment of the trial court. On appeal the case went to the Supreme Court, which rendered its decision on June 28, 2010.

About the Author

The Court issued a 5–4 split decision. Justice Samuel Alito wrote the lead opinion; he was joined by Justices Antonin Scalia, Anthony Kennedy, and Chief Justice John Roberts, with Justice Clarence Thomas writing a separate concurring opinion.

Associate Justice Samuel Anthony Alito Jr. was born in Trenton, New Jersey, on April 1, 1950. He enrolled in Princeton University's Woodrow Wilson School of Public and International Affairs, earning a bachelor's degree in 1972. He then attended the Yale Law School, where he was editor of the *Yale Law Journal*. After completing his legal studies in 1975, he moved to Newark, New Jersey, to launch his legal career—which began with a position as a law clerk for Justice Leonard I. Garth of the U.S. Court of Appeals for the Third Circuit. He then took a position as an assistant district attorney for the district of New Jersey, where he focused his efforts on prosecuting drug traffickers and mobsters—who, he believed, were giving Italian Americans a bad name.

Four years later, he moved to the nation's capital to work as an assistant to the solicitor general for the Department of Justice. In that capacity, he argued cases before the Supreme Court. In 1985 he became the deputy assistant attorney general at the Department of Justice, but in 1987 he returned to New Jersey to work as a U.S. attorney—again with a focus on prosecuting organized crime cases.

In 1990, President George H.W. Bush appointed Alito as a judge on the U.S. Court of Appeals for the Third Circuit, a position he held for sixteen years. During this period he was also an adjunct law professor at Seton Hall University. In 2005, President George W. Bush selected Alito to fill the Supreme Court seat vacated by retiring justice Sandra Day O'Connor. His confirmation hearings were contentious, but in January 2006 he was confirmed by a narrow margin in the Senate.

HISTORICAL DOCUMENT

Otis McDonald, et al., Petitioners v. City of Chicago, Illinois, et al.

[June 28, 2010]

Justice Alito announced the judgment of the Court and delivered the opinion of the Court with respect to Parts I, II–A, II–B, II–D, III–A, and III–B, in which The Chief Justice, Justice Scalia, Justice Kennedy, and Justice Thomas join, and an opinion with respect to Parts II–C, IV, and V, in which The Chief Justice, Justice Scalia, and Justice Kennedy join.

Two years ago, in *District of Columbia* v. *Heller*, we held that the Second Amendment protects the right to keep and bear arms for the purpose of self-defense, and we struck down a District of Columbia law that banned the possession of handguns in the home. The city of Chicago (City) and the village of Oak Park, a Chicago suburb, have laws that are similar to the District of Columbia's, but Chicago and Oak Park argue that their laws are constitutional because the Second Amendment has no application to the States. We have previously held that most of the provisions of the Bill of Rights apply with full force to both the Federal Government and the States. Applying the standard that is well established in our case law, we hold that the Second Amendment right is fully applicable to the States.

I

Otis McDonald, Adam Orlov, Colleen Lawson, and David Lawson (Chicago petitioners) are Chicago residents who would like to keep handguns in their homes for self-defense but are prohibited from doing so by Chicago's firearms laws. A City ordinance provides that "[n]o person shall ... possess ... any firearm unless such person is the holder of a valid registration certificate for such firearm." The Code then prohibits registration of most handguns, thus effectively banning handgun possession by almost all private citizens who reside in the City. Like Chicago, Oak Park makes it "unlawful for any person to possess ... any firearm," a term that includes "pistols, revolvers, guns and small arms ... commonly known as handguns."

Chicago enacted its handgun ban to protect its residents "from the loss of property and injury or death from firearms." The Chicago petitioners and their *amici*, however, argue that the handgun ban has left them vulnerable to criminals. Chicago Police Department statistics, we are told, reveal that the City's handgun murder rate has actually increased since the ban was enacted and that Chicago residents now face one of the highest murder rates in the country and rates of other violent crimes that exceed the average in comparable cities.

Several of the Chicago petitioners have been the targets of threats and violence. For instance, Otis McDonald, who is in his late seventies, lives in a high-crime neighborhood. He is a community activist involved with alternative policing strategies, and his efforts to improve his neighborhood have subjected him to violent threats from drug dealers. Colleen Lawson is a Chicago resident whose home has been targeted by burglars. "In Mrs. Lawson's judgment, possessing a handgun in Chicago would decrease her chances of suffering serious injury or death should she ever be threatened again in her home." McDonald, Lawson, and the other Chicago petitioners own handguns that they store outside of the city limits, but they would like to keep their handguns in their homes for protection.

After our decision in *Heller*, the Chicago petitioners and two groups filed suit against the City in the United States District Court for the Northern District of Illinois. They sought a declaration that the handgun ban and several related Chicago ordinances violate the Second and Fourteenth Amendments to the United States Constitution. Another action challenging the Oak Park law was filed in the same District Court by the National Rifle Association (NRA) and two Oak Park residents. In addition, the NRA and others filed a third action challenging the Chicago ordinances. All three cases were assigned to the same District Judge.

The District Court rejected plaintiffs' argument that the Chicago and Oak Park laws are unconstitutional. The court noted that the Seventh Circuit had "squarely upheld the constitutionality of a ban on handguns a quarter century ago," and that *Heller* had explicitly refrained from "opin[ing] on the subject of incorporation of the Second Amendment." The court observed that a district judge has a "duty to follow established precedent in the Court of Appeals to which he or she is beholden, even though the logic of more recent caselaw may point in a different direction."

The Seventh Circuit affirmed...

II

A

Petitioners argue that the Chicago and Oak Park laws violate the right to keep and bear arms for two reasons. Petitioners' primary submission is that this right is among the "privileges or immunities of citizens of the United States" and that the narrow interpretation of the Privileges or Immunities Clause adopted in the *Slaughter-House Cases, supra,* should now be rejected. As a secondary argument, petitioners contend that the Fourteenth Amendment's Due Process Clause "incorporates" the Second Amendment right.

Chicago and Oak Park (municipal respondents) maintain that a right set out in the Bill of Rights applies to the States only if that right is an indispensable attribute of *any* " 'civilized' " legal system. If it is possible to imagine a civilized country that does not recognize the right, the municipal respondents tell us, then that right is not protected by due process. And since there are civilized countries that ban or strictly regulate the private possession of handguns, the municipal respondents maintain that due process does not preclude such measures. In light of the parties' far-reaching arguments, we begin by recounting this Court's analysis over the years of the relationship between the provisions of the Bill of Rights and the States.

B

The Bill of Rights, including the Second Amendment, originally applied only to the Federal Government. In *Barron ex rel. Tiernan* v. *Mayor of Baltimore*, the Court, in an opinion by Chief Justice Marshall, explained that this question was "of great importance" but "not of much difficulty." In less than four pages, the Court firmly rejected the proposition that the first eight Amendments operate as limitations on the States, holding that they apply only to the Federal Government.

The constitutional Amendments adopted in the aftermath of the Civil War fundamentally altered our country's federal system. The provision at issue in this case, § 1 of the Fourteenth Amendment, provides, among other things, that a State may not abridge "the privileges or immunities of citizens of the United States" or deprive "any person of life, liberty, or property, without due process of law."

Four years after the adoption of the Fourteenth Amendment, this Court was asked to interpret the Amendment's reference to "the privileges or immunities of citizens of the United States." The *Slaughter-House Cases*, involved challenges to a Louisiana law permitting the creation of a state-sanctioned monopoly on the butchering of animals within the city of New Orleans. Justice Samuel Miller's opinion for the Court concluded that the Privileges or Immunities Clause protects only those rights "which owe their existence to the Federal government, its National character, its Constitution, or its laws." The Court held that other fundamental rights—rights that predated the creation of the Federal Government and that "the State governments were created to establish and secure"—were not protected by the Clause.

In drawing a sharp distinction between the rights of federal and state citizenship, the Court relied on two principal arguments. First, the Court emphasized that the Fourteenth Amendment's Privileges or Immunities Clause spoke of "the privileges or immunities of *citizens of the United States*," and the Court contrasted this phrasing with the wording in the first sentence of the Fourteenth Amendment and in the Privileges and Immunities Clause of Article IV, both of which refer to *state* citizenship. Second, the Court stated that a contrary reading would "radically chang[e] the whole theory of the relations of the State and Federal governments to each other and of both these governments to the people," and the Court refused to conclude that such a change had been made "in the absence of language which expresses such a purpose too clearly to admit of doubt." Finding the phrase "privileges or immunities of citizens of the United States" lacking by this high standard, the Court reasoned that the phrase must mean something more limited.

Under the Court's narrow reading, the Privileges or Immunities Clause protects such things as the right

> "to come to the seat of government to assert any claim [a citizen] may have upon that government, to transact any business he may have with it, to seek its protection, to share its offices, to engage in administering its functions ... [and to] become a citizen of any State of the Union by a *bonâ fide* residence therein, with the same rights as other citizens of that State." (internal quotation marks omitted).

Finding no constitutional protection against state intrusion of the kind envisioned by the Louisiana statute, the Court upheld the statute. Four Justices dissented. Justice Field, joined by Chief Justice Chase and Justices Swayne and Bradley, criticized the majority for reducing the Fourteenth Amendment's Privileges or Immunities Clause to "a vain and idle enactment, which accomplished nothing, and most unnecessarily excited Congress and the people on its passage." Justice Field opined that the Privileges or Immunities Clause protects rights that are "in their nature ... fundamental," including the right of every man to pursue his profession without the imposition of unequal or discriminatory restrictions. Justice Bradley's dissent observed that "we are not bound to resort to implication ... to find an authoritative declaration of some of the most important privileges and immunities of citizens of the United States. It is in the Constitution itself." Justice Bradley would have construed the Privileges or Immunities Clause to include those rights enumerated in the Constitution as well as some unenumerated rights. Justice Swayne described the majority's narrow reading of the Privileges or Immunities Clause as "turn[ing] ... what was meant for bread into a stone." (dissenting opinion).

Today, many legal scholars dispute the correctness of the narrow *Slaughter-House* interpretation. . . . Three years after the decision in the *Slaughter-House Cases,* the Court decided *Cruikshank,* the first of the three 19th-century cases on which the Seventh Circuit relied. In that case, the Court reviewed convictions stemming from the infamous Colfax Massacre in Louisiana on Easter Sunday 1873. Dozens of blacks, many unarmed, were slaughtered by a rival band of armed white men. Cruikshank himself allegedly marched unarmed African-American prisoners through the streets and then had them summarily executed. Ninety-seven men were indicted for participating in the massacre, but only nine went to trial. Six of the nine were acquitted of all charges; the remaining three were acquitted of murder but convicted under the Enforcement Act of 1870, for banding and conspiring together to deprive their victims of various constitutional rights, including the right to bear arms.

The Court reversed all of the convictions, including those relating to the deprivation of the victims' right to bear arms. The Court wrote that the right of bearing arms for a lawful purpose "is not a right granted by the Constitution" and is not "in any manner dependent upon that instrument for its existence." "The second amendment," the Court continued, "declares that it shall not be infringed; but this ... means no more than that it shall not be infringed by Congress." *Ibid.* "Our later decisions in *Presser* v. *Illinois,* and *Miller* v. *Texas,* reaffirmed that the Second Amendment applies only to the Federal Government.

C

As previously noted, the Seventh Circuit concluded that *Cruikshank, Presser,* and *Miller* doomed petitioners' claims at the Court of Appeals level. Petitioners argue, however, that we should overrule those decisions and hold that the right to keep and bear arms is one of the "privileges or immunities of citizens of the United States." In petitioners' view, the Privileges or Immunities Clause protects all of the rights set out in the Bill of Rights, as well as some others, but petitioners are unable to identify the Clause's full scope. Nor is there any consensus on that question among the scholars who agree that the *Slaughter-House Cases'* interpretation is flawed.

We see no need to reconsider that interpretation here. For many decades, the question of the rights protected by the Fourteenth Amendment against state infringement has been analyzed under the Due Process Clause of that Amendment and not under the Privileges or Immunities Clause. We therefore decline to disturb the *Slaughter-House* holding.

At the same time, however, this Court's decisions in *Cruikshank, Presser*, and *Miller* do not preclude us from considering whether the Due Process Clause of the Fourteenth Amendment makes the Second Amendment right binding on the States. None of those cases "engage[d] in the sort of Fourteenth Amendment inquiry required by our later cases." As explained more fully below, *Cruikshank, Presser*, and *Miller* all preceded the era in which the Court began the process of "selective incorporation" under the Due Process Clause, and we have never previously addressed the question whether the right to keep and bear arms applies to the States under that theory.

Indeed, *Cruikshank* has not prevented us from holding that other rights that were at issue in that case are binding on the States through the Due Process Clause. In *Cruikshank*, the Court held that the general "right of the people peaceably to assemble for lawful purposes," which is protected by the First Amendment, applied only against the Federal Government and not against the States. Nonetheless, over 60 years later the Court held that the right of peaceful assembly was a "fundamental righ[t] ... safeguarded by the due process clause of the Fourteenth Amendment." We follow the same path here and thus consider whether the right to keep and bear arms applies to the States under the Due Process Clause.

D

1

In the late 19th century, the Court began to consider whether the Due Process Clause prohibits the States from infringing rights set out in the Bill of Rights. Five features of the approach taken during the ensuing era should be noted.

First, the Court viewed the due process question as entirely separate from the question whether a right was a privilege or immunity of national citizenship.

Second, the Court explained that the only rights protected against state infringement by the Due Process Clause were those rights "of such a nature that they are included in the conception of due process of law." While it was "possible that some of the personal rights safeguarded by the first eight Amendments against National action [might] also be safeguarded against state action," the Court stated, this was "not because those rights are enumerated in the first eight Amendments."

The Court used different formulations in describing the boundaries of due process. For example, in *Twining*, the Court referred to "immutable principles of justice which inhere in the very idea of free government which no member of the Union may disregard." In *Snyder v. Massachusetts*, the Court spoke of rights that are "so rooted in the traditions and conscience of our people as to be ranked as fundamental." And in *Palko*, the Court famously said that due process protects those rights that are "the very essence of a scheme of ordered liberty" and essential to "a fair and enlightened system of justice."

Third, in some cases decided during this era the Court "can be seen as having asked, when inquiring into whether some particular procedural safeguard was required of a State, if a civilized system could be imagined that would not accord the particular protection." Thus, in holding that due process prohibits a State from taking private property without just compensation, the Court described the right as "a principle of natural equity, recognized by all temperate and civilized governments, from a deep and universal sense of its justice." Similarly, the Court found that due process did not provide a right against compelled incrimination in part because this right "has no place in the jurisprudence of civilized and free countries outside the domain of the common law."

Fourth, the Court during this era was not hesitant to hold that a right set out in the Bill of Rights failed to meet the test for inclusion within the protection of the Due Process Clause. The Court found that some such rights qualified. But others did not.

Finally, even when a right set out in the Bill of Rights was held to fall within the conception of due process, the protection or remedies afforded against state infringement sometimes differed from the protection or remedies provided against abridgment by the Federal Government. To give one example, in *Betts* the Court held that, although the Sixth Amendment required the appointment of counsel in all federal criminal cases in which the defendant was unable to retain an attorney, the Due Process Clause required appointment of counsel in state criminal proceedings only where "want of counsel in [the] particular case ... result[ed] in a conviction lacking in ... fundamental fairness." Similarly, in *Wolf* v. *Colorado*, the Court held that the "core of the Fourth Amendment" was implicit in the concept of ordered liberty and thus "enforceable against the States through the Due Process Clause" but that the exclusionary rule, which applied in federal cases, did not apply to the States.

2

An alternative theory regarding the relationship between the Bill of Rights and §1 of the Fourteenth Amendment was championed by Justice Black. This theory held that §1 of the Fourteenth Amendment totally incorporated all of the provisions of the Bill of Rights. As Justice Black noted, the chief congressional proponents of the Fourteenth Amendment espoused the view that the Amendment made the Bill of Rights applicable to the States and, in so doing, overruled this Court's decision in *Barron*. Nonetheless, the Court never has embraced Justice Black's "total incorporation" theory.

3

While Justice Black's theory was never adopted, the Court eventually moved in that direction by initiating what has been called a process of "selective incorporation," *i.e.*, the Court began to hold that the Due Process Clause fully incorporates particular rights contained in the first eight Amendments.

The decisions during this time abandoned three of the previously noted characteristics of the earlier period. The Court made it clear that the governing standard is not whether *any* "civilized system [can] be imagined that would not accord the particular protection." Instead, the Court inquired whether a particular Bill of Rights guarantee is fundamental to *our* scheme of ordered liberty and system of justice.

The Court also shed any reluctance to hold that rights guaranteed by the Bill of Rights met the requirements for protection under the Due Process Clause. The Court eventually incorporated almost all of the provisions of the Bill of Rights. Only a handful of the Bill of Rights protections remain unincorporated.

Finally, the Court abandoned "the notion that the Fourteenth Amendment applies to the States only a watered-down, subjective version of the individual guarantees of the Bill of Rights," stating that it would be "incongruous" to apply different standards "depending on whether the claim was asserted in a state or federal court." Instead, the Court decisively held that incorporated Bill of Rights protections "are all to be enforced against the States under the Fourteenth Amendment according to the same standards that protect those personal rights against federal encroachment."

Employing this approach, the Court overruled earlier decisions in which it had held that particular Bill of Rights guarantees or remedies did not apply to the States.

III

With this framework in mind, we now turn directly to the question whether the Second Amendment right to keep and bear arms is incorporated in the concept of due process. In answering that question, as just explained, we must decide whether the right to keep and bear arms is fundamental to *our* scheme of ordered liberty, or as we have said in a related context, whether this right is "deeply rooted in this Nation's history and tradition."

A

Our decision in *Heller* points unmistakably to the answer. Self-defense is a basic right, recognized by many legal systems from ancient times to the present day, and in *Heller*, we held that individual self-defense is "the *central component*" of the Second Amendment right. Explaining that "the need for defense of self, family, and property is most acute" in the home, *ibid.*, we found that this right applies to handguns because they are "the most preferred firearm in the nation to 'keep' and use for protection of one's home and family,"

Heller makes it clear that this right is "deeply rooted in this Nation's history and tradition." *Heller* explored the right's origins, noting that the 1689 English Bill of Rights explicitly protected a right to keep arms for self-defense, and that by 1765, Blackstone was able to assert that the right to keep and bear arms was "one of the fundamental rights of Englishmen."

Blackstone's assessment was shared by the American colonists. As we noted in *Heller*, King George III's attempt to disarm the colonists in the 1760's and 1770's "provoked polemical reactions by Americans invoking their rights as Englishmen to keep arms."

The right to keep and bear arms was considered no less fundamental by those who drafted and ratified the Bill of Rights. "During the 1788 ratification debates, the fear that the federal government would disarm the people in order to impose rule through a standing army or select militia was pervasive in Antifederalist rhetoric." Federalists responded, not by arguing that the right was insufficiently important to warrant protection but by contending that the right was adequately protected by the Constitution's assignment of only limited powers to the Federal Government. Thus, Antifederalists and Federalists alike agreed that the right to bear arms was fundamental to the newly formed system of government. But those who were fearful that the new Federal Government would infringe traditional rights such as the right to keep and bear arms insisted on the adoption of the Bill of Rights as a condition for ratification of the Constitution. This is surely powerful evidence that the right was regarded as fundamental in the sense relevant here.

This understanding persisted in the years immediately following the ratification of the Bill of Rights. In addition to the four States that had adopted Second Amendment analogues before ratification, nine more States adopted state constitutional provisions protecting an individual right to keep and bear arms between 1789 and 1820. Founding-era legal commentators confirmed the importance of the right to early Americans. St. George Tucker, for example, described the right to keep and bear arms as "the true palladium of liberty" and explained that prohibitions on the right would place liberty "on the brink of destruction."

B

1

By the 1850's, the perceived threat that had prompted the inclusion of the Second Amendment in the Bill of Rights—the fear that the National Government would disarm the universal militia—had largely faded as a popular concern, but the right to keep and bear arms was highly valued for purposes of self-defense. Abolitionist authors wrote in support of the right. And when attempts were made to disarm "Free-Soilers" in "Bloody Kansas," Senator Charles Sumner, who later played a leading role in the adoption of the Fourteenth Amendment, proclaimed that "[n]ever was [the rifle] more needed in just self-defense than now in Kansas." Indeed, the 1856 Republican Party Platform protested that in Kansas the constitutional rights of the people had been "fraudulently and violently taken from them" and the "right of the people to keep and bear arms" had been "infringed."

After the Civil War, many of the over 180,000 African Americans who served in the Union Army returned to the States of the old Confederacy, where systematic efforts were made to disarm them and other blacks. The laws of some States formally prohibited African Americans from possessing firearms. For example, a Mississippi law provided that "no freedman, free negro or mulatto, not in the military service of the United States government, and not licensed so to do by the board of police of his or her county, shall keep or carry fire-arms of any kind, or any ammunition, dirk or bowie knife."

Throughout the South, armed parties, often consisting of ex-Confederate soldiers serving in the state militias, forcibly took firearms from newly freed slaves. In the first session of the 39th Congress, Senator Wilson told his colleagues: "In Mississippi rebel State forces, men who were in the rebel armies, are traversing the State, visiting the freedmen, disarming them, perpetrating murders and outrages upon them; and the same things are done in other sections of the country." The Report of the Joint Committee on Reconstruction—which was widely reprinted in the press and distributed by Members of the 39th Congress to their constituents shortly after Congress approved the Fourteenth Amendment—contained numerous examples of such abuses. In one town, the "marshal [took] all arms from returned colored soldiers, and [was] very prompt in shooting the blacks whenever an opportunity occur[red]." As Senator Wilson put it during the debate on a failed proposal to disband Southern militias: "There is one unbroken chain of testimony from all people that are loyal to this country, that the greatest outrages are perpetrated by armed men who go up and down the country searching houses, disarming people, committing outrages of every kind and description."

Union Army commanders took steps to secure the right of all citizens to keep and bear arms, but the 39th Congress concluded that legislative action was necessary. Its efforts to safeguard the right to keep and bear arms demonstrate that the right was still recognized to be fundamental.

The most explicit evidence of Congress' aim appears in §14 of the Freedmen's Bureau Act of 1866, which provided that "the right ... to have full and equal benefit of all laws and proceedings concerning personal liberty, personal security, and the acquisition, enjoyment, and disposition of estate, real and personal, *including the constitutional right to bear arms*, shall be secured to and enjoyed by all the citizens ... without respect to race or color, or previous condition of slavery." Section 14 thus explicitly guaranteed that "all the citizens," black and white, would have "the constitutional right to bear arms."

The Civil Rights Act of 1866, which was considered at the same time as the Freedmen's Bureau Act, similarly sought to protect the right of all citizens to keep and bear arms. Section 1 of the Civil Rights Act guaranteed the "full and equal benefit of all laws and proceedings for the security of person and property, as is enjoyed by white citizens." This language was virtually identical to language in §14 of the Freedmen's Bureau Act. And as noted, the latter provision went on to explain that one of the "laws and proceedings concerning personal liberty, personal security, and the acquisition, enjoyment, and disposition of estate, real and personal" was "the constitutional right to bear arms." Representative Bingham believed that the Civil Rights Act protected the same rights as enumerated in the Freedmen's Bureau bill, which of course explicitly mentioned the right to keep and bear arms. The unavoidable conclusion is that the Civil Rights Act, like the Freedmen's Bureau Act, aimed to protect "the constitutional right to bear arms" and not simply to prohibit discrimination.

Congress, however, ultimately deemed these legislative remedies insufficient. Southern resistance, Presidential vetoes, and this Court's pre-Civil-War precedent persuaded Congress that a constitutional amendment was necessary to provide full protection for the rights of blacks.] Today, it is generally accepted that the Fourteenth Amendment was understood to provide a constitutional basis for protecting the rights set out in the Civil Rights Act of 1866.

In debating the Fourteenth Amendment, the 39th Congress referred to the right to keep and bear arms as a fundamental right deserving of protection. Senator Samuel Pomeroy described three "indispensable" "safeguards of liberty under our form of Government." One of these, he said, was the right to keep and bear arms:

> "Every man ... should have the right to bear arms for the defense of himself and family and his homestead. And if the cabin door of the freedman is broken open and the intruder enters for purposes as vile as were known to slavery, then should a well-loaded musket be in the hand of the occupant to send the polluted wretch to another world, where his wretchedness will forever remain complete.
>
> Even those who thought the Fourteenth Amendment unnecessary believed that blacks, as citizens, "have equal right to protection, and to keep and bear arms for self-defense."

Evidence from the period immediately following the ratification of the Fourteenth Amendment only confirms that the right to keep and bear arms was considered fundamental. In an 1868 speech addressing the disarmament of freedmen, Representative Stevens emphasized the necessity of the right: "Disarm a community and you rob them of the means of defending life. Take away their weapons of defense and you take away the inalienable right of defending liberty." "The fourteenth amendment, now so happily adopted, settles the whole question." And in debating the Civil Rights Act of 1871,

Congress routinely referred to the right to keep and bear arms and decried the continued disarmament of blacks in the South. Finally, legal commentators from the period emphasized the fundamental nature of the right.

The right to keep and bear arms was also widely protected by state constitutions at the time when the Fourteenth Amendment was ratified. In 1868, 22 of the 37 States in the Union had state constitutional provisions explicitly protecting the right to keep and bear arms. Quite a few of these state constitutional guarantees, moreover, explicitly protected the right to keep and bear arms as an individual right to self-defense. What is more, state constitutions adopted during the Reconstruction era by former Confederate States included a right to keep and bear arms. A clear majority of the States in 1868, therefore, recognized the right to keep and bear arms as being among the foundational rights necessary to our system of Government.

In sum, it is clear that the Framers and ratifiers of the Fourteenth Amendment counted the right to keep and bear arms among those fundamental rights necessary to our system of ordered liberty.

2

Despite all this evidence, municipal respondents contend that Congress, in the years immediately following the Civil War, merely sought to outlaw "discriminatory measures taken against freedmen, which it addressed by adopting a non-discrimination principle" and that even an outright ban on the possession of firearms was regarded as acceptable, "so long as it was not done in a discriminatory manner." They argue that Members of Congress overwhelmingly viewed §1 of the Fourteenth Amendment "as an antidiscrimination rule," and they cite statements to the effect that the section would outlaw discriminatory measures. This argument is implausible.

First, while §1 of the Fourteenth Amendment contains "an antidiscrimination rule," namely, the Equal Protection Clause, municipal respondents can hardly mean that §1 does no more than prohibit discrimination. If that were so, then the First Amendment, as applied to the States, would not prohibit nondiscriminatory abridgments of the rights to freedom of speech or freedom of religion; the Fourth Amendment, as applied to the States, would not prohibit all unreasonable searches and seizures but only discriminatory searches and seizures—and so on. We assume that this is not municipal respondents' view, so what they must mean is that the Second Amendment should be singled out for special—and specially unfavorable—treatment. We reject that suggestion.

Second, municipal respondents' argument ignores the clear terms of the Freedmen's Bureau Act of 1866, which acknowledged the existence of the right to bear arms. If that law had used language such as "the equal benefit of laws concerning the bearing of arms," it would be possible to interpret it as simply a prohibition of racial discrimination. But §14 speaks of and protects "the constitutional right to bear arms," an unmistakable reference to the right protected by the Second Amendment. And it protects the "full and equal benefit" of this right in the States. It would have been nonsensical for Congress to guarantee the full and equal benefit of a constitutional right that does not exist.

Third, if the 39th Congress had outlawed only those laws that discriminate on the basis of race or previous condition of servitude, African Americans in the South would likely have remained vulnerable to attack by many of their worst abusers: the state militia and state peace officers. In the years immediately following the Civil War, a law banning the possession of guns by all private citizens would have been nondiscriminatory only in the formal sense. Any such law—like the Chicago and Oak Park ordinances challenged here—presumably would have permitted the possession of guns by those acting under the authority of the State and would thus have left firearms in the hands of the militia and local peace officers. And as the Report of the Joint Committee on Reconstruction revealed, those groups were widely involved in harassing blacks in the South.

Fourth, municipal respondents' purely antidiscrimination theory of the Fourteenth Amendment disregards the plight of whites in the South who opposed the Black Codes. If the 39th Congress and the ratifying public had simply prohibited racial discrimination with respect to the bearing of arms, opponents of the Black Codes would have been left without the means of self-defense—as had abolitionists in Kansas in the 1850's.

Fifth, the 39th Congress' response to proposals to disband and disarm the Southern militias is instructive.

Despite recognizing and deploring the abuses of these militias, the 39th Congress balked at a proposal to disarm them. Disarmament, it was argued, would violate the members' right to bear arms, and it was ultimately decided to disband the militias but not to disarm their members. It cannot be doubted that the right to bear arms was regarded as a substantive guarantee, not a prohibition that could be ignored so long as the States legislated in an evenhanded manner.

IV

Municipal respondents' remaining arguments are at war with our central holding in *Heller*: that the Second Amendment protects a personal right to keep and bear arms for lawful purposes, most notably for self-defense within the home. Municipal respondents, in effect, ask us to treat the right recognized in *Heller* as a second-class right, subject to an entirely different body of rules than the other Bill of Rights guarantees that we have held to be incorporated into the Due Process Clause.

Municipal respondents' main argument is nothing less than a plea to disregard 50 years of incorporation precedent and return (presumably for this case only) to a bygone era. Municipal respondents submit that the Due Process Clause protects only those rights " 'recognized by all temperate and civilized governments, from a deep and universal sense of [their] justice.' " According to municipal respondents, if it is possible to imagine *any* civilized legal system that does not recognize a particular right, then the Due Process Clause does not make that right binding on the States. Therefore, the municipal respondents continue, because such countries as England, Canada, Australia, Japan, Denmark, Finland, Luxembourg, and New Zealand either ban or severely limit handgun ownership, it must follow that no right to possess such weapons is protected by the Fourteenth Amendment.

This line of argument is, of course, inconsistent with the long-established standard we apply in incorporation cases. And the present-day implications of municipal respondents' argument are stunning. For example, many of the rights that our Bill of Rights provides for persons accused of criminal offenses are virtually unique to this country. If *our* understanding of the right to a jury trial, the right against self-incrimination, and the right to counsel were necessary attributes of *any* civilized country, it would follow that the United States is the only civilized Nation in the world.

Municipal respondents attempt to salvage their position by suggesting that their argument applies only to substantive as opposed to procedural rights. Brief for Municipal Respondents 10, n. 3. But even in this trimmed form, municipal respondents' argument flies in the face of more than a half-century of precedent. For example, in *Everson* v. *Board of Ed. of Ewing*, the Court held that the Fourteenth Amendment incorporates the Establishment Clause of the First Amendment. Yet several of the countries that municipal respondents recognize as civilized have established state churches. If we were to adopt municipal respondents' theory, all of this Court's Establishment Clause precedents involving actions taken by state and local governments would go by the boards.

Municipal respondents maintain that the Second Amendment differs from all of the other provisions of the Bill of Rights because it concerns the right to possess a deadly implement and thus has implications for public safety. And they note that there is intense disagreement on the question whether the private possession of guns in the home increases or decreases gun deaths and injuries.

The right to keep and bear arms, however, is not the only constitutional right that has controversial public safety implications. All of the constitutional provisions that impose restrictions on law enforcement and on the prosecution of crimes fall into the same category. Municipal respondents cite no case in which we have refrained from holding that a provision of the Bill of Rights is binding on the States on the ground that the right at issue has disputed public safety implications.

We likewise reject municipal respondents' argument that we should depart from our established incorporation methodology on the ground that making the Second Amendment binding on the States and their subdivisions is inconsistent with principles of federalism and will stifle experimentation. Municipal respondents point out—quite correctly—that conditions and problems differ from locality to locality and that citizens in different jurisdictions have divergent views on the issue of gun control. Municipal respondents therefore urge us to allow state and local governments to enact any gun control law that they deem to be reasonable, including a complete ban on the possession of handguns in the home for self-defense.

There is nothing new in the argument that, in order to respect federalism and allow useful state experimentation, a federal constitutional right should not be fully binding on the States. This argument was made repeatedly and eloquently by Members of this Court who rejected the concept of incorporation and urged retention of the two-track approach to incorporation. Throughout the era of "selective incorporation," Justice Harlan in particular, invoking the values of federalism and state experimentation, fought a determined rearguard action to preserve the two-track approach.

Time and again, however, those pleas failed. Unless we turn back the clock or adopt a special incorporation test applicable only to the Second Amendment, municipal respondents' argument must be rejected. Under our precedents, if a Bill of Rights guarantee is fundamental from an American perspective, then, unless *stare decisis* counsels otherwise, that guarantee is fully binding on the States and thus *limits* (but by no means eliminates) their ability to devise solutions to social problems that suit local needs and values. As noted by the 38 States that have appeared in this case as *amici* supporting petitioners, "[s]tate and local experimentation with reasonable firearms regulations will continue under the Second Amendment."

Municipal respondents and their *amici* complain that incorporation of the Second Amendment right will lead to extensive and costly litigation, but this argument applies with even greater force to constitutional rights and remedies that have already been held to be binding on the States. Consider the exclusionary rule. Although the exclusionary rule "is not an individual right," but a "judicially created rule," this Court made the rule applicable to the States. The exclusionary rule is said to result in "tens of thousands of contested suppression motions each year."

Municipal respondents assert that, although most state constitutions protect firearms rights, state courts have held that these rights are subject to "interest-balancing" and have sustained a variety of restrictions. In *Heller*, however, we expressly rejected the argument that the scope of the Second Amendment right should be determined by judicial interest balancing, and this Court decades ago abandoned "the notion that the Fourteenth Amendment applies to the States only a watered-down, subjective version of the individual guarantees of the Bill of Rights."

As evidence that the Fourteenth Amendment has not historically been understood to restrict the authority of the States to regulate firearms, municipal respondents and supporting *amici* cite a variety of state and local firearms laws that courts have upheld. But what is most striking about their research is the paucity of precedent sustaining bans comparable to those at issue here and in *Heller*. Municipal respondents cite precisely one case (from the late 20th century) in which such a ban was sustained. It is important to keep in mind that *Heller*, while striking down a law that prohibited the possession of handguns in the home, recognized that the right to keep and bear arms is not "a right to keep and carry any weapon whatsoever in any manner whatsoever and for whatever purpose." We made it clear in *Heller* that our holding did not cast doubt on such longstanding regulatory measures as "prohibitions on the possession of firearms by felons and the mentally ill," "laws forbidding the carrying of firearms in sensitive places such as schools and government buildings, or laws imposing conditions and qualifications on the commercial sale of arms." We repeat those assurances here. Despite municipal respondents' doomsday proclamations, incorporation does not imperil every law regulating firearms.

Municipal respondents argue, finally, that the right to keep and bear arms is unique among the rights set out in the first eight Amendments "because the reason for codifying the Second Amendment (to protect the militia) differs from the purpose (primarily, to use firearms to engage in self-defense) that is claimed to make the right implicit in the concept of ordered liberty." Municipal respondents suggest that the Second Amendment right differs from the rights heretofore incorporated because the latter were "valued for [their] own sake." But we have never previously suggested that incorporation of a right turns on whether it has intrinsic as opposed to instrumental value, and quite a few of the rights previously held to be incorporated—for example the right to counsel and the right to confront and subpoena witnesses—are clearly instrumental by any measure. Moreover, this contention repackages one of the chief arguments that we rejected in *Heller*, *i.e.*, that the scope of the Second Amendment right is defined by the immediate threat that led to the inclusion of that right in the Bill of Rights. In *Heller*, we recognized that the codification of this right was prompted by fear that the Federal Government would disarm and thus disable the militias, but we rejected the suggestion that the right was valued only as a means of preserving the militias. On the contrary, we stressed that the right was also valued because the possession of firearms was thought to be essential for self-defense. As we put it, self-defense was "the *central component* of the right itself."

V

A

We turn, finally, to the two dissenting opinions. Justice Stevens' eloquent opinion covers ground already addressed, and therefore little need be added in response. Justice Stevens would " 'ground the prohibitions against state action squarely on due process, without intermediate reliance on any of the first eight Amendments.' " The question presented in this case, in his view, "is whether the particular right asserted by petitioners applies to the States because of the Fourteenth Amendment itself, standing on its own bottom." He would hold that "[t]he rights protected against state infringement by the Fourteenth Amendment's Due Process Clause need not be identical in shape or scope to the rights protected against Federal Government infringement by the various provisions of the Bill of Rights."

As we have explained, the Court, for the past half-century, has moved away from the two-track approach. If we were now to accept Justice Stevens' theory across the board, decades of decisions would be undermined. We assume that this is not what is proposed. What is urged instead, it appears, is that this theory be revived solely for the individual right that *Heller* recognized, over vigorous dissents.

The relationship between the Bill of Rights' guarantees and the States must be governed by a single, neutral principle. It is far too late to exhume what Justice Brennan, writing for the Court 46 years ago, derided as "the notion that the Fourteenth Amendment applies to the States only a watered-down, subjective version of the individual guarantees of the Bill of Rights."

B

Justice Breyer's dissent makes several points to which we briefly respond. To begin, while there is certainly room for disagreement about *Heller*'s analysis of the history of the right to keep and bear arms, nothing written since *Heller* persuades us to reopen the question there decided. Few other questions of original meaning have been as thoroughly explored.

Justice Breyer's conclusion that the Fourteenth Amendment does not incorporate the right to keep and bear arms appears to rest primarily on four factors: First, "there is no popular consensus" that the right is fundamental; second, the right does not protect minorities or persons neglected by those holding political power; third, incorporation of the Second Amendment right would "amount to a significant incursion on a traditional and important area of state concern, altering the constitutional relationship between the States and the Federal Government" and preventing local variations; and fourth, determining the scope of the Second Amendment right in cases involving state and local laws will force judges to answer difficult empirical questions regarding matters that are outside their area of expertise. Even if we believed that these factors were relevant to the incorporation inquiry, none of these factors undermines the case for incorporation of the right to keep and bear arms for self-defense.

First, we have never held that a provision of the Bill of Rights applies to the States only if there is a "popular consensus" that the right is fundamental, and we see no basis for such a rule. But in this case, as it turns out, there is evidence of such a consensus. An *amicus* brief submitted by 58 Members of the Senate and 251 Members of the House of Representatives urges us to hold that the right to keep and bear arms is fundamental. Another brief submitted by 38 States takes the same position.

Second, petitioners and many others who live in high-crime areas dispute the proposition that the Second Amendment right does not protect minorities and those lacking political clout. The plight of Chicagoans living in high-crime areas was recently highlighted when two Illinois legislators representing Chicago districts called on the Governor to deploy the Illinois National Guard to patrol the City's streets. The legislators noted that the number of Chicago homicide victims during the current year equaled the number of American soldiers killed during that same period in Afghanistan and Iraq and that 80% of the Chicago victims were black. *Amici* supporting incorporation of the right to keep and bear arms contend that the right is especially important for women and members of other groups that may be especially vulnerable to violent crime. If, as petitioners believe, their safety and the safety of other law-abiding members of the community would be enhanced by the possession of handguns in the home for self-defense, then the Second Amendment right protects the rights of minorities and other residents of high-crime areas whose needs are not being met by elected public officials.

Third, Justice Breyer is correct that incorporation of the Second Amendment right will to some extent limit the legislative freedom of the States, but this is always true when a Bill of Rights provision is incorporated. Incorporation always restricts experimentation and local variations, but that has not stopped the Court from incorporating virtually every other provision of the Bill of Rights. "[T]he enshrinement of constitutional rights necessarily takes certain policy choices off the table." This conclusion is no more remarkable with respect to the Second Amendment than it is with respect to all the other limitations on state power found in the Constitution.

Finally, Justice Breyer is incorrect that incorporation will require judges to assess the costs and benefits of firearms restrictions and thus to make difficult empirical judgments in an area in which they lack expertise. As we have noted, while his opinion in *Heller* recommended an interest-balancing test, the Court specifically rejected that suggestion. "The very enumeration of the right takes out of the hands of government—even the Third Branch of Government—the power to decide on a case-by-case basis whether the right is *really worth* insisting upon."

* * * * *

In *Heller*, we held that the Second Amendment protects the right to possess a handgun in the home for the purpose of self-defense. Unless considerations of *stare decisis* counsel otherwise, a provision of the Bill of Rights that protects a right that is fundamental from an American perspective applies equally to the Federal Government and the States. We therefore hold that the Due Process Clause of the Fourteenth Amendment incorporates the Second Amendment right recognized in *Heller*. The judgment of the Court of Appeals is reversed, and the case is remanded for further proceedings.

It is so ordered.

Document Themes

McDonald v. City of Chicago had implications for a host of legal issues. One was the role the first clause, the "militia" clause, plays in restricting the right to bear arms. A second is whether the right to bear arms includes a right of self-defense, a "right" that is not mentioned in the Constitution. A third is whether the wording of the Second Amendment is to be interpreted according to the views and standards of 1791. The fourth, and perhaps most crucial, issue is whether the Fourteenth Amendment limits state and municipal action as it applies to the Second Amendment.

Justice Alito and the Court majority agreed with Justice Scalia's view, expressed in *Heller*, that the "militia" clause that begins the Second Amendment is subordinate to the "operative clause" that grants an *individual* right to bear arms, independent of service in a militia. Alito additionally accepts the view that the original public understanding of the right to keep and bear arms meant that firearms could be kept by individuals for purposes of self-defense.

The case, however, was not a referendum on guns and the larger social issue of whether guns should be more strictly controlled. Instead, the case raised the constitutional issue of the applicability of the Second Amendment to the states. Alito makes clear the Court's position early on:

> Two years ago, in *District of Columbia* v. *Heller*, we held that the Second Amendment protects the right to keep and bear arms for the purpose of self-defense, and we struck down a District of Columbia law that banned the possession of handguns in the home. The city of Chicago (City) and the village of Oak Park, a Chicago suburb, have laws that are similar to the District of Columbia's, but Chicago and Oak Park argue that their laws are constitutional because the Second Amendment has no application to the States. We have previously held that most of the provisions of the Bill of Rights apply with full force to both the Federal Government and the States. Applying the standard that is well established in our case law, we hold that the Second Amendment right is fully applicable to the States.

The bulk of the decision, then, is a historical examination of the Supreme Court's piecemeal application of the Fourteenth Amendment in incorporating the provisions of the Bill of Rights into state and local law. What the Alito court concluded was that the Second Amendment right to keep and bear arms is applicable not just to the federal government but to state and local governments as well; if the federal government cannot circumscribe that right, neither can the states. Accordingly, Alito concluded: "A provision of the Bill of Rights that protects a right that is fundamental from an American perspective applies equally to the Federal Government and the States. We therefore hold that the Due Process Clause of the Fourteenth Amendment incorporates the Second Amendment right recognized in *Heller*." The result was to strike down the handgun ban in Chicago and Oak Park.

Additional Reading

Aynes, Richard L., "*McDonald v. Chicago,* Self-Defense, the Right to Bear Arms, and the Future," *Akron Journal of Constitutional Law and Policy* 2 (2011): 181–203.

Horowitz, Emily, "Shooting Blanks: The Supreme Court's Flawed Analysis in *McDonald v. City of Chicago,*" *University of Miami Law Review*66, no. 1 (Fall 2011): 197–231.

"*McDonald v. City of Chicago,*" *Harvard Law Review*124, no. 1 (2010): 229–39.

Rosenthal, Lawrence, and Joyce Lee Malcolm, "Colloquy Debate: *McDonald v. Chicago*: Which Standard of Scrutiny Should Apply to Gun Control," *Northwestern University Law Review*105, no. 1 (2011): 438–66.

Scarola, Matthew, "Analysis: State Gun Regulations and *McDonald,*" *SCOTUSblog*, June 28, 2010.

—Michael J. O'Neal

Peruta v. County of San Diego

Author(s): William A. Fletcher (majority opinion) and Consuelo Maria Callahan (dissenting opinion)
Date: 2016
Genre: Ninth U.S. Circuit Court of Appeals

Summary Overview

Peruta v. County of San Diego (which was consolidated with another case, *Richards v. County of Yolo*) is a key case in contemporary judicial interpretation of the Second Amendment. Specifically, the U.S. Ninth Circuit Court of Appeals took up the issues of concealed carry laws in San Diego and Yolo Counties and whether carrying a concealed weapon was protected by the Second Amendment's right to keep and bear arms.

The court's ruling came in the wake of two landmark U.S. Supreme Court cases, *District of Columbia v. Heller* (2008) and *McDonald v. Chicago* (2010), both of which struck down bans on handgun ownership and affirmed the right of an individual to have a firearm in the home for self-defense. The Court in these cases, however, left open the question of whether that right extended outside the home. The Ninth Circuit affirmed lower court rulings that San Diego County's regulations pertaining to concealed carry licenses are constitutional. The case was appealed to the Supreme Court in 2017, but the Court declined to hear the case.

Defining Moment

According to the California Penal Code, a citizen has to obtain a license to legally carry a concealed firearm. To obtain a license, the applicant must show "good cause," but what constitutes good cause is left up to the discretion of each county's sheriff. The sheriffs of San Diego County and Yolo County define good cause as have a particularized reason for needing a concealed firearm, stating that simply fearing for one's personal safety or wanting to protect one's family was not "good cause."

Edward Peruta and Adam Richards challenged the good cause requirements, arguing that they infringed on their Second Amendment right to keep and bear arms for self-defense. In both cases, the district court granted summary judgment in favor of the counties. (In an interesting aside, before the cases reached the Ninth Circuit, the state of California banned the open carry of firearms, although that ban is likely to face a challenge in light of the Ninth Circuit's 2018 decision in *Young v. Hawaii,* which struck down open carry restrictions in Hawaii, one of the state's in the Ninth Circuit's jurisdiction.)

In 2014, a three-judge panel of the Ninth Circuit ruled that San Diego County's concealed carry law was unconstitutional, then subsequently made a similar ruling in the *Richards* case. The Ninth Circuit then reheard the case en banc (i.e., before the entire bench, not just a panel) and upheld both counties' statutes, holding that "the Second Amendment right to keep and bear arms does not include, in any degree, the right of a member of the general public to carry concealed firearms in public."

About the Author

The majority opinion in *Peruta v. County of San Diego* was written by Justice William A. Fletcher. Fletcher was born on June 6, 1945, in Philadelphia, Pennsylvania. He received his bachelor's degree from Harvard University in 1968 and a second degree as a Rhodes Scholar at Merton College at Oxford University in 1970.

In 1975 he earned his law degree from the Yale Law School. He then clerked for a judge of the U.S. District Court for the Northern District of California, then for U.S. Supreme Court justice William Brennan. In an interesting side note, his mother was a U.S. Ninth Circuit Court of Appeals justice.

From 1977 to 1998, he was a professor of law at the Boalt Hall School of Law at the University of California at Berkeley. President Bill Clinton, Fletcher's Rhodes Scholar classmate, nominated him to a seat on the Ninth Circuit in 1995, although the U.S. Senate never voted on the appointment. In 1997, Clinton re-nominated him, the Senate approved the nomination, and he took his seat in 1998.

The dissent was written by Justice Consuelo Maria Callahan. Callahan was born on June 9, 1950, in Palo Alto, California. She earned her bachelor's degree from Stanford University in 1972, then graduated from the McGeorge School of Law at the University of the Pacific in 1975. Subsequently, in 2004, she received a master of laws degree from the University of Virginia School of Law. After a number of years in public service, she was nominated to the Ninth Circuit Court of Appeals by President George W. Bush in 2003 and took her seat that year after she was unanimously confirmed in the U.S. Senate.

HISTORICAL DOCUMENT

Edward PERUTA; Michelle Laxson; James Dodd; Leslie Buncher, Dr.; Mark Cleary; California Rifle and Pistol Association Foundation, Plaintiffs-Appellants,

v.

COUNTY OF SAN DIEGO; William D. Gore, individually and in his capacity as Sheriff, Defendants-Appellees, State of California, Intervenor.
Adam Richards; Second Amendment Foundation; Calguns Foundation, Inc.; Brett Stewart, Plaintiffs-Appellants,

v.

Ed Prieto; County of Yolo, Defendants-Appellees.
United States Court of Appeals, Ninth Circuit.

W. FLETCHER, Circuit Judge:

Under California law, a member of the general public may not carry a concealed weapon in public unless he or she has been issued a license. An applicant for a license must satisfy a number of conditions. Among other things, the applicant must show "good cause" to carry a concealed firearm. California law authorizes county sheriffs to establish and publish policies defining good cause. The sheriffs of San Diego and Yolo Counties published policies defining good cause as requiring a particularized reason why an applicant needs a concealed firearm for self-defense.

Appellants, who live in San Diego and Yolo Counties, allege that they wish to carry concealed firearms in public for self-defense, but that they do not satisfy the good cause requirements in their counties. They contend that their counties' definitions of good cause violate their Second Amendment right to keep and bear arms. They particularly rely on the Supreme Court's decisions in *District of Columbia v. Heller*, 554 U.S. 570, 128 S.Ct. 2783, 171 L.Ed.2d 637 (2008), and *McDonald v. City of Chicago*, 561 U.S. 742, 130 S.Ct. 3020, 177 L.Ed.2d 894 (2010).

We hold that the Second Amendment does not preserve or protect a right of a member of the general public to carry concealed firearms in public.

I. Procedural History

Plaintiff Edward Peruta lives in San Diego County. He applied for a license to carry a concealed firearm in February 2009, but his application was denied because he had not shown good cause under the policy published in his county. Plaintiff Adam Richards lives in Yolo County. He sought a license to carry a concealed firearm in May 2009, but was told he could not establish good cause under his county's policy. Peruta, Richards, and the other plaintiffs—five residents of San Diego and Yolo Counties, as well as several gun-rights organizations—brought two separate suits challenging under the Second Amendment the two counties' interpretation and application of the statutory good cause requirement under California law.

The district courts granted summary judgment in each case, holding that the counties' policies do not violate the Second Amendment. A divided three-judge panel of this court reversed both decisions. The panel majority held in a published opinion in *Peruta* that San Diego's policy violated the Second Amendment. Although Plaintiffs challenged only the county's concealed firearms policy, the panel held that their challenge should not be "viewed in isolation." Rather, in the view of the panel majority, Plaintiffs' suit should be viewed as a challenge to "the constitutionality of [California's] entire [statutory] scheme." In the majority's view, the Second Amendment required that "the states permit *some form* of carry for self-defense outside the home." Because California's statutory scheme permits concealed carry only upon a showing of good cause and because open carry is also restricted, the panel held that the county's definition of good cause for a concealed carry license violates the Second Amendment. The panel held in *Richards* that, in light of its holding in *Peruta*, the Yolo County policy also violated the Second Amendment.

Yolo County and its sheriff, Ed Prieto, filed a petition for rehearing en banc in *Richards*. San Diego County's sheriff, William Gore, announced that he would not petition for rehearing en banc in *Peruta*. After Sheriff Gore declined to file a petition, the State of California moved to intervene in *Peruta* in order to seek rehearing en banc. The same divided three-judge panel denied California's motion to intervene.

We granted rehearing en banc in both cases.

III. California Firearms Regulation

* * * * *

The sheriff of a county may issue a concealed carry license to a person upon proof of all of the following:

> (1) The applicant is of good moral character.
>
> (2) Good cause exists for issuance of the license.
>
> (3) The applicant is a resident of the county or a city within the county, or the applicant's principal place of employment or business is in the county or a city within the county and the applicant spends a substantial period of time in that place of employment or business.
>
> (4) The applicant has completed a course of training as described in Section 26165.

* * * * *

An affidavit of Blanca Pelowitz, Manager of the San Diego Sheriff's Department License Division, describes the definition of good cause in San Diego County:

Good Cause ... is defined by this County to be a set of circumstances that distinguish the applicant from the mainstream and causes him or her to be placed in harm's way. Simply fearing for one's personal safety alone is not considered good cause. This criterion can be applied to situations related to personal protection as well as those related to individual businesses or occupations.

Good cause is also evaluated on an individual basis. Reasons applicants request a license will fall into one of ... four general categories[.]

The only two general categories potentially relevant to this appeal are:

> Category 2 = Personal Protection Only includes: documented threats, restraining orders and other related situations where an applicant can demonstrate they are a specific target at risk.
>
> Category 4 = Business owners/employees includes a diversity of businesses & occupations, such as doctors, attorneys, CEO's, managers, employees and volunteers whose occupation or business places them at high risk of harm.

The published policy of Yolo County does not define "good cause" but gives examples of where good cause does, or does not, exist. The policy provides as follows:

> Examples of valid reasons to request a permit include, but are not limited to:
>
> Victims of violent crime and/or documented threats of violence.
>
> Business owners who carry large sums of cash or valuable items.
>
> Business owners who work all hours in remote areas and are likely to encounter dangerous people and situations.
>
> Examples o[f] invalid reasons to request a permit include, but are not limited to:
>
> Recreation in remote areas.
>
> Hunting or fishing.
>
> Self protection and protection of family (without credible threats of violence).
>
> Employment in the security field, i.e., security guard, body guard, VIP protection.

Personal safety due to job conditions or duties placed on the applicant by their employer.

IV. Second Amendment and Concealed Carry

Plaintiffs contend that the good cause requirement for concealed carry, as interpreted in the policies of the sheriffs of San Diego and Yolo Counties, violates the Second Amendment. Plaintiffs' arguments in the two cases differ in some particulars, but they essentially proceed as follows. First, they contend that the Second Amendment guarantees at least some ability of a member of the general public to carry firearms in public. Second, they contend that California's restrictions on concealed and open carry of firearms, taken together, violate the Amendment. Third, they contend that there would be sufficient opportunity for public carry of firearms to satisfy the Amendment if the good cause requirement for concealed carry, as interpreted by the sheriffs of San Diego and Yolo Counties, were eliminated. Therefore, they contend, the counties' good cause requirements for concealed carry violate the Amendment. While Plaintiffs base their argument on the entirety of California's statutory scheme, they allege only that they have sought permits to carry concealed weapons, and they seek relief only against the policies requiring good cause for such permits. Notably, Plaintiffs do *not* contend that there is a free-standing Second Amendment right to carry concealed firearms.

We do not reach the question whether the Second Amendment protects some ability to carry firearms in public, such as open carry. That question was left open by the Supreme Court in *Heller,* and we have no need to answer it here. Because Plaintiffs challenge only policies governing concealed carry, we reach only the question whether the Second Amendment protects, in any degree, the ability to carry concealed firearms in public. Based on the overwhelming consensus of historical sources, we conclude that the protection of the Second Amendment—whatever the scope of that protection may be—simply does not extend to the carrying of concealed firearms in public by members of the general public.

The Second Amendment may or may not protect, to some degree, a right of a member of the general public to carry firearms in public. But the existence *velnon*of such a right, and the scope of such a right, are separate from and independent of the question presented here. We hold only that there is no Second Amendment right for members of the general public to carry concealed firearms in public.

A. *Heller* and *McDonald*

The Second Amendment provides: "A well regulated Militia, being necessary to the security of a free State, the right of the people to keep and bear Arms, shall not be infringed." The watershed case interpreting the Amendment is *District of Columbia v. Heller.* The plaintiff in *Heller* challenged a District of Columbia statute that entirely banned the possession of handguns in the home, and required that any lawful firearm in the home be "disassembled or bound by a trigger lock at all times, rendering it inoperable."

Relying on the phrase "shall not be infringed," the Court in *Heller* viewed the Amendment as having "codified a *pre-existing* right." The Court focused on the history leading to the adoption of the Amendment, and on the common understanding of the Amendment in the years following its adoption. The Court concluded that the "pre-existing right" to keep and bear arms preserved by the Second Amendment was in part an individual right to personal self-defense, not confined to the purpose of maintaining a well-regulated militia. The Court struck down the challenged statute, concluding that the Amendment preserves the right of members of the general public to keep and bear arms in their homes for the purpose of self-defense: "[W]e hold that the District's ban on handgun possession in the home violates the Second Amendment, as does its prohibition against rendering any lawful firearm in the home operable for the purpose of immediate self-defense."

The Court in *Heller* was careful to limit the scope of its holding. Of particular interest here, the Court noted that the Second Amendment has not been generally understood to protect the right to carry concealed firearms. The Court wrote:

> *Like most rights, the right secured by the Second Amendment is not unlimited.* From Blackstone through the 19th-century cases, commentators and courts routinely explained that the right was

> not a right to keep and carry any weapon whatsoever in any manner whatsoever and for whatever purpose. *For example, the majority of the 19th-century courts to consider the question held that prohibitions on carrying concealed weapons were lawful under the Second Amendment or state analogues.*

At the end of its opinion, the Court again emphasized the limited scope of its holding, and underscored the tools that remained available to the District of Columbia to regulate firearms. Referring the reader back to the passage just quoted, the Court wrote:

> The Constitution leaves the District of Columbia a variety of tools for combating th[e] problem [of handgun violence], including some measures regulating handguns.

Heller left open the question whether the Second Amendment applies to regulation of firearms by states and localities. The Court answered the question two years later, in *McDonald v. City of Chicago,* holding that the Due Process Clause of the Fourteenth Amendment incorporates the Second Amendment. In substantial part, the Court based its holding on the understanding of a "clear majority" of the states when the Fourteenth Amendment was adopted. The Court wrote:

> A clear majority of the States in 1868... recognized the right to keep and bear arms as being among the foundational rights necessary to our system of Government.

In sum, it is clear that the Framers and ratifiers of the Fourteenth Amendment counted the right to keep and bear arms among those fundamental rights necessary to our system of ordered liberty.

1. History Relevant to the Second Amendment

a. Right to Bear Arms in England

The right to bear arms in England has long been subject to substantial regulation. In 1299, Edward I directed the sheriffs of Safford and Shalop to prohibit anyone from "going armed within the realm without the king's special licence." 4 Calendar Of The Close Rolls, Edward I, 1296-1302, at 318 (Sept. 15, 1299, Canterbury) (H.C. Maxwell-Lyte ed., 1906). Five years later, in 1304, Edward I ordered the sheriff of Leicester to enforce his prohibition on "any knight, esquire or other person from... going armed in any way without the king's licence." 5 Calendar Of The Close Rolls, Edward I, 1302-1307, at 210 (June 10, 1304, Stirling) (H.C. Maxwell-Lyte ed., 1908).

In 1308, Edward II ordered the town of Dover to ensure that "no knight, esquire, or other shall ... go armed at Croydon or elsewhere before the king's coronation." 1 Calendar Of The Close Rolls, Edward II, 1307-1313, at 52 (Feb. 9, 1308, Dover) (H.C. Maxwell-Lyte ed., 1892). In 1310, he issued a similar order to the sheriff of York, demanding that the sheriff prohibit any "earl, baron, knight, or other" from going armed. *Id.* at 257 (Mar. 20, 1310, Berwick-on-Tweed). Two years later, in 1312, Edward II ordered the sheriffs in Warwick and Leicester to seize the weapons of any that "go armed" without special permission from the king. *Id.* at 553 (Oct. 12, 1312, Windsor). These early prohibitions, targeting particular towns and counties, and particular actors, foreshadowed a more general proclamation nearly two decades later, in which Edward II prohibited "throughout [the King's] realm" "any one going armed without [the King's] licence." 4 Calendar Of The Close Rolls, Edward II, 1323-1327, at 560 (Apr. 28, 1326, Kenilworth) (H.C. Maxwell-Lyte ed., 1892).

In 1328, under Edward III, Parliament enacted the Statute of Northampton, an expanded version of Edward II's earlier prohibition. The Statute provided that

> no Man great nor small, of what Condition soever he be, except the King's Servants in his presence, and his Ministers in executing of the King's Precepts, or of their Office, and such as be in their Company assisting them ... be so hardy to come before the King's Justices, or other of the King's Ministers doing their office, with force and arms, nor bring no force in affray of the peace, nor to go nor ride armed by night nor by day, in Fairs, Markets, nor in the presence of the Justices or other Ministers, nor in no part elsewhere, upon pain to forfeit their Armour to the King, and their Bodies to Prison at the King's pleasure.

The Statute of Northampton was widely enforced.

In 1388, for example, Richard II issued to the bailiffs of Scardburgh an

> [o]rder to arrest and imprison until further order for their deliverance all those who shall be found going armed within the town, leading an armed power, making unlawful assemblies, or doing aught else whereby the peace may be broken and the people put in fear ... as in the statute lately published at Northampton among other things it is contained that no man of whatsoever estate or condition shall be bold to appear armed before justices or king's ministers in performance of their office, lead an armed force in breach of the peace, ride or go armed by day or night in fairs and markets or elsewhere in presence of justices etc....

A half-century later, Henry VI issued a similar order, reminding his subjects of the

> statute published in the parliament holden at Norhampton [*sic*] in 2 Edward III, wherein it is contained that no man of whatsoever estate or condition shall go armed, lead an armed power in breach of the peace, or ride or pass armed by day or night in fairs, markets or elsewhere in the presence of the justices, the king's ministers or others under pain of losing his arms and of imprisonment at the king's will....

* * * * *

In 1694, Lord Coke described the Statute of Northampton as providing that a man may neither "goe nor ride armed by night nor by day ... in any place whatsoever." *The Third Part of the Institutes of the Laws of England* 160, ch. 73 (London, R. Brooke, 1797). Coke recounted the case of Sir Thomas Figett, who was arrested when he "went armed under his garments" before a justice of the King's bench. *Id.*at 161-62. William Hawkins wrote in 1716 that, under the Statute of Northampton, "a Man cannot excuse the wearing [of] such Armour in Publick, by alledging that such 932*932 a one threatened him, and that he wears it for the Safety of his Person from his Assault." 1 William Hawkins, *A Treatise Of The Pleas Of The Crown* 489, ch. 28, § 8 (London, J. Curwood, 8th ed. 1824). Blackstone, writing in the 1760s, compared the Statute of Northampton to "the laws of Solon, [under which] every Athenian was finable who walked about the city in armour." 5 William Blackstone, *Commentaries on the Laws of England,* edited by St. George Tucker, 149 § 9 (Phila. 1803).

James II, the last of the Stuart kings and England's last Catholic monarch, sought to disarm his Protestant subjects. James II was driven from the throne in 1688 in the Glorious Revolution. In 1689, under his Protestant successors, William of Orange (William III) and Mary II, Parliament enacted the English Bill of Rights, which, as the Court in *Heller* recognized, has "long been understood to be the predecessor to our Second Amendment." *Heller,* 554 U.S. at 593, 128 S.Ct. 2783. The Bill of Rights provided, with respect to the right to bear arms, "[t]hat the subjects which are Protestants may have arms for their defence suitable to their conditions and *as allowed by law.*" 1 W. & M., c. 2, § 7, in 3 Eng. Stat. at Large 441 (1689) (emphasis added).

To the degree that the English Bill of Rights is an interpretive guide to our Second Amendment, the critical question is the meaning of the phrase "as allowed by law." More narrowly, with respect to the case now before us, the specific question is whether the arms that are "allowed by law"—that is, the arms Protestants had the right to bear—included concealed firearms. The history just recounted demonstrates that carrying concealed firearms in public was not "allowed by law." Not only was it generally prohibited by the Statute of Northampton, but it was specifically forbidden by the statute enacted under Henry VIII, and by the later proclamations of Elizabeth I and James I.

The English writer, Granville Sharp, addressed this precise point in 1782. Sharp is a particularly important source, given that the Court in *Heller* cited his treatise as an authority supporting its understanding of the English Bill of Rights. *See Heller,* 554 U.S. at 594, 128 S.Ct. 2783. According to Sharp, the phrase "as allowed by law" referred to pre-existing restrictions, including the statute passed under Henry VIII prohibiting concealed arms. Sharp wrote:

> [The] latter expression, *"as allowed by law,"* respects the limitations in the above-mentioned

act of 33 Hen. VIII c. 6, which restrain the use of *some particular sort of arms,* meaning only such arms as were liable to be *concealed,* or otherwise favour the designs of murderers, as *"cross-bows, little short hand-guns, and little hagbuts,"* and all guns UNDER CERTAIN LENGTHS, specified in the act....

* * * * *

B. Second Amendment Right to Keep and Bear Concealed Arms

In analyzing the meaning of the Second Amendment, the Supreme Court in *Heller* and *McDonald* treated its historical analysis as determinative. The Court in *Heller* held that the Second Amendment, as originally adopted, "codified a pre-existing right," a "right inherited from our English ancestors." The Court in *McDonald* held, further, that this "pre-existing right" was incorporated into the Fourteenth Amendment, based in substantial part on the importance attached to the right by a "clear majority" of the states. In determining whether the Second Amendment protects the right to carry a concealed weapon in public, we engage in the same historical inquiry as *Heller* and *McDonald.* As will be seen, the history relevant to both the Second Amendment and its incorporation by the Fourteenth Amendment lead to the same conclusion: The right of a member of the general public to carry a concealed firearm in public is not, and never has been, protected by the Second Amendment.

* * * * *

b. Right to Bear Arms in Colonial America

We have found nothing in the historical record suggesting that the law in the American colonies with respect to concealed weapons differed significantly from the law in England. In 1686, the New Jersey legislature, concerned about the "great abuses" suffered by "several people in the Province" from persons carrying weapons in public, passed a statute providing that "no person or persons ... shall presume privately to wear any pocket pistol, skeins, stilladers, daggers or dirks, or other unusual or unlawful weapons within this Province." *An Act Against Wearing Swords, &c.,* N.J. Laws Chap. IX (1689). Other colonies adopted verbatim, or almost verbatim, English law. For example, in 1692, the colony and province of Massachusetts Bay authorized the Justice of the Peace to arrest those who "shall ride or go armed Offensively before any of Their Majesties Justices ... or elsewhere, by Night or by Day, in Fear or Affray of Their Majesties Liege People." *An Act for the Punishing of Criminal Offenders,* Mass. Laws Chap. XI § 6 (1692).

* * * * *

The historical materials bearing on the adoption of the Second and Fourteenth Amendments are remarkably consistent. Under English law, the carrying of concealed weapons was specifically prohibited since at least 1541. The acknowledged predecessor to the Second Amendment, the 1689 English Bill of Rights, protected the rights of Protestants to have arms, but only those arms that were "allowed by law." Concealed weapons were not "allowed by law," but were, instead, flatly prohibited. In the years after the adoption of the Second Amendment and before the adoption of the Fourteenth Amendment, the state courts that considered the question nearly universally concluded that laws forbidding concealed weapons were consistent with both the Second Amendment and their state constitutions. The only exception was Kentucky, whose court of appeals held to the contrary in a two-to-one decision based on its state constitution. Kentucky thereafter amended its constitution to overturn that result. In the decades immediately after the adoption of the Fourteenth Amendment, all of the state courts that addressed the question upheld the ability of their state legislatures to prohibit concealed weapons. Finally, the United States Supreme Court unambiguously stated in 1897 that the protection of the Second Amendment does not extend to "the carrying of concealed weapons."

We therefore conclude that the Second Amendment right to keep and bear arms does not include, in any degree, the right of a member of the general public to carry concealed firearms in public. In so holding, we join several of our sister circuits that have upheld the authority of states to prohibit entirely or to limit substantially the carrying of concealed or concealable firearms.

Our holding that the Second Amendment does not protect the right of a member of the general public to carry concealed firearms in public fully answers the question before us. Because the Second Amendment does not protect in any degree the right to carry concealed firearms in public, any prohibition or restriction a state may choose to impose on concealed carry—including a requirement of "good cause," however defined—is necessarily allowed by the Amendment. There may or may not be a Second Amendment right for a member of the general public to carry a firearm openly in public. The Supreme Court has not answered that question, and we do not answer it here.

* * * * *

Conclusion

We hold that the Second Amendment does not protect, in any degree, the carrying of concealed firearms by members of the general public. This holding resolves the Second Amendment question presented in this case. It also necessarily resolves, adversely to Plaintiffs, their derivative claims of prior restraint, equal protection, privileges and immunities, and due process. In light of our holding, we need not, and do not, answer the question of whether or to what degree the Second Amendment might or might not protect a right of a member of the general public to carry firearms openly in public.

We AFFIRM the judgments of the district courts in both cases.

* * * * *

CALLAHAN, Circuit Judge, dissenting, in which SILVERMAN, Circuit Judge, joins as to all parts except section IV, BEA, Circuit Judge, joins, and N.R. SMITH, Circuit Judge, joins as to all parts except section II.B:

* * * * *

Plaintiffs assert that the counties' concealed weapons licensing schemes, in the context of California's regulations on firearms, obliterate their right to bear arms for self-defense in public. The Supreme Court in *Heller* addressed concealed-carry restrictions and instructed that those restrictions be evaluated in context with open-carry laws to ensure that the government does not deprive citizens of a constitutional right by imposing incremental burdens. In the context of present-day California law, the Defendant counties' limited licensing of the right to carry concealed firearms is tantamount to a total ban on the right of an ordinary citizen to carry a firearm in public for self-defense. Thus, Plaintiffs' Second Amendment rights have been violated. While states may choose between different manners of bearing arms for self-defense, the right must be accommodated.

The majority sets up and knocks down an elaborate straw argument by answering only a narrow question—whether the Second Amendment protects a right to carry concealed firearms in public. But this approach is contrary to *Heller,* and contrary to the prescribed method for evaluating and protecting broad constitutional guarantees. Indeed, the majority's lengthy historical analysis fails to appreciate that many of its cited cases either presumed a right to openly carry a firearm in public or relied on a pre-*Heller* interpretation of the Second Amendment. Because the majority eviscerates the Second Amendment right of individuals to keep and bear arms as defined by *Heller* and reaffirmed in *McDonald,* I respectfully dissent.

I. The Individual Right to Bear Arms Extends Beyond the Home

A. *Under Heller and McDonald, the individual right to bear arms for self-defense extends beyond the home*

Our analysis begins with the text of the Second Amendment and the Supreme Court's opinions in *Heller* and *McDonald,* which instruct that the right to bear arms extends beyond the home.

The Second Amendment guarantees "the right of the people to keep and bear Arms." U.S. Const. amend. II. *Heller* held that the Second Amendment conferred an individual right to keep and bear arms for self-defense. Indeed, *Heller* adopted Justice Ginsburg's definition of "carries a firearm" to mean "wear, bear, or carry ... upon the person or in the clothing or in a pocket, for the purpose ... of being armed and ready for offensive or defensive action in a case of conflict with another person." *McDonald* affirmed that the constitutional right to keep and bear arms applies to the states.

Heller and *McDonald* also instruct that the right to bear arms exists outside the home. Under these cases, the Second Amendment secures "an individual right protecting against both public and private violence," indicating that the right extends in some form to locations where a person might become exposed to public or private violence. The Court reinforced this view by noting that the need for the right is "most acute" in the home, thus implying that the right exists outside the home. *Heller* also identifies "laws forbidding the carrying of firearms in sensitive places such as schools and government buildings" as presumptively lawful. Were the right to self-defense confined to the home, the validity of such laws would be self-evident.

The history of the Second Amendment also indicates that the right to bear arms applies outside the home. The common-law "right of having and using arms for self-preservation and defence," according to Blackstone, protected "the natural right of resistance and self-preservation." Blackstone's Commentaries also made clear that Congress would exceed its authority were it to "pass a law prohibiting any person from bearing arms." Furthermore, the majority of Nineteenth Century courts agreed that the Second Amendment right extended outside the home and included, at minimum, the right to carry an operable weapon in public for the purpose of lawful self-defense. Although some courts approved limitations on the manner of carry outside the home, none approved a total destruction of the right to carry in public.

Our sister circuits either have agreed that the Second Amendment right to bear arms extends outside the home or have assumed that the right exists. Notably, the majority does not refute this analysis, hedging that "[t]he Second Amendment may or may not protect, to some degree, a right of a member of the general public to carry firearms in public." Thus, pursuant to *Heller* and *McDonald*, an individual's right to self-defense extends outside the home and includes a right to bear arms in public in *some* manner.

* * * * *

B. *In the context of California's ban on open carry, the counties' ban on concealed carry for self-defense is unconstitutional*

In the context of California's choice to prohibit open carry, the counties' policies regarding the licensing of concealed carry are tantamount to complete bans on the Second Amendment right to bear arms outside the home for self-defense, and are therefore unconstitutional.

Heller defined the right to bear arms as the right to be "armed and ready for offensive or defensive action in a case of conflict with another person." Here, California has chosen to ban open carry but grants its citizens the ability to carry firearms in public through county-issued concealed weapons licenses. Thus, in California, the only way that the average law-abiding citizen can carry a firearm in public for the lawful, constitutionally protected purpose of self-defense is with a concealed-carry license. And in San Diego and Yolo Counties that option has been taken off the table. Both policies specify that concern for one's personal safety alone does not satisfy the "good cause" requirement for issuance of a license.

California's exceptions to the general prohibition against public carry do little to protect an individual's right to bear arms in public for self-defense. The exceptions for particular groups of law enforcement officers and military personnel do not protect the average citizen. Bearing arms on private property and at places of business does not allow citizens to protect themselves by bearing arms in public. And the exceptions for "making or attempting to make a lawful arrest" or for situations of "immediate, grave danger" offer no solace to an individual concerned about protecting self and family from unforeseen threats in public.

Here, as in *Heller*, the exceptions are limited and do not adequately allow the ordinary citizen to exercise his or her right to keep and bear arms for self-defense within the meaning of the Second Amendment, as defined by the Supreme Court. Thus, the counties' concealed-carry policies in the context of California's open-carry ban obliterate the Second Amendment's right to bear a firearm in some manner in public for self-defense.

* * * * *

C. *Given the right to bear arms for self-defense extends beyond the home, states must accommodate that right to self-defense*

As explained above, given the right to bear arms for self-defense exists outside the home, it follows then that states must accommodate that right. While *Heller* prohibits states from completely banning carrying a firearm in public for self-defense, it leaves states room to choose what manner of carry is allowed. States may choose how to accommodate the right by allowing only open carry, only concealed carry, or some combination of both. However, states may not disallow both manners of carry as the counties and California have done here.

The majority concedes that "[t]he Second Amendment may or may not protect to some degree a right of a member of the general public to carry a firearm in public." Maj. Op. 927. However, it claims that "[i]f there is such a right, it is only a right to carry a firearm openly." Maj. Op. 942. The majority's holding—that California *must* accommodate the right to bear arms in public through open carry—is unsupported by Supreme Court precedent and contrary to federalism principles. The Supreme Court has *never* dictated how states must accommodate a right to bear arms. The majority's cited cases, also cited in *Heller,* make this point clear. Thus, the majority errs by suggesting that states must accommodate the right to bear arms through open carry.

Moreover, the majority's requirement that states accommodate the right to bear arms through open carry is unwise. States may have good reasons for allowing concealed carry but banning open carry. Different states may have different opinions about whether concealed carry or open carry is preferable. The point is that, under *Heller,* states cannot prohibit both open and concealed carry, thus eviscerating the right to bear arms in public for self-defense.

IV. The Counties' Unfettered Discretion to Grant or Deny Concealed Weapons Licenses is Troubling

Finally, while the majority and I would decide this case on Second Amendment grounds, Plaintiffs have raised non-frivolous concerns as to whether the counties' discretion as to who obtains a license violates the Equal Protection Clause and constitutes an unlawful prior restraint. The issues are not ripe for review, but I note that a discretionary licensing scheme that grants concealed weapons permits to only privileged individuals would be troubling. Such discretionary schemes might lead to licenses for a privileged class including high-ranking government officials (like judges), business owners, and former military and police officers, and to the denial of licenses to the vast majority of citizens. ("After the Civil War, many of the over 180,000 African Americans who served in the Union Army returned to the States of the old Confederacy, where systematic efforts were made to disarm them and other blacks. The laws of some States formally prohibited African-Americans from possessing firearms.")

* * * * *

The Second Amendment is not a "second-class" Amendment.

Undoubtedly some think that the Second Amendment is outmoded in a society where our standing army is the pride of our Nation, where well-trained police forces provide personal security, and where gun violence is a serious problem. That is perhaps debatable, but what is not debatable is that it is not the role of th[e] [Supreme] Court to pronounce the Second Amendment extinct.

Today the majority takes a step toward extinguishing the Second Amendment right recognized by the Supreme Court in *Heller* and *McDonald.*

With no clear guidance from the Court regarding how to evaluate laws that restrict and obliterate the right to keep and bear arms for self-defense, the Second Amendment is becoming "[a] constitutional guarantee subject to future judges' assessments" which is "no constitutional guarantee at all."

Accordingly, I dissent.

Document Themes

Justice Fletcher begins by summarizing state law as it pertains to the concealed carrying of firearms. After reviewing the procedural history of the case, the court looks more closely at the "good cause" requirement for carrying a concealed weapon, citing specific examples of cases in which good cause can be demonstrated (e.g., the applicant has been the victim of a violent crime, or a businessperson has to carry large sums of cash). The court then turns to the Second Amendment arguments of the plaintiffs, concluding: "Based on the overwhelming consensus of historical sources, we conclude that the protection of the Second Amendment—whatever the scope of that protection may be—simply does not extend to the carrying of concealed firearms in public by members of the general public." Further: "We hold only that there is no Second Amendment right for members of the general public to carry concealed firearms in public."

In analyzing the issue, the court discusses the two twenty-first-century cases that had on strong bearing on the interpretation of Second Amendment rights, *District of Columbia v. Heller* (2008) and *McDonald v. Chicago* (2010), with emphasis on *Heller*. In *Heller*, the Court states that "the majority of the 19th-century courts to consider the question held that prohibitions on carrying concealed weapons were lawful under the Second Amendment or state analogues." With regard to *McDonald*, the court notes that that the case focused on the Fourteenth Amendment's incorporation of the Second Amendment, commenting that "the right of a member of the general public to carry a concealed firearm in public is not, and never has been, protected by the Second Amendment." After examining historical interpretations of the Second Amendment, the court states its conclusion: "We hold that the Second Amendment does not protect, in any degree, the carrying of concealed firearms by members of the general public."

In a lengthy dissent, Justice Consuelo Callahan writes that "the Defendant counties' limited licensing of the right to carry concealed firearms is tantamount to a total ban on the right of an ordinary citizen to carry a firearm in public for self-defense. Thus, Plaintiffs' Second Amendment rights have been violated." She argues that both *Heller* and *McDonald* extend the right of self-defense beyond the home, writing that "the history of the Second Amendment also indicates that the right to bear arms applies outside the home." She went on to argue that "in the context of California's choice to prohibit open carry, the counties' policies regarding the licensing of concealed carry are tantamount to complete bans on the Second Amendment right to bear arms outside the home for self-defense, and are therefore unconstitutional." She concludes by noting that giving counties an unfettered right to grant or deny concealed carry licenses is "troubling," arguing that "such discretionary schemes might lead to licenses for a privileged class including high-ranking government officials (like judges), business owners, and former military and police officers, and to the denial of licenses to the vast majority of citizens."

Additional Readings

"Interpreting *Peruta v. County of San Diego*," The Federalist Society website, June 14, 2016, https://fedsoc.org/commentary/blog-posts/interpreting-peruta-v-county-of-san-diego.

Kopel, David, "*Peruta v. San Diego*, Analyzed," *Wasington Post*, June 11, 2016, https://www.washingtonpost.com/news/volokh-conspiracy/wp/2016/06/11/peruta-v-san-diego-analyzed/?noredirect=on&utm_term=.d322f0079b80.

Moreland, Maxel, "Does the Second Amendment Protect Concealed Carry?," *University of Cincinnati Law Review* blog, November 8, 2016, https://uclawreview.org/2016/11/08/does-the-second-amendment-protect-concealed-carry/.

"*Peruta v. County of San Diego*," *Harvard Law Review* 130 (January 5, 2017), https://harvardlawreview.org/2017/01/peruta-v-county-of-san-diego/ (case note).

Sarosy, Charlie, "California's Unloaded Open Carry Bans:A Constitutional and Risky, but PerhapsNecessary, Gun Control Strategy," *UCLA Law Review* 61 (2014): 464–504, https://www.uclalawreview.org/pdf/61-2-4.pdf.

—Michael J. O'Neal

Young v. Hawaii

Author(s): Diarmuid Fionntain O'Scannlain (majority opinion)
Date: 2018
Genre: Ninth U.S. Circuit Court of Appeals

Summary Overview

Young v. Hawaii was a case decided by the Ninth U.S. Circuit Court of Appeals (the appellate court with jurisdiction over Alaska, Arizona, California, Hawaii, Idaho, Montana, Nevada, Oregon, and Washington). In its decision, the court reversed a lower court ruling that upheld the state of Hawaii's refusal to grant George Young a permit to openly carry a firearm. The court held that Hawaii violated Young's constitutional rights under the Second Amendment.

Defining Moment

The state of Hawaii has a "Places to Keep" statute, which requires gun owners to keep firearms at their place of business or in their home; essentially, the statute does not allow people to carry firearms in public, although licenses to carry a loaded handgun in public can be granted by the chief of police under certain circumstances. Section 134-9 of Hawaii Revised Statutes specifies these exceptions, which, at the state level, can be made when a person faces an urgent need to protect life or property; the County of Hawaii more narrowly makes an exception only for people who need to carry a firearm as part of their job, and then only when they are on duty.

George Young, a veteran infantry soldier and law enforcement officer, challenged the statute, arguing that he had a Second Amendment right to openly carry a firearm for purposes of self-defense. When he applied for a permit from the County of Hawaii's chief of police, he was denied for failure to satisfy the requirements of section 134-9 of the statutes. Young filed a lawsuit, but his claims were denied in district court. He then appealed to the Ninth Circuit Court of Appeals.

The case was argued before the court in February 2018 and decided on July 24, 2018. The court dismissed the lower court's ruling, holding that Hawaii had in fact violated Young's Second Amendment right to openly carry a firearm for self-defense. Court observers noted that the surprise ruling from the normally liberal California appeals court came one week after the court upheld a lower court's ruling that the state's ban on high-capacity magazines was unconstitutional.

About the Author

The majority opinion in *Young v. Hawaii* was written by Diarmuid Fionntain O'Scannlain, a senior U.S. circuit judge of the U.S. Court of Appeals for the Ninth Circuit. O'Scannlain was born on March 28, 1937, in New York City. In 1957 he received his bachelor's degree from St. John's University. He graduated from the Harvard Law School in 1963 and received a master of laws degree from the University of Virginia Law School in 1992. He began his career as a tax attorney for the Standard Oil Company of New Jersey, but he 1965 he entered private practice in Portland, Oregon. From 1969 to 1971 he was deputy state attorney general of the Oregon State Department of Justice, from 1971 to 1973 he was a public utility commissioner, and from 1973 to 1974 he was director of the Oregon Department of Environmental Quality. After an unsuccessful run for the U.S. House of Representatives, he returned to private practice in 1975.

O'Scannlain's judicial career began in 1986, when President Ronald Reagan appointed him to a seat on the Ninth Circuit Court of Appeals. He achieved senior status as a judge in 2016. He has been a strong proponent of the view that the Ninth Circuit should be split, given its immense geographical size. He wrote a dissent in *Peruta v. San Diego,* a case that had a bearing on *Young v. Hawaii.* In that dissent, he argued that California's concealed carry rules, as they were implemented by the County of San Diego, together with a ban on open carry in most areas of the state, violate the Second Amendment.

HISTORICAL DOCUMENT

O'SCANNLAIN, Circuit Judge.

We must decide whether the Second Amendment encompasses the right of a responsible law-abiding citizen to carry a firearm openly for self-defense outside of the home.

George Young wishes to carry a firearm publicly for personal self-defense in the State of Hawaii. He twice in 2011 applied for a license to carry a handgun, either concealed or openly. His application was denied each time by the County of Hawaii's Chief of Police, Harry Kubojiri, because Young failed to satisfy the requirements set forth in section 134-9 of the Hawaii Revised Statutes ("H.R.S.").

Section 134-9 acts as a limited exception to the State of Hawaii's "Place[s] to Keep" statutes, which generally require that gun owners keep their firearms at their "place of business, residence, or sojourn." The exception allows citizens to obtain a license to carry a loaded handgun in public, either concealed or openly, under certain circumstances. Respecting concealed carry, section 134-9 provides that "[i]n an exceptional case, when an applicant shows reason to fear injury to the applicant's person or property, the chief of police . . . may grant a license to an applicant . . . to carry a pistol or revolver and ammunition therefor concealed on the person." The chief of police may, under section 134-9, grant a license for the open carry of a loaded handgun only "[w]here the urgency or the need has been sufficiently indicated" and the applicant "is engaged in the protection of life and property." The County of Hawaii has promulgated regulations to clarify that open carry is proper only when the license-holder is "in the actual performance of his duties or within the area of his assignment." Police Dep't of Cty. of Haw., *Rules and Regulations Governing the Issuance of Licenses* 10 (Oct. 22, 1997).

Absent a license under section 134-9, a person may only transport an unloaded firearm, in an enclosed container, to and from a place of repair, a target range, a licensed dealer, a firearms exhibit, a hunting ground, or a police station, and may only use those firearms while "actually engaged" in hunting or target shooting.

On June 12, 2012, Young filed this suit *pro se* under 42 U.S.C. § 1983 against the State of Hawaii, its then-Governor, Neil Abercrombie, and its then-Attorney General, David Louie (collectively "the State"), as well as the County of Hawaii, its then-Mayor, William Kenoi, the Hilo County Police Department, and its then-Chief of Police, Harry Kubojiri (collectively "the County"). Primarily alleging that denying his application for a handgun license violates his Second Amendment right to carry a loaded firearm in public for self-defense, Young requested, among other things, injunctive and declaratory relief from the enforcement of section 134-9's licensing requirements.

The State filed a motion to dismiss Young's claims under Federal Rules of Civil Procedure 12(b)(1) and 12(b)(6), and the County filed a motion to dismiss the claims under Rule 12(b)(6). The district court granted both. As for the State of Hawaii, the district court found Young's action to be barred by sovereign immunity. Young's action against the State officials—while not barred by sovereign immunity under *Ex Parte Young*, 209 U.S. 123 (1908)—was dismissed because the district court found their general oversight of the enforcement of Hawaii's laws "insufficient to establish a nexus between [such] officials and the alleged violation of [Young's] civil rights."

Dismissing Young's action against the County on the merits, the district court found that section 134-9 "does not implicate activity protected by the Second Amendment," because that Amendment "establishes only a narrow individual right to keep an operable handgun at home for self-defense." In the alternative, the district court indicated that it would uphold section 134-9's open and concealed carry limitations under intermediate scrutiny. As the court reasoned, the State's "substantial interest in safeguarding the public from the inherent dangers of firearms" was reasonably furthered by policies that "enable[] officials to effectively differentiate between individuals who need to carry a gun for self-defense and those who do not."

Young timely appealed.

II

A

Young's argument is straightforward: he asserts that the County has violated the Second Amendment by enforcing against him the State's limitations in section 134-9 on the open carry of firearms to those "engaged in the protection of life and property" and on the concealed carry of firearms to those who can demonstrate an "exceptional case."

1

The County and the State respond that Young's claim is foreclosed by our en banc decision, which overturned a three-judge panel's decision striking down a concealed carry licensing regime, *see Peruta v. County of San Diego* (*Peruta I*).

In *Peruta II,* we considered a challenge to San Diego's limitations on the concealed carry of handguns outside of the home. California law generally prohibits carrying firearms in public, whether concealed or openly. But San Diego County leaves open the opportunity to carry a concealed firearm upon the demonstration of "good cause." Rejecting Peruta's challenge, our en banc court held that "the Second Amendment right to keep and bear arms does not include, *in any degree,* the right of a member of the general public to carry concealed firearms in public." But, as even the dissent acknowledges, our court explicitly left unresolved the question of whether the Second Amendment encompasses a right to open carry. Young's claim therefore picks up where Peruta's left off and presents an issue of first impression for this circuit: whether the Second Amendment encompasses a right to carry firearms openly in public for self-defense.

2

Our interpretation of the Second Amendment is guided by the Supreme Court's decisions in *District of Columbia v. Heller* and *McDonald v. City of Chicago.* In *Heller,* the Court invalidated a District of Columbia ban on handgun possession in the home, holding that the Second Amendment guarantees an individual right to keep a handgun in one's home for self-defense, and rejecting a collective view of the right. Because the District of Columbia law had completely banned "the quintessential self-defense weapon" within the home, the Court saw no need to clarify further the scope of the right or the level of scrutiny it demands. "Under any of the standards of scrutiny that [the Court has] applied to enumerated constitutional rights," such a severe deprivation must fail.

In *McDonald,* the Court incorporated the Second Amendment against the States through the Fourteenth Amendment, invalidating a Chicago law that effectively banned handgun possession by residents of the city. In determining whether the pre-existing right codified by the Second Amendment was "fundamental to *our* scheme of ordered liberty," the Court stressed the centrality of self-defense: "Self-defense is a basic right, recognized by many legal systems from ancient times to the present day. . . ." Consequently, the Court held it "clear that this right is 'deeply rooted in this Nation's history and tradition,'" thus binding the States alongside the federal government.

As was the case in *Peruta II,* we find ourselves navigating waters uncharted by *Heller* and *McDonald:* the degree to which the Second Amendment protects, or does not protect, the carrying of firearms outside of the home.

B

Our circuit, like others, employs a two-step approach to Second Amendment challenges. We first ask "whether the challenged law burdens conduct protected by the Second Amendment." If so, we must "apply an appropriate level of scrutiny." And because *Heller* makes clear that evaluating restrictions of Second Amendment rights under rational basis review is inappropriate, any means-end scrutiny applied must be some form of heightened scrutiny, such as intermediate or strict scrutiny. Of course, we remain ever mindful not to treat the Second Amendment any differently from other individual constitutional rights. It is not "a second-class right," nor a "constitutional orphan."

Heller and *McDonald* set the goalposts for our inquiry, which requires determining the scope of the Second Amendment with respect to public carry. We must discern the scope of the Amendment not as it appears to us now, but "with the scope [it was] understood to have when the people adopted [it]." Our lodestars are "text and history," because they bear most strongly on what the right was understood to mean, at the time of enactment, to the public. Because "words and phrases were used in their normal and ordinary as distinguished from technical meaning," our approach is not just a textual one, but also a contextual one. History and convention, therefore, illuminate our understanding of the text.

We are not the first circuit to grapple with how far, and to what extent, the Second Amendment applies outside the home. Two circuits, looking closely at the text and history of the Amendment, have held that the Second Amendment indeed protects a general right to carry firearms in public for self-defense. Three others have simply assumed the Second Amendment applies outside the home, without delving into the historical nature of the right.

III

A

We start, as we must, with the text. The Second Amendment provides: "A well regulated Militia, being necessary to the security of a free State, the right of the people to keep and bear Arms, shall not be infringed." It is apparent from the face of the text that the Amendment protects the right not only to "keep" but also to "bear" arms. The latter verb is central to Young's challenge.

Heller provides useful guidance. To "bear," the Court explained, means to "wear" or to "carry . . . upon the person or in the clothing or in a pocket, for the purpose . . . of being armed and ready for offensive or defense action in a case of conflict with another person." And *Heller* explained that "bear arms" did not solely refer to carrying a weapon as part of a militia. Rather, to "bear" an object means to carry it, and "[w]hen used with 'arms,' . . . the term has a meaning that refers to carrying for a particular purpose—confrontation."

The prospect of confrontation is, of course, not limited to one's dwelling. Thus, carrying firearms outside the home fits comfortably within *Heller*'s definition of "bear."

Indeed, the fact that the Second Amendment protects bearing *as well as* keeping arms implies some level of public carry in case of confrontation. A right to "keep" arms, on its own, necessarily implies a right to carry those arms to some extent. For instance, in order to "keep" arms, one would have to carry them home from the place of purchase and occasionally move them from storage place to storage place. The addition of a separate right to "bear" arms, beyond keeping them, should therefore protect something more than mere carrying incidental to keeping arms. Understanding "bear" to protect at least some level of carrying in anticipation of conflict outside of the home provides the necessary gap between "keep" and "bear" to avoid rendering the latter guarantee as mere surplusage.

Heller and *McDonald* suggest a similar understanding of "bear." *Heller* described the "inherent right of self-defense" as "most acute" within the home, implying that the right exists, perhaps less acutely, outside the home. *McDonald* similarly described the right as "most notabl[e]" within the home, implying the right exists, perhaps less notably, outside the home. *Heller* also identified "laws forbidding the carrying of firearms in sensitive places such as schools and government buildings" as presumptively lawful. Why bother clarifying the definition of sensitive public places if the Second Amendment did not apply, at all, to *any* public place?

In short, the text of the Amendment, as interpreted by *Heller* and *McDonald,* points toward the conclusion that "bear" implies a right to carry firearms publicly for self-defense.

B

We next consider the writings of "important founding era legal scholars" to discern the original public understanding of the Second Amendment right, because, as *Heller* explains, "[t]hat sort of inquiry is a critical tool of constitutional interpretation."

Several legal treatises that were in wide circulation throughout the founding era support our textual understanding of "bear arms." In an early American edition of Blackstone's *Commentaries on the Laws of England*—indeed, the "most important" edition, as *Heller* points out—St. George Tucker, a law professor at the College of William & Mary and former influential Antifederalist, insisted that the right to armed self-defense is the "first law of nature" and that "the right of the people to keep and bear arms" is the "true palladium of liberty." And in advocating for the prerogative of the Judiciary to strike down unconstitutional statutes, Tucker wrote: "If, for example, congress were to pass a law prohibiting any person from bearing arms, as a means of preventing insurrections, the judicial courts, . . . would be able to pronounce decidedly upon the constitutionality of these means." Indeed, as Tucker explained, "[i]n many parts of the United States, a man no more thinks, of going out of his house on any occasion, without his rifle or musket in his hand, than a European fine gentleman without his sword by his side."

Blackstone himself espoused a similarly sacred view on the right to bear arms for Englishmen, which was most notably codified in the 1689 English Declaration of Rights as the right of Protestants to "have Arms for their Defense suitable to their Conditions and as allowed by Law." As Blackstone explained, the 1689 Declaration enshrined "the natural right of resistance and self-preservation" and "the right of having and using arms for self-preservation and defence." It followed from Blackstone's premise that such a right, the predecessor to our Second Amendment, "was by the time of the founding understood to be an individual right protecting against both *public* and private violence."

* * * * *

Concluding our analysis of text and review of history, we remain unpersuaded by the County's and the State's argument that the Second Amendment only has force within the home. Once identified as an individual right focused on self-defense, the right to bear arms must guarantee *some* right to self-defense in public. While the concealed carry of firearms categorically falls outside such protection, we are satisfied that the Second Amendment encompasses a right to carry a firearm openly in public for self-defense. Because section 134-9 restricts Young in exercising such right to carry a firearm openly, it burdens conduct protected by the Second Amendment.

* * * * *

So, what constitutes the core of the Second Amendment? As we know, the Second Amendment protects the right "to keep and bear arms." The key inquiry is whether the core of the right encompasses *both* verbs, or only one: keeping *and bearing* arms for self-defense, or, more narrowly, only keeping arms for self-defense within the home.

Heller aids our inquiry but provides no definitive answer. On the one hand, in rejecting the collective view of the right, *Heller* made clear that "self-defense had little to do with the right's *codification;* it was the *central component* of the right itself." On the other hand, *Heller* noted that "whatever else [the Amendment] leaves to future evaluation, it surely elevates above all other interests the right of law-abiding, responsible citizens to use arms in defense of hearth and home." We recognize that several of our sister circuits have interpreted this language to limit the Amendment's core to the home. But we afford little weight to *Heller*'s emphasis on the application of the Second Amendment to the home specifically, for the challenge there exclusively concerned handgun possession in the home. And in any event, it may very well be the case that within the core of the Amendment, self-defense at home is "most acute."

But much of *Heller*'s reasoning implied a core purpose of self-defense *not* limited to the home. The Court cited "at least seven [state constitutional provisions that] unequivocally protected an individual citizen's right to self-defense," which is "strong evidence that that is how the founding generation conceived of the right." Also without any reference to the home, *Heller* noted that "[a] ntislavery advocates routinely invoked the right to bear arms for self-defense," including Joel Tiffany, who wrote "the right to keep and bear arms, also implies the right to use them if necessary in self defence; without this right to use the guaranty would have hardly been worth the paper it consumed." Charles Sumner's famous "Bleeding Kansas" speech, quoted at length in *Heller,* can hardly be read without sensing its vociferous declaration that the Second Amendment's core reaches self-defense on the American frontier: "Never was this efficient weapon [the rifle] more needed in just self-defense, than now in Kansas, and at least one article in our National Constitution must be blotted out, before the complete right to it can in any way be impeached."

Hence, we heed *Heller*'s—and *McDonald*'s—admonition that citizens be allowed to use firearms "for the core lawful purpose of self-defense." While the Amendment's guarantee of a right to "keep" arms effectuates the core purpose of self-defense within the home, the separate right to "bear" arms protects that core purpose outside the home. Indeed, *Heller* tied together the core rights of keeping and bearing firearms in precisely the same manner. When describing the "[f]ew laws in the history of our Nation [that] have *come close* to the severe restriction of the District's handgun ban [within the home]," *Heller* pointed to several state statutes that severely restricted the open carrying of firearms *outside the home*.

We are unpersuaded that historical regulation of public carry requires us to remove the right to bear arms from the Second Amendment's core protection. As the D.C. Circuit has explained, "[t]he rights to keep and to bear, to possess and to carry, are equally important inasmuch as regulations on each must leave alternative channels for both." Regulations on public carry tend to "leave alternative channels" for self-defense outside the home, because "[w]hen a state bans guns merely in particular places, such as public schools, a person can preserve an undiminished right of self-defense by not entering those places," The prevalence of modest regulations on bearing arms, such as a restriction on carrying firearms in a school-zone, does not itself indicate that *bearing* arms is any less protected than *keeping* arms, because the Second Amendment tolerates equally modest restrictions on keeping firearms, such as open surface restrictions in the home. Thus, historical restrictions on public carry "go to show the scope of the right, not its lack of fundamental character."

In sum, we reject a cramped reading of the Second Amendment that renders to "keep" and to "bear" unequal guarantees. *Heller* and *McDonald* describe the core purpose of the Second Amendment as self-defense, and "bear" effectuates such core purpose of self-defense in public. We are persuaded, therefore, that the right to carry a firearm openly for self-defense falls within the core of the Second Amendment.

* * * * *

We do not take lightly the problem of gun violence, which the State of Hawaii "has understandably sought to fight . . . with every legal tool at its disposal." We see nothing in our opinion that would prevent the State from *regulating* the right to bear arms, for the Second Amendment leaves the State "a variety of tools for combatting [the problem of gun violence], including some measures regulating handguns."

But, for better or for worse, the Second Amendment does protect a right to carry a firearm in public for self-defense. We would thus flout the Constitution if we were to hold that, "in regulating the manner of bearing arms, the authority of [the State] has no other limit than its own discretion." While many respectable scholars and activists might find virtue in a firearms-carry regime that restricts the right to a privileged few, "the enshrinement of constitutional rights necessarily takes certain policy choices off the table."

Young has indeed stated a claim that section 134-9's limitations on the issuance of open carry licenses violate the Second Amendment.

REVERSED as to the County, DISMISSED as to the State, and REMANDED for further proceedings consistent with this opinion.

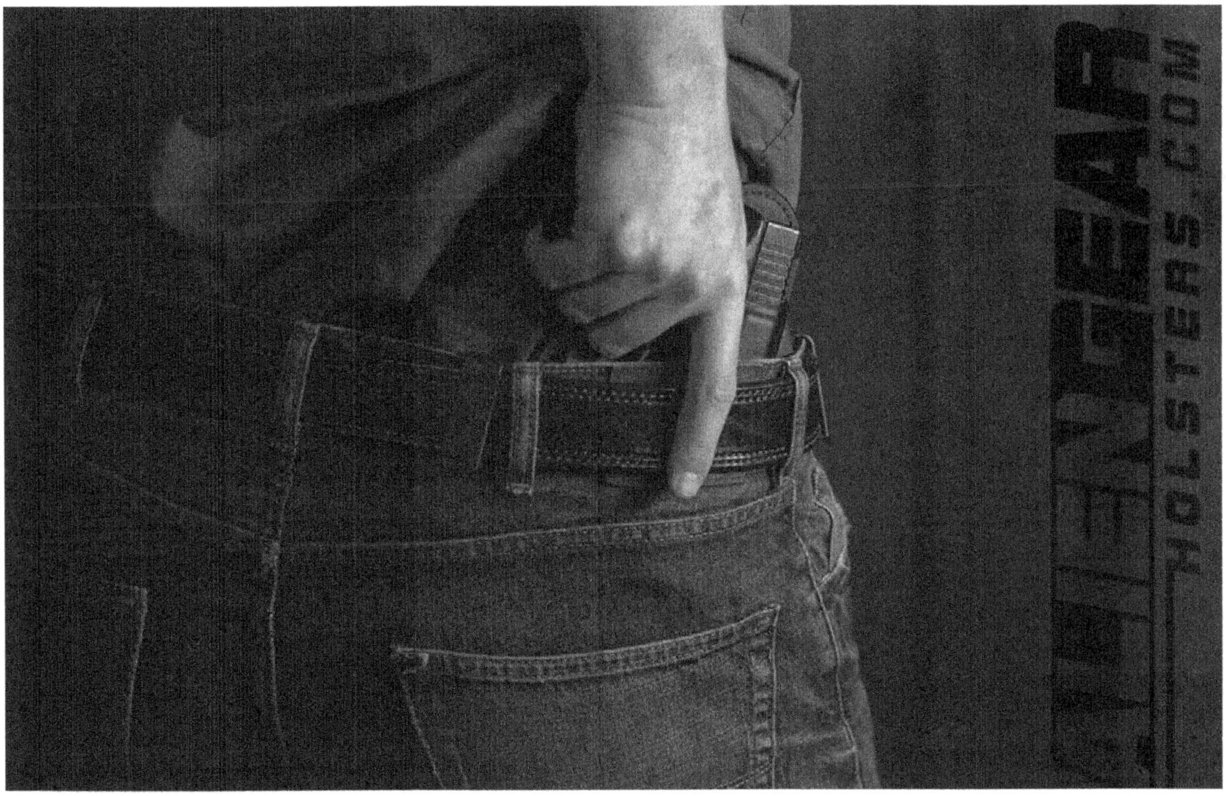

The debate about the open carrying of weapons was part of the Peruta *case. Shown here, a handgun holster for open carry. (By http://aliengearholsters.com.)*

Document Themes

Citing an earlier case, *Peruta v. County of San Diego* (2016), the court acknowledged that the carrying of concealed firearms is not protected by the Second Amendment. However, the court concluded that the Second Amendment does in fact protect the right to openly carry a firearm in public for purposes of self-defense. The court begins by analyzing the text of the Second Amendment and reviewing the relevant history of Second Amendment jurisprudence; in so doing, the court relied heavily on two earlier landmark cases, *District of Columbia v. Heller* and *McDonald v. City of Chicago*. To that end it examines writings from the founding era and nineteenth-century case law. The court was not persuaded by the argument of the county and the state that the Second Amendment applies only to weapons kept in the home. The court went on to reason that once the right to keep and bear arms was identified as an individual right of self-defense, then the same right to self-defense had to apply to in public, outside the home: "We are satisfied that the Second Amendment encompasses a right to carry a firearm openly in public for self-defense. Because section 134-9 restricts Young in exercising such right to carry a firearm openly, it burdens conduct protected by the Second Amendment."

The court then held that because the Hawaii law infringed on the plaintiff's right to carry a firearm openly, it "burdened" conduct protected by the Second Amendment. The court went on to note that any law that restricts open carry to a small subset of the population prevents the ordinary law-abiding citizen from exercising a core right to bear arms for self-defense. The court's conclusion was that to limit the open carry of firearms to those "engaged in the protection of life and property" violated the Second Amendment. Accordingly, the court concluded (quoting U.S. Supreme Court Justice Antonin Scalia in *District of Columbia v. Heller*:

> But, for better or for worse, the Second Amendment does protect a right to carry a firearm in public for self-defense. We would thus flout the Constitution if we were to hold that, "in regulating the manner of bearing arms, the authority of [the State] has no other limit than its own discretion." While many respectable scholars and activists might find virtue in a firearms-carry regime that restricts the right to a privileged few, "the enshrinement of constitutional rights necessarily takes certain policy choices off the table."

Additional Readings

Cooke, Charles C. W., "Gun Carry Laws Don't Invent a New Right," NRA-Institute for Legislative Action website, March 16, 2018, https://www.nraila.org/articles/20180316/gun-carry-laws-don-t-invent-a-new-right.

Frassetto, Mark Anthony, "The First Congressional Debate on Public Carry and What It Tells Us about Firearm Regionalism," *Campbell Law Review* 40 (2018), http://campbelllawreview.com/first-congressional-debate-public-carry-tells-us-firearm-regionalism/.

Meltzer, Jonathan, "Open Carry for All: *Heller* and Our Nineteenth-Century Second Amendment," *Yale Law Journal* 123, no. 5 (March 2014), https://www.yalelawjournal.org/note/open-carry-for-all-heller-and-our-nineteenth-century-second-amendment.

"Open Carry," Giffords Law Center, http://lawcenter.giffords.org/gun-laws/policy-areas/guns-in-public/open-carry/.

Valentine, Matt, "Tallying the Costs of Open Carry," *Atlantic*, January 31, 2016, https://www.theatlantic.com/politics/archive/2016/01/open-carry-laws/436665/.

—*Michael J. O'Neal*

Responses to the Debate

The pattern is a painfully familiar one. A gunman opens fire in a public place, killing many innocent victims. After this tragedy, support for gun control surges. With a closing window for reform, politicians and activists quickly push for new gun laws. But as time elapses, support decreases. Soon enough, the passions fade, and society returns to the status quo.
—Josh Blackman and Shelby Baird, "The Shooting Cycle"

While jurists, such as justices sitting on courts of appeals or of the U.S. Supreme Court, are tasked with the job of interpreting the law in the context of specific cases that come before them, academicians—many of them members of law school faculties, sociologists, and the like—examine the law, and the constitutional underpinnings of the law, from a more theoretical standpoint. Although the academic writer might hold a point of view with the regard to the issue at hand, he or she is at the same time obligated to engage in dispassionate analysis rather than advocacy—although many will engage in advocacy in the press if their research has led them to a firm conclusion about a matter of interest to them.

Presented here are excerpts from articles that appeared in various academic publications that have a bearing on the gun debate. Several are excerpts from law review articles. Josh Blackman and Shelby Baird, for example, wrote in the *Connecticut Law Review* about what they term "the shooting cycle," referring to the stages of public response to a mass shooting; they explore the concept of the shooting cycle in the context of the mass shooting at Sandy Hook Elementary School in Newtown, Massachusetts, in 2012. In the *Yale Law Journal*, Jonathan Meltzer—a prominent name in the gun debate—examines the Supreme Court's decision in *District of Columbia v. Heller* in the context of nineteenth century views regarding the Second Amendment. Meltzer's position is that

> The history relied upon by the Supreme Court, particularly in *Heller*, and the way the Court reads the historical sources, compel two important conclusions about the right to carry weapons. First, the logic, interpretive choices, and dicta of *Heller* suggest that the right to keep and bear arms must extend beyond the home. Second, the right to carry weapons that is guaranteed by the Second Amendment is the right to carry weapons openly.

The Giffords Law Center, too, published a response to the *Heller* case. The law center is named after Gabrielle "Gabby" Giffords, an Arizona congresswoman who survived a severe injury incurred during a mass shooting in a parking lot near Tucson. In the wake of this event, Giffords has become a prominent gun control advocate, and the piece on the law center's website outlines the organization's need for more stringent gun control measures. Robert J. Spitzer—another prominent name in the debate—examines gun law history and Second Amendment rights. Spitzer is also the author of an advocacy piece, "Arming Everyone Is Not the Answer," in which he refutes the view that society would be safer if *more* people carried guns that they could use to stop crimes. These writers represent but a small sampling of the academic writers who have weighed in on the gun debate, often with sharply different opinions about guns, gun control, and the reach of the Second Amendment.

> "To bring gun deaths down, you need to repeal the gun laws that have driven gun deaths up."
> —*Rich Weyland blog post, "An Honest Conversation about Guns"*

> "When adults tell me I have the right to own a gun, all I can hear is my right to own a gun outweighs your student's right to live."
> —*Emma Gonzalez, Florida high school student, speech at gun control rally*

Among members of the public, passions can run high when the issue of gun control arises, very often because of fundamentally different worldviews held by gun-control proponents and those who oppose them. Ann Christiano and Annie Neimand, in an article titled "Most Americans Believe We Should Have Gun Regulation," point to the divide:

> According to Pew Research Center, "50 percent say it is more important to control gun ownership, just slightly more than the 47 percent who say it is more important to protect the right of Americans to own guns." However, 92 percent of Americans agree that there should be background checks for gun buyers. These numbers reveal a country deeply conflicted about the role guns play in keeping us safe.

The authors go on to comment on the sociological divide:

> No one wants to see more lives lost, and both sides make a case for public safety. Yet the discussion in support of commonsense gun laws tends to be shrouded in numbers, infographics, case studies and stories of lives lost, while those opposed make their case with powerful messages about threats to personal safety and liberty—messages that tap into cultural significance they associate with guns, as well as how they see themselves and their world.

The entries in this section reflect this divide over the "cultural significance" associated with guns. Some observers take a position similar to that outlined in Rich Weyland's blog posting, "An Honest Conversation about Guns," arguing that the Second Amendment is inconsistent with *any* gun-control measures. Clayton Cramer explores what he calls "The Racist Roots of Gun Control," and, as one would predict, National Rifle Association chairman Wayne LaPierre vigorously defends guns and gun ownership and resists efforts to impose restrictions on them.

Yet the public reacts strongly in response to mass shootings, particularly those that takes place at schools. In the wake of a school shooting at Marjory Stoneman Douglas High School in Florida, Emma Gonzalez, a student at the school, spoke at a gun control rally in Fort Lauderdale, Florida. She galvanized the crowd with statements like "To every politician who is taking donations from the NRA, shame on you." The student newspaper at the school published a manifesto advocating gun control—to which Donald W. Bohlken responded in the *Des Moines Register* with an editorial titled "Parkland Students' Manifesto Supports Laws That Would Have No Effect on Gun Violence." Some participants in the debate would like to be able to carry weapons onto college campuses, usually identified as "gun-free zones," for self-protection; others respond that "Guns on Campus Make Colleges Less Safe."

> "The Congress hereby declares that the purpose of this title is to provide support to Federal, State, and local law enforcement officials in their fight against crime and violence, and it is not the purpose of this title to place any undue or unnecessary Federal restrictions or burdens on law-abiding citizens with respect to the acquisition, possession, or use of firearms appropriate to the purpose of hunting, trapshooting, target shooting, personal protection, or any other lawful activity."
> —*Gun Control Act of 1968*

The federal government has had difficulty enacting any sort of comprehensive gun control measures in large part because of the sharp divisions that exist between gun control advocates and those who resist gun control measures. This division is as much a cultural one as it is a legal one. It is not too much of an overgeneralization to say that the citizenry in large, densely populated urban areas, compared to people in rural areas, are statistically more likely to favor stiff gun control measures, for the people in these areas are likely to see firsthand the consequences of gun violence. In contrast, people who live in more sparsely populated rural areas, where hunting, target shooting, and other sports involving guns are prevalent, are most like to resist gun control measures.

Despite the political and cultural obstacles the federal government faces in its gun control efforts, significant bills have been passed, starting with the National Firearms Act of 1934, which still makes it illegal to buy and sell fully automatic weapons—that is, machine guns. The Gun Control Act of 1968, passed in the wake of such high-profile gun crimes as the assassination of President John F. Kennedy with a mail-order rifle, regulates the interstate transfer of firearms. The Brady Handgun Violence Protection Act, commonly referred to as the Brady bill or the Brady law, was passed when press secretary James Brady was permanently injured during an assassination attempt on President Ronald Reagan in 1981. The act's formal long title makes its purpose clear: "An Act to provide for a waiting period before the purchase of a handgun, and for the establishment of a national instant criminal background check system to be contacted by firearms dealers before the transfer of any firearm."

The government has responded to gun violence in other ways—by, for example, by efforts on the part of the Centers for Disease Control to collect data on the effects of gun violence, although these efforts were impeded by the "Dickey Amendment," a provision in federal law that stated: "None of the funds made available for injury prevention and control at the Centers for Disease Control and Prevention maybe used to advocate or promote gun control." Another obstacle has been the so-called Tiahrt Amendments, which restrict the ability of law enforcement to investigate gun crimes and to prosecute unscrupulous gun dealers. State governments, however, including that of Florida, have passed "Stand Your Ground" laws that allow a person to respond with force without having a duty to retreat from threats of violence. A more recent issue with which the government is likely to have to contend is that of 3-D printing of plastic guns.

> "Two United States Senators... worked together in good faith, consulting with folks like our Vice President, who has been a champion on this for a long time, to write a common-sense compromise bill that would have required virtually everyone who buys a gun to get a background check. . . . Ninety percent of Americans supported that idea. Ninety percent of Democrats in the Senate voted for that idea. But it failed because 90 percent of Republicans in the Senate voted against that idea. How did this become such a partisan issue?
>
> *—President Barack Obama, press conference, January 5, 2016*

To say that the gun debate in the United States has become politicized would be a gross understatement, for perhaps no issue in American political discourse (other than abortion) is as polarizing as gun control. Although gun violence has been a feature of American life since the nineteenth century, if not before, in the twenty-first century, the issue seems to have taken on new urgency in light of the large and growing number of mass shootings. While there is no widely accepted definition of a "mass shooting," one commonly used measure is that at least four victims are killed or wounded. By this measure, according to the Mass Shooter Tracker website, between 2013 and August 2018, there were 2,230 mass shootings in the United States. Most of these shootings barely made it onto the national news, largely because they were the result of quarrels, domestic disputes, and the like, but those that did, usually because of the sheer carnage involved, were part of the news cycle for days and weeks that followed. Given this intense scrutiny, the topic of guns and gun control was widely discussed in homes, in classrooms, at workplaces, on talk radio, and in newsrooms.

Political positions with regard to the gun debate are likely to be entrenched, in large part because guns and one's attitudes about guns have become defining elements in American culture. For example, according to a 2017 Pew Research Center survey: "Gun ownership spans all types of American communities, but it is particularly common in rural parts of the country. Among adults who live in rural areas, 46% say they own a gun, compared with 28% of adults who live in the suburbs and even fewer—19%—in urban areas." The same survey concluded: "More than eight-in-ten rural gun owners (82%) say the right to own guns is essential to their personal sense of freedom, compared with 59% of gun owners in urban areas." Further, political party can be a predictor of one's attitude toward gun control. Pew Research has determined that 61 percent of gun owners are Republicans and 44 percent of Republicans and independents who lean toward the Republican Party own guns, compared to just 20 percent of Democrats and those leaning toward the Democratic Party. Pew Research concluded: "Republicans and Republican-leaning independents are about twice as likely as Democrats and Democratic leaners to say owning a gun is essential to their freedom (91% vs. 43%)."

The entries in this section provide insight into the politics of the gun debate. President Barack Obama's position in favor of gun control was made clear in a 2017 press conference. Ted Cruz, on the other hand, a Republican, puts up resistance to gun control measures in the wake of the Santa Fe, Texas, school shooting in 2018. Inevitably, when a nominee for a seat on the Supreme Court is put forward, his or her position on the Second Amendment will be examined; one writer here examines Supreme Court nominee Brett Kavanaugh's position on the Second Amendment. Another writer examines the "changing politics" of the gun debate, as red-state Republicans are expressing support for gun control measures while Democratic lawmakers, particularly those in red or purple states, are hinting at opposition to these measures.

> "The challenge in bringing change is that the debate over gun rights isn't really about guns at all. It's about what they represent: cherished freedoms, a reverence for independence. The guns are a rejection of political correctness that creeps into everything."
>
> —*Philip Elliott, Haley Sweetland Edwards, and Charlotte Alter, "The Fight over Gun Control Isn't Really about Guns,"* Time

If journalism is the "first draft" of history, then the first draft of the history of twenty-first-century gun-control efforts in the United States has been repeatedly written in the nation's press, usually in the wake of mass shootings at schools, churches, and such venues as the Las Vegas strip. Writers for the nation's periodical publications, including such venerable magazines as *Time* and the *New Yorker*, respected newspapers such as the *New York Times* and the *Boston Globe*, and publications that lean in one direction or the other politically, such as *Salon* and the *National Review*, weigh in regularly with opinion pieces about the issue. The selections included in this section provide a glimpse into the nature of the analysis and arguments offered by journalists—or those who write for the press—in the debate over guns and gun control.

In a lengthy article in the *New Yorker*, Jill Lepore, a staff writer for the magazine but also a history professor, provides an overview of the passage of the Second Amendment, but she does so in the context of bloody mass shootings, which she dramatically particularizes. In the *Boston Globe*, David Scharfenberg examines the potential effectiveness of gun-control measures, situating them in the context of Australia's gun buyback program enacted in the wake of a mass shooting in that nation in 1996. Writing for the *New York Times*, Nicholas Kristoff provides extensive data on guns, gun laws, suicide rates, and other matters relating to guns and gun violence.

Many gun owners who are suspicious of gun-control efforts feel that the terms of the debate are stacked against them in the press—that much of the mainstream media supports gun control, finds the very existence of the National Rifle Association grotesque, and perhaps even regards many gun owners as "gun nuts." Whether these assumptions are warranted or not, it is true that more conservative elements in the press tend to question the legality and efficacy of many of the gun-control proposals that have been made. Writing for the *National Review*, for example, Stephen P. Halbrook examines a proposal made by retired Supreme Court justice John Paul Stevens to repeal the Second Amendment. In Halbrook's opinion, the proposal is a "pipe dream." Charles W. Cooke, also writing for the *National Review*, launches a broadside against a piece that had appeared in *Salon* magazine that, in his view, entirely misrepresented the position of the nation's founders on the issue of the right to bear arms. The *National Review*'s David French asserts that "no proposed new gun-control law would have prevented the purchase" of the guns recent mass shooters have used. He argues that the only way to stop these shooters is for communities to intervene: "We can't deflect responsibility upwards, to Washington. We're still the first line of defense in our own communities." Writing for the *Christian Science Monitor*, Patrik Jonsson examines the argument for and against concealed carry laws, pointing out that "however persuasive the recent instances of gun violence have been for gun-control proponents, they haven't changed dramatic trend lines in attitudes and gun ownership in America."

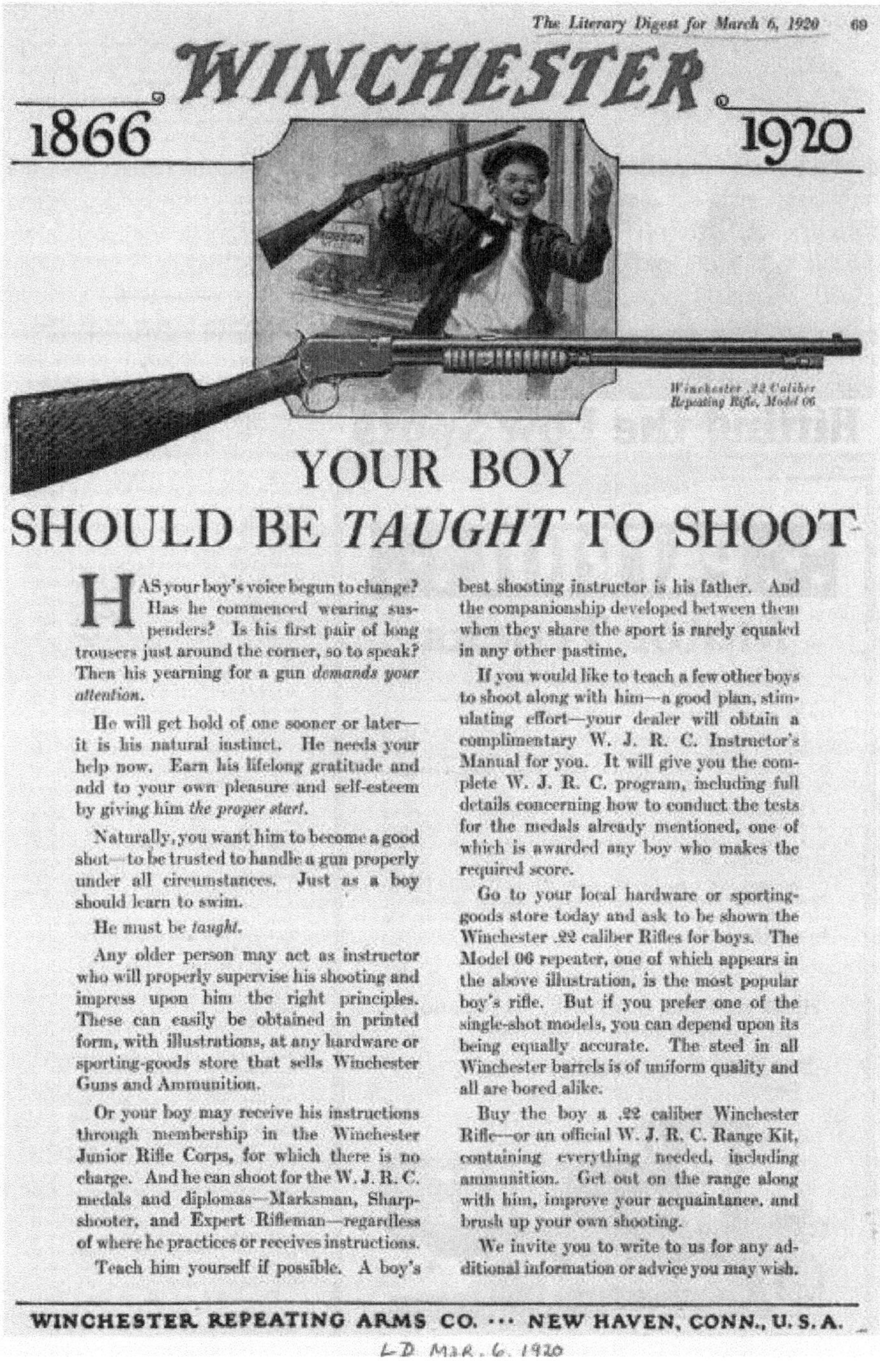

The Literary Digest for March 6, 1920 69

WINCHESTER

1866 1920

Winchester .22 Caliber Repeating Rifle, Model 06

YOUR BOY SHOULD BE *TAUGHT* TO SHOOT

HAS your boy's voice begun to change? Has he commenced wearing suspenders? Is his first pair of long trousers just around the corner, so to speak? Then his yearning for a gun *demands your attention.*

He will get hold of one sooner or later—it is his natural instinct. He needs your help now. Earn his lifelong gratitude and add to your own pleasure and self-esteem by giving him *the proper start.*

Naturally, you want him to become a good shot—to be trusted to handle a gun properly under all circumstances. Just as a boy should learn to swim.

He must be *taught.*

Any older person may act as instructor who will properly supervise his shooting and impress upon him the right principles. These can easily be obtained in printed form, with illustrations, at any hardware or sporting-goods store that sells Winchester Guns and Ammunition.

Or your boy may receive his instructions through membership in the Winchester Junior Rifle Corps, for which there is no charge. And he can shoot for the W. J. R. C. medals and diplomas—Marksman, Sharpshooter, and Expert Rifleman—regardless of where he practices or receives instructions.

Teach him yourself if possible. A boy's best shooting instructor is his father. And the companionship developed between them when they share the sport is rarely equaled in any other pastime.

If you would like to teach a few other boys to shoot along with him—a good plan, stimulating effort—your dealer will obtain a complimentary W. J. R. C. Instructor's Manual for you. It will give you the complete W. J. R. C. program, including full details concerning how to conduct the tests for the medals already mentioned, one of which is awarded any boy who makes the required score.

Go to your local hardware or sporting-goods store today and ask to be shown the Winchester .22 caliber Rifles for boys. The Model 06 repeater, one of which appears in the above illustration, is the most popular boy's rifle. But if you prefer one of the single-shot models, you can depend upon its being equally accurate. The steel in all Winchester barrels is of uniform quality and all are bored alike.

Buy the boy a .22 caliber Winchester Rifle—or an official W. J. R. C. Range Kit, containing everything needed, including ammunition. Get out on the range along with him, improve your acquaintance, and brush up your own shooting.

We invite you to write to us for any additional information or advice you may wish.

WINCHESTER REPEATING ARMS CO. ··· NEW HAVEN, CONN., U. S. A.

LD MAR. 6. 1920

Your boy should be taught to shoot. Printed on image: "Winchester .22 caliber repeating rifle, model 06".

SUPPLEMENTAL HISTORICAL DOCUMENT

Kavanaugh and the Second Amendment

Since Justice Anthony Kennedy announced his plans to retire, analysis of the potential effects of his retirement has mostly focused on areas of the law in which he provided the swing vote for a more liberal result—for example, abortion or gay rights. On those issues, Kennedy's replacement with a more conservative justice could shift the law to the right. But Kennedy sided with his more conservative colleagues in finding a Second Amendment right to have a handgun in the home, and there is no reason to believe that Judge Brett Kavanaugh, if confirmed, is likely to disagree. A more significant question is whether a Supreme Court that included Kavanaugh might take a more expansive view of the Second Amendment and strike down some existing gun laws. Kavanaugh's track record suggests that he might be willing to do so for at least some gun laws, although he does not regard the Second Amendment as creating an absolute right to have or carry a gun. It's not clear, though, what effect Kavanaugh's views would have on the court: The answer may hinge on the votes of his colleagues, and in particular Chief Justice John Roberts and Justice Samuel Alito.

The Second Amendment to the Constitution provides that "the right of the people to keep and bear Arms, shall not be infringed." In 2008, in *District of Columbia v. Heller*, a divided Supreme Court struck down a D.C. law that generally banned the possession of handguns in the home, ruling that the law violated the Second Amendment. Two years later, in *McDonald v. City of Chicago*, the court (again, divided) invalidated a Chicago law similar to Washington's, making clear that the Second Amendment also applies to the states. Since then, the justices have been asked several times to overturn lower-court decisions upholding state gun laws that challengers say violate the Second Amendment, but they have repeatedly declined to step in.

One such occasion came a little over a year ago, when the justices refused to weigh in on a California law that, as a general rule, bars people from carrying guns in public. Justice Clarence Thomas dissented from the denial of review, in an opinion joined by Justice Neil Gorsuch. Thomas lamented the Supreme Court's failure to take up the case, calling the lower court's ruling "indefensible." "The most natural reading," Thomas wrote, of the definition of the right to "bear Arms" should include the right to carry a gun in public. "I find it extremely improbable," Thomas continued, that "the Framers understood the Second Amendment to protect little more than carrying a gun from the bedroom to the kitchen." "Even if other Members of the Court do not agree that the Second Amendment likely protects a right to public carry," Thomas concluded, "the time has come for the Court to answer this important question definitively."

Even more recently, Thomas dissented from the court's announcement that it would not review a challenge to California's 10-day waiting period for gun purchases. The U.S. Court of Appeals for the 9th Circuit rejected a challenge by two California men, who had argued that the waiting period was unconstitutional for, at the very least, state residents who already own a gun or have a license to carry a concealed weapon. When the Supreme Court rejected the men's petition in February 2018, Thomas was sharply critical of both the 9th Circuit's ruling and the Supreme Court's disposition of the case. He argued that the lower courts had generally failed to give the Second Amendment "the respect due an enumerated constitutional right." "If a lower court had treated another right so cavalierly," Thomas continued, "I have little doubt that this Court would intervene. But as evidenced by our continued inaction in this area, the Second Amendment is a disfavored right in this Court," and the justices' "continued refusal to hear Second Amendment cases only enables" the double standard that the lower courts apply to gun-rights cases.

In the wake of the Supreme Court's decision in *Heller*, the District of Columbia went back to the drawing board and passed a law that required gun owners to register their firearms; the law also prohibited both semi-automatic rifles and the possession of magazines with more than 10 rounds of ammunition. A challenge to the law made its way to the U.S. Court of Appeals for the District of Columbia Circuit, where a three-judge panel upheld the ban and most of the registration requirements. Kavanaugh dissented from that ruling; he would have struck down both the ban on semi-automatic rifles and the registration requirements. (He indicated that he would have sent the ban on large-capacity magazines back to the lower court for more fact-finding.)

Kavanaugh reasoned that handguns, which are mostly semi-automatic, are protected by the Second Amendment, and he saw no real difference, from a constitutional perspective, between handguns and semi-automatic rifles. Semi-automatic rifles, he observed, "have not traditionally been banned" and "remain in common use today"; indeed, he noted, handguns are more often used in violent crimes than semi-automatic rifles. The registration requirements, he continued, are unconstitutional because gun owners have traditionally not been required to register all guns that they own legally—"as distinct," Kavanaugh pointed out, "from licensing of gun owners or mandatory recordkeeping by gun sellers."

Although Kavanaugh indicated that he would have struck down the ban on semi-automatic rifles and the registration requirements, his discussion of the proper test to use to review gun laws suggests that he might be willing to uphold some gun laws, such as those requiring a license to carry a concealed weapon, as long as they are consistent with the history and tradition of regulating guns. He contended that a test that assesses "gun bans and regulations based on text, history, and tradition" will often give governments "more flexibility and power" than a balancing test, because "history and tradition show that a variety of gun regulations have co-existed with the Second Amendment right."

Whatever Kavanaugh's position is likely to be on different efforts to regulate guns, he would, if confirmed, be only one of nine justices on the court. We know from his recorded dissents from the denial of review that Thomas would vote to review and overturn some existing gun laws, and we know that Gorsuch—at least to some extent—agrees with him. But it takes four votes to grant review in a case, and we do not know whether Roberts and Alito also agree with Thomas but have opted not to say so publicly, or whether they instead are content to leave the court's gun-rights jurisprudence as it is. We could know more about the future of gun rights relatively soon, as various challenges to gun laws make their way toward the Supreme Court. Indeed, just this week, the 9th Circuit struck downHawaii's ban on carrying weapons openly outside of the home; even if the case goes to the full 9th Circuit, the losing party is almost certain to ask the Supreme Court to weigh in.

This post was originally published at Howe on the Court.

Posted in Nomination of Brett Kavanaugh to the Supreme Court, Judge Kavanaugh's jurisprudence, Featured

Amy Howe, *Kavanaugh and the Second Amendment*, SCOTUSblog (Jul. 27, 2018, 10:51 AM), https://www.scotusblog.com/2018/07/judge-kavanaugh-and-the-second-amendment/

SUPPLEMENTAL HISTORICAL DOCUMENT

"Dickey Amendment"

PUBLIC LAW 104–208—SEPT. 30, 1996
https://www.gpo.gov/fdsys/pkg/PLAW-104publ208/pdf/PLAW-104publ208.pdf

CENTERS FOR DISEASE CONTROL AND PREVENTION DISEASE CONTROL, RESEARCH, AND TRAINING

To carry out titles II, III, VII, XI, XV, XVII, and XIX of the Public Health Service Act, sections 101, 102, 103, 201, 202, 203, 301, and 501 of the Federal Mine Safety and Health Act of 1977, and sections 20, 21 and 22 of the Occupational Safety and Health Act of 1970, title IV of the Immigration and Nationality Act and section 501 of the Refugee Education Assistance Act of 1980; including insurance of official motor vehicles in foreign countries; and hire, maintenance, and operation of aircraft, $2,262,698,000, of which $30,553,000 shall remain available until expended for equipment and construction and renovation of facilities, and of which $32,000,000 shall remain available until September 30, 1998 for mine safety and health activities, and in addition, such sums as may be derived from authorized user fees, which shall be credited to this account: Provided, That in addition to amounts provided herein, up to $48,400,000 shall be available from amounts available under section 241 of the Public Health Service Act, to carry out the National Center for Health Statistics surveys: *Provided further*, That none of the funds made available for injury prevention and control at the Centers for Disease Control and Prevention may be used to advocate or promote gun control.

National Firearms Act of 1934

Author(s): Robert Lee Doughton (sponsor)
Date: 1934
Genre: Legislative act

Summary Overview

The National Firearms Act of 1934 (NFA) was the first modern national gun control law. It was enacted in part to help curb a rising tide of racketeering and gang activity during the Roaring Twenties and beyond; accordingly, it banned weapons that were associated with gangsters, including sawed-off shotguns, machine guns ("Tommy" guns), and silencers. It required that any new gun bear a unique identifying serial number. Further, the law was actually part of the Internal Revenue Code, enabling the federal government to use its taxing powers to control these weapons. Currently, the law is administered by the Bureau of Alcohol, Tobacco, Firearms, and Explosives (ATFE).

Defining Moment

Prior to the major push for gun control legislation in the 1930s that ultimately resulted in passage of the National Firearms Act of 1934 and the Federal Firearms Act in 1938, the Mailing of Firearms Act of 1927 (MFA), also known as the Miller Act, was one of the few successes for gun control advocates. The law, which is still in effect today, prohibits sending through the U.S. Post Office pistols and other firearms that could be concealed on the person.

Consideration of the MFA followed soon after the introduction of another gun control bill supported by Senator John K. Shields, Democrat of Tennessee. The Shields bill would have prohibited the interstate shipment of all handguns except service revolvers, the so-called "big pistols" that Shields considered appropriate for home protection. The bill received legislative consideration in 1921, but extensive opposition developed. Because firearms manufacturing companies were highly concentrated geographically, the bill would have had a significant effect on the industry. Representatives of gun interests argued that the bill's restrictions might jeopardize national defense. Senator Frank Brandegee, Republican from Connecticut, a major gun manufacturing state, strongly opposed the bill and kept it from ever leaving the Judiciary Committee. When Shields lost his reelection bid in 1924, the bill died.

Republican Representative John F. Miller experienced greater success in gaining passage of a gun control bill. Miller's constituents in Seattle, Washington, concerned with the mail-order sales of handguns, pressed him to introduce legislation to prohibit mail shipments of handguns. Unlike the Shields bill, Miller's proposal received wide support. An organized letter writing campaign informed Republican President Calvin Coolidge that the availability of pistols through the mail was tempting young people into criminal activity. A resolution from the United National Association of Post Office Clerks supported the legislation. The opposition of gun advocates could not overcome the strong support for the bill. No representatives from small arms manufacturers appeared at the hearings. One witness, a spokesman for the American Reclamation Society of Detroit, presented an argument that would be heard many times in the coming decades: The small number of firearms in Great Britain was responsible for that nation's low crime rate and therefore more stringent gun control legislation was also needed in the United States.

In the debate on the House floor, congressmen from the gun manufacturing states of Massachusetts and Connecticut offered no opposition to the bill. What opposition developed came from congressmen from southern and western states, who objected to the bill because they believed it violated the Second Amendment right to keep and bear arms. At a time when states rights predominated, they argued that the legislation would result in the proliferation of federal officials intent on violating state sovereignty. Congressman Thomas Blanton, Democrat of Texas, offered an anti-gun control argument that continues to be used: Despite the legislation, criminals would acquire guns, while law abiding citizens would have their constitutional rights violated.

Once the bill was approved by both houses, President Coolidge signed it into law in February 1927. His support of the legislation notwithstanding, Coolidge remained skeptical regarding the prospects for success of gun control legislation, especially in view of the miserable experience with federal enforcement of Prohibition. As the Saturday Evening Post observed, "If the Federal government cannot prevent the landing and distribution of shiploads of rum, how can it stop the criminal from getting the most concealed and vital tool of his trade?" The MFA effectively stopped mail shipments of handguns, but the measure had limited scope. In the meantime, firearms manufacturers were successful in opposing other legislation, and were also able to gain protection from foreign competition when Congress passed the Fordney-McCumber Tariff of 1922 and the Hawley-Smoot Tariff of 1930. The legislative battles of the 1920s established the pattern for future political struggles over gun control proposals.

The post–World War I period witnessed the spread of criminal enterprises. In 1919, the states ratified the Eighteenth Amendment to the Constitution, prohibiting the manufacture, sale, and transportation of liquor. Additionally, Congress passed the National Prohibition Enforcement Act, also called the Volstead Act, on October 28, 1919. One of the unintended consequences of Prohibition, which remained in effect until the amendment was repealed in 1933, was to create an immense black market for liquor, a black market that gangsters and crime families were more than happy to serve—while at the same time peddling drugs and prostitutes. As these enterprises competed for "market share" and tried to protect their turf in the nation's cities, they engaged in a number of highly publicized armed confrontations, often making use of "gangster" weapons such as sawed-off shotguns and machine guns. One of these most widely publicized gangland shootings, the St. Valentine's Day Massacre, took place on February 14, 1929, on Chicago's North Side, when five members of George "Bugs" Moran's gang and others were gunned down. The killing of gangster John Dillinger by federal agents on July 22, 1934, helped galvanize public support for the bill.

In response to the violence, Congress passed the National Firearms Act in 1934. One of the motivations behind the act was to enhance public welfare by curtailing the manufacture and sale of gangster-type weapons. Another, however, was to raise revenue, for the act levied stiff excise taxes both on the manufacture and transfer of NFA firearms. The act required anyone who transferred (i.e., sold, but also loaned or gave away) or owned NFA firearms to register them with the secretary of the treasury. Law enforcement found this requirement to be helpful in identifying and prosecuting criminals. It was noteworthy that no sawed-off shotguns or machine guns were sold in the United States in 1934 after the act was passed.

In 1939, the U.S. Supreme Court, in *United States v. Miller*, upheld the constitutionality of the National Firearms Act, the first time the High Court upheld the government's right to impose restrictions on the scope and meaning of the Second Amendment's right to bear arms.

About the Author

The NFA was sponsored in Congress by Representative Robert Lee Doughton, a Democrat from North Carolina and chairman of the House Ways and Means Committee. Doughton sponsored the bill as a replacement for a far more severe one that had been introduced by Representative Hatton William Sumners—a bill that would have applied to pistols and revolvers. In a brief speech to the House, Doughton stated:

> For some time this country has been at the mercy of the gangsters, racketeers, and professional criminals. The rapidity with which they can go across State lines has become a real menace to the law-abiding people of this country. When the bill was first proposed by the Department of Justice it affected pistols and revolvers, but that provision was eliminated from the bill, and it now only relates to machine guns and sawed-off shotguns and rifles, or guns with barrels less than 18 inches in length, and to mufflers, and to silencers (*Congressional Record*, 73rd Congress, June 13, 1934, 11400).

Doughton, affectionately known as "Farmer Bob," was born in Laurel Springs, North Carolina, on November 7, 1863. In 1911, he began forty-two years of service in the House of Representatives. Among his major legislative accomplishments was the Social Security Act of 1935. He died in his sleep on October 1, 1954.

HISTORICAL DOCUMENT

An Act:

To provide for the taxation of manufacturers, importers, and dealers in certain firearms and machine guns, to tax the sale or other disposal of such weapons, and to restrict importation and regulate interstate transportation thereof.

Be it enacted by the Senate and House of Representatives of the United States of America in Congress assembled,

That for the purposes of the Act.

(a) The term firearm means a shotgun or rifle having a barrel of less than eighteen inches in length, or any other weapon, except a pistol or revolver, from which a shot is discharged by an explosive if such weapon is capable of being concealed on the person, or a machine gun, and includes a muffler or silencer for any firearm whether or not such firearm is included within the foregoing definition.

(b) The term "machine gun" means any weapon which shoots, or is designed to shoot, automatically or semiautomatically, more than one shot, without manual reloading, by a single function of the trigger.

(c) The term "person" includes a partnership, company, association, or corporation, as well as a natural person.

(d) The term "continental United States" means the States of the United States and the District of Columbia.

(e) The term "importer" means any person who imports or brings firearms into the continental United States for sale.

(f) The term "manufacturer" means any person who is engaged within the continental United States in the manufacture of firearms, or who otherwise produces therein any firearm for sale or disposition.

(g) The term "dealer" means any person not a manufacturer or importer engaged within the continental United States in the business of selling firearms. The term "dealer" shall include wholesalers, pawnbrokers, and dealers in used firearms.

(h) The term "interstate commerce" means transportation from any State or Territory or District, or any insular possession of the United States (including the Philippine Islands), to any other State or to the District of Columbia.

(1) The term "Commissioner" means the Commissioner of Internal Revenue.

(j) The term "Secretary" means the Secretary of the Treasury.

(k) The term "to transfer" or "transferred" shall include to sell, assign, pledge, lease, loan, give away, or otherwise dispose of.

SEC. 2. (a) Within fifteen days after the effective date of this Act, or upon first engaging in business, and thereafter on or before the 1st day of July of each year, every importer, manufacturer, and dealer in firearms shall register with the collector of internal revenue for each district in which such business is to be carried on his name or style, principal place of business, and places of business in such district, and pay a special tax at the following rates: Importers o manufacturers, $500 a year; dealers, other than pawnbrokers, $200 a year; pawnbrokers, $300 a year. Where the tax is payable on the 1st day of July in any year it shall be computed for one year; where the tax is payable on any other day it shall be computed proportionately from the 1st day of the month in which the liability to the tax accrued to the 1st day of July following.(b) It shall be unlawful for any person required to register under the provisions of this section to import, manufacture, or deal in firearms without having registered and paid the tax imposed by this section.

SEC. 3. (a) There shall be levied, collected, and paid upon firearms transferred in the continental United

States a tax at the rate of$200 for each firearm, such tax to be paid by the transferor, and to be represented by appropriate stamps to be provided by the Commissioner, with the approval of the Secretary; and the stamps herein provided shall be affixed to the order for such firearm, hereinafter provided for. The tax imposed by this section shall be in addition to any import duty imposed on such firearm.

(b) All provisions of law (including those relating to special taxes, to the assessment, collection, remission, and refund of internal revenue taxes, to the engraving, issuance, sale, accountability, cancellation, and distribution of tax-paid stamps provided for in the internal-revenue laws, and to penalties) applicable with respect to the taxes imposed by section 1 of the Act of December 17, 1914, as amended (U.S.C., Supp. VII, title 26, sees. 1040 and 1383), and all other provisions of the internal-revenue laws shall, insofar as not inconsistent with the provisions of this Act, be applicable with respect to the taxes imposed by this Act.

(c) Under such rules and regulations as the Commissioner, with the approval of the Secretary, may prescribe, and upon proof of the exportation of any firearm to any foreign country (whether exported as part of another article or not) with respect to which the transfer tax under this section has been paid by the manufacturer, the Commissioner shall refund to the manufacturer the amount of the tax so paid, or, if the manufacturer waives all claim for the amount to be refunded, the refund shall be made to the exporter.

SEC. 4. (a) It shall be unlawful for any person to transfer a firearm except in pursuance of a written order from the person seeking to obtain such article, on an application form issued in blank in duplicate for that purpose by the Commissioner. Such order shall identify the applicant by such means of identification as may be prescribed by regulations under this Act: Provided, That, if the applicant is an individual, such identification shall include fingerprints and a photograph thereof.

(b) The Commissioner, with the approval of the Secretary, shall cause suitable forms to be prepared for the purposes above mentioned, and shall cause the same to be distributed to collectors of internal revenue.

(c) Every person so transferring a firearm shall set forth in each copy of such order the manufacturer's number or other mark identifying such firearm, and shall forward a copy of such order to the Commissioner. The original thereof with stamps affixed, shall be returned to the applicant.

(d) No person shall transfer a firearm which has previously been transferred on or after the effective date of this Act, unless such person, in addition to complying with subsection (c), transfers there with the stamp-affixed order provided for in this section for each such prior transfer, in compliance with such regulations as may be prescribed under this Act for proof of payment of all taxes on such firearms.

(e) If the transfer of a firearm is exempted from the provisions of this Act as provided in section 13 hereof, the person transferring such firearm shall notify the Commissioner of the name and address of the applicant, the number or other mark identifying such firearm, and the date of its transfer, and shall file with the Commissioner such documents in proof thereof as the Commissioner may by regulations prescribe.

(f) Importers, manufacturers, and dealers who have registered and paid the tax as provided for in section 2(a) of this Act shall not be required to conform to the provisions of this section with respect to transactions in firearms with dealers or manufacturers if such dealers or manufacturers have registered and have paid such tax, but shall keep such records and make such reports regarding such transactions as may be prescribed by regulations under this Act.

SEC. 5. (a) Within sixty days after the effective date of

this Act every person possessing a firearm shall register, with the collector of the district in which he resides, the number or other mark identifying such firearm, together with his name, address, place where such firearm is usually kept, and place of business or employment, and, if such person is other than a natural person, the name and home address of an executive officer thereof: Provided, That no person shall be required to register under this section with respect to any firearm acquired after the effective date of, and inconformity with the provisions of, this Act.

(b) Whenever on trial for a violation of section 6 hereof the defendant is shown to have or to have had possession of such firearm at any time after such period of sixty days without having registered as required by this section, such possession shall create a presumption that such firearm came into the possession of the defendant subsequent to the effective date of this Act, but this presumption shall not be conclusive.

SEC. 6. It shall be unlawful for any person to receive or possess any firearm which has at any time been transferred in violation of section 3 or 4 of this Act.

SEC. 7. (a) Any firearm which has at any time been transferred in violation of the provisions of this Act shall be subject to seizure and forfeiture and (except as provided in subsection (b)) all the provisions of internal-revenue laws relating to searches, seizures, and forfeiture of unstamped articles are extended to and made to apply to the articles taxed under this Act, and the persons to whom this Act applies.

(b) In the case of the forfeiture of any firearm by reason of a violation of this Act: No notice of public sale shall be required; no such firearm shall be sold at public sale; if such firearm is in the possession of any officer of the United States except the Secretary, such officer shall deliver the firearm to the Secretary; and the Secretary may order such firearm destroyed or may sell such firearm to any State, Territory, or possession (including the Philippine Islands),or political subdivision thereof, or the District of Columbia, or retain it for the use of the Treasury Department or transfer it without charge to any Executive department or independent establishment of the Government for use by it.

SEC. 8. (a) Each manufacturer and importer of a firearm shall identify it with a number or other identification mark approved by the Commissioner, such number or mark to be stamped or otherwise placed thereon in a manner approved by the Commissioner.

(b) It shall be unlawful for anyone to obliterate, remove, change, or alter such number or other identification mark. Whenever on trial for a violation of this subsection the defendant is shown to have or to have had possession of any firearm upon which such number or Possession of, deemed sufficient evidence for mark shall have been obliterated, removed, changed, or altered, such shall be deemed sufficient evidence to authorize conviction, unless the defendant explains such possession to the satisfaction of the jury.

SEC. 9. Importers, manufacturers, and dealers shall keep such books and records and render such returns in relation to the transactions in firearms specified in this Act as the Commissioner, with the approval of the Secretary, may by regulations require.

SEC. 10. (a) No firearm shall be imported or brought into the United States or any territory under its control or jurisdiction (including the Philippine Islands), except that, under regulations prescribed by the Secretary, any firearm may be so imported or brought in when (1) the purpose thereof is shown to be lawful and (2) such firearm is unique or of a type which cannot be obtained within the United States or such territory.

(b) It shall be unlawful (1) fraudulently or knowingly to import any firearm into the United States or any territory under its control or jurisdiction (including the Philippine Islands), in violation of the provisions of this Act; or (2) knowingly to assist in so doing; or (3) to receive, conceal, buy, sell, or in any manner facilitate the transportation, concealment, or sale of any such firearm after being imported or brought in, knowing the same to have been imported or brought in contrary to law. Whenever on trial for a violation of this section the defendant is shown to have or to have had possession of such firearm, such possession shall be deemed sufficient evidence to authorize conviction unless the defendant explains such possession to the satisfaction of the jury.

SEC. 11. It shall be unlawful for any person who is required register as provided in section 5 hereof and who shall not have so registered, or any other person who has not in his possession a stamp-affixed order as provided in section 4 hereof, to ship, carry, or deliver any firearm in interstate commerce.

SEC. 12. The Commissioner, with the approval of the Secretary, shall prescribe such rules and regulations as may be necessary for carrying the provisions of this Act into effect.

SEC. 13. This Act shall not apply to the transfer of firearms (1)to the United States Government, any State, Territory, or possession of the United States, or to any political subdivision thereof, or to the District of Columbia; (2) to any peace officer or any Federal officer designated by regulations of the Commissioner; (3) to the transfer of any firearm which is unserviceable and which is transferred as a curiosity or ornament.

SEC. 14. Any person who violates or fails to comply with any of the requirements of this Act shall, upon conviction, be fined not more than $2,000 or be imprisoned for not more than five years, or both, in the discretion of the court.

SEC. 15. The taxes imposed by paragraph (a) of section 600 of the Revenue Act of 1926 (U.S.C., Supp. VII, title 26, sec. 1120) and by section 610 of the Revenue Act of 1932 (47 Stat. 169, 264), shall not apply to any firearm on which the tax provided by section 3 of this Act has been paid.

SEC. 16. If any provision of this Act, or the application thereof to any person or circumstance, is held invalid, the remainder of the Act, and the application of such provision to other persons or circumstances, shall not be affected thereby.

SEC. 17. This Act shall take effect on the thirtieth day after the date of its enactment.

SEC. 18. This Act may be cited as the "National Firearms Act."

Approved, June 26, 1934.

AUTHENTICATED U.S. GOVERNMENT INFORMATION GPO

I

114TH CONGRESS
1ST SESSION

H. R. 377

To amend chapter 44 of title 18, United States Code, to require homemade firearms to have serial numbers, and for other purposes.

IN THE HOUSE OF REPRESENTATIVES

JANUARY 14, 2015

Mr. HONDA (for himself, Mr. HASTINGS, Ms. KELLY of Illinois, Mr. DANNY K. DAVIS of Illinois, Mr. CONYERS, Mr. LOWENTHAL, Ms. SCHAKOWSKY, and Mr. SWALWELL of California) introduced the following bill; which was referred to the Committee on the Judiciary

---

A BILL

To amend chapter 44 of title 18, United States Code, to require homemade firearms to have serial numbers, and for other purposes.

Be it enacted by the Senate and House of Representatives of the United States of America in Congress assembled,

SECTION 1. SHORT TITLE.

This Act may be cited as the "Homemade Firearms Accountability Act of 2015".

SEC. 2. REQUIREMENT THAT HOMEMADE FIREARMS HAVE SERIAL NUMBERS.

(a) IN GENERAL.—Chapter 44 of title 18, United States Code, is amended by inserting after section 923 the following:

"§ 923A. Serial numbers for homemade firearms

"(a) REQUEST.—A person who has attained 18 years of age and desires to make a firearm, or obtain a unique serial number or other identifying mark for a firearm made by the person after 1968, may request a licensed dealer to issue a unique serial number or other identifying mark for the firearm, which request shall describe the firearm involved, and state whether the firearm will be (or is) a handgun.

"(b) CONSIDERATION.—

"(1) TREATMENT OF REQUEST AS TRANSFER PROPOSAL.—A request made of a licensed dealer pursuant to subsection (a) with respect to firearm shall be treated as a proposed transfer of the firearm from the licensed dealer to the applicant, for purposes of section 922(t) of this title and section 103 of the Brady Handgun Violence Prevention Act.

"(2) ISSUANCE OF SERIAL NUMBER.—A licensed dealer may issue to an applicant a unique serial number and identifying mark for a firearm pursuant to such a request if, applying paragraph (1) of this subsection to the request, section 922(t) or other law would not prohibit the licensed dealer from transferring the firearm to the applicant.

"(3) FEE AUTHORITY.—A licensed dealer may charge an applicant a fee for each serial number and identifying mark assigned and issued under this section, in an amount that is not more than the actual costs associated with assigning and issuing the serial number and identifying mark, and a fee for contacting the national instant criminal background check system with respect to the applicant.

"(c) PROHIBITIONS; REQUIREMENTS.—

"(1) BAN ON MAKING FIREARM BEFORE OBTAINING SERIAL NUMBER.—It shall be unlawful for any person, in or affecting interstate or foreign commerce, to make a firearm, unless the person has obtained a serial number and identifying mark for the firearm under this section.

"(2) BAN ON POSSESSION OR TRANSFER OF FIREARM WITHOUT SERIAL NUMBER.—It shall be unlawful for any person, in or affecting interstate or foreign commerce, to possess or transfer a firearm made by the person after 1968, unless—

"(A) a serial number and identifying mark for the firearm has been issued under this section;

"(B) within 10 days after the issuance, the serial number and identifying mark is stamped on or otherwise permanently affixed to the firearm; and

"(C) if the firearm is made from polymer plastic, 3.7 ounces of material type 17–4 PH stainless steel, on which the unique serial number or identifying mark is stamped or otherwise permanently affixed, are embedded within the plastic.

"(3) EXCEPTIONS.—This subsection shall not apply to—

"(A) a firearm to which a serial number has been assigned pursuant to section 923 of this title or chapter 53 of the Internal Revenue Code of 1986; or

"(B) a licensed manufacturer.

"(d) ADMINISTRATIVE PROVISION.—The Attorney General shall maintain, and make available on request, information on—

"(1) the number of serial numbers and identifying marks issued under this section; and

"(2) the number of arrests for violations of this section.".

(b) PENALTIES.—Section 924(a) of such title is amended—

(1) in paragraph (5), by adding at the end the following: "For purposes of this paragraph, the issuance of a serial number and identifying mark for a firearm in violation of section 923A shall be considered a transfer of the firearm in violation of section 922(t)."; and

(2) by adding at the end the following:

"(8) Whoever knowingly violates section 923A(c) shall be fined under this title, imprisoned not more than 6 months (or, if the firearm involved in the violation is a handgun, 1 year), or both.".

(c) CLERICAL AMENDMENT.—The table of sections for chapter 44 of such title is amended by inserting after the item relating to section 923 the following:

"923A. Serial number requirement for homemade firearms.".

(d) EFFECTIVE DATE.—The amendments made by this section shall take effect on January 1, 2016.

○

Document Themes

The NFA regulated a narrow class of firearms, to the exclusion of ordinary handguns; among these were not only sawed-off shotguns and machine guns but also bazookas, bombs, grenades, and silencers. In defining a firearm, the act states:

> The term firearm means a shotgun or rifle having a barrel of less than eighteen inches in length, or any other weapon, except a pistol or revolver, from which a shot is discharged by an explosive if such weapon is capable of being concealed on the person, or a machine gun, and includes a muffler or silencer for any firearm whether or not such firearm is included within the foregoing definition.

The NFA was and still is administered by the secretary of the treasury, who in turn has delegated authority over enforcement of the act to the Bureau of Alcohol, Tobacco, Firearms, and Explosives. The act created a registration system that requires NFA firearms to be registered to their owners as part of a central registry that the ATFE maintains. Further, the NFA proscribes the manufacture or transfer of an NFA firearm without the approval of the ATFE. It also levies a tax on each permissible transfer or manufacture of an NFA weapon. In 1934, these taxes were stiff: "Importers or manufacturers, $500 a year; dealers, other than pawnbrokers, $200 a year; pawnbrokers, $300 a year." It was felt that these stiff taxes would serve as a deterrent to the manufacture and sale of these dangerous weapons.

In order to ensure that the excise taxes were paid, the act required all owners to register their firearms: "Each manufacturer and importer of a firearm shall identify it with a number or other identification mark approved by the Commissioner, such number or mark to be stamped or otherwise placed thereon in a manner approved by the Commissioner." The act also controlled imports: "It shall be unlawful (1) fraudulently or knowingly to import any firearm into the United States or any territory under its control or jurisdiction (including the Philippine Islands), in violation of the provisions of this Act."

Additional Readings

Chu, Vivian S., "Congressional Authority to Regulate Firearms: A Legal Overview," *Congressional Research Report* #R43033, April 5, 2013.

Clinton, Joshua, and John Lapinski, "Measuring Legislative Accomplishment, 1877–1994,"*American Journal of Political Science,*Vol. 50, no. 1 (2006), pp. 232–49.

Kates, Don B., Jr., "Handgun Prohibition and the Original Meaning of the Second Amendment," *Michigan Law Review*, Vol. 82 (1983): 204–73.

National Firearms Act: Hearings before the Committee on Ways and Means: House of Representative, Seventy-third Congress, Second Session, on H.R. 9066 (Washington, D.C.: U.S. Government Printing Office, 1934), http://www.nfaoa.org/documents/NFA-1934house.pdf.

Schrader, Dorothy, "The Assault Weapons Ban: Review of Federal Laws ControllingPossession of Certain Firearms." Congressional Research Report #95-108, December 1, 1995.

—Michael J. O'Neal

Gun Control Act of 1968

Author(s): Various; Thomas J. Todd (sponsor)
Date: 1968
Genre: Legislative act

Summary Overview

The key feature of the Gun Control Act of 1968 was to regulate the interstate transfer of firearms. The law states that only federally licensed dealers, manufacturers, and importers could legally sell or ship guns over state lines. The law states that its central purpose is "to provide support to Federal, State, and local law enforcement officials in their fight against crime and violence" and not to interfere with the right of law-abiding citizens to acquire firearms "suitable for or readily adaptable to sporting purposes." One of the effects of the law was to implicitly ban the import of "Saturday night specials"—that is, cheap, poorly made handguns often used in the commission of urban crimes and not used for any legitimate sporting purpose. The law additionally identified classes of persons barred from acquiring firearms and provided for enhancing sentencing for anyone who uses a firearm while engaged in illegal drug trafficking.

Defining Moment

The roots of the Gun Control Act of 1968 extend back to the National Firearms Act of 1934. That act required the registration of certain types of firearms. The problem with the 1934 act, however, was that because a convicted felon was not eligible to purchase a firearm, the registration requirement amounted to self-incrimination, which is not permissible under the Fifth Amendment of the Constitution. In 1968 the U.S. Supreme Court heard the case of *Haynes v. United States*, in which the plaintiff challenged the registration requirement. The Court ruled that the registration requirement can in effect force a person accused of a crime to provide evidence—the gun—that may incriminate him. Accordingly, the Court effectively invalidated key portions of the act. Congress passed the Gun Control Act of 1968 to rectify the problem with the National Firearms Act. Thus, the new act did not contain a registration provision but instead focused on interstate transfer of firearms and on identifying classes of people who would be ineligible to acquire a firearm.

Many observers, however, note other defining moments that gave rise to the act, among them the 1963 assassination of President John F. Kennedy, which was carried out with a rifle purchased by mail order. Further, 1968 saw the assassinations of Martin Luther King, Jr., and Senator Robert F. Kennedy, leaving many Americans uneasy about what seemed to be a rising tide of violence. Adding fuel to the fire was the violence surrounding racial unrest in Newark, New Jersey, Detroit, and other cities and protests against the war in Vietnam. Other observers have noted that the act was passed at a time when the Black Panthers were carrying weapons during their marches and demonstrations, many of them military surplus rifles purchased by mail order. Malcolm X, for example, vowed to fight for civil rights "by any means necessary"; he even posed for *Ebony* magazine holding an M1 Carbine rifle. Ironically, in the twenty-first century, political conservatives tend to resist gun control legislation, but in the 1960s, conservatives such as California governor Ronald Reagan supported and promoted it, arguing that such legislation was needed to promote law and order on the streets of the nation's cities. In the eyes of some historians of the period, the Gun Control Act was not an effort to control guns; it was at bottom an effort to control blacks.

About the Author

The Gun Control Act of 1968 was the work of numerous politicians and advocacy groups, but its principal backer, and the one who sponsored the bill in Congress, was Senator Thomas J. Todd, a Connecticut Democrat. Todd was born in Norwich, Connecticut, on May 15, 1907. In 1930 he graduated from Providence College with a degree in philosophy.

After graduating from the Yale University law school in 1933, he worked for the Federal Bureau of Investigation. In later years, he participated in the Nuremberg Trials of Nazi war criminals, earning him a Medal of Freedom in 1946. From 1953 to 1957 he served two terms in the U.S. House of Representatives. In 1958 he won election to the U.S. Senate, where he served until 1971.

His reputation was tarnished when he was censured by the Senate for diverting campaign funds to personal uses. Meanwhile, following the assassination of John F. Kennedy, he worked tirelessly for a gun control bill. Dodd died in Old Lyme, Connecticut, on May 24, 1971.

HISTORICAL DOCUMENT

October 22, 1968
AN ACT

To amend title 18, United States Code, to provide for better control of the interstate traffic in firearms.

Be it enacted by the Senate and House of Representatives of the United States of America in Congress assembled, That this Act maybe cited as the "Gun Control Act of 1968".

PURPOSE

SEC. 101. The Congress hereby declares that the purpose of this titleis to provide support to Federal, State, and local law enforcement officials in their fight against crime and violence, and it is not the purpose of this title to place any undue or unnecessary Federal restrictions or burdens on law-abiding citizens with respect to the acquisition, possession, or use of firearms appropriate to the purpose of hunting, trapshooting, target shooting, personal protection, or any other lawful activity, and that this title is not intended to discourage or eliminate the private ownership or use of firearms by law-abiding citizens for lawful purposes, or provide for the imposition by Federal regulations of any procedures or requirements other than those reasonably necessary to implement and effectuate the provisions of this title.

* * * * *

**§922. Unlawful acts

(a) It shall be unlawful—

(1) for any person, except a licensed importer, licensed manufacturer, or licensed dealer, to engage in the business of importing, manufacturing, or dealing in firearms or ammunition, or in the course of such business to ship, transport, or receive any firearm or ammunition in interstate or foreign commerce;

(2) for any importer, manufacturer, dealer, or collector licensed under the provisions of this chapter to ship or transport in interstate or foreign commerce any firearm or ammunition to any person other than a licensed importer, licensed manufacturer, licensed dealer, or licensed collector;

(3) for any person, other than a licensed importer, licensed manufacturer, licensed dealer, or licensed collector to transport into or receive in the State where he resides (or if the person is a corporation or other business entity, the State where it maintains a place of business) any firearm purchased or otherwise obtained by such person outside that State, except that this paragraph

(A) shall not preclude any person who lawfully acquires a firearm by bequest or intestate succession in a State other than his State of residence from transporting the firearm into or receiving I tin that State, if it is lawful for such person to purchase or possess such firearm in that State,

(B) shall not apply to the transportation or receipt of a rifle or shotgun obtained in conformity with the provisions of subsection (b) (3) of this section, and

(C) shall not apply to the transportation of any firearm acquired in any State prior to the effective date of this chapter;

(4) for any person, other than a licensed importer, licensed manufacturer, licensed dealer, or licensed collector, to transport in interstate or foreign commerce any destructive device, machine-gun (as defined in section 5845 of the Internal Revenue Code of 1954), short-barreled shotgun, or short-barreled rifle, except as specifi-

cally authorized by the Secretary consistent with public safety and necessity;

(5) for any person (other than a licensed importer, licensed manufacturer, licensed dealer, or licensed collector) to transfer, sell, trade, give, transport, or deliver any firearm to any person (other than a licensed importer, licensed manufacturer, licensed dealer, or licensed collector) who the transferor knows or has reasonable cause to believe resides in any State other than that in which the transferor resides (or other than that in which its place of business is located if the transferor is a corporation or other business entity); except that this paragraph shall not apply to

(A) the transfer, transportation, or delivery of a firearm made to carry out a bequest of a firearm to, or an acquisition by interstate succession of a firearm by, a person who is permitted to acquire or possess a firearm under the laws of the State of his residence, and

(B) the loan or rental of a firearm to any person for temporary use for lawful sporting purposes; and

(6) for any person in connection with the acquisition or attempted acquisition of any firearm or ammunition from a licensed importer, licensed manufacturer, licensed dealer, or licensed collector, knowingly to make any false or fictitious oral or written statement or to furnish or exhibit any false, fictitious, or misrepresented identification, intended or likely to deceive such importer, manufacturer, dealer, or collector with respect to any fact material to the lawfulness of the sale or other disposition of such firearm or ammunition under the provisions of this chapter.

(b) It shall be unlawful for any licensed importer, licensed manufacturer, licensed dealer, or licensed collector to sell or deliver

(1) any firearm or ammunition to any individual who the licensee knows or has reasonable cause to believe is less than eighteen years of age, and, if the firearm, or ammunition is other than a s h o t gun or rifle, or ammunition for a shotgun or rifle, to any individual who the licensee knows or has reasonable cause to believe is less than twenty-one years of age.

(2) any firearm or ammunition to any person in any State where the purchase or possession by such person of such firearm or ammunition would be in violation of any State law or any published ordinance applicable at the place of sale, delivery or other disposition, unless the licensee knows or has reasonable cause to believe that the purchase or possession would not be in violation of such State law or such published ordinance;

(3) any firearm to any person who the licensee knows or has reasonable cause to believe does not reside in (or if the person is a corporation or other business entity, does not maintain a place of business in) the State in which the licensee's place of business is located, except that this paragraph

(A) shall not apply to the sale or delivery of a. rifle or shotgun to a resident of a State contiguous to the State in which the licensee's place of business is located if the purchaser's State of residence permits such sale or delivery by law, the sale fully complies with the legal conditions of sale in both such contiguous States, and the purchaser and the licensee have, prior to the sale, or delivery for sale, of the rifle or shotgun, complied with all of the requirements of section 922(c) applicable to intrastate transactions other than at the licensee's business premises,

(B) shall not apply to the loan or rental of a firearm to any person for temporary use for lawful sporting purposes, and

(C) shall not preclude any person who is participating in any organized rifle or shotgun match or contest, or is engaged in hunting, in a State other than his State of residence and whose rifle or shotgun has been lost or stolen or has become inoperative in such other State, from purchasing a rifle or shotgun in such other State from a licensed dealer if such person presents to such dealer a sworn statement

(i) that his rifle or shotgun was lost or stolen or became inoperative while participating in such a match or contest, or while engaged in hunting, in such other State, and

(ii) identifying the chief law enforcement officer of the locality in which such person resides, to whom such licensed dealer shall forward such statement by registered mail;

(4) to any person any destructive device, machinegun (as defined in section 5845 of the Internal Revenue Code of 1954) short-barreled shotgun, or short-barreled rifle, except as specifically authorized by the Secretary consistent with public safety and necessity; and recordkeeping.

(5) any firearm or ammunition to any person unless the licensee notes in his records, required to be kept pursuant to section 923 of this chapter, the name, age, and place of residence of such person if the person is an individual, or the identity and principal and local places of business of such person if the person is a corporation or other business entity.

* * * * *

(d) It shall be unlawful for any person to sell or otherwise dispose of any firearm or ammunition to any person knowing or having reasonable cause to believe that such person—

(1) is under indictment for, or has been convicted in any court of, a crime punishable by imprisonment for a term exceeding one year;

(2) is a fugitive from justice;

(3) is an unlawful user of or addicted to any controlled substance (as defined in section 102 of the Controlled Substances Act (21 U.S.C. 802));

(4) has been adjudicated as a mental defective or has been committed to any mental institution;

(5) who, being an alien, is illegally or unlawfully in the United States;

(6) who has been discharged from the Armed Forces under dishonorable conditions;

(7) who, having been a citizen of the United States, has renounced his citizenship; or

(8) is subject to a court order that restrains such person from harassing, stalking, or threatening an intimate partner of such person or child of such intimate partner or person, or engaging in other conduct that would place an intimate partner in reasonable fear of bodily injury to the partner or child, except that this paragraph shall only apply to a court order that—

(A) was issued after a hearing of which such person received actual notice, and at which such person had the opportunity to participate; and

(B)

(i) includes a finding that such person represents a credible threat to the physical safety of such intimate partner or child; or

(ii) by its terms explicitly prohibits the use, attempted use, or threatened use of physical force against such intimate partner or child that would reasonably be expected to cause bodily injury.

* * * * *

(c)(1) Whoever, during and in relation to any crime of violence or drug trafficking crime (including a crime of violence or drug trafficking crime which provides for an enhanced punishment if committed by the use of a deadly or dangerous weapon or device) for which he may be prosecuted in a court of the United States, uses or carries a firearm, shall, in addition to the punishment provided for such crime of violence or drug trafficking crime, be sentenced to imprisonment for five years, and if the firearm is a short-barreled rifle, short-barreled shotgun, or semiautomatic assault weapon, to imprisonment for ten years, and if the firearm is a machinegun, or a destructive device, or is equipped with a firearm silencer or firearm muffler, to imprisonment for thirty years. In the case of his second or subsequent conviction under this subsection, such person shall be sentenced to imprisonment for twenty years, and if the firearm is a machinegun, or a destructive device, or is equipped with a firearm silencer or firearm muffler, to life imprisonment without release. Notwithstanding any other provision of law, the court shall not place on probation or suspend the sentence of any person convicted of a violation of this subsection, nor shall the term of imprisonment imposed under this subsection run concurrently with any other term of imprisonment including that imposed for the crime of violence or drug trafficking crime in which the firearm was used or carried.

SUPPLEMENTAL HISTORICAL DOCUMENT

"New Gun Control Provisions Passed In Spending Bill"

NPR, March 25, 2018

NPR's Sarah McCammon asks Pennsylvania Congressman Ryan Costello about provisions in the omnibus bill to improve criminal background checks for gun buyers and allow CDC research into gun violence.

SARAH MCCAMMON, HOST:
We're going to start the program with a story that dominated the news this weekend, and that's the renewed focus on American gun laws. Hundreds of thousands of people marched across the country in support of tighter gun restrictions. But what you might not have heard is that Congress and the president passed a couple of new rules about guns in the spending bill that was signed into law on Friday. One is meant to close a loophole that allowed the mass shooter in Sutherland Springs, Texas last year to pass a background check. The other frees the Centers for Disease Control to study gun violence. We wanted to know more about all of this, so we called up Congressman Ryan Costello. He's a Republican from Pennsylvania.

Congressman Costello, welcome back to the program.

RYAN COSTELLO: Great to be with you.

MCCAMMON: One of the new provisions in the spending bill is something that you've supported in the past. It's called FixNICS. That's the National Instant Criminal Background Check system run by the FBI. How does this law work to strengthen background checks?

COSTELLO: Because the background check system that we have right now is incomplete and sometimes inaccurate. Oftentimes, federal agencies or local law enforcement agencies do not upload that data. That was the case in Texas with the church shooting. And we've also found that states, really, are not on the hook for providing any sort of verification whether or not they are in compliance. And so FixNICS is intended to require public reporting and verification from various agencies to confirm that they are uploading the data because our background check system is only effective when we have accurate and comprehensive data submitted into it.

MCCAMMON: Republicans have been hesitant to pass any sort of gun control measures and FixNICS isn't a new idea. Why did this finally pass now?

COSTELLO: Because previously it was—listen. This is common sense. Everybody—virtually everyone supports this bill. It was previously coupled with concealed-carry reciprocity, which stands for the proposition that if you are in a state where you need to go through—let's just call it very reduced permitting in order to carry a concealed weapon or perhaps no permitting at all, then you could go into another state, and that other state would have to honor, by reciprocity, your home state. Democrats objected to that. Some Republicans such as myself voted against that as well. And so, as a consequence of FixNICS being coupled with concealed carry, that was not a bill that had the kind of broad bipartisan support that could make its way forward into the omnibus bill. However, the FixNICS component to that was something that the great majority of all legislators, Republican and Democrat, do support.

MCCAMMON: Also in this bill is language allowing the Centers for Disease Control to conduct research on gun violence, something that hadn't been happening under current law previously. Do you support that change?

COSTELLO: I do. I also support legislation that would clarify that as well in addition to this. Now, some gun-safety advocates will say that this change does not really do all that much. All it does is say that the CDC can, if it would like to, engage in such research, which is an improvement over the debate over whether that was permitted or not. There was some question or confusion over that. I actually think the CDC should move forward with research in this area. When you look at the role of technology and what are used or immersed on a day-today basis with—and social media, YouTube videos and just the acceleration of society. I think it is very important. But nevertheless, the omnibus bill clarifies that the Dickey Amendment does not prohibit the CDC from engaging in such research.

MCCAMMON: It doesn't fund that research though. Should Congress pass funding for research on gun violence by the CDC?

COSTELLO: I believe that it should. Yes. It didn't in this bill. The CDC obviously could go ahead and allocate research to that funding, but that, even, can be a little bit tricky. That can really be up to a determination by each respective administration. I think there should be money for that. Yes.

MCCAMMON: There were...

COSTELLO: I would...

MCCAMMON: ...Of course...

COSTELLO: ...I would probably be—whether or not I'm in the minority or majority on that is an open question.

MCCAMMON: There were, of course, massive demonstrations yesterday calling for stricter gun laws. Gun control advocates say the new provisions in the spending bill aren't enough. Are there other gun restrictions you and others in your party might support?

COSTELLO: Well, let me say what I support and what I think everyone can agree to and that is there is a bill, the Thompson-King bill, in the House that's similar to the Toomey-Manchin Bill in the Senate, and specifically, when we're talking about background checks, purchasing a gun over the Internet in a catalog or at a gun show should require a background check. At present, there is no federal law that requires that. That is a state-by-state law.

I think that in this day and age, when my wife—and I love her—buys what she buys on Amazon—you know, the way folks shop on a day-to-day basis, the Internet is really such an open-ended way to circumvent background checks, and that's one law that I do think should come from the federal government, and that's universal background checks.

MCCAMMON: Quickly, Congressman, I have to let you go in just a moment, but before I do, I need to ask you—there are reports you won't seek re-election this year. Is that the case?

COSTELLO: So I will be making an announcement on that a little bit later this evening or early tomorrow morning. All right. But certainly, I appreciate you asking the question.

MCCAMMON: All right. Thank you. That's Representative Ryan Costello, Republican from Pennsylvania.

https://www.npr.org/2018/03/25/596880465/new-gun-control-provisions-passed-in-spending-bill

Document Themes

The act begins with a statement of purpose, which is to "support to Federal, State, and local law enforcement officials in their fight against crime and violence." Congress assures the public that the purpose of the act is not to burden law-abiding citizens or "to discourage or eliminate the private ownership or use of firearms by law-abiding citizens for lawful purposes." Among those purposes, the act mentions "hunting, trapshooting, target shooting, personal protection, or any other lawful activity."

The chief provision of the act is to make it unlawful for anyone "except a licensed importer, licensed manufacturer, or licensed dealer" to import, manufacture, or deal in firearms or ammunition or to ship, transport, or receive firearms or ammunition in interstate or foreign transactions. Further, it would be unlawful for any of these licensed persons to ship firearms in interstate commerce to anyone not licensed. The act goes on to detail other provisions having to do with the residence of gun purchasers and the movement of firearms across state lines. The law makes it unlawful to provide "false, fictitious, or misrepresented identification, intended or likely to deceive such importer, manufacturer, dealer, or collector" when acquiring a firearm.

The act contains a number of other provisions. The definition of "firearm" was expanded to include a wider range of weapons. It banned importing firearms that were not suitable for sporting purposes, effectively—but not explicitly—banning Saturday night specials. It set a minimum age of eighteen to buy a gun. It required firearms to be marked with a serial number for tracking purposes. And it banned fugitives, felons, drug users, persons who had been committed to a mental health institution, persons dishonorably discharged from the military, non-citizens, persons who have restraining orders against them, and anyone with a domestic violence conviction from acquiring a firearm. Additionally, in response to the growing prevalence of drugs and drug trafficking, the act provided for "enhanced sentencing" of persons who committed acts of violence in connection with the illegal drug trade.

Additional Readings

Cook, Philip, "The Saturday Night Special: An Assessment of Alternative Definitions from a Policy Perspective," *Journal of Law and Criminology*, Vol. 72, no. 4 (Winter 1981), pp. 1735–45.

Patterson, Samuel C., and Keith R. Eakin,."Congress and Gun Control."In *The Changing Politics of Gun Control*, ed. John M. Bruce and Clyde Wilcox (Lanham, MD: Rowman & Littlefield Publishers, 1998).

Proposed Amendments to the Gun Control Act of 1968 toProhibit the Sale of "Saturday Night Special" Handguns: Hearings on S. 2507 Before the Subcommittee toInvestigate Juvenile Delinquency of the Senate Committee on theJudiciary, 92nd Cong., 1st Sess. (1971).

Santaella-Tenorio, Julian, Magdalena Cerdá, Andrés Villaveces, and Sandro Gale, "What Do We Know About the Association between Firearm Legislation andFirearm-Related Injuries?," *Epidemiologic Reviews*, Vol. 38 (2016), pp. 140–57.

Spitzer, Robert J.,*The Politics of Gun Control*(Chatham, NJ: Chatham House Publishers, 1995).

Zimring, Franklin E., "Firearms and Federal Law: The Gun Control Act of 1968," *Journal of Legal Studies* 4 (January 1975): 133–98.

—*Michael J. O'Neal*

Undetectable Firearms Act

Author: 100th Congress
Date: 1988
Genre: Legislative act

Summary Overview

The Undetectable Firearms Act of 1988, also known as the Terrorist Firearms Detection Act, banned the manufacture, importation, possession, receipt, and transfer of plastic and ceramic guns that are undetectable by magnetometers and X-ray machines in airports and other public places. The act specified that a firearm must contain a minimum of 3.7 ounces of metal to make it detectable.

When Congress began consideration of a ban on plastic weapons, the National Rifle Association (NRA) expressed its opposition. In Senate hearings, an NRA representative labeled proposed legislation a "Trojan horse" intended to compromise the gun ownership rights of law-abiding citizens. The organization claimed that simply because terrorists might employ a product does not justify denying its use to the general public. Gun supporters claimed that the new weapons, which were not yet in production, had definite advantages over existing firearms. They would be lighter and more easily used, and would not rust. However, supporters of a ban defined the issue not as one of gun control, but of safety, for the guns were considered a major threat to the security of citizens if they could not be detected by standard equipment.

In February 1988, Vice President George H. W. Bush brought the issue into the national headlines. Participating in a debate among candidates for the Republican nomination for president sponsored by Gun Owners of New Hampshire, Bush showed the audience a small .22-caliber plastic pistol lent to him by the Treasury Department. While reiterating his support for the right of citizens to bear arms, he stated that Congress must deal with new firearms that are virtually undetectable by existing devices. The audience showed its approval and the other candidates quickly agreed with Bush, indicating widespread support for legislation banning plastic guns.

However, Senator James A. McClure, Republican of Idaho, one of the original authors of the Firearms Owners Protection Act, had introduced a weakened measure as an alternative to the one sponsored by Senators Strom Thurmond, Republican of South Carolina, and Howard Metzenbaum, Democrat of Ohio. McClure's proposal, supported by the NRA, would ban guns made entirely of plastic, but would allow the production of firearms with minimum amounts of metal. The NRA expressed its concern that the Thurmond-Metzenbaum legislation would lead to a ban on some existing weapons. Police organizations objected to the McClure proposal, claiming that the standard would allow the production of guns that could not be detected by existing devices.

Representatives of 12 police organizations met with Republican President Ronald Reagan's Attorney General, Edwin Meese, who had expressed his support for the alternative measure. Although the Justice Department initially indicated that advances in electronic equipment would improve the ability to detect weapons, thus obviating the need for stricter standards, the Reagan administration ultimately agreed to change its position and support the more restrictive provisions. In discussions among representatives of the Justice, Treasury, and Transportation Departments and a Law Enforcement Steering Committee representing law enforcement organizations, a compromise level of 3.7 ounces of metal was reached. When the NRA was assured that no existing gun would be banned under this standard, the organization dropped its opposition to the measure.

With all concerned groups supporting the same principle, the House of Representatives and the Senate passed slightly different versions of the bill in May 1988. The final legislation, approved by both houses in October and signed by President Reagan in November 1988, required all guns to set off metal detectors at a level equivalent to a firearm containing 3.7 ounces of stainless steel, or to be detectable by X-ray machines. In 1998 Congress renewed the Act for an additional five years, and in 2003 Congress approved a ten-year renewal. In 2013 Senator Charles Schumer, arguing that some plastic guns still could pass through screening undetected, proposed a revised version of the Act that would mandate non-detachable metal parts to firearms. The National Rifle Association strongly objected to any expansion in the law and so Congress renewed the legislation for another ten years without changes.

Richard Feldman, former lobbyist for the now disbanded American Shooting Sports Council, has noted that the Glock 17—the Austrian-manufactured handgun that was the original focus of controversy—always could be detected by airport or building security X-ray machines and that the controversy revolved around the political motives of gun control and gun rights groups alike.

Additional Reading

Feldman, Richard. *Ricochet: Confessions of a Gun Lobbyist*. Hoboken, N.J: John Wiley & Sons, 2008. Print.

Sugarmann, Josh. *National Rifle Association: Money, Firepower & Fear*. Washington, D.C: National Press Books, 1992. Print

National Rifle Association, "NRA Statement on the Reauthorization of the 'Undetectable Firearms Act,' HR 3626," www.nraila.org/articles/20131203/nra-statement-on-the-reauthorization-of-the-undetectable-firearms-act-hr-3626.

SUPPLEMENTAL HISTORICAL DOCUMENT

3D-printed gun controversy: Everything you need to know

Marrian Zhou, August 16, 2018

The debate over 3D-printed guns has hit its melting point.

The battle about how to handle blueprints for plastic guns has raged for years, but it flared up in a big way in July after the US State Department settled a legal case and let an organization called Defense Distributed go ahead and release plans online.

That prompted eight state attorneys general to sue the State Department, on July 30. The same day, 20 state attorneys general sent a letter (PDF) to the State Department and Justice Department, saying the guns should be stopped.

On July 31, a Seattle judge granted a temporary restraining order to block the publication of blueprints until a hearing set for Aug. 10. But it's now rescheduled to Aug. 21, according to court records released on Friday.

Eleven more states on Aug. 2 joined the plaintiffs—making it a 19-state lawsuit against the State Department and Defense Distributed.

The back-and-forth underscores the broader fight pitting First and Second Amendment rights protecting free speech and gun ownership against public safety and the need to protect against easy access to weapons. It also comes amid a broader discussion of gun control in light of an increasing number of public shooting incidents.

This isn't a simple case, so CNET's here to break it down for you.

So what are 3D-printed guns?

As the name implies, they're parts for guns made using a 3D printer and plans created on a computer or downloaded online.

They may be made of plastic, but the guns are capable of firing standard handgun rounds. But they're not complete. One plan for a plastic gun still requires a metal nail that serves as a firing pin and a six-ounce piece of steel that's included solely to enable metal detectors to spot the guns (which keeps the weapons from running afoul of the US Undetectable Firearms Act).

The controversy over 3D-printed guns stretches as far back as 2012, when Cody Wilson announced plans to make such a weapon. It took him and members of his open source organization, Defense Distributed, just eight months.

By May 2013, Wilson debuted the world's first 3D-printed handgun, the Liberator.

What exactly can you print?

The Liberator is the closest thing to a completely plastic gun, but it still needs a steel nail to serve as the firing pin. The rest of Defense Distributed's blueprints relate to the frame of a gun, also known as a receiver. Those receivers serve to house the complete gun, which enthusiasts still need to assemble themselves, according to Popular Mechanics.

It's important to note that these receivers don't have critical parts like bolts, barrels, stocks or other parts. So it's not like you can 3D print a gun and start firing it right away.

3D printers can also produce metal gun parts as well, though it's much more expensive and dangerous to use this type of industrial 3D printer, because of the high melting points of metals. They're also not easily accessible.

Why are people worried?

Wilson published his designs online. That means anyone can download the blueprints and print out the gun parts as long as they have access to a computer and a 3D printer.

These guns are also theoretically untraceable.

The Undetectable Firearms Act makes it a federal offense to "manufacture, import, sell, ship, deliver, possess, transfer or receive" a firearm capable of defeating airport metal detection.

While the completed Liberator is a detectable firearm, as long as you stash the firing pin and the small piece of steel elsewhere, you can carry the gun and walk right through airport security checkpoints.

Also, because these guns are homemade, they don't carry an industrial serial number (so they're what's called "ghost guns"). Besides that, people don't have to go through a background check to get one, like they'd have to do to buy a commercial firearm.

On top of that, criminals can more easily get rid of the weapons, denying law enforcement the opportunity to gather material evidence. Plastic is easier to destroy than metal. The melting point for 3D-printing plastic is roughly 464 Fahrenheit (240 Celsius), while that of steel is 2,500 Fahrenheit (1,371 Celsius).

"3D-printed guns represent one dimension of a larger problem of do-it-yourself homemade firearms which is an increasing threat to public safety," said Kristen Rand, legislative director of the gun control advocacy organization Violence Policy Center, in an email statement. "It is important that policymakers act now to address this burgeoning threat before it is too late."

There're already easier ways to get a firearm or a homemade one, such as stealing a gun from a legal firearm owner, purchasing one from the black market and make one yourself with a 80-percent-finished receiver—it's not considered a firearm if the receiver isn't finished. Thus, 3D-printed guns can't become a norm yet.

However, if 3D printers become cheaper, better and more accessible in the future, we can't dismiss the possibility that 3D-printed guns will change the landscape of illicit arms trade.

Who is Cody Wilson?

Wilson learned about 3D printers during his second year at the University of Texas Law School in 2012, according to *The Washington Post*. He was reportedly inspired by Julian Assange and WikiLeaks to create an open-source platform.

"We wanted to be the Wiki for guns," Wilson told the *Post*.

Then he reportedly launched Defcad.com, an unregulated file-sharing website that eventually became the first community around 3D printed guns.

Wilson is no stranger to the media. He's also known for starting a crowdfunding site called Hatreon, in 2017. After neo-Nazi groups got kicked off crowdfunding sites like Patreon and GoFundMe, as well as payment services like PayPal and Apple Pay, they turned to Hatreon to finance their cause.

Regarding his blueprints for 3D-printed guns, Wilson told *The New York Times* that he wanted to promote decentralized solutions in an ever-centralizing world.

"I think the state should be as weak as possible relative to the individual," Wilson told the publication. "The proper posture of the state is one that at least is in fear of its citizen, not one that lords over it."

CNET asked Wilson earlier in July if he worries about people with bad intentions getting their hands on his gun designs. He said, "no concerns regarding public access." At the time, he also told *ArsTechnica* that he'd been cashing in from selling the Ghost Gunner, a home tool that lets people make a key gun part out of metal and use that part to build an untraceable firearm.

Wilson also reportedly drew an analogy to World War II, when the Allies tried to deliver weapons behind enemy lines.

"Instead of dropping the gun on Europe," he told the *Times*. "We dropped it on the internet."

His critics, however, have called his method "open-source terrorism," the *Times* reported.

Wilson didn't immediately respond to a request for comment.

Cody Wilson fires his 3D-printed handgun, the Liberator

Defense Distributed has already made plans for this open-source weapon—dubbed a Wiki Weapon—available online for free, and continues to refine and test the design to improve reliability.

Wilson reappeared in the news last month after he won a settlement with the State Department on the distribution of his blueprints online and said he'd resume publication on Wednesday, Aug. 1. He said he'd make the plans available for anyone to download for free.

How does the State Department figure into this?

The State Department, currently overseen by Secretary of State Mike Pompeo, regulates the exports of defense products in accordance with the ITAR—International Traffic in Arms Regulations—which was why the department had the run-in with Defense Distributed in the first place, according to a State Department spokesperson.

Several months after the Liberator debuted in 2013, the State Department said Defense Distributed violated ITAR by publishing its designs for the gun online, since the internet doesn't have borders, and issued a restraining order. The company then removed the files, according to *ArsTechnica*.

Defense Distributed didn't give up, right?

Yep. Two years later, the company teamed up with the Second Amendment Foundation and sued the State Department, arguing the government can't prevent publication before it occurs and making it an issue related to the First Amendment's freedom of speech protection.

In July, the State Department agreed to waive its prior restraint order against Wilson and Defense Distributed, allowing his organization to freely publish designs and other technical files about 3D printed guns, according to SAF's release.

"The Department of Justice suggested that the State Department and the US government settle this case, and so that is what was done," said Heather Nauert, a spokesperson for the State Department, during the Department press briefing on Tuesday. "We were informed that we would have lost this case in court, or would have likely lost this case in court based on First Amendment grounds."

The State Department also voluntarily settled with Defense Distributed and SAF because it will soon transfer the responsibility of regulating exports and manufacturing of commercially available firearms to the Commerce Department. As a result, the issue raised in the lawsuit won't fall under the jurisdiction of the State Department in the near future, according to a State Department official.

"We took the device—the advice of the Department of Justice, and here we are right now," said Nauert.

The Justice Department declined to comment.

How do the states play into this?

Eight US state attorneys general, Massachusetts, Connecticut, New Jersey, Pennsylvania, Oregon, Maryland, New York and the District of Columbia, on Monday filed a lawsuit to block the distribution of 3D-printed gun designs online due to a State Department settlement with the gun Wilson and his company Defense Distributed.

"The federal government is trying to allow access to online plans that will allow anyone to anonymously build their own downloadable, untraceable, and undetectable gun," said Massachusetts Attorney General Maura Healey, in a release. "This is an imminent threat to public safety and violates the law. We have a responsibility to ensure that these files are not made easily available to the public."

Their complaint asked the court to declare that the public release of Wilson's 3D-printed gun blueprints is an unlawful, unconstitutional violation of the Tenth Amendment and prohibit anyone from releasing the designs once the injunction is established.

The attorneys said the Trump administration has infringed on their states' exercise of police power and enforcement of public safety laws by letting people prohibited from owning a firearm, including children, felons and the mentally ill, have access to these plans.

Simultaneously, 20 state attorneys general sent a letter to the State Department and the Department of Justice asking for the same thing.

On Tuesday, Seattle Federal Judge Robert S. Lasnik granted a temporary restraining order against the 3D-printed gun blueprints. Though Wilson's blueprints went live online as of July 27, earlier than the scheduled Aug. 1.

More states on Thursday joined the lawsuit against the State Department and Defense Distributed. Now the plaintiffs have expanded to 19 US states.

The hearing to determine whether this order should become a preliminary injunction—a court order that prohibits the parties to do something until a final ruling is made—is set on Friday, Aug. 10.

What was Wilson's response?

Wilson has started a campaign and fundraiser on his website to unblock his Defcad.com. Defense Distributed's LEGIO, the company's "political and technical fraternity," is collecting membership fees from $5 to $1,000.

Wilson didn't immediately respond to a request for comment, but he further stated his stance during his latest interview on *Fox News* Sunday.

"I literally believe in the Second Amendment to the point of that it's alright and it should be expected there will be social costs for protecting a right like this," Wilson said. "Of course we should expect, and have a mature attitude that bad things can happen."

He also criticized politicians for just realizing the loophole in the regulations of 3D printed guns—the blueprints can be downloaded by anyone and are "protected by the First Amendment," as Wilson claimed.

"I'm sorry that a bunch of politicians woke up to the reality of this just last week," he said. "But this is the way that it's always been."

The Justice Department is representing the State Department in this lawsuit, and the Justice Department declined to comment.

A State Department official told CNET in an email that the department has no role in domestic gun control policies and the broader question of this technology's potential. He said the agency has already completed the actions required under the settlement agreement.

"I think it would be wise for news organizations and people having conversations about this to be aware that at least since the year 2013, these have been available, these Computer Assisted Designs for making these 3D guns—have been available online for several years," said Nauert.

This isn't a new debate, right?

Nope. Wilson's plastic gun designs has been online for years. Download counts at Defcad.com suggest the gun plans had already been downloaded over 20,000 times.

And it wasn't the first controversy on 3D printed firearms.

In 2012, MakerBot's Thingiverse website hosted design files for producing a key component of an AR15 semi automatic rifle with a 3D printer. Anyone could download Michael "HaveBlue" Guslick's design for the lower receiver and produce it.

MakerBot later removed the designs for a printable AR15 and other weapon components from its 3D-printing file library.

Where's Congress in the midst of all this?

The Congress renewed the Undetectable Firearms Act in 2013, which required all firearms to contain at least 3.7 ounce of steel so they could be detected.

But it didn't say which part has to be metal.

In the heat of the 3D-printed gun controversy, US Democratic Senator Bill Nelson of Florida on Tuesday filed legislations—the Untraceable Firearms Act and the 3D Printed Gun Safety Act—to make it illegal for anyone to intentionally publish a digital file online that programs a 3D printer to automatically manufacture a firearm, according to a release emailed by Nelson's representative. The bills were also backed by Senators Richard Blumenthal, Ed Markey, Chuck Schumer, Jack Reed, Dianne Feinstein, Bob Menendez and others.

"Just think about all the work we're doing to hardening our schools in the wake of the Parkland shooting," Nelson said in the release. "None of that will do any good if you can simply print one of these undetectable plastic guns at home."

The legislations also require every firearm to have a serial number and to have at least one main component, such as the frame or the barrel, made of metal—an effort to prevent people from detaching a small metal part from a plastic gun to go through security and then reattach it afterwards.

Nelson asked the Senate for "unanimous consent"—the bill can be approved right away unless any one senator objects. After he made the request, Republican Senator Mike Lee of Utah objected based on free speech concerns.

"Any legislation that comes forth from this body that begins with the following words will attract my attention and should attract the attention of anyone who's concerned about our first amendment and other constitutional rights," said Sen. Lee on the Senate floor. "It begins with the words it shall be unlawful for my person to intentionally publish. That ought to be concerning to us, to each and every one of us, Democrats and Republicans alike."

As a result, Nelson's legislations will have to undergo the normal process of passing a bill, which can take from two weeks to several months, or sometimes, years.

What is President Trump's reaction?

President Trump weighed in on Tuesday in a tweet, "I am looking into 3D Plastic Guns being sold to the public. Already spoke to NRA, doesn't seem to make much sense!"

Trump is incorrect in his point about 3D plastic guns being sold to the public. The designs of these guns were given out for free. The tweet didn't specify which part didn't make sense.

NRA and the White House haven't responded to requests for comment.

Did the Department of Justice ever respond?

Yes and no.

On Aug. 16, US Attorney General Jeff Sessions warned in that anyone who used a 3D printer to manufacture an "undetectable" gun would be prosecuted to the fullest extent of the law, according to Reuters.

"We will not stand for the evasion ... of current law and will take action to ensure that individuals who violate the law by making plastic firearms and rendering them undetectable, will be prosecuted to the fullest extent," Sessions said in a statement.

The statement came a day after the DOJ asked a court to allow online distribution of 3D-printed gun designs, which enable the manufacture undetectable and untraceable gun parts, Reuters reported.

The DOJ didn't immediately respond to a request for comment.

On Aug. 9, Defense Distributed, SAF and Conn Williamson submitted a response to a lawsuit filed by a coalition of states seeking to prevent the posting of the plans online, saying the DOJ had long argued that publishing weapon plans was protected by the First Amendment.

The defendants attached DOJ memos, including a 1997 report to Congress, which said people who publish bomb-making information are protected by the Constitution and shouldn't be found at fault even if someone is harmed if the plans are used.

Separately, 22 state attorneys general sent a letter to Sessions and Secretary of State Mike Pompeo asking them to block the publication of 3D-printed gun blueprints. The states haven't received a response.

https://www.cnet.com/news/the-3d-printed-gun-controversy-everything-you-need-to-know/

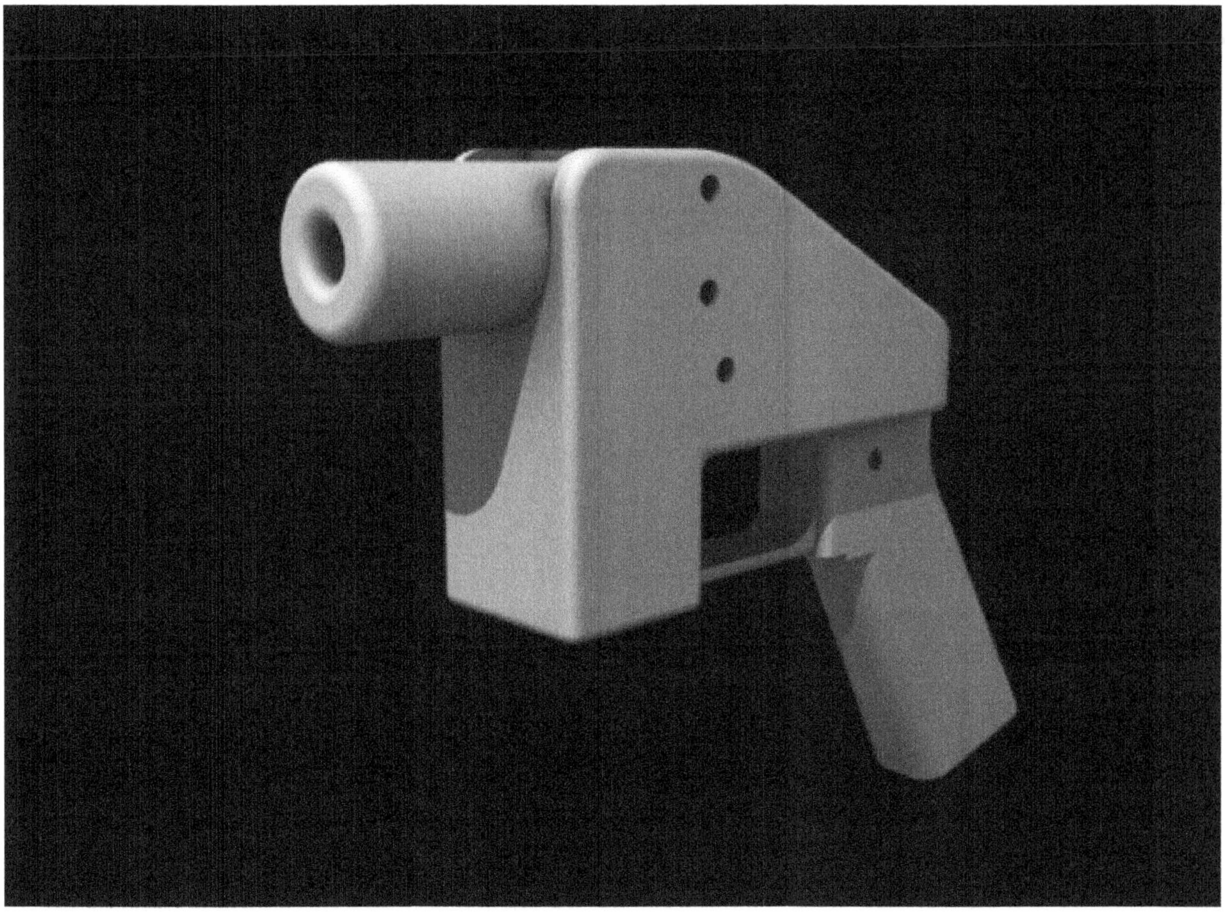

Digital Liberator pistol by Defense Distributed (By Kamenev.)

Brady Handgun Violence Protection Act

Author(s): Charles Schumer (reintroduced to the House of Representatives and Howard Metzenbaum (reintroduced to the Senate)

Date: 1993

Genre: Legislative act

Summary Overview

Congress passed the Brady Handgun Violence Protection Act of 1993, commonly referred to as the Brady bill, in the wake of an assassination attempt on President Ronald Reagan in 1981. "Brady" is James Brady, Reagan's press secretary, who was wounded by one of the assailant's bullets and remained permanently disabled until his death in 2014. Meanwhile, Brady's wife, Sarah Brady, served as chair of the Brady Campaign to Prevent Gun Violence as the couple lobbied for stricter handgun control and restrictions on assault weapons, and "Brady" and the "Brady bill" have become almost synonymous with gun-control efforts. The fundamental purposes of the act are made clear in its formal long title: "An Act to provide for a waiting period before the purchase of a handgun, and for the establishment of a national instant criminal background check system to be contacted by firearms dealers before the transfer of any firearm."

Defining Moment

The defining moment behind the Brady bill is readily identified. On March 30, 1981, President Ronald Reagan exited the Hilton Hotel in Washington, D.C., after having addressed the Building and Construction Workers Union. From a distance of about ten feet, John Hinckley, Jr., fired on the president with a .22-caliber Röhm RG-14 revolver. His first shot hit press secretary James Brady; other shots wounded a police officer and a Secret Service agent. Hinckley's target, though, was the president, who was wounded when a shot ricocheted off the presidential limousine and struck him. Hinckley was quickly wrestled to the ground and arrested. Ultimately, he was found not guilty by reason of insanity.

Hinkley, it turned out, had become obsessed with the movie *Taxi Driver*, in which Robert DeNiro plays the part of a cab driver who stalks a presidential candidate in an effort to impress a young prostitute played by Jodie Foster. Hinkley in turn became obsessed with Foster and believed that he could impress her and win her love by carrying out a high-profile assassination. In 1980 he began following President Jimmy Carter from state to state and was arrested at an airport in Nashville, Tennessee, for carrying guns at a Carter campaign stop, but the Secret Service was never notified. His guns were confiscated, but he went to a pawnshop Dallas and purchased more guns, including the one he used in the Reagan assassination attempt. He later wrote a letter to Jodie Foster stating that his assassination attempt on President Reagan was for her.

Meanwhile, Brady never fully recovered from his injuries. The shooting left him partially paralyzed, with slurred speech. His wife, Sarah Brady, served as chair of the Brady Campaign to Prevent Gun Violence. The history of this organization dates back to 1974, when the National Council to Control Handguns was formed. That organization operated under the name Handgun Control, Inc., from 1980 to 2000; in 2001 it was renamed the Brady Campaign to Prevent Gun Violence; at the same time, the Center to Prevent Handgun Violence was renamed the Brady Center to Prevent Gun Violence.

About the Author

An initial version of the Brady bill stalled in the U.S. Senate in 1991, but in 1993, New York Democratic Representative Charles Schumer reintroduced the bill in the House of Representatives, while Ohio Democratic Senator Howard Metzenbaum reintroduced it in the Senate. Ultimately, the bill passed in both the houses of Congress, and President Bill Clinton signed the bill into law on November 30, 1993.

"Chuck" Schumer was born on November 23, 1950, in Brooklyn, New York. He graduated from Harvard Law School in 1974 and was subsequently elected to the New York State Assembly. In 1980, when he was just twenty-nine years old, he was elected to the U.S. House of Representatives, where he served for eighteen years. In 1998 he was elected to the U.S. Senate and became New York's senior senator when Daniel Patrick Moynihan retired in 2000. He won reelection in 2004, 2010, and 2016.

Howard Metzenbaum was born in Cleveland, Ohio, on June 4, 2017. He graduated from Ohio State University in 1939, then from OSU's School of Law in 1941. He served in the Ohio House of Representatives from 1943 to 1947, then in the Ohio Senate from 1947 to 1951. In 1976 the governor appointed him to fill a U.S. Senate seat vacated by the resignation of Robert Taft, Jr. He was reelected in 1982 and 1988; his tenure in the Senate ended in 1994. He died in Florida on March 12, 2008.

HISTORICAL DOCUMENT

One Hundred Third Congress of the United States of America

AT THE FIRST SESSION

Begun and held at the City of Washington on Tuesday, the fifth day of January, one thousand nine hundred and ninety-three

An Act

To provide for a waiting period before the purchase of a handgun, and for the establishment of a national instant criminal background check system to be contacted by firearms dealers before the transfer of any firearm.

Be it enacted by the Senate and House of Representatives of the United States of America in Congress assembled,

TITLE I—BRADY HANDGUN CONTROL

SEC. 101.SHORT TITLE.

This title may be cited as the 'Brady Handgun Violence Prevention Act'.

SEC. 102. FEDERAL FIREARMS LICENSEE REQUIRED TO CONDUCT CRIMINAL BACKGROUND CHECK BEFORE TRANSFER OF FIREARM TO NON-LICENSEE.

(a) INTERIM PROVISION-

(1) IN GENERAL-Section 922 of title 18, United States Code, is amended by adding at the end the following:

'(s)(1) Beginning on the date that is 90 days after the date of enactment of this subsection and ending on the day before the date that is 60 months after such date of enactment, it shall be unlawful for any licensed importer, licensed manufacturer, or licensed dealer to sell, deliver, or transfer a handgun to an individual who is not licensed under section 923, unless—

'(A) after the most recent proposal of such transfer by the transferee—

'(i) the transferor has—

'(I) received from the transferee a statement of the transferee containing the information described in paragraph (3);

'(II) verified the identity of the transferee by examining the identification document presented;

'(III) within 1 day after the transferee furnishes the statement, provided notice of the contents of the statement to the chief law enforcement officer of the place of residence of the transferee; and

'(IV) within 1 day after the transferee furnishes the statement, transmitted a copy of the statement

to the chief law enforcement officer of the place of residence of the transferee; and

'(ii)(I) 5 business days (meaning days on which State offices are open) have elapsed from the date the transferor furnished notice of the contents of the statement to the chief law enforcement officer, during which period the transferor has not received information from the chief law enforcement officer that receipt or possession of the handgun by the transferee would be in violation of Federal, State, or local law; or

'(II) the transferor has received notice from the chief law enforcement officer that the officer has no information indicating that receipt or possession of the handgun by the transferee would violate Federal, State, or local law;

'(B) the transferee has presented to the transferor a written statement, issued by the chief law enforcement officer of the place of residence of the transferee during the 10-day period ending on the date of the most recent proposal of such transfer by the transferee, stating that the transferee requires access to a handgun because of a threat to the life of the transferee or of any member of the household of the transferee;

'(C)(i) the transferee has presented to the transferor a permit that—

'(I) allows the transferee to possess or acquire a handgun; and

'(II) was issued not more than 5 years earlier by the State in which the transfer is to take place; and

'(ii) the law of the State provides that such a permit is to be issued only after an authorized government official has verified that the information available to such official does not indicate that possession of a handgun by the transferee would be in violation of the law;

'(D) the law of the State requires that, before any licensed importer, licensed manufacturer, or licensed dealer completes the transfer of a handgun to an individual who is not licensed under section 923, an authorized government official verify that the information available to such official does not indicate that possession of a handgun by the transferee would be in violation of law;

'(E) the Secretary has approved the transfer under section 5812 of the Internal Revenue Code of 1986; or

'(F) on application of the transferor, the Secretary has certified that compliance with subparagraph (A)(i)(III) is impracticable because—

'(i) the ratio of the number of law enforcement officers of the State in which the transfer is to occur to the number of square miles of land area of the State does not exceed 0.0025;

'(ii) the business premises of the transferor at which the transfer is to occur are extremely remote in relation to the chief law enforcement officer; and

'(iii) there is an absence of telecommunications facilities in the geographical area in which the business premises are located.

'(2) A chief law enforcement officer to whom a transferor has provided notice pursuant to paragraph (1)(A)(i)(III) shall make a reasonable effort to ascertain within 5 business days whether receipt or possession would be in violation of the law, including research in whatever State and local recordkeeping systems are available and in a national system designated by the Attorney General.

'(3) The statement referred to in paragraph (1)(A)(i)(I) shall contain only—

'(A) the name, address, and date of birth appearing on a valid identification document (as defined in section 1028(d)(1)) of the transferee containing a photograph of the transferee and a description of the identification used;

'(B) a statement that the transferee—

'(i) is not under indictment for, and has not been convicted in any court of, a crime punishable by imprisonment for a term exceeding 1 year;

'(ii) is not a fugitive from justice;

'(iii) is not an unlawful user of or addicted to any controlled substance (as defined in section 102 of the Controlled Substances Act);

'(iv) has not been adjudicated as a mental defective or been committed to a mental institution;

'(v) is not an alien who is illegally or unlawfully in the United States;

'(vi) has not been discharged from the Armed Forces under dishonorable conditions; and

'(vii) is not a person who, having been a citizen of the United States, has renounced such citizenship;

'(C) the date the statement is made; and

'(D) notice that the transferee intends to obtain a handgun from the transferor.

'(4) Any transferor of a handgun who, after such transfer, receives a report from a chief law enforcement officer containing information that receipt or possession of the handgun by the transferee violates Federal, State, or local law shall, within 1 business day after receipt of such request, communicate any information related to the transfer that the transferor has about the transfer and the transferee to—

'(A) the chief law enforcement officer of the place of business of the transferor; and

'(B) the chief law enforcement officer of the place of residence of the transferee.

'(5) Any transferor who receives information, not otherwise available to the public, in a report under this subsection shall not disclose such information except to the transferee, to law enforcement authorities, or pursuant to the direction of a court of law.

'(6)(A) Any transferor who sells, delivers, or otherwise transfers a handgun to a transferee shall retain the copy of the statement of the transferee with respect to the handgun transaction, and shall retain evidence that the transferor has complied with subclauses (III) and (IV) of paragraph (1)(A)(i) with respect to the statement.

'(B) Unless the chief law enforcement officer to whom a statement is transmitted under paragraph (1)(A)(i)(IV) determines that a transaction would violate Federal, State, or local law—

'(i) the officer shall, within 20 business days after the date the transferee made the statement on the basis of which the notice was provided, destroy the statement, any record containing information derived from the statement, and any record created as a result of the notice required by paragraph (1)(A)(i)(III);

'(ii) the information contained in the statement shall not be conveyed to any person except a person who has a need to know in order to carry out this subsection; and

'(iii) the information contained in the statement shall not be used for any purpose other than to carry out this subsection.

'(C) If a chief law enforcement officer determines that an individual is ineligible to receive a handgun and the individual requests the officer to provide the reason for such determination, the officer shall provide such reasons to the individual in writing within 20 business days after receipt of the request.

'(7) A chief law enforcement officer or other person responsible for providing criminal history background information pursuant to this subsection shall not be liable in an action at law for damages—

'(A) for failure to prevent the sale or transfer of a handgun to a person whose receipt or possession of the handgun is unlawful under this section; or

'(B) for preventing such a sale or transfer to a person who may lawfully receive or possess a handgun.

'(8) For purposes of this subsection, the term 'chief law enforcement officer' means the chief of police, the sheriff, or an equivalent officer or the designee of any such individual.

'(9) The Secretary shall take necessary actions to ensure that the provisions of this subsection are published and disseminated to licensed dealers, law enforcement officials, and the public.'.

(2) HANDGUN DEFINED- Section 921(a) of title 18, United States Code, is amended by adding at the end the following:

'(29) The term 'handgun' means—

'(A) a firearm which has a short stock and is designed to be held and fired by the use of a single hand; and

'(B) any combination of parts from which a firearm described in subparagraph (A) can be assembled.'.

(b) PERMANENT PROVISION- Section 922 of title 18, United States Code, as amended by subsection (a)(1), is amended by adding at the end the following:

'(t)(1) Beginning on the date that is 30 days after the Attorney General notifies licensees under section 103(d) of the Brady Handgun Violence Prevention Act that the national instant criminal background check system is established, a licensed importer, licensed manufacturer, or licensed dealer shall not transfer a firearm to any other person who is not licensed under this chapter, unless—

'(A) before the completion of the transfer, the licensee contacts the national instant criminal background check system established under section 103 of that Act;

'(B)(i) the system provides the licensee with a unique identification number; or

'(ii) 3 business days (meaning a day on which State offices are open) have elapsed since the licensee contacted the system, and the system has not notified the licensee that the receipt of a firearm by such other person would violate subsection (g) or (n) of this section; and

'(C) the transferor has verified the identity of the transferee by examining a valid identification document (as defined in section 1028(d)(1) of this title) of the transferee containing a photograph of the transferee.

'(2) If receipt of a firearm would not violate section 922 (g) or (n) or State law, the system shall—

'(A) assign a unique identification number to the transfer;

'(B) provide the licensee with the number; and

'(C) destroy all records of the system with respect to the call (other than the identifying number and the date the number was assigned) and all records of the system relating to the person or the transfer.

'(3) Paragraph (1) shall not apply to a firearm transfer between a licensee and another person if—

'(A)(i) such other person has presented to the licensee a permit that—

'(I) allows such other person to possess or acquire a firearm; and

'(II) was issued not more than 5 years earlier by the State in which the transfer is to take place; and

'(ii) the law of the State provides that such a permit is to be issued only after an authorized government official has verified that the information available to such official does not indicate that possession of a firearm by such other person would be in violation of law;

'(B) the Secretary has approved the transfer under section 5812 of the Internal Revenue Code of 1986; or

'(C) on application of the transferor, the Secretary has certified that compliance with paragraph (1)(A) is impracticable because—

'(i) the ratio of the number of law enforcement officers of the State in which the transfer is to occur to the number of square miles of land area of the State does not exceed 0.0025;

'(ii) the business premises of the licensee at which the transfer is to occur are extremely remote in relation to the chief law enforcement officer (as defined in subsection (s)(8)); and

'(iii) there is an absence of telecommunications facilities in the geographical area in which the business premises are located.

'(4) If the national instant criminal background check system notifies the licensee that the information available to the system does not demonstrate that the receipt of a firearm by such other person would violate subsection (g) or (n) or State law, and the licensee transfers a firearm to such other person, the licensee shall include in the record of the transfer the unique identification number provided by the system with respect to the transfer.

'(5) If the licensee knowingly transfers a firearm to such other person and knowingly fails to comply with paragraph (1) of this subsection with respect to the transfer and, at the time such other person most recently proposed the transfer, the national instant criminal background check system was operating and information was available to the system demonstrating that receipt of a firearm by such other person would violate subsection (g) or (n) of this section or State law, the Secretary may, after notice and opportunity for a hearing, suspend for not more than 6 months or revoke any license issued to the licensee under section 923, and may impose on the licensee a civil fine of not more than $5,000.

'(6) Neither a local government nor an employee of the Federal Government or of any State or local government, responsible for providing information to the national instant criminal background check system shall be liable in an action at law for damages—

'(A) for failure to prevent the sale or transfer of a firearm to a person whose receipt or possession of the firearm is unlawful under this section; or

'(B) for preventing such a sale or transfer to a person who may lawfully receive or possess a firearm.'.

(c) PENALTY- Section 924(a) of title 18, United States Code, is amended—

(1) in paragraph (1), by striking 'paragraph (2) or (3) of'; and

(2) by adding at the end the following:

'(5) Whoever knowingly violates subsection (s) or (t) of section 922 shall be fined not more than $1,000, imprisoned for not more than 1 year, or both.'.

SEC. 103.NATIONAL INSTANT CRIMINAL BACKGROUND CHECK SYSTEM.

* * * * *

(e) ADMINISTRATIVE PROVISIONS-

(1) AUTHORITY TO OBTAIN OFFICIAL INFORMATION- Notwithstanding any other law, the Attorney General may secure directly from any department or agency of the United States such information on persons for whom receipt of a firearm would violate subsection (g) or (n) of section 922 of title 18, United States Code or State law, as is necessary to enable the system to operate in accordance with this section. On request of the Attorney General, the head of such department or agency shall furnish such information to the system.

(2) OTHER AUTHORITY- The Attorney General shall develop such computer software, design and obtain such telecommunications and computer hardware, and employ such personnel, as are necessary to establish and operate the system in accordance with this section.

(f) WRITTEN REASONS PROVIDED ON REQUEST- If the national instant criminal background check system determines that an individual is ineligible to receive a firearm and the individual requests the system to provide the reasons for the determination, the system shall provide such reasons to the individual, in writing, within 5 business days after the date of the request.

(g) CORRECTION OF ERRONEOUS SYSTEM INFORMATION- If the system established under this section informs an individual contacting the system that receipt of a firearm by a prospective transferee would violate subsection (g) or (n) of section 922 of title 18, United States Code or State law, the prospective transferee may request the Attorney General to provide the prospective transferee with the reasons therefor. Upon receipt of such a request, the Attorney General shall immediately comply with the request. The prospective transferee may submit to the Attorney General information to correct, clarify, or supplement records of the system with respect to the prospective transferee. After receipt of such information, the Attorney General shall immediately consider the information, investigate the matter further, and correct all erroneous Federal records relating to the prospective transferee and give notice of the error to any Federal department or agency or any State that was the source of such erroneous records.

(h) REGULATIONS- After 90 days' notice to the public and an opportunity for hearing by interested parties, the Attorney General shall prescribe regulations to ensure the privacy and security of the information of the system established under this section.

(i) PROHIBITION RELATING TO ESTABLISHMENT OF REGISTRATION SYSTEMS WITH RESPECT TO FIREARMS- No department, agency, officer, or employee of the United States may—

(1) require that any record or portion thereof generated by the system established under this section be recorded at or transferred to a facility owned, managed, or controlled by the United States or any State or political subdivision thereof; or

(2) use the system established under this section to establish any system for the registration of firearms, firearm owners, or firearm transactions or dispositions, except with respect to persons, prohibited by section 922 (g) or (n) of title 18, United States Code or State law, from receiving a firearm.

(j) DEFINITIONS- As used in this section:

(1) LICENSEE- The term 'licensee' means a licensed importer (as defined in section 921(a)(9) of title 18, United States Code), a licensed manufacturer (as defined in section 921(a)(10) of that title), or a licensed dealer (as defined in section 921(a)(11) of that title).

(2) OTHER TERMS- The terms 'firearm', 'handgun', 'licensed importer', 'licensed manufacturer', and 'licensed dealer' have the meanings stated in section 921(a) of title 18, United States Code, as amended by subsection (a)(2).

(k) AUTHORIZATION OF APPROPRIATIONS- There are authorized to be appropriated, which may be appropriated from the Violent Crime Reduction Trust Fund established by section 1115 of title 31, United States Code, such sums as are necessary to enable the Attorney General to carry out this section.

SEC. 104. REMEDY FOR ERRONEOUS DENIAL OF FIREARM.

(a) IN GENERAL- Chapter 44 of title 18, United States Code, is amended by inserting after section 925 the following new section:

'Sec. 925A. Remedy for erroneous denial of firearm

'Any person denied a firearm pursuant to subsection (s) or (t) of section 922—

'(1) due to the provision of erroneous information relating to the person by any State or political subdivision thereof, or by the national instant criminal background check system established under section 103 of the Brady Handgun Violence Prevention Act; or

'(2) who was not prohibited from receipt of a firearm pursuant to subsection (g) or (n) of section 922,

may bring an action against the State or political subdivision responsible for providing the erroneous information, or responsible for denying the transfer, or against the United States, as the case may be, for an order directing that the erroneous information be corrected or that the transfer be approved, as the case may be. In any action under this section, the court, in its discretion, may allow the prevailing party a reasonable attorney's fee as part of the costs.'.

SUPPLEMENTAL HISTORICAL DOCUMENT

"Our Manifesto to Fix America's Gun Laws,"

The Guardian, March 23, 2018

March for Our Lives—live updates
by Editorial staff of the *Eagle Eye*
Fri 23 Mar 2018 01.00 EDT Last modified on Sat 24 Mar 2018 11.39 EDT

As a student publication, the *Eagle Eye* works to tell the stories of those who do not have a voice. Today, we are the ones who feel our voice must be elevated.

In the wake of the tragedy that occurred at our school on 14 February at Marjory Stoneman Douglas, our lives have changed beyond what we ever imagined. We, along with our publication, have been transformed. We will remain so for the rest of our lives.

We have a unique platform not only as student journalists, but also as survivors of a mass shooting. We are firsthand witnesses to the kind of devastation that gross incompetence and political inaction can produce. We cannot stand idly by as the country continues to be infected by a plague of gun violence that seeps into community after community, and does irreparable damage to the hearts and minds of the American people.

That's why the *Eagle Eye* has come together and proposed these following changes to gun policy. We believe federal and state governments must put these in place to ensure that mass shootings and gun violence cease to be a staple of American culture.

We will be marching this Saturday, 24 March, for those that we loved and lost, and we write this in the hope that no other community or publication will ever have to do the same.

The changes we propose:

Ban semi-automatic weapons that fire high-velocity rounds

Civilians shouldn't have access to the same weapons that soldiers do. That's a gross misuse of the second amendment.

These weapons were designed for dealing death: not to animals or targets, but to other human beings. The fact that they can be bought by the public does not promote domestic tranquility. Rather, their availability puts us into the kind of danger faced by men and women trapped in war zones.

This situation reflects a failure of our government. It must be corrected to ensure the safety of those guaranteed the rights to life, liberty and the pursuit of happiness.

Ban accessories that simulate automatic weapons

High-capacity magazines played a huge role in the shooting at our school. In only 10 minutes, 17 people were killed, and 17 others were injured. This is unacceptable.

That's why we believe that bump stocks, high-capacity magazines and similar accessories that simulate the effect of military-grade automatic weapons should be banned.

In the 2017 shooting in Las Vegas, 58 people were killed and 851 others were injured. The gunman's use of bump stocks enabled vast numbers of people to be hurt while gathered in one of the most iconic cities in America. If it can happen there, it can happen anywhere. That's why action must be taken to take these accessories off the market.

Establish a database of gun sales and universal background checks

We believe that there should be a database recording which guns are sold in the United States, to whom, and of what caliber and capacity they are.

Just as the department of motor vehicles has a database of license plates and car owners, the Department of Defense should have a database of gun serial numbers and gun owners. This data should be paired with infractions of gun laws, past criminal offenses and the status of the gun owner's mental health and physical capability.

Together with universal background checks, this system would help law enforcement stop a potentially dangerous person before they commit a gun crime.

Change privacy laws to allow mental healthcare providers to communicate with law enforcement

As seen in the tragedy at our school, poor communication

between mental healthcare providers and law enforcement may have contributed to a disturbed person with murderous tendencies and intentions entering a school and gunning down 17 people in cold blood.

We must improve this channel of communication. To do so, privacy laws should be amended. That will allow us to prevent people who are a danger to themselves or to others from purchasing firearms. That could help prevent tragedies such as the Parkland massacre.

Close gun show and secondhand sales loopholes

Thanks to loopholes, people who otherwise wouldn't be able to buy firearms are able to purchase them at gun shows and secondhand sales. The existence of these loopholes reflects the ineptitude of state and federal legislators.

If we are serious about preventing people from purchasing deadly weapons, we must monitor sales that take place at gun shows and on secondhand markets. This is especially urgent given the danger posed by mentally unstable and violent individuals armed with firearms.

Allow the CDC to make recommendations for gun reform

The Centers for Disease Control and Prevention should be allowed to conduct research on the dangers of gun violence. The fact that they are currently prohibited from doing so undermines the first amendment. It also violates the rights of the American people.

It is hypocritical to rally people to protect the second amendment, while remaining silent on the ways that blocking research violates one of our most basic constitutional freedoms.

Raise the firearm purchase age to 21

In a few months from now, many of us will be turning 18. We will not be able to drink; we will not be able to rent a car. Most of us will still be living with our parents. We will not be able to purchase a handgun. And yet, we will be able to purchase an AR-15.

Why is it that we will be able to legally obtain a weapon that has the ability to fire over 150 rounds and kill 17 people in about six minutes? That is unacceptable. It makes no sense that to buy a handgun, you have to be 21, but a gun of mass destruction and devastation like the AR-15 can be purchased when one is just becoming an adult.

With the exception of those who are serving the United States in the military, the age to obtain any firearm must be raised to 21.

Dedicate more funds to mental health research and professionals

Federal and state government should earmark more funds specifically for mental health services. Those with mental health issues, especially those who express aggressive, violent, suicidal and/or homicidal thoughts should have the opportunity to receive the help they need regardless of their economic status.

Schools specifically should receive more funds in order to hire more psychologists and guidance counselors who can aid students suffering from PTSD, depression and other debilitating mental illnesses.

Many of those who commit mass shootings suffer from these kinds of illnesses. It is essential that more funds be dedicated to mental health research.

Increase funding for school security

We believe that schools should be given sufficient funds for school security and resource officers to protect and secure the entire campus. As a school of over 3,000 students, teachers and faculty, Marjory Stoneman Douglas high school was only supplied funds to hire one on-campus armed resource officer by the state.

Without backup, this officer's hesitation proved to be disastrous and allowed for the senseless deaths of people who were killed on the third floor of the 1200 building.

Though this idea has been proposed in the past, these funds should not be appropriated from the already scarce funding for public education. Governments should find resources to secure the millions of children that attend public schools without taking away from the quality of education that is offered at these institutions.

The Eagle Eye *is the newspaper of Marjory Stoneman Douglas high school. Editorial staff: Madyson Kravitz, Dara Rosen, Taylor Yon, Leni Steinhardt, Emma Dowd, Brianna Fisher, Zoe Gordon, Kyra Parrow, Carly Novell, Rebecca Schneid, Kevin Trejos, Suzanna Barna, Nikhita Nookala, Richard Doan, and Christy Ma*

https://www.theguardian.com/us-news/commentisfree/2018/mar/23/parkland-students-manifesto-americas-gun-laws

Document Themes

Much of the Brady bill as passed deals with the technical issues associated with instituting and implementing the system. The chief provision, however, is that before a person can buy a firearm from a federally licensed dealer, manufacturer, or importer, a background check has to be conducted. Eligibility is determined by the FBI's National Instant Criminal Background Check System (NICS), although the original bill imposed a five-day waiting period until the NICS could be implemented in 1998. Two other databases are accessed when a person purchases a gun from a licensed dealer: that of the National Crime Information Center and the Interstate Identification Index. Additionally, the bill prohibits the transference of a firearm to any person who has been convicted of a crime punishable by a prison sentence of more than a year; to a fugitive from justice; to a drug addict or user of controlled substances; to anyone adjudicated as a mental defective or who has been committed to a mental institution; to an illegal immigrant; to anyone dishonorably discharged from the military; to any former U.S. citizen who has renounced U.S. citizenship; to a person under a restraining order to protect a domestic partner or has been convicted of domestic violence.

Generally, Brady background checks can be completed within minutes with the FBI still on the telephone with the gun dealer, but occasionally a gun buyer may have to wait three business days to complete the purchase. Unlicensed private sellers who are not engaged in the business of dealing in firearms are not subject to the provisions of the Brady bill.

It should be noted that the 1994 bill remained in effect until 1997, but that year, the U.S. Supreme Court, in *Printz v. United States*, struck down the law's background check requirement on Tenth Amendment grounds, ruling that the federal government cannot compel state law enforcement to take any particular action. A new version of the bill was passed in 1998; this version covered all guns, instituted an instant background check of states' and FBI databases to identify criminals, and required a three-day waiting period.

Additional Readings

"Effectiveness of the Brady Act and Background Checks,"Giffords Law Center to Prevent Gun Violence, http://lawcenter.giffords.org/effectiveness-brady-actbackground-checks/.

Gardiner, Richard E., and Stephen P. Halbrook, "NRA and Law Enforcement Opposition to the Brady Act: From Congress to the District Courts," *Journal of Civil Rights and Economic Development*, Vol. 10, no. 1 (Fall 1994), pp. 13–41.

Jacobs, James B., and Kimberly A. Potter, "Keeping Guns out of the Wrong Hands: The BradyLaw and the Limits of Regulation," *Journal of Criminal Law and Criminology*, Vol. 86, no. 1 (Fall 1995), pp. 93–120.

Ludwig, J., and P.J. Cook, "Homicide and Suicide Rates Associated with Implementation of the Brady Handgun Violence Prevention Act," *JAMA*, Vol. 284, no. 5 (August 2000), pp. 585–91, https://www.ncbi.nlm.nih.gov/pubmed/10918704.

Marshall, Michael, "Study Shows Brady Bill Had No Impact on Gun Homicides," University of Virginia School of Law website, March 13, 2003, https://www.law.virginia.edu/news/2003_spr/cook.htm.

—*Michael J. O'Neal*

About 700 people gathered outside the Minnesota capitol building to denounce all efforts to restrict guns. Speakers called for new laws to protect gun owners like "Stand Your Ground" laws. Their criticism was directed at liberals and also Republican politicians who they see as weak advocates for gun rights. (By Fibonacci Blue.)

Florida Legislation "Justifiable Use of Force" ("Stand Your Ground" Law)

Author(s): Dennis K. Baxley (sponsor)
Date: 2005
Genre: State law

Summary Overview

In 2005, the state of Florida passed a statute referred to as "Justifiable Use of Force." Essentially, the statute was what has come to be called a "Stand Your Ground" law, meaning that a person can legally use deadly force if he or she "reasonably believes that using or threatening to use such force is necessary to prevent imminent death or great bodily harm." Florida's Stand Your Ground statute was the nation's first of its kind. This type of law in effect repeals "duty to retreat" laws, which state obligate a person who is facing an imminent threat of personal harm to retreat from the threat as much as possible before responding with force. The relevance of Florida's Stand Your Ground statute to the gun debate is simply that the use of deadly force is likely (but not necessarily) to involve a firearm, so the statute is intended to clarify when a person can use a firearm in self-defense.

Defining Moment

Before Florida's Stand Your Ground statute was enacted, a person had to first use every reasonable means to retreat from danger before using deadly force in self-defense. In various appellate decisions, for example, Florida courts ruled that a person had to "retreat to the wall" before making use of deadly force. This duty to retreat was derived from common law rather than from statute. The only exception to the duty to retreat rule recognized by the Florida courts was the so-called Castle Doctrine, which stated that if the person who used deadly force was not the aggressor and was assaulted in his or her home, the person had no duty to retreat. Later, the courts applied the Castle Doctrine to places of business. Even still, the Castle Doctrine required that the owner or occupant of the "castle" reasonably believe that the use of deadly force was necessary to prevent death or serious bodily harm.

As of 2018, twenty-four states had adopted Stand Your Ground laws, although other states have adopted similar doctrines through judicial interpretation of self-defense laws. Other states continue to adhere to the duty-to-retreat doctrine.

"Stand Your Ground" laws have been controversial, in large part because they have led to gun violence that, in the eyes of some observers, may not have been necessary and that has led to tragic results. One of the most prominent instances took place on February 26, 2012, when George Zimmerman, an armed security guard, shot to death seventeen-year-old Trayvon Martin in Sanford, Florida, in the belief that he had to "stand his ground" in the face of threatened violence from Martin. The statute in Florida, which was updated in 2017 to make it easier for a defendant to claim self-defense, came under intense scrutiny in 2018 when a sheriff near Clearwater, Florida, declined to file charges against one Michael Drejka, who shot to death an unarmed Markeis McGlockton. McGlockton appeared to be trying to protect his girlfriend from being harassed by Drejka during a dispute over a handicapped parking space. After McGlockton pushed Drejka forcefully to the ground, Drejka pulled a gun and shot McGlockton, who was standing several steps away, in the chest. The sheriff commented that state law shielded Drejka, but others argue that this was an unnecessary gun death and that he should have been charged with homicide.

About the Author

The Florida statute was sponsored in the legislature by Republican state senator Dennis K. Baxley. Baxley was born on August 22, 1952, in Ocala, Florida. In 1974 he earned degrees in psychology and sociology from Florida State University. He then attended Miami-Dade Community College to earn a degree in mortuary science. He is the founder of Hiers-Baxley Funeral Services. He later served on the Belleview city commission, then as the town's mayor. He served in the Florida House of Representatives from 2000 to 2007, then again from 2010 to 2016. It was during his first stint in the legislature that he sponsored the Justifiable Use of Force statute.

HISTORICAL DOCUMENT

The 2018 Florida Statutes

Title XLVI

CRIMES

Chapter 776

JUSTIFIABLE USE OF FORCE

776.013 Home protection; use or threatened use of deadly force; presumption of fear of death or great bodily harm.—

(1) A person who is in a dwelling or residence in which the person has a right to be has no duty to retreat and has the right to stand his or her ground and use or threaten to use:

(a) Nondeadly force against another when and to the extent that the person reasonably believes that such conduct is necessary to defend himself or herself or another against the other's imminent use of unlawful force; or

(b) Deadly force if he or she reasonably believes that using or threatening to use such force is necessary to prevent imminent death or great bodily harm to himself or herself or another or to prevent the imminent commission of a forcible felony.

(2) A person is presumed to have held a reasonable fear of imminent peril of death or great bodily harm to himself or herself or another when using or threatening to use defensive force that is intended or likely to cause death or great bodily harm to another if:

(a) The person against whom the defensive force was used or threatened was in the process of unlawfully and forcefully entering, or had unlawfully and forcibly entered, a dwelling, residence, or occupied vehicle, or if that person had removed or was attempting to remove another against that person's will from the dwelling, residence, or occupied vehicle; and

(b) The person who uses or threatens to use defensive force knew or had reason to believe that an unlawful and forcible entry or unlawful and forcible act was occurring or had occurred.

(3) The presumption set forth in subsection (2) does not apply if:

(a) The person against whom the defensive force is used or threatened has the right to be in or is a lawful resident of the dwelling, residence, or vehicle, such as an owner, lessee, or titleholder, and there is not an injunction for protection from domestic violence or a written pretrial supervision order of no contact against that person; or

(b) The person or persons sought to be removed is a child or grandchild, or is otherwise in the lawful custody or under the lawful guardianship of, the person against whom the defensive force is used or threatened; or

(c) The person who uses or threatens to use defensive force is engaged in a criminal activity or is using the dwelling, residence, or occupied vehicle to further a criminal activity; or

(d) The person against whom the defensive force is used or threatened is a law enforcement officer, as defined in s. 943.10(14), who enters or attempts to enter a dwelling, residence, or vehicle in the performance of his or her official duties and the officer identified himself or herself in accordance with any applicable law or the person using or threatening to use force knew or reasonably should have known that the person entering or attempting to enter was a law enforcement officer.

(4) A person who unlawfully and by force enters or attempts to enter a person's dwelling, residence, or occupied vehicle is presumed to be doing so with the intent to commit an unlawful act involving force or violence.

(5) As used in this section, the term:

(a) "Dwelling" means a building or conveyance of any kind, including any attached porch, whether the building or conveyance is temporary or permanent, mobile or immobile, which has a roof over it, including a tent, and is designed to be occupied by people lodging therein at night.

(b) "Residence" means a dwelling in which a person resides either temporarily or permanently or is visiting as an invited guest.

(c) "Vehicle" means a conveyance of any kind, whether or not motorized, which is designed to transport people or property.

Document Themes

The core of Florida's "Justifiable Use of Force" statute is contained in paragraphs (1) and (2). The statute specifies, first, that a person who is in a dwelling or residence has no duty to retreat and can stand his or her ground by using or threatening to use force under two major conditions. The first allows nondeadly force when a person reasonably believes that he or she has to use force to defend him or herself against an intruder's use of force. The second allows the use of *deadly* force if the person reasonably believes that doing so is necessary to prevent imminent death or great bodily harm, or to prevent the imminent commission of a felony. The statute goes on to examine the issue of "reasonable fear." A person who uses deadly force is *presumed* to be acting reasonably if the person against whom the force is used was unlawfully or forcibly entering a home or car or was attempting to in effect kidnap the occupant. Further, the person who uses defensive force is presumed to have acted reasonably if he or she had reason to believe that someone was about to commit a crime or had already done so.

The remained of the statute specifies exceptions: The person entering the dwelling has a legal right to do so (e.g., a landlord); the person entering the dwelling is asserting custody rights over a child or grandchild; the person entering the dwelling is a law-enforcement officer carrying out his or her duties; the person using defensive force is engaged in unlawful activity.

Additional Readings

Elkin, Elizabeth, and Dakin Andone, "What You Need to Know about 'Stand Your Ground' Laws," CNN, July 29, 2018, https://www.cnn.com/2018/07/29/us/stand-your-ground-law-explainer-trnd/index.html.

Headley, Andrea, and Mohamad G. Alkadry, "The Fight or Flight Response: A Look at Stand YourGround," *Ralph Bunche Journal of Public Affairs*, Vol. 5, no. 1 (Spring 2016), https://digitalscholarship.tsu.edu/cgi/viewcontent.cgi?article=1035&context=rbjpa.

Humphreys, David K., Antonio Gasparrini, and Douglas J. Wiebe, "Evaluating the Impact of Florida's 'Stand Your Ground' Self-defense Law on Homicide and Suicide by Firearm: An Interrupted Time Series Study," *JAMA Internal Medicine*, Vol. 177, no. 1 (January 2017), pp. 44–50.

Lave, Tamara Rice, "Shoot to Kill: A Critical Look at-Stand Your Ground Laws," *University of Miami Law Review* 67 (2013): 827–60.

"Stand Your Ground Laws," FindLaw website, https://criminal.findlaw.com/criminal-law-basics/stand-your-ground-laws.html.

Ward, Cynthia, "'Stand Your Ground" and Self Defense," *American Journal of Criminal Law*, Vol. 43, no. 2 (2013): 89–138.

—Michael J. O'Neal

Protection of Lawful Commerce in Arms Act

Author(s): Larry Craig (sponsor)
Date: 2005
Genre: Legislative act

Summary Overview

The Protection of Lawful Commerce in Arms Act (PLCAA), passed in 2005, represented the culmination of political efforts to extend legal protection to gun manufacturers and dealers from lawsuits filed against them by cities, states, and individuals who held the industry at least partly responsible for the effects of gun violence. The PLCAA barred civil suits against gun and ammunition manufacturers, distributors, dealers, trade associations, and importers, but it made narrow exceptions for cases involving defective guns or expressly criminal behavior by those otherwise protected, as, for example, when a gun is knowingly sold to someone not legally eligible to purchase it. The law halted over a dozen lawsuits that were pending around the country.

Defining Moment

Beginning in roughly the early 1980s, growing numbers of gun violence victims were turning to the courts to seek compensation for injuries. The victims filed claims not only against their attackers but also against gun manufacturers and sellers, who were likely to have deeper pockets than the criminals who committed the crimes. These victims also believed that such lawsuits would help promote safer firearm designs, prevent future sales of guns to criminals, and shift some of the blame for gun violence to the gun industry.

But it was not just individuals who were bringing suit against the gun industry; by the mid-2000s, more than thirty municipalities, along with the state of New York, were filing suits in an effort to recoup the costs of law enforcement and emergency medical services connected with gun violence. New York, for example, charged the gun industry with creating a public nuisance by selling products used in the commission of crimes. The state argued that the industry's sales practices allowed guns to be sold in an illegal secondary market, where they can be purchased by criminals.

Several of the lawsuits called for injunctions that would force the firearms industry to incorporate safety features and to restrict sales in ways that would reduce gun violence. Among the theories of liability were strict liability for abnormally dangerous activities, defective design, negligent marketing, oversupply, overpromotion, failure to supervise retails dealers, public nuisance, and deceptive trade practices. It was in response to this rising tide of lawsuits that Congress passed the PLCAA.

About the Author

The PLCAA was sponsored in Congress by Republican Larry Craig, a U.S. senator from Idaho. Craig was born on July 20, 1945, in Council, Idaho, and raised on a family ranch. He enrolled at the University of Idaho, where he was elected president of his fraternity and of the student body. He began his career in politics in 1974, when he was elected, at age twenty-eight, to the Idaho state senate; he won reelection twice before running successfully for Congress in 1980. His tenure in the House was marred by two scandals. The first took place in 1982, when a former congressional page alleged that he had sex with three House members; suspicion fell on Craig, who preemptively denied the charge. The House Ethics Committee conducted an investigation and found that the allegations had no merit.

Craig was elected to the U.S. Senate in 1990, winning reelection in 1996 and 2002. Again, his reputation was marred by scandal after he was arrested on suspicion of lewd conduct in a men's rest room at the Minneapolis–St. Paul airport on June 11, 2007. The claim was that he was exhibiting behaviors used by men to seek anonymous sex. Ultimately, he pled guilty to a misdemeanor charge of disorderly conduct, but the incident became nightly fodder for late-night comedians. Throughout the scandal, Craig denied taking part in any improper sexual encounters. In September of that year, he announced that he would resign from the Senate, but he later withdrew the announcement. He was admonished in the Senate for improper conduct, and when his term expired in 2009, he did not seek reelection. He then opened a consulting firm focusing on energy issues.

HISTORICAL DOCUMENT

One Hundred Ninth Congress of the United States of America
At the First Session
Begun and held at the City of Washington on Tuesday, the fourth day of January, two thousand and five
An Act

To prohibit civil liability actions from being brought or continued against manufacturers, distributors, dealers, or importers of firearms or ammunition for damages, injunctive or other relief resulting from the misuse of their products by others.

Be it enacted by the Senate and House of Representatives of the

United States of America in Congress assembled,

SECTION 1.SHORT TITLE.

This Act may be cited as the "Protection of Lawful Commerce in Arms Act".

SEC. 2.FINDINGS; PURPOSES.

(a) Findings

Congress finds the following:

(1)

The Second Amendment to the United States Constitution provides that the right of the people to keep and bear arms shall not be infringed.

(2)

The Second Amendment to the United States Constitution protects the rights of individuals, including those who are not members of a militia or engaged in military service or training, to keep and bear arms.

(3)

Lawsuits have been commenced against manufacturers, distributors, dealers, and importers of firearms that operate as designed and intended, which seek money damages and other relief for the harm caused by the misuse of firearms by third parties, including criminals.

(4)

The manufacture, importation, possession, sale, and use of firearms and ammunition in the United States are heavily regulated by Federal, State, and local laws. Such Federal laws include the Gun Control Act of 1968, the National Firearms Act [26 U.S.C. 5801 et seq.], and the Arms Export Control Act [22 U.S.C. 2751 et seq.].

(5)

Businesses in the United States that are engaged in interstate and foreign commerce through the lawful design, manufacture, marketing, distribution, importation, or sale to the public of firearms or ammunition products that have been shipped or transported in interstate or foreign commerce are not, and should not, be liable for the harm caused by those who criminally or unlawfully misuse firearm products or ammunition products that function as designed and intended.

(6)

The possibility of imposing liability on an entire industry for harm that is solely caused by others is an abuse of the legal system, erodes public confidence in our Nation's laws, threatens the diminution of a basic constitutional right and civil liberty, invites the disassembly and destabilization of other industries and economic sectors lawfully competing in the free enterprise system of the United States, and constitutes an unreasonable burden on interstate and foreign commerce of the United States.

(7)

The liability actions commenced or contemplated by the Federal Government, States, municipalities, and private interest groups and others are based on theories without foundation in hundreds of years of the common law and jurisprudence of the United States and do not represent a bona fide expansion of the common law. The possible sustaining of these actions by a maverick judicial officer or petit jury would expand civil liability in a manner never contemplated by the framers of the Constitution, by Congress, or by the legislatures of the several States. Such an expansion of liability would constitute a deprivation of the rights, privileges, and immunities guaranteed to a citizen of the United States under the Fourteenth Amendment to the United States Constitution.

(8)

The liability actions commenced or contemplated by the Federal Government, States, municipalities, private interest groups and others attempt to use the judicial branch to circumvent the Legislative branch of government to regulate interstate and foreign commerce through judgments and judicial decrees thereby threatening the Separation of Powers doctrine and weakening and undermining important principles of federalism, State sovereignty and comity between the sister States.

(b) Purposes

The purposes of this chapter are as follows:

(1)

To prohibit causes of action against manufacturers, distributors, dealers, and importers of firearms or ammunition products, and their trade associations, for the harm solely caused by the criminal or unlawful misuse of firearm products or ammunition products by others when the product functioned as designed and intended.

(2)

To preserve a citizen's access to a supply of firearms and ammunition for all lawful purposes, including hunting, self-defense, collecting, and competitive or recreational shooting.

(3)

To guarantee a citizen's rights, privileges, and immunities, as applied to the States, under the Fourteenth Amendment to the United States Constitution, pursuant to section 5 of that Amendment.

(4)

To prevent the use of such lawsuits to impose unreasonable burdens on interstate and foreign commerce.

(5)

To protect the right, under the First Amendment to the Constitution, of manufacturers, distributors, dealers, and importers of firearms or ammunition products, and trade associations, to speak freely, to assemble peaceably, and to petition the Government for a redress of their grievances.

(6)

To preserve and protect the Separation of Powers doctrine and important principles of federalism, State sovereignty and comity between sister States.

(7)

To exercise congressional power under article IV, section 1 (the Full Faith and Credit Clause) of the United States Constitution.

SEC. 3.PROHIBITION ON BRINGING OF QUALIFIED CIVIL LIABILITY ACTIONS IN

FEDERAL OR STATE COURT.

(a) In general

A qualified civil liability action may not be brought in any Federal or State court.

(b) Dismissal of pending actions

A qualified civil liability action that is pending on October 26, 2005, shall be immediately dismissed by the court in which the action was brought or is currently pending.

SEC. 4.DEFINITIONS.

(1) Engaged in the business

The term "engaged in the business" has the meaning given that term in section 921(a)(21) of title 18, and, as applied to a seller of ammunition, means a person who devotes time, attention, and labor to the sale of ammunition as a regular course of trade or business with the principal objective of livelihood and profit through the sale or distribution of ammunition.

(2) Manufacturer

The term "manufacturer" means, with respect to a qualified product, a person who is engaged in the business of manufacturing the product in interstate or foreign commerce and who is licensed to engage in business as such a manufacturer under chapter 44 of title 18.

(3) Person

The term "person" means any individual, corporation, company, association, firm, partnership, society, joint stock company, or any other entity, including any governmental entity.

(4) Qualified product

The term "qualified product" means a firearm (as defined in subparagraph (A) or (B) of section 921(a)(3) of title 18), including any antique firearm (as defined in section 921(a)(16) of such title), or ammunition (as defined in section 921(a)(17)(A) of such title), or a component part of a firearm or ammunition, that has been shipped or transported in interstate or foreign commerce.

(5) Qualified civil liability action

(A) In general

The term "qualified civil liability action" means a civil action or proceeding or an administrative proceeding brought by any person against a manufacturer or seller of a qualified product, or a trade association, for damages, punitive damages, injunctive or declaratory relief, abatement, restitution, fines, or penalties, or other relief, resulting from the criminal or unlawful misuse of a qualified product by the person or a third party, but shall not include—

(i)

an action brought against a transferor convicted under section 924(h) of title 18, or a comparable or identical State felony law, by a party directly harmed by the conduct of which the transferee is so convicted;

(ii)

an action brought against a seller for negligent entrustment or negligence per se;

(iii)

an action in which a manufacturer or seller of a qualified product knowingly violated a State or Federal statute applicable to the sale or marketing of the product, and the violation was a proximate cause of the harm for which relief is sought, including—

(I)

any case in which the manufacturer or seller knowingly made any false entry in, or failed to make appropriate entry in, any record required to be kept under Federal or State law with respect to the qualified product, or aided, abetted, or conspired with any person in making any false or fictitious oral or written statement with respect to any fact material to the lawfulness of the sale or other disposition of a qualified product; or

(II)

any case in which the manufacturer or seller aided, abetted, or conspired with any other person to sell or otherwise dispose of a qualified product, knowing, or having reasonable cause to believe, that the actual buyer of the qualified product was prohibited from possessing or receiving a firearm or ammunition under subsection (g) or (n) of section 922 of title 18;

(iv)

an action for breach of contract or warranty in connection with the purchase of the product;

(v)

an action for death, physical injuries or property damage resulting directly from a defect in design or manufacture of the product, when used as intended or in a reasonably foreseeable manner, except that where the discharge of the product was caused by a volitional act that constituted a criminal offense, then such act shall be considered the sole proximate cause of any resulting death, personal injuries or property damage; or

(vi)

an action or proceeding commenced by the Attorney General to enforce the provisions of chapter 44 of title 18 or chapter 53 of title 26.

(B) Negligent entrustment

As used in subparagraph (A)(ii), the term "negligent entrustment" means the supplying of a qualified product by a seller for use by another person when the seller knows, or reasonably should know, the person to whom the product is supplied is likely to, and does, use the product in a manner involving unreasonable risk of physical injury to the person or others.

(C) Rule of construction

The exceptions enumerated under clauses (i) through (v) of subparagraph (A) shall be construed so as not to be in conflict, and no provision of this chapter shall be construed to create a public or private cause of action or remedy.

(D) Minor child exception

Nothing in this chapter shall be construed to limit the right of a person under 17 years of age to recover damages authorized under Federal or State law in a civil action that meets 1 of the requirements under clauses (i) through (v) of subparagraph (A).

(6)Seller

The term "seller" means, with respect to a qualified product—

(A)

an importer (as defined in section 921(a)(9) of title 18) who is engaged in the business as such an importer in interstate or foreign commerce and who is licensed to engage in business as such an importer under chapter 44 of title 18;

(B)

a dealer (as defined in section 921(a)(11) of title 18) who is engaged in the business as such a dealer in interstate or foreign commerce and who is licensed to engage in business as such a dealer under chapter 44 of title 18; or

(C)

a person engaged in the business of selling ammunition (as defined in section 921(a)(17)(A) of title 18) in interstate or foreign commerce at the wholesale or retail level.

(7) State

The term "State" includes each of the several States of the United States, the District of Columbia, the Commonwealth of Puerto Rico, the Virgin Islands, Guam, American Samoa, and the Commonwealth of the Northern Mariana Islands, and any other territory or possession of the United States, and any political subdivision of any such place.

(8) Trade association

The term "trade association" means—

(A)

any corporation, unincorporated association, federation, business league, professional or business organization not organized or operated for profit and no part of the net earnings of which inures to the benefit of any private shareholder or individual;

(B)

that is an organization described in section 501(c)(6) of title 26 and exempt from tax under section 501(a) of such title; and

(C)

2 or more members of which are manufacturers or sellers of a qualified product.

(9) Unlawful misuse

The term "unlawful misuse" means conduct that violates a statute, ordinance, or regulation as it relates to the use of a qualified product.

SUPPLEMENTAL HISTORICAL DOCUMENT

"New Gun Policies Won't Stop Mass Shootings, but People Can"

David French

National Review, February 15, 2018

It is the responsibility of a free people to be aware, to have courage, and to care for one another.

The United States is facing a puzzling paradox. Even as gun crime has plunged precipitously from the terrible highs of the early 1990s, mass shootings have increased. Consider this, 15 of the 20 worst mass shootings in U.S. history have occurred since the Columbine school shooting in 1999. The five worst have all occurred since 2007, and three of those five were in 2016 and 2017.

It's horrifying, and governmental solutions are hard to find. Twitter's fondest wishes to the contrary, the unique characteristics of mass shootings mean that they often escape the reach of public policy. The Washington Post's Glenn Kessler (hardly an NRA apologist) famously fact-checked Marco Rubio's assertion that new gun laws wouldn't have prevented any recent mass shootings and declared it true. Time and again, existing laws failed, or no proposed new gun-control law would have prevented the purchase.

The reason is obvious. Mass shootings are among the most premeditated of crimes, often planned months in advance. The shooter at Marjory Stoneman Douglas High School reportedly wore a gas mask, carried smoke grenades, and set off the fire alarm so that students would pour out into the hallways. Though we'll obviously learn more in the coming days, each of these things suggests careful preparation. A man who is determined to kill and who is proactive in finding the means to kill will find guns. He can modify guns. He can find magazines.

But that doesn't mean there's nothing we can do. When policies fail, people can and should rise to the occasion. Looking at the deadliest mass shootings since Columbine, we see that the warning signs were there, time and again. People could have made a difference.

Syed Farook and Tashfeen Malik spent at least a year preparing for their attack in San Bernardino, Calif. Farook may have even discussed the attack three years before the murders. A neighbor reportedly witnessed suspicious activity at the the shooters' home, but was afraid to report what she saw.

The story of Devin Patrick Kelley — the church shooter in Sutherland Springs, Texas — is full of warning signs, acts of aggression, and missed opportunities. He was violent, he never should have passed a background check, and he "displayed a fascination with mass murders."

Adam Lanza's family struggled with him for years before he committed mass murder at Sandy Hook. His mother was "overwhelmed" by his behavior, and he lived in deep isolation — blocking anyone from entering his room and even covering his windows with black plastic bags.

Seung-Hui Cho, the Virginia Tech killer, was known to be profoundly troubled. He stalked and threatened female schoolmates. In 2005, a court ruled that he was "an imminent danger to others," but he was released for outpatient care.

The FBI twice investigated Omar Mateen, the Orlando Nightclub shooter, and he once claimed that he was affiliated with al-Qaeda and Hezbollah.

The list could go on and on. In fact, evidence of extended mental-health problems, aberrant behavior, or political radicalization is so common that the absence of such evidence in the Las Vegas shooting renders it the mysterious black swan of mass killings.

In 2015 Malcolm Gladwell wrote an extended essay in the *New Yorker* about school shootings and offered a provocative thesis:

Gladwell argues that each new shooting lowers the threshold for the shooters to come. Each new shooting makes it easier for the next shooter to pick up his gun.

Others have used the term "contagion" to describe the wave of copycat killers. Again, each killing inspires the next, and as the killings increase so does the inspiration.

What does this mean? It means that Americans need to be aware that this contagion exists, that this "ever-evolving riot" is under way. We can't deflect responsibility upwards, to Washington. We're still the first line of defense in our own communities. We cannot simply assume that the kid filling his social-media feed with menacing pictures is just in "a phase" or that strange obsessions with murder or mass death are morbid, but harmless.

We've trained ourselves to mind our own business, to delegate interventions to professionals, and to "judge not" the actions of others. But in a real way, we are our brother's keeper; and an ethic of "see something, say something" is a vital part of community life.

Instead, we all too often retreat into our lives — either afraid that intervention carries risks or falsely comforted by the belief that surely someone else will do the right thing. We've seen this dynamic in other crimes. The worst of the sexual predators revealed (so far) by the #MeToo movement, Harvey Weinstein and Larry Nassar, could have been stopped so much earlier if the people around them had shown just an ounce more courage in the face of known complaints and known misconduct. We didn't need better laws to stop rape. We needed better people.

One of the greatest challenges for any society is stopping a man who is determined to commit murder, and we'll never fully succeed. Even the most vigilant community will still suffer at the hands of evil men. But it's days like these, when children lay dead in school, that we must remind ourselves that we're all in this together. We have responsibilities, not just to mourn and comfort the families of the lost, but to think carefully about our own communities and the circle of people in our lives — and to take action to guard our own children and our own schools.

It is the duty of a free people to be aware, to have courage, and to care for one another. For me, that's a reminder that I can't consider a troubled person someone else's problem. I can't assume it won't happen in my school or in my town. Rather than tweet impotently, I've armed myself to protect my family and my neighbors; in my past role as a member of a school board, I've worked to better secure my kids' school; and I've vowed that if — God forbid — I ever see evidence or warning signs of the darkness of a killer's heart, I'll have the courage to seek the intervention that can save lives.

That's not public policy. It's personal responsibility. It's also the best way to confine the contagion that's killing our kids.

https://www.nationalreview.com/2018/02/new-gun-policies-wont-stop-mass-shootings-but-people-can/

Document Themes

The chief congressional findings in the PLCAA include, first, the possibility that liability will be imposed on an entire industry for harm that is done by others, which Congress regarded as an "abuse of the legal system." Second, the lawsuits that had been filed or were being considered by various levels of government "are based on theories without foundation in hundreds of years of the common law and jurisprudence of the United States." Third, Congress regarded the efforts to use the judicial branch of government to deal with gun violence in this manner as an attempt "to circumvent the Legislative branch of government."

The act goes on, then, to state its purposes, the chief of which is:

> To prohibit causes of action against manufacturers, distributors, dealers, and importers of firearms or ammunition products, and their trade associations, for the harm solely caused by the criminal or unlawful misuse of firearm products or ammunition products by others when the product functioned as designed and intended.

Thus, if a person fires a gun and the gun operates as intended, the gun manufacturer cannot be held liable for any harm that results from the "criminal or unlawful misuse" of the gun; if, in contrast, a person fires a gun and the gun explodes in his or her hand, then the gun user would have a legitimate cause of action against the manufacturer.

A second purpose harkens back to Congress's finding that "the Second Amendment to the United States Constitution provides that the right of the people to keep and bear arms shall not be infringed." Accordingly, a secondary purpose of the act is "to preserve a citizen's access to a supply of firearms and ammunition for all lawful purposes, including hunting, self-defense, collecting, and competitive or recreational shooting."

The act specifies a number of exceptions—that is, causes of action that are not barred by the law. These exceptions include cases in which someone has knowingly transferred a gun that will be used in the commission of a crime or knew that it would pose a serious risk to the purchaser or others. Also excepted are the manufacture or sale of a product that violates state or federal law, that breaches a contract or warranty (i.e., a defective weapon), or that results in injury or damage resulting from a defect in the firearm's design. A final exception included any transaction that violates the Gun Control Act or the National Firearms Act.

Additional Reading

Center for American Progress, "Immunizing the Gun Industry: The Harmful Effect of the Protection of Lawful Commerce in Arms Act," January 15, 2016, https://cdn.americanprogress.org/wp-content/uploads/2016/01/14133650/PLCAA.pdf.

Chu, Vivian S., "The Protection of Lawful Commerce in Arms Act: An Overview of Limiting Tort Liability of Gun Manufacturers," Congressional Research Service, December 20, 2012, https://fas.org/sgp/crs/misc/R42871.pdf.

Crow, Alden, "Shooting Blanks: The Ineffectiveness of the Protection of Lawful Commerce in Arms Act," *SMU Law Review* 59 (2006): 1813–39.

Federalist Society, "The Truth about PLCAA," April 26, 2016, https://fedsoc.org/commentary/blog-posts/the-truth-about-plcaa.

Kurtzleben, Danielle, "Fact Check: Are Gun-Makers 'Totally Free of Liability for Their Behavior'?," *NPR*, October 6, 2015, https://www.npr.org/sections/itsallpolitics/2015/10/06/446348616/fact-check-are-gun-makers-totally-free-of-liability-for-their-behavior.

Lopez, German, "Bernie Sanders's Vote to Protect Gun Companies from Lawsuits, Explained," *Vox*, April 14, 2016, https://www.vox.com/2015/10/14/9533389/bernie-sanders-gun-lawsuits-democratic-debate.

Sugarman, Stephen D., "Torts and Guns," University of California–Berkeley, https://www.law.berkeley.edu/wp-content/uploads/2015/04/guns-420-posting-version-1.pdf.

Vernick, John S., LainieRutkow, and Daniel A. Salmon, "Availability of Litigation as a Public Health Tool for Firearm Injury Prevention: Comparison of Guns, Vaccines, and Motor Vehicles," *American Journal of Public Health*, Vol. 97 (November 2007), pp. 1991–97.

—Michael J. O'Neal

"An Honest Conversation about Guns"

Author(s): Rich Weyland
Date: 2018
Genre: Blog post

Summary Overview

In light of various high profile mass shootings in the opening years of the twenty-first century, and particularly in 2017 and 2018, the topic of guns and gun control was widely debated among politicians, commentators, and the citizenry. The following entry, written in question-and-answer format, was posted on *Spouting Off*, a blog written by Indiana author Rich Weyland. The post, in which the author responds to questions about gun control, defends a strong position in opposition to gun control measures. The author's position is that any gun regulation is an unconstitutional infringement on the right to bear arms.

Defining Moment

Although the issue of gun control has been around for many years, it took on new urgency beginning in 1999 with the mass shootings at Columbine High School in Colorado. As the new century unfolded, further mass shootings took place. One of the most horrific took place at Sandy Hook Elementary School in Connecticut, where twenty children and six staff members lost their lives at the hands of a crazed twenty-year-old armed with a semi-automatic rifle. In October of 2017, the deadliest mass shooting in U.S. history occurred when a man armed with twenty-four firearms opened fire on a crowd of people attending a concert on the Las Vegas Strip, killing fifty-eight people and injuring 851. Matters reached a crescendo in 2018 with a mass shooting that took the lives of seventeen people at a high school in Parkland, Florida, sparking mass demonstrations by students across the country calling for stiffer gun regulation. It was in this context that the conversation recorded in the *Spouting Off* blog took place.

About the Author

Richard F. Weyland received his BS and MS degrees in physics from the University of Illinois and has worked in the computer industry for over forty years. He worked for various communications and computer companies before starting his own consulting firm in 1992. The company has consulted for technology companies from the Fortune 500 down to tiny start-ups.

Weyland most recently has been a digital forensic analyst and testifying computer expert in intellectual property lawsuits. He is currently the president of the Trade Secret Office, Inc., a software startup that has created a trade secret asset management system.

Weyland is co-author of *Trade Secret Asset Management 2018*, as well as a number of book chapters and magazine articles on intellectual property law, especially trade secrets. He has also written several science fiction novels. Weyland and his wife live in the deep woods outside Bloomington, Indiana.

HISTORICAL DOCUMENT

The following reproduces much of a late-night conversation I had with a friend about guns and gun control. The friend is not particularly anti-gun, but he seemed interested in probing my position on these matters while no doubt sometimes playing devil's advocate.

You don't think we need more gun laws?

No, I think we have way too many already, and they violate the Constitution's Second Amendment. "The right of the people to keep and bear arms shall not be infringed."

But that's in the context of a militia, and the militia is the National Guard.

No, it's not, for two reasons. One, the same people who wrote the Second Amendment wrote the Militia Act of 1792 three years later. It defined the militia as all able-bodied men between the ages of 18 and 45. So if you say the Second Amendment applies only to the militia, that still means everybody between 18 and 45.

Second, Blackstone's *Commentaries on the Laws of England* was written about 25 years before the Constitution. It was so fundamental in its analysis of the law it is still just called Blackstone. He wrote on statutory interpretation. The Second Amendment is, in his terms, composed of a predicate clause and an operational clause. The predicate clause is those "Whereas this and whereas that" clauses that begin many acts passed by Congress. The operational clause is the "Therefore be it enacted" part. Blackstone's formulation, and it has been followed in statutory interpretation every since, is that the operational clause—"the right of the people to keep and bear arms shall not be infringed"—stands alone, and the predicate clause—"A well-regulated militia being necessary to the security of a free state"—is not used, *unless* the operational clause is ambiguous, in which case the predicate clause is used to resolve the ambiguity. The operational clause of the Second Amendment is *not* ambiguous.

It also says the militia has to be well-regulated, so it anticipates some regulations on guns.

No, it doesn't. "Well regulated" at the time meant, and still does mean, "operating to a standard." This is why clocks that were accurate enough to use to operate the railroads in the nineteenth century were called "Regulator" clocks. They kept the time to the standard specified for railroad operations. Such clocks were always marked as being Regulator clocks. So with the militia. The militia was to be organized and drilled to a standard, set by the Congress under authority of Article 1, Section 8 of the Constitution, but the actual organization and drilling was left to the states. In any case, since it is the predicate clause, and the operational clause of the Second Amendment is not ambiguous, it isn't relevant.

But I can own guns. How are my rights being infringed?

First, you can only own certain guns.

Well, you don't want people having Tommy guns.

You asked how your rights under the Second Amendment are being infringed. That's one way. You can't own machine guns, at least not without a lot of paperwork and taxes and hoo-ha, and no more can be made for civilian use, which makes them tremendously expensive. You can't own sawed-off shotguns, or short-barreled rifles, called SBRs.

The second way it's being infringed is by paperwork. You have to fill out a Form 4473, and the gun store has to call the FBI and ask if it's OK to sell you a gun.

But that's not infringing your rights.

The hell it isn't. A "fringe" is an edge. The Second Amendment basically says your right to keep and bear arms can't be "edged about." This is clear in other contexts. If you said your neighbor's deck was infringing on your yard, you don't mean he planked over your whole yard, or that his deck wouldn't be infringing if it only covered half your yard. No, you mean it hangs over the property line anywhere, at all, even a couple inches. Same thing here. Words mean things. Same word, same meaning.

Look at it another way. We have freedom of religion spelled out in the First Amendment. Now if the government said, "Well, that doesn't mean polytheistic religions, or religions that believe in reincarnation, or the Mormons, because those people are crazy," people would go absolutely nuts. But that's the way it is with guns. "Well, that doesn't mean machine guns, or short-barreled rifles or shotguns." That's simply wrong. It's unconstitutional on its face.

And filling out a Form 4473, and calling the FBI before selling you a gun? OK, so let's say you need to fill out a Form 4474 before going into a church, and the priest has to call the FBI for permission every time you want to receive communion. Huh? Or same thing with freedom of speech. Well, you know, normal speech like standing on a street corner is OK, but you need to fill out a Form 4475 before getting an Internet connection, and have WordPress call the FBI for approval every time you post to your blog. You know, because those "large magazine" "fully automatic" web blogs are dangerous. They could be used to overthrow the government.

You don't think the government should have records of who buys a gun?

The government should never have any records about who buys a gun, ever. Right now, for the most part, they don't. The stores keep the 4473s, and the government doesn't get them and isn't supposed to keep records on the NICS calls. But I don't trust them. So no, the government shouldn't have any records of gun sales.

But what if someone who isn't in NICS as a prohibited person goes to a gun store and gets a trunkful of guns, and then goes into the city, like Chicago, say, and sells them to gang members, and one of those guns kills a child? How are they supposed to track the gun's provenance?

I don't care.

You don't care if someone kills a child?

No, I don't care what hypothetical you offer, I don't want the government keeping records of who has guns. In the twentieth century, 15 million people worldwide were killed by criminals, and 50 million people died in wars, but ***100 million people*** were killed by ***their own*** governments, ***always*** after they were disarmed. ***That*** is what I worry about most. That is clearly the biggest danger to me, to you, to children, to everybody. That the government knows who has guns, and goes and rounds up the guns. Once disarmed, we are, like the 100 million people killed by their own governments in the twentieth century, at the mercy of government.

Do you know how many gun murders there are in the United States per year?

I don't know. A hundred thousand, hundred and fifty thousand, maybe.

Nope. There are about 33,500 gun deaths per year in the United States. About two-thirds of those are suicides, half of them by men over 45. There are about 500 accidental shootings, usually someone shooting himself while cleaning a gun that hasn't been properly unloaded. Most of those are probably suicides, too, as, if you commit suicide, your wife doesn't get the life insurance payment, but, if you 'accidentally' shoot yourself in the head cleaning your gun, she does.

What you get down to is about 11,000 gun homicides per year. At that rate, it would take ***nine thousand years*** to equal the 100 million people killed by their own governments in the twentieth century. Guns aren't anywhere near as dangerous as governments.

That was mostly by communist governments, by the way. If you want to make something that's very dangerous illegal, you should probably start with communism.

So you would have everybody walking around with a gun all the time.

If they want to. We would be safer, not less safe. If a criminal knew that, if he pulled a gun out and started shooting, five or ten or twenty people would shoot back, he wouldn't do it. These people are cowards. When confronted with an armed response, these shooters almost always surrender or shoot themselves.

What about the Las Vegas shooting? He was too far away to hit with a handgun.

I'm not so sure. That was a country western concert. Had it not been a gun-free zone, there probably would have been two hundred or more people there carrying. You're telling me that if two hundred people started shooting back, that ***somebody*** wouldn't have hit him, or that he wouldn't have stopped shooting and sought cover with bullets flying all around him?

Sounds like the Wild West, or the Roaring 20s.

The biggest, most sensational shooting in the Wild West was the Gunfight at the OK Corral. Very famous, everybody's heard about it. Three men dead. It was written up in the San Francisco paper, 800 miles away. That's not even a hot weekend night in the Englewood district of Chicago.

As for the Roaring 20s, the biggest gangland shooting from the period was the St. Valentine's Day massacre in 1929. Again, very famous, everybody's heard about it. Seven dead. It was in newspapers coast to coast. Again, when that happens in Chicago now, it barely makes the *Chicago* papers.

The Wild West and the Roaring 20s sound pretty good in that context.

But we have to do something.

No, we don't. Or at least, not what you think. More people get killed by drunk drivers. Thirty times as many people get killed by medical mistakes. Go after those.

If you really want to bring shooting deaths down, give law-abiding people their Second Amendment rights back. The criminals don't obey gun laws anyway. Get the gun laws out of the way of allowing law-abiding people to defend themselves. 98% of mass shootings since 1950 occurred in so-called gun-free zones. They're not really gun-free zones, because the criminals carry guns into them whenever they want. What they really are is unarmed-citizen zones. No wonder they attract nut cases.

To bring gun deaths down, you need to repeal the gun laws that have driven gun deaths up.

Besides which, it's my Constitutional right. Says so, right there: "shall not be infringed."

Well, the Constitution isn't hard and fast.

Oh, yes, it is. It's a ***contract***, among the sovereign states, from which the federal government derives all its power. Now if you want to change it, that's fine. There's a way to do that. Propose an amendment that would change the Second Amendment, then get that passed according to the rules. That would allow public discussion on all these issues.

And if it doesn't pass, then the Second Amendment stands, as written.

And that means all these unconstitutional gun laws have got to go.

SUPPLEMENTAL HISTORICAL DOCUMENT

"The Politics of Gun Control Is Changing"

Josh Kraushaar

National Journal, February 27, 2018.

To understand how the renewed debate over gun control will play out politically, just look at the divergent reactions of two leading lawmakers involved in the gun debate: Democratic Sen. Heidi Heitkamp and Republican Rep. Brian Mast.

Mast, an Army veteran and longtime National Rifle Association member, publicly called for a sweeping ban on assault weapons in the wake of the deadly school shooting just miles from his district. Despite representing Republican-friendly turf, where President Trump won 53 percent of the vote in 2016, he's now one of the GOP's leading gun-control advocates.

Heitkamp, who stuck out as one of the few Democrats to oppose expanded background checks after the Sandy Hook school shooting, has been notably quiet about her position on gun control post-Parkland. Even as other red-state colleagues (like Sens. Joe Manchin of West Virginia and Claire McCaskill of Missouri) have expressed support for some small-scale regulations, the North Dakota senator hasn't joined them as she prepares for a competitive reelection race this year.

The battle over guns is as much a regional battle as a partisan one—and the country's geographic divide over the issue is what will make passing significant gun-control legislation so difficult. But it's also undeniable that there's been a clear boost in support for new gun regulations, making the politics of this moment more treacherous than ever for Republicans.

The shift on gun control from leading Republicans who need suburban votes has been head-snapping. Florida Gov. Rick Scott, preparing for a high-profile Senate race this year, broke with the NRA in calling for raising age limits on purchasing assault rifles. Sen. Marco Rubio of Florida, whose political appeal is centered in the GOP-friendly suburbs, came out for a panoply of small-scale gun-control proposals in CNN's televised town hall last week.

And it's not just centered in Florida; the shifts are taking place in suburban areas across the country. Rep. Ryan Costello, a suburban Philadelphia congressman facing a tough reelection campaign, didn't rule out supporting a ban on assault weapons in a recent MSNBC interview. Rep. Leonard Lance of New Jersey, also vulnerable in the midterms, is calling for improved background checks and an end to a ban on gun-violence research. In a swing suburban Denver seat, Republicans are even dishing oppo on a Democratic opponent over his work for a law firm that once lobbied for gun interests.

These shifts follow polling showing a notable spike in support for increased regulations and a growing intensity from supporters of gun control. Typically, gun owners are significantly more mobilized than gun-control activists, which gives the NRA an edge in its lobbying efforts. But a new CNN poll suggests the intensity gap has reversed, at least for now: 31 percent of respondents said they held a "very unfavorable" view of the NRA, while 21 percent held a "very favorable" opinion. (In 2016, most national polls showed the NRA with a net-positive favorability rating.) Overall, 70 percent of respondents said they support stronger gun-control laws—the most since December 1993 and an 18-point spike from an October survey conducted shortly after the Las Vegas massacre. An outright 51 percent majority of voters "strongly" supports more gun restrictions.

Dig deeper into the data, and it's clear that white women—amply represented in suburban swing districts—are driving this change. In October, Quinnipiac found 42 percent of white women said the NRA supports policies that are "good" for the country; only 34 percent agreed in this month's poll. CNN's survey found a huge gender gap: 56 percent of men viewed the NRA favorably, compared to 36 percent of women.

That momentum, however, is tempered by the continued resistance to gun control in rural and small-town America. Red-state Democrats, particularly those senators up for reelection this year, have remained conspicuously quiet about support for new gun regulations. Conor Lamb, the party's star recruit in an upcoming House election in working-class Western Pennsylvania, is as pro-gun as most conservative Republicans. Senate Democratic operatives tasked with winning back a majority are reluctant to publicly weigh in on the issue—at least so far.

In my last column on gun-control politics, I concluded that the party that was divided—the Democrats at the time—was the one losing the public debate on the subject. After Parkland, however, we're seeing fresh splinters within the Republican Party between its suburban House members and its NRA-supportive base. That's a major shift, one that suggests the long-term politics of the issue is moving in the Democratic Party's favor.

Ultimately, Democrats may need to win back control of the House and have their red-state Senate races behind them for any significant gun legislation to get passed through Congress. But it's far more likely that this renewed anti-gun activism will have lasting consequences, even if it faces short-term roadblocks. As Parkland school survivor Delaney Tarr acknowledged to *The Washington Post*: "This is a marathon, not a sprint."

https://www.nationaljournal.com/s/664593/politics-gun-control-is-changing?unlock=RZ4P0XSC71YC7N59

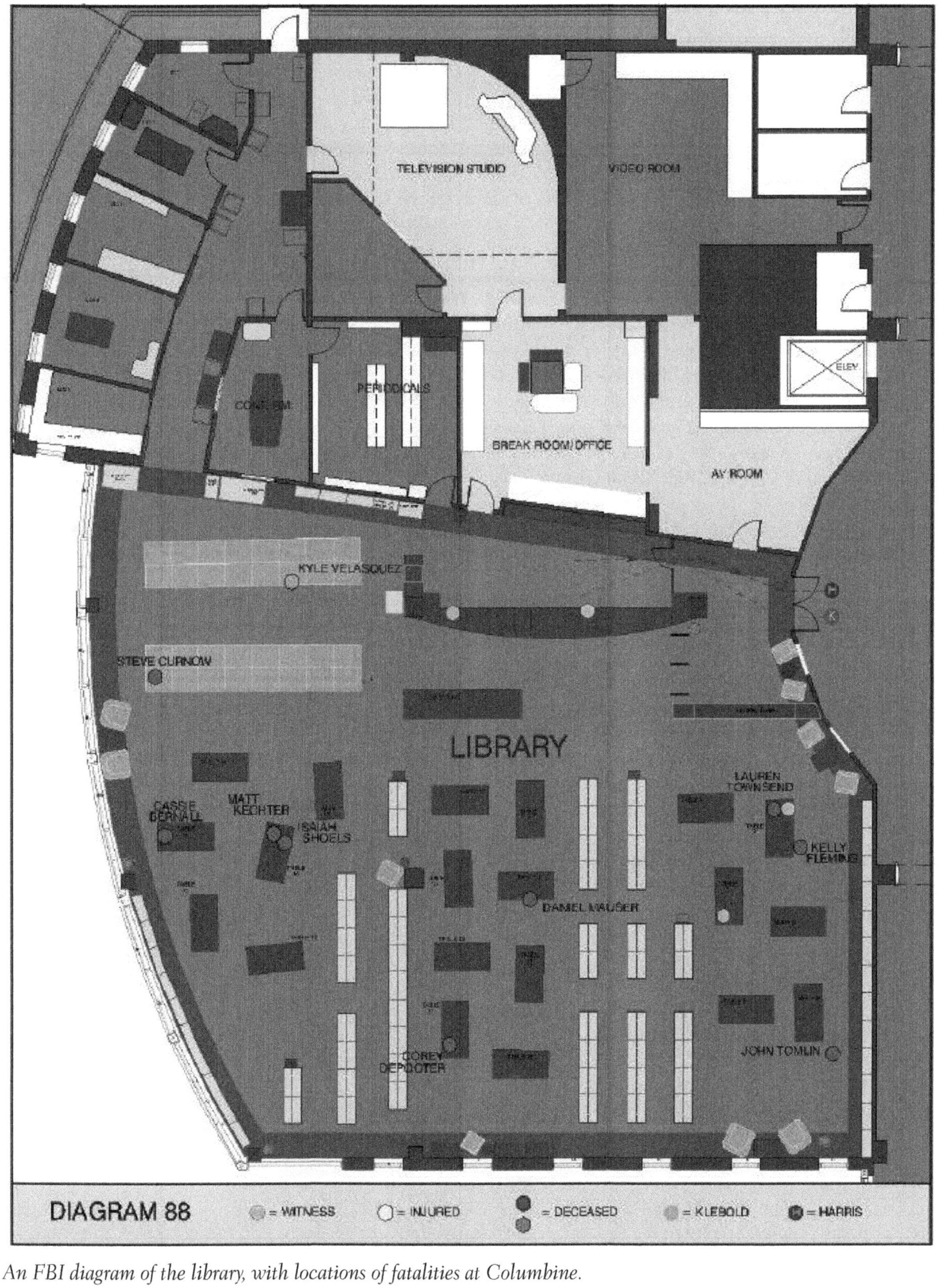

An FBI diagram of the library, with locations of fatalities at Columbine.

Document Themes

Put simply, the dominant theme of "An Honest Conversation about Guns" is that all gun-control laws are ineffective and unconstitutional. The conversation begins by examining the Second Amendment and the issue of whether the amendment applies just to the militia. The respondent points out that the Militia Act of 1792 applied to *all* able-bodied men between the ages of 18 and 45, not just to those in the militia. The respondent then examines the problem of the two loosely connected clauses of the Second Amendment. He refers to Sir William Blackstone's *Commentaries*, the leading legal text of the time. Blackstone distinguished between predicate clauses and operational clauses in statutory interpretation. The respondent argues that the operational clause of the Second Amendment, "the right of the people to keep and bear Arms, shall not be infringed" stands alone. The predicate clause takes effect only if the operational clause is ambiguous—which in the Second Amendment would appear not to be the case. Additionally, the respondent clarifies from a historical standpoint what "well regulated" meant in the context of the militia.

The conversation then turns to the issue of "infringement" on a right. The respondent notes, first, that a person cannot own certain types of , which he sees as a form of infringement. Paperwork and registration requirements are another form of infringement. The respondent categorically rejects the notion that the government should maintain a registry of guns and gun owners, pointing out that people exercise their *First* Amendment freedom of religion without having to fill out a form before going into a church. The respondent points out that an "infringement" does not mean that the right has been trampled or entirely denied; even the smallest restriction meets the definition of "infringement." Thus, he concludes that any restriction on a person's ability to buy a gun is an unconstitutional infringement on a right granted by the Second Amendment.

The conversation then turns to government despotism. The respondent points out that while in the United States there are approximately 11,000 gun homicides each year, the number of people killed by, for example, medical mistakes or drunk drivers is much higher. More significantly, in the twentieth century, 100 million people were killed by their own governments, primarily in Communist nations, leading to the conclusion that outlawing Communism would save more lives than outlawing guns. The respondent states: "Guns aren't anywhere near as dangerous as governments."

The discussion then takes up the issue of open and concealed carrying of guns. The respondent takes the position that if more people were armed, the public would be safer: "If a criminal knew that, if he pulled a gun out and started shooting, five or ten or twenty people would shoot back, he wouldn't do it." He further asserts that "98% of mass shootings since 1950 occurred in so-called gun-free zones. They're not really gun-free zones, because the criminals carry guns into them whenever they want. What they really are is unarmed-citizen zones." In response to the contention that arming people would create a "Wild West" or "Roaring Twenties" atmosphere, the respondent points out that the most notorious shootings from those eras were insignificant in comparison with the shootings taking place today.

The respondent concludes by commenting that the Constitution is a contract among the states; he rejects the questioner's assertion that the Constitution is not "hard and fast." If the public wants to eliminate the rights granted by the Second Amendment, then the way to do so is to amend the Constitution.

Additional Reading

Gillespie, Nick, "Gun Control Isn't the Answer," *Daily Beast*, June 14, 2016, https://www.thedailybeast.com/gun-control-isnt-the-answer.

"Gun Control Isn't the Answer," *National Review*, February 16, 2018, https://www.nationalreview.com/2018/02/parkland-florida-school-shooting-gun-control-not-answer/.

Libresco, Leah, "I Used to Think Gun Control Was the Answer. My Research Told Me Otherwise," *Washington Post*, October 3, 2017, http//wapo.st/2OsiMNZwapo.st/2.

Rossman, Sean, "High Schoolers Still Like Their Guns, Even after Parkland," *USA Today*, March 23, 2018, https://www.usatoday.com/story/news/nation-now/2018/03/23/kids-gun-control-stance-after-parkland/444834002/.

APPENDIXES

Chronological List

Web Resources

American Civil Liberties Union
aclu.org
Home page of the American Civil Liberties Union, the leading organization working to protect civil rights in the United States.

Brady Campaign to Prevent Gun Violence
http://www.bradycampaign.org/
The Brady Campaign is the most recent iteration of a gun-control group formed in 1974.

Bureau of Justice Statistics
https://www.bjs.gov/
The Bureau of Justice Statistics is a data collection arm of the U.S. Department of Justice's Office of Justice Programs. Founded in 1979, the bureau collects and analyzes statistics related to the nation's justice system.

Cato Institute
https://www.cato.org/
The Cato Institute describes its work as broadening public-policy debate on "individual liberty, limited government, free markets and peace." Cato is thought of as a libertarian think tank, and strongly rejects government infringement on individual rights.

Center for American Progress
https://www.americanprogress.org/
According to its website, the center seeks to "combine bold policy ideas with a modern communications platform to help shape the national debate, expose the hollowness of conservative governing philosophy, and challenge the media to cover the issues that truly matter."

Congressional Research Service
http://www.loc.gov/crsinfo/
The CRS no longer releases its reports to the general public, but many can be found fairly easily online. The U.S. State Department and independent groups, including the Law Librarian's Society of Washington, D.C., and the National Council for Science and the Environment post the full text of some CRS reports relating to each group's area of interest.

Consumer Federation of America
https://consumerfed.org/
The Consumer Federation of America, formed in 1968, acts on behalf of consumers through "advocacy, research, education, and service."

FactCheck.org
www.factcheck.org
According to its website, FactCheck.org is a "nonpartisan, nonprofit 'consumer advocate' for voters that aims to reduce the level of deception and confusion in U.S. politics

Heritage Foundation
https://www.heritage.org/
The Heritage Foundation, one of the nation's best-known think tanks on the right, says its mission is to "formulate and promote conservative public policies based on the principles of free enterprise, limited government, individual freedom, traditional American values, and a strong national defense."

History
https://www.history.com/topics/united-states-constitution/2nd-amendment
Tells the story of America through topics of interest, such as the Declaration of Independence, major wars, and notable Americans. Features videos from The History Channel and other resources.

History Matters
historymatters.gmu.edu
An online resource from George Mason University that provides links, teaching materials, primary documents, and guides for evaluating historical records.

Hypertext History

digitalhistory.uh.edu

Offers an online history textbook, Hypertext History, which chronicles the story of America, along with interactive timelines. This online source also contains handouts, lesson plans, e-lectures, movies, games, biographies, glossaries, maps, music, and much more.

Library of Congress

memory.loc.gov/ammem/index.html

Covers the various eras and ages of American history in detail, including resources such as readings, interactive activities, multimedia, and more.

National Archives

docsteach.org

Centered on teaching through the use of primary source documents. This online resource provides activities for many different historical eras dating to the American Revolution as well as thousands of primary source documents.

National Conference of State Legislatures

http://www.ncsl.org/

A bipartisan organization for state, commonwealth and territorial legislators and their staffs, the National Conference of State Legislatures "provides research, technical assistance and opportunities for policymakers to exchange ideas on the most pressing state issues."

National History Education Clearinghouse

teachinghistory.org

A project funded by the US Department of Education that aims to assist teachers of all levels to augment their efforts in teaching American history. It strives to amplify student achievement through improving the knowledge of teachers.

National Rifle Association

https://home.nra.org/

The National Rifle Association, one of the nation's oldest advocacy groups, was formed in 1871 to "promote and encourage rifle shooting on a scientific basis."

PBS

pbs.org/wgbh/americanexperience

Offers an array of source materials linked to topics featured in the award winning American Experience history series.

Pew Research Center

http://www.pewresearch.org/

The Pew Research Center, a nonpartisan organization that's a subsidiary of the Pew Charitable Trusts, calls itself a "fact tank." It conducts public opinion polling and social science research, and publishes reports and information on various issues through seven distinct projects:

ProCon.org

www.procon.org

This independent, nonprofit website lays out the arguments on both sides of a host of controversial issues. Its mission statement: "We promote critical thinking, education, and informed citizenship."

Regulations.gov

www.regulations.gov

Regulations.gov was set up in 2003 to better equip citizens to find, view and comment upon the vast array of federal regulations.

Smithsonian Institution

smithsonianeducation.org

An online resource for educators, families, and students offering lesson plans, interactive activities, and more.

Teaching American History

teachingamericanhistory.org

Allows visitors to learn more about American history through original source documents detailing the broad spectrum of American history. The site contains document libraries, audio lectures, lesson plans, and more.

The Gilder Lehrman Institute
gilderlehrman.org

Offers many options in relation to the history of America. The History by Era section provides detailed explanations of specific time periods while the primary sources present firsthand accounts from a historical perspective.

The National Constitution Center
https://constitutioncenter.org/

Explore the Constitution's history and what it means today with leading constitutional scholars from across the legal and philosophical spectrum.

U.S. History
ushistory.org/us

Contains an outline that details the entire record of American history. This resource offers historical insight and stories that demonstrate what an American truly is from a historical perspective.

Urban Institute
https://www.urban.org/

The Urban Institute says it is a "nonprofit, nonpartisan policy research and educational organization" focusing on "the social, economic, and governance problems facing the nation." It has its roots in the Great Society era of government anti-poverty programs; it was chartered by a blue-ribbon commission assembled by President Lyndon Johnson to examine problems and issues faced by the nation's urban populations.

Bibliography

Allen, William B., and Kevin A. Cloonan, *The Federalist Papers: A Commentary*, 2nd ed. (New York: Peter Lang, 2004).

Aynes, Richard L., "*McDonald v. Chicago,* Self-Defense, the Right to Bear Arms, and the Future," *Akron Journal of Constitutional Law and Policy* 2 (2011): 181–203.

Baron, Dennis, "Guns and Grammar: the Linguistics of the Second Amendment," University of Illinois English Department, https://www.english.illinois.edu/-people-/faculty/debaron/essays/guns.pdf

Billias, George, *Elbridge Gerry: Founding Father and Republican Statesman* (New York: McGraw-Hill, 1976).

Blocher, Joseph, "Firearm Localism," *Yale Law Journal* 123, no. 1 (October 2013), https://www.yalelawjournal.org/article/firearm-localism.

Boissoneault, Lorraine, "In the Congressional Fight over Slavery, Decorum Went out the Door," *Smithsonian. com*, February 10, 2017, https://www.smithsonianmag.com/history/tempers-ran-so-hot-congress-one-senator-was-nearly-beaten-death-180962111/

Bradsher, Greg, "A Founding Father in Dissent: Elbridge Gerry Helped Inspire Bill of Rights in His Opposition to the Constitution," *Prologue Magazine*, Vol. 38, no. 2 (Summer 2006), https://www.archives.gov/publications/prologue/2006/spring/gerry.html.

Brown, David W., "How Alexander Hamilton Solved America's Gun Problem—228 Years Ago," *The Week*, June 15, 2016, http://theweek.com/articles/629815/how-alexander-hamilton-solved-americas-gun-problem--228-years-ago.

Carrington, Paul D., "The Constitutional Law Scholarship of Thomas McIntyre Cooley," *American Journal of Legal History* 41 (1997): 368–99.

Carter, Gregg Lee, *The Gun Control Movement* (New York: Twayne, 1997).

Center for American Progress, "Immunizing the Gun Industry: The Harmful Effect of the Protection of Lawful Commerce in Arms Act," January 15, 2016, https://cdn.americanprogress.org/wp-content/uploads/2016/01/14133650/PLCAA.pdf.

Charles, Patrick J., *Armed in America: A History of Gun Rights from Colonial Militias to Concealed Carry* (New York: Prometheus Books, 2018), Chapter 3, "American Constitutionalism and the Second Amendment."

______, "Historical Thoughts on the Evolution of Firearms Regulations in the Late Nineteenth Century," Chapter 4 of *Bearing Arms: A History of Gun Rights from Colonial Militias to Concealed Carry* (Prometheus Books, 2017), http://wagv.org/wp-content/uploads/patrick-charles-evolution-of-firearms-regulations-in-the-late-nineteenth-century.pdf.

Chu, Vivian S., "Congressional Authority to Regulate Firearms: A Legal Overview," *Congressional Research Report* #R43033, April 5, 2013.

Clinton, Joshua, and John Lapinski, "Measuring Legislative Accomplishment, 1877–1994,"*American Journal of Political Science*, Vol. 50, no. 1 (2006), pp. 232–49.

______, "The Protection of Lawful Commerce in Arms Act: An Overview of Limiting Tort Liability of Gun Manufacturers," *Congressional Research Service*, December 20, 2012, https://fas.org/sgp/crs/misc/R42871.pdf.

Colonial Williamsburg website, "St. George Tucker," http://www.history.org/almanack/people/bios/biotuck.cfm.

Conley, Patrick T., and John P. Kaminski, eds., *The Bill of Rights and the States: The Colonial and Revolutionary Origins of American Liberties* (Madison, WI: Conter for the Study of the American Constitution, 1992).

Cook, Philip, "The Saturday Night Special: An Assessment of Alternative Definitions from a Policy Perspective," *Journal of Law and Criminology*, Vol. 72, no. 4 (Winter 1981), pp. 1735–45.

Cooke, Charles C. W., "Gun Carry Laws Don't Invent a New Right," NRA-Institute for Legislative Action website, March 16, 2018, https://www.nraila.org/articles/20180316/gun-carry-laws-don-t-invent-a-new-right.

Cornell, Saul, "The Early American Origins of the Modern Gun Control Debate: The Right to Bear Arms, Firearms Regulation, and the Lessons of History," *Stanford Law and Policy Review* 17 (2006): 567–92.

______, "The Right to Keep and Carry Arms in Anglo-American Law: Preserving Liberty and Keeping the Peace," *Law and Contemporary Problems* 80, no. 2 (2017): 11–54

______, "St. George Tucker and the Second Amendment: Original Understandings and Modern Misunderstandings," *William and Mary Law Review*, 47, no. 4 (February 2006), 1123–55)

______, *A Well-Regulated Militia: The Founding Fathers and the Origins of Gun Control in America* (New York:

Oxford University Press, 2006).

Cornell, Saul, and Nathan Kozuskanich, eds., *The Second Amendment on Trial: Critical Essays on District of Columbia v. Heller* (Amherst, MA: University of Massachusetts Press, 2013).

Cottrol, Robert J., "*Presser v. Illinois*," in *The Oxford Guide to United States Supreme Court Decisions*, edited by Kermit L. Hall (New York: Oxford University Press, 1999), p. 244.

Cottrol, Robert J., and Raymond T. Diamond., "The Second Amendment: Toward an Afro-Americanist Reconsideration," in *Guns: Who Should Have Them*, edited by David B. Kopel (Amherst, NY: Prometheus Books, 1995), pp. 127–57.

Crow, Alden, "Shooting Blanks: The Ineffectiveness of the Protection of Lawful Commerce in Arms Act," *SMU Law Review* 59 (2006): 1813–39.

Cullen, Charles T., *St. George Tucker and Law in Virginia, 1772–1804* (New York: Garland Publishing, 1987).

Cushman, Clare, *The Supreme Court Justices: Illustrated Biographies, 1789–1995*, 2nd ed. (Supreme Court Historical Society, Congressional Quarterly Books, 2001).

"The Debate over a Bill of Rights," Center for the Study of the American Constitution website, https://csac.history.wisc.edu/document-collections/constitutional-debates/bill-of-rights/.

District of Columbia v. Heller Oral Argument, C-SPAN, March 18, 2008, https://www.c-span.org/video/?204466-1/district-columbia-v-heller-oral-argument.

Dorf, Michael, "Federalist 46 and the Second Amendment," Dorf on Law website, February 21, 2018, http://www.dorfonlaw.org/2018/02/federalist-46-and-second-amendment.html

Douglas, Davison M., "St. George Tucker," *Encyclopedia Virginia*, 2017, https://www.encyclopediavirginia.org/Tucker_St_George_1752_x2013_1827.

Dunne, Gerald T., *Justice Joseph Story and the Rise of the Supreme Court* (New York: Simon & Schuster, 1970).

"Effectiveness of the Brady Act and Background Checks," Giffords Law Center to Prevent Gun Violence, http://lawcenter.giffords.org/effectiveness-brady-actbackground-checks/.

Elkin, Elizabeth, and Dakin Andone, "What You Need to Know about 'Stand Your Ground' Laws," *CNN*, July 29, 2018, https://www.cnn.com/2018/07/29/us/stand-your-ground-law-explainer-trnd/index.html.

Epps, Garrett, "The Second Amendment Does Not Transcend All Others," *Atlantic*, March 8, 2018, https://www.theatlantic.com/politics/archive/2018/03/second-amendment-text-context/555101/.

Federalist Society, "The Truth about PLCAA," April 26, 2016, https://fedsoc.org/commentary/blog-posts/the-truth-about-plcaa.

Finkelman, Paul, "A Well Regulated Militia: The Second Amendment in Historical Perspective," *Chicago-Kent Law Review* 76, no. 1 (October 2000): 195–236.

Frank, John P., Leon Friedman, and Fred L. Israel, eds., *The Justices of the United States Supreme Court: Their Lives and Major Opinions* (Langhorne, PA: Chelsea House Publishers, 1995).

Frassetto, Mark Anthony, "The First Congressional Debate on Public Carry and What It Tells Us about Firearm Regionalism," *Campbell Law Review* 40 (2018), http://campbelllawreview.com/first-congressional-debate-public-carry-tells-us-firearm-regionalism/.

Frye, Brian L., "The Peculiar Story of *United States v. Miller*," *NYU Journal of Law & Liberty* 3, no. 1 (2008): 48–82.

Gardiner, Richard E., and Stephen P. Halbrook, "NRA and Law Enforcement Opposition to the Brady Act: From Congress to the District Courts," *Journal of Civil Rights and Economic Development*, Vol. 10, no. 1 (Fall 1994), pp. 13–41.

Gentile, Gian, Michael E. Linick, and Michael Shurkin, *The Evolution of U.S. Military Policy from the Constitution to the Present* (Santa Monica, CA: RAND Corporation, 2017), Chapter 2, "The Constitutional Moorings for the Evolution of U.S. Military Policy."

Gillespie, Nick, "Gun Control Isn't the Answer," *Daily Beast*, June 14, 2016, https://www.thedailybeast.com/gun-control-isnt-the-answer.

"Gun Control Isn't the Answer," *National Review*, February 16, 2018, https://www.nationalreview.com/2018/02/parkland-florida-school-shooting-gun-control-not-answer/.

Halbrook, Stephen P., "St. George Tucker's Second Amendment: Deconstructing 'the True Palladium of Liberty,'" *Tennessee Journal of Law and Policy* 3, no. 2 (2014): 1–36

______, "The Right of Workers to Assemble and to Bear Arms: *Presser v. Illinois*, One of the Last Holdouts Against Application of the Bill of Rights to the States," *University of Detroit Mercy Law Review*, Vol 76 (Summer 1999): 943–89.

______, That Every Man Be Armed: The Evolution of a Constitutional Right, rev. ed. (Albuquerque, NM: University of New Mexico Press, 2013).

______, *The Founders' Second Amendment: Origins of the Right to Keep and Bear Arms* (Oakland, CA: The Independent Institute, 2008), Chapter 14.

Hall, Kermit L., ed., *The Oxford Companion to the Supreme Court of the United States* (New York: Oxford University Press, 1992).

Hardy, David T., "The Rise and Demise of the Collective Right Interpretation of the Second Amendment," *Cleveland State Law Review* 59 (2011): 315–59.

Headley, Andrea, and Mohamad G. Alkadry, "The Fight or Flight Response: A Look at Stand Your Ground," *Ralph Bunche Journal of Public Affairs*, Vol. 5, no. 1 (Spring 2016), https://digitalscholarship.tsu.edu/cgi/viewcontent.cgi?article=1035&context=rbjpa

Hobson, Charles F., ed. *St. George Tucker's Law Reports and Selected Papers, 1782–1825* (Chapel Hill, NC: University of North Carolina Press, 2013).

Horowitz, Emily, "Shooting Blanks: The Supreme Court's Flawed Analysis in *McDonald v. City of Chicago*," *University of Miami Law Review*66, no. 1 (Fall 2011): 197–231.

Horowitz, Valerie L., ed., *The Unsigned Essays of Supreme Court Justice Joseph Story: Early American Views of Law* (Clark, NJ: Lawbook Exchange, 2015).

Humphreys, David K., Antonio Gasparrini, and Douglas J. Wiebe, "Evaluating the Impact of Florida's 'Stand Your Ground' Self-defense Law on Homicide and Suicide by Firearm: An Interrupted Time Series Study," *JAMA Internal Medicine*, Vol. 177, no. 1 (January 2017), pp. 44–50.

"Institute of Bill of Rights Law Symposium: St. George Tucker and His Influence on American Law" in the *William and Mary Law Review* 47, no. 4 (February 2006): 1111–1426.

"Interpreting *Peruta v. County of San Diego*," The Federalist Society website, June 14, 2016, https://fedsoc.org/commentary/blog-posts/interpreting-peruta-v-county-of-san-diego.

Jacobs, James B., and Kimberly A. Potter, "Keeping Guns out of the Wrong Hands: The BradyLaw and the Limits of Regulation," *Journal of Criminal Law and Criminology*, Vol. 86, no. 1 (Fall 1995), pp. 93–120.

Jancer, Matt, "Gun Control Is as Old as the Old West," *Smithsonian.com*, February 5, 2018, https://www.smithsonianmag.com/history/gun-control-old-west-180968013/.

Johnson, Nicholas J., David B. Kopel, George A. Mocsary, and Michael P. O'Shea, *Firearms Law and the Second Amendment: Regulation, Rights, and Policy* (Alphen aan den Rijn, Netherlands: Wolters Kluwer Law & Business, 2017).

Jones, Alan, "Thomas M. Cooley and the Michigan Supreme Court: 1865–1885," *American Journal of Legal History* 10 (1966): 97–121.

Kates, Don B., Jr., "Handgun Prohibition and the Original Meaning of the Second Amendment," *Michigan Law Review*, Vol. 82 (1983): 204–73.

Knowlton, Jerome C., "Thomas McIntyre Cooley," *Michigan Law Review* 5 (March 1907): 309–25.

Kopel, David B., "English Legal History and the Right to Carry Arms," *Washington Post*, October 31, 2015.

______, "*Peruta v. San Diego*, Analyzed," *Wasington Post*, June 11, 2016.

______, "The Second Amendment in the Nineteenth Century," *BYU Law Review* 4 (1998): 1359–1554.

Kurtzleben, Danielle, "Fact Check: Are Gun-Makers 'Totally Free of Liability for Their Behavior'?," *NPR*, October 6, 2015.

Lave, Tamara Rice, "Shoot to Kill: A Critical Look at Stand Your Ground Laws," *University of Miami Law Review* 67 (2013): 827–60.

Leary, John C., "John Norton Pomeroy, 1828–1885: A Biographical Sketch," *Law Library Journal* 47 (1954): 138.

Levy, Robert A., and William H. Mellor. "Gun Owners' Rights," in *The Dirty Dozen: How Twelve Supreme Court Cases Radically Expanded Government and Eroded Freedom* (New York: Sentinel), Chapter 6, pp. 107–126.

Libresco, Leah, "I Used to Think Gun Control Was the Answer. My Research Told Me Otherwise," *Washington Post*, October 3, 2017.

Lieber, David A. "The Cruikshank Redemption: The Enduring Rationale for Excluding the Second Amendment from the Court's Modern Incorporation Doctrine," *Journal of Criminal Law and Criminology*, Vol. 95, no. 3 (Spring 2005): pp. 1079–1125.

Lopez, German, "Bernie Sanders's Vote to Protect Gun Companies from Lawsuits, Explained," *Vox*, April 14, 2016.

Ludwig, J., and P.J. Cook, "Homicide and Suicide Rates Associated with Implementation of the Brady Handgun Violence Prevention Act," *JAMA*, Vol. 284, no. 5 (August 2000), pp. 585–91.

Madison's Speech Proposing Amendments to the Constitution, June 8, 1789, Teaching American History.org, http://teachingamericanhistory.org/bor/madison_17890608/.

Mahon, John K., *The American Militia: Decade of Decision 1789–1800* (Gainesville, FL: University of Florida Press, 1960.

______, *History of the Militia and the National Guard* (New York: Free Press, 1983).

Malcolm, Joyce Lee, "The Supreme Court and the Uses of History: *District of Columbia v. Heller*," *UCLA Law Review*, 56 (2009): 1377–98.

______, *To Keep and Bear Arms: The Origins of an Anglo-American Right* (Cambridge, MA: Harvard University Press, 1996).

Marshall, Michael, "Study Shows Brady Bill Had No Impact on Gun Homicides," University of Virginia School of Law website, March 13, 2003.

McClellan, James, *Joseph Story and the American Constitution: A Study in Political and Legal Thought, with Selected Writings* (Norman, OK: University of Oklahoma Press, 1971).

"*McDonald v. City of Chicago*," *Harvard Law Review*124, no. 1 (2010): 229–39.

Meltzer, Jonathan, "Open Carry for All: *Heller* and Our Nineteenth-Century Second Amendment," *Yale Law Journal* 123, no. 5 (March 2014).

Michigan Law: University of Michigan, "Thomas M. Cooley," *History and Traditions*, http://www.law.umich.edu/historyandtraditions/faculty/Faculty_Lists/Alpha_Faculty/Pages/Cooley_ThomasM.aspx.

Mocsary, George A., "Explaining Away the Obvious: The Infeasibility of Characterizing the Second Amendment as a Nonindividual Right," *Fordham Law Review* 76 (2008): 2113–75.

Mondschein, Ken, "'A Well-Regulated Militia': The Medieval Origins of the Second Amendment," Medievalists.net, April 23, 2018.

Moreland, Maxel, "Does the Second Amendment Protect Concealed Carry?," *University of Cincinnati Law Review* blog, November 8, 2016.

National Firearms Act: Hearings before the Committee on Ways and Means: House of Representative, Seventy-third Congress, Second Session, on H.R. 9066 (Washington, D.C.: U.S. Government Printing Office, 1934).

"Open Carry," Giffords Law Center, http://lawcenter.giffords.org/gun-laws/policy-areas/guns-in-public/open-carry/.

Paludan, Phillip S., "John Norton Pomeroy, State Rights Nationalist," *American Journal of Legal History* 12, no. 4 (October, 1968): 275–93

Papers of the War Department, 1784–1800, http://wardepartmentpapers.org.

Patterson, Samuel C., and Keith R. Eakin,."Congress and Gun Control."In *The Changing Politics of Gun Control*, ed. John M. Bruce and Clyde Wilcox (Lanham, MD: Rowman & Littlefield Publishers, 1998).

Peacock, Anthony A., *How To Read The Federalist Papers* (Washington, D.C.: Heritage Foundation, 2010).

"*Peruta v. County of San Diego*," *Harvard Law Review* 130 (January 5, 2017), https://harvardlawreview.org/2017/01/peruta-v-county-of-san-diego/ (case note).

Pfau, Michael, "Time, Tropes, and Textuality: Reading Republicanism in Charles Sumner's 'Crime Against Kansas,'" *Rhetoric & Public Affairs*, Vol. 6, no. 3 (Fall 2003), pp. 385–413.

Pierson, Michael D., "'All Southern Society Is Assailed by the Foulest Charges': Charles Sumner's 'The Crime against Kansas' and the Escalation of Republican Anti-Slavery Rhetoric," *New England Quarterly*, Vol. 68, no. 4 (December 1995), pp. 531–57.

Posner, Richard A., "In Defense of Looseness," *New Republic*, August 27, 2008.

Powell, H. Jefferson. "Enumerated Means and Unlimited Ends." *Michigan Law Review* 94, no. 3 (December, 1995): 651-673.

Presser, Stephen B., "Review: Resurrecting the Conservative Tradition in American Legal History," *Reviews in American History* 13, no. 4 (1985): 526–533.

Proposed Amendments to the Gun Control Act of 1968 to Prohibit the Sale of "Saturday Night Special" Handguns: Hearings on S. 2507 Before the Subcommittee to Investigate Juvenile Delinquency of the Senate Committee on the Judiciary, 92nd Cong., 1st Sess. (1971).

Regan, Donald H. "How to Think About the Federal Commerce Power and Incidentally Rewrite *United States v. Lopez*." *Michigan Law Review* 94, no. 3 (December, 1995): 554-614.

Report of the House Select Committee, July 28, 1789, Teaching American History.org, http://teachingamericanhistory.org/bor/houseselect_17890728/.

Rosenthal, Lawrence, and Joyce Lee Malcolm, "Colloquy Debate: *McDonald v. Chicago*: Which Standard of Scrutiny Should Apply to Gun Control," *Northwestern University Law Review*105, no. 1 (2011): 438–66)

Rossman, Sean, "High Schoolers Still Like Their Guns, Even after Parkland," *USA Today*, March 23, 2018.

Santaella-Tenorio, Julian, Magdalena Cerdá, Andrés Villaveces, and Sandro Gale, "What Do We Know About the Association between Firearm Legislation and Firearm-Related Injuries?," *Epidemiologic Reviews*, Vol. 38 (2016), pp. 140–57.

Sarosy, Charlie, "California's Unloaded Open Carry Bans: A Constitutional and Risky, but Perhaps Necessary, Gun Control Strategy," *UCLA Law Review* 61 (2014): 464–504, https://www.uclalawreview.org/pdf/61-2-4.pdf.

Scarola, Matthew, "Analysis: State Gun Regulations and *McDonald*," *SCOTUSblog*, June 28, 2010.

Schrader, Dorothy, "The Assault Weapons Ban: Review of Federal Laws ControllingPossession of Certain Firearms." Congressional Research Report #95-108, December 1, 1995.

Scott, Kyle, *The Federalist Papers: A Reader's Guide* (New York: Bloomsbury Academic, 2013).

Seddig, Robert G., "Henry Baldwin," *The Oxford Companion to the Supreme Court of the United States*, edited by Kermit L. Hall (New York: Oxford University Press, 1992).

Shalhope, Robert E., "The Ideological Origins of the Second Amendment," *Journal of American History*, Vol. 69 (1982): 599–614.

Shusterman, Hoah, "What the Second Amendment Really Meant to the Founders," *Washington Post*, February 22, 2018.

Siegel, Stephen A., "Historicism in Late Nineteenth-Century Constitutional Thought," *Wisconsin Law Review* (1990): 1431–1547.

Sinha, Manisha, "The Caning of Charles Sumner: Slavery, Race, and Ideology in the Age of the Civil War," *Journal of the Early Republic*, Vol. 23 (Summer 2003), pp. 233–62.

Slusser, Daniel Lawrence, "In Defense of Southern Honor: Preston Brooks and the Attack on Charles Sumner," *The Forum: Journal of History*, Vol. 2, no. 1 (2010), pp. 98–110.

Smith, Richard W. "Interpreting the Constitution from Inside the Jury Box: Affecting Interstate Commerce as an Element of the Crime." *Washington and Lee Law Review* 55, no. 2 (Spring, 1998): 615-658.

Solum, Lawrence B., "*District of Columbia v. Heller* and Originalism," *Northwestern University Law Review*, 103, no. 2 (2009): 923–82.

Spitzer, Robert J. "Gun Laws Are as Old as Gun Ownership," American Constitution Society website, May 18, 2015.

______, *Gun Control: A Documentary and Reference Guide* (Westport, CT: Greenwood Press, 2009).

______, *Guns across America: Reconciling Gun Rules and Rights* (New York: Oxford University Press, 2015).

______, *The Politics of Gun Control*, 5th ed. (Boulder, CO: Paradigm Publishers, 2012).

"Stand Your Ground Laws," FindLaw website, https://criminal.findlaw.com/criminal-law-basics/stand-your-ground-laws.html.

Story, Allan C., ed., *Presser v. State of Illinois* U.S. Supreme Court Transcript of Record with Supporting Pleadings (Detroit, MI: Gale, 2011).

Stowell, Ethan T. "Top Gun: The Second Amendment, Self-Defense, and Private Property Exclusion," *Regent University Law Review*, Vol. 26 (2014): pp. 521–55.

Sugarman, Stephen D., "Torts and Guns," University of California–Berkeley, https://www.law.berkeley.edu/wp-content/uploads/2015/04/guns-420-posting-version-1.pdf.

Sullivan, William, "Is the Second Amendment for Just the Militia?," *American Thinker*, April 5, 2018.

Swisher, Carl B., *The Taney Period, 1836–1864*. Vol. 5 of *History of the Supreme Court of the United States* (New York: Macmillan, 1974).

Tracinski, Robert, "How the Second Amendment Prevents Tyranny," *The Federalist*, March 22, 2018.

Urofsky, Melvin I., *The Supreme Court Justices: A Biographical Dictionary* (New York: Garland Publishing, 1994).

Valentine, Matt, "Tallying the Costs of Open Carry," *Atlantic*, January 31, 2016.

Van Buskirk, Judith L., "William Rawle," *The Yale Biographical Dictionary of American Law*, ed. Roger K. Newman (New Haven, CT: Yale University Press, 2009), pp. 447–48.

Vandercoy, David E., "The History of the Second Amendment," *Valparaiso University Law Review* 28, no. 3 (Spring 1994): 1007–39.

Vernick, John S., Lainie Rutkow, and Daniel A. Salmon, "Availability of Litigation as a Public Health Tool for Firearm Injury Prevention: Comparison of Guns, Vaccines, and Motor Vehicles," *American Journal of Public Health*, Vol. 97 (November 2007), pp. 1991–97.

Vile, John R, *A Companion to the United States Constitution and Its Amendments*. 3d ed. Westport, Conn.: Praeger, 2001.

Volokh, Eugene, "The Amazing Vanishing Second Amendment," *New York University Law Review* 73 (June 1998): 831–40.

Ward, Cynthia, "'Stand Your Ground" and Self Defense," *American Journal of Criminal Law*, Vol. 43, no. 2 (2013): 89–138.

"William Joseph Gaston," *Dictionary of North Carolina Biography*, edited by William S. Powell (Chapel Hills, NC: University of North Carolina Press, 1979–1996).

Winkler, Adam, "Scrutinizing the Second Amendment," *Michigan Law Review* 105 (2007): 683–733.

Yassky, David S., "The Second Amendment: Structure, History, and Constitutional Change," *Michigan Law Review* 99 (December 2000): 588–668.

Zimring, Franklin E., "Firearms and Federal Law: The Gun Control Act of 1968," *Journal of Legal Studies* 4 (January 1975): 133–98.

Acknowledgments

A View of the Constitution of the United States. William Rawle. 1829. http://press-pubs.uchicago.edu/founders/print_documents/amendIIs9.html

All Guns Are Not Created "All Guns Are Not Created Equal." Kevin M. Sweeney and Saul Cornell. *Chronicle of Higher Education*. January 28, 2013. Published by permission. https://www.chronicle.com/article/All-Guns-Are-Not-Created-Equal/136805

Amendment II. U.S. Constitution. https://constitutioncenter.org/interactive-constitution/amendments/amendment-ii

"Barack Obama's Speech on New Gun Control Measures." Barack Obama. January 5, 2016

Blackstone's *Commentaries*: With Notes of Reference, to the Constitution and Laws, of the Federal Government of the United States; and of the Commonwealth of Virginia. St. George Tucker. 1803

"The crime against Kansas." Charles Sumner. May 19, 1856. https://archive.org/stream/crimeagainstkans00sumn/crimeagainstkans00sumn_djvu.txt

"Defending an Under-21 Firearm Ban Under the Second Amendment Two Step." Amit Vora. *Stanford Law Review*. May 1, 2018. Published by permission.

"Dickey Amendment." Public Law 104–208—Sept. 30, 1996. https://www.gpo.gov/fdsys/pkg/PLAW-104publ208/pdf/PLAW-104publ208.pdf

District Of Columbia, et al., Petitioners v. Dick Anthony Heller. Justice Antonin Scalia. Supreme Court Of The United States

Familiar Exposition of the Constitution of the United States. Joseph Story. 1840. http://www2.law.ucla.edu/volokh/beararms/comment.htm#TUCKER

Federalist Paper 24: The Powers Necessary to the Common Defense Further Considered. PUBLIUS (Alexander Hamilton). *Independent Journal*. https://www.congress.gov/resources/display/content/The+Federalist+Papers#TheFederalistPapers-24

Federalist Paper 25: The Same Subject Continued: The Powers Necessary to the Common Defense Further Considered. PUBLIUS (Alexander Hamilton). *New York Packet*. https://www.congress.gov/resources/display/content/The+Federalist+Papers#TheFederalistPapers-25

Federalist Paper 46: The Influence of the State and Federal Governments Compared. PUBLIUS (James Madison). *New York Packet*. https://www.congress.gov/resources/display/content/The+Federalist+Papers#TheFederalistPapers-46

The General Principles of Constitutional Law in the United States of America. Thomas M. Cooley and Andrew C. McLaughlin. (Boston: Little Brown, 1898), pp. 297–99.

Gun Control Act of 1968: Public Law 90-617 and 90-618. 90th Congress. https://www.gpo.gov/fdsys/pkg/STATUTE-82/pdf/STATUTE-82-Pg1213-2.pdf

Gun Control: Statutory Limitations on Disclosure. William J. Krouse. *Congressional Research Service*. May 27, 2009. https://fas.org/sgp/crs/misc/RS22458.pdf

"Gun Regulation and the Second Amendment: Moving Forward After *District of Columbia v. Heller*." *Giffords Law Center*. Law Center Against Violence. https://lawcenter.giffords.org/wp-content/uploads/2012/05/DC_v_Heller_Gun_Regulation_Brochure.pdf

House of Representatives Debate, Second Amendment. *The Congressional Register*. August 17, 1789

An Introduction to the Constitutional Law of the United States, 3rd. edition. John Norton Pomeroy. Boston: Houghton Mifflin, 1875, p. 157; originally published in 1868. August 1875. https://www.constitution.org/cmt/pomeroy/pomeroy.htm

Johnson v. Tompkins et al. Circuit Court of Pennsylvania. April 1833

"Justifiable Use of Force" ("Stand Your Ground Law," 2005). Florida Legislation. http://www.leg.state.fl.us/statutes/index.cfm?App_mode=Display_Statute&Search_String=&URL=0700-0799/0776/Sections/0776.013.html

Militia Act of 1792. 2nd Congress. May 2, 1792. http://www.constitution.org/mil/mil_act_1792.htm

N.R.A. News Conference. Wayne LaPierre. *National Rifle Association*. December 21, 2012. Published by permission. https://assets.documentcloud.org/documents/547481/n-r-a-news-conference-december-21-2012.pdf

National Firearms Act Of 1934 [H.B.9741]. 73rd Congress. gpo.gov. June 26, 1934. https://archive.org/stream/NationalFirearmsActOf1934/National_Firearms_Act_of_1934_djvu.txt

"New Gun Control Provisions Passed In Spending Bill." NPR's Sarah McCammon, Pennsylvania Congressman Ryan Costello. NPR.org. March 25, 2018. Published by permission. https://www.npr.org/2018/03/25/596880465/new-gun-control-provisions-passed-in-spending-bill

"Open Carry for All: *Heller* and Our Nineteenth-Century Second Amendment." Jonathan Meltzer. *Yale Law Journal*, Vol. 123 (2014). March 1, 2014. Published by permission. https://www.yalelawjournal.org/note/open-carry-for-all-heller-and-our-nineteenth-century-second-amendment

Otis Mcdonald, et al., Petitioners v. City Of Chicago, Illinois, et al. Supreme Court (Justice Antonin Scalia). Supreme.justia.com. June 28, 2010. https://supreme.justia.com/cases/federal/us/561/742/opinion.html

"Our Manifesto to Fix America's Gun Laws." Editorial staff of the Eagle Eye. *Eagle Eye*. https://issuu.com/melissafalkowski4/docs/4thquarterfull

Peruta v. County of San Diego. United States Court of Appeals, Ninth Circuit (W. Fletcher, Circuit Judge). June 16, 2015

"Protection of Lawful Commerce in Arms Act" Public Law 92. 109th Congress. Congressional Record: Protection of Lawful Commerce in Arms Act. January 4, 2005. https://www.gpo.gov/fdsys/pkg/PLAW-109publ92/html/PLAW-109publ92.htm

"Public Safety and Recreational Firearms Use Protection Act." 103rd Congress. Congressional Record: Public Safety and Recreational Firearms Use Protection Act. https://www.govtrack.us/congress/bills/103/hr4296/text

"The Racist Roots of Gun Control". Clayton E. Cramer. *Kansas Journal of Law & Public Policy*, Winter 1995. Published by permission. https://www.firearmsandliberty.com/cramer.racism.html

The right to keep and bear arms report of the Subcommittee on the Constitution of the Committee on the Judiciary, United States Senate, Ninety-seventh Congress, second session. 97th Congress. Washington, D.C. :U.S. G.P.O.,1982. 1982. https://babel.hathitrust.org/cgi/pt?id=mdp.39015005397099;view=1up;seq=1

"St. George Tucker and the Second Amendment: Original Understandings and Modern Misunderstandings." Saul Cornell. *William and Mary Law Review*, 47, no. 4 (2006), 1123-55. Published by permission. http://scholarship.law.wm.edu/cgi/viewcontent.cgi?article=1231&context=wmlr&sei-redir=1

State v. Chandler. Supreme Court. 1850. http://www.guncite.com/court/state/5la489.html

State vs. Robert S. Huntly. Supreme Court. June 1843. https://constitution.org/2ll/2ndcourt/state/190st.htm

3D-printed Gun Controversy: Everything You Need to Know. Marrian Zhou. *Cnet*. August 16, 2018. https://www.cnet.com/news/the-3d-printed-gun-controversy-everything-you-need-to-know/

"Tiahrt Restrictions Repeal Act." 115th Congress. March 14, 2018. https://www.congress.gov/bill/115th-congress/house-bill/5271/text

United States v. Cruikshank. Supreme Court. February 18, 1905. https://supreme.justia.com/cases/federal/us/92/542/

United States v. Lopez. Supreme Court. April 26, 1995. https://supreme.justia.com/cases/federal/us/514/549/case.html

United States v. Miller. Supreme Court. *Legal Information Institute*, Cornell Law School. May 15, 1939. https://www.law.cornell.edu/supremecourt/text/307/174\

Young v. Hawaii. Ninth Circuit Court of Appeals. July 24, 2018. http://cdn.ca9.uscourts.gov/datastore/opinions/2018/07/24/12-17808.pdf

Index

G

H

N

O

P

Y

Z

FASKEN LEARNING RESOURCE CENTER
9000089779

REFERENCE

KF The gun debate /
3941
.A68
G86
V. 2